GLOBALIZATION

GLOBALIZATION

Capitalism and its Alternatives

LESLIE SKLAIR

OXFORD

UNIVERSITY PRESS

OXFORD
UNIVERSITY PRESS

Great Clarendon Street, Oxford OX2 6DP

Oxford University Press is a department of the University of Oxford.
It furthers the University's objective of excellence in research, scholarship,
and education by publishing worldwide in

Oxford New York
Auckland Bankok Buenos Aires Cape Town
Chennai Dar es Salaam Delhi Hong Kong
Istanbul Karachi Kolkata Kuala Lumpur Madrid
Melbourne Mexico City Mumbai Nairobi
São Paulo Shanghai Taipei Tokyo Toronto.

Oxford is a registered trade mark of Oxford University Press
in the UK and in certain other countries

Published in the United States
by Oxford University Press Inc., New York

British Library Cataloguing in Publication Data
Data available

Library of Congress Cataloging in Publication Data
Data available

ISBN 0-19-924744-7

3 5 7 9 10 8 6 4 2

Typeset in Swift and Meta
by RefineCatch Limited, Bungay, Suffolk
Printed in Great Britain by
T.J. International Ltd.,
Padstow, Cornwall

PREFACE AND ACKNOWLEDGEMENTS

This book is a new version rather than a third edition of what was previously published under the title *Sociology of the Global System*. The main differences from the 1995 edition of that book are (i) updating of sources and information on all the topics discussed (over 400 post-1995 references, over 200 of these published in 2000 or later); (ii) new sections on the history and theory of globalization, especially in Chapter 3; (iii) new sections on the crises of class polarization and ecological unsustainability of capitalist globalization in Chapter 3; (iv) a new case study on Enron in India in Chapter 4; (v) a new section on the physical space for transnational practices and urban globalization in Chapter 5; (vi) a new section on genetically modified crops in Chapter 6; (vii) a new case study on the global tobacco industry in Chapter 7; (viii) a new section on the media in China in Chapter 9; (ix) a new Chapter 10 on challenges to capitalist globalization; and (x) a new Chapter 11 on the globalization of human rights. In addition there are about twenty new tables and figures.

Oxford University Press subjected the book to an extensive and welcome peer review process, and I am very grateful to the four anonymous persons who reviewed the proposal for OUP and made several valuable suggestions for revisions, and those who commented on the new chapters. Sidney Tarrow made some penetrating criticisms of Chapter 10, but we still disagree on social movements. I am also very grateful to the copyright holders who permitted me to reprint pictures and cartoons. The professionalism of all at OUP was of great help as I completed the book.

My intellectual debts continue to mount. Since 1995, new cohorts of research students have challenged me and given me the great benefit of their own research as they successfully completed their Ph.D.s. My thanks are offered to Drs Ana Bergareche, Herry-Priyono, Boris Holzer, Yun-tae Kim, Carolina Ladino, Ka-ho Mok, Alex Pereira, Peter Robbins, Alejandra Salas-Porras, and Emily Scraggs. The ongoing research projects of Michelle Bellars, Mario Brincat, Reeve Bustami, Joabe Cavalcanti, Geraldine Chan, Claudia Granados, Robyn Gutteridge, Aparna Joshi, Nan-Yeong Park-Matthews, Luis Ramirez, and Jill Timms have also influenced the development of my thinking, as have the students on my two Master's courses, Approaches to Globalization and Sociology of Development. The issues discussed in this book have also been sharpened by many fruitful encounters in universities and research centres around the world in recent years. I thank the organizers of sessions at the University of Southern California, University of Calgary, the international conference on globalization in Hainan Island China; IME2000 conference in Tijuana, Mexico; the University of California Riverside; the Fathom Globalization Forum at Columbia University in New York; ULU Marxist Society; Hellenic Observatory Athens; Netherlands Institute for Advanced Studies Wassenaar; the University of Mauritius; the Global Studies Association in Manchester; the University of Buenos Aires; IHDP in Rio; and the Central European University in Budapest. A special mention is due to Aparna Joshi, Luis Ramirez, Danielle Hidalgo, Herry-Priyono, and Emily Calkins for their really invaluable help at various periods during 2000–1 in tracking down sources, suggesting improvements, designing tables and figures, and making the manuscript ready for the printers. Luis, in particular, helped me greatly in the final stages, as did Evangelis Kalpadakis with the index.

My beloved family, Doro (who makes it all possible), Jessie, Aphra, and Tillie (at home and abroad), provide daily confirmations that my ideas about changing the world are not always as obvious to intelligent and sensitive people as they are to me and although it sometimes may not sound like it, I do love arguing with them.

LESLIE SKLAIR

London, October 2001

CONTENTS

DETAILED CONTENTS

BOXES, FIGURES, TABLES

Although we have tried to trace and contact copyright holders before publication, in some cases this has not been possible. If contacted we will be pleased to rectify any errors or omissions at the earliest opportunity.

SELECTED ABBREVIATIONS

AFL	American Federation of Labor
AI	Amnesty International
ANC	African National Congress
APEC	Asia–Pacific Economic Cooperation
ASEAN	Association of South East Asian Nations
ASH	Action on Smoking and Health
BA	bureaucratic authoritarianism
BIAC	Business and Industry Advisory Committee
BR	biotechnology revolution
CAD/CAM	computer aided design/manufacturing
CBI	Confederation of British Industry
CDI	Comecon direct investment
CEDAW	Convention on the Elimination of All Forms of Discrimination Against Women
CEO	chief executive officer
CIS	Commonwealth of Independent States
Comecon	Council for Mutual Economic Cooperation
COMESA	Common Market for Southern and Eastern Africa
DPC	Dabhol Power Company
ELI	export-led industrialization
EOZ	export-oriented zone
EPZ	export processing zone
ERT	European Round Table
ESR	economic and social rights
FAO	Food and Agriculture Organization
FDI	foreign direct investment
FG500	*Fortune* Global 500
FIVIMS	Food Insecurity Vulnerability Information Mapping Systems
FW	First World
G7	group of seven
GATT	General Agreement on Tariffs and Trade
GDI	Gender Development Index
GEM	Gender Empowerment Measure
GM	genetically modified
GNI	gross national income
GNP	gross national product

GR	green revolution
HDI	Human Development Index
HPI-1	Human Poverty Index (developing countries)
HPI-2	Human Poverty Index (industrialized countries)
ICC	International Covenant on Civil and Political Rights
ICE	International Covenant on Economic, Social and Cultural Rights
ICFTU	International Confederation of Free Trade Unions
ILO	International Labour Organization
IMF	International Monetary Fund
INGO	international non-governmental organization
ISI	import substitution industrialization
IT	information technology
JC	*Journal of Communication*
LETS	Local Exchange Trading System
MAI	Multilateral Agreement on Investment
MSAN	most seriously affected nation
NAFTA	North American Free Trade Agreement
NAM	Non-aligned Movement
NATO	North Atlantic Treaty Organization
NGO	non-governmental organization
NIC	newly industrializing country
NIDL	New International Division of Labour
NSM	new social movement
NSW	New Second World
OECD	Organization for Economic Cooperation and Development
OPEC	Organization of Petroleum Exporting Countries
P-CC	producer-consumer co-operative
PRC	People's Republic of China
SADC	Southern Africa Development Council
SAP	structural adjustment programme
SEZ	special economic zone
SLORC	State Law and Order Restoration Council
SOE	state-owned enterprise
TCC	transnational capitalist class
TCS	*Theory, Culture and Society*
TIE	Transnational Information Exchange
TNAA	transnational advertising agencies
TNC	transnational corporation
TNP	transnational practices
TRIPS	trade-related intellectual property rights
TW	Third World

UN	United Nations
UNCTAD	United Nations Conference on Trade and Development
UNCED	United Nations Conference on Environment and Development
UNHCR	United Nations High Commissioner for Refugees
UNCTC	United Nations Centre on Transnational Corporations
UNDP	United Nations Development Programme
UNESCO	United Nations Educational, Scientific and Cultural Organization
UNRISD	United Nations Research Institute for Social Development
USAID	United States Agency for International Development
USCIB	United States Council for International Business
USDA	United States Department of Agriculture
USSR	Union of Socialist Soviet Republics
USTR	United States Trade Representative
VALCO	Volta Aluminium Company
WCTH	World Conference on Tobacco and Health
WDI	World Development Indicators
WFTU	World Federation of Trade Unions
WHO	World Health Organization
WTO	World Trade Organization

Chapter 1

INTRODUCTION

THE PROBLEM OF GLOBALIZATION

When the first edition of *Sociology of the Global System* was published at the end of 1990 globalization was a relatively new and controversial idea in academia and in the advanced echelons of the corporate elite. Now globalization has become the focus of intense intellectual debate and political struggle all over the world. The approach to globalization that I put forward in 1990 argued that there was one dominant global system structured around the transnational corporations, a transnational capitalist class and the culture-ideology of consumerism. In the early 1990s it was not clear to everyone that this apparently one-sided conception of globalization was the most fruitful approach to take. However, by the beginning of the twenty-first century, in the aftermath of the battle of Seattle and many other challenges to capitalist hegemony, it is difficult to deny the centrality of the struggle between the forces for and against capitalist globalization.

The changes in the title and the focus of this book are acknowledgements that the decade of the 1990s was decisive for the ongoing theory and practice of globalization and a prediction that the first decade of the twenty-first century will see the flowering of alternative non-capitalist forms of globalization. Many writers proclaimed that the collapse of the Soviet Union signalled the triumph of capitalism in its world historic struggle with communism. But as the 1990s unfolded, it became more and more obvious that for the time being one specific version of capitalism, namely global capitalism, had triumphed against one specific version of communism, Stalinism. As Singer commented: 'The Year 1989, with the East European regimes tumbling in quick succession, could have been greeted as a sign that people do count and that obsolete systems are, ultimately, swept away. Instead it was hailed, illogically, as proof that our system will go on for ever' (Singer 1999: 1). Despite intense illogical efforts to prove that there is no viable alternative to capitalist globalization, many people resisted the appropriation of globalization by what I term the transnational capitalist class.

Competing alternative global systems, organized across borders and challenging capitalist globalization, have been theorized and researched in a rich body of writings within the various but converging frameworks of transnational social movements, transnational advocacy networks, and transnationalism from below. The argument of this book is that as the dominance of the capitalist global system spreads and deepens, these spreadings and deepenings simultaneously sow the seeds of the transformations of the dominant system by providing resources, forms of organizational capacities, and clarity of purpose for competing forms of globalization. While there are many ways to express this dialectic, the theme of the globalization of human rights within an emerging socialist form of globalization seems to me to be the most powerful and most accurate representation of the central world-historical direction of change. Movements for human rights focused on democracy, community, gender, ethnicity, religion, education, age, ecology, disability, sexuality, and more, have all been nurtured and undermined by capitalist globalization. The struggle for economic human rights by socialists of different types has taken the movements for the more traditional forms of human rights into new, globalizing spheres that directly challenge global capitalism. I focus on the two most serious crises of capitalist globalization—class polarization and ecological unsustainability (introduced in Chapter 3)—precisely because they directly undermine these human rights. This book tries to explain how and why this happens and to suggest some outcomes of the struggles against these crises, outcomes that provide alternatives to capitalist globalization.

GLOBALIZATION AND EVERYDAY LIFE

The study of globalization appears rather abstract and 'out there' rather than part of our daily lives. This is not surprising and, indeed, is a fundamental part of the problem and salience of globalization for an understanding of some of the determining circumstances under which we live. This is the reason why it is important to think about both the subjective and the objective sides of globalization. These are not two separate issues, but merely two perspectives on the same phenomenon. The subjective side looks at globalization from the point of view of the individual whose life is affected by globalization and whose own decisions (for example, media use, job situation, voting behaviour, consumption choices) in their turn play a part in affecting the structures of globalization; the objective side starts from the forces of globalization themselves (mass media corporations, global economic forces, institutions that structure politics, global marketing) and how they create and condition opportunities for individual choice for different groups of people. It is, frankly, silly to suggest (as some of the agency-versus-structure debates in sociology have done) that we have to chose one or the other. We obviously have to consider both. However, there are serious methodological and other problems in the social sciences in general and in globalization research in particular, when we do try to study empirically both the subjective and the objective sides of the question, rather than simply theorize speculatively about it (which is also necessary).

Many people who are sympathetic to the idea of globalization find most accounts of it excessively structuralist and abstract, focusing on impersonal global forces against which the individual has no say. This is exemplified in the declining influence of Wallerstein's world-system theory, with its obvious globalizing tendencies from the outside and the current popularity of a more reflexive approach to globalization, encapsulated in the idea of globalization as reflexive modernity. On this view, globalization involves 'emergent forms of world interdependence and planetary consciousness' (Giddens 1990: 175). Apart from presenting serious problems of methodology, the assertion that there are emergent forms of world interdependence and planetary consciousness is as yet misconceived for most of the world's people. Watching soap operas like *Neighbours* or *Friends* or *Oshin* or cheering on a team as you watch the World Cup on TV in a village or shanty town or global city does not necessarily mean that the individual viewer has planetary consciousness, whatever that is. What it does mean, however, is that when the viewer actually starts to become conscious of the global prestige of the lifestyles these media events embody and desires and eventually buys products displayed, then an objective relationship is established with the transnational corporations, the core of the capitalist global system. Whether or not any given individual or group has planetary consciousness or consciousness of the global whole is an open empirical question, though not one which many theorists of globalization have actually studied empirically.[1] The findings of studies on this question would help to evaluate the validity of the idea that the best way to study globalization is through cultural forms (an approach I criticize in a subsequent chapter). Perhaps some people would recognize and confirm such consciousness in some contexts and on some occasions (when the media are full of some global issue) but not in other contexts and at other times. This would be very interesting to research and would, of course, tell us much about the subjective side of globalization. But we cannot assume the existence of such consciousness and we certainly cannot assume it exists just because millions of people watch similar TV programmes and adverts, idealize the same stars, and buy the same products all over the world. Objective facts on media use, name recognition of celebrities, and global sales are in the public record.[2] These are what the objective side of globalization is about, and they do not depend for their validity on anyone's global consciousness.

The approach of this book, in contrast to the idealist slant of concepts like global consciousness, is more decidedly materialist.

CAPITALIST GLOBALIZATION

With few exceptions social scientists have not yet come to regard the whole world as a legitimate object of knowledge. There are very good reasons for this. The study of even a single society is considered to be extraordinarily difficult because of the complexity of social relations and the obvious problems of trying to generalize about people, their groupings, and the structures within which they act.

Comparative sociology, politics, anthropology, international relations, and so on are supposed to generate universal propositions on the basis of systematic comparisons of a variety of different societies, and so they might have been expected to stimulate thinking about global systems. In fact the opposite happened. Because of the obsession of most comparativists with problems of measurement, all sight of global systems was lost in the mists of dubious generalization about a host of discrete variables from societies whose only conceptual connection was that someone (often a foreign observer) had produced facts or numbers about one phenomenon that could be correlated with facts or numbers from other societies purporting to be about the same phenomenon. This drew attention away from the whole and focused it on the part, as all empiricist research tends to do. So the social sciences groan under the weight of occupational, educational, demographic, gender, ethnic, and many more categories of data collected cross-culturally, but offering little if any insight into global systems as such.

Does any global system really exist? Like all ideas it exists in the minds of people who think it, but it is further from the world of everyday immediate experience than other ideas such as power or friendship. Some ideas are found to have or are intended to have no scientific validity at all. The point of this book is to demonstrate that the concept of global systems does have genuine scientific validity and, indeed, that it is increasingly necessary for the analysis of a growing number of rapidly changing phenomena. Naturally, people who chose to ignore these phenomena will have no need for the idea (just as those who choose to ignore societal phenomena have no need for an idea of society) but in both cases this leads to a dramatic impoverishment of their views of the real world.

As globalization has come to be identified in the minds of most people with the capitalist system, it is necessary to make the basic distinction between globalization as a generic term, and various forms of globalization, notably capitalist globalization, the critical object of this book, and socialist globalization, the dialectical subject of this book. It is not difficult to understand why globalization and capitalist globalization (and the global system and the capitalist global system) have been identified and confused. The rise of massive globalizing corporations, the rapid spread of so-called free trade, the oft-cited weakening of states and governments, the penetration of mass media (promoting what I have termed the culture-ideology of consumerism) to all corners of the globe, and the denationalization and privatization of former state monopolies have all been seen as consequences of capitalist globalization and the powers of a capitalist global system that began to emerge fully in the second half of the twentieth century. Figure 1.1, from *The Economist* magazine (a leading proponent of capitalist globalization) illustrates the assurance and control of the capitalist class at the end of the twentieth century. The dominance and sheer productive might of capitalist globalization, even though it was not frequently identified as such, deflected theoretical and empirical attention away from possibilities of other types of globalization. In particular, when the Soviet Union and its empire in Eastern Europe collapsed around 1990 (see Chapter 8 below), the prospect for anything remotely like socialist globalization was out of the question. The decade of the 1990s proved decisive in at least one respect. The capitalist triumphalism that

Figure 1.1 Global issues mastered every week
Source: promotional circular © *The Economist* Newspaper Limited, London.

immediately followed the end of the Soviet Union was extremely short-lived, and by the end of the twentieth century an anti-globalization movement (or, more accurately, a dynamic network of anti-capitalist movements and organizations) had emerged as an active opponent of capitalist globalization.

The collapse of Stalinism paradoxically highlighted the fact that the two main crises of capitalist globalization—class polarization and ecological unsustainability—could never be solved. The confusion between globalization and capitalist globalization (its historically contingent dominant form) understandably helped to create an anti-globalization movement. The central task of this book is to demonstrate that capitalist globalization is an historical form but not the only possible viable form of globalization. My own conception of socialist globalization is an attempt to make globalization a dialectical subject, a subject that can be created through theory and practice. The first stage of this process is to theorize capitalist globalization as a critical object. The second stage is to theorize the socialist alternative (see Chapter 11 below). As we are presently living within an inter-state system, it is necessary to begin with an analysis of the relationships between globalization as such, capitalist globalization, and the state system.

GLOBALIZATION, CAPITALIST GLOBALIZATION, AND THE STATE SYSTEM

What, then, does the idea (or concept, or abstraction) of globalization refer to? Because the world is divided into nominally sovereign states, some with relatively clear and unified national cultures, these states are usually identified as the basic elements of global systems. State-centrism, thus, is the framework for analysing the world in terms of the state system. Globalization, on the other hand, is the framework for analysing the world in terms of the global system. The state-centrist analysis of state systems is what the thriving academic discipline of International Relations tends to do. Nevertheless, even here the notion that there are some important international relations that are not necessarily between states is generally accepted.[3] This was the position of John Burton, an influential figure in the creation of the modern discipline of International Relations. In a series of books from the 1960s he searched for a theory of world society. Burton (1972: 19, 20) argued: 'We are choosing an approach when we choose to speak of world society and not inter-national relations' and that studies based on states 'cannot give us that understanding we seek of world society' either within or between states. What he labels the billiard-ball model only recognizes governmental interaction. Historically, world society has become a believable idea only in the last few hundred years, and science, technology, industry, and universal values are creating a world that is different from any past age. The geographical image of states must be replaced by the behavioural image of systems. However, for Burton, 'world society appears to be at a transition stage at which it is neither a world comprising only of states, nor a world comprising only systems' (p. 51).

Burton's approach pays little attention to such problems as the globalization of capital, class struggle, or ideology, and he often appears to confuse society and system at both the descriptive and the conceptual levels. This is a consequence of the primacy he gives to communications over power. Nevertheless, his attempt to move International Relations from the study of relations between nations to the study of world society (leaving aside the essential vagueness of this latter idea), did represent a progressive problem shift for all those interested in transnational as well as international relations.

In parallel but quite independent of Burton, other scholars began to make an explicit attempt to replace the state-centric model with a transnational relations model, focused more on transnational interactions and organizations. In an important collection of essays, Keohane and Nye disclosed that they began to think along these lines under the influence of the sociologist Raymond Aron, whose book *Peace and War*, translated in 1966, introduced the idea of transnational society. They found this unsatisfactory because 'it did not direct attention to governmental manipulation of transnational relations . . . [and they have] grown progressively more interested in the interaction between governments and transnational society and in transnational coalitions among subunits of governments' (Keohane and Nye 1973: p. vii).

The transnational relations approach, therefore, is not a specific theory but more of an injunction to researchers to pay more attention to non-governmental entities, particularly when they are interacting with governments. This is an important point but, as with Burton's world society, there is an essential vagueness about the central concept, transnational relations. One consequence of this is that no systematic research programme has resulted from this approach. Its eclecticism is what attracts many scholars. The proponents of the transnational relations approach have a tendency to analyse interactions within systems rather than effects of practices and though they claim to be transcending the state-centric model, they more often than not permit the state to set the agenda for them. This is because, for the most part, they conceptualize the state and its agencies as by far the most important actors in the global system. In this they may or may not be correct, empirically, and they may or may not be theorizing in the most fruitful manner, but the very structure of the approach suggests an ambiguity about this key issue. And this persists in the work of political scientists, sociologists, and others who have been impressed by the approach.[4]

Of particular interest for the argument here are various attempts to theorize the relations between transnational corporations and states (Strange 1996) and state and class (notably Cox 1987). The work of Cox provided the impetus for what became known as the Gramscian turn in International Relations (see Gill 1993). Nevertheless, state-centrism is still the norm in International Relations, International Political Economy, and macro-sociology though, as works like Strange (1996), Wade (1990), and Evans (1995) indicate, the distinction between the powers of the state and what the state actually does is of prime importance. All states can and most do legislate in a wide variety of spheres. As we shall see in Chapter 3 most theorists of globalization argue that the powers of states have been limited to a greater or lesser extent by forces that they cannot or will not control. The difference between cannot and will not is central to my concept of the relations between class and state. For example, theorists of the Third Way assume that governments cannot do much about globalization but they are quite optimistic about their ability to lessen the shocks of it for those most seriously affected (Giddens 2000). The theory of the transnational capitalist class argues, on the contrary, that globalizing elements in governments and bureaucracies who are members of the transnational capitalist class (TCC) are complicit in capitalist globalization (Sklair 2001). On this analysis, often governments will go along with globalization not because they cannot resist it but because they perceive it to be in their own interests.

In order to avoid the confusion that persists in most of the literature, for example in the otherwise very useful collections of readings on globalization edited by Jameson and

Miyoshi (1998) and Lechner and Boli (2000), I distinguish between *inter-national*, *trans-national*, and *globalist* approaches to globalization. These distinctions signal the differences between the state-centrist conception of an inter-national system based on states, the transnational conception of global systems based on globalizing forces and institutions, and the globalist conception of global systems based on an already more or less completed global project. The approach of this book, global systems theory, represents a dialectical synthesis in the attempt to transcend the contradictions of a state-centrism that fails to recognize the global, and a globalism that fails to recognize the persistence of states. The global, therefore, is an aspiration rather than a completed project and while there are few forces or institutions or phenomena that can be said to be genuinely global, there are increasing numbers that are globalizing. As I have argued in a parallel project, major transnational corporations are the most important and most powerful globalizing institutions in the world today and by virtue of this fact they make the capitalist global system the dominant global system (Sklair 2001).

Classical Marxists refuse to accept, either empirically or theoretically, that the state is the most important actor in the global system. For Marxists, the global system is the capitalist global system, and the most important actors are members of the capitalist class in the most powerful states. In practice, however, most contemporary Marxism is state-centrist to a greater or lesser extent. This is illustrated by the debates about the relative autonomy of the state. Few Marxists now hold to the traditional claim that the state is nothing but the executive committee of the bourgeoisie. Apparent contradictions between state actions and the interests of the capitalist class can be explained in terms of the struggles of the competing fractions of the bourgeoisie and the bureaucracy. Neo-Marxists have gone much further and claim that in advanced capitalist societies the state and its various bureaucracies have distinctive levels of relative autonomy from the different fractions of the bourgeoisie. Theoretical innovations such as corporatism and regulation theory open up the possibility that state functionaries can successfully play off one section of the bourgeoisie (as well as competing classes) against others, domestically or transnationally, in their own interests. These are all empirically observable phenomena in states all over the world and when they occur it seems obvious that extreme globalists are mistaken in their belief that the state is dead or that it is about to disappear. To this extent, the globalist approach to globalization is not convincing.

Where a country is largely isolated from the rest of the world, the state-centrist approach does seem more plausible than for countries located within an identifiable system of global relationships. Nevertheless, state-centrists, transnational relations advocates, and Marxists of several persuasions, while acknowledging the growing importance of the global system in one form or another, all continue to prioritize the system of nation-states; they all fall back on it to describe what happens in the world, and to explain how and why it happens. The renaissance of historical sociology in the 1970s, for example, was largely powered by the idea of bringing the state back in (see Evans *et al.* 1985), though it is doubtful that it was ever outside the main frames of reference in twentieth-century social science. My argument for the transnational approach to globalization is that state-centrism, in whatever form, takes us quite far but not far enough.

TRANSNATIONAL PRACTICES

The argument of this book is that we need to move to what we can term global systems theory if we are to understand the contemporary world and explain what is happening in it. We cannot ignore the nation-state, but this book attempts to offer in addition a conception of globalization based on transnational practices (TNPs).[5] Globalization, therefore, is defined as a particular way of organizing social life across existing state borders. Research on small communities, global cities, border regions, groups of states, and virtual and mobile communities of various types provides strong evidence that existing territorial borders are becoming less important and that transnational practices are becoming more important. The balance of power between state and non-state actors and agencies is changing. This is what is meant by the transnational approach to globalization.

TNPs are analytically distinguished on three levels, economic, political, and culture-ideology, what I take to constitute the sociological totality. In the concrete conditions of the world as it is, a world largely structured by global capitalism, each of these TNPs is typically, but not exclusively, characterized by a major institutional form. The transnational corporation (TNC) is the major locus of transnational economic practices; the transnational capitalist class is the major locus of transnational political practices; and the major locus of transnational culture-ideology practices is to be found in the culture-ideology of consumerism. Not all culture is ideological, even in capitalist societies. The reason why I run culture and ideology together is that consumerism in the global system can only be fully understood as a culture-ideology practice. When we buy something that has been imported we are engaged in a typical economic transnational practice. When we are influenced to vote or support a cause by those whose interests are transnational we are engaged in a typical political transnational practice. When a global brand establishes a set of meanings for us and our friends and many others we do not know personally, we are engaged in a typical culture-ideology transnational practice.

The TNPs make sense only in the context of a global system. Global systems theory based on transnational practices is an attempt to escape from the limitations of state-centrism and to avoid the exaggerations of globalism. In order to do this, it is necessary to spell out exactly what these limitations and exaggerations are. The capitalist global system is marked by a very great asymmetry. The most important economic, political, and culture-ideology goods that circulate around the world tend to be owned and/or controlled by small groups in a relatively small number of places, mainly in and around global cities. Until recently it was both convenient and accurate to use the term Western to describe this asymmetry, and the idea of Western imperialism was widely acknowledged as a way of analysing the global system. Other terms, such as superpower, the triad of centre, semi-periphery, and periphery states, and hegemon state are also common. However, these terms appear to be losing their theoretical point as globalization threatens to displace state-centrism as the most fruitful approach for analysing the world today.[6]

Nevertheless, the inter-state system has been the spatial reference point for most of the crucial transnational practices that go to make up the structures of the global system, in the sense that transnational practices intersect in particular places and these places usually come under the jurisdiction of particular nation-states. But it is not the only reference point, and some argue that it can distort the ways we try to understand the world today (Strange 1996, Sklair 2001). The argument of this book is that the most important global force at the beginning of the twenty-first century is the capitalist global system. Transnational corporations provide the material base for a transnational capitalist class that unquestionably dictates economic transnational practices, and is the most important single force in the struggle to dominate political and culture-ideology transnational practices. There are several other systems, regionally important, ethnically, culturally, and/or theologically based but none has, as yet, dominated the global system as capitalism did in the twentieth century. Resistances to capitalism, particularly in the form of radical social movements, have been and continue to be numerous and influential, though few offer genuine alternatives to capitalist society and none has had the pervasive success in state-building or the creation of institutions that capitalism enjoyed in the twentieth century. As I shall argue in the latter part of this book, this phase may be coming to an end.

The success of historical systems is often bound up with the success of the states that are their dominant powers. Britain in the nineteenth century was the leading power of the imperialist system, and the United States of America in the twentieth century was the leading power of the international capitalist system. Through their (respective) imperialist and neo-imperialist trajectories the ruling classes of these two countries etched the forms of home-grown capitalism onto what has become the capitalist global system. Mighty domestic economies, progressive ruling classes (in comparison with most others actually existing), and at least some desirable culture-ideology features particularly attractive to modernizing elites were combined with the willingness to use military force to open doors to them all over the world. This ensured the creation, persistence, and often aggrandisement of dominant social classes everywhere willing and eager to adopt their ways.

These dominant classes provided many members of what was to become the transnational capitalist class. The TCC consists of those people who see their own interests and/or the interests of their social and/or ethnic group, often transformed into an imagined national interest, as best served by an identification with the interests of the capitalist global system. In particular, the interests of those who own and control the major transnational corporations dictated the interests of the system as a whole. The fundamental in-built instability of the capitalist global system, and the most important contradiction with which any theory of the global system has to grapple, is that the dominant ideology of the system is under constant challenge. The substantive content of the theory, how those who own and control the transnational corporations harness the transnational capitalist class to solidify their hegemonic control of consumerist culture and ideology, is the site of the many struggles for the global system. Who will win and who will lose these struggles is not a foregone conclusion.

The role of elites in Britain and the USA in the history of capitalism and the very existence of the TCC that the capitalist classes in Britain, the USA, and other places helped create, have historically built in the asymmetries and inequalities that now characterize capitalist globalization. Just as the leaders of dominant states (whether acting directly in the interests of the capitalist class or not) can call on superior economic, political, and culture-ideology resources in their dealings with those who challenge their interests, the transnational capitalist class enjoys similar dominance. The transnational approach to globalization that provides the framework for this book, therefore, is an attempt to replace the state-centrist paradigm of the social sciences with a paradigm of transnational practices, practices that cross state borders but do not originate with state actors, agencies, or institutions. It is not the state as such that drives globalization, but the transnational capitalist class (the institutional focus of political TNPs). The state, as we shall see, has a place in the transnational capitalist class via globalizing bureaucrats, politicians, and professionals. This class derives its material base from the transnational corporations (the institutional focus of economic TNPs) and the value-system of the culture-ideology of consumerism (culture-ideology TNPs).

STRUCTURE OF THE BOOK

This book is intended to serve both as an introduction to the study of globalization and as a more detailed statement of the transnational practices approach to globalization. In this chapter I have attempted to provide a general introduction to what globalization is all about and to persuade you that there is some merit (as well as many dangers) in taking a distinctive and focused view of globalization rather than, as so many writers do, simply assuming that everything comes under this vast conceptual umbrella. Chapter 2, 'Thinking about the Global', pursues this idea and shows how difficult it is to think about the whole world, through an analysis of various ways that the global system has been classified. All these classifications have been useful, but none has really been able to cope with the central issue of globalization, namely what is the relationship between globalization (however defined) and the ongoing system of states. Chapter 3 shows how theories of development became embryonic theories of globalization and provided some ideas for what I call the competing conceptions of globalization. This helps to explain why globalization as a field of study is so contentious in terms of the unresolved issues of previous theoretical struggles. Here, my own competing conception of globalization is introduced, and the framework it provides serves as the problematic for the rest of the book. The main implications of my own competing conception of globalization are that (i) capitalist globalization is only one form of globalization, (ii) it is fatally flawed because of the twin crises of class polarization and ecological unsustainability, and (iii) socialist globalization is one viable alternative form of globalization. Here I reverse the conventional discourses of the crisis of communism or socialism, or the crisis of the Third World, crises that only capitalism is said to be able to resolve, by posing the question: why is capitalism always in crisis? The specific crises of capitalist globalization, class polarization and ecological sustainability, are traced back to the contradictions at the heart of globalizing corporations, the transnational capitalist class and the culture-ideology of consumerism. Chapter 4 sets out the substantive implications of the concept of transnational practices, in particular the ways in which economic transnational practices based in TNCs established capitalism as the major force for globalization in the second half of the twentieth century. Chapter 5 extends this analysis through corporations, class, and consumerism. Chapter 6 reflects both my own interest in the sociology of development and the central place of what we can still usefully label the Third World in the study of globalization and the critique of capitalist globalization. 'Transnational Practices in the Third World' shows both the effects of capitalist globalization in Third World countries and the difficulties of the state-centrist analysis of so-called 'developing countries' in the era of capitalist globalization. Chapter 7 explores the culture-ideology of consumerism and the central role of the mass media in capitalist globalization. Chapter 8 deals with communist and post-communist societies in the capitalist global system and Chapter 9 looks in more detail at China, the only non-capitalist society left that could in practical terms resist capitalist globalization. Chapter 10 connects challenges to capitalist globalization with the critique of capitalism through the discourse of crisis. Oppositions crystallized around a multitude of issues: notably protectionism, new social movements, and the Green movement. From these sources an embryonic anti-capitalist and anti-globalization movement has emerged to challenge the transnational capitalist class in its various guises. This leads logically to the question that frames Chapter 11: how will capitalist globalization end? This is a question that requires conceptual and substantive work to provide even the first glimmers of an answer. The globalization of human rights as the foundation for a new form of socialist globalization provides the context for this discussion. The concluding chapter returns to the centrality of the TNCs and the new focus on the globalization of genuine human rights as a counter-hegemonic global system. The book concludes with another voice adding to the rapidly growing minority of those who refuse to accept that there is no alternative to capitalist globalization.

NOTES

1. There is, however, an emerging research literature on the local effects of global processes (Lechner and Boli 2000: part III). For an exemplary empirical study on the middle class in India, see Ganguly-Scrase and Scrase (1999).

2. For copious information on these, and other global forces, see the regular reports from UNESCO, annual reports of media and entertainment corporations, global trade journals, and business magazines. Balnaves *et al.* (2001) is a useful point of departure.

3. International Relations is, of course, an increasingly complex and multi-faceted discipline. These paragraphs attempt only to draw out some sociological implications of developments in this area.

4. For an attempt to resuscitate the transnational relations perspective, see Risse-Kappen (1995). Buzan and Little (2000) claim to offer a new approach to International Relations theory. Despite its many fine qualities, it fails to cope adequately with the challenge of globalization and reproduces many of the problems of international relations without taking us forward to transnational practices or even transnational relations, as Risse-Kappen *et al.* try to do.

5. I use the term practice in the active sense of *praxis* associated with critical theorists of the Frankfurt School, in contrast to the more passive term *relations* used in conventional sociology, political science, International Relations, etc.

6. The book was largely completed before the attacks on New York and Washington on 11 September 2001 and the subsequent 'war against terrorism'. These terrible events make it all the more necessary to think of our world in globalizing rather than state-centrist terms.

Chapter 2
THINKING ABOUT THE GLOBAL

There are no entirely satisfactory terms for comparing countries, societies, or the even more unsatisfactory units of nations or nation-states, as my critique of state-centrism has argued. However, for convenience, I use the purely descriptive terms First World (FW) in comparison with Third World (TW). Two further points should be noted at this stage: (i) the differences between different societies conventionally classified as First World (for example, Sweden and Portugal) and Third World (for example, South Korea and Ethiopia) can be as important as their similarities; and (ii) I have rejected the more common term 'developing societies' for the simple reason that so many TW societies are clearly not developing in many respects, and this formulation begs the question of what they are developing towards.

The main difference between the First World of advanced industrial societies and the Third World of less developed societies commonly revolves around the issue of the level of industrialization and its consequences. For example, the distribution of the labour force between agriculture and industry has always been regarded as an important indicator of economic growth, if not development, precisely because most of the present advanced industrial societies exhibited a marked tendency to reduce their agricultural labour force while increasing their industrial and subsequently their service sector labour force. This is why industrialization is seen to be so important in theories of development.[1] Standard of living is another key measure that distinguishes First World from Third World. Whether measured by per capita GNP or calorific intake or any other indicator, it gives a quick if not always entirely accurate or meaningful basis on which to rank societies.

However obvious and relevant these measures might seem, they are all theory-laden in the sense that they all assume, usually without any argument or justification, a particular theory of economic growth and/or development. I do not make this point to suggest that all these theories are wrong in every detail, but to underline the importance of looking behind the apparently innocent measures on which so much of the literature on development and social change and, now, globalization, which seems to have replaced development as a focus of study, is based (Roberts and Hite 2000). We must know what we are letting ourselves in for, theoretically, when we use such measures. This is far from an argument that we should avoid such measures (let alone empirical research itself) but rather a call for a continual critical assessment of the measures, and for better measures.[2] With this caution in mind, let us turn to the question of how social scientists have classified what we now commonly refer to as the global system.

CLASSIFYING THE GLOBAL SYSTEM

The global system used to be most commonly classified in terms of First, Second, and Third Worlds, and while these are very convenient and for many purposes useful labels, it is certain that they conceal as much as they reveal. The three worlds formula was introduced in the 1950s to distinguish the advanced industrialized countries (First World) from the communist Soviet Union and Eastern Europe (Second World) and the rest, the poorer and relatively unindustrialized, less developed countries (Third World). The attempt to lump together countries that appeared to be at very different stages of development under the umbrella of the Third World was problematic, and when communism was abandoned in Eastern Europe and the former Soviet Union, the rationale for the Second World appeared to have vanished. However, the three worlds formula still has its uses. In this book the postcommunist societies of Eastern Europe and the former Soviet Union will be termed the New Second World (NSW) and where generalizations can usefully be made about the First, Second, and Third Worlds, the labels will be retained. This is clearly both a theoretical and a practical decision: theoretical in that, in terms of the theory of capitalist globalization, the three worlds formula implies that important generalizations can still be made about how the aggregate entities of First, New Second, and Third Worlds relate to the system as a whole; and practical in that for many purposes these categories are useful despite the regional, societal, and local differences they mask. Nevertheless, if we are to begin to describe the global system in a more theoretically fruitful manner we are going to have to look behind these labels. There are at least five main classifications of the global system in current usage and as presently constructed they are all more or less state-centred. These can be roughly characterized as: income-based; trade-based; resource-based; quality of life-based; region and bloc-based.

INCOME-BASED CLASSIFICATIONS

This is the simplest, most widely used, and in some ways the most misleading of the classifications. Economists and economic historians have been interested in measuring poverty and wealth on a per capita basis for some time, and such data has been available for some of the advanced industrial countries for many years. The lack of adequate statistical services in some Third World countries has meant that accurate population numbers, let alone GNP per capita numbers, have not always been available. This situation has been improving since the 1970s, and international agencies have been systematically organizing the collection of such data. From 1978 to 1995 the World Bank published an annual *World Development Report* that included tables on a large number of World Development Indicators, based for the most part on UN and internal World Bank data sources. Since 1996 the Tables have been published annually in a separate volume, *World Development Indicators* (WDI), and many of them can be downloaded from the World Bank website. This is certainly the most useful, easily accessible, and up-to-date compilation of data and it provides the basis for an enormous volume of research on a very wide variety of issues. In 2001, for example, more than 500 Indicators were used to chart change on a variety of development goals. A CD-Rom version of WDI gives access to over 1,000 data tables and 500 time-series indicators for over 200 countries and regions.

The World Bank ranks all the countries of the world according to their GNP per capita,[3] though countries with populations of less than one million (of whom there were 35 in 1988, and 74 with populations of less than 1.5 million or with sparse data in 2000/1) are excluded from the main tables. All World Bank financial data are converted into US dollars and this is, indeed, one serious problem with them as the bank itself has acknowledged. The 1978 Report had 125 countries with GNP per capita figures ranging from the poorest ($70 in Bhutan) to the richest ($15,480 in Kuwait). The countries of the world were divided as follows: low income with GNP per capita up to $250 (34 countries); middle income over $250 per capita (58 countries); industrialized countries (19); capital surplus oil exporters (3); and centrally planned economies, communist countries (11). There were several anomalies in this classification. In the first place, while countries listed from 1 to 92 were in strict GNP per capita order, countries 93, 94, and 95 (South Africa, Ireland, and Italy) all had lower per capita figures than 92 (Israel). No fewer than 14 middle-income countries had higher per capita figures than 'industrialized' South Africa, and five of these were 'richer' than Ireland. Further, the per capita figures for the oil exporters and the centrally planned economies would distribute the countries in these categories fairly widely throughout the list.

By 1983, the categories had changed somewhat, though the anomalies remained. The poorest 34 countries were still identified as low-income economies; the next 60 countries were divided into 39 lower-middle income and 21 upper-middle income economies. Four high income oil exporters, 19 industrial market economies, and 8 Eastern European non-market economies completed the list of 125 countries. The main differences between the 1978 and the 1983 lists were definitional (the splitting up of the middle-income group) and political. South Africa was expelled from the industrial group and relegated to the upper-middle-income group and replaced, incidentally, by Spain, while Taiwan was expelled altogether from the list. The People's Republic of China was integrated into the low-income group as the twenty-first poorest country in the world. The two most populous countries in the world, China and India, were also separated out from the rest of the low-income economies for averaging purposes, as were oil exporters and oil importers in the middle-income economies group.

By 1988 the total number of countries had risen to 129, split into 39 low-income, 34 lower-middle, 24 upper-middle, 4 high-income oil exporters, 19 industrial market, and 9 centrally planned economies, renamed non-reporting non-members (aptly, as there was little information on them outside the demographic and social indicators tables). Again, a certain amount of category switching had taken place. For example, Hungary, Poland, and Romania were inserted into the upper-middle-income group, where their apparent per capita income scores would locate them in any case, whereas Angola, Cuba, and North Korea were transplanted from lower-middle income to non-reporting non-members. Further, all the low- and middle-income groups were also categorized as developing economies subdivided into oil exporters, exporters of manufactures, highly indebted countries, and sub-Saharan Africa (new sub-categories of great ideological significance), for the purposes of averaging.

In 1994, when the dust had begun to settle after the collapse of communism in Eastern Europe and the former Soviet Union, 132 countries in all appeared in the main tables, with another 75 classified separately as other economies for lack of data. In the 1994 Report there were 42 low-income economies, the poorest being Mozambique with a per capita income estimated at $60 per year as against an average of $390 overall. The 67 middle-income countries (46 lower and 21 higher middle) averaged $2,490 per capita, while the 23 higher-income countries averaged $22,160 (the richest country in the world on this criterion was Switzerland with an average per capita income of $36,080).

In 2000, the creation of new states and improvements in data gathering produced a world of 207 economies. There were 64 low-income economies (average per capita income of $775 or less), 55 lower-middle-income economies (up to $2,995), 38 middle-income economies (up to $9,226) and 50 upper-income economies. On the basis of these classifications, it can be concluded that the World Bank appears to have abandoned crude political judgements in presenting inter-country comparisons. It takes its economic classification to the logical state-centrist conclusion of offering a 75 per cent discount on all its many rather expensive publications to those who live in low-income countries, 35 per cent to those in most middle-income countries, and no discount to those in the rest of the world (**worldbank.org/publications**).

However, even if some previous anomalies have disappeared, the assumptions on which it bases its classifications remain. These assumptions are that:

(a) GNP per capita can be determined for all of the countries concerned in such a way that meaningful comparisons can be drawn;

(b) per capita income is an adequate criterion for drawing comparisons;

(c) the 'national' economy is the best unit of analysis.

Economists at the World Bank and elsewhere have laboured hard and long to put international data on a sound footing and the Technical Notes that follow the tables in the Reports are full of acknowledgements of the difficulties of the problems involved. These difficulties, however, are not simply technical in the sense of translating one country's GNP or GNI into terms that will bear comparison with those of other countries, but a matter of political economy, in the sense that some measures best represent some socio-economic systems while they discriminate against, perhaps by undervaluing the products of, other socio-economic systems or classes of people within a system. A glaring example of this is the neglect of the domestically consumed products of farmers (particularly women) in the Third World.

Women's work in the countries of the Third World is generally rendered invisible by normal national accounting procedures because it usually takes place outside the conventional sphere of wage labour, mostly on the family farm and in the home. This invisibility results in serious understatements of the great economic significance of female labour, especially in the production, collection, preparation, and processing of food. Thus, male-dominated organizations, such as national statistical services and the World Bank, undercount the real economic activity of Third World countries (see Boserup 1989, first published in 1970).[4]

It is no accident that the global standard used by the World Bank and most other organizations is the US dollar. It is a simple indication of the facts that the US market is still the biggest in the world (despite the fact that its share of the global economy is in decline) and that the economic activities in which globalizing corporations are mainly involved tend to determine how global economic activity gets measured, that is more often than not in US dollars. Lurking behind these measures, therefore, is a congerie of theories of economic growth and/or development based on the characteristics of capitalist globalization and its main actors.

Income-based classifications of the economies of communities in which the market is not the dominant feature, therefore, are inherently problematic, because where they are used as the basis of inter-country comparisons, which is by far the most common use that is made of them, they predispose the results of such comparisons to certain conclusions which are usually prejudiced by unspoken theory-laden assumptions. However, as long as we are aware of these provisos, and are able to correct the most crass biases at the empirical and conceptual levels, there is clearly a use to which such classifications can be put. For example, the countries of the world can also be split into groups according to population as well as per capita income. The logic behind this is obvious. It is clearly very relevant to an appreciation of the relative levels of economic growth and development within and between countries to know how many people the social product, however large or small, has to be divided among. The sometimes massive variations between different parts of the same country are also important.[5].

If we correlate population categories (1 to 20 million, 20 to 50 million, 50 to 100 million, and 100 million plus) with World Bank GNP per capita categories (roughly lower-, middle-, and higher-income countries) around 1990 we find that two-thirds of countries were relatively small (up to about 20 million in population) and two-thirds of these were quite poor (GNP per capita of less than $1,500). Almost half of the relatively rich countries (GNP per capita of more than $8,000) had relatively large populations (over 50 million). The only real conclusion that we can draw from such an exercise is that there appears to be no simple relationship between population and the wealth of a country, which might give a little pause to those who dogmatically believe that poverty is a direct consequence of 'overpopulation'.

Average GNP per capita measures also obscure the fact that often differences within countries are just as important as differences between them, a key tenet of global system theory. While the World Bank tries to build in some measures of income and wealth distribution within countries, such data is hard to come by and not always very reliable. This issue is further discussed in the section on quality of life below.

TRADE-BASED CLASSIFICATIONS

Though clearly important, income and population size are not the only important characteristics of communities and countries. The structure of the economy and society can be broken down in a variety of ways for a variety of purposes. Those who investigated the factors that accompanied economic growth and development in the second half of the twentieth century often looked to the historical experiences of the contemporary advanced industrial societies for clues, and they generally found that patterns of foreign trade were very important. Aaronson (2001) makes the connection between trade and the American dream, and this has been generalized worldwide through the neo-liberal dictum that trade is always good and that it always raises the standard of living of everyone involved. Rosen (2002), in her study of trade policy and the apparel industry in the USA, shows how it has produced winners (apparel manufacturers) and losers (workers in sweatshops). These issues are certainly controversial, and challenges to neo-liberal trade policy make up a large part of the anti-globalization argument (Hines 2000, Starr 2000).

The history of capitalist expansion is bound up with the fact that capitalists from the First World imported raw materials from the Third World and exported manufactured goods and capital. The so-called terms of trade, more accurately labelled unequal exchange, ensured that for the most part the prices of raw materials fell relative to the prices of manufactured goods. A further important feature of this system of trade was that while those companies exporting manufactured goods (mainly based in First World countries) were often involved in many diverse lines of business, the raw materials exporters often specialized in one or two major staples. Mono-crop economies are particularly vulnerable to instabilities in the world market directed not by some hidden hand, but by the actions of profit-maximizing capitalists mostly based in First World countries and often acting in unison through cartels. Despite fluctuations, the prices paid to producers in the Third World for most commodities have declined since the 1980s, notably for coffee, cocoa, cotton, tea, sugar, and rubber, as Table 2.1 shows.

Since the 1950s, world trade has been regulated informally by international bodies representing the governments of the most economically important countries. Formally, the system has been regulated by the General Agreement on Tariffs and Trade (GATT), in a contentious series of negotiating rounds in which the poor countries of the Third World generally considered themselves to have been badly treated by the rich countries of the First World (see Brown 1993: ch. 7). In April 1994, 125 governments signed a global trade treaty in Morocco to set up the World Trade Organization (WTO) to replace GATT in 1995. WTO has accelerated the pressures to liberalize trade in goods and services and to protect intellectual property rights. It has tougher dispute-settlement powers than GATT and there is no single country veto power in WTO. In the view of a scholar-enthusiast: 'Technology had unmasked the failure of socialism . . . the sterile debate between North and South, between rich and poor, long sustained by East–West rivalry, had already become empty as country after country in the South embraced market-based policies and accepted the utility of multilateral rules to reinforce them' (Hart 1997: 75–6). Hart quotes the words of Renato Ruggiero, Director-General of WTO in his address to the first ministerial meeting in Singapore: 'a world trading system which has the support of a knowledgeable and engaged global community will be in a far stronger position to manage the

Table 2.1 Primary commodity prices in 1990 $US (1980, 1990, 2000)

Type of commodity	1980	1990	2000
Coffee, robusta (cents/kg)	450	118	90
Coffee, Arabica (cents/kg)	481	197	190
Cocoa (cents/kg)	362	127	90
Cotton (cents/kg)	284	182	129
Tea, average, 3 auctions	230	206	186
Tobacco ($/mt)	3,161	3,392	2,960
Sugar (cents/kg)	88	28	18
Rubber (cents/kg)	198	86	68
Bananas ($/mt)	526	541	420
Oranges ($/mt)	542	531	360

Note: mt = metric tons.   *Source*: data compiled from World Bank (2001: table 6.4).

forces of globalization for everyone's benefit' (ibid.: 77, n. 1). As we shall see below, this optimism was quickly dissipated, but the hold of the major TNCs on world trade seems unlikely to be weakened.[6]

Even those writers who specifically warned against using the historical experiences of contemporary rich countries as a guide for the Third World could not resist drawing some conclusions from the realm of foreign trade. It seemed very obvious, first of all, that a country does not get rich by importing manufactured goods if it can possibly manufacture them itself. This truism was elevated to the status of a theory of and a strategy for development, particularly in Latin America, and became known as import substitution industrialization (ISI). But though they no longer imported some categories of finished products, many Third World manufacturers found they were importing the components, materials, and technology for these products instead. When ISI began to fail, or at least brought with it as many problems as it was solving, a new theory and strategy began to emerge based not on imports but on exports. The idea behind this was the mirror image of ISI. What had enriched the rich was not their insulation from imports (rich countries do, in fact, import huge amounts) but their success in manufactured exports, where higher prices could be commanded than for Third World raw materials. This thinking led to the theory and strategy of export-led industrialization (ELI).

ISI and ELI have been used as complementary and contradictory developmental strategies (see Gereffi and Wyman 1990). Let it suffice to say, at this point, notwithstanding the criticisms that have been made of the assumptions on which both ISI and ELI theories are based, export–import structure is now a key characteristic of the economic growth and by implication developmental prospects of all countries. That this should be so is not simply a matter of cognitive theory choice, but also a matter of the economic, political, and culture-ideology interests of theoreticians and practical actors all over the world. This is not entirely unconnected to another feature of the economies of many Third World countries that has become of great salience in recent years, namely their foreign debt and the effect that servicing the debt, particularly in times of unpredictable interest rates, has on economic and social planning (Dent and Peters 1999).

RESOURCE-BASED CLASSIFICATIONS

No country in the world is entirely self-sufficient in all the materials it uses. Even the largest and most richly resource-endowed countries, such as the USA and China, must import some raw materials, for example, oil and rare metals. The USA is particularly vulnerable in this respect, both because it has little of some crucial resources, and because its vast productive machine uses so much of everything. In a book significantly entitled *American Multinationals and American Interests*, Bergson and his colleagues worked out the percentage of key minerals and metals supplied by imports in 1976. The list included columbium, sheet mica, strontium (100 per cent); manganese, cobalt, tantalum, chromium (90 per cent +); asbestos, aluminum, fluorine, bismuth, platinum (80 per cent +); and tin, mercury, nickel (70 per cent +). It is no wonder that the USA keeps such a large navy patrolling the trade routes of the world (Bergson *et al.* 1978: table 5–1). During the 1990s the USA and Japan both consumed more than they produced of aluminium, cadmium, copper, lead, mercury, nickel, tin, zinc, and iron ore (World Resources Institute and USA National Mining Association data). In 1998 the US imported 16% of its copper, 25 per cent of its aluminium, 18 per cent of its steel, and 15 per cent of its natural gas (Ciccantell 2001: table 4). Though it is the most resource-rich economy in the world, because it is so productive over such a wide variety of products the USA is still resource-dependent to an appreciable degree.[7]

The list leaves out what is the single most important import for the USA and many other countries, namely oil. Gail reported that a Gallup Poll in May 1978 showed that 40 per cent of Americans did not know that the USA imported oil at all, and that hardly any of them knew that it imported about half its crude oil and refined products at that time. Knowledge on the issue was increased by the Iranian hostage crisis in 1979–80 and the Gulf War in 1990. However, in the twenty-first century as in the twentieth century the fact remains that the 'U.S. economy is now absolutely dependent on imported oil' (Gail 1978: 18). Since 1990, the USA has imported between 40 and 50 per cent of its oil, though it now imports relatively less oil from the Gulf and more from Canada, Mexico, and other sources (Ciccantell 2001). The proportion of imports in total commercial energy use in the USA rose from about 14 per cent in 1990 to over 20 per cent by the end of the decade. This is largely because the per capita use of energy in the USA rose from about 7,700 kg. of oil equivalent in 1990 to over 8,000 in 1997 and in that period carbon dioxide emissions also rose from 19.3 to 20 metric tons per person (World Bank 2001: table 10)

Geological chance put massive reserves of oil within the boundaries of some barren and desolate desert kingdoms and political will has, through the organized power of OPEC, turned some of their rulers into the richest men in the world and their oil companies into major globalizing TNCs (Al-Moneef 1999). However important the possession of oil is for a country, the cases of Nigeria, Mexico, and Egypt demonstrate that oil alone is no guarantee of general prosperity;[8] the effect of having to rely on imported oil is of great significance for development. So clear did this become after the 1974 oil crisis, when the upward spiral of oil prices began, that international agencies invented a new category of country: most seriously affected nations (MSANs), i.e. those countries, mainly in Africa, who could no longer afford to buy oil. Inability to buy oil is widely interpreted to mean inability to sustain even a very low level of industrialization. Development prospects for such countries are extremely bleak.

Oil, natural gas, and coal make up about 75 per cent of global energy consumption, nearer 90 per cent in the oil-importing Third World, though traditional sources such as firewood do not normally figure in such calculations. This is typical. Firewood is a major and usually free source of energy for cooking, heating, and small-scale industry in poor rural communities all over the world and supplies are dwindling. But it is of little commercial potential. While there has been some work on alternative less costly and less environmentally destructive sources of energy, it is nevertheless legitimate to ask why global lenders have flooded the Third World with loans rather than with funds to develop these other sources of energy and why there appears to be so little serious attention paid to such alternatives in the rest of the world. It is also relevant to note that, on average, in 1997 each person in the USA consumed almost double the energy as the average Swede, seventeen times as much as the average Tanzanian, and over forty times as much as the average Bangladeshi (World Bank 2001: table 10). Of course, the average person is not a real person and there are certainly some Tanzanians and Bangladeshis who consume more energy than some Swedes or North Americans, though not many. (The average inhabitant of Singapore consumes even more energy than that of the USA.)

Food is another vital resource, and for the hungry it is infinitely more important than oil. Some countries chose to import food items that they could easily grow for themselves because governments find it commercially advantageous to grow crops for export and to import the food they need where it tends to be less costly relative to their exports. There are few governments that chose to rely on imports of basic cereals (wheat, rice, etc.) if they can avoid it. More or less all the countries in the world that are heavily dependent on cereal imports on a per capita basis are poor countries, or rich countries with relatively little arable land (like Japan).

It would, therefore, be instructive to classify the countries of the world in terms of their oil and cereal resources, as measured by the degree to which they are self-sufficient or seriously dependent on others for their supplies. We must be careful not to speak of oil and cereal needs, which may be very different from consumption. This point is made not in the interests of pedantry, but because it bears directly on the criticisms of current approaches to the global system that lie at the heart of this book. To anticipate the argument a little, consumption patterns of the majority of people (not only in the Third World) are so ill-matched to their needs because both consumption and needs are generally structured by the transnational practices promoted in the interests of those who control the capitalist global system. When we begin to appreciate more clearly and with greater precision how and why so many communities in the world are locked into a global system that is so patently against the interests of the majority of their people, we may find one of the keys to the development puzzle, and a valuable clue as to how capitalist globalization currently works. A resource-based classification of the countries of the world represents a step towards this goal (see Cole, in Norwine and Gonzalez 1988).

QUALITY OF LIFE-BASED CLASSIFICATIONS

The structure of the economy is clearly the basis on which to build a classification of the countries of the world in terms of their economic growth, or lack of it. Development in the global system implies something more. For many years national and international agencies have been collecting data on significant social indicators, and it is now possible, with all the provisos about the nature of the data that I have already made, to make some, albeit rough and preliminary, ranking of the countries of the world on the most widely accepted social and welfare criteria. The point of this exercise is to begin to derive a picture of how economic growth and development, as they have been generally defined, are related. The social welfare indicators that are most commonly agreed to be of relevance here are the degree of literacy, the distribution of health and educational services, the infant mortality rate, and the life expectancy of the population. To this list it would be very desirable to add the distribution of income, housing, consumer durables, and a wide range of human rights, but there is, as yet, not much reliable information available on these for many communities in the poorer parts of the world.

Scholars from various disciplines have been working on these problems since the mid-1940s (see Estes, in Norwine and Gonzalez 1988). The first substantial efforts came from international organizations, particularly United Nations agencies and the OECD. In 1979, Morris published a Physical Quality of Life Index but as this was exclusively based on health and educational criteria, it is of limited utility. In an attempt to extend the scope of quality of life methodology, Estes constructed an Index of Social Progress based on forty-four welfare-relevant social indicators, which includes items normally ignored by economically based measures (like the status of women and children, politics, effects of disasters, cultural diversity, and defence expenditures). The changing distributions between 1970 and 1980 on this Index have been calculated for over 100 countries, with some surprising results. For example, Costa Rica and some of the countries of Eastern Europe ranked higher than the UK and the USA.

Gonzalez (Norwine and Gonzalez 1988: table 4.2) usefully compares four different indexes for a large sample of countries. He finds, not surprisingly, that the two based mainly on economic indicators tend to rank the USA very high (first and second), while the other two more widely based classifications rank it lower (sixth and twenty-fourth). This is clearly a very controversial question, and it has been much discussed in the context of the basic needs approach to development. Basic needs theorists argue that it is more fruitful to stress results rather than inputs in order to measure the adequacy of development policy. For example, life expectancy is a better measure of health services than numbers of people per doctor, and calorie supply per capita actually available for consumption is a better measure of nutrition than total production of food. Thus, the basic needs approach switches attention from 'how much is being produced . . . to what is being produced, in what ways, for whom and with what impact' (Hicks and Streeton 1979: 577).

This approach has been most fruitfully developed by the United Nations Development Programme (UNDP) in its *Human Development Report* (published annually since 1990). The UNDP team began by developing a Human Development Index (HDI) based on three basic indicators, longevity (measured by life expectancy at birth), knowledge (adult literacy and mean years of schooling), and income (real income per capita). This Index was thus wider than the World Bank's single GDP per capita measure and narrower than the other Quality of Life Indexes discussed above. While the HDI certainly had its problems, in terms of the data available it was a significant improvement on previous attempts to begin to measure human development.

During the 1990s further refinements of the HDI were made in two important spheres. First, separate measures of poverty and deprivation were distinguished for developing (HPI-1) and industrialized (HPI-2) countries. The HPI-1 index measures human poverty in developing countries on three criteria of deprivation: longevity (those who do not survive to 40 years of age), knowledge (adult illiteracy rate), and economic provisioning (people lacking access to health services and safe water). For industrialized countries, the HPI-2 index measures deprivation in these three spheres also, but the survival age is 60, the knowledge test is adult functional illiteracy, and the economic test is income poverty. 'The HPI-2 values show that human poverty is not confined to developing countries' (UNDP 2000a: 151).[9] On these measures the USA, UK, and Ireland have double the level of human poverty (around 15 per cent of the population) as do Norway, Sweden, and Denmark. The distinction between income poverty and human poverty (focusing on the lack of human capabilities) has been elaborated further (see UNDP 2000b: esp. ch. 10).

UNDP reports have always recognized intra-country differences. In the early 1990s on average US whites had a slightly higher HDI than all Japanese, US blacks scored much lower, on a par with all in Trinidad and Tobago, and US hispanics scored even lower, about the same as Estonians. Gender differences were also found to be substantial. US white females scored highest on HDI, followed closely by white males, with black females some way behind and black males behind them. Significant disparities were also found between the separate states in India and Mexico and so on (UNDP 1993: 17–19 and *passim*). Findings like these led to the introduction of the Gender Development Index (GDI) and Gender Empowerment Measure (GEM) in 1995. In the 2000 Report substantial differences were also recorded between rural and urban areas (for example in Uganda), between regions (in China, see also Chapter 9 below), and between language and ethnic groups (in Guatemala, South Africa, India, and Namibia). It was reported that some developing countries (for example, Bahamas, Barbados, Venezuela, Costa Rica, and Mexico) out-performed some industrialized countries (Spain, Portugal, Italy, Greece, and Japan) on measures of gender equality (UNDP 2000*a*: 152–5). These findings confirm that national averages tend to reinforce some misleading stereotypes about our world. The UNDP human development indexes can truly be said to be the first large-scale transnational, as well as inter-national, development ranking system and is therefore of particular value for research on globalization.

As I suggested at the beginning of this discussion on classifying the global system, all measures are theory laden. This is particularly the case for quality of life, because the ways in which quality of life is measured, and specifically the role and definition of basic needs, virtually define our conceptions of development within the global system. As I shall argue below (see Chapter 11), it is now time to replace the welfare capitalist conception of needs with a socialist conception of human rights and responsibilities.

REGION AND BLOC-BASED CLASSIFICATIONS

This type of classification is one that in the early 1990s appeared to be less relevant for the twenty-first century than it had been in the twentieth century. This is the classification based on socio-political blocs and regions. The major economic regions of the world at present are NAFTA (North America), the European Union, Japan (sometimes with, sometimes without the rest of South-East Asia), and China. But first, let us examine the blocs. The main bloc-based classification reflects the economic, political, and culture-ideology struggle between capitalism and communism for control over the global system. So important was it considered to be that the decades since the end of the Second World War until 1990 were commonly referred to as the epoch of the Cold War between capitalism and communism (Halliday 1999).

It is interesting to note that in the 1978 World Bank Report some communist countries were given a special category, centrally planned economies. In the 1983 Report this was changed to Eastern European non-market economies and by 1988 the communist countries were either scattered in the developing economies groups or under the anodyne label of non-reporting non-members. These changes were partly to handle the massive, though poor, People's Republic of China, incorporated into the low-income economies, and the dropping of the geographical reference is a nod of recognition in the direction of the African and Asian and other countries who then claimed to be socialist (very few still do). By the early 1990s ruling groups in all the countries of Eastern Europe had abandoned communism and were trying, in a variety of ways, to insert themselves into the capitalist global system. The scope and volume of the transnational practices of agents and agencies in these countries with those in the countries and institutions of the capitalist system increased dramatically in the 1990s. Chapter 8 discusses in more detail some of the causes and consequences of this tremendous transformation and the prospects for capitalist globalization in the New Second World.

Communism found its first means of expression in the various Internationals that were established by Marx and Engels and their followers from the 1860s on, but it was not until the Bolshevik Party, the first communist party to seize state power, ushered in the birth of the Soviet Union that we can realistically speak of a communist bloc. In 1949, the Soviet Union organized the Council for Mutual Economic Cooperation (Comecon), paralleling the Organization for European Economic Cooperation, which had been formed in 1948 as a framework within which the United States could distribute aid to rebuild the war-shattered West European economies. This body was renamed the Organization for Economic Cooperation and Development (OECD) in 1961 and its membership and functions were extended to promote the global leadership of the capitalist Western democracies. It has the reputation of a rich countries club, though some poorer European countries (Greece, Portugal, Hungary, and the Czech and Slovak Republics) and Third World countries (South Korea, Turkey, and Mexico) have now joined. The OECD is one of the major bodies promoting capitalist globalization and any country that wishes to join must sign up to that agenda, as its website makes clear.

The most visible public presence of the communist and capitalist blocs, however, was through their military alliances. The Warsaw Pact of Eastern European communist countries was a Soviet-dominated military alliance, established in 1955 in response to the entry of West Germany into US-dominated NATO (North Atlantic Treaty Organization). NATO had been formed after the Second World War in order to tie North America and Western Europe together in a military alliance against the perceived threat of world domination by the Soviet Union. The opposition of these two blocs had a profound effect on the geopolitics and political economy of the global system in the second half of the twentieth century. However, since 1990 the Warsaw Pact has collapsed and NATO has changed quite dramatically, with some former Eastern European communist states likely to join. Although the military hegemony of NATO, based largely on phenomenal nuclear overkill capacity, remains unsurpassed, other blocs have arisen to challenge it on a variety of strategic issues.

One such alternative bloc, identified by the World Bank and the rest of the world, is OPEC (Organization of Petroleum Exporting Countries) established in 1960. Throughout the 1970s it exerted tremendous influence on the world economy through its control of the level of production and the price of oil. This control eroded in the 1980s and 1990s because of internal struggles in the Arab world, as Iraq and Iran, and then Iraq and Kuwait and a coalition of Western states led by successive US governments, went to war. While OPEC has not acted as a powerful bloc since the early 1980s, its members retain the ability to do so in the future. Cooley (2001: 178) provides an informative review of some recent literature on the oil states. He suggests that conceiving:

oil-led development and state-building in the later oil states (post-1973) as direct attempts to emulate the organizational patterns of the original OPEC group and use the myths of wealth and redistribution that are popularly associated with oil development as a corner-stone of the state-building project . . . [former Soviet republics] are increasingly evoking the oil-rich Persian Gulf states as non-socialist alternatives to western models of deepening market reforms and expanding democratic participation.

The idea of collective economic and political action is exactly what is meant when we speak about blocs. The rise of Pacific Asia as a global economic force was expressed in the formation of APEC (Asia Pacific Economic Cooperation) and ASEAN (Association of South East Asian Nations) and these organizations have had a good measure of success in furthering their own agendas (see Preston 1998). ASEAN plus Three (Japan, China, South Korea) is another possibility.

Nevertheless, most blocs start from a position of weakness, not strength. The feeble achievements of the Non-aligned Movement (NAM) and the Group of 77 confirmed this in the political sphere (Williams 1991, Lavelle 2001). NAM originated in the Bandung Conference of 1955, where a large number of poor African and Asian countries called for a better economic deal from the rich countries of the world. The Group of 77, named for 77 poor southern countries unaligned with either the Soviet or the US camp, came together in 1964 through their common membership of the United Nations. The Group, now with over 100 members, also presses for a better deal from the rich countries of the world, mainly in the north. The only common interest of these southern countries is their general view that they are being more or less exploited by the rich countries of the north. An expression of this was the call for a New International Economic Order in the 1980s and similar initiatives since then. These produced torrents of words but little effective action. Such practical failures make it difficult to sustain economic community, political unity, or culture-ideology sympathy. After several false starts COMESA (Common Market for Southern and Eastern Africa) has emerged as a bloc of twenty-one mostly very poor countries with a combined population of almost four hundred million. All these people shared a combined gross domestic product in 2000 of about $160 billion (less than the annual revenues of General Motors or Wal-Mart Stores or Exxon Mobil or Ford Motor or DaimlerChrysler).

Many scholars who accept the declining significance of these blocs and of the nation-state, particularly with the rise of the global economy and mass culture, are uncertain about the existence of a truly global system. For them regionalization appears to be a more satisfactory context in which to answer the big questions that globalization raises (see Bhalla 1998). This thinking is clearly linked to ideas about the hegemony of the superpowers that have dominated analysis of the international system for centuries (Bornschier and Chase-Dunn 1999). In the 1970s there emerged a new mode of thinking that came to be known as Trilateralism. This was roughly the view that the anti-communist powers (USA, Western Europe and Japan) each have their own regional natural spheres of interest and that world peace and prosperity depended on these three regional powers being able to work out their differences peacefully in the interests of capitalist management of the global system (Sklar 1980). The point of this, of course, was eventually to destroy the global advance of communism. Since the demise of the Soviet empire and the opening up of China, the trilateralism argument has been developed in a variety of directions.

The regional economic unions operate more or less like blocs. Prime amongst these at the present historical juncture is the EU, whose progress towards economic and political integration has been too slow for the cosmopolitans, and too fast for the chauvinists in the member countries. Other economic unions, some short-lived and some longer-lived, in Africa, Asia, and South America have had a modicum of influence locally, but none can be said to have had a major influence in global terms. This is largely explicable from the realization that most, if not all, of these regional unions begin from a position of economic and political weakness.[10]

Two exceptions, one actual the other potential, are the North American Free Trade Agreement (NAFTA) and what is coming to be known as Greater China. NAFTA is a trading pact, but with environmental and labour side agreements, binding the USA, Canada, and Mexico together (see Wallach and Naiman 1998). Other Central and South American countries have expressed the wish to join in the near future. The second substantial bloc has come to be known as Greater China, a concept for which forty-one different variations have been found. Greater China includes the People's Republic of China, Hong Kong (reunited with China in 1997 but still administratively separate), and Taiwan. Together these have a formidable economic potential awaiting the end of political differences (Harding 1993).[11]

Regional responses to globalization are very varied. Most commentators argue that while the regions of Western Europe, Japan and East Asia, and North America have been able to take advantage of globalization and increase prosperity, most of the rest of the world has not been able to do so and that many communities (even in the rich regions) have suffered from globalization.[12] Brecher and Costello (1994) put forward the radical argument that globalization involves a race to the bottom as corporations and governments scramble to reduce living standards for vulnerable groups of workers and citizens in order to compete successfully in the global economy. In aggregate terms it is certainly true to say that some regions have lost out as far as the spoils of globalization are concerned (Africa, south Asia, postcommunist Europe, and parts of Latin America), but overemphasis on this tends to miss the very important fact that all over the world there are groups who have done very well out of globalization. The polarization crisis is more intense within countries and cities than between them.

While much of the research on the relationship between the global and the regional, and, indeed, the other concrete areas of interest that have been identified, provides very useful empirical examples and counter-examples for global theorists to consider, there is a general failure to conceptualize and research empirically global forces that drive certain kinds of development. Part of the problem is that most of the available data is in terms of states and national economies (ideas that are very difficult to abandon but sometimes quite misleading when you want to study globalization). Research operationalized in terms of communities, cities, industrial districts, sub-national and supra-national regions is increasing rapidly and provides much of the evidence for the arguments of the following chapters.

The countries and communities of the world, irrespective of bloc or region, appear to be more and more bound up with one another through the extension of transnational practices, some of which are directly identifiable as practices of global capitalism and some not. Even the conventional wisdom that the world is best understood in terms of the triad of economic regions based on North America, the European Union, and Japan has come under empirical challenge. Using a sensitive method to analyse the intensity of international trade and foreign direct investment flows between 1985 and 1995, Poon *et al.* (2000) demonstrate that investment intensity patterns did not conform to any bloc-like formation in this period, but showed what they term globally diffused network regions.

CONCLUSION

These five more or less state-centric classifications of per capita income, trade, resources, quality of life, and regions and blocs serve different purposes in theory and practice. They can be used, for example, to organize the evidence for and justify morally one or other theory of development or why there is no development. As I have emphasized, it is very important to be aware of the assumptions that lie behind these classifications and the theories based on them. These theories often guide the practice of those who make and carry out the policies that have led to so much apparent economic growth and so little actual development in many Third World countries.

These classifications, then, give us a wealth of empirical data but the result is conceptual confusion and general inconclusiveness when we try to explain anything in terms of such state-centred categories. The tremendous variation in the conditions of First, New Second, and Third World countries, and between communities within them, might lead the faint-hearted to conclude that the capitalist global system is so hopelessly complex that there is no point in trying to conceptualize it at all. This is precisely the limitation of state-centrist approaches and why all analyses that begin and end with states have such difficulty in finding explanations of what is going on in the world. To illustrate this point, let us consider the phenomenon that motivates so much research on the global system, namely the gap between rich and poor.

Capitalist globalization produces class polarization. This is a combination of widening gaps between the rich and the poor, both within countries and between countries, and absolute increases in the numbers of very rich and very poor. Such an outcome might tempt us to subscribe pessimistically to the view that the countries of the Third World are passive victims of the exercise of the exploitative power of First World countries. This view is a direct consequence of the state-centrist approach, and has to be rejected on the grounds that it is theoretically mechanical and empirically false. There are under-privileged individuals and groups in the First World, as well as in the Third and New Second Worlds. It is not a geographical accident of birth that determines whether an individual or group is going to be rich or poor, but a question of class location that may change during the lifetime of individuals and groups. Of course, there are relatively as well as absolutely very many more poor people in the Third World than in the First World but this is not only a question of geography but also of transnational class location.

The poor in all countries struggle against the domestic and global forces that oppress them and their resistance takes many forms, and in the Third World this has often taken the form of struggles for national liberation (see Bayat 2000). Capitalism typically uses the myth of the nation-state, sometimes in the form of reactionary nationalist ideologies, to deflect criticism of and opposition to its hegemonic control of the global system onto the claims of competing 'nations'. Dividing the world up into nation-states, as it is for most practical purposes for most people, is therefore a profoundly ideological strategy. It is not common sense, and the fact that for most people it is still one of the fundamental taken-for-granted assumptions of daily life is a measure of the tremendous success and power of capitalist globalization.

In contrast, ideologies not based on the nation-state tend to be of two types: those that necessarily exclude outsiders and create an in-group; and those that are inclusively transnational and cosmopolitan, and promote the common human characteristics of all those who share the planet. A powerful example of the first type is ethnic exclusivism, whose extreme form is found in the Fascist idea of race pride. Similarly, some religious fundamentalisms classify all non-believers (generally an ascribed rather than an achieved status) as devilish.

The second type includes the several versions of democratic socialism (as opposed to chauvinist bureaucratic communism, taken to its most extreme form in Stalinism). The intractable nature of the crises of capitalist globalization suggests that the central issue in turning democratic socialism into a global project is the globalization of human rights. Socialist globalization is based on the belief that the survival of humanity is incompatible with capitalist exploitation, imperialism, and the patriarchal and/or racist nation-state. Many tactical and strategic differences separate those who hold these views, particularly between women and men, between different ethnic and religious groups, and between libertarians and those who attach great importance to the construction of rule-bound democratic organizations and institutions. It is certainly the case that the global capitalist project is a great deal more consistent at this point in time than any socialist globalization project. It is also certainly the case that capitalist globalization has brought to hundreds of millions of people a standard of living that their parents would never have believed possible. In this sense, for many people all over the world it is a proven success, while its socialist alternative is, to many other people all over the world, an obscure jumble of aspirations. Capitalist globalization produces the material conditions for socialist globalization, but closes down the political and culture-ideology spaces for it.

In the next chapter the roots of globalization are identified in theories of development, and these are critically analysed as a prelude to competing conceptions of globalization.

NOTES

1. Unlike many writers on capitalism and globalization, I do not focus my analysis on Fordism, post-Fordism, and/or regulation. The reasons are simple. First, as with all ideal types, Fordism and post-Fordism conceal much more than they reveal and neither has ever been as clear-cut as its proponents suggest (see Lyddon 1996); second, the state-centrism of the regulation school fatally flaws its attempts to explain capitalist globalization.

2. Polly Hill convincingly points up the 'poor quality of official statistics' in her iconoclastic critique of development economics (Hill 1986: ch. 3), and I shall follow her contradictory example in making use of them while expressing scepticism.

3. In 2001 the Bank announced several changes in terminology, most importantly that GNP was to be relabelled GNI (Gross National Income).

4. A Women in Development Unit was established at the World Bank in 1986 but its career has been quite controversial. For critical studies of World Bank policy-making on gender, see Mies (in Sklair 1994: ch. 6), and O'Brien et al. (2000). The '50 years is Enough' campaign to replace the World Bank and the IMF with more responsive development agencies can be followed on the Internet.

5. For example, between north-east Brazil and the Sao Paulo–Rio industrial belt; between the north and the south of Italy; and between the coastal provinces and the interior of China (see Chapter 9 below). There are, of course, rich and poor in all regions.

6. For a reliable account of the global trade and investment system, see Brewer and Young (1998). Dunkley (2000) and Barker and Mander (2000) offer more critical perspectives.

7. For a thoughtful critique of the concept of resource dependence see Russett (1984).

8. In Nigeria, for example, there is a chronic shortage of petrol. This is because the domestic price is heavily subsidized, encouraging substantial illegal sales to neighbouring countries from where black market supplies are reimported at a huge premium.

9. The Child Poverty Action Group in the UK reported in August 2001 that infant mortality was 70 per cent higher in the poorest compared with the richest families and that around 2.4 million children lacked basic necessities (a warm home or three adequate meals a day, for example). Overall income inequality was higher in 1999/2000 than in 1997, though efforts of New Labour to target poor families apparently began to reduce inequalities in 2001.

10. See Stallings (1995) and Bhalla (1998) on regional responses to global change.

11. See also Hodder (1996) and Yeung and Olds (2000) on globalizing Chinese business firms from China and elsewhere.

12. Of course, it is true that on average the world is much more prosperous now than at any time in previous history (see, e.g. Easterlin 2000), but that is a different issue as we shall see in the next chapter.

Chapter 3

FROM DEVELOPMENT TO GLOBALIZATION

Globalization is a relatively new idea in the social sciences though people who work in and write about the mass media, transnational corporations, and international business have been using it for some time. The central feature of the idea of globalization is that many contemporary problems cannot be adequately studied at the level of nation-states, that is, in terms of each country and its inter-national relations (state-centrism) but need to be seen in terms of transnational processes, beyond the level of particular countries (globalization). Some globalists (notably, Ohmae 1995) have even gone so far as to predict that global forces, by which they usually mean transnational corporations and other global economic institutions, are becoming so powerful that the nation-state is finished. This is not a necessary consequence of most theories of globalization, though many argue that the significance of the nation-state is declining (even if the ideology of nationalism is still strong in some places).[1]

Perhaps the last refuge of globo-sceptics is the legal system, but even here, as one prominent legal theorist confidently explains in the first sentence of a collection on global law without a state: 'This book deals with legal pluralism in an emerging world society. Its central thesis is that globalization of law creates a multitude of decentred law-making processes in various sectors of civil society, independently of nation-states' (Teubner 1997: p. xiii). This, too, is the thrust of most conventional business and management writers who venture across borders. For example: 'Global business activities have altered the traditional relationship between organizations and nation-states. Whereas the values of nation-states traditionally were the major influences on organizations based there, today business activities and the organizations that stimulate them are conduits for global culture more than they are recipients of national culture' (Parker 1998: 226).

All these views are relatively new and though it is important not to be taken in by the fashion among globalization theorists to find evidence of it in all previous history, in order to understand globalization it is first necessary to understand previous attempts to theorize the global (even if the theorists did not explicitly characterize their own theorizing as global). Most of this theorizing can be considered under the umbrella term of theories of development.

THEORIES OF DEVELOPMENT AS EMBRYONIC THEORIES OF THE GLOBAL

There are many accounts of theories of development and I claim no privilege for the classification adopted here. It does, however, cover the main theories that attracted a following in the twentieth century and continue to do so. This book is not intended as a textbook of theories, so there is no detailed exegetical analysis of each one. My purpose here will be to give a very brief sketch of what each of the theories attempts and to direct the interested reader to other sources that give detailed accounts and critiques of them. The theories are identified by the following labels: imperialism; modernization; neo-Marxism; modes of production.

IMPERIALISM

The theory of imperialism (or colonialism, where the imperialists actually settled in the colony) tries to explain the structure of the modern world in terms of the struggles between the major powers to find new markets, sources of raw materials, investment opportunities, and to extend their political and cultural influence. It puts the necessity for capitalist expansion at the centre of the theory. Although Marx himself did discuss the issue of colonialism in various places, it was Lenin's book *Imperialism, the Highest Stage of Capitalism* (1916), that first put forward a systematic theory of the international relationships of monopoly capitalism. As is often the case in the creation of new ideas, there were many scholars working along the same lines as Lenin, particularly those trying to analyse the experience of the British Empire at the end of the nineteenth century, like J. A. Hobson, whose book *Imperialism* appeared in 1902.

The Marxist theory of imperialism has been robustly challenged and robustly defended from many directions,[2] and it has left its mark on most subsequent theories of the global system. It raises two questions crucial for the understanding of the modern world. First, is the theory historically true in the sense that the phenomenon of imperialism is best explained in terms of the expansion of the world capitalist system? This is still a crucial question because, with the end of direct colonial rule (political imperialism) in most of the Third World by the 1970s, the idea that imperialism was finished was widely believed. However, if imperialism is a consequence of capitalist expansionism and not simply a colonial system of government, then some form of economic imperialism could persist after independence for ex-colonies, thus neo-imperialism. Second, if this is true, can capitalism develop the Third World? Bill Warren, a self-styled orthodox Marxist, took this question by the scruff of the neck in his book *Imperialism: Pioneer of Capitalism* (1980), and argued to the consternation of a wide variety of antagonists that the problem with the Third World is not that there is too much capitalism but too little. Many contemporary Marxists (notably those associated with the New York-based journal *Monthly Review*) consider globalization simply as a new version of imperialism, and in one sense they are correct. The drivers of capitalist globalization do work in many respects as the classical theory of imperialism suggested that international capitalists in the nineteenth and the beginning of the twentieth centuries did. However, with the possible exception of the theory of Rosa Luxemburg, all these arguments are shackled by their state-centrism.[3] We shall return to these issues below when neo-Marxist theories are discussed.

MODERNIZATION

Modernization theories of the global system are largely based on the distinction between the traditional and the modern. The central idea of the theory is that development revolves around the question of attitudes and values (rather than the material interests entailed in capitalist expansionism). Traditional societies are run by traditionally minded individuals, typically those who are inward-looking, not prepared to innovate, and influenced by magic and religion; while modern societies are run by modern-minded individuals, outward-looking, keen to try out new things, influenced by rational thought and practical experience. This theory is partly derived from Max Weber's attempts to relate the rise of capitalism (the epitome of modern society) with the Protestant ethic and to show how other different belief systems (like the religions of the Orient) inhibited the rise of modern society. Modernization theory, like the Weber thesis, has its strong supporters and detractors.[4]

A revised, neo-modernization approach has been constructed to cope with the rise of the east Asian 'tigers' and the impact of Confucianism (see Berger and Hsiao, 1988; Kim, in Sklair 1994: ch. 5). The focus of research on the successes of these economies can be contrasted with the growing volume of research on the costs of rapid industrialization since the 1980s (for example, Bello and Rosenfeld 1990; Jenkins, in Sklair 1994: ch. 4) and in postcommunist Europe (Manser 1993). There are two main problems with the theory, now generally acknowledged. The first is that the distinction between traditional and modern is too crude to be theoretically useful, and that there may well be clear material interests behind at least some so-called traditional and modern attitudes and values. The second main criticism is that modernization theory tends to ignore the role that class and other interests play in the promotion or inhibition of development.[5]

The main strength of the theory is that it directs attention to the entrepreneurial and/or innovative personalities who seem to be so important in the developmental process, but even here the theory does tend to ignore the inconsistencies and contradictions that are inherent in explanations based on individual characteristics. The search for a theory that will combine structural explanations in terms of societal forces and psychological explanations in terms of individual attributes is as far from success in this as in all other fields of social research.

The idea of neo-evolutionism is often coupled with the theory of modernization. Neo-evolutionism provides an historical context for the analysis of traditional and modern societies, in the sense that modern societies are said to evolve from traditional ones through the processes of social differentiation. For example, in so-called traditional societies the political and the economic and the educational functions all tend to be fulfilled by the same elementary institution, whereas in so-called modern societies we have separate social structures and organizations to deal with politics, the economy, education, and so on. Modern societies are therefore institutionally differentiated, on the analogy of biological organisms, from the relatively simple to the relatively complex. This is called neo-evolutionism because the nineteenth-century evolutionism that found a single path along which societies would evolve (usually from the primitive to the civilized) was considered unacceptable. Neo-evolutionism rejects this unilinear dogma, and argues that there are many possible paths from the traditional to the modern, though there is a strong supposition that the capitalist road via pluralist democracy resulting in something like the contemporary USA and Western Europe, are the best and most efficient of the alternatives.[6] In the 1950s and the 1960s, as an offshoot of the sociological functionalism of Talcott Parsons, theories of modernization and neo-evolutionism dominated the social science study of development. However, by the mid-1960s, with anti-imperialist wars raging in Africa, Asia, and Latin America, various neo-Marxist theories were beginning to challenge the functionalist orthodoxies.

NEO-MARXISM

Marx did not himself create a systematic theory of the global system, though his work certainly guided Lenin and others in their attempts to construct a theory of imperialism. The Leninist theory of capitalist expansionism is generally considered to be the orthodox Marxist position. But even if Lenin was correct in his analysis of the capitalist-imperialist roots of the First World War, by the 1950s and 1960s the capitalist global system and the Third World had both changed so much that many Marxists felt the need to generate new theories to explain what was happening and to show the way forward from a political point of view. This is why these theories are labelled neo-Marxist.

The single most influential neo-Marxist conceptual innovation for the analysis of development within the global system in general in the last few decades has been dependency theory, or what might be more accurately termed the dependency metatheory. The dependency metatheory, created by a group of social scientists in Latin America (the dependentistas), came to prominence in the 1960s and, despite formidable criticism since then, has obstinately refused to disappear. It is useful to distinguish three theories connected with the metatheory. These are the theories of dependent underdevelopment, dependent development, and dependency reversal (see Sklair 1988*a*). The dependentistas argued that the capitalist global system, largely but not exclusively through transnational corporations (TNCs), operated actively to underdevelop the Third World and that no genuine development was possible as long as this system survived.[7] While substantial general support for the dependency approach was accumulated, most scholars now acknowledge that the dependentistas were never able to explain satisfactorily the economic growth and social and industrial development that had clearly taken place in some Third World countries (Roberts and Hite 2000: part III). The widespread acceptance of a new name for them, the Newly Industrializing Countries (NICs), was undoubtedly an implicit recognition of the inadequacy of Frank's version of dependency theory as dependent underdevelopment (but see Frank 1984). Other writers in the dependency tradition saw this, but were unwilling to discard the dependency approach entirely. Cardoso called what was plainly development to pragmatists, associated dependent industrialization (see Cardoso and Faletto 1979), and in the hands of Evans (1979) this evolved into a more general theory of dependent development.

Dependency theorists, therefore, were still trying to answer the question that had troubled Marxists since the turn of the century, namely: can capitalism develop the Third World? Frank and those who agreed with his theory of the development of underdevelopment unequivocally denied that capitalism could ever develop the Third World.

The best it could do would be to permit a small degree of enclave development, which only reproduced First World–Third World exploitation within Third World cities and rural areas. Dependent development theorists, on the other hand, acknowledged capitalist development in the Third World, particularly in the NICs, but it was a peculiar, dependent kind of development. The problem is that dependent development seems to be possible not only in the Third World but also in underprivileged areas everywhere, including the First World. This conceptual inflation reduces the effectiveness of the idea by playing into the hands of critics who maintain that the concept of dependency is unviable because it closes off the theoretical space for explaining growth and development, however limited, where it does occur. To those who argue along these lines, the idea of dependent development seems entirely ad hoc, dragged in to explain away phenomena that the theory seems to forbid.

One possible exit from this cul de sac was the idea (it did not become a fully articulated theory) of dependency reversal. This suggested that certain Third World countries, or sectors within them, which were once in the thrall of dependency could escape and reverse their previous disadvantage (Doran *et al.* 1983). This is an interesting and, in the case of institutions rather than countries, an eminently testable idea. For example, there has been a good deal of solid research on the changing nature of the mining industries in the Third World, once entirely and now less entirely dominated by First World TNCs. Some of this research suggests that in certain cases, for example the bauxite and aluminium industry, the global disposition of power is still very much in favour of the First World TNCs, while in other cases, for example petroleum and perhaps copper, the balance of power has shifted in recent decades, and the First World TNCs have to work harder for their share of the profits.[8]

The fundamental flaw of dependency reversal is that it tends to take development strategies for granted while it assesses the benefits or costs of particular activities. The price that an institution (or a whole country) might have to pay for success in reversing a particular state of dependency might in the long run not be worth paying. For example, a Third World producer might win the battle to process a mineral or an industrial crop on site, but if this leads to a crisis in foreign currency because the machinery and the technology necessary for the task have to be imported, then it may result in greater dependence eventually. Nevertheless, if there is any sense in which capitalism can develop the Third World, and there is evidence that this is happening in some countries or in some sectors, then the theoretical elaboration of the idea of dependency reversal may be useful.

Dependency theorists frequently argue that the best alternative to global capitalism for Third World countries is through what Amin (1997) terms strategic delinking. But this seems to me to create as many problems as it solves. It would have to be the state that delinks (strategically or not). All states have the capacity to delink at present (and in some spheres some do this). The problem is to explain why most states do not delink in most spheres, indeed why most states appear to be increasing and intensifying the links to capitalist globalization they already have.[9]

In parallel with the dependency framework, but distanced theoretically and empirically from it by conceptual innovations and differences of interpretation, is the world-systems approach whose origins can be found in the works of Immanuel Wallerstein, particularly his three volumes on *The Modern World-System* (1974, 1980, 1988).

The world-system theorists have developed a systematic and far-reaching analysis based on a dynamically changing division of labour between core, peripheral, and semi-peripheral countries in the capitalist world-system. As this approach has served as a bridge between theories of development and theories of globalization, it will be considered in more detail later.

MODES OF PRODUCTION

There are, however, many who call themselves Marxists, who appear to have rejected entirely the whole problematic of dependency. They argue that the reasons for under-development in any given Third World country lie mainly in the mode of production of the country itself rather than in the position of the country within the wider capitalist system. More specifically, the prospects for revolution can be deduced from the mode of production within a particular social formation (society) and the class forces that are struggling for power (see Taylor 1979). So while dependency theorists argue for delinking from the world capitalist system, some mode of production theorists argue that capitalist industrialization is the only reliable path to development and, eventually, socialist revolution in the Third World (Warren 1980). On this theory, global capitalism provides the necessary impetus for revolution in the countries where TNCs are most active. So, where neo-Marxists argue that the revolutionary forces in the Third World need not wait for Western-style capitalism in order to produce successful communist revolutions, mode of production theorists maintain the orthodox Marxist thesis that communism can only come about when the organized working class, the proletariat, destroys the class power of the bourgeoisie through anti-capitalist revolution. Marx himself even suggested that this need not necessarily be a violent revolution, but might be achieved by democratic means in advanced societies.

Modes of production theorists may have more in common with the dependentistas than they seem to realize. Their arguments suggest that the lack of development in the Third World is due to obstacles, both internal and externally imposed, to capitalist industrialization. This is really not very different from what dependency theories argue. The mode of production approach produces a type of dependency reversal theory in its insistence that capitalist industrialization can succeed in the Third World. In this they agree with the advocates of capitalist globalization who continually proclaim that TNCs are the only reliable vehicles for development though, of course, there is a serious disagreement about the nature and likely outcome of the process. The disagreement revolves around the role of the class struggle in the Third World, and it is not only with representatives of the transnational capitalist class, but also with dependency theorists. Marxists criticize neo-Marxists for concentrating too much on questions of international exchange and terms of trade (exploitation by the First World of the Third World) and too little on questions of production and ownership (capital accumulation and class struggle).

These theories of development and their implicit or explicit approaches to the analysis of the global system all remain quite controversial, each with its own adherents and detractors, and each guiding substantive research in a variety of problem areas. The inability of critics to kill off previous theories entirely, and of theories to defend themselves against their critics to the satisfaction of all concerned, led several writers to conclude that development theory is in crisis (see Booth 1994). The way out of the crisis, in my view, is to refocus our attention away from state-centrist ideas of Western cultures bringing modernization to traditional societies or First World countries exploiting Third World countries, to the analysis of transnational practices in the global system. In order to do this it is necessary to show how transnational practices have been monopolized by key institutions in the capitalist global system. It is at this point that the argument begins to move from development to globalization.

COMPETING CONCEPTIONS OF GLOBALIZATION

There is no single agreed definition of globalization, indeed, some argue that its signifi-cance has been much exaggerated. As the ever-increasing numbers of books and articles discussing different aspects of it suggest, it appears to be an idea whose time has come in sociology in particular and in the social sciences in general. Waters (1995: 1) was being too cautious when he suggested that it may be 'the concept of the 1990s'. Arguments about globalization look set to last well into the twenty-first century.[10]

One problem in understanding much of the globalization literature, as I pointed out in Chapter 1, is that not all those who use the term distinguish it clearly enough from internationalization, and some writers appear to use the terms interchangeably. In this book a clear distinction will be drawn between the inter-national, the transnational, and the global. The hyphen in inter-national is to signify that this conception of globalization is founded on the existing even if changing system of states. The transnational signifies the emergence of forces and institutions not founded on the state system though they are constrained by and simultaneously transcend it in specific ways. The global signifies an already achieved state of globalization but, in my view, this is still fairly uncommon. Thus, for example, most major transnational corporations are certainly globalizing, but few if any are actually global yet, in the sense that they can operate entirely free of states and the inter-state system. However, the power of these globalizing corporations and the transnational capitalist class that owns and controls them all over the world ensures the hegemony of capitalist globalization in the present era (Sklair 2001).

These issues are difficult to theorize and to research empirically. The social sciences are largely based on concepts of society that identify the unit of analysis with a particular country (for example, British, Japanese, US, Russian, Indian society), sub-systems within countries (British education, the Japanese economy, American culture, Russian politics, Indian religion) or comparisons between single countries and groups of them (modern Britain and traditional India, declining America and ascendant Japan or vice versa, rich and poor countries, countries of the North and the South). This general approach, state-centrism, is still useful in many respects and there are clearly good reasons for it. Not the least of these is that most historical and contemporary sociological data has been col-lected on nation-states. However, most globalization theorists argue that the nation-state is no longer the only important unit of analysis and some argue that it is now less important in some fundamental respects than other, globalizing, forces. These global-izing forces include mass media and the corporations that own and control them, trans-national corporations (some of which are richer than the majority of countries) and even social movements that spread ideas like global environmental responsibility, universal human rights, and the worldwide call for democracy and human dignity. Sassen expresses the tentative nature of this new perspective well: 'My working hypothesis is that while globalization leaves national territory basically unaltered, it is having pronounced effects on the exclusive territoriality of the national state—that is, its effects are not on the boundaries of national territory as such but on the institutional encasements of the national territory' (Sassen 2000b: 372).

Yearley (1996: ch. 1) identifies two main obstacles to making sociological sense of globalization, namely the connection between the discipline of sociology and the nation-state, and the fact that countries differ significantly in their geographies. Despite these difficulties (really elaborations of the local-global problem which will be discussed below) he makes the telling point that a focus on the environment encourages us to work down to the global from the universal, a necessary corrective to state-centrist conceptions which work up to the global from the nation-state or even from individualistic notions of global consciousness.

The actual study of globalization revolves primarily around two main classes of phenomena that have become increasingly significant in the last few decades. These are, first, the emergence of a global economy based on new systems of production, finance, and consumption driven by globalizing transnational corporations (TNC) (Dunning 1997, Dicken 1998). The second is the idea of global culture, focused on transformations in the global scope of particular types of TNC, those who own and control the mass media (Herman and McChesney 1997), notably television channels and the transnational advertising agencies. This is often connected with the spread of particular patterns of consumption and a culture and ideology of consumerism at the global level. While not all globalization researchers entirely accept the existence of a global economy or a global culture, most accept that however we define globalization, significant economic, political, and culture-ideology changes are taking place all over the world because of it.

The largest TNCs have assets and annual sales far in excess of the GNP of most of the countries in the world. Fewer than sixty countries out a total of around 200 have GNPs of more than $US20 billion (World Bank 2001). By contrast, the *Fortune* Global 500 (hereafter FG500)[11] list of the biggest TNCs by turnover, published in July 2001, reports that 245 had annual revenues in excess of $20 billion (the top fifty-one exceeded $50 billion). Thus, in this important sense such well-known names as Exxon Mobil, Wal-Mart Stores, and General Motors (the top three), plus Shell, Toyota, Unilever, Volkswagen, Nestlé, Sony, Pepsico, Coca-Cola, Toshiba, and the huge Japanese trading houses (and many other corporations most people have never heard of) have more economic power at their disposal than the majority of the countries in the world. Another, perhaps more effective, measure is the comparison between corporate revenues and state revenues (what governments raise in taxes and other receipts). While the six biggest are states, thirty-five of the top fifty are, in fact, corporations (see Figure 3.1). These figures prove little in themselves; they simply indicate the gigantism of TNCs relative to most countries.

Not only have TNCs grown enormously in size in recent decades but their global reach has expanded dramatically. Many major TNCs (for example, IBM, Microsoft, Mitsubishi, Samsung, Nestlé, ICI, Unilever, and Dow Chemical) regularly earn more than half of their revenues outside their countries of origin.[12] The FG500 includes many companies from the Third World, for example in 2001 the national oil companies of Brazil (Petrobras), India (Indian Oil), Mexico (Pemex), Malaysia (Petronas), and Venezuela (PDVSA), owned by

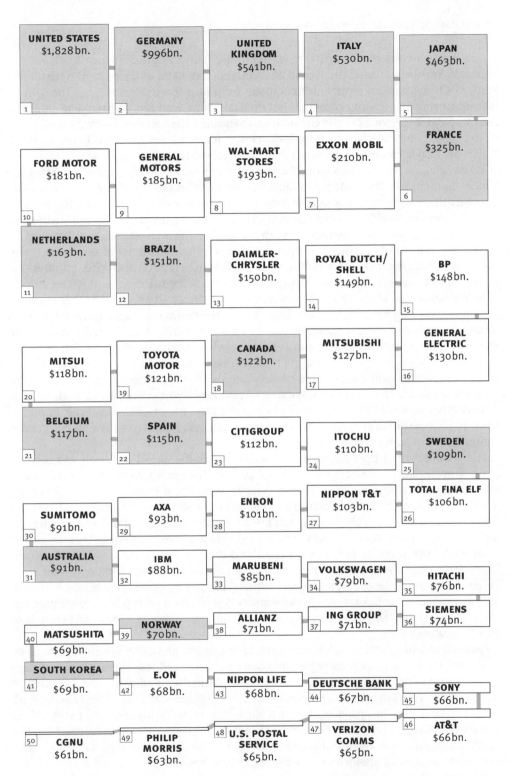

Figure 3.1 World's biggest economic entities by revenues (in US$ bn., 2000)

Source: www.odci.gov/cia/publications/factbook/indexgeo.html (state budgets) accessed summer 2001; corporate revenues from *Fortune* Global 500 (23 July 2001) from an idea of Charles Gray.

the state but usually run like private corporations; banks in Brazil (Banco Bradesco and Banco do Brasil) and China (Industrial and Commercial, Bank of China, and Agricultural Bank of China), and an electronics company from Singapore (Flextronics). The Korean manufacturing and trading conglomerates (chaebol) are well represented (eleven in the 2001 list) and some, for example Hyundai and Samsung, have attained global brand-name status. Major Chinese state corporations, eleven in 2001 (plus one TNC based in Hong Kong), are also becoming prominent (Sklair and Robbins 2002).

Those who are sceptical about globalization argue that the facts that most TNCs are legally domiciled in the USA, Japan, and Europe and that they trade and invest mainly between themselves means that the world economy is still best analysed in terms of national corporations. The global economy, they claim, is a myth (for example, Hirst and Thompson 1996). But this deduction entirely ignores the well-established fact that an increasing number of corporations operating outside their countries of origin see themselves as globalizing, as is obvious if we read their annual reports and other publications rather than focus exclusively on aggregate data on foreign investment.[13] You cannot simply assume that all TNCs headquartered in the USA, or Japan, or any other country, somehow express a national interest. They do not; they primarily express the interests of those who own and control them, even if historical patterns of TNC development have differed from country to country and region to region. Analysing globalization as a relatively recent phenomenon, originating from the 1960s, allows us to see more clearly the tensions between traditional inter-national patterns of TNC development and new transnational corporate structures and dynamics. It is also important to realize that, even in state-centrist terms, a relatively small investment for a major TNC can result in a relatively large measure of economic presence in a small, poor country or in a poor region or community in a larger and less poor country.

The second central phenomenon of globalization is the global diffusion and increasingly concentrated ownership and control of the electronic mass media, particularly television (Herman and McChesney 1997, Barker 1997). The number of TV sets per capita grew so rapidly in Third World countries during the last decades of the twentieth century (from fewer than ten per thousand population in 1970 to sixty per 1,000 in 1993, according to UNESCO) that many researchers argued that a globalizing effect because of the mass media was taking place, even in the Third World (see, for example, Sussman and Lent 1991, Balnaves et al. 2001). However, this still leaves many households without regular access. In India, for example, it was estimated that of one billion population in 2000 only about half of the households in the country had television sets (about 70 million) but about 40 per cent of those are connected to the channels offered by tens of thousands of cable operators.

Ownership and control of television, including satellite and cable systems, and associated media like newspaper, magazine and book publishing, films, video, tapes and compact discs and DVD, and a wide variety of other marketing media, are concentrated in relatively few very large TNCs. The predominance of US-based corporations is being challenged by Japanese, European, and Australian groups globally, and even by corporations based in the Third World, like the Brazilian media empire of TV Globo (Nordenstreng and Schiller 1993, Herman and McChesney 1997: ch. 6). The mass media, particularly television, spreads the culture-ideology of consumerism, but not in the same ways and not evenly throughout the world.

The remainder of this chapter will present the main approaches that social scientists have adopted to study globalization, offering a critique of each of them and laying the foundations for the argument that while each has its own merits, the most theoretically coherent and empirically convincing approach is the one elaborated in this book: global systems theory based on transnational practices.

There are several ways to categorize theory and research on globalization. One approach is to compare mono-causal with multi-causal explanations of the phenomenon, as does McGrew (1992). This is a useful way of looking at the problem but it has two main drawbacks. First, it ends up by putting in the same bag thinkers with entirely different types of explanations, for example those who see globalization as a consequence of the development of material-technological forces and those who see it as a consequence of ideological and/or cultural forces. Second, few if any thinkers present an entirely mono-causal explanation of anything; most of the thinkers McGrew identifies as mono-causal do try to show the relevance of a variety of factors even if they tend to prioritize some factors over others, while those he identifies as multi-causal do not always argue that everything causes everything else. They, too, prioritize, though perhaps to a lesser extent than the former group. Globalization, by its very nature, is a big and complex subject.

A second approach is to compare the disciplinary focus of globalization studies. This is certainly an interesting and fruitful avenue to explore: each discipline has made distinct-ive contributions to the study of globalization (to some extent all the social sciences have contributed to the debate, but in addition to sociology international relations, geography and political economy can be singled out). These contributions are commonly borrowed by sociologists of globalization, and vice versa, and this will be reflected in my own categorization.

A third approach focuses on attitudes to globalization, as in Held *et al.* (1999) who distinguish three types. These are hyperglobalists (those who see globalization as a dom-inant and unstoppable phenomenon and predict the end of the nation-state), sceptics (those who deny the novelty and to some extent the existence of globalization, the global economy, and so on), and transformationalists (those who accept globalization and see widespread predictable and unpredictable effects—their own position). The problem with the transformationalist thesis, unsurprisingly, is that it tries to explain almost everything in terms of almost everything else. It is certainly comprehensive, but it lacks conceptual specificity (being very eclectic) and historical specificity (seeing globalization in almost every historical period).

All of these classifications are useful for a variety of purposes, but I have chosen to categorize approaches to globalization on the basis of who or what is said to be driving globalization. This gives four research clusters in which groups of scholars are working on similar research problems, either in direct contact with each other or, more com-monly, in indirect contact. Given the relative novelty of globalization as a problem area in social science, with the exception of the world-system school, none of these approaches has really solidified into a commonly agreed set of propositions or has an institutional form.

The four sources of globalization research are:

- the world-systems approach;
- the global culture approach;

- the global polity and society approach;
- the global capitalism approach.

WORLD-SYSTEMS

The world-systems approach is based on the distinction between core, semi-peripheral, and peripheral countries in terms of their changing roles in the international division of labour dominated by the capitalist world-system. World-systems as a model in social science research, inspired by the work of Immanuel Wallerstein, has been developed in a large and continually expanding body of literature since the 1970s (see Wallerstein 1974, 1980, 1988; and Shannon 1996, and Hall 2000 for good overviews).

Unlike the other approaches it is not only a collection of academic writings but also a highly institutionalized academic enterprise. It is based at the Braudel Center for the Study of Economies, Historical Systems, and Civilizations (named for the great French historian Fernand Braudel) at Binghamton University (NY state) established by Waller-stein, with several other outposts, notably a new Center for Interdisciplinary Research on World-Systems directed by Chase-Dunn at the University of California Riverside. The Braudel Center is noted for a lively interchange between permanent and visiting scholars within a structure of interrelated research projects, including joint academic ventures with the Max Planck-Institut in Germany and the Maison des Sciences de l'Homme in France. The results of these projects frequently appear in the Journal of the Center, *Review*, first published in 1977. The world-systems theorists have also established a section in the American Sociological Association, Political Economy of the World-System, which organizes regular conferences and publications. Its newsletter is a useful guide that complements material from the Braudel Center on the activities of the world-systems network of theorists and researchers, and it has a book series.[14] Though the work of world-systems theorists cannot be said to be fully a part of the globalization literature as such (see King 1991), the institutionalization of the world-systems approach undoubtedly prepared the ground for globalization in the social sciences.

In some senses, Wallerstein and his school could rightly claim to have been global all along—after all, what could be more global than the world-system? However, there is no specific concept of the global in most world-systems literature. Reference to the global comes mainly from critics and, significantly, can be traced to the long-standing problems that the world-system model has had with cultural issues. Wallerstein's essay on 'Culture as the Ideological Battleground of the Modern World-System', the critique by Boyne, and Wallerstein's attempt to rescue his position under the title of 'Culture is the World-System' (all in Featherstone 1990), illustrate the problem well. Two further shortcomings of world-systems theory have been critically exposed. It is said, first, to neglect class struggle and, second, to distort the history of capitalism and thus the progressive role of capitalism in development (see Shannon 1996: chs. 6–7). Though argument continues on all these points, for more than twenty years this school of thought has been the most systematic available for the analysis of the global system, and those working within its orbit have produced and continue to produce an impressive array of theory and research.

The world-systems approach, like the dependency approach, has always had difficulty in dealing with development, or at least industrialization in the Third World. Wallerstein elaborated the concept of the semi-periphery, and this idea has been picked up by many scholars as a useful tool in analysing the so-called Newly Industrializing Countries (NICs) and, increasingly, those countries that are on the fringes of the First World, but not exactly in the Third World, like Ireland, Portugal, and the Balkan states (see O'Hearn 1998 on the 'Celtic Tiger'). Critics of world-systems theory have suggested that the idea of the semi-periphery is an ad hoc invention to deal with those cases that do not fit neatly into the· core-periphery framework. This criticism is strengthened to some extent by the observation that much creative work in this genre in recent years has been precisely in the elaboration of dependent development in the countries of the semi-periphery.

An implicit attempt to make connections between the dependency theory and world-systems was formulated on the basis of an influential conceptual innovation, the new international division of labour (NIDL) theory, particularly as elaborated by Fröbel and his colleagues (1980). This theory drew attention to the consequences of changes in global production strategies of the TNCs since the 1960s. In common with Wallerstein and the world-systems theorists, the proponents of the NIDL share a general conception of the capitalist world-system divided into core, semi-periphery, and periphery in which a division of labour has evolved to maximize the profits of transnational corporations and to solve the problems of the major capitalist societies. In common with the dependentistas the NIDL theorists see little prospect for any genuine Third World development in these changes in global capitalist strategies. The idea of the new international division of labour excited a great deal of research interest in the 1970s and 1980s (for example, the volumes edited by Nash and Fernandez-Kelly 1983; Sanderson 1985) but has been overtaken by the wider and less state-centric debates around globalization (see Roberts and Hite 2000: Part IV).

The theory of the new international division of labour was criticized for its uncompromising condemnation of TNC operations in the Third World, on the grounds that there is not very much that is new about it, and that it relies on an empirical base that is far too limited. Much of this criticism appears quite justified. Nevertheless, the activities of TNCs wherever they are and in whatever industry, are increasingly being integrated into global processes of supply, production, and marketing. The theorists of the new international division of labour rendered great service by highlighting these phenomena even if they did so in a rather one-sided and state-centrist manner. By concentrating too much on the TNCs' search for cheap labour, the NIDL failed to connect economic with political and culture-ideology transnational practices. It is true that much foreign investment is for the domestic markets of host countries, and that the export-processing industries that are at the centre of the NIDL thesis account for only a small part of TNC foreign investment in the Third World but, as I have argued for the cases of Ireland, China, and Mexico (Sklair 1988*b*, 1991, 1993), the symbolic significance of export-oriented development strategies is extremely important in the contemporary global system. To this extent, the neo-Marxist, world-systems, and NIDL theorists are in general agreement.

Chase-Dunn, in his suggestively entitled book, *Global Formation* (1989), does try to take the argument a stage further by arguing for a dual logic approach to economy and polity. At the economic level, he argues, a global logic of the world economy prevails whereas at the level of politics a state-centred logic of the world-system prevails. However, as the world economy is basically still explicable only in terms of national economies (countries of the core, semi-periphery, and periphery), Chase-Dunn's formulation largely reproduces the problems of Wallerstein's state-centrist analysis.

There is, therefore, no distinctively global dimension in the world-systems model; it appears locked into the inter-national focus that it has always emphasized. Wallerstein himself rarely if ever uses the word globalization. For him, the economics of the model rests on the inter-national division of labour that distinguishes core, semi-periphery, and periphery countries. The politics are mostly bound up with anti-systemic movements and superpower struggles. And the cultural, in so far as it is dealt with at all, covers debates about the national and the universal and the concept of civilization(s) in the social sciences. Many critics are not convinced that the world-systems model, usually considered to be economistic (that is, reducing all questions to economic factors) can deal with cultural issues adequately. Wolff tellingly comments on the way in which the concept of culture was inserted into Wallerstein's world-system model: 'An economism which gallantly switches its attentions to the operations of culture is still economism' (in King 1991: 168). Wallerstein's attempts to theorize race and nationalism in terms of the geoculture of the world-system (Wallerstein 1991: part II) might be seen as a dilution of his economism, but few would argue that cultural factors are an important part of the analysis.

There is one main exception to the state-centrism of world-systems theory, namely research on the idea of commodity chains (networks of labour, production, and marketing of goods). This work has shifted attention away from the national to the transnational to some extent (Gereffi and Korzeniewicz 1994), reinforced by a new focus on value chains (Gereffi and Kaplinsky 2001) . However, in general, the global and the inter-national are generally used interchangeably by world-systems theorists.[15] This is certainly one possible use of global but it seems quite superfluous, given that the idea of the international is so common in the social science literature. Nevertheless, whatever the fate of world-systems analysis, it is unlikely that ideas of globalization would have spread so quickly and deeply in sociology and related disciplines without the impetus it gave to looking at the whole world.

GLOBAL CULTURE

A second model of globalization derives specifically from research on the globalization of culture. The global culture approach argues that globalization is driven by a homogenizing mass media-based culture, and that this threatens national and/or local cultures and identities. As we shall see below, this is complementary to rather than in contradiction with the global polity and society approach, which focuses more on ideas of an emerging global consciousness and their implications for global community, governance, and security.

The first major statement of the global culture approach to globalization was a collection of articles in book form from the journal *Theory, Culture and Society* (*TCS*) edited by Featherstone (1990) under the title *Global Culture*. While it does not have the institutional solidity of the Braudel Center, *TCS* has also brought together groups of like-minded scholars through the journal and conferences, which has resulted in an intellectual critical mass for the development of a culturalist approach to globalization. Of the writers associated with *TCS* who have made notable contributions to this effort,

Robertson, who has been credited with introducing the term globalization into sociology (Waters 1995: 2), and Appadurai are probably the most influential.[16]

Appadurai has developed a fivefold conceptual framework for the analysis of global cultural flows. His categories are ethnoscapes (flows of people), mediascapes (flows of images), technoscapes (flows of machinery), finanscapes (flows of money), and ideoscapes (flows of ideas). This formulation has proved a useful tool for some researchers grappling to organize large masses of empirical research findings, for example, in the absorbing study by Olds (2001) of urban mega-projects in Vancouver and Shanghai.

Although these researchers cannot be identified as a school in the same way as world-systems researchers can be, there are some common themes running through their works. First, they are all interested in the question of how specific identities can survive in the face of an emerging global culture. Second, they tend to prioritize the cultural over the political and/or the economic. A distinctive feature of this model is that it problematizes the existence of global culture, as a reality, a possibility, or a fantasy. The inspiration for this debate is the emergence of what Marshall McLuhan famously called the global village, the very rapid growth that has taken place over the last few decades in the scope and scale of the mass media (McLuhan 1987). The basic idea is that the spread of the mass media, especially television and now the Internet, means that everyone in the world can be exposed to the same images, almost instantaneously. This, the argument goes, turns the whole world into a sort of global village. The debate has been enlivened by studies of the cultures of globalization (Jameson and Miyoshi 1998) in the plural, and attempts to connect globalization, modernity, and post-colonialism (see Lazarus 1999).

A subset of the global culture approach, characterized as globo-localism, derives from a group of scholars from various social science backgrounds whose main concern is to try to make sense of the multifaceted and enormously complex web of local-global relations. There is a good deal of overlap between this and the globalization of culture model, but the globo-local researchers tend to emphasize the territorial dimension. There is no single common theoretical position in the work of these theorists (see, for example, Mlinar 1992). What unites them is the urge to theorize and research questions of what happens to territorial identities (within and across countries) in a globalizing world.[17]

The fundamental problem with the cultural approach to globalization (indeed the cultural approach to anything) is that it is cultural, and always risks losing sight of the material realities that lie behind the cultural and symbolic phenomena that are being researched. Guerlain expresses this well:

One day culturalists claim that Japanese culture explains the economic successes of Japan and then a few years later culture also explains the setbacks. Soon everyone is likely to explain Chinese successes by some cultural characteristic of China, though these same cultural traits were there too when China was written off as a communist basket case. Indeed if tomorrow Indonesia or Brazil came to be major international players their culture, indeed their diversity – which is no less impressive than the American one – would become an explanation and a model for other countries to emulate. (Guerlain 1997: 50)

Without doubt, the main research question for cultural globalization is the autonomy of local cultures in the face of an advancing global culture. Competing claims of local cultures against the forces of globalization have forced themselves onto the sociological, cultural, and political agendas all over the world. This is largely continuous with the focus of the third globalization model based on the idea of global polity and society.

GLOBAL POLITY AND SOCIETY

Inspiration for this general conception of globalization is often located in the pictures of planet earth sent back by space explorers. A classic statement of this was the report of Apollo XIV astronaut Edgar Mitchell in 1971: 'It was a beautiful, harmonious, peaceful-looking planet, blue with white clouds, and one that gave you a deep sense . . . of home, of being, of identity. It is what I prefer to call instant global consciousness.'[18] This individualistic conception of global consciousness, derived from simply being in or gazing at the world (usually via the media) can be contrasted with a collective conception derived from being with and mobilizing fellow human beings to solve global problems (see Chapters 10–11 below).

Had astronaut Mitchell penetrated a little through the clouds he would also have seen horrific wars in Vietnam and other parts of Asia, bloody repression by various dictatorial regimes in Africa and Latin America, dead and maimed bodies as a result of sectarian terrorism in Britain and Ireland, as well as a terrible toll of human misery from hunger, disease, legal and illegal drug abuse, and carnage on roads all round the world as automobile cultures intensified their own peculiar structures of globalization.

Global polity and society theorists argue that the concept of global polity and/or society has become a believable idea only in the modern age and, in particular, science, technology, industry, and universal values are increasingly creating a world that is different from any past age. The globalization literature is full of discussions of the decreasing power and significance of the nation-state and the increasing significance (if not actually power) of supra-national and global institutions and systems of belief. For these theorists, while globalization itself can have many causes, the most desirable driver for the future will be the organization of global governance through, for some, global civil society.

A significant literature connects globalization with modernity, around the theme that modernity has become a progressively global phenomenon. Ideas of space–time distanciation (Giddens 1990) and of time–space compression (Harvey 1989) were generated to illustrate how processes of globalization compress, stretch, and deepen space–time for people all over the world thus creating some of the conditions for a global polity and society.

Giddens, in particular, developed these themes in his analysis of the relations between globalization and modernity. He defined globalization in terms of four dimensions, the nation-state system, the world military order, the international division of labour, and the world capitalist economy. He explains globalization as a consequence of modernity itself and characterizes the transformation of key social relations in terms of globalizing tendencies of modernity and localized events in daily life. The transnational or global society thrust of Giddens's concept of globalization is clear from his reference to emergent forms of world interdependence and planetary consciousness.

In his attempt to order the field of globalization studies, Spybey (1996) contrasts the view that 'modernity is inherently globalizing' (Giddens 1990: 63) with the view that globalization pre-dates modernity (Robertson 1992). While Spybey comes down in favour of Giddens's thesis that globalization is best conceptualized as reflexive modernization, he is less clear about why these differences matter and, in the end, as with so many debates in the social sciences, the main protagonists seem to be saying more or less the same things in rather different languages. However, there is one important point in this debate that is separable from the often convoluted arguments about modernity and postmodernity. Is globalization a new name for a relatively old phenomenon (which appears to be the argument of Robertson and, paradoxically, many globo-sceptics)? Is it a relatively new, largely twentieth-century phenomenon but a form of modernity (the argument of Giddens)? Or is it very new and primarily a consequence of post-1960s capitalism (the argument of this book)?

Why does this matter? It matters because if we want to understand our own lives and the lives of those around us, in our families, communities, local regions, countries, supra-national regions, and, ultimately, how we relate to the global, then it is absolutely fundamental that we are clear about the extent to which the many different structures within which we live are the same in the most important respects as they have been, or are different. Hirst and Thompson, in their attempt to demonstrate that globalization is a myth and that the global economy does not really exist, argue unconvincingly that there is 'no fundamental difference between the international submarine telegraph cable method of financial transactions [of the early twentieth century] and contemporary elec-tronic systems' (Hirst and Thompson 1996: 197). The fundamental difference is, precisely, in the way that the electronics revolution (a post-1960s phenomenon) has transformed the quantitative possibilities of transferring cash and money capital into qualitatively new forms of corporate and personal financing, entrepreneurship, and, crucially, the system of credit on which the global culture-ideology of consumerism largely rests. These phenomena are all new and fundamental for understanding not only what is hap-pening in the rich countries, but in social groups anywhere who have a part to play in this global system. In this sense, ideas of a global polity and society are very provocative, but while it is relatively easy to establish empirically the objective dimensions of globaliza-tion as they involve the large majority of the world's population, the idea of global polity and/or global society, based on subjective relationships to globalization, planetary consciousness, and the like, is highly speculative.

There appears to be, however, a real psychological need for many progressive writers to believe in the possibilities of a global society (which I share). As McGrew (1992) shows, this theme is elaborated by scholars grappling with the apparent contradictions between globalization and local disruption and strife based on ethnic and other particularistic loyalties. It is in this type of approach that a growing appreciation of the ethical problems of globalization is particularly to be found. The reason for this is simple: now that humankind is vulnerable to destruction through nuclear and toxic catastrophes, a demo-cratic and just human society on the global level, however utopian, seems to be the best long-term guarantee of the continued survival of humanity.

GLOBAL CAPITALISM

A fourth approach locates the main driver of globalization in the structures of an ever-more globalizing capitalism (for example, Ross and Trachte 1990, McMichael 2000, Robinson 1996, and my own work). While all of these writers and others who could be identified with this approach develop their own specific analyses of globalization, they all strive towards a concept of the global that involves more than the relations between nation-states and state-centrist explanations of national economies competing against each other.

Ross and Trachte focus specifically on capitalism as a social system which can best be analysed on three levels, namely the level of the internal logic of the system (inspired by Marx and Adam Smith), the structural level of historical development, and the level of the specific social formation, or society. They explain the deindustrialization of some of the heartland regions of capitalism and the transformations of the Third World in these terms and argue that the globalization of the capitalist system is deeply connected to the capitalist crises of the 1970s and after. This leads them to conclude that 'We are only at the beginning of the global era' (Ross and Trachte 1990: 230), a prediction that looked far-fetched in 1990 but sounds commonplace today.

McMichael (2000) focuses on the issue of Third World development and provides both theoretical and empirical support for the thesis that globalization is a qualitatively new phenomenon and not simply a quantitative expansion of older trends. He contrasts the Development Project of the late 1940s up to the early 1970s, modelled on the parallel development of national economies under an international development regime, with the Globalization Project from the 1980s onwards, modelled on development through integration into a globalized world market and directed by a public-private coalition of Global Managers. He explains: 'As economic activity became embedded more deeply in global enterprise, the reach of the global economy strengthened at the expense of national economies. This situation was not unique to the 1980s, but the mechanisms of the debt regime institutionalized the power and authority of global management within states' very organization and procedures. This was the turning point in the story of development' (McMichael 2000: 139).

To these writers on globalization and capitalism we can add other Marx-inspired scholars who see capitalism as a global system, but do not have any specific concepts of globalization. The most important of these is the geographer, David Harvey, whose Marx-ist analysis of modernity and postmodernity is significant for the attempt to build a bridge between the debates around economic and cultural globalization (Harvey 1989, especially ch. 15). However, it should be noted that most Marx-inclined writers appear to be very sceptical about the value of globalization as a concept, preferring to see it as yet another mystification thrown up by capitalist ideologues to confuse the masses (see, for example, Petras and Veltmeyer 2000).

I locate my own work since 1990 within the Marx-inspired conception of globalization. In the first version of this book in 1990 I proposed a more explicit model of the global capitalism model within a framework for analysis of globalization, namely global sys-tems theory, based on the concept of transnational practices, practices that originate with non-state actors and cross state borders. They are analytically distinguished in three spheres: economic, political, and culture-ideology. The research agenda of this theory is concerned with how TNCs, the transnational capitalist class, and the culture-ideology of consumerism operate to transform the world in terms of the global capitalist project. In this book, the argument is taken further into alternative forms of globalization. These will be discussed in the following chapters.

SUMMING UP THE APPROACHES

This selective account of the state of globalization studies to date has focused on what distinguishes transnational (globalizing) from national and inter-national forces, processes, and institutions. It is almost exclusively based on the European and North American literature and it does not preclude the possibility of other and quite different conceptions of globalization being developed elsewhere. Despite the view, particularly evident in the accounts of global culture theorists (see Waters 1995) that globalization is more or less the same as Westernization or Americanization or McDonaldization (Ritzer 1996), more and more critics are beginning to deconstruct this one-way traffic bias in the globalization literature (see Guerlain 1997). This critique is well represented in the empirical cases and analytical points of those who are 'Interrogating Theories of the Global' (in King 1991: ch. 6), contributions in Jameson and Miyoshi (1998), and in the post-colonial critique (surveyed in Lazarus 1999), all of who provide necessary correctives to European-North American orthodoxies. Mittelman's (2000) development of the concept of a global division of labour and power is also relevant here. These and others are doing important research on globalization, though their work does not necessarily fit into the four approaches identified above. It is very likely that an introduction to globalization studies to be written ten years from now will reflect non-Western perspectives much more strongly.[19]

Each of the four approaches to globalization has its own distinctive strengths and weaknesses. The world-system model tends to be economistic (minimizing the importance of political and cultural factors), but as globalization is often interpreted in terms of economic actors and economic institutions, this does seem to be a realistic approach. The globalization of culture model, on the other hand, tends to be culturalist (minimizing economic factors), but as much of the criticism of globalization comes from those who focus on the negative effects of homogenizing mass media and marketing on local and indigenous cultures, the culturalist approach has many adherents. The global polity and society approach tends to be both optimistic and all-inclusive, an excellent combination for the production of world-views, but less satisfactory for social science research programmes. Finally, the global capitalism model, by prioritizing the capitalist global system and paying less attention to other global forces, runs the risk of appearing one-sided. However, two questions remain: how important is that one side (global capitalism)? And, what, exactly, is wrong with capitalist globalization? These are the central questions that this book poses and tries to answer.

The answer to the first question is implicit on almost every page in the book. Global capitalism, driven by the TNCs, organized politically through the transnational capitalist class, and fuelled by the culture-ideology of consumerism, is the most potent force for change in the world today. This is hardly a controversial proposition. The second question is more problematic. Attitudes to capitalist globalization range from happy fatalism (things are getting better all the time) through optimistic fatalism (things will surely get better for those who are hurting) to depressed fatalism (things will get worse for those who are hurting and may never get much better but there is nothing anyone can do about it). However, Marx-inspired crisis theory suggests that the problems with capitalism are a consequence of contradictions within the capitalist mode of production itself. Global system theory complements this argument by globalizing it. As capitalism globalizes, its crises intensify. Two main crises can be identified, the crisis of class polarization and the crisis of ecological unsustainability.[20]

THE CLASS POLARIZATION CRISIS

The crisis of class polarization—the growing numbers of the very rich and the very poor and the widening gaps between them—is at the focus of radical critiques of capitalist globalization. Singer attacks this question in terms of inequality:

inequality appears at the very center of the major issues of our time: international exploitation, racism, gender discrimination, and the hierarchical division of labor. And when polarization rhymes with stagnation, it is no longer possible to pretend that, because of the expanding pie, equality is irrelevant. Egalitarianism—not to be confused with levelling and uniformity—must be at the very heart of any progressive project. (Singer 1999: 6)

What makes this a *class* crisis? The facts are as follows. According to the World Bank, agencies of the UN, and most other sources, between 1970 and 2000 the distribution of income on a per capita basis between the richest and the poorest countries and between groups within most countries became more unequal (Korzeniewicz and Moran 1997). The UNDP presented a sobering historical perspective in its 2000 Report: 'Global inequalities in income increased in the 20th century by orders of magnitude out of proportion to anything experienced before. The distance between the incomes of the richest and poorest country was about 3 to 1 in 1820, 35 to 1 in 1950, 44 to 1 in 1973 and 72 to 1 in 1992' (UNDP 2000a: 6). No doubt the exact proportions can be challenged (see Atkinson and Bourguignon 2000) but the recent trend is undeniable. The usual way to measure inequalities within countries is by comparing deciles (10 per cent) or quintiles (20 per cent) of the total distribution of incomes. The top 10 per cent of the world's income earners got relatively more and the bottom 10 per cent got relatively less, while the average per capita income (gross national product divided by population) roughly doubled in the last quarter of the twentieth century. Was the whole world becoming richer or poorer? The rich in most countries certainly became richer, both relative to the poor and absolutely. Relative to the rich the poor were becoming poorer, while some of them were becoming richer in absolute terms. Other groups of poor people, notably landless peasants, including many women and their children, and the families of the urban unemployed, became absolutely poorer in this period too.

UN Research Institute for Social Development (UNRISD 2000: table 1.3) estimated that the numbers of people living on less than $1 per day had increased from 1,196,500,000 in 1987 to 1,214,200,000 in 1998. Reductions had been recorded in East Asia and the Pacific, the Middle East and North Africa, increases in postcommunist Europe and Central Asia, Latin America, Caribbean, South Asia and sub-Saharan Africa. 'The incidence of poverty has increased in the past few years not because the world as a whole is getting poorer, but because the benefits of growth have been unevenly spread. There has been a striking increase in inequality' (UNRISD 2000: 11).

Most countries for which there is data appeared to have made some progress between 1975 and 2000, but in different ways. The exceptions are in sub-Saharan Africa (because of

HIV/AIDS) and in postcommunist Europe (because of economic stagnation). The different criteria that UNDP generated for developing (HPI-1) and industrialized (HPI-2) countries permit a finer analysis of world poverty. Data on eighty-five Third World countries illustrates a wide range of deprivation among them. For example, 3.9 per cent of the population of Uruguay were in severe poverty in the late 1990s compared with 64.7 per cent in Niger. Overall, the HPI-1 measure of more than one-third of the developing countries exceeded 33 per cent (that is, at least one-third of the people in these countries were in extreme poverty). Variations between the general HDI measure and HPI-1 show that while Mexico and Trinidad and Tobago, for example, shared the same HDI, Mexico had double the proportion in extreme poverty; and while Guatemala and Tanzania differed widely on HDI , they had the same proportion in extreme poverty (29 per cent).

HPI-2 (industrialized country) rankings showed that Norway, Sweden, and Netherlands had the lowest proportions in poverty (but still around 7–8 per cent of their populations), while the UK, Ireland, and the USA, despite very high overall HDI scores, had around 15 per cent in poverty. Disparities also exist within countries, between regions and districts, especially between urban and rural communities (poverty levels are often double in rural compared with urban areas, and large differences exist between provinces in China). Many ethnic and language groups (e.g. Mayan communities in Guatemala, African males in South Africa, scheduled tribes in India, and San speakers in Namibia) suffer relative deprivation. Imaginative research in Vietnam in the early 1990s showed that members of ethnic minorities were typically up to twice as far from post offices, schools, hospitals, and district centres as members of the ethnic majority (UNDP 2000a: 32). The Gender Index (GDI) for 143 countries is lower in every case than HDI, proving that gender inequality is more or less universal. However, some countries have improved their positions on this measure, though this might be due to men losing some of their advantages as much as women doing better.

In a grim report on human poverty UNDP lists the income or consumption share of the poorest 20 per cent of the population in fourteen countries in four continents. On these figures, the people in the poorest quintile in Brazil who share just 2.5 per cent of total income appear to be worst off. Comparable figures for South Africa are 2.9, for Russia 4.2, and for Thailand 5.6. In words that echo the empirical reality that underlies what I am conceptualizing as the crisis of class polarization, UNDP concludes: 'Economic growth cannot be accelerated enough to overcome the handicap of too much income directed to the rich. Income does not trickle down; it only circulates among elite groups' (UNDP 2000b: 43). The poorest people in the world suffer on many counts. For example, with respect to clean water and sanitation:

When the International Drinking Water Supply and Sanitation Decade started in 1981, it was estimated that 2.4 billion people needed both an improved water supply and improved sanitation [equivalent to facilities for 660,000 people per day for ten years, while actual numbers provided for were 370,000 and 200,000 per day] ... The corresponding figures for the 1990s, the decade of Safe Water 2000, were 220,000 per day with improved water and 210,000 per day with improved sanitation. (Mara and Feacham 2001: 13–14)

The numbers served are impressive, but far from adequate to solve the problems. In 2001 it was estimated that over 1 billion people still lack adequate water supply, with most of the growth likely to occur in urban areas. Mara and Feacham suggest that providing access by 2025 to all of them is a possible target. However, 2.4 billion people need improved sanitation (most of these in rural areas). To meet this projected need proper toilets will have to be provided for 460,000 people every day for the next twenty-five years. This level of provision is not feasible.

Faced with such overwhelming evidence from a variety of sources, even the WTO Annual Report for 1998 had to admit the reality of polarization, albeit in a convoluted statement: 'Empirical evidence tends to show that trade liberalization may entail non-trivial adjustment costs for certain groups' (quoted in Hines 2000: 157). Non-trivial adjustment costs meant that in Mexico, for example, real incomes of workers were estimated to have declined by 84.6 per cent between 1976 and 1998. In 1981 the minimum wage bought 38 kilos of tortillas (the staple food of the poor), by January 2000 only 9.3 kilos. The Independent Peasants Union estimated that 26 million rural dwellers (one quarter of the population) could not afford an adequate diet. Meanwhile, foreign investment, social polarization, and crime boom and welfare provision collapses. Mexican society is becoming increasingly militarized, with gated communities, armed guards, and invasive police and military power (Ochoa and Wilson 2001). This description can be reproduced in many Third World countries, as the World Bank, UNRISD, and UNDP reports cited above confirm.

Poverty in the Third World is now relatively well known to the reasonably informed lay reader. What is less well known is that in the First World, particularly in the USA and some parts of Europe, and more recently in Japan, the economic position of many workers and the workless poor has deteriorated since the 1960s as the HDI-2 data shows (see Walker 1999 for a snapshot of the situation). Thomas (2001) argues convincingly that the neo-liberal vision of global governance and development cannot provide human security (satisfaction of basic needs) and as poverty and inequality deepen this represents a crisis for the system. As we have seen, there is plenty of evidence for the crisis, though it is important also to recognize the significance of the other side of the crisis, the growing numbers of the very rich (Bhalla 1998).[21] Box 3.1 illustrates the dramatic extent of polarization between rich and poor for a number of Third World countries with respect to health and education.

The distinctiveness of the class polarization thesis is that it recognizes both increasing emiseration and increasing enrichment, thus in all countries, rich and poor, privileged communities are to be found. In Douala, a large city in Cameroon, Denver (the reference is to the TV show *Dynasty*) is an upmarket neighbourhood that 'aims to be the preferred place of residence of the newly rich: young entrepreneurs, businessmen, corporate executives, and high-level administrators in the Ministry of Finance' (Monga 2000: 205). This Denver stands in stark contrast to the nearby settlement of Bepanda Yon-yon, typical of squalid neighbourhoods all over Africa. The key symbol of the difference, Monga reports, is the air conditioner.

As Dockemdorff *et al.* (2000) demonstrate, despite the success of Santiago de Chile as a modern business metropolis, there is severe residential polarization in terms of poverty (many of the poor work in the formal sector by the way), education, infrastructure, and other services. 'The new location trends for office buildings are perhaps the most significant example of segregation. Ninety-six per cent of the total office space constructed between 1990 and 1998 is shared between [the richest] five of the 34 communas. . . . This shows how the globalization process is restructuring cities, by creating new service zones

---

Box 3.1 **Polarization in health and education in Third World societies (late 1990s)**

- In Sao Paulo (Brazil) and Accra (Ghana) death rates from infectious disease are twice as high for those living in the poorest areas compared with the richest areas.

- In the Philippines, South Africa, and Nepal infant mortality rate for the poorest 20% of children is twice as high as for the richest 20%.

- In NE and SE Brazil the under-5 mortality rate for the poorest 20% of children is over six times that of the richest 20% of children.

- In Peru, rates of underweight and stunting amongst the poorest 20% are about five times those amongst the richest 20%.

- In Indonesia only 21% of births of the rural poor and 49% of births of the urban poor were attended by medical personnel, compared with 78% and 93% for the rural and urban rich.

- 59% of deaths among the poorest 20% of the world population were caused by communicable diseases, for the rich 8%.

- In India, 15–19-year-olds from the richest 20% of households have completed on average ten years of schooling, children from the poorest 40% of households have on average no schooling.

- 39% of poor 6–14-year-olds in Nigeria were in school, compared with 91% of rich 6–14s; in Madagascar, 47% compared with 90%.

- In Ecuador, 75% of households among the poorest fifth lack piped water, compared with 12% among the richest fifth.

- In Sao Paulo the 9% living in the richest areas consume five times as much water per capita as the 41% living in the poorest areas; in Accra water consumption per capita is three times higher for the one-third of people living in the richest areas compared to those living in the poorest areas.

- In Guatemala, the richest 20% of under-5s have a 47% rate of stunting, whereas the poorest 20% have a 70% rate of stunting; 25% of the richest 20% of children under 5 are underweight, compared with 41% of the poorest 20%.

- In Morocco, 15% of the wealthiest under-5s quintile suffer from stunting, 39% of the poorest quintile; 6% of the richest children under 5 in Morocco are underweight and 23% of the poorest are underweight.

- In Peru, 10% of the richest children under 5 suffer from stunting, compared with 51% of the poorest; 5% of the wealthiest quintile of children under 5 are underweight, 22% of the poorest.

Source: adapted from **http://worldbank.com/poverty/date/trends/social.pdf**

---

with new location patterns, complemented by high quality infrastructure' (Dockemdorff *et al.* 2000: 179). While the proportions may be extreme, the pattern is familiar (compare Marcuse and van Kempen 2000: ch. 12).

Mexico, Chile, and Cameroon are not untypical. The way that capitalist globalization tries to cope with the crisis of class polarization is put very starkly but in terms that many will recognize by Tehranian (1999: 15): 'Pancapitalism has found an ingenious solution to these problems: gated ghettos, factories, and residential communities. In Mexico City, New York, Los Angeles, Chicago, Bombay, and Calcutta, the ghettos for the poor are more or less defined and cordoned off geographically. It is unsafe for outsiders to wander of into these areas.'[22] Residential segregation is, of course, nothing new, but the increase of high-security housing for the rich, often electronically protected against the poor, is a feature of many societies. For example, Blakely and Snyder (1997) show that by 1997 about 9 million Americans were living in gated communities of various types. Chaplin (1999) goes some way to provide a convincing explanation for this. The middle and upper classes (she is writing of India, but it is generally true) have little interest in putting pressure on their municipal authorities to provide services for the urban poor and certainly would not want to pay for the expensive infrastructure involved. In cities in India, as well as in Brazil and other deeply divided countries, quite luxurious enclaves coexist uneasily with slum and ghettos. This polarization provokes several distinct political responses, and models of the passive poor, the surviving poor, the politically active poor, and the resisting poor have been generated to explain these (Bayat 2000).

Another indication of widening gaps between the new rich and the very poor is the increasingly important phenomenon of tourism within Asia, Latin America, and Africa (see Ghimire 2001). Not unnaturally, as more and more people in the Third World become richer they will want to spend at least some of their money on leisure. In Chapters 7 and 9 the spread of the culture-ideology of consumerism in the Third World and in China is discussed, and the growth of internal tourism is a component of this facet of the spread of capitalist globalization.

Similarly, the digital divide highlights polarization between richer and poorer in terms of access to electronic technologies, particularly the Internet (Mansell and Wehn 1998, Main 2001). In regional terms there is plenty of evidence of the digital divide. In 1998, North America had 168 times more Internet hosts than Africa, and Africa had 396 times more people per host than North America (Madon 2000: 86; see also M'Bayo 1997). Lists comparing the connectivity of different countries are common, but state-centrism, as usual, can be misleading. In the USA, for example, there is a definite hierarchy of Internet use, not all cities are network cities there (Townsend 2001) and neither are they in most other countries (see also, Graham 1999). Within communities, it is obvious that some groups have more access than others, even in the USA where the relative affordability of home Internet use means that around 60 per cent had access in 2001. On the other hand, in some parts of the Third World there is a good deal of pathbreaking research taking place on cheap, user-friendly electronics. For example, scientists in India have developed a palmtop, the Simputer, with software that translates English into a variety of Indian languages (**www.simputer.org**). This runs on AAA batteries and gives relatively inexpensive online access. In Brazil, the government is developing a Computador Popular (the locals call it the Volkscomputor) that will cut the cost of basic computing. But these machines will still cost around $200, beyond the means of most people in these countries, though the Simputer is designed for communal use.

Despite these and many other initiatives there is clearly a polarization crisis on a global scale. But is this a class crisis? As most of the evidence makes clear it is the lack of economic resources that is the main reason why so many of the poor are getting poorer while access to economic resources explains why the rich are getting richer. While there are more poor women than men, more poor members of some ethnic minorities than of the majority groups, and more poor people in rural than urban areas, their relative poverty is not due to their gender, their ethnicity, or their location but to their lack of access to education, well-paying jobs, land, fair prices for their crops, and to their poor health, malnutrition, and hunger. That the children of the very poor generally find it very difficult to escape from poverty themselves goes a long way towards explaining why these cycles of deprivation are so difficult to break down. It is their relationship to the means of production, to capital in its various forms, that locks most of the poor into

---

Box 3.2 **Polarization in the USA**

- The *Washington Post* carried an article on 1 March, 1998, saying that the richest 1% of the US population possesses more wealth than the total wealth of 90% of the total population.

- The bottom 25% of US families witnessed a 9% decline in income between 1979 and 1995, with the richest 25% of families enjoying a 26% increase during the period, according to a *USA Today* report in 1997.

- The income of the richest 5% of families was 5.7 times that for the bottom 20% of families in 1995.

- Official statistics released in 1997 show that the top 20% of US families shared 49% of the country's total income in 1996, with the income level for the bottom 20% families falling by 1.8%.

- The current income level for the top 20% of the population is nine times more than the figure for the bottom 20%, up significantly from the 3.5 times figure in 1979. In addition, some 75% of American workers earn less today than in 1979.

- 16% of the US population lived below the poverty line in 1974, with the figure rising to 19% in 1997.

- Results from the most recent census show a disparity in the economic status of blacks, with the average net property value of black families standing at only a tenth of the level for white families. A *USA Today* article published in April 1997 noted that the income level for Afro-American families stands at only 63% of the level for white families.

- The *Wall Street Journal* (3 Sept. 1997) reported that the income level for a black person is 19% lower than that for a white person with the same education level. It also noted that the proportion of poverty-stricken black families is 15% higher than for poor white families, with the total number of the former more than double the figure for the latter.

Source: adapted from 'Human Rights Records in the United States' (Ren Yanshi, Beijing, 1 March 1999)
http://mprofaca.cronet.com/hr_in usa.html

---

poverty, thus it is at its base a class crisis. As Box 3.2 illustrates, class polarization appears to be as true for one of the richest and best-endowed societies in the world, the USA (ironically the source is from China), as it is for poorer countries.

THE CRISIS OF ECOLOGICAL UNSUSTAINABILITY

While the literature on all aspects of globalization has been expanding very rapidly in the last decade, it is probably no exaggeration to say that the literature on global environmental change has led the way. Much of this literature highlights what Held *et al.* in their survey of globalization describe as 'a catastrophe in the making' (1999: ch. 8).

The facts of ecological stress at the planetary level are clear, though their significance is not universally agreed. Scientific research, the mass publicity that it attracted, and consequent state and private funding, combined to provide a framework for the study of global environmental change in the context of sustainable development (World Resources Institute 1992; McManus 1996). Some advances have been made, for example in the control of CFC gases and some stewardship of some parts of the atmosphere, oceans, forests, and other natural resources, though argument still rages over the so-called global commons (Redclift and Woodgate 1995: vol. ii, part I). Nevertheless, in an unprecedented joint millennium report, with the ominous subtitle *People and Ecosystems: the Fraying Web of*

Table 3.1 Indicators of ecological crisis

	Agro	Coastal	Forest	Fresh Water	Grassland
Food/Fibre production	Decreasing (Good)	Decreasing (Fair)	Increasing (Good)	Mixed (Good)	Decreasing (Fair)
Water Quality	Decreasing (Poor)	Mixed (Fair)	Decreasing (Fair)	Decreasing (Poor)	(Not assessed)
Water Quantity	Decreasing (Fair)	(Not assessed)	Decreasing (Fair)	Decreasing (Fair)	(Not assessed)
Biodiversity	Decreasing (Poor)	Decreasing (Fair)	Decreasing (Poor)	Decreasing (Bad)	Decreasing (Fair)
Carbon Storage	Mixed (Fair)	(Not assessed)	Decreasing (Fair)	(Not assessed)	Decreasing (Good)
Recreation	(Not assessed)	Unknown (Good)	(Not assessed)	(Not assessed)	Decreasing (Good)
Shoreline Protection	(Not assessed)	Decreasing (Poor)	(Not assessed)	(Not assessed)	(Not assessed)
Wood Fuel Production	(Not assessed)	(Not assessed)	Unknown (Fair)	(Not assessed)	(Not assessed)

Note: decreasing/mixed/increasing refer to condition of ecosystem; text in brackets refers to the estimated capacity of the ecosystem for sustainability.

Source: data compiled from 'The Ecosystem Scorecard' *World Resources 2000–01*, reprinted by permission of the publisher.

Life, UNDP, UNEP, World Bank, and the World Resources Institute all but acknowledge that the present global system is unsustainable, though the fact that it is a capitalist system is ignored (World Resources Institute 2000). Table 3.1, taken from this report, presents some key indicators of ecological crisis.

Agricultural lands, rainforests and other wooded areas, grasslands, and sources of fresh water are all at risk. Many rivers and other aquatic ecosystems are suffering severe ecological distress. The most dramatic cases are that of the Aral Sea where of twenty-four pre-existing fish species twenty have already disappeared, and the Rhine River where forty-four species became rare or disappeared between 1890 and 1975. Other rivers (the Colorado, Danube, Pearl River) also show signs of severe stress because of biodiversity loss, change of species composition, and loss of fisheries (World Resources Institute 2000: 115). Table 3.2 illustrates this last point for the oceans, the unsustainability of fisheries in the world's oceans at the present rate of exploitation. Ocean fishing is a very important source of food and income for poor people living near coastlines and the overfishing by large commercial fleets increases the pressure on the livelihoods of the poor.

While the details of the impending ecological crisis are not widely known, most people appear to be more aware of human impacts on the environment than ever before. This is due to at least three major factors.

(i) A series of high-profile international meetings since the 1970s, notably the United Nations Conference on Environment and Development in Rio in 1992 and the controversy over the implementation of the Kyoto agreement on global climate change, have made it difficult for intellectual and political elites to ignore the crisis. This is clear from even a casual look at daily papers and magazines and TV all over the world. To take just

Table 3.2 State of the world's ocean fisheries

Ocean	Status of the fisheries	Fully fished by:
Atlantic Ocean	I–F	1983
North-east Atlantic	OV	1983
North-west Atlantic	OV	1971
Eastern Central Atlantic	OV	1984
Western Central Atlantic	OV	1987
South-east Atlantic	OV	1978
South-west Atlantic	I	1997
Pacific Ocean	I–F	1999
North-east Pacific	OV	1990
North-west Pacific	I	1998
Eastern Central Pacific	OV	1988
Western Central Pacific	I	2003
South-east Pacific	I	2001
South-west Pacific	OV	1991
Indian Ocean	I	–
Eastern Indian	I	2037
Western Indian	I	2051
Mediterranean and the Black Sea	F	–
Antarctic	OV	1980

Note: OV, Overfished; F, Fully fished; I, Catch is increasing.

Source: Adapted from tables in *World Resources 2000–01*, reprinted by permission of the publisher.

one example from the academic research sphere, in the introduction to a special number of the *Journal of Social Issues* on 'Promoting Environmentalism', Zelezny and Schultz (2000) document the increasingly critical treatment of the environment in several special issues since the 1960s. Then, the main problem was conceptualized as the effects of the physical environment on human beings, now the focus is on what we are doing to the environment. The number of academic journals and research institutes on the environment has accelerated rapidly since the 1960s, reflected in the impressive three volumes on *Sociology of the Environment* edited by Redclift and Woodgate (1995).

(ii) There is clearly a growing disquiet about daily environmental degradation, serious incidents, and the difficulty of making environmental choices. The destruction of the ozone layer, decreasing biodiversity, worsening land, air, and water pollution in many places; sudden environmental catastrophes such as those at Bhopal and Chernobyl, devastating oil spills; floods, droughts, and hurricanes attributed to global warming; and advice on what we have to do to save the planet, are regularly reported in the mass media and popular scientific publications (see Brower and Leon 1999).

(iii) The rise in the last few decades of green movements in the North (McCormick 1992; Vig and Axelrod 1999) and the South (Wignaraja 1993, Goldfrank *et al.* 1999: part III) exerts a continuous pressure for action on the environment. The significance of the increasing convergence of environmental campaigns and movements around the world lies in the recognition that there are winners and losers in most struggles over the environment (see Redclift and Woodgate 1995: vol. iii). Dwivedi (2001: 16) correctly points up the common perception of the differences between activists in the North and the South: 'it is not as much life-styles as life chances that constitute the battleground of environmental politics in the South.' He cites the movements around Chipko and the Narmada dam in India, the Chico dam in the Philippines, rubber tappers in Brazil, the Zapatistas, the Ogoni in Nigeria, and Green Belt activists in Kenya. Forsyth (2001) takes the argument a little further in his analysis of environmental movements in Thailand. His research demonstrates that environmentalism (in South-East Asia at least) cannot simply be dismissed as a pastime of the urban elite. He distinguishes three categories of environmental issues: green (wildlife, forestry, wilderness, etc.); brown (industrial and urban pollution); and a growing discourse of 'red-green' environmentalism (poverty reduction and social development as environmental priorities). Using newspaper framings of environmental conflicts from the *Bangkok Post* (an English language paper but written mainly for Thais) from the 1980s and 1990s, he shows the centrality of deforestation for all groups, but each framed the issues in a different way.[23] Those pursuing the red-green agenda on reforestation (and dams) highlighted threats to farming communities, acknowledging that environmental issues have winners and losers, and these tend to be class-based.

O'Brien and Leichenko (2000), in their assessment of the impacts of climate change, develop the winners and losers approach (this is, of course, a very general proposition) into the concept of double exposure, when some regions, sectors, ecosystems, and social groups are exposed simultaneously to adverse impacts from climate change and economic globalization. This usefully combines the analysis of the crises of class polarization and ecological unsustainability (though they do not use these terms). As they observe, winners can eventually become losers, though losers usually remain losers.[24]

While many TNCs (both the major globalizing corporations and smaller consumer-sensitive companies) have begun to institutionalize in-house mechanisms for dealing with resource and pollution issues, many other TNCs, their subcontracting partners, and local firms ignore good practice in production and waste disposal, even where required to do so by law, and pose ongoing threats to the global environment. More generally, the role of capitalist globalization in promoting unsustainable patterns of consumption with little thought for the environmental consequences has been critically scrutinized (Durning 1992, Redclift 1996). This latter issue raises fundamental questions about the capitalist global project and the central place of consumption, for both economic growth and ideological credibility. Even Wallerstein (in Goldfrank *et al.* 1999: 7) has come to the conclusion that 'the implementation of significant ecological measures, seriously carried out, could well serve as the coup de grace to the viability of the capitalist system'.[25]

Global capitalism, through the unceasing public pronouncements of members of the transnational capitalist class, acknowledges many of these issues, but as problems to be solved rather than crises. Corporate executives, world leaders, those who run the major international institutions, globalizing professionals, the mainstream mass media, all accept that the rich are getting richer, some of the poor are getting poorer, and the gaps between the rich and the poor are widening in our globalizing world. This is rarely seen as a class polarization crisis, but that is what it is. Summits and conferences are held, expert commissions are established, targets are set, Action Programmes are put into practice, some targets are missed and some are achieved, and the process grinds on. Public representatives of the transnational capitalist class accept that there are environmental problems and that something has to be done about them. The transnational capitalist class even accommodates some mild criticism of consumerism and globalization, but the fatal connection between the capitalist mode of production and the holistic ecological crisis is almost entirely suppressed. Addiction research might help us to understand the psychological processes involved in burying what most of us know to be true about class polarization and ecological unsustainability to the deepest reaches of the unconscious. This analysis from India makes the point well:

Since independence a preference for giganticism has come to dominate our development paradigm. Our planners, politicians and experts have opted wholesale for large dams and gigantic industrial units, and have dug mines and exploited forests in pursuit of their elitist vision of progress and development. The cumulative ill-effects of all this development are now assuming disastrous proportions for a large section of the population, particularly for its most depressed strata—the tribals, the peasants and labourers—along with the already depleting natural resource base and our scarce financial recources. (Action Committee for National Rally against Destructive Development (1989), quoted in Dwivedi 1998: 148)[26]

The following chapters will set out the role of capitalist globalization in the creation and intensification of these crises. In order to do this, it is necessary to focus on the significance of transnational corporations for capitalist globalization.

NOTES

1. In an interesting critique of state-centrism, Radice (2000) points out that much of the argument against globalization as such rests on a rather naive progressive nationalism. To which I can add that if Ohmae had not existed then globo-sceptics would have had to invent him!.

2. See Owen and Sutcliffe (1972), with its still useful annotated bibliography; and the more recent survey by Brewer (1990).

3. 'Rosa Luxemburg stands at the apex of the attempt to make operational the Marxist concept of class as the primary social referent, and to break once and for all the old alternative stranglehold of nation. In this respect her contribution is second to none' (Nettl 1969: 519). This is precisely what the theory of socialist globalization attempts to do, but in order to do this, the Marxist concept of class needs to be globalized (see Sklair 2001: ch. 2).

4. This is a very bare summary. For a balanced account of modernization theory and its main critics, see the textbook by Harrison (1988). Some of the main sources are reprinted in Roberts and Hite (2000: part II).

5. It is interesting to note that the widespread criticisms of modernization theory and the inadequacy of the traditional/modern dichotomy appeared to have been forgotten by subsequent theorists of modernity. Notable in this respect is the attempt to theorize globalization as late and reflexive modernity (Giddens 1990); see also Lazarus (1999).

6. The best single source for these views is the book of readings edited by Eisenstadt (1970). See also Harrison (1988).

7. There are several excellent guides to this literature, notably Kay (1989) for a distinctive Latin American perspective. Packenham (1992) usefully discusses the politics of dependency theory, and Frank (1984) has a large bibliography, for and against.

8. See, in general, Moody (1998). I look in more detail at the bauxite-aluminium and the power industry in Chapter 4. My own research in the 1980s and early 1990s attempted to establish criteria for evaluating positive and negative developmental effects of TNC investment in the Third World (Sklair 1991, 1993) and Sklair (1994).

9. Beeson (2000) presents an interesting analysis of attempted selective delinking in Malaysia.

10. Lechner and Boli (2000) usefully reproduce fifty-four basic sources. See also two comprehensive multi-disciplinary surveys, Scholte (2000) and Held *et al.* (1999) and the collection edited by Smith and Guarnizo (1998). In addition to the multitude of US and Euro-centred publications on globalization, see Jameson and Miyoshi (1998) and the post-colonialist analysis in Lazarus (1999). The extensive bibliographies in these and other sources cited in the text complement the brief interpretation of competing conceptions of globalization that follows.

11. *Fortune* magazine publishes annual lists of the biggest TNCs in the USA and around the world, ranked by revenues. Other sources do the same, but the *Fortune* 500 and Global 500 labels have stuck. The cut-off point for entry to the FG500 in 2001 was $10.3 billion.

12. While important, this measure is not a decisive indicator of whether a TNC is globalizing for the simple reason that the enormous size of the domestic market of some countries (notably the G7) means that TNCs domiciled in these countries may have huge amounts of foreign earnings from a relatively small proportion of their total revenues. For an attempt to construct measures of the extent to which TNCs are globalizing, see Sklair (2001).

13. All parts of all economies are clearly not equally globalizing. However, there is evidence that sourcing, production, and marketing processes within TNCs are being deterritorialized from countries of origin and operate in a globalizing economic system. This is the real issue for economic globalization (Dicken 1998, Sklair 2001, Gereffi and Kaplinsky 2001).

14. See Hall (2000); and also the *Journal of World-Systems Research* (**csf.colorado.edu/wsystems/jwsr.html**).

15. It may be the case that radical social scientists from the USA, so conscious of the power and ruthlessness of the American state, have difficulty in abandoning state-centrism entirely.

16. Both have chapters in Featherstone (1990). See also Robertson (1992) and Appadurai (1996).

17. The textbook by Scholte (2000), for example, is organized in terms of the triad of globalization, superterritorialization, and territorialization.

18. This is quoted in many different places. My source is, significantly, from the back page of the 25th Anniversary Issue of *Earthmatters*, the magazine of Friends of the Earth, UK. The quote is superimposed on a very cloudy map of planet earth.

19. See also the special issues of *Third World Quarterly* on globalization (21/2 2000), *International Sociology* (journal of the International Sociological Association) and *Global Networks* (journal of the Global Studies Association). All have lively websites.

20. Marxist economists will protest that the main crisis of capitalism is the falling rate of profit, though there has always been controversy even among Marxists over this (see *Historical Materialism* issues 4 and 5, 1999, Brenner 2001). Even if the rate of profit does decline it will not destroy capitalism, though its effects, class polarization and ecological unsustainability, could. For the roots of the debate on legitimation crisis, see Habermas (1976).

21. See also Vandersluis and Yeros (2000), an interesting collection that condemns globalization for failing to realize humanist ideals, a theme revisited in Chapter 10 below.

22. The fantasies of popular culture, for example Ridley Scott's film *Blade Runner* and Tom Wolf's novel *Bonfire of the Vanities*, express fears about the crisis very well. The relationships between globalization, polarization, and crime are explored by Findlay (1999).

23. See also Holzer (2001) on the significance of environmental framing.

24. Rubinoff (2001) similarly shows how the global demand for prawns (shrimp) has created unprecedented prosperity for some aquaculturalists at the cost of serious disruption to the traditional ecological balance in Goan coastal villages.

25. Hughes (2000) makes a relatively convincing argument that Marx was aware of the potential ecological crisis of capitalism. See also O'Connor (1994), Redclift and Woodgate (1995: vol.i, part II), and the journal *Capitalism, Nature, Socialism*.

26. According to research on how far the media was meeting its obligations to report on basic education needs in India, in one year's newspaper articles 8,550 were on foreign investment, 3,430 on foreign trade, 990 on education, and only 60 on rural primary education (cited in UNDP 2000a: 104).

Chapter 4

TRANSNATIONAL CORPORATIONS AND CAPITALIST GLOBALIZATION

The impact of transnational corporations in the global system, especially *Fortune* Global 500 corporations, is plain for all to see. Tourists and business travellers will more often than not travel on a plane manufactured by one of the few corporations that dominate the aerospace industry, operated by one of the airlines that dominate the civil airline industry (nine airlines were big enough to make the FG500 in 2001). They will mostly occupy hotel rooms subcontracted to or owned or managed by the local affiliate of one of the few chains that dominate the global hotel industry.[1] The cars they rent will be products of the few TNCs that dominate the global auto industry, and the agency may well be part of one of the small group of companies that dominate the car rental industry. And they will pay for some or all of this with one of the credit cards or travellers cheques issued by the few TNCs that control global personal finance.[2]

The traveller will be able to watch television programmes and films produced and distributed by the major media conglomerates, will be able to buy globally branded products, at a price, and will usually be able to get around using English, the major global language. The traveller is also liable to be bombarded with advertisements for global consumer goods placed by the local affiliates of the transnational advertising agencies. While TNCs from the United States no longer dominate these sectors as they once did, they are still the leaders in a wide variety of fields and even when they are not the leaders it is often what are labelled American-style (a problematic idea) cultural products or local adaptations of them that are on offer.

This much is obvious at the level of perception. However, it would be simplistic to conclude that the two Mcs (McLuhan and McDonald's) have succeeded in shaping the global village in the form of a fast food outlet or that the real world is in the process of being reconstructed as a universal theme park along the lines of Disneyland.[3] The reality is much more complex than this, though we would be well advised to remember the central insight of McLuhan, that the world is becoming a global village, and of McDonald's, that global packaging creates global desires.

In the previous chapters I dealt briefly with some of the major ways in which the global system has been categorized. Now is the time to act on the reasons why I find most of these approaches unsatisfactory. Lying behind my summary evaluations of these theories is the conviction that most of them are fixated around the unhelpful ideas that the state is the most appropriate unit of analysis and that First World states exploit Third World countries. The view that is propounded here is that it is more fruitful to conceptualize the global system in terms of transnational practices. Those who dominate in the realms of economic, political, and culture-ideology transnational practices in one community, city, subnational region, country, supranational region or, indeed, globally, may exploit, ignore, or help those in other places. The state-centrist approach can lead to empirical enlightenment in some cases, as I tried to show in the previous chapters, but at the expense of some theoretical confusion. The crux of the matter lies in moving beyond state-centrism to a theory of globalization based not in states and the inter-state system, but in transnational practices.

ECONOMY, POLITY, CULTURE-IDEOLOGY

The bearers of transnational practices within the capitalist global system stand in determinate relationships to all other categories of actors. Groups may be included or excluded from profitable participation in the system. One of the most important historic tasks of capitalist imperialism was to include various previously excluded groups within its realm of influence. This inclusion was, however, partial and differences emerged between the economic, political, and culture-ideology spheres.

In the economic sphere, the capitalist global system offers a more or less circumscribed place to the wage-earning majorities in most countries. The workers, the direct producers of goods and services, have occupational choices that are generally free within the range offered by local economic conditions, but they do change over time and place. For example, as capitalist globalization reduced the numbers of manufacturing jobs in most high-wage countries, workers there have been forced to seek jobs in other, often less well-paid and less secure sectors. Throughout the First World, many older workers displaced from traditional industries (like mining and metal industries) were faced with permanent unemployment. The other side of the coin is that some of the manufacturing jobs lost in relatively high-wage countries have turned up in relatively low-wage countries. This has, undoubtedly, over the last few decades, brought many people from the Third World countryside into urban areas, whether forced off their lands by hunger or predatory landlords, or as willing migrants in search of a better life.

Transnational migration, by no means a novel phenomenon, is also a prominent feature of many communities. In the twentieth century large numbers of people migrated from poor countries to richer countries in search of work and from dangerous regions to safer places in search of personal security. Millions moved from Europe and Asia to the Americas; from black Africa to white-ruled Southern Africa; from Central America and the Caribbean to North America; from the Caribbean and the Indian subcontinent to Britain; and from southern and eastern to north-western Europe. The rapid increase in such migration since the 1950s has prompted one commentator to speak of the creation of new global diasporas (Cohen 1997; see also Portes 2001). In addition, since the 1980s, there has been massive internal migration in search of employment opportunities, notably within China (Cannon 2000, and see Chapter 9 below). Faist asks why there are so few migrants from so many places and why there are so many from a few places. In contrast to much previous research on the issue that limits itself to sending and receiving communities, he elaborates the conception of transnational social spaces to capture the 'dense circular flows of persons, goods, ideas, and symbols within a migration system' (Faist 2000: 2), across generations.

While Faist's work focuses on the flows between Turkey and Germany since the 1960s, the idea of transnational social spaces seems to me an important addition to the battery of concepts available for globalization scholars. As was discussed in the section on the global culture approach to globalization in Chapter 3, much of the research effort in this genre has revolved around the idea of deterritorialized spaces of flows. Faist, correctly in my view, criticizes this as a not very fruitful set of abstractions, preferring to elaborate transnational social spaces as a series of bridges and doors (the image of Georg Simmel) located in actual places (Faist 2000: ch. 7, especially fig. 7.1). The places are legally within sovereign states, of course, but can only be grasped sociologically as transnational spaces, less structure than process, as in his discussion of the growth of migrant transnationalizing civil societies (323 ff.)[4] These territorialized spaces, therefore, are where transnational practices occur, but they are not in their most important respects defined by the nation-states in whose legal territories they happen to be located. This is the challenge, theoretically and actually, of non-state actors in the global system (see also Higgott *et al.* 2000, Pries 2000).

In those states with substantial migrant minorities as well as in those without, the inclusion of the subordinate classes in the political sphere is very partial. To put it crudely, the capitalist global system has very little need of the subordinate classes in this sphere. In the parliamentary democracies the parties must be able to mobilize the masses to vote every so often, but very few countries make voting compulsory. In many parliamentary democracies voter turn-out tends to be around half to three-quarters of the electorate in general elections and very much less in local elections. While conventional political organization is usually unfettered, the structural obstacles to genuine opposition to the capitalist system are such that there are rarely any serious challenges to it. For example: 'The presidential debates [between Clinton and Dole] were in fact sponsored by an entity called the Commission of Presidential Debates involving executives from an array of big-business firms—Philip Morris, AT&T, Prudential, IBM, Ford, and General Motors', and they excluded the alternative candidates Ralph Nader and Ross Perot (Boggs 2000: 64). Boggs concludes that this is a result of a deeply ingrained culture of antipolitics in the USA,[5] and though he considers it exceptional in this respect, many other countries are not far behind.

While the capitalist class is increasingly organized transnationally, the obstacles to transnational class formation among subordinate groups are formidable.

This is partly because, in the era of globalization, the lines among enemies, friends and allies are blurred, unlike the situation three or four decades ago when the targets of the struggle were much clearer. At the same time, the exclusionary processes of globalization, especially the continuous post-Fordist restructuring, fragment large sections of the subordinate groups, especially the unorganized, peripheral and migrant workers. Thus, resistance to globalization among subordinate groups often remains unco-ordinated, diffuse and weak. (Embong 2000: 1000)

Where serious challenges to capitalist globalization do emerge, for example in the case of the election of the socialist Salvador Allende as president of Chile in 1970, the threat is removed by violent overthrow of the constitutional power by the capitalist class through the army and the police, with the support of other key sectors of the establishment. In the Chilean case, as is well known, this was done with the active collaboration of the US government and TNCs.[6] The destabilization of socialist governments in Mozambique and Nicaragua by terrorism sponsored by hostile states (apartheid South Africa and the USA) is also well documented (see Chapter 8 below) as is terrorism against these states. In one-party states, spontaneous political participation by the masses is usually actively discouraged and realistic threats to the prevailing order tend to be focused on changing the people at the top, *coup d'état*, rather than on changing the conditions under which global capitalism operates.

The culture-ideology sphere is, however, entirely different. Here, the aim of the capitalist global system is total inclusion of all classes, and especially the subordinate classes in so far as the bourgeoisie can be considered already included. The culture-ideology project of global capitalism is to persuade people to consume not simply to satisfy their biological and other modest needs but in response to artificially created desires in order to perpetuate the accumulation of capital for private profit, in other words, to ensure that the capitalist global system goes on for ever. The culture-ideology of consumerism proclaims, literally, that the meaning of life is to be found in the things that we possess. To consume, therefore, is to be fully alive, and to remain fully alive we must continuously consume, discard, consume. The notions of men and women as economic or political beings are marginalized by global capitalism, quite logically, as the system does not even pretend to satisfy everyone in the economic or the political spheres. Men, women, children, even pets, are consumers. The point of economic activity for ordinary members of the system is simply to provide the resources to be consumers, and the point of political activity is to ensure, usually through political inactivity, that the conditions for consuming are maintained. This system has been evolving for centuries, first for aristocracies and members of the bourgeoisie all over the world, then spreading to the working classes in the First World, and slowly but surely penetrating to all those with disposable income everywhere.

This is why I have persisted in using the label culture-ideology, risking the sin of inelegance for the possibility of clarity. Culture always has an ideological function for consumerism in the capitalist global system, so all transnational cultural practices in this sphere are at the same time ideological practices, thus culture-ideology. This is not an empirical assertion—it is no doubt sometimes false and usually impossible to prove one way or the other. The idea of culture-ideology transnational practices and, in particular, the idea of the culture-ideology of consumerism in the capitalist global system, are conceptual tools in the theory of the global system. Global capitalism does not permit culture-ideology neutrality. Those cultural practices that cannot be incorporated into the culture-ideology of consumerism become oppositional counter-hegemonic forces, to be harnessed or marginalized, and if that fails, destroyed physically. Ordinary so-called counter-cultures are regularly incorporated and commercialized and pose no threat, indeed through the process of differentiation (illusory variety and choice), they are a source of great strength to the capitalist global system.[7] The celebrations of the twentieth anniversary of the student and worker revolts of 1968 became media events and were relentlessly commercially exploited with the willing and presumably lucrative participation of many of those who had then been (and still are) dedicated to the overthrow of the capitalist system. Consumerist appropriations of the bicentennial of the American and French Revolutions are other interesting examples. We shall have to wait for the year 2017 to see what the culture-ideology of consumerism makes of the hundredth anniversary of the Bolshevik revolution!

The culture-ideology of consumerism is, as it were, the fuel that powers the motor of global capitalism. The driver is the transnational capitalist class. But the vehicle itself is the mighty transnational corporation. As those who own and control the TNCs are the main drivers of capitalist globalization, they merit a central place in my analysis.

HISTORY AND THEORY OF THE TRANSNATIONAL CORPORATION (TNC)

As D. K. Fieldhouse (1986) remarks in his critique of the concept, the term multinational corporation was first coined by David Lilienthal (the head of the great US public utility the Tennessee Valley Authority) in 1960, long after its reality had made itself felt. Notwithstanding its apparent novelty, the multinational (or, hereafter, transnational) corporation dates back to at least 1867. Until the 1940s it was predominantly a European phenomenon, and 'is neither homogeneous in function nor consistent in character' (Fieldhouse 1986: 24).

Despite Fieldhouse's erudite attempt to consign the concept to the dustbin of history, most observers agree that it is both sufficiently homogeneous in function and consistent in character to be useful. While TNCs are certainly to be found in a wide variety of economic sectors they share the same basic function of capital accumulation on a global scale, and the same consistent character of having to work out global strategies to ensure their continued growth. However, Fieldhouse does have a point. TNCs are not all of a piece. Take the question of size.

In the mid-1970s, eight companies shared 30 per cent of the global oil market, seven companies shared 25 per cent of the global copper market, and in their respective global markets six bauxite companies shared 58 per cent, seven iron ore companies shared 50 per cent, and a few tea, coffee, banana, and tobacco companies shared 60 per cent or more of their markets (see Dunning 1981: ch. 1). This left thousands of other, smaller TNCs scrambling for tiny market shares in most business sectors. Thus, the first major distinction to be made is between the major TNCs, the FG500, and the rest. The rest is, of course, made up of many different types of TNCs. For example, a relatively small company in terms of employees or sales or assets may still hold a dominant place in the global distribution of a crucial commodity or service, usually by virtue of its technological superiority over its competitors.

RESEARCH ON TNCs

Research on the transnational corporations is dominated by no single methodology or substantive focus, but borrows from more or less all of the varying traditions in the social sciences. By volume, most of the research on the TNCs has actually been done by economists, business historians, and organization theorists and some of this work has been influential on the ways other disciplines have approached them. In 1992 the United Nations Library on Transnational Corporations was launched, collecting together more than 8,000 pages in twenty volumes (Dunning 1992–4). The UN Library was organized in terms of key themes: the first four volumes were on the Theory of TNCs, Historical Perspectives, TNCs and Economic Development, and TNCs and Business Strategy. The rest focused on finance, organization, trade, TNC-government relations, regional integration, industries, law, etc.[8]

For all their excellent qualities it must be said that the twenty volumes of the UN Library on TNCs are dominated by the paradigm of conventional economics, are somewhat conservative in outlook (by which I mean they focus on the economic efficiency and structure of TNCs), and generally present a picture that pre-dates the debates around the role of TNCs in capitalist globalization, the issue that concerns us here. For the roots of this debate we must consider more radical approaches to the TNCs (by which I mean those that focus on the social, political, and cultural as well as the economic effects). For example, Jenkins (1987) distinguishes several theory-research traditions in the role of TNCs in development; Stopford and Strange (1991) present a firm–firm, firm–state, and state–state framework that has proved fruitful for those interested in the relationships between the local and the global (for example, Dicken 1998), and my own research on the FG500 (Sklair 2001) has focused on criteria for measuring and evaluating globalizing corporations. While acknowledging that there is no best way to organize this vast literature, for my purposes the main types of enquiry that connect TNCs and globalization can be categorized in terms of general theories, sectoral, country/regional, and issue-based studies, and company histories. A further category is what can be labelled as promotional literature. While there is a considerable overlap between all of these categories, in most of the works the primary emphasis is clear enough.

General theories focus on the substantive and theoretical structures of TNCs and their consequences for economic internationalization or globalization, rather than experiences in a particular industry or country. The most useful conventional survey is the UN Library volume edited by Dunning cited above but, with the exception of Hymer and Vernon, not too many of the contributors have influenced the debate outside the narrow confines of economics. Discussion of the transaction costs of operating abroad has dominated the economic discussion of TNCs, but analysis of these costs tends to be restricted to their effects on the corporations, not on the people and communities where they are doing their business. In addition, many scholars have attempted to distinguish between different types of cross-border corporations, and this has led to rather confusing proliferation of terms, including international, multinational, multi-domestic, transnational, global and globalizing enterprises and/or corporations. For example, in their influential *Managing across Borders: The Transnational Solution*, Bartlett and Goshall (1989) appear to suggest that transnational corporations are more globalizing than global corporations! There are also many somewhat more polemical radical contributions to this literature. Notable is the pioneering work in the dependency tradition on global reach by Barnet and Muller (1974), that has a good claim to parentage of a flood of anti-corporate and anti-globalization books (such as Korten 1995 and Klein 2000). Despite their differences in tone and depth of analysis, all of these works agree on the centrality of the TNC for understanding the capitalist global system. By explicitly identifying categories of corporations like the FG500, they also convey the impression that a qualitatively new force is at work in the global system.

Sectoral case studies focus on TNCs in specific industries. The sectors of the global economy are usually divided into manufacturing, service, and natural resource-based industries, but it is becoming increasingly difficult to categorize most of the major TNCs in such broad terms. In the FG500, for example, companies are distributed among 40–50 separate industries. A classification I used in my own research divided the FG500 into five business sectors: consumer goods and services, financial services, heavy industry, infrastructure, and electronics (Sklair 2001: ch. 3). There are many examples of studies of TNCs in these five sectors that indicate the rich variety of research available.[9] The main issues for the debate around globalization and the TNCs in sectoral terms have been the developmental and/or damaging effects of certain industries. Examples include the global financial system, the environmental hazards of a globalizing automobile industry (with obvious connections to the culture-ideology of consumerism), and the impact of mining and oil exploration on vulnerable communities and fragile ecologies (Madeley 1999). As more and more TNCs begin to take full advantage of the new global trading and investment regime being imposed by the WTO new issues are bound to emerge in more sectors. For example, the challenge by the South African government to the pharmaceutical industry over generic HIV/AIDS drugs is bound to be taken up in many other countries, likewise the threats and promises of genetically modified crops will certainly impact TNCs in the biosciences (see Gibbs 2000, Isserman 2001).

One further aspect of sectoral studies is that in the 1990s the numbers of major mergers and acquisitions rose to unprecedented levels, and this activity appears to be continuing into the new century. Most of these mergers and acquisitions are within sectors, notably in the oil, telecommunications, and financial services industries, but some significant cross-sector activity has occurred. Since the 1990s the world of media has been dominated by a small group of globalizing conglomerates with interests in a variety of business sectors. For example, in 2000 AOL (an Internet company) and Time-Warner (an entertainment company) merged, thus creating the first global mass media content and delivery conglomerate. This is, of course, highly significant for the theory of capitalist globalization and, in particular, the culture-ideology of consumerism (see Table 4.1).

Even where they do not actually merge or acquire, TNCs have also created unprecedented levels of strategic alliances and global networks. These can be between different parts of the same TNC, between different parts of more than one TNC, and between two or more TNCs as a whole for a particular purpose (see Dicken 1998: ch. 7). This has led some to assert that a new form of global economy, alliance capitalism, is emerging (Gerlach 1992; Dunning 1997; Portnoy, in Higgott *et al.* 2000: ch. 9). This is, of course, exactly what the theory of capitalist globalization would predict. TNCs are loosening their ties with their countries of origin and seeking alliances all over the world with other companies for commercial advantages.

Country and/or regional case studies focus on the impact of the TNCs as a whole (or specific industries) on one country or region. There are now few areas in the world where the impact of the TNCs has not been researched. Orthodox economists, organization theorists, and business historians have tended to study the impact of TNCs from First World countries on other First World countries, mostly the impact of TNCs from the USA or Europe or Japan on other host countries in the First World. The well-known Harvard project of the 1960s and 1970s, directed by Raymond Vernon, which was very influential in putting the study of TNCs (actually multinational corporations) on the map, was focused on the First World. Other scholars working in and around International Political Economy, on the other hand, have tended to study the impacts of TNCs from the First World on the countries of the Third World. Much of this work has been carried out either within the dependency framework or as critical reaction to it.[10] This is also the case for

Table 4.1 Globalizing media conglomerates

Business	AOL Time Warner	Disney	Bertelsmann	Viacom	News Corporation	Vivendi Universal
TV and Cinema	12 companies including Warner Bros and Hanna-Barbera, CNN, Time Warner Cable	The Disney Channel, ESPN, ABC plus other major television networks. Walt Disney Pictures, Touchstone, Miramax Films, Buena Vista and four other movie companies	Owns UK's Channel 5, plus 22 television stations and 18 radio stations in 10 countries (RTL network)	Owns CBS with 200 affiliated TV stations and global distribution, for example through MTV (c.350 million households), also owns Nickelodeon. Paramount, United Cinemas International. Blockbuster Video, and 104 cinemas	Owns Fox TV, the largest in the US with 22 stations; 14 Fox companies including 20th Century Fox, Sky digital TV, Star TV broadcasts to over 300 million people across Asia, and Phoenix satellite TV and four other channels cover China.	Owns Canal + with more than 14 million subscribers in 11 European countries; Universal Studios; and cinema chains such us the Odeon chain, Cineplex, United Cinema International
Internet and Telecommunications	AOL, Compuserve, Netscape. Trial-running telephone service over the internet in the US	18 Online ventures including Infoseek	Bertelsmann Broadband, Lycos, Barnes & Noble.com and numerous other online ventures			VivendiNet, MP3.com plus 2 major French mobile phone companies and Vivendi Telecom International with operations in several countries.
Printed press and publishing houses	*Time, Fortune* and 33 other titles with a total of 120 million readers. 24 book brands	5 magazine publishing groups, 4 newspapers, Disney Books	The world's biggest publisher: Random House. Gruner & Jahrs publishes 80 magazines worldwide and owns 9 newspapers	Publishes more than 2000 book titles annually	Owns *New York Post* in USA, *The Times, The Sun* and *News of the World* in the UK, plus newspapers in Australia, New Zealand, Fiji and Papua. HarperCollins and seven other publishing houses.	Owns Havas, group of 60 publishing houses selling 80 million books and 40 million CD-ROMS a year
Radio and Recording Companies	52 record labels	29 radio stations, 6 music labels	Bertelsmann Music Group (BMG) operates in 54 countries. US labels own 200 labels worldwide	180 radio stations in the USA	–	Universal Music Group has over 20% share of the global music market, major labels are Polygram and Motown; operates in 63 countries
Other Businesses	Theme parks, 4 sports teams, Warner Bros merchandising stores in 30 countries	Disney theme parks, MGM studios, 27 hotels, several sports clubs, 720 Disney Stores worldwide	Bertelsmann Service Group	Infinity Outdoor, the largest advertising company in the world.	Australian National Rugby League, the LA Dodgers, and UK football clubs	5 Theme Parks plus Vivendi Environment, the water and utility group including UK train service Connex

Source: Adapted table from *New Internationalist* April 2001, **www.newint.org**, reprinted by permission of the publisher.

research on export-processing and special economic zones, for example, Fröbel *et al.* (1980) on the NIDL, Sklair (1993) on the maquila industry in Mexico, Green (1998) on free zones in the Caribbean, and Pereira (2000) on a zone operated by the Singapore government in China. I predicted in my original studies on the maquilas in Mexico in 1989 and the Special Economic Zones in China in 1991, that the whole world would become an export-processing zone for TNCs. What I did not predict was that it would happen so quickly!

Since the emergence of the European Union, NAFTA, and ASEAN as serious political-economic blocs in the 1980s and 1990s, the study of the relationships between regionalization, globalization, and the TNCs has blossomed (see Robson 1993, Amin and Thrift 1994, Brewer and Young 1998). There are three central propositions that normally underpin this area of research. First, TNCs operating within one region can sensibly be studied as a unit in comparison with TNCs (even the same ones) operating in other regions. Second, major TNCs, especially in Europe, can provide a powerful impetus for economic integration, particularly through lobbying for legislation that serves their interests (see Pedler and Van Schendelen 1994). And third, regionalization can be seen as a form of globalization by virtue of the fact that most foreign direct investment by TNCs is concentrated in the three main regional blocs (see Chapter 2 above). While the details of these arguments need not detain us here, it is important to note that such debates reinforce both the centrality of the TNCs for globalization and the problems of overemphasizing the geographical over the strategic aspects of capitalist globalization (Poon *et al.* 2000).

Issue-based studies of TNCs focus mainly on three main problem areas. These are gender, environment, and corporate citizenship. The common theme that connects these is the growing conviction that TNCs have a responsibility for protecting the rights of all those affected by what they do. The spread of the TNCs has brought significant changes to the sexual division of labour all over the world. Globalizing industries, notably electronics and apparel, employ many more women than men whether in export-processing zones or whether they are located in poor and not so poor countries (Rosen 2002: ch. 2). Much of the research on women and economic globalization has focused on TNCs in export-processing zones (see Nash and Fernandez-Kelly 1983, Lim 1985, and Elson and Pearson 1989; Visvanathan *et al.* 1997: part 3). While most of these studies have been hostile to the TNCs, accusing them of various types of sexual exploitation and exposing the fact that women in these factories are typically paid less and treated worse than male employees (see Chapter 6 below), the fact that TNCs have offered opportunities for some measure of economic and possibly social advancement to millions of women all over the world has not been given the attention it deserves. This is partly due to a lack of appreciation that under the conditions of capitalist globalization all workers, men and women, are exploited and that gender exploitation may work both ways. This argument does not undermine the findings on sexual discrimination in TNC workplaces and the particular disadvantages of women workers; it merely draws attention to the fact that different groups of workers (men and women, young and older, white and non-white, immigrant and local-born) are routinely played off against each other by TNCs and by members of the transnational capitalist class.

The literature on the environmental impacts of TNCs has grown very rapidly in recent decades in parallel with the recognition that the planet is facing an ever more serious ecological crisis.[11] There are two diametrically opposing theses expressed in this literature. First, many governments, inter-state organizations (notably UN agencies), environmental NGOs, and TNCs argue that together they can tackle and solve environmental problems without much sacrifice to the consumerist way of life of the better-off and without jeopardizing the prospects for development of the poor. I have labelled the coalition that is driving this wishful thinking the sustainable development historical bloc. The second thesis is that there is a genuine ecological crisis driven by the culture-ideology of consumerism as propagated by the transnational capitalist class, working mainly through the TNCs. To put this in dramatic terms, the survival of the planet and life on earth depends on breaking the economic power of the TNCs, the political power of the transnational capitalist class, and the culture-ideology power of consumerism, in short, replacing capitalist globalization with something better. This is clearly going to be a long-term project (see Chapters 10 and 11 below). Suffice to say at this point that the ever-increasing volume of research on positive corporate responses to environmental problems and the contrasting anti-corporate and anti-globalization movements literature will undoubtedly provide much food for thought for those thinking about globalization in the twenty-first century.

Issues of corporate citizenship are often found in writings on the environmental impact of TNCs but they have become so important that they deserve their own place in the discussion.[12] The question at the centre of this discussion is: are TNCs (indeed businesses as such) responsible only to their owners or do they have wider responsibilities, to their employees, the people in whose communities they operate, their consumers, and, for globalizing corporations, the whole world? This question is intimately bound up with how governments (from city authorities, through sub-national to national governments and international jurisdictions) regulate or chose not to regulate the activities of TNCs. Orthodox economists and management theorists tend to argue that corporations will perform better when they are allowed to regulate themselves, and that they will behave well without being forced to by restrictive legislation (Moran 1993, Braithwaite and Drahos 2000). Radical anti-globalization theorists take the opposing view, and argue that most TNCs will do more or less anything they can get away with in order to make profits (Korten 1995). No doubt many corporations behave badly and many behave well, but it is certainly too simplistic nowadays to argue that companies will do anything for profits. The contemporary level of monitoring of corporate activities is historically unprecedented. There are thousands of organizations actively seeking out corporate malpractices all over the world (Starr 2000, Corporate Watch website). The use of the Internet means that individuals and groups in even very remote parts of the world can report on what they see to a global audience almost instantaneously.[13] The proprietors of the mass media, always hungry for sensational content, cannot always be sure that negative stories about their corporate friends will never see the light of day, though big advertisers can usually protect themselves from too much adverse publicity (Beder 1997). Revelations about child labour and sweatshops in the global networks of apparel companies such as Nike and The Gap, environmental offences by oil and mining companies, and the ongoing saga of the infant formula companies in the Third World (see Chapter 7 below) have all appeared on prime-time TV and in newspapers and magazines all over the world. This type of negative publicity often has adverse effects on the stock prices of these companies, and shareholders (including senior executives) can suffer significant losses. The reputation of a company, particularly a globalizing TNC, is a very valuable asset. Therefore, global corporate citizenship is a topic that will continue to attract a good deal of interest, from the corporations themselves as well as from their opponents.

Company histories come in a variety of forms. There are many extremely hostile studies of TNCs that target them as violators of human rights, bad employers, destroyers of the environment, and hypocrites. Outstanding examples of this genre are the study of Procter & Gamble by the *Wall Street Journal* writer Alecia Swasy (1994) and Kluger's (1997) study of Philip Morris. There are also many academic studies of companies or aspects of company history, mostly critical rather than hostile, usually with negotiated access to company files and often based on interviews with executives (and occasionally with workers). The articles and review sections of business history journals indicate the range of research available. Good examples of the genre are the study of technology and work-place relations in News Corporation by Marjoribanks (2000), and Cowie's (1999) analysis of the seventy-year history of RCA. (Friendly company-sponsored histories, while often very revealing and perhaps more useful than intended, will be discussed as promotional literature.) Of particular value for the study of capitalist globalization are studies (like those of Marjoribanks and Cowie) that explain how TNCs have changed from domestic firms to globalizing corporations, why these changes took place and their outcomes: global expansion in the case of News Corporation and acquisition by Thomson Electronics in the case of RCA. We can expect more studies that take the histories of major companies up to the twenty-first century in the near future to provide valuable information and conceptual apparatus for the analysis of the connections between TNCs and capitalist globalization.

Promotional literature is the final category of publications on the TNCs that will be considered here. Financial publications, the global business press, and many general magazines are full of material whose main aim is to further the interests of the TNCs. Much of it is clearly apologist, particularly that produced directly by TNCs or by public relations firms on their behalf (exposed in Beder 1997, Monbiot 2000). However, there have been some TNC-sponsored volumes based on more serious research, for example when academics join forces with TNC executives to state the case for the multinationals (Madden 1977; Mertz 1984) and, increasingly, as companies seek to celebrate their environmental successes (for example, Willums and Goluke 1992). While company-commissioned corporate histories can be regarded as a specialist type of promotional literature, they are often useful precisely because they give an insight into how TNCs wish to present themselves to others. In particular, most such works from the early 1990s onwards do make specific reference (usually at the end) to the globalizing of the corporation. A few examples will suffice to make this point. Under the title 'Familiar Visions Far From Home', we learn how the visionary founder of Waste Management Inc. set out to make it a world class company: 'the business environment of the wider world is where corporate greatness increasingly will be judged' (Jacobson 1993: 280). The corporate autobiography of Helmut Maucher, former CEO of Nestlé, is even more explicit. The concluding chapter, 'The Global Vision for the Next Millennium', pictures Nestlé feeding the whole world (Maucher 1994).[14]

This survey of the rich variety of literature on TNCs points in several directions, but one thing is clear. If we are to understand capitalist globalization we must understand transnational corporations and their transnational economic practices, alone or (increasingly) in alliance with others, namely foreign direct investment.

TNCs AND FOREIGN DIRECT INVESTMENT

The history of the TNC is, of course, bound up with the history of foreign direct invest-ment (FDI). Although FDI had been substantial from the beginning of the twentieth century, it really took off in the 1950s, as a result of the flow of funds from the United States into Europe after the Second World War. US-based firms already had considerable sums invested in European subsidiaries since the second half of the nineteenth century, and post-1945 investments served both to rebuild what had been destroyed and to extend it. A political motive was clearly bound up with this economic activity. US foreign policy was based on the necessity of stopping the worldwide advance of communism in Europe and elsewhere through the economic development of areas under threat. US firms did not meekly follow the foreign policy line of their government against their own interests. There were large profits to be made from investing in a whole host of European industries and TNC executives and their local affiliates worked closely with globalizing politicians, bureaucrats, and professionals to make this happen.

In the 1950s and the 1960s many US firms grew so large so fast that Europeans began to speak of the American takeover of their economies. The widely read and influential book of the French politician and columnist, Servan-Schreiber, translated as *The American Chal-lenge* (1968), summed up these fears about the loss of economic independence. This and many other books and newspaper and magazine articles recommended that European industry and commerce should learn from the methods of the Americans and try to beat them at their own game. It is interesting to note that at the turn of the new millennium politicians, bureaucrats, and intellectuals in France were still displaying great suspicion about American influence in Europe. In the late 1990s France was the first government to break ranks on the OECD-sponsored Multilateral Agreement on Investment, and social movements against globalization, McDonald's, and *le fast food* were thinly veiled attacks on the Americanization of Europe.[15] This populist rallying loses some credibility when it is discovered that the entrepreneur Ong Beng Seng from Singapore owned Planet Hollywood; Silas Chou of Hong Kong owned Tommy Hilfiger; Vincent Tan and Khoo Kay Peng, both from Malaysia, owned Kenny Rogers Roasters and Laura Ashley respectively. 'Western icons; Asian owners—such are the fruits of the global marketplace' (Backman 1999: 1).

American economic activity in the international arena (or American economic imperi-alism, as it was increasingly being labelled) began to be identified as a problem in urgent need of resolution. For many, the TNCs were the problem. Since the 1970s, almost all the major international agencies in the economic and trade fields have been producing recommendations on how to regulate the activities of the TNCs in recognition that both the rich countries in which the bulk of FDI was located and the poorer countries needed protection (Mander and Goldsmith 1996). TNC investments might appear minor relative to the total GNP of most large and rich countries, but they are extremely important in the context of specific economic sectors in poor countries as well as in struggling regions all over the world. The UN Department of Economic and Social Affairs took a special interest in these issues and a series of intensively researched reports in the 1970s led to the creation of a Commission on Transnational Corporations and a research centre. This eventually became institutionalized as the UN Centre on Transnational Corporations, with the difficult task of trying to reconcile the interests of TNCs, communities eager for their investments and those adversely affected. As part of a reorganization at the United Nations, the UNCTC was dissolved in the early 1990s and became the Transnational Corporations and Management Division of the UN Department of Economic and Social Development. Subsequently it was relocated from New York to Geneva and incorporated into the United Nations Conference on Trade and Development (UNCTAD) as the Division on Investment, Technology and Enterprise Development. The UNCTC influential quinquennial publication *Transnational Corporations in World Development* was replaced by an annual *World Investment Report*. While it still produces reviews of the place of TNCs in the global economy and a journal, *Transnational Corporations* (largely an outlet for conventional academic and policy-oriented articles), its role as an independent monitor of the practices of TNCs appears to be over (see Robbins 1996).

Activity at the quasi-governmental level, like the UN and OECD, has been more than paralleled by a plethora of unofficial pressure groups that monitor the activities of the TNCs, wherever they may be. Church, consumer, and other campaigning groups frequently expose abuses of TNC power. The Amsterdam-based Transnational Information Exchange (TIE) was a pioneer of counter-strategies to combat the overwhelming resources that the TNCs can muster when they are attacked. These strategies are based on research to identify the interests behind the target companies 'to such an extent that their image, reputation and credibility are jeopardized by continued support of corporate denial of justice' (TIE 1985: 33). Some of the campaigns that TIE has been involved in with other networks have lasted many years, such as the Nestlé Infant Formula boycott, the campaign to force corporations to divest in South Africa, the struggles on behalf of Coca-Cola workers in Guatemala and Control Data workers in Korea, as well as several campaigns against TNC policies in the United States. The US-based International Labor Rights Fund is also very active in these areas (**www.laborrights.org**). The Washington-based Public Citizen (part of the network founded by Ralph Nader), the New York based Interfaith Center on Corporate Responsibility, the Boston-based INFACT, the Penang-based International Organization of Consumer Unions, and the Cambridge (UK)-based Baby Milk Action, have all also helped to organize successful campaigns, and there are thousands of similar small transnational networks now monitoring the TNCs in various parts of the world. Most of these organizations have regular newsletters, and many have influential magazines, for example Public Citizen's *Multinational Monitor*. The flood of environmentalist and consumer-advice literature that began in the 1980s often contains material critical of the TNCs (see Starr 2000).

The views of the TNCs can be found in a variety of sources, for example in their public interest advocacy advertising in the world's mass media (Sethi 1977, Brown *et al.* 2001), and in countless government sponsored settings (Monbiot 2000, Sklair 2001). The contest between the TNCs and their critics is, however, very unequal. Mander (1978: 19–20) noted, in all seriousness, that in the USA: 'During the early 1970s, all environmental groups together spent about $500,000 per year in advertising in order to offset an average of about $3 billion in corporate expenditures on the same subjects. This ratio was relatively small, only 6,000 to 1, which may help explain the early success of the environmental movement.' While some of the environmental and human rights organizations now have much greater budgets, the ratio is still weighted heavily in favour of the corporations and business in general (see Beder 1997; Rucht, in Smith *et al.* 1997: ch. 11; Sklair 2001: chs. 6–7).

These struggles pit the small people against the might of the transnational corporations, some of whom are richer than most countries (see Table 3.1 above). Nevertheless, even the poorest or smallest countries can, theoretically at least, frustrate the expansion plans of any one of these TNC giants by the simple, if often costly, expedients of refusing them permission to trade or manufacture within their territory or by nationalizing (expropriating) their property if they are already in business there. There is a large literature on this question, and this raises the thorny issue of the relations between TNCs and governments.

TNCs AND GOVERNMENTS

The theory of capitalist globalization presented here is a direct challenge to the conventional idea that there are different national styles of capitalism (Anglo-American, Japanese, German, French, Chinese, and so on) and that these are consequences of the relations between big business and governments, the historical trajectories of each country (path dependency) and styles of regulation and corporate governance. Obviously there is some truth in all this. There are some differences between big business and the organization of capitalism from place to place, between cities, regions, countries, areas settled by different ethnic groups, and so on, just as there are obviously differences between different industries, companies of different sizes, and companies operating under totally different systems of regulation, wherever they are located. The issue is not whether there are differences (of course there are) but what is the significance of these differences. Most theorists and researchers who accept the reality of globalization (as I showed in Chapter 3, it has been defined in a variety of ways) accept that there has been a fundamental change in the relations between transnational corporations and governments (or the state, not exactly the same thing). The globalizing challenge to the conventional view is that most governments and the states they purport to govern have less power over domestic and foreign TNCs than they once had (this cannot be denied, in my view) and, more controversially, that most governments appear to be quite satisfied with this state of affairs and some even want to push it further. My explanation for this is bound up with the structure of the transnational capitalist class, and the role of the state fraction (globalizing politicians and bureaucrats) within it.

Nevertheless, state-centrist path dependency arguments comparing national capitalisms are still very popular and some exponents are beginning to deal seriously with globalization. Let me take one example of this genre and try to highlight its strengths and weaknesses with respect to the relations between TNCs, the state, and governments. Cioffi (2000) meets head on the argument that state regulation of business has declined under the pressure of globalization. His study of financial market regulation, company law, and labour law aims to demonstrate that, indeed, state regulation still matters very much. He distinguishes three types of political economies, neo-liberal (in the USA and UK), neo-corporatist (Germany), and statist (France and Japan). He is careful to note that pension reform might have explosive effects on financial regulation everywhere soon, but claims that this has not yet happened. Harmes (1998) suggests that this process might be further advanced than Cioffi accepts, and this would be a strong argument for the impact of financial globalization. Unsurprisingly, Cioffi finds much evidence of differences between regulations in all three spheres for all three types of economies, and if one is interested in the differences then Cioffi is a useful guide. However, when he comes to discuss actual outcomes of these regulatory regimes a rather different picture emerges. He is correct to single out the French case as crucial. France in the latter part of the twentieth century did stand out (with Japan) as an apparent exception in some respects to the onward rush to neo-liberal capitalist globalization. He explains that the hands-off attitude of the French government to the BNP–Paribas–Société Génerale hostile takeover battle in the late 1990s 'signalled the French government's policy choice to allow market forces, and in particular a new market for corporate control, to reshape French finance. . . . The French state could have blocked any of the bids and imposed a resolution, but chose not to' (Cioffi 2000: 587). What he fails to do is to ask why the French government chose not to act in this and, subsequently, other cases. My answer to this crucial question would take the form that the state and corporate fractions of the transnational capitalist class in France did act, but they acted in the interests of the globalizing corporations, presented as the best option for their conception of the French national interest.

Case studies in Pedler and Van Schendelen (1994) and Balanya et al. (2000) on lobbying in the EU in general, and Apeldoorn (2000) on the European Round Table of Industrialists (ERT) demonstrate that major globalizing corporations play an increasingly political role in Europe, as do their equivalents in other parts of the world. The campaigning journalist George Monbiot in his book *The Captive State: The Corporate Takeover of Britain* has compiled a Fat Cats Directory of all the appointments made by New Labour after the 1997 election (Monbiot 2000: ch. 6). His playful listing of Previous Gluttony and Subsequent Creamery masks a deadly serious purpose, namely to demonstrate how far those who own and control corporate wealth in Britain were given the tasks of regulating (and deregulating) their own interests. The former chair of British Airways and President of the CBI was put in charge of the national energy tax review; the President of the Country Landowners Association was appointed chair of the government's Countryside Agency; the former chair of BP and a vice-chair of ERT was appointed Minister for Trade and Competitiveness, and on and on.[16] Cioffi appears to be totally immune to the idea that what major corporations do can have any connection with class interests, though he does to some extent acknowledge the denationalization of TNCs in the global economy. 'The BNP–Paribas, Total–Fina–Elf Aquitaine, and Carrefour–Promodes mergers represent a new breed of nationally-based firms shaped more by market forces than state fiat and oriented towards European and international competition rather than national markets and state economic management' (Cioffi 2000: 591). The fact that Petrofina was actually domiciled in Belgium further undermines the idea of 'national firms'.[17]

It was not always thus. In development studies, for example, the relations between TNCs and governments have been seen more in the context of Third World governments seizing the assets of foreign companies, expropriation. The experience of expropriating governments is very mixed.[18] While there do seem to be systematic differences between extractive industries like petroleum and metal ore mining, and manufacturing industries, like consumer goods, the general conclusion is that where the TNCs are patient and persistent they usually at least recover the value of their seized assets. Either they have a sufficient stranglehold over processing and marketing, the case in the extractive industries as the experience of the copper industry in Chile shows (Moran 1974) or they have sufficient control over intra-firm transfers, particularly transfer pricing.[19] As Sigmund (1980) demonstrated for Latin America, when compensation was finally paid, it often overstated the value of the assets. Here different elements in the transnational capitalist class are clearly seen working through the agency of the home country state in defence of their interests. The most thoroughly studied case is indigenization in Nigeria, and I shall discuss this below.

Most of this research, as is immediately obvious, is posed within the logic of state-centrism. There have, however, been some attempts to go beyond this and to develop conceptions of the TNC not as representatives of the power of the state, as tends to happen within state-centrist analyses, but as independent of and even, on occasion, opponents of the state. While all TNCs are domiciled for legal purposes if no other in particular countries, many have argued that some TNCs are actually more powerful than most nation-states. Barnet and Muller's thesis of the global reach of the TNCs (1974), and Vernon's sovereignty at bay thesis (1971) both highlighted the increasingly powerful positions of TNCs in their dealings with governments decades before the idea of corporate globalization was common currency. Though emanating from totally different perspectives and rejecting the globalist prediction of the disappearance of the state (Vernon suggested that the state could defend its interests against the TNCs), they illustrate just how widespread such ideas were (and still are).

As Figure 3.1 showed, the largest TNCs have annual sales far in excess of the budgets of most governments. The dependency perspective focused attention on the unequal relationship between mighty TNCs and the ruling groups in their powerful home countries that looked after their interests all over the globe, on the one hand, and the relatively weak and powerless Third World countries in which they were involved, on the other. Norman Girvan's (1976) study of mining TNCs in the Caribbean evocatively labels this relationship corporate imperialism. However, as argued in Chapter 3, the dependency perspective failed to explain how the practices of the TNCs and those who act as their agents in the Third World actually operated to produce underdevelopment. This is particularly relevant where something like the kinds of development that are taken for granted in the First World have occurred regionally or in particular industries in some Third World countries. The four tigers of South-East Asia registered impressive rates of economic growth and, more unevenly, social progress and became a model of what might be achieved by countries in the Third World within the capitalist global economy (though none was a conventional 'country'). Two projects in the infrastructure sector in countries aspiring to NIC status, the Volta dam project in Ghana and the Enron power project in India, make an instructive comparison.

THE VOLTA DAM AND THE ENRON PROJECT

Ghana has large accessible bauxite and hydro-electric potential, both of which have been at the centre of the country's development planning. When Ghana became independent in 1957 the US-based aluminium corporations, Kaiser and Reynolds, outbid British-based interests to develop the bauxite industry. The plan was that foreign capital would build a dam on the Volta River to generate power, and that the private sector would own the smelter.[20] The original idea that Ghana should take a 40 per cent stake in the project vanished early on. As the magazine *West Africa* (1980: 523) put it: 'By stripping the Volta scheme of all the ancillary facilities which could have stimulated a Ghanaian industrial revolution, Kaiser and Reynolds succeeded in creating the conditions for one of the most prosperous aluminium smelters in the world . . . at what was then the lowest power rate in the world.'

The Volta Aluminium Company (VALCO) was set up in 1959. Girvan identified four main aspects of this project:

1 Resource accessibility. Ghana agreed to provide cheap power, but the Ghanaians never expected the smelter to take as much as 65 per cent of the dam's power. Many other industrial projects never got off the ground because of energy shortages, and Ghana was subsequently forced to import power from the Ivory Coast.

2 Bauxite supply. VALCO acquired monopoly rights over ore that they did not exploit for marketing reasons; and the company operated as an enclave industry.

3 Payment stream. VALCO became 'the most spectacular beneficiary of the tax regime in Ghana devised to attract foreign investment'. Revenues from the bauxite were used to service the debt incurred to build the dam that provided the TNCs with the cut-price power to smelt the ore.

4 Status of the Master Agreement. The agreement was geared to the details on the prevention of nationalization and left little room for re-negotiation (West Africa 1980: 573).

By 1974 Kaiser operated in twenty-five countries and was running 'a crazy shipping system which sends Ghanaian bauxite to Scotland, Guinean alumina to the US, Jamaican alumina to Ghana and Ghanaian aluminium all round the world. Such policies only make sense to the corporate investors and stem from the perceived need to avoid integrating the industry in any but the core capitalist countries' (West Africa 1980: 612). As Madeley (1999) shows, this is not an uncommon outcome for mining projects in the Third World. Despite the cheap Volta power (and water supply) that permitted expansion on smelting, the TNCs refused to build an alumina plant to process local bauxite. Eventually, Ghana was forced to build one itself (Tsikata 1986: ch. 1). Over the years, the British taxpayer has paid hundreds of millions of pounds to provide electricity below cost for British Aluminium to smelt Ghanaian bauxite in Scotland. The Kaiser Corporation had a similar deal in New Zealand.

The real developmental loss for Ghana was that most of the power from the Volta went to VALCO, so there was little left for local use. In 1980, only 5 per cent of Ghana's people had access to electricity.[21] So while it would be difficult to argue that there were no benefits for Ghana, or for other Third World countries in similar projects, it is quite clear that the interests of the TNCs in obtaining cheap power in Ghana as part of their global industrial strategy ran counter to the interests of Ghanaian development. As the authors of a study on the effects of the Volta hydro project conclude, although there were some benefits, many of the tens of thousands of local people who were resettled lost out. 'The concept of turning the resettlements into "bridgeheads" of modernization amidst rural underdevelopment has failed' (Diaw and Schmidt-Kallert, 1990: 218).[22] As Valco and similar projects failed to deliver what was necessary to give the people of Ghana the tools for their own development the World Bank and the IMF moved in, with generally negative consequences.[23] As Brydon and Legge (1996: 4) point out, from a country that was once widely regarded as having good developmental prospects: 'In the 1990s, however, Ghana is seen not as a pioneer of African independence with visionary implications for change in the world order, but rather as an exemplary member of the club of poorer nations, a member who is taking the [World Bank and IMF] medicine and following the rules.'[24]

The case of Enron in India suggests that similar problems exist for similar projects today. The Enron project in Dabhol, a coastal city in Maharashtra (one of the richest provinces in India) was one of eight fast-track foreign investment infrastructure projects set up as a result of the Indian government liberalizing economic reforms of 1991.[25] At that time Enron, based in Houston, Texas, was relatively small but it was also one of the most globalizing energy companies (by 2001 it was the biggest energy company in the world with revenues in excess of $100bn., and ranked sixteen in the FG500). In terms that vividly recall the Volga dam project, the Dahbol Power Company (DPC) was created as a joint venture of Enron (80 per cent), GE Capital and Bechtel (with 10 per cent each) and the financing of the project was (to put it mildly) not very advantageous for the Indian government or the Maharashtra State Electricity Board, contracted to buy power from the company at up to ten times the rate of domestically generated power. The contract also meant the import of practically all the equipment and fuel needed for the project, no explicit technology transfer, and a serious drain on India's reserves of foreign currency. The contract promised a cash flow of over $30bn. to the company up to the 2020s, the largest foreign investment project ever in India.

A Memorandum of Understanding between Enron and the state electricity board was signed just three days after the Enron team arrived for the first time in India. After a detailed review the World Bank refused to finance the project, no doubt worried about the foreign currency problem and India's ability to service its considerable debt. Central to this assessment was the fact that the Dhabol plant would run on LNG (natural gas) that would have to be imported rather than the cheaper coal that India had in abundance. The state assumed that the higher cost of this power would be met by demands for electricity by consumers willing to pay the higher prices (the Bank questioned this assumption and argued that demand growth had been inflated). Basically, the technical and financial arguments of the World Bank were ignored and the project was pushed through with financing from the Industrial Development Bank of India. There is documentary evidence that the authorities lied over a series of issues regarding the project before and after the dispute with the World Bank. Enron's response was most revealing: 'I feel that the World Bank opinion can be changed. We will engage a PR firm during the next trip and hope-fully manage the (Indian) media from here on' (letter from Vice President of Enron to Chairman of state electricity board in 1993, quoted in Mehta 2000: 47). This rather gnomic statement was somewhat clarified by the testimony of an Enron employee to the Committee on Appropriations of the U.S. House of Representatives:

Working through this process (of evolution of Enron's Dabhol project) has given the Indian author-ities a real and concrete understanding of the kinds of legal and policy changes needed in India, and has given the Indian banks a real and concrete understanding of sound project lending practices. Moreover, our company spent an enormous amount of its own money—approximately $20 million—on this education and project development process alone, not including any project costs' (quoted Mehta 2000: 121)

Mehta, who is not opposed in principle to (indeed welcomes) foreign private capital in the power, petroleum, and telecom sectors (Mehta 2000: 16), explains that in mid-1992 a high-powered government of India team had visited the USA specifically to find private companies willing to engage in power projects and that Enron had shown a keen interest. This, no doubt, explains why the power purchase agreement was rushed through in terms very much to the benefit of the company and in obvious contravention of the laws of India. The company's 'education' budget no doubt also helps to explain how and why it weathered the storms that were to follow.

In 1995, amid claims that Enron had broken Indian laws, compromised national and local politicians and officials, violated human rights, and generally ignored the people most directly affected, the project was suspended by the newly elected state government controlled by an anti-Congress Party coalition. Enron reacted by threatening legal action against the authorities for breach of contract and renegotiations were announced. The project resumed unchanged and legal challenges from various organizations continued.[26] The excessive tariff that the state electricity board paid to DPC continued to infuriate critics of the project. Tariff payments from May 1999 to December 2000 averaged over twice as much per unit as the original estimate. Rao sensibly argues that amendments to electricity legislation in India have left monopolies and neither public nor private companies want to give these up: 'the attempt seems to be to replace statewide government monopolies by private monopolies' (Rao 2000: 1590).

Throughout the 1990s public opposition to the project had grown, fanned undoubtedly by the struggle between the Congress Party and the BJP. This came to a head in 1997 when the local police and a battalion of the State Reserve Police paid for by the company violently suppressed popular demonstrations against the project and terrorized its opponents. Both Amnesty International and Human Rights Watch carried out on-the-spot investigations of the affair, and there is overwhelming evidence to support the charges of police brutality and other extra-legal actions by the state. Despite this, the project continued to enjoy high-level support both in India and abroad. When he retired from the diplomatic service the US ambassador to India, Frank Wisner, joined the board of Enron, no doubt to continue to be diplomatic by other means.[27] Most commentators agree that rather than Enron changing its practices to adapt to Indian law it is Indian law that has consistently changed to accommodate Enron (and big business in general).

It is not, therefore, surprising to discover that the magazine *Multinational Monitor* selected the Enron project in India for inclusion in its Ten Worst Corporations list several times in the 1990s. Nevertheless, it is only fair (and usually instructive) to investigate how accused parties see themselves. This is easy to do in the case of Enron. The company's website asserts:

We treat others as we would like to be treated ourselves. We do not tolerate abusive or disrespectful treatment. Ruthlessness, callousness, and arrogance don't belong here. We work with customers and prospects [sic] openly, honestly, and sincerely [. . .] We have an obligation to communicate. Here, we take the time to talk with one another . . . and to listen. We believe that information is meant to move and that information moves people.

We are satisfied with nothing less than the very best in everything we do (accessed 10 Jan. 1999)

To what extent did these issues reflect on Enron as a globalizing corporation? Despite all that can be learned from websites of the people most directly affected by the power station, and from Amnesty International and Human Rights Watch, in 1999 *Fortune* ranked Enron as one of the best companies to work for in the USA and *Forbes* magazine named Enron the top power company in the world. Mehta's judgement on the ongoing saga or disgrace of the DPC, for all its passion, is impressively dispassionate. He does not blame Enron for grabbing all that it can from the project (and from others he documents in his book); that is how TNCs make profits and satisfy their shareholders. The bulk of the responsibility, he argues, lies at home: 'There was a complete failure of every conceivable institutional structure—the government, the press, courts as well as of institutions—constitutional, statutory or those emerging from the executive' (Mehta 2000: 177). And, as he demonstrates, the Enron project is only one, albeit the biggest, of these failures.[28]

The root cause of these failures is forcefully expressed in a statement in 1995 by the National Alliance for Peoples Movement in India: 'Earlier the government used to plan projects for drinking water, irrigation, roads, education, health, etc. The focus of government today is on projects like national highways, airports, modern sophisticated seaports, telecommunications and electricity for big industries. In other words, [these are facilities] that foreign MNCs demand' (quoted in Dwivedi 1998: 159–60).

How, then, can the government of a poor country maximize its benefits from FDI? The theory of the obsolescing bargain (Vernon 1971) is an attempt to answer this question. The argument is that over a period of time, and particularly as a new technology matures, host countries are more able to drive harder bargains with the TNCs that wish to invest in them. This may be the case in some industries, or for some products, but as both Moran's study of the copper industry in Chile (1974) and Girvan's of the Caribbean bauxite industry (1976) demonstrate in rather different ways, the stranglehold that globally integrated corporations can exert on distribution and marketing may nullify what appears on the ground to be a better bargain for the host. What Raikes and Gibbon (2000: 62–3) argue for export agriculture in Africa: 'competition between international buyers of Africa's export crops is structurally very limited, with only a handful of importing enterprises exercising a high degree of market power', is generally true all over the Third World. Thus, as most governments dismantle their barriers to TNCs, some more reluctantly than others, state-centrism becomes less and less fruitful as an approach.

The theory being propounded here sees the global system as primarily a capitalist global system, the main forces of which are the transnational corporations, the transnational capitalist class, and the culture-ideology of consumerism. This indicates that in order to lay bare the workings of capitalist globalization we must focus on the TNCs. As the analysis of the Volta dam and the Enron project suggests, economic transnational practices in the Third World are largely what the TNCs and their local associates, often in conjunction with other members of the transnational capitalist class, are doing in the economic, the political, and the culture-ideology spheres. To this extent, therefore, Mehta's 'sneaking admiration' for Enron is a little misplaced. TNCs set themselves standards and we are entitled to assess their performance.

One test of the real power of governments over TNCs is the phenomenon of indigenization, the compulsory transfer of the assets and control of foreign companies to local agents. The case of oil-rich Nigeria has attracted a good deal of scholarly attention in this respect, and is worth looking at more closely.

INDIGENIZATION IN NIGERIA

The status of TNCs can change in the countries where they have made direct investments. Expropriation suggests that little or no compensation has been paid by the expropriator to the TNC; nationalization and forced divestment leave the question open; and indigenization suggests that foreign TNC personnel and control are changed to indigenous personnel and control. Divestment indicates that it is the TNC that is the prime mover in the process of disengaging.

Kobrin studied no less than 511 acts of forced divestment involving 1,500 firms in seventy-six Third World countries from 1960 to 1976. His underlying hypothesis was that 'in the vast majority of countries where forced divestment is used selectively its being chosen vis-a-vis alternate regulatory or administrative policies is, inter alia, a function of firm and industry-specific characteristics' (Kobrin 1980: 69). His results refute the commonly expressed irrational economic nationalism explanation of forced divestment in the countries of the Third World. Third World states, he argues, tend to take over foreign investments that they consider important for national development. Indigenization implies that there are local agents, official or private, standing in the wings ready to take over the indigenized companies. My argument is that what at first sight appears to be a paradigm case of indigenous, national forces dispossessing transnational corporations is in fact a clear illustration of the emergence of the transnational capitalist class.

Like many former colonies Nigeria has had a long history of incorporation into the capitalist global system (see Shenton and Freund 1978). Thanks to its oil income, Nigeria, with a population of over one hundred million (by far the most populous country in Africa) is one of the richest countries, on a per capita income basis, in the continent. The legacy of British colonialism and the fact of oil money are mixed blessings. Scholars have documented significant levels of TNC participation in agriculture (Oculi, in Lubeck 1987: ch. 6), the oil industry (Ihonvbere and Shaw 1988), import substituting manufacturing industries (Biersteker, in Lubeck 1987: ch. 8), and in the mining, service, financial, and infrastructure sectors (in Onimode *et al.* 1983).

The Nigerian case is illustrative of a common pattern. As a proportion of the total economy, TNC investment is small, but as a proportion in some important industries, for example oil, machinery, and financial services, it is substantial. In the technologically advanced sectors, the TNCs are dominant. Nigerian scholars have pointed to major structural distortions in economy and society for which the TNCs are at least partly responsible. For example:

Proposals for domestic production of iron and steel, petro-chemicals, machine-tools and the like are typically discouraged or delayed by the mnc's in preference for quick profit-yielding manufacturing of semi-luxury consumer goods like lace, car assembly, beer, carpets, and so on. This is largely the result of a wooly acceptance of import-substitution industrialisation, which implies that import substitutes based on the imported semi-luxury consumption habits, rather than the basic needs of the mass-majority, would enjoy industrial priority. (Onimode *et al.* 1983: 122)

Onimode *et al.* show that the TNCs have also exerted influence by manipulating class contradictions through a compliant comprador bourgeoisie and a denationalized labour aristocracy. This has encouraged corruption and 'cultural degradation . . . foreign intellectual domination, the imposition of imperialist values and the ossification of national culture' (p. 125). These are the circumstances under which successive Nigerian govern-ments have attempted to indigenize, under slogans of gaining control over their economic and ultimately their developmental destinies.

Indigenization occurred in Nigeria in three phases. The first decree was issued in 1972 by the military regime in alliance with the local bourgeoisie, who clearly expected to benefit from the initiative. This first wave of indigenization had few practical effects, and most foreign TNCs in Nigeria managed to evade serious loss of control by enlisting members of the local bourgeoisie to front for them, a universal practice where there are restrictions on foreigners engaging in certain economic activities. The second decree, in 1977, represented a further attempt by the military government to wrest control from the TNCs, particularly to counter the defensive measures that the TNCs had developed to nullify the effects of the first decree. Because it appeared tougher, the second decree encouraged the TNCs to develop even more defences to protect their interests. Biersteker (in Lubeck 1987: ch. 8) lists the most important of them. In addition to fronting, TNCs resorted to public sale of shares to dilute ownership and retain effective control, tech-nical agreements with Nigerian partners, negotiation of exemptions from the author-ities, the two-company strategy, changes in voting rules to disenfranchise local partners, dividing boards of directors, bringing in expatriate executives, bribery, and simply ignor-ing the law. A further decree in 1982, this time initiated by a civilian government, reinforced state control of the banking and finance sectors and went a little way to encourage Nigerian capital to invest more in the manufacturing sector. However, the TNCs are still as strong as they ever were and the notion that the Nigerian government, let alone the average Nigerian, has any more control of the economy than before indigenization, is very doubtful.[29]

This is confirmed in the case of the music industry in Africa, discussed through the lens of Afropop and the paradoxes of imperialism by Lazarus (1999: ch. 4). He cites the analysis of Christopher Waterman on the record industry in Nigeria, in terms that almost exactly parallel the findings discussed above.

The vigor of the record industry continues to be strongly affected by shifts in Nigeria's balance of trade and in import–export laws, which restrict the flow of raw materials and machinery. Indigen-ization has not shifted the balance of power between local and foreign concerns, rather it has served to 'rationalize the relationship between the Nigerian bourgeoisie and its patron, international cap-ital.' It is very difficult for entrepreneurs without ties to foreign corporations to break into the record manufacturing business. (in Lazarus 1999: 201)

All agree that the main beneficiaries of the indigenization process have been the state functionaries and those few Nigerians who were invited to sit on the boards of TNCs in Nigeria (see Ake 1985). The companies that were indigenized did not cease to be trans-national, and did not cease to engage in transnational practices. Those who owned and/or controlled them were thus also engaging in transnational practices and were thus, poten-tially at least, local affiliates of the transnational capitalist class. Their new transnational roles would naturally increase the likelihood that they would identify their interests with the capitalist global system, objectively if not subjectively. This is a crucial point in the argument that links indigenization with the creation of the transnational capitalist class. Subjectively, patriotic Nigerians who have taken control of indigenized TNCs will see their own and Nigeria's best interests served by the success of their enterprises. They may be hostile to the capitalist global system and feel that they and Nigeria are victims of exploitation within it, but objectively, as participants in the system through their own transnational practices, they identify their interests and those of their country with it. In a study of business associations in Kano (Nigeria) and Dar es Salaam (Tanzania) it is noted that foreign agencies, USAID for example, have funded such bodies. 'The strong ties between business associations and foreign actors illustrate that the capitalist movement in Tanzania [and Nigeria too] is closely linked to wider international forces aimed at encouraging entrepreneurialism, and developing market forces' (Heilman and Lucas 1997: 165). Indigenization can actually create the conditions for a transnational capitalist class in what appears to be the most unfruitful soil.

Few will wonder why the products and lifestyles of the industrialized world seem desirable and relatively accessible to many in Third World countries. However, the extent to which this is due to the deliberate efforts of capitalists to sell their products and services is often difficult to determine. It is for this reason that the basic unit of analysis of these processes in global system theory is not the state or the inter-state system, but transnational practices and how they operate through the TNCs, the transnational capitalist class, and the culture-ideology of consumerism to sustain capitalist globalization. Investigating how economic, political, and transnational practices work enriches our vision of the world and makes it easier to see clearly the sources of our present ills. While there is obviously some value in comparing the successes of some countries with the failures of others, or the prosperity of the First World with the poverty of the Third World, this does not take us very far. The TNCs, the transnational capitalist class, and the culture-ideology of consumerism intensify the two main crises of capitalism, class polarization and ecological unsustainability all over the world and can only be explained in terms of the transnational practices that produce them.

NOTES

1. According to industry sources, the six biggest are Cendant (domiciled in the USA) with over half a million rooms worldwide; Bass Hotels and Resorts (UK), Marriott International (USA), Accor (France), Choice Hotels and Best Western (both US-based) all have over 300,000 rooms. See also, Judd and Fainstein (1999).

2. Table 2.6 in Nolan (2001) is a useful list of market dominance by the few largest corporations in a variety of industries.

3. The scholarly literature on Disney includes Sorkin (1992), Achille (in Pedler and Van Schendelen 1994: ch. 4), Buckingham (1997), and Fogelson (in Judd and Fainstein 1999: 89–106). Davis (1996) analyses the FG500 corporate grip on theme parks.

4. There is an interesting theoretical parallel between Faist's evidence on *transnationalizing* civil societies and scepticism on transnational civil society and my evidence on *globalizing* corporations and scepticism on global corporations. Also relevant here is the theoretical construction of 'transnationalism from below' (see Smith and Guarnizo 1998).

5. See also the exceptionally interesting ethnographic study of Eliasoph (1998).

6. Documented by Kaufman (1988: 4–37) under the euphemistic heading 'Direct constraints of official and non-official U.S. origin'. For the continuing baleful influence of this in Chile, see Weeks (2000).

7. An excellent illustration of this is the 'conquest of the cool' (Frank 1998).

8. The introductions to all twenty volumes are conveniently collected in Dunning and Sauvant (1996). Individual volumes are cited as appropriate and identified in the list of references by editor.

9. Dicken (1998) provides a reliable survey and copious references for a similar classification.

10. Notable examples of such studies include Moran (1974) on copper TNCs in Chile, Kowaleski (1982) on TNCs in the Caribbean. See also, Li and Li (1999) on TNCs in China, Buckley and Clegg (1991) on TNCs in Africa, and Hood and Young (2000: part III).

11. For case studies of environmental impacts of eight TNCs, see Sklair (2001: ch. 7). See also, Karliner (1997) and Madeley (1999).

12. For a review of the literature on how corporate citizenship has become a globalizing practice see Sklair (2001: ch. 6). *The Journal of Corporate Citizenship* (Issue 1, 2001) promises to be a valuable resource for studying these issues.

13. Research on the Internet is booming. See, for example, Ferdinand (2000), Gereffi (2001), Langman *et al.* (2002), Madon (2000), Miller and Slater (2000), Walch (1999). Edelman (1998) shows how peasant associations in Central America are using it to good effect.

14. For more examples see the chapter on 'global visions' in Sklair (2001).

15. Opposition to capitalist globalization is often confused, deliberately in some cases, with anti-Americanization (see Chapter 7 below). As Guerlain (1997: 30) asserts: 'The French—if one can thus call the very small number of people who are opinion makers in France—often choose America as the anti-model or scapegoat of choice in the realm of culture.' See also the attempt by Zeitlin and Herrigel (2000) to deconstruct Americanization in the realm of management and technology.

16. As Braithwaite and Drahos (2000) show in their large study of global business regulation, generally the leading companies in most industries influence how they are regulated.

17. Cioffi's work is representative of the University of California Berkeley Roundtable on the International Economy and he refers to its publications in his paper.

18. Kobrin (1980) and Jodice (1980) test different views on expropriations in several industries while Minor (1994) documents the decline of expropriations. Hines (2000) puts forward the site-here-to-sell-here principle in his argument on the need to replace globalization with localization. I shall return to this in Chapter 10.

19. For a variety of arguments and data on transfer pricing see the chapters in Moran (1993).

20. This account is based on four unsigned articles in *West Africa* (1980), the collection edited by Tsikata (1986), and the books by Graham (1982) and Diaw and Schmidt-Kallert (1990).

21. Nash (2001: ch. 3) reports that while the state of Chiapas produces 52 per cent of Mexico's electricity, 35 per cent of the people in the state have no electricity supply.

22. A judgement on the Narmada dam in India concurs: 'Alongside large-scale destruction and/or transfer of natural resources these activities and projects frequently involve displacement of local communities. In other words, such productive activities plant the seeds of conflict by their very nature' (Dwivedi 1998: 139).

23. Owusu (2001) shows that one result of a structural adjustment programme (SAP) in Ghana was a boom in processed wood production and export, suggesting that governments can derive benefits and that there are winners from SAPs, as well as losers. This is not to be scoffed at—China alone imported almost $4 billion worth of solid wood in 2000 for its housing boom (Freese 2001).

24. For an (unofficial) World Bank evaluation of 220 SAPs in Africa and elsewhere, see Dollar and Svensson (2000), who argue that failures can usually be explained by domestic factors, that is the programme is rarely at fault. For an interesting analysis of what people in Africa think about SAPs, see Mattes and Bratton (2001).

25. This account is based on Wagle (1996), Mehta (2000), Rao (2001), and reports by Amnesty International (1997) and Human Rights Watch (1998). Enron collapsed spectacularly at the end of 2001 amidst accusations of mismanagement and fraud. The future of the Dhabol project is uncertain.

26. The BJP won the state election largely on opposition to the project. Mehta (2000: 221–2) reproduces a letter from a BJP notable claiming that corruption was at the root of the Enron problem, but there is no evidence of any significant change in this respect when the BJP came to power.

27. More evidence of the transnational capitalist class in action. In Britain, the former Conservative secretary for energy, Lord Wakeham, also joined the Enron Board after his party's disastrous defeat in the 1997 election. Though it had no previous experience in the water and sewerage industry, Enron was permitted by the New Labour government to acquire Wessex Water (in south-west England) despite the protests of the Wessex Customer Services Committee.

28. Of course, most projects are on a much smaller scale, but many reflect similar problems. See for example the revealing study of TNC development of the island provinces of Bohol and Cebu in the Philippines as a by-product of a water treatment and supply project (Fisher and Urich 2001).

29. Henley (in Stopford and Strange, 1991: 286, n. 2) reports a TNC executive in an insurance firm in Nigeria to the effect that indigenization 'made no perceptible differences to the management of the company or, more surprisingly, to the subsidiary's profitability to the parent company'.

Chapter 5

TRANSNATIONAL PRACTICES: CORPORATIONS, CLASS, AND CONSUMERISM

THE CONCEPTUAL SPACE FOR TRANSNATIONAL PRACTICES (TNP)

The concept of transnational practices refers to the effects of what people do when they are acting within specific institutional contexts that cross state borders. Transnational practices create globalizing processes. TNPs focus attention on observable phenomena, some of which are measurable, instead of highly abstract and often very vague relations between conceptual entities. Not only is it impossible to theorize fruitfully on the basis of abstract relations which are nothing but abstract relations, it is only possible to theorize fruitfully on the basis of abstractions that refer directly to observable phenomena in material reality. Globalizing processes are abstract concepts, but the transnational practices that create them refer directly to what agents and agencies do and derive meaning from the institutional settings in which they occur, and because of which they have determinate effects. TNPs do not, themselves, constitute a theory. They do, however, provide a conceptual framework within which a theory may be constructed. At this point, I shall briefly elaborate the theory of the global system based on the three spheres of economic, political, and culture-ideology transnational practices.

The global system is most fruitfully conceptualized as a system that operates at three levels, and knowledge about which can be organized in three spheres, namely the economic, the political, and the culture-ideology. Each sphere is typically characterized by a representative institution, cohesive structures of practices, organized and patterned, which can only be properly understood in terms of their transnational effects. The dominant form of globalization in the present era is undoubtedly capitalist globalization. This being the case, the primary agents and institutional focus of economic transnational practices are the transnational corporations.

However, there are others. The World Bank, the IMF, WTO, commodity exchanges, the G7 (political leaders of the seven most important economies), the US Treasury, and so on are mostly controlled by those who share the interests of the major TNCs and the major TNCs share their interests. In a revealing report on 'IMF: Efforts to Advance U.S. Policies at the Fund' by the US General Accounting Office (GAO-01–214, 23 January 2001) we discover that the US Treasury and the Executive Director actively promoted US policies on sound banking, labour issues, and audits of military expenditures. The report concluded that it was difficult to determine the precise significance of US influence, because other countries generally support the same policies. This phenomenon is widely known as the Washington Consensus, a term coined by John Williamson of the Institute for International Economics.

By 'Washington' Williamson meant not only the US government, but all those institutions and networks of opinion leaders centered in the world's defacto capital—the IMF, World Bank, think-tanks, politically sophisticated investment bankers, and worldly finance ministers, all those who meet each other in Washington and collectively define the conventional wisdom of the moment . . . [One may roughly] summarize this consensus as . . . the belief that Victorian virtue and economic policy—free markets and sound money—is the key to economic development. (C. Thomas 1999: 225, n. 2; see also Makinson 2000)

This is the transnational capitalist class at work. The underlying goal of keeping global capitalism on course is in constant tension with the selfish and destabilizing actions of those who cannot resist system-threatening opportunities to get rich quick or to cut their losses. It is, however, the direct producers, not the transnational capitalist class who usually suffer most when this occurs as, for example, the tin miners of Bolivia and the rest of the world found out when the London Metal Exchange terminated its tin contract in 1985 (Crabtree 1987) and when the Association of Coffee Producing Countries collapsed late in 2001. In the 1990s the World Bank loaned large sums for coffee production in Vietnam, now the second largest coffee bean exporter in the world. The result, predict-ably, was massive oversupply and prices plunged to their lowest level since the 1970s. The major coffee processors, like Nestlé and the coffee shop chains springing up all over the world, refuse to pay more for their coffee beans while charging premium prices for their beverages. Coffee farmers and their families will go hungry.[1] The miners and peasant producers who lose out from capitalist globalization parallel those who also lose out when firms close factories and make relatively well-paid (usually unionized) workers redundant in one place and relocate to other places where they pay lower wages and avoid unions. Big capitalists, however, often make substantial profits from these forms of economic restructuring. This is where the New International Division of Labour meets the race to the bottom (Frobel et al. 1980, Brecher and Costello 1994).

It may be helpful to spell out who determine priorities for economic, political, and culture-ideology transnational practices, and what they actually do. Those who own and control the TNCs organize the production of commodities and the services necessary to manufacture and sell them. The state fraction of the transnational capitalist class produces the political environment within which the products and services can be suc-cessfully marketed all over the world irrespective of their origins and qualities. Those responsible for the dissemination of the culture-ideology of consumerism produce the values and attitudes that create and sustain the need for the products. These are ana-lytical rather than empirical distinctions. In the real world they are inextricably mixed. TNCs get involved in host country politics, and the culture-ideology of consumerism is largely promulgated through the transnational corporations involved in mass media and advertising.[2] Members of the transnational capitalist class often work directly for TNCs, and their lifestyles are exemplary for the spread of consumerism. Nevertheless, it is useful to make these analytical distinctions, particularly where the apparent and real empirical contradictions are difficult to disentangle.

The thesis on which this conceptual apparatus rests and on which any viable theory of the current dominant global system depends is that capitalism is changing qualitatively from an inter-national to a globalizing system. This is the subject of a heated debate in academic, political, and cultural circles. The idea that capitalism has entered a new global phase (whether it be organized or disorganized) clearly commands a good deal of support though, unsurprisingly, there are considerable differences on the details. The conception of global capitalism of Ross and Trachte (1990) convincingly locates the emergence of global capitalism in a series of technological revolutions (primarily in transportation, communications, electronics, biotechnology), and this provides a key support to the global system theory being elaborated here. My focus on transnational corporations draws on a large and rich literature on the global corporation, again full of internal disputes, but based on the premise, well expressed by Howells and Wood (1993: 4) that 'the production processes within large firms are being decoupled from specific territories and being formed into new global systems' (also Dicken 1998, Sklair 2001).

From the business periodical literature there are hundreds, probably thousands, of examples of the impact of globalization to chose from to fortify the thesis. The cover feature on 'The Stateless Corporation' in *Business Week* (14 May 1990: 98–106) was an early influential statement of this perspective, and in one of its regular forays into the big questions, *Fortune* magazine identified globalization as the first of four business revolutions happening simultaneously, the other three being computers, flexible management, and the information economy (13 Dec. 1993: 32–7). And this has intensified in the twenty-first century. So, while some industrial and social phenomena seem to resist globalization and the state has obviously not disappeared, there is sufficient general support for the thesis that capitalism is entering something like a global phase to justify this enquiry.

The theory of capitalist globalization revolves around the necessity for global capitalism to continually increase production and cross-border trade, to guarantee the political conditions for these to occur uninterruptedly all over the world, and to create in people the need to want to consume all the products that are available, on a permanent basis. There are, of course, other forces at work in the global system, and in some respects global capitalism has had to come to terms with them, particularly when they challenge capitalist globalization. It is often argued that globalization can be resisted locally (see Featherstone 1990, Jones 1998) but this is very difficult to pin down. In order to start to do this, and to provide a real setting for global system theory, it is necessary to articulate where exactly globalization and resistance to it take place.

THE PHYSICAL SPACES FOR TRANSNATIONAL PRACTICES

The physical spaces for transnational practices in the capitalist global system are wherever those who own and control the TNCs operate, wherever members of the transnational capitalist class meet, and wherever the culture-ideology of consumerism penetrates. It is frequently argued that globalization takes place mostly in and around cities (Short and Kim 1999, Marcuse and van Kempen 2000) and an interesting body of research on urban social movements in the context of globalization is emerging (see Hamel *et al.* 2000, Guidry *et al.* 2000). With the tremendous growth of urbanization in the second half of the twentieth century, particularly in the Third World, it is not only the cities of Europe and North America that are of interest. As Figure 5.1 shows, most cities with over 10 million inhabitants are now in Asia and Latin America.

The idea of world or global cities has dominated the debate about the relationship between globalization and urbanization. In the most influential formulation of this idea, Friedmann (in Knox and Taylor 1995, first published in 1982) argued that world cities can be identified in terms of a set of interrelated criteria. These were: the extent to which a city is a major financial center, has global or regional TNCs and international institutional headquarters, has rapid growth of business services, is an important manufacturing centre, and is a major transport node. Paul Waley (in Marcuse and van Kempen 2000: 153–4) expresses this very well in his analysis of the development of Tokyo after the Second World War: '[The] coming-of-age of leading Japanese enterprises as transnational corporations intensified pressure to create a fitting urban backdrop, a corporate global city whose physical appearance matched the pretensions of its leading corporate establishments.' In the 1980s, Friedmann constructed a world-city hierarchy with primary and secondary cities in the core and semi-periphery countries. Subsequent research on global cities focused on the global role of particular cities (London, New York, Los Angeles, and Tokyo attracted most attention), and the inter-connections between the global economy, regions, cities, and communities (see Knox and Taylor 1995, Sassen 2000a). These formulations have been criticized on several counts, mainly because they appear to

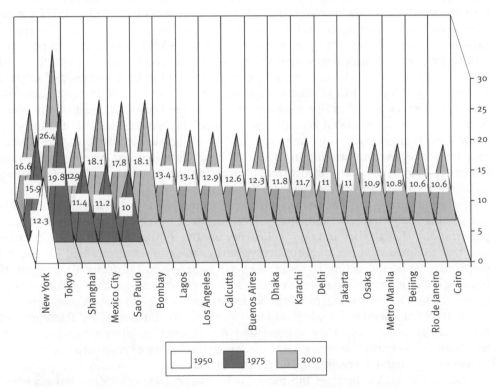

Figure 5.1 Cities with 10 million or more inhabitants (1950, 1975, 2000)

Source: Adapted table from Population Division of the Department of Economic and Social Affairs of the United Nations Secretariat (2002), *World Urbanization Prospect: the 1999 Revision* **www.un.org/esa/population/publications/wup/1999/urbanization/pdf** (28 January 2002), reprinted by permission of the publisher.

attribute too much to a few cities,[3] but they remain the starting point for this aspect of global studies.

Global cities, however, are not located exclusively in the First World. Now Shanghai, Bombay, Calcutta, Dhaka, Karachi, and others in Asia; Mexico City, Sao Paulo, Buenos Aires, and Rio in Latin America; Lagos and Cairo in Africa (and many other smaller cities) combine world-class telecommunications and the skyscrapers that accommodate the regional headquarters of TNCs and global institutions with shanty towns lacking basic amenities of sewerage, clean running water, and a dependable electricity supply, not to speak of adequate schools and medical services.

Sanjoy Chakravorty, for example, shows how the New Calcutta markets itself as the gateway to the Asian Tigers. To understand Calcutta (indeed to understand most major cities) it is vital to consider the spatial distribution of the informal sector, in this case especially domestic labour. The reforms of July 1991 removed entry barriers for foreign investment in India with major effects for urban space, notably in Haldia, a new industrial enclave outside Calcutta where colonies (as the districts are called) are actually named after corporations. Chakravorty contrasts the planning disasters of New Calcutta (for example, construction of a new town that lies empty because government employees refused to relocate there) with the slum-free electronic enclave of Salt Lake new town, where the biggest complaint is the shortage of servants. 'Certainly, the bourgeois planning apparatus has worked and continues to work for the benefit of the upper classes' (in Marcuse and van Kempern 2000: 74). Indeed, mini-slums may be thoughtfully incorporated to solve the Salt Lake servant problem! (p. 76, n. 21). Ribeiro and Telles also focus on what they term emerging dualization in Rio. The city has experienced a tremendous increase in home-owning (in 1940, 30 per cent of households owned and 64 per cent rented; by 1980, the percentages were 57 and 34). The deindustrialization that followed Brazil's insertion in the global economy destroyed the jobs of large numbers of salaried and public employees and created a huge rise in numbers of self-employed, mainly informal workers. The rich live in the central city, the poor (and most of the black population) live in peripheral zones. In 1992, favela youth descended on the glittering South Zone beaches prompting the local residents to organize against what they saw as invasion. Power is concentrating in the hands of 'an elite that acts together with local governments in large urban restructuring projects in the city center, further augmenting social segmentation' (in Marcuse and van Kempern 2000: 92).

However, Marcuse and van Kempern (2000: 7) themselves argue that 'Globalization is not automatically translated into spatial patterns, even in the case of a growing social polarization'. Though they and their colleagues use the term globalizing cities they caution that the pattern is not uniform everywhere (some cities, Calcutta and Rio among them, may be de-globalizing in some respects). A purely spatial focus, they argue, is limiting because it encourages static conceptions of walling and quartering. The concept of city can also be misleading, for cities do not prosper or decline though groups within them do: 'What is a crisis for one group may be prosperity for the others' (Marcuse and van Kempern 2000: 265). They suggest that the concept of layered city is a better metaphor, recognizing the potentially polarizing significance of residential, workplace, transportation, child, recreational, and commercial layers.

Cities are so visible because the mass media, particularly television, has achieved almost universal coverage throughout the Third World, and there are now few people who have no access at all to TV images of global cities. This has added to the long-standing magnetic pull of the cities for rural dwellers, many of whose livelihoods have been threatened or actually destroyed by global agri-business (Bonanno *et al.* 1994, Watts and Goodman 1997). Rural migrants into the cities serve as channels of transmission for transnational practices between cities and countryside, within countries and between them (see Faist 2000).

In an important revision of the world city hypothesis, Hill and Kim (2000) argue that major cities like Tokyo and Seoul do not fit the model based on the convergence in economic base, spatial organization, and social structure. They distinguish between two world city types, namely the market-centred bourgeois city (New York is the prototype) and the state-centred political bureaucratic city (of which Tokyo is the prototype). The globalist paradigm is flawed, they claim, because it does not see the role of the state in all world cities, as states all try simultaneously to be national and global. In rather different terms, McNeill (2000) draws a similar conclusion from his nuanced study of the establishment of the Guggenheim museum franchise in Bilbao, an effect of globalization but one in which urban, regional, and national identities are all being negotiated. A new kind of Western entrepreneurial city is emerging: 'increasingly carceral, dividing and separating populations like never before along class, race and sexual lines' (Hall and Hubbard 1998: 1), with serious consequences for the future of civil society (Douglass and Friedmann 1998).

The physical spaces for transnational practices are located all over the planet. They are in inner-city neighbourhoods where recent migrants live next to the bright lights of newly developed business districts or recreated tourist sites where global cultural forms are being inexorably spread all over the world (Judd and Feinstein 1999).[4] But they are also in rural areas within easy reach of cities where peasants are drawn into cash crop production by the promise of riches from agro-TNCs, and they are in mines and plantations far from cities where government agencies, TNCs, and their local affiliates are restructuring communities. They are even in the sea, where states and industries go to 'war' over cod and tuna (Bonanno and Constance 1996). It is to these types of economic transnational practices that we now turn.

ECONOMIC TRANSNATIONAL PRACTICES

Economic transnational practices are economic practices that transcend state boundaries. These may seem to be entirely contained within the borders of a single country even though their effects are transnational. For example, within one country there are consumer demands for products that are unavailable, in general or during particular seasons, from domestic sources. Retailers place orders with suppliers who fill the orders from foreign sources. Neither the retailer nor the consumer needs to know or care where the product comes from, though some countries now have country of origin rules making mandatory the display of this information. Many campaigning groups make sure that customers know, for example, that some products come from sweatshops in Asia or the USA (Bonacich and Applebaum 2000, Rosen 2002). There may be a parallel situation in the supplier country. Local producers may simply sell their products to a domestic marketing board or wholesaler and neither know nor care who the final consumer is. Transnational corporations, big or small, enter the scene when sellers, intermediaries, and buyers are parts of the same transnational network (Morgan 2001).

Hundreds of thousands of companies based all over the world export goods and services. In the USA alone in the late 1990s there were more than 200,000 exporting companies according to the website of the US Department of Commerce. Of this large number of exporters only about 15 per cent operated from multiple locations, but these accounted for about 80 per cent of exports from the USA and almost half of manufacturing exports were from the top fifty firms. They, of course, are the major TNCs, comprising the less than 1 per cent of US manufacturers that export to fifty or more countries. Over half of all US export value derives from their transnational economic practices and, significantly, much of their business is comprised of intra-firm transactions. The picture is similar in many other countries with firms that export manufactured goods. The global economy is dominated by a few gigantic transnational corporations marketing their products, many of them global brands, all over the world, some medium-sized companies producing in a few locations and selling in multiple markets, while many more small firms sell from one location to one or a few other locations.

One important consequence of the expansion of the capitalist world economy has been that individual economic actors (like workers and entrepreneurs) and collective economic actors (like trade unions and TNCs) have become much more conscious of the transnationality of their practices and have striven to extend their global influence. As capitalist globalization spread, anti-globalization researchers and activists focused on imports and exports, and vested some products with great political and culture-ideology significance. Increasing numbers of consumers now register where what they are buying comes from, and producers now register where what they are producing will go to, and this knowledge may affect their actions. An important example of this process is the rapid growth of ethical and organic marketing between Third World producers and First World consumers (Barrientos 2000, Raynolds 2000). These transnational practices must be seen within the context of an unprecedented increase in the volume of economic transnational practices since the 1950s, as evidenced by the tremendous growth of cross-border trade. According to the World Bank, global exports rose from $US94 billion in 1965, to $1,365 billion in 1986, $3,500 billion in 1993 and over $5,400 billion in 1999. Foreign investment and other types of capital flows have increased even more rapidly (Streeton, in Bhalla 1998: ch. 1). This means that even some quite poor people in some poor countries now have access to many non-local consumer goods, and through their use of the mass media are becoming more aware of the status-conferring advantages that global branded goods and services have over others. These new economic communities are generally referred to as emerging markets (see Sidaway and Pryke 2000), signifying that their main interest for capitalist globalization is their potential for the profitable sale of goods and services. Transnational corporations are routinely conceived of as the surest route to economic development on a global scale (Hood and Young 2000). This, of course, largely depends on people having the money to buy goods and services, and the primary source of money for most people in the world is their jobs.[5]

JOBS

The most obvious and tangible effect of economic TNPs is the creation of jobs when a foreign corporation opens a factory or an office abroad. These jobs are almost always seen as benefits, both by the workers who flock to take them up and by the governments that have established incentive programmes to attract them in the first place or to keep them when the corporations threaten to move.[6] Jobs are only one, albeit the most visible, benefit of economic TNPs. Other benefits include the exports due to foreign firms, and the backward linkages that they set up in the host economy (that is the locally produced goods and services they purchase, either from existing firms or from firms established primarily to supply the TNCs). Backward linkages also create jobs, for example in the most favourable cases local firms will grow to supply the TNCs with valuable components and services. But while this does happen frequently in the First World, it is not so common in Third World locations.

But these jobs have costs. As noted above, governments all over the world offer fiscal incentives to attract foreign firms to open factories. For example, in 1958 the government of the Irish Republic decreed that profits from exports by companies in the Shannon Industrial Estate would be exempt from tax for twenty-five years, and profit tax remission for firms outside Shannon was to be 100 per cent for a period of ten years. This was extended subsequently several times, as is quite common all over the world. Further costs are the bureaucracies set up to woo and service foreign manufacturers, and imported components that foreign firms use to produce what they do. It is difficult to know whether FDI would take place without incentives and to work out the actual cost to the local populations of the tax remissions and infrastructural investments made by the host governments of the communities and countries where TNCs enjoy these privileges. The relentless drive to attract more and more foreign investment (high tech by preference, but practically any would do) that began seriously in the 1970s continues, and there are now very few countries anywhere in the world that do not have some incentives to attract FDI. The decline in restrictive investment regimes and the increase in positive incentives for TNCs all over the world, particularly in the Third World, were documented in the World Investment Reports of UNCTAD throughout the 1990s. This is a measure of the potency of economic transnational practices in the global system.

Thus, a seemingly simple and straightforward phenomenon like a TNC opening a factory or an office in a foreign country has very wide ramifications. It is clearly a central economic transnational practice.[7] Let us pursue this further.

Much of the expansion in manufacturing employment in the global system since the 1950s has come from relatively few industries, such as automobiles, apparel, electronics, household goods, and toys. In some, though not all, countries where agents of the developmental state have tried to promote export-led industrialization, the most dynamic parts of their economies have tended to be those with TNC participation. Globosceptic state-centrist theorists make much of the fact that two of the most successful of these economies, namely South Korea and Taiwan, had relatively little FDI and that state agencies exerted control of credit and foreign currency. This is true, but both benefited decisively from access to the US market and both, especially South Korea, developed formidable TNCs of their own. The Asian financial crisis of the late 1990s (see Jomo 1998) and the increasing role of financial globalization in most of the economies of Asia in the 1990s have gone some way to dismantle the Asian developmental state though Woo-Cumings (1999) and others argue that it is being 're-invented' (see also Robinson and White 1998). The global transformation from state-driven planning to marketization that began in the 1980s took hold in Asia in the 1990s. The growing access of Asian corporations (parastatal and private) to global capital markets, reduced their dependency on the state for capital, and the developmental state in Asia is increasingly being seen as incompatible with financial globalization (Pang 2000). The pressures on business brought about by increasingly global markets for capital (Jomo 1998) and labour (Rowley and Benson 2000) have forced some unwelcome changes on Asian developmental states. The NICs, once held up as the model for successful development, are having to change.[8]

But the growth of new industry jobs in the Third World has hardly kept pace with the loss of jobs in traditional indigenous industries, and TNCs have directly caused the loss of at least some of these indigenous jobs by forcing domestic competitors out of business. For example, electronics TNCs from the USA, Europe, and Japan have pre-empted the creation of a domestically owned electronics industry in all but a few countries. However, a domestic, if not entirely domestically controlled, electronics industry can survive as a result of the stimulus given by foreign firms, as Grieco (1984) illustrates in the case of India's restrictive foreign investment regime in general, and its struggle with IBM, in particular. However, as Evans (1995) demonstrates, by the 1990s even an Indian government claiming economic nationalist credentials had succumbed to the economic transnational practices of capitalist globalization, and had opened up its economy.

There are two substantive issues to be considered in this situation: first, the desirability in terms of economic efficiency of incentives for foreign firms; and second, which incentives are most liable to be effective in attracting and retaining TNCs. While it might seem simple common sense to argue that, for example, tax relief on profits must be an important factor in the decision of a manufacturer to produce offshore, this is not always the case. For many foreign investors involved in export-processing in low-wage locations, foreign plants are cost centres, rather than profit centres for tax purposes (though considerable monetary profits are often made). Where profits are declared, tax relief tends to represent an extra bonus rather than a necessary incentive to foreign investors.

Workers and governments in most countries are interested not only in how many jobs are created for how long and at what cost, but also what kinds of jobs are created. Ironically, one of the main criticisms levelled at transnational corporations in Asia, Africa, and Latin America is that their operations are predominantly of the export-processing variety. This usually means that they are paying low wages, mainly to women workers (so-called nimble-fingered young women) in monotonous and often physically debilitating jobs, the products of which constitute a small proportion of the value-added of the final commodity. In such enterprises top managers and technicians tend to be expatriates and little if any advanced training is offered to the local workers. In many cases this type of foreign investment will not upgrade the host economy in any meaningful sense. As most of these zones are in Third World countries, these issues will be taken up in the next chapter.

The size and character of the host market (local, regional, or national) and the types of foreign companies that investment agencies set out to attract, are important considerations for the assessment of the developmental effects of foreign investment. TNC factories and offices tend to outperform local firms in most economic sectors in most Third World countries and in some First and New Second World industries. However, many exporters import the materials and components used to make their exported goods rather than buy them locally. This reduces the magnitude of local value added, a key measure of the benefit of foreign investment. What the TNCs spend locally can be broken down into three components, namely wages and salaries, utility and service costs, and material linkages.

Jobs created by FDI in the New Second and Third Worlds have one key advantage for the host economy compared with those created in the First World, namely foreign currency. Few countries outside the First World have transferable currencies. The hard currencies of the First World, especially US dollars, Japanese yen, and the Euro, can be used freely in international trade, while the soft currencies of the rest of the world's countries are generally not acceptable for the settlement of international accounts. If a soft-currency country wants to import something, it must earn or borrow one of the hard currencies to pay for it (or engage in barter trade). Usually, the hard currency exchanged by foreign investors to pay wages, salaries, and utility and other costs has a significance in New Second and Third World countries that it does not have in First World countries. Thus, the more hard currency TNCs can be persuaded to spend in soft currency countries, the greater the economic impact.

The sectoral composition of the labour force has not changed a great deal in the poorest countries, particularly those with large populations, mainly because the absolute numbers of village dwellers tends to hide even quite large increases in absolute numbers of industrial and service workers in the cities. Despite this, in more or less every country the proportion of service workers in the labour force (including police, armed forces, and other state employees) has increased in the last few decades. Many of these service workers work in the informal sector, defined as all those people not in the formal waged economy. A considerable literature has grown on the subject of such workers, particularly women, and how they interact with those in the formal economy in the local context and relate to the global economy (see Scott, in Elson 1995: ch. 5). There are many conflicting interpretations of the informal sector, but the structural approach is of most interest to globalization theorists. Structuralists see the informal sector as an integral part of the capitalist economy, locally and globally. So the informal sector is theorized not as a more primitive form of economic life, but as that part of a capitalist economy unregulated or only partly regulated by the state, with its own structures of wealth and exploitation (Portes and Castells 1989). Globalization presents costs and benefits for women and men working in the spaces around the formal and the informal sectors, creating winners and losers. As Figure 5.2 illustrates, in apparel sweatshops in Los Angeles, California, the sale of 10,000 dresses produces $1,000,000, from which the retailer takes $500,000 while 10,000 workers share $50,000, 5 dollars per worker per dress. As Bonacich and Applebaum (2000) show, despite hard working conditions, there can be a considerable level of solidarity and organization among informal workers.

Carr *et al.* (2000) analyse the impact of the Internet on women home-based workers within the framework of global value chains. Their cases of networks in manufactured goods (fashion garments), agricultural products (non-traditional exports), and non-timber forest products (shea butter) demonstrate the uneven distribution of power and rewards between richer and poorer participants and between women and men in the global value

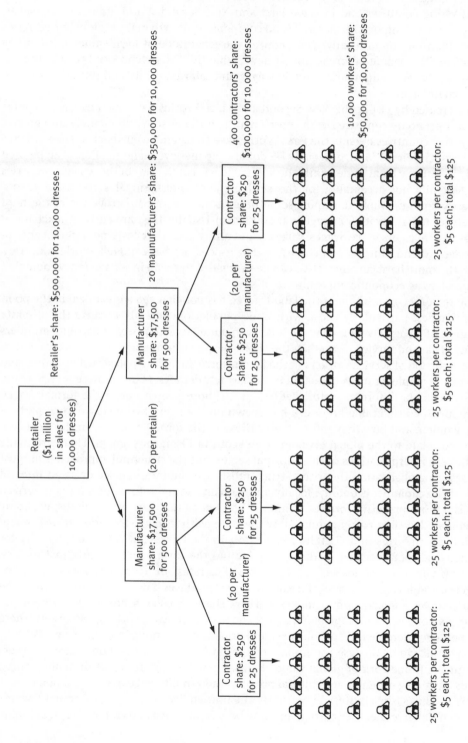

Figure 5.2 Accumulation of wealth from 10,000 dresses selling for $100 each

Source: Bonacich and Applebaum (2000: 207), © 2000 The University of California Press and authors.

chains. Employee networks are putting the Internet to effective use for the spread of information and for organizing purposes locally and transnationally (Shostak 1999). These informal (unregulated) producers and service-providers that TNCs routinely use as parts of their direct and indirect transnational production and distribution chains lead us back to the question of linkages as a significant transnational practice.

LINKAGES

The local purchase of materials and components, backward linkages, is usually in hard currency, but linkages also have a more general industrial significance in all three Worlds alike. Linkages may be either backward, when the purchasing firm, which need be neither foreign nor an exporter, buys what it needs locally, or forward, when the seller firm supplies a local firm with what it needs to produce something else. The ideal state of affairs from the point of view of host countries is where foreign firms actually stimulate the creation and growth of the suppliers of their needs, particularly those materials and components that have a high value-added quality (like electronic components or valuable raw materials) within the local economy. Forward linkages, where the output of these foreign firms (for example semiconductors for consumer electronic goods or textiles for the apparel industry) goes into the local economy for further processing, are an added bonus. These are what Hirschman calls input-provision, derived demand, or backward linkage effects and output-utilization or forward linkage effects (Hirschman 1958: ch. 6). These linkages constitute the first criterion of what I have labelled a successful development effect (Sklair 1993: ch. 9). Though not all linkages are necessarily beneficial to the host economy, and those in different industries may have different characteristics, linkages can be crucial in the transformation of economic growth into general development. Suffice it to say that even in the midwest region of Ireland, widely regarded as the first successful free zone in the world, whose agencies have an unsurpassed international reputation, linkages have been uninspiring. My own research showed that the foreign exporting sector bought very little that was of Irish manufacture, and even when it did these were low value-added goods, like packaging materials and industrial consumables (Sklair 1988b). In the export-oriented zones in Egypt, China, and Mexico (Sklair 1993) backward linkages were even lower than in Ireland, perhaps in the region of 1 or 2 per cent of total purchases.

It is important to look behind the aggregate figures of local sourcing to try to identify where linkage effects could realistically be expected to result from the transnational practices of established and potential TNCs, and what the host authorities could realistically hope to do about it in terms of their transnational practices. In Ireland, three separate initiatives were established in the midwest region to tackle this problem. The Shannon Development Company had a Matchmaker service to match up the capacities of local suppliers with the needs of industrial purchasers, the Irish Development Authority Project Identification Unit supplied local firms with information on the purchasing requirements of the TNCs, and the Irish Goods Council did the same thing. By the year 2000, the Irish development agencies had given up the struggle for export-oriented industrialization based on manufacturing TNCs, and in the midwest the emphasis was on the information economy. This, however, was based on call centres rather than state-of-the-art electronic TNCs.[9] These activities are mirrored in many sites of investment all over the world where TNCs are seen as potential purchasers of local goods.

The effort to create backward linkages reveals some important economic transnational practices. The logic of transnational production either forbids, permits, or encourages backward linkages. Where a product is entirely integrated within the TNC or its network of captive suppliers, or where the intermediate components or materials used are of such a specialized nature that there are simply no available suppliers outside the existing TNC network, then backward linkages are literally forbidden by the logic of global production. For TNCs involved in more traditional product lines that are in no way state of the art, where materials and components are more readily available, on the surface at least, the logic of TNC production appears to permit backward linkages. This is seen, correctly, as potentially very rewarding for domestic industry, and in some First World countries and in the NICs the supply of materials and components, for example for TNCs in the automobile industry, has certainly been economically rewarding (usually because of local content requirements, on which see below). In most Second and Third World countries this has not generally happened. The reasons are that local production is not of the quality required by the world market, prices are too high and delivery is unreliable.

No one familiar with the performance of some domestic industry in most countries outside and some inside the First World would be surprised by this but, even so, one might wonder why the figures for local sourcing are quite so low when local materials and components are available. The logic of global production is again operating, but through transfer pricing and the use of captive suppliers. By the very nature of the case, notably the obsession of most firms with commercial secrecy, this is difficult to research. Only when local factories actually begin to produce what TNCs need at competitive price, quality and delivery, will host country governments be in a position to challenge the TNCs on linkages. Where this has already happened, particularly in the case of automobile parts, it tends to be connected with local content requirements. TNCs tend to get round this by buying up or establishing their own local suppliers (Bennett and Sharp 1985; Zapata *et al.* 1990). However, in such cases, TNCs can occasionally be seen actually to encourage backward linkages (Sklair 1993: 245–6).

The job creation and job destruction effects of TNCs have very wide ramifications and they are sociologically and developmentally among the most important economic transnational practices. This will be illustrated further in the next chapter, with particular reference to the developmental effects of TNC practices and the sexual division of labour they have created, in the Third World.

POLITICAL TRANSNATIONAL PRACTICES

In 'Transnationalism and the New Tribe', Field described the historical occurrence of what he labelled transnational individuals and the growth of the tendency towards purposeful transnational philanthropy in the United States (Field 1973: 11–12). In Field's view, by the late nineteenth century the organizational revolution had transformed transnationalism from an individual to a company affair, and two levels of culture emerged, global and local, with a New Tribe of those imbued with transnational global culture. What is missing from Field's account is the connection between political transnational practices and the capitalist global system. The reason for this is that Field's New Tribe was imbued with the rather vague mission of transmitting Western techniques to traditional societies (reminiscent of modernization theory) and although this opens the door to many fascinating details about the structures of culture contact, it is at a rather high level of generality for explanatory purposes and it seriously underplays the role of the class responsible for capitalist globalization.

Nevertheless, there is a considerable degree of interest in transnational political practice at this level, particularly in the development of non-governmental organizations (NGO). At the end of the 1980s the *Yearbook of International Organizations* (Union of International Associations 1988–9) listed thousands of bodies classified as federations of international organizations, universal membership organizations, intercontinental membership organizations, regionally defined membership organizations, organizations emanating from places, persons, and other bodies, and organizations having a special form, including foundations and funds. The subject guide traverses the spectrum from abattoir to zymurgy (the art of fermentation); a sample page from the universal membership organizations section details the International Association of Legal Science, World Alliance of Reformed Churches, and Association of Geoscientists for International Development (see also Smith, in Smith *et al.* 1997: ch. 3).

Most of these are what Willetts (1982) termed 'Pressure Groups as Transnational Actors'. Willetts identifies two main categories, namely sectional groups (including TNCs, trade unions, professional associations, and recreational clubs), and promotional groups (welfare agencies, religious organizations, communal groups, political parties, and specific-issue groups). Any such classification is bound to be somewhat arbitrary and, as Willetts acknowledges, many groups can be placed in more than one category. Over 1,000 NGOs were involved in the creation of the UN and there are currently around 1,500 NGOs attached in some way to the UN.

It is difficult to assess the importance of such organizations. (I return to this subject in Chapters 10 and 11 below, when I assess the potential of these and similar organizations and movements to challenge capitalist globalization, particularly in terms of the globalization of human rights.) Here the emphasis will be on political practices in general, then in the next section on the transnational capitalist class (TCC) and the groups and organizations with which it has its most significant contacts. A terminological point is in order here. The term transnational capitalist class is used in the singular. This is to signify that the concept of the TCC entails global capitalist interests. There are, of course, cases where the interests of the class as a whole, to promote global capitalism, are transcended by other interests for individual members, where Jews refuse to do business with Germans, or Arabs with Jews, or Protestants with Catholics, or white people with non-white people, for example. The strength and unity of the transnational capitalist class are, therefore, always open to empirical questions.[10]

The possibility of genuinely global politics, transnational rather than inter-national, what Beck (1999) calls global subpolitics, is often called into question by the apparent uniqueness of political life and structures in every country, region, and community. Chirot puts the paradox well when he says: 'efforts to understand the general forces at work throughout the world should not overlook the specific historical and cultural influences that make seemingly similar global forces have such different effects in various parts of the world' (Chirot 1991: p. xi). The bewildering complexity of politics in the Third

World (see, for example, Randall and Theobold 1998), let alone the other two, bears this out.

Questions of ethnic solidarity and ethnic strife (often related to religion) probably present the most serious actual and theoretical challenge to politics at the global level. UNRISD (2000: 57) presents a very useful typology of societal ethnic structure based on five types of polarity with varying degrees of potential for dividing people and, by implication, reducing the prospects for the formation of transnational in contrast to cross-national bonds. Societies marked by unipolarity are those where the largest of many ethnic groups constitute 70 per cent or more of the population (examples are Botswana and China); bipolarity is where the two largest groups constitute at least 80 per cent of the population (as in Rwanda, Belgium, and Fiji), and tripolarity is where there are three large groups in a multi-ethnic population (Switzerland, Nigeria, and Malawi). Fragmented multipolarity where no group dominates (as in Cameroon, Tanzania, and PNG), and concentrated multipolarity where one large group dominates but there are many others (as in India, Kenya, and Ethiopia) complete the typology. While ethnic differences and ethnic conflicts are important issues in many societies and fundamental in some, their existence does not negate the force of capitalist globalization though it can help to explain the forms that it takes and the effects that it has. Transnational communities that result from migration (Smith and Guarnizo 1998, Faist 2000) provide many examples of this.

Most attempts to theorize global politics are really inter-national and state-centrist or focus on relatively ineffective international organizations at a relatively high level of generalization but this appears to be an inherent characteristic of such theorizing rather than contingent weakness (as in Buzan and Little 2000). This being the case, the analytic entry point of transnational political practices at the conceptual level and the substantive institutional focus on the transnational capitalist class seem to be more realistic bases for deconstructing the apparent uniqueness of national politics in a globalizing world. Global system theory predicts that the transnational capitalist class is growing stronger and more united and, as I shall go on to argue, this can be best explained by the increasing success of the transnational corporations in propagating the culture-ideology of consumerism.

THE TRANSNATIONAL CAPITALIST CLASS

The transnational capitalist class is not made up of capitalists in the traditional Marxist sense.[11] Direct ownership or control of the means of production is no longer the exclusive criterion for serving the interests of capital, particularly not the global interests of capital.

The transnational capitalist class (TCC) is transnational in at least five senses. Its members tend to share global as well as local economic interests; they seek to exert economic control in the workplace, political control in domestic and international politics, and culture-ideology control in everyday life; they tend to have global rather than local perspectives on a variety of issues; they tend to be people from many countries, more and more of whom begin to consider themselves citizens of the world as well as of their places of birth; and they tend to share similar lifestyles, particularly patterns of luxury consumption of goods and services. In my formulation, the transnational capitalist class includes the following four fractions:

- TNC executives and their local affiliates (corporate fraction);
- globalizing state and inter-state bureaucrats and politicians (state fraction);
- globalizing professionals (technical fraction); and
- merchants and media (consumerist fraction).

This class sees its mission as organizing the conditions under which its interests and the interests of the global system (which usually but do not always coincide) can be furthered within the transnational, inter-state, national, and local contexts. The concept of the transnational capitalist class implies that there is one central transnational capitalist class that makes system-wide decisions, and that it connects with the TCC in each community, region, and country.

Political transnational practices are not primarily conducted within conventional political organizations. Neither the transnational capitalist class nor any other class operates primarily through transnational political parties. However, loose transnational political groupings do exist and they do have some effects on, and are affected by, the political practices of the TCC in most countries. There are no genuine transnational political parties, though there appears to be a growing interest in international associations of parties, which are sometimes mistaken for transnational parties. The post-Comintern Communist Movement, the Socialist International, international Fascist organizations, and various liberal and neo-liberal multi-state parties have never had much success.

There are, however, various transnational political organizations through which fractions of the TCC operate locally, for example, the Rotary Club and its offshoots and the network of American, European, and Japan-related Chambers of Commerce that straddles the globe. As Errington and Gewertz (1997) show in their study of a Rotary Club in Melanesia as well as my own research on AmCham in Mexico (Sklair 1993: *passim*), these organizations work as crucial transmission belts and lines of communication between global capitalism and local business. For example, a visit to the website of BISNIS (Business Information Service for the Newly Independent States) of the USA Trade Center in the Russian Far East tells us that in addition to two International Businesss Associations there were eight Rotary Clubs operating in this remote region in 2001.

At a more elevated level are the Trilateral Commission of the great and good from the United States, Europe, and Japan whose business is 'Elite Planning for World Management' (Sklar 1980); the World Economic Forum which meets at Davos in Switzerland and the annual Global conferences organized by *Fortune* magazine that bring together the corporate and the state fractions of the TCC. Many other similar but less well-known networks for capitalist globalization exist, for example the Bilderberg Group and Caux Round Table of senior business leaders. There are few major cities in any First or Third World (and now New Second World) country that do not have members of or connections with one or more of these organizations. They vary in strength from the major First World political and business capitals, through important Third World cities like Cairo, Singapore, and Mexico City, to nominal presences in some of the poorer countries in Africa, Asia, and Latin America. They are backed up by many powerful official bodies, such as foreign trade and economics departments of the major states. Specialized agencies of the World Bank and the IMF, WTO, US Agency for International Development (USAID), development banks, and the UN work with TNCs, local businesses, and NGOs (willing and not so willing) in projects that promote the agenda of capitalist globalization (Fox and Brown 1998, O'Brien *et al.* 2000).

The political practices of the transnational capitalist class will be analysed in terms of two issues. First, how it operates to change the nature of the political struggle between capital and labour, and second, the downgrading of indigenous practices.

LABOUR AND THE TRANSNATIONAL CAPITALIST CLASS

The relative strength of the transnational capitalist class can be understood in terms of the relative weakness of transnational labour. Labour is represented by some genuinely transnational trade unions.[12] The World Federation of Trade Unions (WFTU) was founded in 1945, with 350 delegates representing 67 million workers in 56 countries. This immediately postwar show of labour unity included members from the CIO (Congress of Industrial Organizations), one of the two main union movements in the USA (but not the other, the AFL (American Federation of Labor)), Britain, the Soviet Union, China, and India. WFTU split under the pressure of the Cold War in 1949, when the British TUC and the CIO from the United States (followed by the AFL) set up in opposition the International Confederation of Free Trade Unions (ICFTU). ICFTU followed a strict international and national no-contact policy with the WFTU, which it saw as entirely Soviet-dominated. In the 1980s, the WFTU had over 200 million members in seventy countries (most of Eastern Europe and communist unions in Western Europe and Japan), though the Italian communist trade union had withdrawn and the French began to distance themselves in the mid-1970s, ostensibly to improve the climate for domestic solidarity. ICFTU had about 90 million members (in ninety-two countries, including Western Europe, the Americas, and most of the Third World). The World Council of Labour, a Christian-oriented movement, had about 15 million members (Press and Thomson 1989). The collapse of the Soviet Union and communism in general in Eastern Europe in the 1990s led to the collapse of the WFTU, and splits that developed as a result of this in the ICFTU suggest that labour solidarity in opposition to capitalist globalization is an uncertain prospect (Ashwin, in Cohen and Rai 2000).

In addition, there are some industrially based transnational union organizations, for example the International Metalworkers Federation, and the International Union of Food and Allied Workers' Associations. These have been involved in genuine transnational labour struggles, and have gained some short-term victories. However, they face substantial difficulties in their struggles against organized capital, locally and transnationally (Leisink 1999; Ashwin, and Munck, both in Cohen and Rai 2000) and they have little influence.

However, there is a good deal of research on how the labour movement reacts to globalization (see Munck and Waterman 1999). The level of unionization to be found in TNC-owned industry in different countries varies widely as do the prospects for successful campaigns. Wills (1999) and Herod (2001), in case studies from Europe and the USA respectively, both emphasize the need for strategic flexibility. In some circumstances organizing globally promises better prospects of success, in others organizing locally does. The question cannot be realistically discussed, however, unless there is some meas-ure of the genuine independence of the union. We must distinguish at least three cases: first, where unions are prohibited or repressed; second, where unions are the creatures of governments or companies; third, where genuinely independent unions actually oper-ate.[13] While most TNCs in most countries will follow the local rules regarding the unions, host governments, particularly those promoting export-processing industries (not always under pressure from foreign investors), have often suspended national labour legislation in order to attract TNCs and/or to keep production going and foreign currency rolling in. Some cases will be discussed in the next chapter. With very few exceptions, most global-izing bureaucrats and politicians wanting to take advantage of the fruits of capitalist globalization will be unhelpful towards labour unions, if not downright hostile to them when they dare to challenge the transnational capitalist class (see, for example, Marjoribanks 2000).

DOWNGRADING OF INDIGENOUS PRACTICES

Even the most casual observer of transnational practices in the economic, political, and culture-ideology spheres cannot but be struck by the fact that indigenous practices are often unfavourably compared with foreign practices. Despite conceptual difficulties of the indigenous-foreign distinction (similar to traditional-modern), such comparisons are common between countries, cities, neighbourhoods, and regions. The downgrading of indigenous practices in many parts of the world is a subtle and circular process in which the newcomer has all the advantages and the incumbent all the handicaps. The necessity for and the presence of foreign companies, for example, are constant reminders of the deficiencies of the domestic economy. The new methods that TNCs bring are defined as more efficient (if not necessarily more desirable) than the traditional methods of produc-tion current in the host economy, and where entirely new products enter, this only underlines the inadequacies of the host. These can all have a depressing effect on local industry (see Barnes and Kaplinsky 2000).

Although academic researchers have questioned the notion of dualism (so-called trad-itional and modern sectors of an economy), as rather too clear-cut and simplistic, there may be an element of the self-fulfilling prophecy at work here. The more powerful the belief that indigenous practices are inferior and unreliable, the more likely are they actually to become so. An excellent illustration of this process occurs, rather unexpect-edly, in one of the great texts of the anti-colonial and anti-racist movements, Fanon's *The Wretched of the Earth*. He writes:

if the building of a bridge does not enrich the awareness of those who work on it, then that bridge ought not to be built and the citizens can go on swimming across the river or going by boat. The bridge should not be 'parachuted down' from above; it should not be imposed by a deus ex machina upon the social scene; on the contrary, it should come from the muscles and brains of the citizens. Certainly, there may well be need of engineers and architects, sometimes completely foreign engin-eers and architects; but the local party leaders should always be present, so that the new techniques can make their way into the cerebral desert of the citizen, so that the bridge in whole and in part can be taken up and conceived, and the responsibility for it assumed by the citizen. In this way, and in this way only, everything is possible. (Fanon [1968], in Lazarus 1999: 103)

It is necessary to distinguish between economic, political, and culture-ideology practices here. In terms of economic logic, an indigenous enterprise may be fulfilling the needs of the local consumers through efficient use of domestic inputs, while in terms of political (transnational) logic it is perceived as quite inefficient because of its lack of international competitiveness. In more dramatic terms, the downgrading of local industries reflects the success of the transnational capitalist class in dragging them into the global economy and thereby transforming them, even in a rather minimal sense, into transnational industries.

The presence of expatriate managers and technicians in foreign firms in even the most industrially advanced economies serves to intensify the distinction between superior foreign and inferior indigenous industry. Recruitment of top management appears to be through two circuits, but with a predominantly one-way flow. Transnational companies, particularly those with global reputations, have less difficulty in recruiting the available staff, either from indigenous firms or from other foreign companies. Indeed, there is some evidence of a transnational staff circuit as random conversations in airports and more systematic interviews with TNC executives confirm. The larger transnationals commonly train key staff at headquarters (usually in the USA, Japan, and Europe) and for some a job with a major TNC is the first step in a global career. There is a good deal of evidence to suggest that managerial and technical talent flows from the indigenous sector to the transnational companies rather than vice versa, particularly but not exclusively in the Third World. Gershenberg (1987) argued this for Kenya as Okada (1983) did for Indonesia, though my own later research on Mexico (Sklair 1993) suggests that this may be more of a two-way process in some industries. *Fortune* (18 August 1997: 50) reported that Microsoft had subsidiaries in sixty countries employing 6,200 people of whom only five were expatriates! While this sounds exceptional, local economies may derive benefits from this type of brain drain, even sufficient to offset the costs, if there is seen to be fair competition between the TNCs and the indigenous firms for trained managerial, technical, and craft personnel. The optimum situation would be a policy that would encourage the TNCs to train young people rather than entice away those already trained and working in the indigenous sector. Some of these young people are, of course, tomorrow's transnational capitalist class.

The downgrading of indigenous industry may be compensated for by the more progressive business environment that foreign companies promote, and particularly the high-technology companies of US, European, or Japanese origin. Transnational corporations can give a competitive stimulation to existing local companies by demonstrating the business potential of new lines or products, and they can also directly influence the market for new indigenous firms, as Evans (1995) has shown for the computer industries in several countries. In general, higher expectations of transnational firms for business services and a better-educated workforce may provoke the state into public spending that might otherwise not have taken place. For example, some governments would probably not have spent as much on telecommunications and infrastructure as they have done without the stimulus of a foreign-dominated export sector that produces hard-currency earnings and the expectation that such facilities, however expensive, would attract even more companies. The managers and workers of those firms may well benefit from this in the long run, as well as the TNCs. It must be noted, however, that the managers and workers of those indigenous firms that go under will not see this as an undiluted benefit and that state subsidies to attract FDI will not benefit the poor much.

There can also be a knock-on effect of the higher and more innovative technology that some foreign firms employ, all through society. This generates a climate for the technological upgrading of industry as a commercial proposition, and it also ensures that hardware and software are conveniently available, at a price, for those who wish to take advantage of them in any sphere. The presence of famous name globalizing firms undoubtedly encourages some enterprising local businesses to take opportunities that are offered for joint ventures and other forms of strategic alliances.

In these ways the transnational capitalist class downgrades certain indigenous practices by comparison with new and more glamorous transnational practices (some of which, paradoxically, might have originated locally as hybrid cultural practices). This creates what used to be termed a comprador mentality, the attitude that the best practices were invariably connected with foreigners who were the bearers of capitalist practices. Comprador mentality was either a cost or a benefit, depending on your position in the ideological struggle between those who believed that capitalism would inevitably damage Third World development prospects in the long run, and those who believed that there would be no development prospects without capitalism. This struggle revolved around the opposing material interests of competing classes and groups, and it still does.

Capitalist globalization has created new groups of what can be termed indigenous globalizers, aspiring members of the transnational capitalist class who have replaced the old compradors. They identify with global capitalism rather than any particular powerful country or corporation. Like all globalizers they are intellectually and geographically mobile. They make their connections with their countries of residence through the globalizing politicians and professionals who are officially responsible for regulating business, politics, and culture-ideology at the level of the national and local state.

The thesis that defines my approach to political transnational practices is that the state is a site of struggle between globalizers and localizers, principally between globalizing bureaucrats and politicians (indigenous globalizers) on the one hand and localizing bureaucrats and politicians on the other. This can be illustrated briefly with references to two examples that are very different in substance but identical in principle. In 2001 the only major supplier of non-genetically modified soybeans was Brazil. A powerful globalizing group within the federal government led by the agriculture minister pushed hard for the introduction of GM soybeans, arguing that Brazil must enthusiastically adopt biotechnology if it is to be a leading agricultural exporter in the twenty-first century. This group was supported by farmers in Brazil as well as US government agencies, the American Soyabean Association and major TNCs. Monsanto controlled two-thirds of seed production in the country through acquisitions of local companies, and opened a $US550 million factory in September 2001 (with incentives from the Brazilian government) to produce GM pesticide in anticipation of the permission to grow the GM soybeans. The company had been encouraged by the fact that the agriculture minister had announced that the GM crop would go ahead at a meeting for investors in New York in July 2001. However, the localizing group led by the attorney general reacted swiftly to this announcement and the minister was warned that he could be prosecuted if he authorized the GM crop. The localizers were supported by the Brazilian consumer association (Idec), with transnational links to the anti-GM movement outside the Americas (Branford 2001, see also Reisner 2001). The Brazilian state is thus the site of a political struggle between globalizers and localizers over whether people worldwide will have a choice to eat meat and poultry that has not been fed GM fodder.

The second example concerns the accession of China to the WTO. The Chinese government had applied to join GATT, the predecessor of WTO, in 1986 but no agreement had been reached by 1995, when the WTO was established. A cordial relationship grew between Presidents Clinton and Jiang Zemin, and Sino-US talks on WTO membership went well. China had accelerated its opening up of the economy to the outside world in the 1990s, reducing tariffs, negotiating over the sensitive telecommunications market, and forging positive trade relations with many existing WTO members (see Nolan 2001: esp. ch. 11). However, not all of China's leaders were enthusiastic for membership, particularly as domestic economic difficulties began to throw doubt on the wisdom of more opening up and political difficulties within the USA arose. In the midst of these problems, Premier Zhu Rongji visited the USA in April 1999 and offered significant trade concessions, but these did not satisfy the Republicans who pressured Clinton to demand even more. Lai (2001: 240) documents how Zhu called on US business leaders to intervene: 'Many US corporations and business associations expressed their disappointment over the impasse of the talks, and urged Clinton and their elected representatives to reach an agreement with China.' This situation, not surprisingly, caused controversy in China.

Lai identifies two sources of opposition. The first congregated around the National People's Congress (China's 'Parliament') led by Li Peng, and combined both Communist Party leaders and other NPC elements. The second group comprised six ministries and one State Council bureau, all threatened by increased foreign competition that would result from implementation of WTO rules. However, the globalizers in the political centre (led by President Jiang Zemin and orchestrated by the Ministry of Foreign Trade and Economic Cooperation) held firm. Despite a major international incident (the allegedly accidental bombing of the Chinese embassy in Belgrade) and the efforts of the localizing opposition in China to stir up anti-American and anti-capitalist sentiment, the USA and China signed an agreement for WTO membership on 15 November 1999 in Beijing, ratified in 2001. The nature of the political system in China facilitated the efforts of President Jiang and his group to marginalize the opposition groups politically, though perhaps not in the wider society. Nolan (2001: 925 ff.) discusses popular anti-globalization books in China, including *China Can Say No?* (1996) and *The Globalization Trap and China's Realistic Choices* (2000) and predicts a series of shocks to the system when China does join the WTO. What these examples from Brazil and China make clear is that the state is a site of struggle between globalizers and localizers and that both claim to be working for the national interest. The supporters of GM soybeans in Brazil and the supporters of WTO membership in China all argued that what they wanted was in the long run best for the country as a whole, even when they acknowledged (as both groups did) that some would suffer. The state will always be a central site of struggle for capitalist globalization, struggles that produce winners and losers.

There are those who see the destiny of the world as bound up with the adoption of all that is modern, often embodied in the products and practices of the TNCs. On the other hand, there are those who are deeply suspicious of the modernization represented by the TNCs, particularly where this is perceived as Western or US dominance in culture, industry, warfare, science, and technology. A battery of concepts, some of which have migrated from social science jargon to the mass media, identify those on either side of the divide.

The academically discredited distinction between traditional and modern is still common currency, while the notions of inward-oriented and outward-oriented describe those who look for guidance and sustenance to the resources of their own groups as opposed to those who look outside, usually to the West. Much the same idea is expressed by the distinction between local and cosmopolitan orientation. The question of the indigenous globalizers in the Third World will be resumed in the next chapter.

The price that the state will pay to sustain the costs of foreign investment will depend largely on the powers of indigenous globalizers, the local members of the transnational capitalist class. Whatever the price happens to be at a given time, and this can vary dramatically, it will be a price worth paying for some and not for others. What accounts for the complexity of the problem of evaluation is not only the economic and social costs involved themselves, but the interests, conflicting or in harmony, of those who pay the costs and those who reap the benefits. It may be an over-simplification to conceptualize all the different interests in terms of class struggle, particularly as some of the interest groups involved and some of the alliances of interests forged may defy analysis in conventional Marxist terms, particularly in the Third World (see Maxfield and Schneider 1997, Woo-Cumings 1999). Nevertheless, there are class interests involved even though they may not always conveniently reduce to one labouring class versus one capitalist class.

The transnational capitalist class supported by the strata that the TNCs have created (globalizing bureaucrats, politicians, and professionals) and even in some circumstances privileged fractions of the labour force, will all increasingly identify their own interests with those of the capitalist global system. Those on the fringes of the TCC will often be forced to make a choice between acting on behalf of it against what many would define as the interests of their own communities, as the transnational practices of capitalist globalization penetrate ever deeper into the areas that most heavily impact on their daily lives. The specific function of those who are directly responsible for transnational political practices is to create and sustain the organizational forms within which this penetration takes place and to connect them organically with those indigenous practices that can be incorporated and mobilized in the interests of the capitalist global system. In order to do this the transnational capitalist class must promote, all over the world, a specific structure of culture-ideology transnational practices, namely the culture-ideology of consumerism. It is no accident that the age of capitalist globalization should have begun to flower in the second half of the twentieth century, just when the electronic revolution that heralded the age of the globalizing mass media took root (see Schiller 1999).

CULTURE-IDEOLOGY TRANSNATIONAL PRACTICES

There are many theorists who argue that the driving force for globalization lies not in the economic nor in the political sphere, but in the realm of culture and ideology. Those for whom this idea is a novelty may be surprised to learn that it was the writings and political practice of a Marxist, and a communist militant at that, which were largely responsible for the present currency of this view among radical thinkers. Antonio Gramsci, who spent most of his adult life (1926–37) in Mussolini's prisons in Fascist Italy, elaborated on

Marx's insight that the ruling ideas of an epoch are the ideas of its ruling class, to create a theory of hegemony and a theory of classes of intellectuals whose function it is in any literate society to propagate or to challenge these leading ideas. Gramsci's *Prison Notebooks* represent not only a stirring monument to the human spirit under adversity but a significant turning point in the history of Marxist ideas and their contemporary relevance. This is partly because in the sphere of culture and ideology the material conditions have changed to such an extent that what Gramsci was arguing about hegemonic processes in the 1930s has become more, not less, relevant today than it was then. To put the point graphically, while Marx and his nineteenth-century comrades would have no great difficulty in recognizing the economic and the political spheres today, despite the major changes that have undoubtedly taken place in the last 150 years, in the culture-ideology sphere the opportunities for hegemonic control on a global scale have changed out of all recognition.

In one of the first quantitative studies of what he terms the communication explosion, Cherry (1978) argued that global telecommunications were based on a tripod skeleton of three main circuits, transatlantic/Europe, Far East/Europe, and North/South America. Shipping, air transport, telephone, and telegraph generally followed these routes. The Pacific satellite system, just emerging when he was writing in the 1970s, turned the tripod into a quadripod. This is, of course, not an analysis of the technical possibilities, for modern telecommunications and transportation of goods and people can go virtually anywhere by any route. It is an analysis of actual communications practices in terms of traffic created by capitalist globalization. Under the umbrella of the United Nations, dozens of agencies are involved in the organization of global communications. The Rome Plan of 1963, revised in the Mexico City Plan of 1967, divided the world into thirty-four communications zones. The fact that Europe was split into ten zones reflected the politics of the capitalist global system rather than its technology, and suggested that 'the world is not shrinking everywhere like a deflated balloon, but very irregularly, more like a dried apple, furrowed and distorted' (Cherry 1978: 135).

The 1980s witnessed an unprecedented increase in the scale and scope of the electronic media of communication, as well as genuine innovations in their nature. Technological advances and price reductions in producer and consumer electronics led the TNCs from the USA, Europe, and Japan that for the most part control the electronic media, to become globalizing corporations in ways that would have been technically impossible, and in some cases even unthinkable, a few decades previously (see Schiller 1999). This gave the potential for distribution of messages and images on a scale never before achieved. While of course there are continuities with the past, it is clear that the new forms of communication are of fundamental significance (Sussman and Lent 1991, Tehranian 1999, Thusu 2000). The fact that this is happening within and as a result of capitalist globalization indicates that a qualitatively new relationship between culture and ideology is being forged.

All those who argue that it is the medium not the message that characterizes this revolution are in my view entirely wrong. The fact that a greater variety of messages may be broadcast on a vastly greater scale does not alter the fact that the central messages come from those who own and control the major corporations. McLuhan's famous 'the medium is the message' is true only to the extent that transnational corporations increasingly control the media to propagate their message, as McLuhan himself occasionally acknowledged. A telling indicator of this is the phenomenal increase since the 1980s in commercial sponsorship of what used to be considered purely cultural events, such as operas, museum exhibits, science, and education, and their incorporation into capitalist globalization (Shaw 1993, Sklair 2001: ch. 6) and the commercialization and globalization of sport, notably the Olympic Games and the World Cup, by some of the world's largest TNCs (see Maguire 1999, Sugden and Tomlinson 1998). The television networks in the USA paid over $600m. for the Winter and Summer games of 1988 and Coca-Cola and Visa paid $22m. and $15m. respectively for exclusive use of the five-ring symbol. The four-year cycle is now estimated to create revenues of around $4 billion. The 2008 summer games has a budget of almost $2 billion and the International Olympic Committee announced in July 2001, when the summer Olympics was awarded to Beijing, that over one billion dollars was already under contract. This is driven by a variety of interests around the media and urban boosterism and is a direct consequence of how the culture-ideology of consumerism works to create global mega-events. An excellent example of this process was the campaign to stage the 2004 Olympics in Cape Town (Hiller 2000).

The recognition that transnational practices in the culture-ideology sphere were seriously asymmetrical had to be addressed in a way that was not necessary for economic and political TNPs. The reason for this is the peculiar status of culture-ideology in the reproduction of capitalist globalization. Here it is useful to distinguish between private and public media. The main difference between them is that private media are used mainly to transmit commercial data and documents, often under conditions of extreme security, while public (mass) media are used mainly to broadcast entertainment, always under conditions of the greatest visibility to the paying public. Both forms were revolutionized in the 1980s by the development and dissemination of new information and communication technologies, such as cable and satellite television, video, and the Internet. The capacity for total packaging of cultural products was institutionalized in entirely new forms creating new commercial opportunties (Footer and Graber 2000).

Bagdikian (1989) characterized those who control this system as the lords of the global village. They purvey their product (a relatively undifferentiated mass of news, information, ideas, entertainment, and popular culture) to a rapidly expanding public, eventually the whole world. He argued that national boundaries are growing increasingly meaningless as the main actors (five groups at the time he was writing) strive for total control in the production, delivery, and marketing of what we can call the culture-ideology goods of the capitalist global system (see Table 4.1 above). Their goal is to create a buying mood for the benefit of the global troika of media, advertising, and consumer goods manufacturers. 'Nothing in human experience has prepared men, women and children for the modern television techniques of fixing human attention and creating the uncritical mood required to sell goods, many of which are marginal at best to human needs' (Bagdikian 1989: 819). Two symbolic facts: by the age of 16, the average North American youth has been exposed to more than 300,000 television commercials; and the former Soviet Union sold advertising slots on cosmonaut suits and space ships! (For many others, see Durning 1992.) In order to connect and explain these facts, we need to generate a new framework, namely the culture-ideology of consumerism.

THE CULTURE-IDEOLOGY OF CONSUMERISM

The transformation of the culture-ideology of consumerism from a sectional preference of the rich to a globalizing phenomenon can be explained in terms of two central factors, factors that are historically unprecedented. First, capitalism entered a qualitatively new globalizing phase in the 1960s. As the electronic revolution got under way, the productivity of capitalist factories, systems of extraction and processing of raw materials, product design, marketing and distribution of goods and services began to be transformed in one sector after another. This golden age of capitalism began in the USA, but spread a little later to Japan and Western Europe and other parts of the First World, to the NICs, and to some cities and enclaves in the Third World. Second, the technical and social relations that structured the mass media all over the world made it very easy for new consumerist lifestyles to become the dominant motif for these media. Therefore, in the second half of the twentieth century, for the first time in human history, the dominant economic system, capitalism, was sufficiently productive to provide a basic package of material possessions and services to almost everyone in the First World and to privileged groups elsewhere. Capitalism, particularly in its neo-liberal phase from the 1980s, promised that eventually the rising tide would raise all boats, that is, everyone else in the world would get rich as long as they did what the transnational capitalist class told to them to do. A rapidly globalizing system of mass media was also geared up to tell everyone what was available and, crucially, to persuade people that this culture-ideology of consumerism was what a happy and satisfying life was all about. In a powerful empirical study of the increasing hours and more intensive nature of work in the United States since the 1950s, Schor (1991) demonstrated how capitalist consumerism led North Americans (and, I would argue, other groups elsewhere) into a sort of Faustian bargain whereby those who can find work trade off their time for more and more consumer goods and services.

Mass media perform many functions for global capitalism. They speed up the circulation of material goods through advertising, which reduces the time between production and consumption. They begin to inculcate the dominant ideology into the minds of viewers, listeners, and readers from an early age, in the words of Esteinou Madrid, 'creating the political/cultural demand for the survival of capitalism' (1986: 119). The systematic blurring of the lines between information, entertainment, and promotion of products lies at the heart of this practice. This has not in itself created consumerism, for consumer cultures have been in place for centuries.[14] What it has created is a reformulation of consumerism that transforms all the mass media and their contents into opportunities to sell ideas, values, products, in short, a consumerist world-view. Elements of this are found in Boorstin's idea of the consumption community (1968), integral to his thesis of American distinctiveness. Muniz and O'Guinn (2001) take this forward in the concept of brand community. Their ethnographic studies of owners of Macintosh computers and Saab and Ford Bronco cars illustrate the existence of three traditional markers of community, namely shared consciousness, shared rituals and traditions, and a sense of moral responsibility. They conclude, somewhat controversially: 'We believe brand communities to be real, significant, and generally a good thing, and evidence of the persistence of community in consumer culture' (p. 428).

Contemporary consumer culture would not be possible without the shopping mall, both symbolically and substantively. As Crawford (in Sorkin 1992: 3–30) argued, the merging of the architecture of the mall with the culture of the theme park has become the key symbol and the key spatial reference point for consumer capitalism, not only in North America but increasingly all over the world. What Goss (1993) terms the magic of the mall has to be understood on several levels, how the consuming environment is carefully designed and controlled, the seductive nature of the consuming experience, the transformation of nominal public space into actual private terrain. Although there are certainly anomalies of decaying city districts interspersed with gleaming malls bursting with consumer goods in the First World, it is in the poorer parts of the Third World that these anomalies are at their most stark. Third World malls until quite recently catered mainly to the needs and wants of expatriate TNC executives and officials, and local members of the transnational capitalist class. The success of the culture-ideology of consumerism can be observed all over the world in these malls, where now large numbers of workers and their families flock to buy, usually with credit cards, thus locking themselves into the financial system of capitalist globalization. The integration of the medium of the mall and the message of the culture-ideology of consumerism had a formative influence on the trajectory of global capitalism. The medium looks like the message because the message, the culture-ideology of consumerism, has engulfed the medium. The problem, therefore, is not *Understanding Media* (the title of McLuhan's great if somewhat misconceived book) but understanding capitalist globalization, the system that produces and reproduces both the message and the media that incessantly transmit it.

A fundamental problem that has plagued media studies is the precise relationship between, on the one hand, the media and the messages they relay and, on the other, the audiences that receive these messages and the meanings they take from them and/or read into them. As we shall see below, it is naive to assume that most media messages actually do have the effects that their creators intend, even when the audiences are deemed to be unsophisticated and lacking in education. A growing body of theory and research has tested these ideas in a wide variety of social, cultural, and geographical settings (see, for example, Ang 1990; Dowmunt 1993; Liebes and Katz 1990; Tomlinson 1991). Ang, and Liebes and Katz, who carried out research projects on attitudes to the soap opera *Dallas*, discovered that different audiences read the same programmes very differently. While Ang's notion of a critical enthnography of reception and the social dynamics of meaning-making of Liebes and Katz problematize the message-reception issue very fruitfully, my contention here is that this research is mainly directed to a second order of meanings, no more and no less important than the first order of meaning of these media products. However, it is the first order of meanings, the culture-ideology of consumerism, with which I am concerned here. This provides the framework for the second order of meanings which raises different, more nuanced, and sometimes contradictory issues.

The connections between capitalist globalization and the culture-ideology of consumerism must be laid bare. In an attempt to do this, Featherstone (1987:21) develops a useful composite picture of contemporary consumer culture. He writes:

1. Goods are framed and displayed to entice the customer, and shopping becomes an overtly symbolic event.

2. Images play a central part, constantly created and circulated by the mass media.

3. Acquisition of goods leads to a 'greater aestheticisation of reality'.

The end result of these processes is a new concept of lifestyle, enhanced self-image. This 'glosses over the real distinctions in the capacity to consume and ignores the low paid, the unemployed, the old' (ibid.: 22), though the ubiquity of the culture-ideology of consumerism actually does include everyone (or, at least, all those with the potential to buy) however poor, because no one can escape its images. And, it must be added, very few people would choose to escape its images and what they represent in terms of the good, or better, life.[15] Monga (2000: 193) insightfully analyses this issue through the stories of women from Africa who eventually found asylum in France and USA (and many more who did not). 'Though the perspectives of these women are in themselves of interest, what is of real import is their fundamental goal: survival in a rapidly changing world where the rhetoric of globalisation poorly conceals the reality of the increasing marginalisation of Africa and its inhabitants [including men]'. This is concretely expressed in three strategies for African women and their children mainly through migrating to the USA. The first is through the sale of beauty products for immediate income. The cosmetics industry in the USA, uniquely, has designed a range for black women, so women in Africa are keen to get hold of them, usually through high end informal sector locations. These locations are also socio-economic markers of a system based on credit in which authentic products straight from the USA are at a premium. The second strategy is education of children, a route to intermediate material well-being. The possibility of working through college in the USA makes this an attractive option. While France focuses on rhetoric for African women, the USA focuses on marketable skills, and the myth of America as the land of opportunity contrasts with the racism that black people often find in France. The third, long-term strategy, is the Americanization of children, through giving birth in the USA. This involves the rapid Americanization of names in Africa (usually taken from TV characters) and, Monga argues, illustrates a deeper desire to participate in the global village. She quotes Zhan to the effect that the 'success of American brand-name products abroad is due not to their "Americanism" per se but to their ability to match the demands of a diverse market throughout the world' (cited in Monga 2000: 202, n. 10). Monga is entirely on the mark when she argues: 'whereas women from Africa turn to American culture, some members of the African-American community look to African, or African-inspired culture as a means of expressing their need for self-affirmation and social recognition, often utilizing the same cultural markers as African women: first names, apparel, and art objects' (Monga 2000: 204).

The issue of Americanization is clearly a central dilemma of any critique of consumerism (and also of the politics of the consumer movement). Many scholars (pre-eminently Ewen 1976) point up the distinctive role of the United States in the campaign to make consumer culture universal. Through Hollywood, and the globalization of the movies, via Madison Avenue, from where Ewen's captains of consciousness created the modern advertising industry, to the more geographically diffuse but ideologically monolithic television networking conceptualizers, the consumerist elites of the transnational capitalist class in the United States has assumed leadership of the culture-ideology of consumerism in the interests of global capitalism in the twentieth century.[16]

A good illustration of this is in the origin of the soap opera, one of the most highly developed media forms through which mass consumerism is projected. It began in the 1920s when Glen Sample, an American advertising agent, had the idea of adapting a newspaper serial for the radio, a medium already dominated by commercial interests.

The programme, *Betty and Bob*, was sponsored by a flour manufacturer, and Sample used the same idea to promote Oxydol washing powder for Procter & Gamble, under siege from Unilever's Rinso in the US market. Oxydol won out, and the so-called soap opera that was used to sell it gave its name to a genre, massively reinforced by its wholesale adoption by television all over the world since the 1950s.[17]

The universal availability of the mass media has been rapidly achieved through relatively cheap transistor radios, cassette recorders, and televisions, which now totally penetrate the First World, almost totally penetrate the urban Second and Third Worlds, and are beginning to penetrate deeply into the countryside even in the poorest places. Thus, the potential of global exposure to global communication, the dream of every merchant in history, has arrived. The socialization process by which people learn what to want, which used to occur mainly in the home and the school, is increasingly taking place through what the theorists of the Frankfurt School had so acutely termed the culture industry (reprinted in Bernstein 1992).[18]

CONSUMERISM AND THE INFORMATION TECHNOLOGY REVOLUTION

There is general agreement that on all key measures there has been an enormous growth not only in the availability but also in the use of the mass media over the last few decades. Even in many poor Third World societies substantial growth has occurred. The motor of this growth has been the rapid spread of television, and personal computers among the better-off. The prices of these goods have declined substantially in relative terms over time, though the culture-ideology of consumerism, by celebrating the new, means that people spend much more on them overall. This development parallels (not accidentally) the enormous growth of the TNCs themselves since the 1950s, both in scope and geographical spread.

The systematic study of information technology (IT) is growing very rapidly. Although there is general agreement that its potential for human progress is enormous, there is a good deal of doubt that those who control it will actively seek the public good over their own private interests where these conflict (see *Journal of Communication* 1989; Sussman and Lent 1991; Tehranian 1999). Through IT, for example, many financial institutions and aid agencies analyse, disseminate, and predict information about the likelihood of crop surpluses and crop failures and consequently famine in the poorest regions of the world. However all this activity has as much, perhaps more effect on commodity prices as actually reducing suffering.

In the 1980s TNCs from the USA controlled over three-quarters of the total volume of transborder data flows, including transmission, storage, and processing (see Mowlana 1985: ch. 5). In 2001, of the nine FG500 firms in computer manufacturing, six were from the USA and three from Japan, and all three major computer services and software firms were US-based.[19] The popularity of Manuel Castells's theory of the information age characterized by the network society (Castells 2000) among global business elites (as well as among many social scientists) speaks volumes for the central place of the IT revolution in capitalist globalization. The contribution of firms outside the First World is mainly restricted to assembly and fabrication of electronic products, usually on contract or as quasi-captive suppliers to TNCs, but there are some exceptions.[20]

Nevertheless, control does not entail specific effects in the economic, political, and culture-ideology spheres. In order to demonstrate a connection and to begin to document specific effects it is first necessary to show how the structural conditions of the capitalist global system are inherent in the ways in which the communications TNCs operate. Hamelink makes what appears to be the useful distinction between the information-independent and the information-dependent countries. He points to the increase in global cultural synchronization through which information dependent countries are made more similar in commercially relevant areas to the information-independent countries from which most of the messages they receive about the world emanate.

Global use of data flows – particularly through transnational corporations – is thus likely to have an impact on the synchronization of techniques (e.g. via the standardization of equipment), symbols (e.g. through the use of the universal computer language) and social relations (e.g. through the organisation of industrial production and job patterns). (Hamelink 1984: 72)

From the 1970s on there was a considerable surge of scholarly and public interest in the private media and, latterly, in their role in the Third World. UNESCO-sponsored research, particularly associated with the International Commission for the Study of Communication Problems, led to the publication of *Many Voices, One World* (MacBride Commission 1980), which set the agenda for the 1980s and provided a spur to World Communications Year in 1983, continuing World Conferences on Strategies and Policies for Informatics, and other initiatives (see Tehranian 1999). Three interconnected themes informed these activities, namely the continued control of cultural industries by a small group of immensely powerful TNCs; the effects of this control on those societies too poor to have much of an independent presence in these industries; and the opportunities that the new technologies offer for the development of the Third World. Given the disparities between the information capacities of First and Third World societies, and the technical nature of these disparities, 'a vital question becomes, do transnational data flows increase the informational advantage and social impact of transnational corporations?' (Hamelink 1984: 14). By the 1990s, this question had been taken up by many prominent members of the transnational capitalist class (notably Bill Gates of Microsoft) and transformed into the issue of the digital divide, one of the key elements of class polarization intensified by capitalist globalization.

These are all important questions but, once again, the methodology of state-centrism serves to blur rather than clarify the issues. The national origins of the agents of media control is not the point. American media, Japanese media, European media are convenient labels but they have no theoretical purchase in the capitalist global system. Media corporations in and of the Third World, and even some in and of the New Second World, have relatively independent systems of communication and, of course, more or less all sovereign states exert some control over the mass media within their own territory, though far less than was the case even in the 1980s. The issue is not whether nationals or foreigners control the media, but whether the interests of those who do control the media, nationals or foreigners, are driven by capitalist globalization. Many researchers have shown that mass media can now be replaced to some extent by media targeted to specific niche markets. New media technologies, especially the Internet, can provide a framework for the growth of virtual ethnic communities across national borders, unhindered by physical distance. This is true and important, but it is the material interests behind the culture-ideology of consumerism, not the nationality or ethnicity of the lords and stewards of the global village, that is the issue. (These questions will be further analysed through a discussion of what has been labelled cultural, and more specifically, media imperialism, in Chapter 7).

Hamelink sums up the impact of informatics in the First World in a manner that suggests a gloomy future for the Third World, caught in the TNC-woven web of private and public communications. Despite its state-centrism, it is worth quoting at length as it catches some of the transnational practices intrinsic to the project for global consumerism of the culture industries.

In developed countries it can be observed that the widespread utilization of informatics [IT]:
—offers some new job opportunities but on balance creates more unemployment;
—offers some decentralization in social decision-making, but on balance reinforces centralized administration and tends to erode democracy;
—offers potentially to enhance citizen participation in local government, to inform citizens of their rights and duties, and to provide new information-services to citizens, but on balance it reinforces local dominant coalitions, makes local government more expensive to run, makes it less responsive to the general public, and tends to exclude many interests;
—offers potentially more security for data processing and transmission, but on balance threatens privacy in unprecedented ways;
—offers the suggestion of more social equity, but on balance adds to existing social disparities the phenomenon of information inequality. (Hamelink 1984: 89)

While acknowledging the digital divide, writing more than a decade later scholars like Mansell and Wehn (1998) and Madon (2000) are rather more optimistic about the prospects for harnessing information technology for the needs of development. By the 1990s, low-cost electronic networks were expanding rapidly throughout the Third World, even in Africa. The electronic network launched by the Commonwealth Secretariat (COMNET-IT) in 1990 has done much to bring governments (if not citizens) together. Madon identifies six key areas in which the Internet facilitates development: economic productivity (websites help business in the Third World become more global); health (the HealthNet system already links sixteen African and four Asian countries); education (outward from universities and research centres to the general population); poverty alleviation and empowerment (for example, the USAID project in the Horn of Africa); democracy (the growing network of networks); and sustainable development (through UNCED and many other projects). The issue is not simply numbers connected (provision), but accessibility and contribution to human progress (outcomes). As P. Thomas (1999) shows in his study of the WTO and telecommunications in India, some local companies win and some lose in the globalization process. This is not surprising— according to Aufderheide (1999) the passage of the 1996 Telecommunications Act in the USA, allegedly designed to enhance market competition, actually resulted through deregulation in further concentration of the media in the hands of fewer but bigger media giants.

A focus of much current research is the emancipatory power of the Internet (Walch 1999, Miller and Slater 2000). On its democratic potential, Ferdinand (2000: 1) confidently asserts: 'As a means of communication it [Internet traffic] has the potential to revolutionize political activity far more profoundly that the telephone or television ever did, for unlike them it offers the possibility of direct two-way interaction between the citizens and politicians.' As I discussed in Chapter 3, the reality of the digital divide within and between countries tempers this judgement. M'Bayo (1997) points out that there are more telephone lines in Manhattan (New York) than in the whole of sub-Saharan Africa and that half of the population of the world have never made a telephone call. To some this is an outrage, but to globalizing corporations it is a splendid business opportunity. Iridium (Motorola) and several other major TNCs have rapidly moved into Africa to exploit this potential. M'Bayo usefully lays out the choices that must be made between land-based and wireless networks, and their respective prospects and problems. The prospects include the Teledesic proposal (in which Bill Gates has a stake) for an Internet in the sky via fibre optics, Iridium has a plan to launch over sixty satellites, and AT&T is developing Africa One based on an undersea fibre optic cable around Africa. The Internet Society (ISOC) is beginning to train network service providers, and the Leland Initiative of USAID is working in twenty countries to help Africans gain access to the information highway. This five-year $15 million project to connect African countries to the Internet comes with the condition that governments allow service delivery by private providers and permit the free flow of information. Projects supported by the International Telecommunications Union and the World Bank also encourage the private sector.

M'Bayo is realistic about the obstacles, notably the lack of finance for survival let alone advanced telecommunications. Africa has neither the technical nor the administrative infrastructure to support such developments at present. Main (2001) echoes M'Bayo's hopes that the Internet will evolve into a global information infrastructure that will include the Third World, but is rather sceptical about the prospects of this happening under capitalist globalization. Commerce drives the global information infrastructure and owners require returns on their investment—privatization and global competition disadvantage most Third World governments.

According to Main, there are several basic problems that distinguish the First World and the Third World with respect to this apparently progressive agenda. First, connectivity: in most Third World countries average waiting time for a phone connection is years rather than months and the cost of connecting to the Internet is high (e.g. in Guatemala the annual fee is about the annual per capita income!). In addition, there are various technical issues that need to be resolved (undersea cable or satellites). Language and content are also problematic. There is tremendous variation even in some small countries and this poses problems for local suppliers. The elitist nature of the Internet (the digital divide) is in constant tension with the empowerment thesis, especially in poorer countries (Mansell and Wehn 1998).

The stirrings of a global debate on the creation of new consumption needs provides a complex set of tests for these hypotheses. Consumption tends to be more class-specific in poor societies than in rich societies. In poor societies not many people have much discretionary income left after they have satisfied their basic needs of food and shelter, if indeed they can satisfy these at all. In rich societies, on the other hand, most people do have enough discretionary income left (or have easy access to credit) after they have paid for their food and shelter, though the numbers who do not appear to be growing at an alarming rate in some rich countries, as the growth in what is euphemistically termed exclusion in the USA and the UK and other countries seems to suggest. Recall Boxes 3.1 and 3.2 that showed how the poorest groups in some poor and rich societies have fared since the 1980s.

The creation of needs depends on multi-layered structures and dynamics connecting individual characteristics of the consumer with processes operating at the societal level. Capitalist globalization propagates an integrated culture and ideology of consumerism through the manipulation of existing consumption needs and the creation of new ones. The creation of these new consumption needs by the corporate mass media tends to be neither random nor arbitrary, but structured in terms of a consumerist world-view. In one interesting analysis of this issue, Sauvant and Mennis (in Kumar 1980: ch. 11) argue that the TNCs act as transmission belts along which the contents of what they label the TNC business culture are carried from the rich countries to the poor countries of the world. In their view, this results in inappropriate sociocultural patterns that impede independent development. Despite a state-centrism that conceals the agency of many groups in poor countries in the process of transmission of these sociocultural patterns (the culture-ideology of consumerism, to be concrete) the idea of the TNCs as transmission belts is a useful and evocative one. Some major and many not so major TNCs in and around IT have their origins in the countries of the Third World (Mansell and Wehn 1998: chs. 7–9, Sklair and Robbins 2002: Table 5).

The relationship of the TNCs, the transnational capitalist class, and consumerism, and their influence over the popular masses, lies at the centre of the debate over economic, political, and culture-ideology transnational practices. It is precisely the business culture introduced and propagated by the TNCs that is considered by many to be the sine qua non for modernization (as opposed to dependency reversal or radical development). The struggle to create a new modernist concept and practice of consumerism is one of the crucial conjunctures of economic, political, and culture-ideology transnational practices, lying at the heart of the crises of class polarization and ecological unsustainability.

THE THEORY OF THE GLOBAL SYSTEM: A SUMMARY

The theory of the global system can be summarized, graphically, as follows. All global systems rest on economic transnational practices and at the highest level of abstraction these are the building blocks of the system. Concretely, in the capitalist global system they are mainly located in the major transnational corporations. Transnational political practices are the principles of organization of the system. Members of the transnational capitalist class drive the system, and by manipulating the design of the system they can build variations into it. Transnational culture-ideology practices are the nuts and bolts and the glue that hold the system together. Without them, parts of the system would drift off into space. This is accomplished through the culture-ideology of consumerism. Different forms of globalization would require different institutional structures for their transnational practices, as I elaborate in Chapter 11.

In order to work properly the dominant institutions in each of the three spheres have to take control of key resources. Under the conditions of capitalist globalization, the transnational corporations strive to control global capital and material resources, the transnational capitalist class strives to control global power, and the transnational agents and institutions of the culture-ideology of consumerism strive to control the realm of ideas.[21] Effective corporate control of global capital and resources is almost complete. There are few important natural resources that are entirely exempt from the formal or effective control of the TNCs or official agencies with whom they have strategic alliances. The transnational capitalist class and its local affiliates exert their rule through its connections with globalizing bureaucrats and politicians in pro-capitalist political parties or social democratic parties that choose not to fundamentally challenge the global capitalist project. The local affiliates of the TCC exert authority in non-capitalist states indirectly to a greater or lesser extent. This is the price levied as a sort of entrance fee into the capitalist global system. In the last resort, it is the corporate control of capital and labour that is the decisive factor for those who do not wish to be excluded from the system.

The struggle for control of ideas in the interests of capitalist consumerism is fierce; the goal is to create the one-dimensional man within the apparently limitless vistas of consumerism that Marcuse (1964) prophesied. Ideas that are antagonistic to the global capitalist project can be reduced to one central counter-hegemonic idea, the rejection of the culture-ideology of consumerism itself, and they get little exposure in the mass media, as opposed to alternative media where they are at the core of an exciting cultural diversity for minority groups all over the world. Without consumerism, the rationale for continuous capitalist accumulation dissolves. It is the capacity to commercialize and commodify all ideas and the products in which they adhere, television programmes, advertisements, newsprint, books, tapes, CDs, videos, films, the Internet, and so on, that global capitalism strives to appropriate. Habermas (1989) pointedly termed this 'the colonization of the lifeworld'. How this is accomplished outside the First World is the subject of the next four chapters.

NOTES

1. For a theoretical analysis of falling commodity prices see Raikes and Gibbon (2000).

2. In her provocative essay on 'advertising citizenship' Meijer (1998: 240) criticizes Slater's belief that advertising is incapable of instilling good narratives of the self, good lifestyles and good advice (from Slater 1997). 'But why [she asks] should it not be capable of changing you for the good?' The answer is simple: of course it could, but under the conditions of capitalist globalization it rarely does.

3. Taylor (2000) distinguishes panregional, major regional, and minor regional centres, some of which are not very important world cities. Short *et al.* (1996) criticize the methodology of global city research; and Townsend (2001) stresses the inadequacy of original formulations on global cities in the Internet age.

4. Scarpaci (2000) is a useful collection on the transformation of socialist cities, most trying to be tourist cities in a period of rapid globalization.

5. The two-volume collection edited by Simai (1995) on global employment is a very useful source for these economic transnational practices.

6. This happens all over the world. In 2000–1 the British government was reported to have offered grants of £40 million to subsidize the Renault–Nissan car plant in the north-east region of England.

7. There is a vast multi-disciplinary literature on what I term economic TNPs. In addition to the UNCTC twenty volume library (Dunning 1992–4), there are useful surveys from international finance (Strange 1998), politics and international relations (Shaw 1999), geography (Dicken 1998), history (Teichova *et al.* 1986), law (Wiener 1999), anthropology (Rothstein and Blim 1992), and business studies (Parker 1998).

8. For example, the research of Pereira (2000), based on his Ph.D. thesis at LSE, analyses the attempt of the Singapore government to export its developmental state strategy to China (and Vietnam, India, Thailand, and Indonesia). Despite the ultimate failure of the Suzhou industrial park in China, this is one possible future for the NICs in the global arena.

9. There were many successful electronic assembly TNCs operating in the region. I am grateful to

officials and corporate executives involved in FDI in the Shannon area for interviews (in March 2000) on the changes since the 1980s.

10. For an example of a very critical test case, the experience of US-domiciled TNCs in Iran in the 1980s, see Bassiry and Dekmejian (1985).

11. For a book-length analysis see Sklair (2001) where several fruitful precursors to the concept of the transnational capitalist class are discussed. Embong (2000) is a useful critique of transnational class theory, and van der Pijl (1998) provides an historical perspective.

12. This section is based on Press and Thomson (1989: chs. 1 and 2), updated in Ashwin (in Cohen and Rai 2000: 101–16). Munck (in Cohen and Rai 2000: 83–100) observes that Castells, in his impressive three volumes on the information age, says practically nothing about trade unions and the labour movement while devoting a whole volume (Castells 1997) to identity-based social movements. See also Radice (2000).

13. Sometimes all three situations coexist, as in the maquilas in Mexico. For stimulating discussions on the labour movement in Nigeria see Otobo (1987), in Russia, Clarke *et al.* (1993). See also, Munck and Waterman (1999: part IV).

14. In addition to the references in the text, see McKendrick *et al.* (1982) on the development of consumerism in eighteenth-century England; Belk (1988), Slater (1997), and the new *Journal of Consumer Culture* (ed. Slater and Ritzer).

15. See Wernick's (1991) stimulating, *Promotional Culture: Advertising, Ideology and Symbolic Expression*. The British Library CIP Data on this book gives the title as 'Promotional Culture: Advertising and ideology in late capitalism', suggesting that 'symbolic expression' sold more books than 'late capitalism' in that particular promotional culture!

16. The creation of consumer engineering in the United States (see Sheldon and Arens 1932, as discussed by Ewen 1976) confirms that this phenomenon pre-dated the golden age of the 1950s.

17. See M. Mattelart (1986: ch. 1), where she illuminates the crucial role of the media in creating the housewife as consumer. See also, on fotonovelas, Flora and Flora (1978) and Barker (1997: ch. 3). I return to this issue in Chapter 7.

18. For the more popular postmodern turn on consumerism, see Baudrillard (1988), Foster (1985), Jameson (1991). While stimulating, the literature on postmodernism so celebrates its own contradictions that it is often difficult to know whether it supports or undermines any given position, perhaps that is the point?

19. IBM dominated computer manufacturing with revenues of over $88b. in 2001, followed by Fujitsu, almost $50b. The joint revenues of the merging Hewlett-Packard and Compaq were $90b.

20. For example, in South-East Asia, TV Globo in Brazil, and the software industry in Bangalore, India.

21. Commodification of one of the prime idea-producing institutions, the university, is proceeding rapidly, see Schiller (1999: ch. 4), Monbiot (2000: ch. 9), Currie (2002).

Chapter 6

TRANSNATIONAL PRACTICES IN THE THIRD WORLD

There is a strong tendency in some quarters to assume that all the effects of capitalist globalization in the Third World are unwelcome and malign, just as there is a strong tendency in other quarters to assume that they are all welcome and benign. Transnational corporations, the transnational capitalist class, and the culture-ideology of consumerism are all seen as evil attempts to undermine the freedom and cultural autonomy of weak and poor victims, or the only true paths to development and the only reliable vehicles for releasing the poor from their misery.

These are very significant differences. Nevertheless, there is one point on which both interpretations tend to agree, namely the general unstopability of the spread of capitalist globalization, particularly in the poorer and hence more vulnerable parts of the world. This is a very central issue for any theory of globalization in so far as it distinguishes between a dismal chronicle of inevitability, which is absolutely not my intention, and an attempt to illuminate what is happening by a theory of what makes it happen and, by implication, what could bring about other outcomes.

It must be immediately obvious that such arguments will be somewhat confused unless a definition of development can be agreed. This realization has led to a great deal of debate, and although it cannot be said that a general consensus has been reached on how best to define development, a good deal of light has been shed on the processes involved in different types of development (Allen and Thomas 2000, Roberts and Hite 2000). A viable distinction can be made between economic growth (measured on such criteria as GNP per capita, proportion of the labour force engaged in industry, and the proportion of manufactured goods in total exports) and development, which has somewhat wider social implications. The crucial difference between economic growth and development, as I am using the term here, is that development may include everything that is already included in economic growth plus criteria of distribution of the social product and active protection of human rights (see Chapter 11 below for elaboration). It is not possible to be much more precise than this without becoming hopelessly entangled in a series of impossible dilemmas. This approximate definition, not unlike others in hotly contested areas of enquiry, is also a guide to further research.

The ultimate strength of capitalist globalization is that it continually works, and works very hard, to persuade people that the system is natural, fair, and fundamentally better than any realistic alternative. Global capitalism is successful to the extent that it does persuade people that there is no alternative and to the extent that it manages to distort alternatives that gain a public hearing and viewing. Where the capitalist state has to use force, the army or the police, then this is clearly a failure of hegemony, though where people are persuaded that the use of force is legitimate, this may actually increase the legitimacy of the system.

Until the 1980s, most Third World countries were one-party states of one type or another and many were ruled through the routine exercise of physical force by the army and the police. Waves of democratization swept over Africa, Asia, and Latin America in the 1980s and 1990s—over 100 countries had competitive elections in 1993 (Pateman 1996). While they produced a variety of political systems based on rather different principles of democracy and with varying degrees of baggage from the past (Robinson 1996, Randall and Theobold 1998, Weeks 2000), the democratic surplus certainly outweighed the democratic deficit in most Third World countries.[1] Authoritarianism and military rule are not in the long-term interests of a global capitalism trying to promote the culture-ideology of consumerism. Under pressure from well-targeted campaigns TNCs from the USA and Europe were encouraged to divest from countries whose leaders flouted democratic conventions and such action undermined racist and dictatorial regimes. The best example of this is the campaign against apartheid in South Africa organized around the Sullivan Principles of business practice. As Massie (1997: p. xxviii) demonstrates: 'Former officials from the white regime now readily acknowledge that South Africa could not have sustained its racial policies without the financial, technological, and psychological support of foreign companies and countries.' A convincing analysis of the crucial role of the campaign for British bank divestment in South Africa concludes that 'the country was excluded from access to new long-term international loan finance; this created a siege economy, and the resultant outflow of capital eroded white living standards and morale. Apartheid was now economically damaging to those whom it had been designed to benefit' (John 2000: 433). Apartheid was defeated, but such campaigns do not always work.

The case of Burma is a good example. On 8 September 1988 the State Law and Order Restoration Council (SLORC) was established by military coup in Burma and on 30 November 1988 the Union of Myanmar Foreign Investment Law came into force (McCarthy 2000). This gave incentives for FDI to effect the transition from a planned socialist economy to a free market system. General Ne Win's Burmese Way to Socialism introduced in 1962 had led to international isolation and increasing autarchy, and the country was excluded from the lavish anti-communist aid available from Western governments and agencies. However, Burma fared little better under the new regime. In December 1997 SLORC changed its title to the State Peace and Development Council, though the policies remained the same. The 1988 FDI law focused on high-tech, hard-currency investment and personnel (companies had to bring their own technical staff with them). The Union of Myanmar Holding Corporation, owned by the Ministry of Defence (capitalized at about 20 per cent of Burma's GNP in the 1990s), was the main partner for most joint ventures. The major restriction on FDI was that foreign currency had to be exchanged at the official rate of 6 to the US dollar (the unofficial rate was 300–400). However, ways were found to lessen the currency burden; PepsiCo, for example, bought mung beans for export with its local revenues. Wages in Burma are much lower than in many of its neighbours ($20–30 against $200 a month in Thailand, for example) and this is certainly an incentive, as is the lack of workers' rights (that led to the US government withdrawing some trading privileges in 1989). There are several foreign banks represented in the country, despite a lack of business. The regime has been forced to turn a blind eye to the black market in currency and other goods, infrastructure is very poor, and World Bank/IMF aid is blocked by the US government. Despite a worldwide campaign to persuade TNCs, governments, and international agencies to disinvest from Burma, very little has been achieved. Most TNCs, Japan, and other Asian governments have discretely helped the regime. Beer (in Zunes *et al.* 1999: ch. 9) makes the important point that the internal opposition to the regime is divided between groups waging violent armed struggle (outside urban areas) and groups engaged in peaceful, non-violent resistance (in the cities, and for the international community). While pro-democracy activists have forced some consumer goods companies open to boycott (like PepsiCo, Carlsberg, Heineken, Liz Clairborne, and Levi Strauss) to divest, they have been replaced by others.

Official FDI data is deceptive. McCarthy reports that by 1998 about $7b. worth of foreign investment had been approved, but this included abandoned projects (for example, Amoco's $335m. loss). However, most Chinese FDI is not counted. Oil and gas is the biggest sector and this is shoring up the regime (Total and Unocal[2] share around 60 per cent). Hotels and tourism are booming, and there is also some investment in fisheries and real estate. Not surprisingly, there is a 'comparative lack of willingness by foreign investors to enter into 100 per cent, foreign-owned enterprise. Most investors chose to embrace the system of organized corruption and obscure regulations by partnering the SLORC on a joint-venture or production-sharing basis' (McCarthy 2000: 247). Daewoo, Rothmans, Tiger Beer, and others from Singapore, and Japanese companies (e.g. Mitsubishi) have pressured their governments to resume concessionary loans. The home countries of the biggest investing TNCs in 1996 were Singapore, the UK, France, Thailand, Malaysia, the USA, and Japan. The response of the international community has varied from constructive engagement (ASEAN) to US sanctions on new investment from 1997 (a gap that China has begun to fill). The limited engagement of the EU, Japan, and the USA pre-1997 was based on the argument that economic development would lead to the growth of the middle class and that this would create irresistible pressures for democratization. McCarthy argues convincingly that this argument is flawed because both a Chinese and an indigenous military middle class already exist in Burma and they are not likely to struggle for democracy. US sanctions have had little material effect (in contrast to the situation for Cuba). When Burma joined ASEAN in 1997 expectations for reform rose but (as of late 2001) little has changed. The support of neighbouring countries has been a crucial advantage for the regime in Burma, in contrast to the apartheid regime in South Africa that was surrounded by enemies (Sidaway 1998). Most TNCs will continue to seek profits, irrespective of the nature of the regimes governing the sites where they operate, unless they are forced to divest.

Capitalism depends on both the reality and the illusion of choice, but people are not fools and the capitalist global system offers many genuine choices. This creates many contradictions and paradoxes. In the previous chapter some general contradictions and paradoxes of economic, political, and culture-ideology transnational practices were discussed. In this chapter the focus will be on the economic TNPs of transnational corporations, and the political TNPs of the transnational capitalist class in the Third World. (The culture-ideology of consumerism in the Third World will be the subject of the next chapter.)

ECONOMIC TRANSNATIONAL PRACTICES IN THE THIRD WORLD

The analysis of economic TNPs, and particularly the role of the transnational corporations, begins with a paradox. Historically, what came to be known as the Third World attracted only a tiny proportion of all the foreign investment that has ever taken place, while the economies of many poor countries, and even some rich ones, are commonly said to be dominated by foreign capital and/or foreign firms. Not many *Fortune* Global 500 corporations have the relative economic impact on the USA, for example, as a few copper TNCs have had on Chile, or fruit companies on Central America, or mining corporations in Southern Africa.

Up to the early years of the twentieth century, the typical pattern of foreign investment was the portfolio type, where private capitalists individually, or through financial organizations, would invest funds in enterprises abroad such as railways or mines or trading companies, and simply collect the dividends as they came in. Naturally, some of these investors, particularly those who were speculating in the more unpredictable ventures, lost money, but by and large the European and American coupon clippers as they were called, did very well out of their overseas investments.

Portfolio investment had low visibility in the sense that it was very difficult for the general population to discover who actually owned how much of the resources and enterprises in their countries and communities. There was often very little foreign involvement in the day-to-day running of the enterprises. Nevertheless, some large firms, whose names and identities were (and in some cases still are) well known, were directly active overseas in the nineteenth century. These included the great British trading companies in West Africa (the predecessors of Unilever), the North American fruit companies in Central America, whose activities gave rise to the expression banana republic, and the East India Company, which was to provide the basis for British colonial administration in India. This type of investment, which involves the establishment of an enterprise over which the parent company exercises decisive management control, is termed foreign direct investment (FDI), and it is FDI with which this chapter is mainly concerned.

For most of the second half of the twentieth century, a serious contradiction lay at the heart of much of the critical research on economic transnational practices in the Third World. The rhetoric of most Third World governments, and radical researchers on the iniquities of FDI in general (and sometimes specific TNCs), seemed at odds with the almost universal scramble of these same Third World governments, advised (in some cases) by the same radical researchers to create policies to attract more and more FDI into their countries. The best way to approach this contradiction is to see it as a genuine clash of radical theory and pragmatic experience. The theory taught that development for a Third World country was not possible within the orbit of capitalist imperialism, a dependency theory of the type discussed in Chapter 3; while experience taught that FDI often led to some development, and some groups certainly seemed to benefit from it.

TRANSNATIONAL CORPORATIONS IN THE THIRD WORLD

TNCs, like all businesses, are not charitable foundations but organizations devoted to the pursuit of profit. It is irrelevant to criticize TNCs operating in the Third World or anywhere else because they are out to make profits. However, the means by which TNCs make profits in the Third World is a legitimate area of interest. Radical critics argue that they make their profits by exploiting cheap labour to produce goods that people often don't really need. This may be true to some extent but it fails to grasp the totality of how capitalist globalization works in the Third World.

In 1995 members of the US Congress were having one of their regular debates about whether or not to continue funding the International Development Association, the arm of the World Bank that provides cheap loans to the governments of the poorest countries in the world. The World Bank took out full-page advertisements in the major Washington newspapers, proclaiming:

It doesn't just lend money, it helps developing countries become tomorrow's markets. Just ask McDermott International Inc. of New Orleans, Louisiana. Thanks to smart World Bank investment in Africa five years ago, McDermott brought home a $255 million contract for offshore oil and gas construction that produced work for over 1,000 Americans. And that's just one success story. Developing countries now purchase almost $200 billion in US exports, creating nearly 4 million American jobs. (Quoted in Hildyard 1996: 176)

GE, GM, Motorola, IBM, AT&T, Allied Signal, Cargill, Westinghouse, and many more have benefited from World Bank funds. Hildyard argues that the apparently absurd thesis that official aid functions largely as an export subsidy for companies in the northern industrialized countries is well founded. Evaluating aid in sub-Saharan Africa, Rimmer puts this very bluntly. Aid dependence, he argues, cuts both ways: 'Africa depends on the aid agencies and the agencies substantially depend on Africa. . . . [if aid was reduced] Much reduced also would be the livings obtained from aid by the exporters, contractors, consultants, NGO personnel and academics who are "aid's real constituencies in the West" [the quote is from Van de Walle]' (Rimmer 2000: 122; see also Wagle (1996) on Enron in India). While this sounds rather far-fetched, the fact is that in 1999 around 40 per cent of the $957b. US food aid budget (PL 480) was distributed by private agencies (USAID website).

While official aid is usually for public works, increasingly the World Bank and other aid projects are being privatized (for example, road-building in India, China, Mexico, and Chile), and this has led to less strict guidelines on disclosure, accountability, and environmental impact (Fox and Brown 1998). The major TNCs and their local affiliates responsible for these projects, thus, are the new arbiters and beneficiaries of development. They are not risking their own money for most of the bills are paid out of the taxes of ordinary workers in the countries whose governments fund the international financial institutions.

It is not just the World Bank and similar institutions that are facilitating and subsidizing the entry of TNCs into the Third World (we would expect them to be doing just that) but also agencies of the United Nations. For example, the Global Sustainable Development Facility run by the UNDP (under the slogan 2B2M: 2 Billion People to the Market by

2020) signed up an impressive group of major corporations at $50,000 each (including Rio Tinto, ABB, Novartis, Dow Chemical). Karliner (1999: 320) comments: 'the most pressing needs of the world's poorest citizens are in arenas of little or no interest to global corporations: the provision of basic health, education and food resources', and concludes that this is one important move in the corporate effort to co-opt the UN to capitalist globalization (see also Balanya *et al.* 2000: ch. 18). UNDP was forced to discontinue this programme, partly due to NGO outrage, and a more general Global Compact was launched in July 2000. This partnership of UN agencies, businesses, and NGOs is intended to promote good corporate practices on environmental protection, human rights, and labour standards (Utting 2000). Utting, a Project Leader at the prestigious UN Research Institute for Social Development, gives convincing reasons to be sceptical about its potential contribution to genuine development.[3]

The logic of transnational production and marketing for consumer goods is at least partly based on standardization. Naturally, there are many TNCs that run specific production lines to serve specific markets, but it is usually the case that a TNC will prefer to enter a new market with a standard product rather than incur the costs of retooling, redesign, and perhaps restructuring of distribution. Therefore, it follows logically that it will normally be in the interests of the TNCs to try to create the market for their standard products in new locations irrespective of the social needs of the indigenous populations, if and when these differ from corporate interests. The increasing universality of this state of affairs can be illustrated for two quite different industries. Both Murray (1998) on the globalization of Chilean fresh fruit producers and marketers, and Miozzo (2000) on the auto industry in Argentina (and countless other examples) show how patterns of production and distribution are increasingly having to be integrated into global networks, in my terms transnational economic practices at work.

TNC production and trade create new consumption needs in Third World countries as well as everywhere else. Armstrong and McGee (1985), for example, show how cities in Asia and Latin America played a crucial role in the dissemination of so-called Western cultural values, particularly the ideology of consumerism, and the central function of the TNCs in this. These processes have not been universally welcomed. A typical criticism is:

> The presence of transnational corporations in the manufacturing sectors of Third World countries facilitates the transmission of their business culture, their management concepts and operational techniques, to Third World partners and to local entrepreneurs ... Their sales campaigns have resulted, for example, in increasing consumption of white bread, confections and soft drinks among the poorest people in the world by convincing people that status, convenience, and sweet taste are more important than nutrition. (Jefkins and Ugboajah 1986: 170–1)

Jefkins and Ugboajah illustrated this charge with many telling examples from advertisements on Nigerian radio and television. This of course is happening all over the world.

A study of laundry cleaning products (detergents and soaps) in Barbados (James 1983), gives details of how TNCs go about transforming consumption needs and capturing Third World markets. In the early 1970s the local firm that had been producing soap since 1943 was closed down by the action of its major shareholder, who also owned an import agency. For the previous few years the soap factory had been losing business because of imports of synthetic detergents, mainly through Lever Bros. the local branch of Unilever.[4] The importer had decided to clear the way for a more profitable relationship with Lever

Bros. by eliminating the local laundry soap competition entirely. The consequence of this was that by the end of the decade the Unilever detergent and one other brand had captured 90 per cent of the market in Barbados. Both brands had heavy advertising expenditure and James demonstrates empirically that consumers ranked the brands according to the claims of the advertisers (soil and stain removal etc.), despite the fact that independent tests showed very little actual difference between the brands. The Unilever product actually cost twice as much per ounce in Barbados as it did in England, and by driving out cheaper local alternatives the end result for the lower-income consumer in Barbados was a product that was too expensive, too well packaged, and often surplus to requirements. It is difficult to disagree with James (1983: 148) when he argues:

it is the existence of Lever Bros. which itself sets a limit to the extent of the trade-offs by ensuring the dominance of the type of products in which multinational companies in general, and Lever Bros. in particular, have a comparative advantage, namely, brand differentiated goods which are intensively promoted. That is to say, the barriers to entry to the industry are such as to ensure the dominance of the highly priced and expensively packaged products. Those involved in packaging and distributing the unbranded varieties wrapped in plastic are small-scale operators lacking both the necessary resources and marketing skills to capture a larger share of the detergent market. One of them expressed the fear that Lever's would cut off his sources of supply if his share of the market expanded sizeably. As far as competing local production is concerned, a number of industrialists interviewed said that they had considered the possibility but stressed the superior marketing skills of Lever Bros., diseconomies of small scale production and consumer preference for imported goods as the major disincentives.

It is most unlikely that this is a special case, either in terms of product (detergents are a typical branded and highly competitive consumer product) or location (Barbados has no exceptional rules to encourage or discourage TNC products or advertising). In a subsequent work, James (2000: 4) argues that 'globalization is penetrating increasingly into consumption systems that diverge from and are hence often lacking in, at least some of the elements required for modern products to yield the utilities that are expected of them'. He shows how TNC products marketed to the Third World are becoming less and less appropriate to the needs of consumers. Nevertheless, case studies from India (detergents) and Brazil (TV programmes) show that local products can recapture markets from foreign products. This suggests that local exponents of the culture-ideology of consumerism are becoming more competitive (sports shoes of the smaller and less glamorous TNC, Bata, compete well with the more expensive Nikes and Reeboks in some markets).

There is no straightforward way to deal with the question of appropriate products. The TNCs will naturally and in many cases justifiably argue that what their critics consider to be the creation of new needs in Third World countries in order to boost profits is, in fact, a response to changing consumer needs that arise in societies that are in the process of urbanization and industrialization. I shall discuss in detail the underlying issue of the culture-ideology of consumerism, and the role of the TNCs in it, in the next chapter.

However we may criticize the practices of the TNCs in the Third World, for most people whatever they do will be secondary to the major benefit they bring, namely the creation of employment.

TNC EMPLOYMENT

As the discussion in the previous chapter indicated, a central effect of economic trans-national practices for capitalist globalization is job creation and job destruction by TNCs. There are some TNCs that have been operating in Latin America, Africa, and Asia for decades and have won enviable reputations as model employers. At the other extreme, there are cases, for example in Export Processing Zones, where minimum wages fall below the levels necessary for a decent standard of living, where unions are forbidden, and benefits, job security, and conditions of work are very poor by any standards (Bailey *et al.* 1993, Klein 2000).[5]

Some years ago Vaitsos (1974: 345) made the important point that 'In the same product lines where foreign investors generally specialize, national firms do not necessarily behave differently and in some cases they might promote the direct use of less labor. In such cases the issue is not the foreignness of the ownership of the firm but the foreign-ness of the product and its technology to the conditions characterizing the producing country'. For most TNCs, plant size and branch of industry are more important determin-ants of their employment practices than the bare fact of foreign ownership. The biggest, FG500 corporations, often take the question of corporate identity very seriously and, although the wages they offer are not necessarily any better than those of other com-panies, their facilities and non-wage benefits do tend to be superior.[6] Such firms strive, though not always successfully, to inculcate feelings of membership of a global family among their mainly female employees through company magazines, competitions related to work and non-work activities, and widespread uses of company logos on small gifts and prizes.

TNCs have been responsible for the introduction of new industries and thus new cat-egories of manufacturing (and also some non-manufacturing) employment into many Third World communities over recent decades. There are several global industries in which TNC employment is significant in the Third World. In consumer electronics, toys, apparel, automobile parts, and sports goods, a major part of production is carried out in the overseas assembly plants of TNCs and their subcontractors. This has repercussions all through the labour force. Operatives who have never previously held factory jobs need to be trained, expatriates are replaced with indigenous managerial and technical personnel, and indigenous capacity springs up in unfamiliar and/or high-technology industries. Almost all of what was said about this in Chapter 4 is relevant wherever TNCs create jobs, but there are some additional factors to be considered in the Third World.

We may distinguish the following cases:

(a) Where TNCs introduce industries where there were none at all before. Export Process-ing Zones (EPZ) have often been established in industrially virgin territory, for example, Special Economic Zones in China, some of the maquila towns along Mexico's border with the United States, and the Bataan EPZ in the Philippines.

(b) Where TNCs introduce new types of economic activities into Third World com-munities that are already industrializing, notably technological upgrading of manufacturing and services.

(c) Where TNCs directly or indirectly intervene in the structure of Third World industries through the processes of acquisition of indigenous companies, predatory pricing, and restrictive practices to destroy local competition, and enticements designed to attract key personnel from domestic to TNC employment. Since the 1980s many TNCs have benefited from privatizations of state-owned companies. In an instructive case study of telecommunications in Jamaica and Trinidad and Tobago, McCormick (1997) shows how undemocratic these deals can be.

(d) There may also be differences between TNC employment in wholly owned subsidiaries and in joint ventures, licensing agreements, and other forms of foreign investment.

While investment in the Third World levelled off somewhat in the 1980s (UNCTC 1988), the growth of export-oriented employment, mainly due to increased TNC activity in export processing (often referred to as production-sharing in the business press) continued to be rapid. According to *Fortune* (14 Dec. 1992: 62–70) firms were increasingly moving offshore for skilled and technical workers (3M in India, Hewlett-Packard in Mexico, ABB in Thailand, for example). Fierce competition existed between typing mills in the Philippines (10,000 characters for 50 cents US) and China (only 20 cents)! The process accelerated throughout the 1990s. In 2000 *Business Week* reported:

What was once seen as a blue-collar phenomenon is now spreading to the service sector. U.S. data-processing companies are using high-speed data lines to ship document images to low-wage countries such as India and Mexico. Some 45,000 people work in these and other service jobs in maquiladoras, twice the number in 1994, when NAFTA took effect. They do everything from processing used tickets for America West Airlines Inc. to screening U.S. credit-card applications for fraud. And the work is getting more advanced. As U.S. companies tap bilingual Mexicans, 'we have people getting on the phone and calling customers' in the U.S., says Ray Chiarello, CFO of 2,800-employee Electronic Data Management International in Cuidad Juarez. (Bernstein 2000: 52)

This race to the bottom is yet another consequence of capitalist globalization in which the class polarization crisis is reflected in increased profits for TNCs and their local affiliates and near-subsistence wages and insecurity for the workers who get these jobs. The argument of Zhu (2000), that TNCs have not always brought better conditions for workers in China, can be generalized globally.

A further complexity is that some commentators are beginning to argue that because of changes in relative wage rates between First and Third World workers, the declining proportion of labour to total costs of production, and technological innovations, jobs are coming back home, mainly to the USA and Europe. However, as I argue in my own research on the maquila industry in Mexico (dominated by TNCs from the USA), though some jobs have been repatriated it is unlikely that this will ever be a very significant trend (Sklair 1993: ch. 11). Faltermayer (1991) writing in *Fortune*, made the telling point that while some US companies were coming back home this was only happening in niche markets. He gave several good reasons for this. US workers' wages had stagnated since the late 1960s while pay had risen in dollar terms in some Third World countries; productivity gains and reduction of the workforce in the USA had reduced the importance of labour costs in some industries; quick response and delivery for home-based manufacturers reduced the friction of distance; there were definite advantages to having design and production capacities close by each other; there were specific problems of doing business in some Third World countries; and, lastly but not very convincingly, patriotism.[7] *Forbes* later reported that thanks to NAFTA an apparel manufacturer had repatriated jobs from Sri Lanka to northern Mexico, a trend that had accelerated to the degree that Mexico had surpassed Hong Kong and China to become the top source of US apparel imports (10 Feb. 1997: 76). The research of Bonacich and Applebaum (2000) confirms these trends for the apparel industry in California, where foreign export zones are repatriated as sweatshops in the USA, and as Rosen (2002: ch. 12) demonstrates, while the profits of apparel manufacturers in the USA rose dramatically in the mid-1990s, the wages of their workers declined.

A consensus is growing that the main problem for the global economy 'will be finding enough highly skilled and computer-literate workers to staff rapidly growing information industries. . . . demand for skilled workers will exceed supply by 20 per cent in Western Europe in 2002. And engineers comprise some 40 per cent of China's enormous crop of annual graduates' (*Business Week*, 31 Jan. 2000: 39). In the light of these predictions, the strategy of Microsoft to employ local talent all round the world makes sense. Bill Gates and his senior executives 'contend that the same model has worked for years in the U.S., Japan, and Europe, so why shouldn't it in developing countries too?' (*Fortune*, 18 Aug. 1997: 55).

Nevertheless, more jobs are still being exported from places where labour is dearer to places where labour is cheaper. In some of the lower-wage countries the growth of this type of employment has been the only real employment growth in recent decades. This comment in an ILO/UNCTC study of export-processing zones in the Caribbean is very typical: 'In spite of the small number of jobs generated so far, the rate at which EPZs create employment is, however, so high that they rank as the most dynamic agents for job creation compared with other sources of national employment' (Long 1986: 60). Despite NAFTA, this is still true for apparel manufacturing in Caribbean zones (Green 1998). The point to note here is that it is the lower-wage sectors for which this is the case and the crucial impact of the TNCs has been to create intense pressure to keep down labour costs in order to attract foreign investment. It is, therefore, not surprising to discover that in some, though not all, export-oriented zones (EOZs) the rights of workers to organize is curtailed, either formally or in practice, and that Trade Unions are either suppressed or manipulated through government–TNC collaboration (see current ICFTU website). The case of export zone factories in Guatemala reported by Petersen (1993) is extreme but by no means unique.[8]

There is a good deal of controversy over this issue. Fröbel *et al.* (1980), who developed the idea of the new international division of labour, used the export-processing zones and the world market factories in them to illustrate their thesis that the NIDL was an extremely exploitative system. They identified the main characteristics of this system as disposable cheap labour, minimal skill transmission because of the fragmentation of work, and maximum locational flexibility (footloose factories). In similar vein, the International Confederation of Free Trade Unions, the non-communist bloc transnational labour movement, issued a pessimistic report on export-processing zones in 1983, focusing on the suppression of trade union rights. ICFTU listed the problems of EPZs as a disappointing level of job creation, an extremely unbalanced structure of employment, low wages and poor working conditions, minimal job security, long hours and high intensity of production, minimal social services, poor living conditions, health and safety risks, special labour legislation and suppression of unions, and cases of non-ratification of

ILO Conventions (ICFTU 1983). Similarly, among researchers (with the partial exception of some free-market economists), it was rare to find a good word about EPZs in the 1980s. By the 1990s, however, the mood began to change as more and more of the Third World was being turned into free zones of various types and as whole countries began to dismantle their restrictions on foreign direct investment. Among researchers the emphasis began to shift from outright hostility to a more pragmatic evaluation of the costs and benefits of TNC investment.[9]

There has also been a great deal of valuable research on workers in the informal sector or second economy in many societies, in the First and Third Worlds (Portes and Castells 1989, Rowbotham and Mitter 1994, Drakakis-Smith 2000: ch. 5) and in the New Second World (Łoś 1990). While the original studies of the informal economy tended to see it as a phenomenon distinct from the formal economy, in the 1990s researchers began to focus more on its direct and indirect links with the formal sector in urban, national, and global economic systems (see, for example, Teltschler 1994). The informal sector can be fruitfully analysed as one part, albeit with distinctive features, of the global economy in which there are empirically demonstrable connections between street vendors and small workshops in the back streets of cities and the globalizing operations of transnational corporations. The main differences discerned are the relative lack of employment and welfare protections for subordinate workers in the informal as compared with the formal sector (Portes and Castells 1989) though, of course, many workers in the formal sector in the Third World have very limited levels of protections. The research focus on the vulnerability of workers in the Third World has been firmly on women.

TNCs AND THE SEXUAL DIVISION OF LABOUR

Gender plays a particularly important role for many writers on globalization for two main reasons. First, much of the critique of globalization originates from the version of the new international division of labour (NIDL) formulated by Fröbel *et al.* (1980) that emphasizes the role of young women working for TNCs in export-processing enclaves of various types (Nash and Fernandez-Kelly 1983, Mitter 1986). While many have questioned the economic significance of these new patterns of employment, there is no doubt as to their symbolic importance in publicizing capitalist globalization, not only in academic circles but also through the mass media, and its economic, political, and culture-ideology consequences.

Second, the feminization of poverty thesis drew attention to the adverse consequences for urban and rural women and their families of global structural adjustment policies from the 1980s on (Tinker 1990, O'Brien *et al.* 2000: ch. 2). These policies were imposed by transnational financial and aid institutions (notably the World Bank) through national governments in many poor countries. This is one sphere in which the local consequences of global economic and social policies have been comprehensively researched. There is a growing consensus that these processes of globalization effect men and women differently, notably that they tend to create more burdens for women and more opportunities for men (Beneria and Feldman 1992; Elson 1995; Kawewe and Dibie 2000; Pearson, in Allen and Thomas 2000: ch. 18). Brydon and Legge (1996), for example, critically analyse the programme in Ghana and the subsequent, not very effective, Programme of Actions to Mitigate the Social Costs of Adjustment.

Mies's thesis of housewifization attempts to explain this in terms of the impact of colonialism and global capitalism, arguing that the position of women in the new international division of labour can be theoretically linked with the feminization of poverty. When women are defined as housewives and sex objects, they are the optimal labour force for global capital (Mies 1998). She provides empirical evidence and conceptual insights of relevance for the significance of gender for both class polarization and ecological unsustainability and reinforces the argument that more research effort should be devoted to the effects of capitalist globalization on households (Visvanathan *et al.* 1997: part 2).

The spread of the transnational corporations has brought significant changes to the sexual division of labour in the Third World. As noted above, in most export-oriented zones around the world most of the employees are young unmarried women, and TNCs and local investment agencies publicly express a preference for them. From the maquilas along the Mexico–US border to the electronics and garment factories of South-East Asia, reports of 75 per cent of jobs taken by young females in the foreign-owned sector are common,[10] though since the 1980s the proportion of male workers in some zones has been on the increase, for example in Mexico and East Asia (see Sklair 1993: ch. 8).The entrance of women into the manufacturing workforce, particularly into its most modern sectors, is clearly having important consequences in many Third World countries. This state of affairs produces a dilemma. In most countries women are glad to have jobs in factories and to earn cash, however tedious the work and low the wages (relative to male wages, that is, but not necessarily to previous or alternative female wages).[11] The geographical distribution of foreign direct investment (FDI) in many Third World countries has meant job openings for women in cities and small country towns and rural areas. FDI in some countries of the Third World has resulted in a predominantly male state sector industrial labour force being augmented by many more women in private, especially foreign-owned, industry. The entry of the TNCs, therefore, has had effects on the sexual division of labour as well as on the division of labour in general (Brydon and Chant 1989: ch. 7).

The impact on patriarchal social relations of new industries introduced into Third World communities by TNCs has stimulated a great deal of interesting research from all over the world (Garnsey and Paukert 1987; Elson 1995; Kothari and Nababsing 1996; Visvanathan *et al.* 1997: part 3). There are three analytically separate but empirically intertwined dimensions to be considered. These are:

(*a*) the sex composition of the TNC shop floor labour force in the Third World;

(*b*) the opportunities for women to be upwardly mobile within TNCs compared with domestically owned industries;

(*c*) the impact of both of these factors on the position of women outside the sphere of employment in Third World countries.

(*a*) The sex composition of the TNC shop floor labour force, particularly in export zones, has to be seen in the context of a substantial body of evidence to suggest that, in general, industrial employers in the Third World tend to prefer men over women (Anker and Hein 1986), though the research of Garnsey and Paukert (1987: 12–24) showed that there were relatively more women working in industry in Asia than in Africa and Latin

America in the 1980s. The reasons why the TNC-dominated export-processing industries employ many more women than men have stimulated a great deal of argument and it is not always possible to generalize cross-culturally. For example, in Mauritius, women originally had a legislated lower minimum wage than men (Hein, in Anker and Hein 1986: ch. 7), whereas in Mexico there is no legal difference though men do tend to monopolize the higher paying jobs (Sklair 1993: ch. 8). So while differential wage rates might explain the preponderance of women in the Mauritius EPZ,[12] they do not explain it in the Mexican maquilas. However, as is widely attested, irrespective of minimum wages, women do tend to earn less than men in the First as well as the Third World.[13]

A more convincing explanation is that the industries that are most common in the EPZs, apparel and electronics assembly, are industries that employ many more women than men wherever they are (Mitter 1986; Visvanathan *et al.* 1997). Why do these industries employ mostly women? The answer to this question is usually in terms of the boring, monotonous, and repetitive nature of the work and the widespread belief that women make a more docile, patient (long-suffering?) labour force, less likely to join unions and/or organize to improve their conditions. Despite some evidence to the contrary of Third World women in EOZs organizing fierce resistance to exploitation, sexual as well as economic, the overwhelming weight of evidence supports the view that most women workers in EOZs, while not necessarily enthralled by their jobs, are glad to have them and tend to prefer them to the alternatives on offer. This issue will be revisited below.

(b) While TNCs are not universally renowned for their commitment to feminist principles, there is a sense in which the generally more egalitarian employment practices of the USA and Europe spill over into the Third World through TNC direct investment. The increasing though still very minimal participation of women in managerial, technical, and higher professional occupations within the corporation has already attracted a good deal of attention, but there is little research specifically on the phenomenon of the female salariat in TNCs in the Third World (see Garnsey and Paukert 1987: 57–67). My own research in Mexico showed that that female managers tended to be found in those departments that were concerned with inter-personal relations within the plant (personnel, public relations, training) and that women who started off in these areas and succeeded were occasionally promoted to higher levels of management. There was also a route through from secretarial and personal assistant positions to higher levels, particularly for English-speakers in TNC-related businesses.

Cultural attributes (English language skills, style of life, adoption of cosmopolitan rather than local attitudes and values) appear to be just as important as more formal job skills in the promotion of women as well as men in the TNCs in Third World countries. A woman's chance of advancement is probably no worse in the TNCs than in domestic industry. It is difficult to know whether the increasing participation of Third World women in managerial, technical, and professional employment in TNCs in the Third World is simply part of the indigenization process of replacing expatriate with local personnel, or whether it is a qualitatively different phenomenon in its own right.

(c) One entirely unresolved issue revolves around the question of the balance of costs and benefits for women due to the entry of the TNCs in the Third World. Some have argued that the TNCs have disrupted traditional family life where they have hired more women than men, for example along Mexico's northern border. As Tiano (1994) has shown, this view conceals some implicit and contradictory sexist assumptions. Work on TNC investment in Asia has similarly brought to the surface some of the problems and contradictions of the analysis of patriarchal societies from a progressive feminist perspective. There is clearly a connection between the preference of TNCs to hire women over men in EPZs in order to procure a more docile labour force (regularly cloaked in the rationale that nimble-fingered girls are more suited for assembly work), and the cruder forms of patriarchy all over the world.

However, as Lim (in Tinker 1990) has argued, it is difficult to generalize on the impact of TNC employment on different groups of women even within the same society. Research on Malaysian and Singaporean women export-industry workers (a category that mostly includes TNC workers) shows that ethnicity and the availability of alternative employment can be key factors in the social and moral evaluation of women workers (men, too), and that there are substantial variations in the conceptions of factory work for women (whether in TNCs or not) across different communities. This does not necessarily disprove the contention that TNCs exploit women workers in particular in the Third World, though it does modify the thesis to the extent that in some Third World countries TNCs do provide some good jobs for women that help them to fulfil relatively freely chosen cultural needs (see also Pearson, in Sklair 1994: ch. 16).[14]

The point, however, is not whether exploitation of women or men occurs in TNC factories, for they are capitalist businesses predicated on the exploitation of all the factors of production. The point is, to what extent is the abuse of women and men as workers over and above capitalist exploitation in particular societies and communities more characteristic inside than outside TNCs? Are TNCs guilty of more abuse than domestic companies? The International Labour Organization (ILO), the Asian Regional Team for Employment Promotion, and others conducted worthwhile research on these issues in the 1980s and 1990s. The Multinational Enterprises Project of the ILO produced a series of reports on the employment effects of the TNCs, mostly in Third World countries and although some abuses were documented, the general conclusions of Fröbel *et al.*, Fernandez-Kelly, ICFTU, and other critics inspired by the dependency approach were not entirely supported.

For example, in an ILO study of export zones in Sri Lanka, South Korea, the Philippines, Malaysia, and India, Maex (1983) demonstrated that poor wages and conditions are explained better by the characteristics of the workforce in zone industries (mainly young women), than by their location or the ownership of the plants. Young women are not poorly paid because they work for TNCs in export zones, they are poorly paid wherever they work, but TNCs may well employ young women in the zones because they are cheaper to employ than older men in some countries. Further, as Dror (1984: 706) pointed out: 'With few exceptions, the incentive package does not include easily identifiable features pertaining directly to labour, such as suspension of labour laws, prohibition of trade union activity or lower (minimum) wage.' Nevertheless, his four case studies (Mauritius, Pakistan, Philippines, and Sri Lanka) revealed a variety of repressive labour practices. In Pakistan: 'The wholesale exemption of EPZ enterprises from the provisions of so many labour laws leaves many issues to the mercy of the individual contract of employment' (p. 709), while in the Philippines: 'The Bataan administrator said that some EPZ employes were paying 75 per cent of the minimum wage for six months, then dismissing the workers and hiring others at the 75 per cent rate' (p. 711). In addition, complaints of involuntary overtime, violence to women on the shop floor, and summary dismissal without compensation have been consistently reported from the 1960s, for example in Mauritius, Bangladesh, and Sri Lanka (Kothari and Nababsing 1996), in the Mexican maquila industry (Sklair 1993, Pena 1997), in China's Special Economic Zones (Sklair 1991), and on the websites of several campaigns against sweatshops (Bonacich and Applebaum 2000).

Trade unions have been particularly strong in the Bataan EPZ in the Philippines, but this is unusual in export zones (see Mitter 1986: 74-9). It is not surprising that the typical EPZ worker does not join a union. Most unions are male-dominated and tend to be completely unresponsive to the needs of women workers. The absence of strong unions has been connected with the alleged propensity of TNCs to hop from one cheap labour zone to another (Fröbel et al. 1980), though Dror found little evidence of footloose industries. Despite some notorious examples of TNCs abandoning their Third World (and sometimes First World) workers without legal compensation, there is no evidence to suggest that TNC plants inside or outside zones are statistically any more likely to close down than domestic companies. To add to the complexity, Maex (1983: 53) found that wages in Asian EPZs tended to be somewhat lower than national averages, while Dror (1984: 715) suggested that 'in most EPZs remuneration is often somewhat higher than in comparable occupations in the same country'. As Nababsing comments: 'The growing importance of hiring workers on a piece-rate basis and the weight of overtime work in the EPZ sector makes the concept of minimum wages somewhat irrelevant' (in Kothari and Nababsing 1996: 137). My own research in Mexico (1993: chs. 7-9) similarly shows the impact of gender and ownership on wages to be very complex.

We are, therefore, forced to conclude that it is impossible to generalize about TNC employment practices in export zones per se, though we can generalize about the effects of TNC employment practices on particular industries and particular workforces. Subcontractors for TNCs in the Third World, for example, have poor records overall. To recall Vaitsos's point, it is not the foreignness of the firm that makes the difference but the nature of the product and its place in the global commodity chain, its transnationality, within the capitalist global system.

TRANSNATIONAL PRESSURES ON TNCs

Many TNCs embark on offshore production to escape from their domestic unions, particularly in the USA. This is another area of considerable controversy. While some argue that the anti-labour nature of many of the governments in low-wage countries makes the task of the TNCs even easier, others argue that the TNCs tend to bring a more progressive atmosphere into labour relations. It must be said, however, that it is not only recently authoritarian Third World regimes, desperate for FDI, that have sometimes been prepared to sacrifice the interests of their workers in order to attract the jobs created by the TNCs.

This, of course, has always been a central dilemma of capitalist globalization and one that the critics of TNC practices in the Third World cannot escape. The problematic global economic situation of the 1980s and 1990s sharpened the horns of this dilemma for TNCs, governments, and workers in the Third World. While there is no convincing evidence that TNCs can bring salvation to the Third World, in many poor countries they are seen as responsible for the only bright spots in the economy and society. This is why the strategy of export-led industrialization fuelled by foreign investment and technology has been so powerful.[15] The most visible aspect of this is the jobs that the TNCs have created. Irrespective of the fact that many, perhaps most of these jobs are low paid, dirty (even the gleaming electronics industry is on the defensive against charges of health and safety problems for its workforce), and monotonous, they are very widely sought after and they often carry high prestige. It is not only the numbers of TNC jobs but their specific character in Third World contexts that imbues them with prestige. At the bottom of the TNC hierarchy, the workers on the shop floor, there is clearly a reputational element at work, in so far as being an employee in a company that has a global brand name appears to mean something positive for most people. Further, the huge resources of the larger TNCs always promise skill enhancement and local promotion, even if they do not deliver them very frequently. The evidence on this question is sketchy (Enderwick 1994). TNCs are sensitive to home country criticisms that they are exporting jobs, and the less menial the jobs, the more vulnerable the TNCs.

Globalizing business labels this process production-sharing. The argument is that companies from the First World will contribute high-value high technology and components for the production process, while workers from the Third World will contribute low-value, low-skill labour. Any upgrading of skills in Third World TNC production is liable to be challenged by home country constituencies, at the same time as it is welcomed by those in the host country. This is a zero-sum game (particularly in the USA and Europe) in that each occurrence of technical upgrading of a TNC plant in a Third World country is at the same time proudly announced for host country consumption by the TNC, and seized upon in the home country as evidence of job destruction. The usual defence of TNCs who export jobs from the First to the Third (and increasingly New Second) World is that the export of these jobs is necessary to protect higher-skill jobs at home. Technological developments, in particular computer-aided design and manufacturing (CAD/CAM), introduce further complexities.

The fashion garment industry provides many example of this process. Here, information on current consumer preferences can be transmitted by computer almost instantaneously from the marketplace to the factory, wherever it might be, and even design modifications or completely new designs can be electronically fed into CAD/CAM equipment in the factory for instant production (Dicken 1998: ch. 9). This has led to some repatriation of the apparel industry from the Third World back to the First. For small producers subcontracting to TNCs, the technology and the expertise required to make it work are prohibitively expensive, so it tends to be controlled by the TNCs or by the gargantuan retailers that they supply (Bonacich and Applebaum 2000). This means that garment workers (and probably those in other industries too) in the Third World who benefited from the search for cheap labour by the TNCs in the past can no longer assume that their jobs will always be safe from relocation back to the First World just as workers in the First World are always at risk themselves.[16] However, it is too soon to say with any degree of certainty to what extent computerization spells the end of TNC jobs in the Third, or in the First World.

The case of the Mexican maquila industry illustrates this well (Sklair 1993, Tiano 1994, Pena 1997). The maquila (export-oriented assembly) industry was introduced along

Mexico's northern border in the mid-1960s and was extended to the rest of the country in 1972. The Mexican government set up the maquila programme to create jobs, earn dollars, and introduce new technology. For the US firms, including many FG500 corporations, the main point was that labour was much cheaper in Mexico. From very small beginnings, by the start of the twenty-first century there were 3,000 maquila plants employing over one million workers producing a great variety of goods along the Mexico–US border and in the interior of the country. And every time the Mexican economy goes into crisis and the peso loses value, the maquila industry booms. Cooney (in Ochoa and Wilson 2001: 55) reports that in 1995 the Mexican economy contracted by 6.2 per cent while the maquila industry expanded by 30 per cent. The maquilas have been accused of causing job losses in the USA because of companies moving to Mexico. US proponents of the maquilas argue that these jobs are bound to go anyway and that the advantage of the maquila industry on the border is that it has always used a high proportion of US materials, components, and services. They have claimed that far from destroying jobs the maquilas may actually create new jobs in the USA. It may be difficult to persuade TV assembly workers in the USA whose plant has closed and relocated to Mexico that the maquila industry creates jobs for them. However, it is not so difficult to persuade relatively well-paid workers who makes highly sophisticated electronic components in a US factory that supplies assembly plants in Mexico that the maquila industry protects their jobs (Cowie 1999).

Proponents have also had to persuade successive Mexican governments that the maquilas are good for Mexico. Many US-owned maquilas claim to be in the market for locally produced materials and components, backward linkages. As I explained in the previous chapter, few export zones anywhere have a good record on linkages, but few have a worse record than the maquila industry. The inability of Mexico to produce (or to sell) materials and components to the TNCs is a fact that Mexican and US facilitators tend to obscure when presenting their case in Mexico! Clearly, both sides cannot win. Either the maquilas continue to buy from the USA and protect the jobs of US suppliers, or they buy in Mexico, and these jobs are lost, however many others are created.

Another supposed benefit for Mexico is the replacement of US managers, technicians, and highly trained personnel by Mexicans. This has happened to an appreciable extent in US-owned maquilas that have great incentives to employ Mexican managers and technicians who speak Spanish, are familiar with local conditions, and are much cheaper than equivalent US personnel. Technology transfer has also taken place in a number of technologically sophisticated maquilas. But, again, any gain for Mexican workers will usually mean a loss for workers in the USA.

Every case has its special characteristics. For Mexico, the shared border with the USA and dramatic periodic devaluations of the peso explain the rapid growth in the 1980s and 1990s. Other features, for example, the gradual increase in the numbers of indigenous managers and technicians in the maquilas, were more typical of the spread of economic transnational practices in employment and other areas globally. The North American Free Trade Agreement (NAFTA) signed by the USA, Canada, and Mexico in 1992 promised great benefits to Mexico from its association with its two much richer northern neighbours, and the volume of transnational practices in the economic, political, and culture-ideology spheres have certainly increased. However, there are many on both sides of the border who are yet to be convinced that the workers and the environment of the USA and

Canada, let alone Mexico, will benefit (Wallach and Naiman 1998, Ciccantell 2001). The radical consensus is:

The introduction of the North American Free Trade Agreement (NAFTA) in 1994 sought to accelerate transnational access to the Mexican economy by deregulating financial services and chipping away at sectors of the economy that had been protected historically, such as corn and petroleum. The extent of this global penetration has served to disrupt broad sectors of Mexican society and tear an already threadbare social fabric. (Ochoa and Wilson 2001: 4)[17]

Gradually, TNCs appear to have seen the benefits (or in some countries accepted the inevitability) of employing host country managers and technicians to run their plants. It is likely that the chief executive of a large TNC plant in a Third World country will still be from the First World, but it is now quite common to see host country nationals occupying senior positions. Studies from the 1980s showed that up to 40 per cent of expatriate US executives failed on foreign assignments, and had to be sent home, and that expatriate managers were increasingly considered by the TNCs to be a source of avoidable trouble and expense (Kobrin 1988). The rise of the international business schools in recent decades along with large numbers of Third World students in the universities and technical institutes of the First World, despite rapidly rising costs, have provided increasing pools of potential local employees for the TNCs, and recruitment is brisk. The spectacular rise in numbers of business magazines (often with a global focus) in most Third World countries charts these changes. The number of business schools in Third World cities is also rising rapidly and they provide recruits for domestic industry and TNCs. In many Third World countries young graduates from such institutions find posts with high degrees of responsibility in national development agencies. The extent to which business schools all over the world have an agenda broadly in line with capitalist globalization is, therefore, a matter of great significance (see Merkle 1980, O'Connor 1999).

There is also considerable pressure on TNCs to promote socially and environmentally responsible business practices in the Third World (assuming, of course, that they are already doing this elsewhere). Multitudes of NGOs, national governments, international agencies (notably those attached to the UN) and even some business groups, hold conferences and workshops and training sessions to imbue TNC managers with these practices and sometimes to monitor their performances. Practically every major TNC will have some group somewhere investigating what it is doing. Dealing with these groups can take up much valuable management time and energy but ignoring them can lead to damage to corporate reputations and loss of value in the stock market. Few major corporations ignore these risks, and most train their personnel in damage-limitation techniques (Sklair 2001: chs. 6–7).

TRAINING AND TECHNOLOGY

The role of the TNCs in training is quite controversial. Not everyone accepts the received knowledge that TNCs are good at training managers, and that these managers spread their know-how throughout Third World host societies. For example, in the case of Kenya, Gershenberg (1987) found that publicly owned firms and to a lesser extent TNCs in equity joint ventures with the Kenyan government were more likely to foster local management training and dissemination of know-how than private firms. Although there is an important ethnic factor in this research, namely the predominance of Asian over African managers in the sample, the finding is still significant. A study on Indonesia suggested that TNCs were more liable to take managers from local firms than to do their own training (Okada 1983). This finding is supported by evidence from the beverage industry in South Africa in the mid-1990s. Coca-Cola and Pepsi-Cola are locked in combat over this and other Third World markets (see, on the cola wars, Chapter 7 below). Pepsi established a joint venture with local black partners and the CEO is quoted as saying: 'Our commitment is to create the most dynamic and most admired black-managed and black-owned company in South Africa.' New Age Beverages, owned 75 per cent by a local firm and 25 per cent by PepsiCo, recruited the top executive of the most prominent black-owned business in South Africa, National Sorghum Breweries (Associated Press, 6 June 1994).

The main point of managerial and technical recruitment from local firms is often posed in terms of the need to transfer technology to the host society. There is a large literature on technology transfer, though most of it is from the perspective of those who do the transferring rather than the recipients. There are, however, a few exceptions. Adikibi (1983) analysed how the TNCs that controlled the modern tyre sector in Nigeria produced to global standards and did so with a good complement of indigenous managers and technicians. There was no doubt that these people could produce tyres, but when the TNCs withdrew from Nigeria during the Biafran war, production ceased in the factories because of the ways in which the TNCs had organized the division of labour on the shop floor. The indigenous personnel, while they were fully trained in the specific features of their own parts of the process, were excluded from positions that gave access to the whole of the production process. Thus, the TNCs protected their monopoly in technique while appearing to transfer the technology to local people.

This is neither uncommon (Sano 1983) nor surprising, in light of the technological dependence of most Third World firms and the technological dominance of the TNCs (Stewart 1978: ch. 5). For many TNCs, protection of technology is a matter of corporate life and death. However, the situation is changing. In the 1960s and 1970s when nationalizations were rife, exposure to hostile action by host governments might have been substantially increased if the host governments believed that their nationals could run the plants. Therefore, many TNCs felt that there were risks inherent in training local technicians and managers too well. Such considerations are more relevant for understanding the ways in which TNCs set out to create comprador bourgeoisies (and comprador proletariats in some cases) in the past, than they are today. This is testament to the globalizing mission of the transnational capitalist class in the Third World and the creation of a cadre of indigenous globalizers.

Technology transfer and the creation of linkages can also be closely connected. Backward and forward linkages with local firms are often very practical expressions of how TNCs can transfer technology positively to individuals and firms in the Third World. Both backward and forward linkages can have substantial financial, employment, and technical effects. Hill (1982), in a study on the Philippines, illustrated a typical pattern where local linkages were created by assemblers who established joint ventures with licensees or foreign firms. However, in these cases, local sourcing of parts often conceals import content through assembly kits for various products. Lall's study of the Indian truck industry (1985: ch. 5) was more encouraging on the potential for employment creating backward linkages. After the economic reforms in the early 1990s foreign TNCs have become increasingly connected with Indian companies (compare Stoever 1989 and Evans 1995) and, as we saw in the case of Enron, with state and provincial authorities.

My own studies of export-oriented zones, particularly in China and Mexico, suggest that backward and forward linkages tend to be very meagre, and these cases are rather more typical of the Third World as a whole than relatively highly developed enclaves like Singapore, Hong Kong, and the computer industry in India. The developmental effects of TNC investment must be worked out on a case-by-case basis and cannot be judged in isolation from the development goals of the competing groups and classes in the countries and communities concerned. The six criteria of positive development that I have used in my own research (linkages, retained foreign currency earnings, genuine technology transfer, upgrading of personnel, conditions of work, and environmental impact) is one way to tackle this problem (Sklair 1993, and Henderson, in Sklair 1994: ch. 13).

Nevertheless, TNCs do introduce much usable technology into the Third World, and while it may not lead to the conquest of global markets it may still have a very positive effect on industry and employment in particular countries. The ILO Multinational Enterprises programme, noted above in connection with export-processing zones, also sponsored a series of studies on the employment generation effects of technology choice by TNCs in the Third World. Studies in Singapore, Nigeria, Brazil, India, and Kenya uncovered a very wide range of technologies in use and, if indirect employment is taken into account, a considerable job creation effect is visible. Though technological change does tend to lead to more capital-intensive than labour-intensive development, there can be substantial employment created indirectly through backward and forward linkages. The Kenya study, for example, reported that employees left a TNC car assembly plant to set up their own roadside workshops (ILO 1984: ch. 3).

In the case of joint ventures (and similar arrangements) there are different issues at stake. Here, the transfer of technology is often the main point of the exercise. In a study of thirty-three European chemical and pharmaceutical joint ventures in Indonesia, Thailand, Philippines, Singapore, and Malaysia, Lasserre (1982) discovered that home country technicians were not trained to train in specific sociocultural settings. Training, in any case, was very limited, local staff visits to home country plants were not very involving, and on-the-job training tended to consist of little more than watching expatriates at work. Thus, 'although on paper there is a training effort, the results are far from satisfactory' (Lasserre 1982: 57). The work of Zweig (2000) on management training centres in China suggests that problems such as these persist (see Chapter 9 below).

This is not very surprising when we consider that most joint ventures appear not to be entirely voluntary. One study, based on sixty-six Third World firms and the evidence from other studies (Beamish 1985), found three main reasons for setting up joint ventures: host government pressure; the need for the partner's skills; and the need for other attributes or assets. In addition, Beamish showed that the creation of joint ventures was often due to non-tariff barriers threatening the market position of the TNCs. In subsequent research on joint ventures in China, Beamish (1993) demonstrated that the balance of power in joint ventures cannot always be taken for granted, particularly in China. Corporations with global brands and/or valuable technologies have established mutually valuable partnerships with government enterprises and recently privatized companies in many countries. As more and more Third World countries are drawn into the WTO network, and more and more trade barriers fall, more joint ventures may become genuine business propositions.

THE GLOBAL FOOD SYSTEM

The global food system is dominated by a few highly industrialized TNCs based in North America, Japan, and Europe that control the production, processing, and marketing of most of what the First World eats and drinks (Bonanno *et al.* 1994). Six companies were listed in the FG500 food consumer products group in 2001: Nestlé, domiciled in Switzerland, was first with revenues of almost $50b., Unilever (UK/Netherlands), Conagra and Sara Lee (USA), Groupe Danone (France), and Snow Brand Milk Products (Japan). In the food production group IBP (USA) led the pack with revenues of almost $17b., followed by Montedison (Italy), and Archer Daniels Midland and Farmland Industries (both from the USA).[18]

At the other end of the scale the global food system also includes billions of peasants labouring in small family farms and millions of small local food and drink companies. In many parts of the world food production and processing constitute the bulk of the industrial sector. In the 1980s, food products accounted for about 30 per cent of Third World manufacturing output and an even higher proportion of employment. This is not surprising, for one would suppose that every country has to satisfy the basic needs of its people for food as a first priority. As many Third World countries are slowly but surely moving from economies based predominantly on agriculture into manufacturing and service industries and as Third World populations are moving in great numbers from rural to urban areas, there are concomitant changes in the structures of food provision in these countries and in some First World regions too (Bernstein *et al.* 1990, Bonanno *et al.* 1994, Watts and Goodman 1997, Mies and Bennholdt-Thomsen 1999: ch. 3). More and more workers in the Third World are choosing or are being forced into non-agrarian livelihoods in rural areas or to migrate to urban areas. The former phenomenon has attracted much less attention from researchers than the latter but it is just as important.

Bryceson (in Bryceson and Jamal 1997: ch. 1) conceptualizes it as de-agrarianization, long-term processes of occupational adjustment, reorientation of income-earning opportunities, social identification, and spatial relocation. As economic crises and structural adjustment programmes have caused contractions in urban employment opportunities and as some rural communities have had more investment, there are winners as well as losers. 'Houses, roads, mills, and other village infrastructure have been built, generating employment in construction, operation and maintenance' (Bryceson and Jamal 1997: 8). Though rural dwellers juggle various occupations, many remain subsistence farmers in the last instance. De-agrarianization also has important effects on rural dwellers as consumers. Free goods (what people can grow for themselves) are increasingly replaced by market-provisioned goods (water, energy, fodder); the demand for traditional handicrafts changes (handicraft skills can be enhanced or destroyed); and there is likely to be development of the local service economy (notably petty trade). Bryceson concludes that in Africa at least, the 'formal sector rather than the informal sector is now the residual' (ibid.: 14). This, of course, creates severe fiscal problems for states in Africa.[19]

Briefly put, all these changes in employment and residence mean that fewer and fewer people in the Third World are able or willing to procure their own food directly from the land and so they are becoming more and more dependent on bought and processed food and drink. This has, of course, been the case in the advanced industrial societies for a very long time, but with the difference that the food industry and particularly global brands today are concentrated in the hands of a relatively small number of TNCs. This has introduced a qualitatively new circumstance that was not operating when today's First World countries were making their transitions to industrialization and urbanization (Leopold 1985). For example, the surprising rise of obesity in some parts of the Third World has been directly connected with the introduction of new, usually high-sugar, high-fat, high-salt processed foods into traditional diets.

The focus of much research and thinking about food in the Third World is the idea of entitlements (notably analysed by Sen in the 1980s) which directs attention to the poverty of hungry people rather than supplies of food. The political issue revolves around the distinction between growth-mediated security (the thesis that rapid economic expansion will eventually eradicate poverty and solve the food problem) and support-led security (immediate public measures to ensure that every single person receives an entitlement of food).[20] Sen and his colleagues conclude, with a high degree of restraint: 'in the absence of public involvement to guarantee that the fruits of growth are widely shared, rapid economic growth can have a disappointingly poor impact on living conditions' (Drèze and Sen 1991: 4).

Food security is derived through land (self-sufficient production) or through income (purchasing power) but, as Alamgir and Arora (1991) demonstrate with a mass of data, the problem is that the poor do not have enough land and that the landless are often the jobless. They show a worsening trend of land distribution in the 1970s and 1980s, particularly in Latin America, and in Food Security Status tables for over seventy Third World countries, more than fifty were in the very poor category (Alamgir and Arora 1991: Annex III). On the global food system they comment: 'It is easier for large buyers [primarily the TNC food traders] than poor developing countries to buy into the market and ensure delivery' (ibid.: 162).

In 1997 the FAO convened an Inter-Agency Working Group on Food Insecurity Vulnerability Information Mapping Systems (FIVIMS). About fifty countries at risk nominated national focal points, and over twenty agencies and organizations are involved. In 1999, FAO published the first global food insecurity report: 'Chronic food insecurity is represented by estimates of the number of people whose food intake does not provide enough calories to meet their basic energy requirements—i.e. the undernourished. Measurements of nutritional status or undernutrition, on the other hand, are based on information about people's actual physiological condition' (FAO 1999: 6). These may be due to lack of food, inadequate purchasing power, or inappropriate utilization in households. Food insecurity and poor conditions of health and sanitation are the major causes of poor nutritional status.

Why was a global mapping system necessary? The answer is simple. According to experts at the World Food Summit in Rome in 1996, there were about 840 million people in developing countries subsisting on diets deficient in calories. About 170 million children under 5 were underweight (around 30 per cent of children in the Third World). Best estimates indicate that 250 million children suffer from vitamin A deficiency, 800 million people suffer from iodine deficiency, and 2 billion people are affected by iron deficiency and anaemia (one reason why many poor people in poor countries appear lethargic to the casual observer).[21] That is why FIVIMS is necessary in a world in which food mountains are destroyed and farmers in rich countries are paid not to grow crops, in a system of capitalist globalization that boasts the most efficient and productive agribusiness in human history.[22] The UNDP estimated in 1998 that it would take about $13 billion extra annually to achieve basic health and nutrition in all developing countries. This is the same as is spent every year on perfume in Europe and the USA, less than is spent on pet food, and about one-third of what is spent on business entertainment in Japan. World military expenditure in comparison was $780 billion, sixty times as much (C. Thomas 1999: table 1). Senauer and Sur (2001) estimate that economic growth rates of between 6 and 7 per cent would be necessary to end world hunger by 2025 (3–4 per cent by 2050). It is very unlikely that even the lower figure can be achieved, especially in the regions most in need and, as they note, their analysis focuses on availability and ignores access to and use of food crops. Prospects are bleak.

FIVIMS identified six groups particularly vulnerable to severe hunger and malnutrition: victims of conflicts (refugees and war damaged), migrant workers and their families, marginal people in urban areas (unemployed and homeless), at-risk social groups (indigenous peoples, ethnic minorities, illiterate households), low-income households, and dependent people living alone or in large families (FAO 1999: 15). The range of the vulnerable suggests that such people might be found all over the world, and this is borne out by the data. About 34 million of the world's undernourished people do not live in the Third World, mostly in postcommunist Europe. Even in the USA groaning under masses of discarded food and an epidemic of obesity, over 4 million households suffer from hunger for at least part of the year and about 800,000 from severe hunger. But most people even in the Third World are not starving, and this is partly due to the fact that there is a large quantity of food and food aid circulating. As Bush (1996) argues, food and the lack of it can be a political weapon (locally and globally).

It is widely believed, and widely propagated by the popular mass media, that famine and malnutrition in Third World countries are caused by shortages of food. This is true, of course, but only in a limited sense. Brown (1993: 30), working from FAO data from the 1980s, shows that of the forty-three Third World countries that had insufficient food, thirty of these actually exported food and some of these were amongst the poorest. The first *State of Food Insecurity in the World* report (FAO 1999) provides a great deal of data that fully confirms the thesis of the polarizing effects of capitalist globalization on the availability of food between regions and countries. It shows that in the 1990s, while the total number of undernourished people in the world probably declined by about 40 million, some thirty-seven countries accounted for reductions of 100 million while across the rest of the Third World the undernourished increased by about 60 million (FAO 1999: 4). Table 6.1 compares the prevalence of undernourishment in Third World regions and some countries in 1978/81 and 1995/7. While the position of the hungry in some countries in this period has improved, in others it has deteriorated.

The entitlement of the hungry and the availability of food are not necessarily related in a simple fashion but two facts stand out: it is women who produce most of the domestically consumed food in the Third World and it is women and children who bear the brunt of famines and malnutrition.

Table 6.1 Undernourishment in the Third World (1978/81 and 1995/7)

Region, Subregion, Country	Undernourished in total population (%)	
	1979/81	1995/7
TOTAL DEVELOPING WORLD	29	18
ASIA AND PACIFIC	32	17
East Asia	29	14
China	30	13
North Korea	19	48
Mongolia	27	48
Oceania	31	24
Papua New Guinea	31	24
South-East Asia	27	13
Indonesia	26	6
Laos	32	33
South Asia	38	23
Nepal	46	21
Sri Lanka	22	25
AMERICAS AND CARIBBEAN	13	11
[NORTH AMERICA]	5	5
Caribbean	19	31
Cuba	3	19
Dominican Republic	25	26
Haiti	47	61
Central America	20	17
Honduras	31	21
Nicaragua	26	31
South America	14	10
Argentina	1	1
Guyana	13	16
Venezuela	4	15
NEAR EAST AND NORTH AFRICA	9	9
Total Near East	10	12
Afghanistan	33	62
Iraq	4	15
Lebanon	8	2
North Africa	8	4
Algeria	9	5
Libyan Arab Jamahiriya	0	1
SUB-SAHARAN AFRICA	37	33
Central Africa	36	48
Cameroon	20	32
Central African Republic	22	42
Chad	69	46
East Africa	35	42
Burundi	38	63
Kenya	25	41
Uganda	31	28
Southern Africa	32	44
Angola	29	43
Madagascar	18	39
Mauritius	10	6
West Africa	40	16
Côte d'Ivoire	7	15
Ghana	61	11
Liberia	22	42

Note: Undernourishment is defined in terms of total number of calories available from local sources, average minimum calories requirement for total population, and distribution (see FAO 1999: 6–7). Countries represent best cases and worst cases within regions.

Source: data compiled from FAO (1999: 29–30).

WOMEN AND FOOD

'Women produce between 60 and 80 percent of the food in most developing countries and are responsible for half of the world's food production.'[23] Food production in the Third World cannot be understood in isolation from the relationship between the sexual division of labour and the sources of economic power. In land-scarce societies, like many regions of Latin America and Asia, men will tend to monopolize the land, both through male peasant appropriation of family plots and the big landlord system of production. In sub-Saharan Africa, where land hunger is less common, women tend to be left alone to cultivate and market their produce. However, where agriculture starts to become mechanized, usually under the auspices of the colonial powers and/or foreign investors, men begin to take more interest and to appropriate the economic gains for themselves (see Boserup 1989[1970], Mies and Bennholdt-Thomsen 1999).

Patrilocal residence, where women join the households of their husbands rather than vice versa, and the persistence of domestic production, where families consume most of what they produce rather than buy and sell in the market, have always been seen as obstacles to capitalist development in the Third World and as strong reinforcements for the maintenance of feudal-patriarchal relations. Ever since the earliest days of colonialism, however, capitalism has developed mechanisms to integrate such recalcitrant modes of production and social formations into profitable systems of production and distribution all over the world. Third World rural economies were brought into the colonial systems of Britain and other imperialist states by making it more difficult for their populations to live outside the market, typically by imposing taxes on rural communities. This forced them to produce crops for the market, often for export markets, putting pressure on their capacity to produce crops for domestic consumption. The global commodity system was largely based on persuading and/or forcing the peoples of the non-industrial countries to produce the food and industrial raw materials that were necessary for the continuous growth of capitalism and industrialization in the First World. The theory of unequal exchange (Emmanuel 1972) explains how these raw materials generally lost value over time relative to the manufactured goods made out of them. Wallerstein and the world-systems school built from these foundations the framework of the international (then the new international) division of labour into core, semi-periphery, and periphery to indicate where (that is, in which countries) these stages in production and trade took place (Wallerstein 1974, Fröbel *et al.* 1980).

So, in order to achieve this the colonial authorities had to engineer a switch from subsistence production of basic food crops to the production of cash crops for the international market and to replace the natural economy of the non-industrial society with the money economy of the capitalist industrial society. This has undoubtedly led to the enrichment of some rural and urban groups in the Third World, those who have successfully adapted to the changing demands of the global marketplace. However, it has also resulted in further impoverishment for subsistence farmers (see Waters 2000) and for many in the Third World, loss of self-sufficiency in food and greater dependence on food imports from the First World. Such economic transformations undermined the political independence of Third World governments and the autonomy of women where this was based on some degree of control over land.

Historically, this is a surprising and disturbing conclusion. In the nineteenth century, the effects of economic development, colonialism, and capitalism were widely thought to be wholly favourable to women. The assumption that modernization would help to liberate women from the semi-servitude of primitive patriarchal societies was deeply embedded in the consciousness of charitable institutions and individuals in the West, not least the Christian missionaries who flocked to save souls, introduce underwear, and establish proper moral codes in the colonies of the imperialist powers. However, these optimistic hopes, while not entirely misconceived, appear to have ignored the many formidable traditional obstacles to the emancipation of women that still remain in most Third World societies, as well as new obstacles created by the so-called modernization processes themselves.

FAO (2001) reports that the number of female-headed households in rural areas in the Third World is increasing substantially (31 per cent of total households in sub-Saharan Africa, 17 per cent in Latin America and the Caribbean, and 14 per cent in Asia) as men migrate in search of employment. Despite this women are denied access to the basic resources that would assist them in caring for themselves and their families. They have minimal access to land, little access to credit, agricultural inputs, education or training or extension services, to decision-making, and to the benefits of research and appropriate technology.[24]

Thus, women's work in domestic food production has remained largely invisible and unrewarded (see Boserup 1989; FAO 2001) while the glorious role of the agri-TNCs is broadcast from TV, radio, newsprint, and billboards all over the Third World. Agribusiness is global!

AGRIBUSINESS

According to United Nations studies in the 1970s less than one-third of the food consumed in the Third World was processed (Fath 1985). Affiliates of TNCs accounted for about one-eighth of Third World food-processing industry, and about 90 per cent of this was in branded goods and the export sector. TNCs tended to be active in wheat and corn milling, animal feed, poultry, processed dairy products, canned fruit and vegetables, breakfast cereals, margarine and table oils, confectionery, soft drink concentrates, beer, coffee, and cocoa products. In the export sector, TNCs are still central in bananas, fish, canned fruit, and tea; quite important in vegetable oils, cocoa, coffee, and flowers; but no longer central in sugar and beef products (see Raikes and Gibbon 2000). Pradip Thomas expresses very well how capitalist globalization is transforming agriculture. He highlights:

[the] clash between two, very different approaches to agricultural production and consumption: the dominant global model that is based on the free market model of agriculture, with its accent on comparative advantage, export-oriented exploitation of cash crops, high-cost inputs, concentration of power in the hands of agribusinesses, the privatization of land holding and monopoly control over seed, germ plasm and micro-organisms produced/manipulated through the help of genetic engineering techniques; and the subsistence model, followed by a large percentage of India's farmers, which is based on immediate food security, sustainable, ecologically friendly farm, water, land

and resource management, farmers' rights with respect to breeding of plant varieties, co-operative trading and resource management. (P. Thomas 1999: 282)

World food standards are set by the Codex Alimentarius Commission, established in 1963 and run jointly by FAO and WHO. As the diets of the world's peoples are increasingly filled with processed foods and drinks, issues such as food labelling, pesticide residues, and additives become ever more pressing. The Codex Commission and its various committees are largely dominated by TNCs and industry federations working closely with First World governments, while Third World governments and NGOs are very poorly represented (Avery *et al.* 1993). For example, in the 1989–91 session almost half of the US delegation and over 60 per cent of the Swiss delegation actually represented industry, and industry took up 41 per cent of the places on the Food Additives and Contaminants Committee and 46 per cent on the Committee on Nutrition. This raises the question: who does Codex serve: consumers or industry? Avery and her colleagues argued that 'lack of money remains a serious barrier to participation for many groups and nations. Moreover, the issue of conflicts of interests raised by the large number of industry representatives present at its meetings, and the decline of democratic control over food standards, have so far been addressed by the Codex internal reform only cursorily' (1993: 5). Evidence from the Codex website reveals that the situation is not much changed at the start of the twenty-first century. For a body that exercises increasing global control over our food and drink, the questions remain.

In no single Third World country will the TNCs entirely dominate the production and marketing of food and, indeed, compared with some industries, the role of the TNCs in food looks quite minor. However, as a result of capitalist globalization First World supermarket chains have tightened their grip over Third World agriculture. 'A small number of brand manufacturers who retain strong images globally (like Nestlé) remain influential, and all retailers have to deal with them on inferior terms. But a majority have to compete for "preferred supplier" status, on terms dictated by supermarket chains which have rationalised relations with suppliers through JIT [Just in Time] ordering' (Raikes and Gibbon 2000: 69). FG500 for 2001 indicated that twenty-four food and drug stores with combined revenues in excess of $500 billion dominated the globalized food trade.

Individual TNCs tend to dominate specific product markets rather than whole industries. In Mexico in the 1970s, for example, there were no foreign dairy bottlers and only one ice creamer, but ten out of twelve canned milk producers were foreign. The primary interest of the TNCs in Mexico, as everywhere else in the Third World, is in the urban middle-class market. For example, Nestlé refused to develop an inexpensive infant milk for the Mexican government low-cost food agency, and Nabisco refused to develop a soy-based breakfast cereal for government distribution. What Van Whiting argued in the 1980s is still, by and large, true today: 'Rather than investing in research and development of new products for the poor, foreign firms invest in advertising existing products for the well-to-do' (in Newfarmer 1985: 370). While Mexico exports food, but not much processed foods, foreign food processors are net importers, and where TNCs use local raw materials the contracting arrangements tend to drive the poorer peasants off the land (see Llambi, in Bonanno *et al.* 1994: ch. 9).

The relationship between cash crops, particularly those for export, and subsistence crops for local consumption has occasioned an intense and sometimes bitter debate that has been going on for decades, if not centuries, and goes to the very heart of the capitalist global system and its transnational contradictions (Waters 2000). In the 1980s the debate revolved round what has been labelled the World Bank complementarity thesis. In an exemplary study of cotton in the Ivory Coast, Bassett (1988) argued that the World Bank operated on the basis of four hypotheses, all of which were false. First, the trickle-down fertilizer hypothesis predicts that local food crops will benefit from increased fertilizer use on the cash crop. In the study area what actually happened was that food crops were displaced from the head to the end of the fertilizer rotation in more than half the cases. The second hypothesis is that cash cropping increases the general mechanization of agriculture. What actually happened was that mechanization was concentrated on land-clearing incentives, representing an 'extraordinary subsidy to the relatively wealthy progressive farmer' (Bassett 1988: 52). The third prediction is that cash crops will create regional food markets. The rice that the peasants in the research area bought came from Burma, Thailand, and China, not from the Ivory Coast or its neighbours. Finally, the complementarity thesis predicts that services and subsidies for export crops will also benefit food crops. They did not, for the obvious reason that the cash crop companies have little interest in developing food crops for local consumption.

In this case, subsistence requirements could still be met from cotton income. However, as there was no clearly demonstrated link between cash crop promotion and improvements in food crops to make up for the shortfall in the cropping area that results from giving over the land to cash crops, the issue of food security must be raised. The World Bank *World Development Report* for 1988 showed that between 1970 and 1986 the Ivory Coast, often regarded as one of Africa's success stories, more than tripled its cereals imports, its external debt rose more than thirtyfold, and food production per capita barely kept up with population growth. Like other Third World countries its quest for World Bank-induced export earnings through cash crops was purchased at a high price with no apparent significant complementarity in food crops. By the mid-1990s, the food situation in the Ivory Coast had deteriorated. Between 1980 and 1995 the proportion of the population undernourished rose from 7 to 15 per cent, and 24 per cent of under-5s were underweight (FAO 1999: table 2).[25]

Not everyone, however, fully accepts that TNC involvement in Third World agriculture always does lead to food insecurity. Scott (in Abel and Lewis 1985: 483–99) argued that the criticisms of TNCs in food-processing export industries in the Third World often fail to distinguish between national and personal food security. Foreign investment, Scott claims, may reduce food insecurity in a variety of ways, for example by increasing export diversification. But what is possible in theory does not always happen in practice and many Third World countries that were recently more or less self-sufficient in basic foodstuffs are now increasingly dependent on imports. This is not entirely explained by huge increases in population, as is widely propagated by the mass media and widely believed.[26] Many very poor countries, and even some whose people suffered famines in the 1980s, like Ethiopia, actually turned over land to cash crops for export. In Egypt, for example, huge imports of cheap grain from the USA made it uneconomical for local farmers to grow grain, threatening the livelihood of subsistence producers (Nash (2001: 86) reports the same from 1990s Mexico). Large tracts of land that once grew food for local consumption began to grow strawberries, luxury vegetables, and other cash crops for export (see

Steif 1989). Egypt is a good example of the food security problem because it appears to be in quite a favourable position. Official UN data for 1987 showed that its food supply was 131 per cent of calorific requirements and its food production was 135 per cent of the base years 1979–81 (Alamgir and Arora 1991: 219). Brown (1993: 30), also citing official figures, puts Egypt in the category of countries having enough food thanks to net imports. In 2000, about half of the wheat consumed in Egypt was imported (see United States Department of Agriculture (USDA) website).

In different circumstances this might be a great success story—after all one of the world's largest food grain importers is Japan. Egypt's grain imports more than doubled between 1970 and 1986, from under four million to almost nine million metric tons (about 180 kilos per head), foreign debt increased twenty-five-fold, to over $22 billion, and when the IMF forced the government to increase the price of bread, there were riots in the streets.[27] Throughout the 1990s Egypt continued to be a major importer of grain, around 6–7 million metric tons annually. According to the FAO fewer than 4 per cent of Egyptians were undernourished, compared with more than 35 per cent in twenty-five other countries in Africa and Asia (FAO 1999: 8–9). Nevertheless, FAO also reported that 15 per cent of children in Egypt were stunted because of a lack of adequate nutrition. The global food system can by no stretch of the imagination be said to have improved Egypt's long-term food security. How, we may ask, can a country like Egypt, by no means the poorest or most vulnerable in the Third World, find itself in this position?

There are many answers to this question at many levels. The role of the TNCs in solving or intensifying the problems of hunger and nutrition in the Third World is extremely controversial and the arguments have raged since the 1980s (see Tullis and Hollist 1986, Bernstein *et al.* 1990, Bonanno *et al.* 1994, McMichael 1994). For example, the TNCs that control the world trade are criticized if they do not sell grain to the Third World, and they are criticized if they do (Kneen 1995). Everyone agrees, however, that a few TNCs do control the global trade in grain, as well as the trade in other basic commodities. Andrae and Beckman (1985), in a provocative study of Nigeria, label the global grain system a wheat trap. Intensification of capitalist globalization since the 1980s suggests that the trap is even tighter today than it was then. As Friedmann argues: 'The history of agriculture in international capitalism is one of impoverishment of direct producers, though to different degrees and in different ways' (in Bernstein *et al.* 1990: 25). Two authors from the International Fund for Agricultural Development put the consequences of this system even more starkly when they wrote: 'It costs US$800 to carry a ton of food to the Ethiopian highlands to feed a family for a year, while, with half as much, the same family could improve its own production capacity and feed itself for twenty years' (Alamgir and Arora 1991: 125).

Let us focus our attention on where Third World grain imports come from and how they happen to be available in such massive quantities. For this, we need to look at the history of the United States Public Law 480 (PL 480). *Foreign Agriculture*, a US Department of Commerce magazine, under the unequivocal title 'U.S. Food Aid Builds Cash Markets in Developing Countries' (Feb. 1984: 20–1) provides an account of PL 480 in celebration of its thirtieth anniversary. 'PL 480 was enacted as a means of exporting surplus U.S. commodities to dollar-short nations' and 'has become an important vehicle for developing commercial export markets, for meeting humanitarian food needs, and for spurring economic and agricultural growth in the developing world' (ibid.: 20). Between 1954 and

1984, over 300 million tons of agricultural products valued at $33 billion were sent to more than 100 countries under the programme. Over 70 per cent were distributed under Title I, concessional sales, of which 80 per cent went to the Third World, representing almost one-third of total US direct aid to them. The main recipients were India ($6 billion), Egypt ($2.7b.), South Korea ($1.9b.), and Indonesia ($1.7b.). 'Aid often is a springboard to trade . . . PL 480 has established itself as one of the United States' most successful market development tools' (ibid.). Korea, Taiwan, and Mexico bought significant amounts of US produce, and Egypt, Indonesia, the Dominican Republic, Morocco, Tunisia, and Peru were beginning to do so in the mid-1980s. At that time, about half of US grain exports were sent under PL 480.

By 2000, the food aid budget had escalated to $957 billion and the message was the same: 'Several of the leading importers of U.S. agricultural products, such as Egypt and Thailand, are former recipients of food assistance. Food aid positively affects almost every state in the union, with benefits not only to farmers but also to food processors, packers, transporters, railroads, stevedores, ocean carriers and others' ('About PL 480 Title II', USAID website).[28]

All the expertise of a fully computerized trade and product information service is available for US exporters and no corner of the global marketplace is left un-intelligenced. The USA spent hundreds of millions of dollars on a Targeted Export Assistance Program, under the interestingly labelled Food Security Act of 1985, to help US producers disadvantaged by unfair competition from abroad. The Country Briefs section of *Foreign Agriculture* for September 1986 lists the following:

Jamaica's programme for local milk production is an 'excellent opportunity to export high-quality U.S. dairy cattle' (ibid.).

Egypt's growing demand for protein meals for animal feed is welcomed as the US is the largest supplier of feeds. A new floating elevator at Abu Keer near Alexandria (built with USAID funds) will facilitate bulk shipments.

Korea's growing rapeseed imports are causing anxiety, as they could cut into US soybeans sales.

Taiwan's cattle industry is expanding, opening the door for US alfalfa sales.

Foreign Agriculture was replaced by *AgExporter* in 1989 and continued to celebrate the links between US agricultural exports and the aid programme. In the 2001 issues we find a good deal about wood exports to the Caribbean and China (January), leather exports to Vietnam (June), food exports of various kinds to Central America and organic produce to Asia (July). A most informative article in September reports that snack food exports from US companies to the Philippines doubled from around $25m. to almost $50m. between 1995 and 2000 (USDA website).

These examples suggest what the cynical reader must have already suspected, and what the open-minded reader may well be beginning to suspect. Is the global food strategy of the US government designed to undermine the capacity of Third World countries to feed themselves, and render them dependent on cash crop earnings to buy food from ever-bulging US silos supplied by fully mechanized US farms? When anything is being grown in the Third World, the US government seems to stand ready to supply all the technical inputs required. This is an understandable conclusion, but it is flawed in one essential respect, namely its state-centrism. The US government as such has no interest in rendering the Third World unable to feed itself. Apart from the assumed humanitarian philosophies of most of its politicians and citizens, nothing is better designed to drive the masses in poor countries into the arms of communists or other malcontents than short-ages of food.[29] It is quite absurd to suggest that the US government, or the government of any other food surplus state, plans such things.

It is not absurd, however, to suggest that, implicitly, TNCs might see their best interests served in such a strategy.[30] TNCs in the grain business, financing its production, trans-porting it around the world, building handling facilities, processing it, breeding fine seeds, developing GM crops, might well consider that the inhibition of Third World grain production will maximize their profits. They might also, and in a perverse way, quite sensibly believe that if US farmers can produce grain cheaper (in economistic if not ecological terms) than farmers in the Third World then it will also be in the interests of poor people to participate in such a global food system. In this they will find enthusiastic allies within the Third World in the political sphere, in the bureaucracy, and in business circles, who might prefer cash crops. As Tullis and Hollist pointed out in the introduction to their book on the international political economy of food: 'Urban-biased policy makers frequently have fostered an increase in exports in order to earn foreign exchange without much regard for impacts on rural employment, nutrition, migration, or domestic food security. Until now, fostering economic growth through export expansion has been the easiest and safest thing to to do politically' (1986: p. viii). We can be sure that most members of the transnational capitalist class in the Third World are urban-based and urban-biased and that they cultivate their allies in the rural sector with care.

Cash crop exports are politically safe in the sense that hard-currency earnings allow Third World governments to buy in cheap grain to feed their urban populations, and relieves them of the problems of ensuring adequate food supplies from what sometimes appears to be a permanently disgruntled peasantry. Cash crops can also, of course, be commercially very lucrative, but only when they are acceptable on the world market. This is rarely under the control of the direct producer, the farmer, but is increasingly coming under the control of the TNC conglomerates that manage the global food system. The case study by Sanderson (in Tullis and Hollist 1986: ch. 5) on the emergence of the World Steer is a good illustration of this process.

The world steer, like the world car, emerged over the last decades through an inter-national standardization of producer technology and a specific set of social relations. These are transnational in scope (combining feedlot technology developed by TNCs in the USA, antibiotics developed by TNCs in Europe, and the market in Japan for boxed beef); and based on international standards for consumption and trade. This is not synonymous with First World domination, for domestic firms in Brazil, Mexico, and Argentina are also participants in the political economy of the world steer. 'The homogenization of tastes for certain products (and the productive processes they imply) shows that there is little difference in the creation of a luxury commodity for foreign consumers and its creation for domestic elites at the expense of the rural poor' (Tullis and Hollist 1986: 127). There are two very important points here. First, the global standardization of taste is global only in a class sense. Capitalist agribusiness has yet to make high-quality beefsteak available on a regular basis for all the inhabitants of the rich countries, let alone those in the poor countries.[31] Second, the system tends to work for better-off foreign consumers and domestic elites by making life more difficult for the rural poor. For example, as Mexico exports more and more live cattle for processing in the USA, the hides and by-products traditionally used by poor Mexican consumers and artisans are now being reimported for sale at much higher prices.[32] This raises two questions. Why should the TNCs produce what the poor need? Who is to determine what the poor in the Third World really do need?

Mindful of questions such as these, many Third World governments have tried to establish food policies in order to ensure an acceptable level of food security over the medium and long term. With few exceptions, they have turned to the TNCs for help in this daunting task. Consequently, some transnational economic practices have increased the capacity of Third World countries to feed themselves. But even in such cases, there are those who argue that it is the interests of the capitalist global system that are being primarily served, even if some of those who are being exploited do derive some benefits. In this limited way, some development eventually filters down—the largely discredited but still very popular trickle-down theory beloved of neo-liberal economists and policy makers.

Sano's book on food in Nigeria demonstrates how a government's attempt to cut its food imports by stimulating domestic production led to an increasing dependence on other imports, especially fertilizer and machinery. The TNCs control research and production of new seed varieties and, as many studies have argued, the so-called Green Revolution was managed in large part through the TNCs and ended up benefiting the rich farmer and merchant classes, and increasing the poverty of the rural masses.[33] Even some apparently successful agricultural projects are suspect: 'though they might be instrumental in reducing the level of food imports in the course of the next five to ten years, they will increase Nigerian dependency on foreign-manufactured commodities and know-how . . . imports like fertilizers, pesticides and agricultural machinery' (Sano 1983: 66). In this case, dependency moves from the primary level of food imports to a secondary level of technical inputs, and then to a tertiary level of import substitution plants run by the TNCs. As with import substitution in Latin America and parts of Asia, the heavy costs of imports sustained by these projects seriously reduced their economic benefits for Nigerian farmers and the poor in general. All too familiar are state government claims that 'contracts for machinery and equipment were primarily awarded to foreign firms at overvalued prices, even when the items were available in Nigeria, and that the training of the Nigerian staff in the project was insufficient to enable it to take over the project' (Sano 1983: 71).

GENETICALLY MODIFIED CROPS

The criticisms that Sano made of the Nigerian food system in the 1980s are ominously echoed by critiques that are made today of the concerted attempt to solve the food problems of the world by genetically modified (GM) crops. TNCs, notably Monsanto, despite the support of many globalizing politicians, bureaucrats, and professionals, have been roundly condemned for the methods they have used to introduce GM crops and their attendant technical inputs into traditional agricultural systems. Leaving aside the crucial and still very controversial question of whether or not GM crops actually could put an end to hunger and malnutrition on planet Earth, their social relations of production and distribution under the conditions of capitalist globalization suggest that they are more likely to increase than eliminate the crises of class polarization and ecological unsustainability (see Chataway *et al.* 2000; Lappe and Bailey 1999). 'What is particularly interesting about genetic engineering in agriculture is the wide variety of social movements opposed to it' (Reisner 2001: 1401).

In an important study on agricultural biotechnology for the Third World, Arends-Kuenning and Makundi (2000) argue that as the benefits of the Green Revolution (GR) are slowing down the new Biotechnology Revolution (BR) could be of great significance. These differ in that while the GR was mainly carried through by the public and non-profit sector, the BR is dominated by the private commercial sector. The most controversial aspect of the BR is the ability to produce genetically engineered (transgenic) crops. While most of the attention has been on the terminator gene and other scares (see A. Reisner, in Isserman 2001), genetic engineering can also produce plants with added micronutrients like vitamin A, iron, and zinc (all deficient in poor people's diets) and vaccines, for example against polio.

The first transgenic crop was virus-resistant tobacco in China. By the late 1990s, soybeans accounted for over half of all transgenic crops, corn about 11 per cent, plus small amounts of cotton, canola, potatoes, squash, and papaya. Over 70 per cent of GM crops are bred for herbicide tolerance, 22 per cent for insect resistance, and most of the rest for both. As of 1998, of the twenty-two proprietors registering new varieties, nineteen were private corporations and three were public (Arends-Kuenning and Makundi 2000).

About 10 per cent of transgenic trials take place in the Third World. China, for example, is expected to enter joint ventures with private corporations for transgenic rice resistant to stem borers. From 1996 to 1999 the global transgenic crop area rose from 2.8 to about 40 million hectares (more than 70 per cent was in the USA, 17 per cent in Argentina, and 10 per cent in Canada). Arends-Kuenning and Makundi point out that the similarity between the transgenic crop patterns in the First and the Third Worlds is disturbing in that many Third World staples are ignored, suggesting an inappropriate transfer of technology. Of the three most important Third World crops (rice, wheat, and corn) only corn is being developed and even here it is not certain that this will be very useful for farmers in the Third World given the common pests, lack of scientific infrastructure, and distribution systems found in the poorer countries.

The main lessons learned from the GR were that public and non-profit bodies helped reduce numbers of hungry people from 1,000 million in the 1960s to around 800 million in the 1990s, despite doubling of the world population. Poor farmers could have benefited from the GR, though few did because of lack of education, dependence on irrigation and chemical fertilizers, and lack of access to credit (see also FAO 2001). Further, the GR often ignored the needs of women. For example, in Tunisia women preferred hard varieties of wheat for couscous instead of the new soft varieties; and short-stalked rice and wheat (less vulnerable to storms) meant less straw for thatching, mat-making, and fodder, all important sources of income for rural women. However, in northern India the GR motivated men to seek education and they, in turn, looked for educated wives, encouraging families to invest in education for their daughters. The GR also had some serious ecological effects, with evidence to suggest damage to the water table and soils, and health risks resulting from chemical inputs.

Like the Green Revolution, the Biotechnology Revolution has benefits and costs; it also produces winners and losers (Lappe and Bailey 1999). Genetically engineering crops to resist specific insects and fungi could clearly be very beneficial (late potato blight destroys about 15 per cent of the world crop, and in storage a substantial proportion of rice and other grains is destroyed by insects). But the TNCs driving the BR tend to regard such projects as risky and unprofitable, so their focus is on First World problems (as is the case in medical and pharmaceutical research). Most work on problems of the Third World is left to public and non-profit organizations, what the International Rice Research Institute in the Philippines calls New Frontier Projects. At present, Arends-Kuenning and Makundi argue, conventional plant breeding would do more for the yields of poor farmers than transgenics. However, innovations like the new golden rice containing beta-carotene (vitamin A) and potatoes containing vaccines clearly have great potential as does the promise of drought-resistant crops that would reclaim many hitherto unfavourable soils. The Rockefeller Foundation, the Swiss government, and the EU funded a scheme enabling the major life sciences company Astra-Zeneca to give golden rice seedlings free to farmers in the Third World, who will be allowed to earn up to $10,000 without paying royalties. The company will offset this by marketing golden rice in the First World in a range of functional foods (reported in *Financial Times*, 16 May 2000). However, safety precautions around GM crops that are being demanded in the First World are unlikely to be implemented in the Third World (Gibbs 2000, Isserman 2001).

As Table 6.2 shows, most of the patents on gene sequences of food crops are held by private corporations. More than 75 per cent of investment in biotechnology is in the private sector, controlled by six large agribusiness corporations. All over the world, state funding of research is falling, and not very efficient research centres in the Third World are prey to loss of funding in any case. The WTO intellectual property rules (TRIPS) stimulated private investment, Structural Adjustment Programmes encouraged privatization, and increasing commercialization of Third World agriculture attracted TNCs into the most profitable sectors. Arends-Kuenning and Makundi (2000: 333) explain:

Table 6.2 Holders of patents for food crop gene sequences

Company	Crop	% of gene sequence patent applications
Dow	maize	30.3
Du Pont	maize	26.9
	wheat	40.6
Monsanto	maize	4.7
	potato	5.6
	wheat	27.1
AstraZeneca	maize	3.8
	potato	3.2
Rybozyme	potato	71.7
Aventis	wheat	4.9
Novartis	wheat	4.2
Top 5	maize	84.9 (of 2,181)
Top 5	potato	85.7 (of 1,110)
Top 5	wheat	79.6 (of 288)

Note: with the exception of Rybozyme all these are FG500 companies (Monsanto dropped out of the FG500 in 1999).

Source: data compiled from the *Guardian* (15 Nov. 2000).

The private sector does not have incentives to develop varieties that are useful to poor people who cannot afford them or to undertake long-term scientific research that might have a payoff far down the road . . . Because the private sector is guided by profit, it neglects 'orphan crops' [cassava, cowpeas, lentils, millet, sweet potatoes] whose improvement might bring great social benefits but which are not profitable for private sector companies.

These crops were also neglected in the GR. Some of the poorest countries in the world rely on potatoes, for example, but little research is being done on them. The transfer of a virus-resistant potato to Mexico by Monsanto is one exception, but Monsanto has protected its future interests very tightly. In joint ventures between public/non-profits and TNCs, it is often unclear who owns what. Some Third World governments are belatedly trying to protect their plants from TNC predators, for example the struggles over basmati rice in Pakistan (now patented by RiceTec Inc. in Texas) and the neem tree in India. The onward march of biotechnology threatens more of these struggles (Shiva and Moser 1995).

Biotechnology, like all technologies, has its benefits and costs, and produces winners and losers. Given the potential (as yet unrealized) of biotechnology to improve world food supplies and to combat dietary deficiencies and disease relatively cheaply and efficiently, it does no service to those in need to reject it out of hand. There are scientific questions to be answered and, if past experience is any guide, the results will be less awful than the pessimists predict, and less wonderful than the optimists predict. What does seem clear, though, is that the biotechnology that capitalist globalization is creating, driven by the market, will not benefit the poor as much as a biotechnology driven by democratic decision-making. Pitting poor Indian peasants against mighty US agribusiness distorts the real issue.

Criticisms of TNCs based on their foreignness are often confused with those based on transnational practices, which domestic firms may share. The choice in the Third World is not always exclusively between foreign exploitative private capitalism and domestic altruistic social movements, in the food or in any other industry. The battle over GM crops in India is between efficient foreign TNCs (Monsanto, for example) working with technically sophisticated indigenous private companies (Maharashtra Hybrid Seed Corporation, its joint venture partner), against groups that reject GM crops in principle based in national and state governments, agricultural associations, and peasant movements (see Joshi forthcoming). The point at issue, in India and everywhere else, is not whether a corporation and its practices are foreign, but to what extent they work in the interests of capitalist globalization (as with the Enron project) or in the interests of the majority of the population. The jury is still out on GM crops, but the issue raises questions about transnational political practices and the transnational capitalist class, to which I now turn.

POLITICAL TRANSNATIONAL PRACTICES IN THE THIRD WORLD

The central problematic for the analysis of political globalization in the Third World is the issue of development strategies, how to move from the underdeveloped or developing state through the NIC stage to, eventually, the goal of advanced industrialization and genuine development. Capitalist globalization, socialist globalization, communism, and developmentalism all make their claim for posterity precisely by promising all those who will listen that they have the magic formula for this transition.[34] Many groups at many levels organize politically to implement development strategies. They operate locally (community organizations, local business groups, and local authorities), nationally (government agencies, industry associations, and national NGOs), internationally (UN, international development banks), and transnationally (globalizing NGOs, the transnational capitalist class). The development strategies that have been most clearly articulated and most actively propagated by modernizing elites of one type or another are usually discussed under the rubric of the developmental state (see Grabowski 1994, Robinson and White 1998, Woo-Cumings 1999). As governments and various other ruling-class elements are almost always the main public actors in the pursuit of development strategies, most of this research is, not unexpectedly, state-centric and much of this focuses on business–state relations (see Maxfield and Schneider 1997).

The basic problem of any government in any society is to secure its own power and/or to get re-elected, with or against modernizing and traditional elites. While conventional theories of modernization and more recent theories of globalization have identified TNCs as carriers of democratic values and practices to the Third World, such views have been powerfully criticized from many quarters. The theory of bureaucratic authoritarianism (BA) elaborated by O'Donnell (1979) was one of the strongest and most influential challenges to the idea that the TNCs have exerted a benevolent influence on economic and political development, particularly in Latin America. BA refers to the tendency of ruling classes in Third World societies to turn to authoritarian solutions with the active or tacit support of foreign corporations in order to implement their development strategies, particularly the project of export-led industrialization which focuses more on social discipline than democratic practices.

This argument suggests that the participation of the TNCs in Third World countries can only be assured when they have an acceptable business climate in which to operate, and that BA regimes are more likely to provide such a climate. Therefore, whether or not TNCs actually intervene in the internal politics of countries in which they invest (sometimes they do, and sometimes they do not), their very presence was said to have predisposed towards BA regimes. It is of great significance that most of the NICs made their most marked economic progress when their polities were strong one-party states, not necessarily totalitarian in the classic sense, but certainly lacking in most of the genuinely pluralistic institutions that characterize advanced industrial societies. This led many people to argue that, under the conditions of capitalist globalization, industrialization was only possible for Third World countries where bureaucratic authoritarian regimes could organize the economy and, particularly, discipline the labour force, to satisfy the demands of the transnational corporations, their local affiliates, and the global market. Bello and Rosenfeld (1990) put forward the thesis that this form of authoritarian development was unsustainable, in political and ecological terms, and the East Asian crisis of the 1990s suggested that there is some truth to this. However, others have argued that TNCs are indifferent to democracy rather than hostile to it (see Becker, in Becker et al. 1987: ch. 3). Perhaps it would be more accurate to say that the TNCs are indifferent to democracy in the Third World as long as the people do not elect genuinely left-wing governments! Experience since the 1990s has shown that TNCs can cope with apparently left-of-centre governments all over the world without too much difficulty.

The most notable feature of transnational political practices in the last decades of the twentieth century was the tremendous upsurge in redemocratization or the transition to democracy in previously authoritarian states. More or less democratic elections took place in the NICs, all over Africa, in Latin America, parts of Asia, and in the New Second World. Research on the prospects for genuine democracy in the Third World (see, for example, Munck 1989, Robinson 1996, Randall and Theobold 1998) and the relationships between capitalism, development, and democracy (Rueschmeyer *et al.* 1992, Robinson and White 1998) moved up the scholarly agenda.

The idea that regimes in Third World countries have institutionalized specific mechanisms for dealing with TNCs, and vice versa, has been conceptualized in terms of the triple alliance between the host state, the TNCs, and the outward-oriented elements in the indigenous bourgeoisie. Studies by Evans (1979) on Brazil, Gillespie (1984) on Egypt, and Ihonvbere and Shaw (1988) on Nigeria, focused on the ways in which transnational triple alliances operated in the countries of the Third World. Building on Cardoso and Faletto (1979) Evans used the idea of the triple alliance to give a concrete class structure to dependent development, but the state loomed large in the analysis. The trends to more and more TNC power and influence that Evans and others discerned in the 1960s have intensified as capitalist globalization has spread. Thus: 'the insertion of Brazil in global markets appears to increasingly subordinate it to the interests of world financial circuits and promote the loss of the state's capacity to control its own development' (Ribeiro and Telles, in Marcuse and van Kempen 2000: 78).

The theory of the comprador bourgeoisie, central to the dependency approach, has fallen into disuse in recent years though there have been various attempts to reconceptualize what it refers to. Sklar's postimperialism theory identified a new class, a managerial bourgeoisie (in Becker *et al.* 1987). This new class was said to have a local wing and a corporate international wing. Compradors identified with the interests of foreign investors whether they were directly employed by them or not, and facilitated the transformation of traditional patterns of consumption and behaviour in the Third World.

This is one important part of what I intend by the concept of the transnational capitalist class (TCC), but with two important differences. First, the theoretical functions of the TCC and the managerial bourgeoisie are quite different. Sklar and Becker argue that the managerial bourgeoisie is the key class in a postimperialist world where the struggle between capital and labour has become less important. This class, in their formulation, encapsulates the best interests, in a developmentalist sense, of the nation. It is engaged in a non-deadly, if not always exactly friendly struggle for business with transnational capital abroad and a relatively consensual, if not always cooperative project for national development at home. The concept of the TCC, on the contrary, is embedded in a theory of the capitalist global system, operating through the transnational practices of the TNCs, as they attempt to achieve a reformation of capitalist hegemony in the Third World.

Second, Sklar's concept lacks a genuinely global dimension, partly because it neglects the culture-ideology sphere and, in particular, it misses the fundamental significance of the culture-ideology of consumerism. This class, whatever we call it, cannot be properly understood and its historic role cannot be adequately explained, outside the critical contradictions of capitalist accumulation on a mass scale, globally: class polarization and ecological unsustainability.

The central issue is whether or not a Third World bourgeoisie can become hegemonic in its own realm and drive towards real development (as in Becker's analysis of Peru's New Bourgeoisie) or whether the only realistic option for Third World bourgeoisies, under the present system of capitalist globalization, is to throw their lot in with the TNCs, as Evans argued for the triple alliance in Brazil. The logical extension of this argument is that some form of interdependence might be possible, where Third World actors could carve out niches for themselves in the crevices that the hegemon TNCs leave unattended. And this is precisely the conclusion that Evans reached in his more recent work on the globalizing of the computer industries of India, Brazil, and South Korea (Evans 1995).[35] He is not alone in this opinion, for it is a short step from the interdependence thesis to a full-blown production-sharing conception of the global system, the positive capitalistic version of international division of labour theory (critically discussed in Sklair 1993: ch. 1) that eliminates any idea that the capitalist mode of production has any exploitative features, globally or locally.

This is also the case for the working class and other subordinate classes. It is not only members of the transnational capitalist class that engage in transnational political practices. Where the TNCs are active in Third World direct investment, in the form of factory production, they naturally augment (and sometimes create) an industrial proletariat. In some cases, TNC jobs are among the best-paid and most highly valued in Third World communities. This led in the 1980s to a new lease of life for the old concept of labour aristocracy and it was attached to the workers who had these jobs (see Lloyd 1982). Since then, the bulk of research on labour and globalization has focused much more on the loss of job security and increasing casualization of the labour force all over the world, the race to the bottom (Brecher and Costello 1994). It is certainly true that in a globalizing world there are multiple labour forces and multiple worlds of labour. 'Nationalization—the use of national political and regulatory resources to constrain the boundaries of markets to overlap with actual national geographical frontiers—leaves labor deeply committed to the nation as its home, however. This is the nub of labor's problems today' (Ross 2000: 89). I return to this issue in Chapter 10 when I discuss the prospects for social movements against capitalist globalization, coalitions of many categories of workers and others whose interests would be best served by other forms of globalization.

THE TRANSNATIONAL CAPITALIST CLASS IN THE THIRD WORLD

The term comprador, from the Portuguese to buy, has its origins in the employment of the domestic servants of white colonialists in India and China. These people would handle the household accounts of their employers and act as go-betweens with the local population. In China, the European trading houses began to employ local Chinese to act as their agents from the middle of the nineteenth century, and the term began to be attached to those who would serve the interests of the foreigner before the interests of their co-nationals.[36] For radicals and nationalists in the Third World, therefore, comprador is a term of abuse and, as a consequence, has lost most of the little value it ever had for analysis. The transnational capitalist class performs quite a different theor-etical function and has fewer of the pejorative connotations that have bedevilled the comprador class. The transnational capitalist class is not identified with any foreign country in particular, or even necessarily with the First World, or the white world, or the Western world. Its members identify with the capitalist globalization and reconceptual-ize their several local and other interests in terms of the capitalist global system.[37] Their political project is to transform the imagined national interests of their countrymen and women in terms of capitalist globalization. What I referred to previously as the com-prador mentality, the slavish attachment to things foreign, is not a necessary component of the ideology of the TCC, but it does occur, especially as Americanization.

Although the comprador class in one form or another has existed for centuries, the transnational capitalist class is a relatively new phenomenon. The basic difference between the two is that whereas the compradors are entirely beholden to TNCs and foreign interests, members of the TCC who originate from outside the First World and/or who are not white may, under certain circumstances, begin to dictate their own terms to those who own and control the TNCs and other important institutions. That this is rarely understood is a direct consequence of the combined influence of state-centrism and the dependency thesis, both of which consistently confuse the power of the TNCs with the power of First World states (usually America) and the weakness of the Third World with the presumed weakness of economic institutions located there. Of course, most TNCs originate in the First World and most Third World economic institutions are weak, but this ignores important exceptions. The numbers of TNCs based in Third World countries, particularly the NICs, has grown rapidly since the 1970s (Lall 1983, Yeung 1994). Now, some Third World globalizing corporations are extremely large and wield considerable influence (Sklair and Robbins 2002).[38] Reporting on big business in Asia, Backman (1999: section 5) speaks of 'President of the Country; Chairman of the Board' (ch. 13) and 'President Soeharto and the *Fortune* 500' (ch. 14).

It is not the nationality of economic institutions or of the classes that dominate them that is the primary consideration in explaining how the global system works, but rather the structural locations of institutions and classes in the system. Frank and Wallerstein's version of the international division of labour may have been accurate for some countries during some periods, but the transformation of capitalism on a global scale in the latter part of the twentieth century has rendered it increasingly less so. This has been obscured because the connections between accumulation in the context of states and the growth of the transnational capitalist class have been rather different in the First and the Third (and also now the New Second) Worlds for a variety of reasons, of which the form of corruption is one.[39]

Members of the transnational capitalist class in the Third World will undoubtedly be connected with foreign TNCs and their local affiliates, though they will not necessarily work for them. They frequently work through their own companies, which may be in a position to compete with TNCs anywhere in the world, or as globalizing bureaucrats, politicians, professionals, or members of consumerist elites. In so far as these people own or control major assets within the capitalist global system or share the interests of those who do, they are members of the transnational capitalist class. The TCC includes frac-tions of old indigenous elites and comprador bourgeoisies, as well as new globalizing capitalists and their allies. Studies such as those of Zaalouk (1989) on Egypt, and Zeitlin and Ratcliff (1988) on Chile illustrate very well the different historical trajectories of capitalist classes in different communities and countries, but they also illuminate the emergence of new groups that become the local affiliates of the transnational capitalist class.

The four groups of people who constitute the local membership of the transnational capitalist class in the Third World have some distinctive characteristics. Expatriate TNC executives in the Third World tend to be from manufacturing or technical backgrounds while their local affiliates tend to be legal, administrative, or financial specialists, though this is changing as more local people are being entrusted with top managerial responsibility by the TNCs (recall the case of Microsoft from Chapter 5). Increasing numbers of TNC executives have come through assembly operations and other corporate functions in First and Third World countries and tend to be increasingly aware of corporate global strategy.

Globalizing state bureaucrats must be seen in the context of the protectionist, import-substituting past of most Third World countries, and periods of open hostility between government and business in some. There is substantial evidence that the balance of power has swung decisively from locally oriented and internally directed to globally oriented and externally directed state bureaucrats since the 1980s all over the Third World. How else can we explain the significant moves towards liberalization of foreign investment regimes in the Third World and postcommunist Europe since the 1980s. Two specific examples bear this out. In Mexico, the decision to join the GATT in 1986 and the coalition between some factions in government and business to push forward the Free Trade Agreement with the USA and Canada (NAFTA) illustrate the trend away from localizers towards globalizers. 'Thus the NAFTA negotiations consolidated and formalized a powerful policymaking coalition between a small number of outward-oriented big business elites and Mexican government technocrats' (Thacker 1999: 72).[40] While it is difficult to imagine a transnational capitalist class in China, the social structures of the open-door policy and the powerful impetus for joining the WTO also illustrate that globalizing bureaucrats and politicians inspired by globalizing corporations, from China and abroad, are in the ascendance (see Nolan 2001, and Chapter 9 below).

In parallel with globalizing bureaucrats, globalizing politicians are to be found in increasing numbers all over the Third World. Not all of these people are wholehearted globalizers, but advancement in modernizing political parties appears to depend more and more on toeing the line on the central issues of economic policy and the political and culture-ideology consequences of it. Similarly, globalizing professionals (lawyers, journalists, consultants, academics, etc.), in so far as they serve the global interests of capital, find places in the transnational capitalist class.[41] Finally, consumerist elites, by which I mean globalizing merchants and those involved in media promotion of consumerism, free market capitalism, modernization in the image of globally branded lifestyles and consumption patterns, play a key role in the transnational capitalist class. (This issue, fundamental to the theory of capitalist globalization, is discussed more fully in the next chapter.)

These, then, are the component parts of the TCC and, if my analysis is correct, ruling groups in the Third World are being transformed as a consequence of the changing nature of the insertion of their communities, countries, and regions into the capitalist global system. How do these groups work in the interests of global capitalism? In one interesting project, Geyikdagi (1984) examined the attitudes of political elites in the Middle East to the TNCs. He found two types, the highly suspicious and the willing business partners. Regimes of the latter type, it appears, tended to be very susceptible to coups. Since the 1960s Third World governments have become better disposed to TNCs 'as they have experienced the benefits derived from foreign investment' (Geyikdagi 1984: 15). It is not clear whether personal benefits or benefits to the development of the host country, or both, is meant. Whatever the case, not only governments in the Middle East appear to be more pragmatic now than in the recent past and although anti-TNC rhetoric has not entirely vanished in public utterances, the line is substantially moderated in regulations for and negotiations with the TNCs.[42] Despite the political problems that basically anti-Western regimes have in dealing with TNCs from the USA and Europe, the desire of elites for leading-edge technology is the crucial test, as Bassiry and Dekmejian (1985) illustrate in the case of the TNCs and the Iranian revolution.

This is only possible where governments and bureaucracies harbour potential members of the transnational capitalist class willing to deal with the TNCs. Even when the political relations between Third World and First World governments are hostile, these individuals can be isolated from particular transnational corporations. Such is the efficacy of propaganda for capitalist globalization that it is rarely capitalism itself that is targeted in such cases, but the symbols of First World, usually American or Japanese or European countries' national power. Local members of the transnational capitalist class can exact a much higher price for their services than the comprador class ever could, for two reasons. First, the stakes are bigger than ever before, because of the expansion of globalizing corporations and their interests in Third World markets. Second, transnational capitalists from the Third World have more choice in deciding whom to deal with than before. This does not necessarily put the economy of the country of origin of the individual member of the TCC in a better position, for the benefits of this changing situation may accrue to the Swiss banking industry, or the real estate markets in California and New York and the Côte d'Azur, as well as the purveyors of super-luxury consumer goods, as in the case of the 'new tribe' of M'Benzis (Mercedes-Benz owners) in Africa. Research on capitalist classes in Africa provide interesting test cases for the emergence of a transnational capitalist class in the Third World.

THE AFRICAN BOURGEOISIE

Lubeck (1987) contrasts the force of internal against external factors in explaining capital accumulation in Africa, showing how the autonomy of indigenous accumulation is opposed to some form of dependency in terms of the economic rationality of the capitalist class in a poor society. It is in the interests of this class that workers can afford to buy the types of products that are easily available in their local markets. Thus:

the internally oriented bourgoisie possesses an objective interest in wage-led rather than externally-determined demand for its products ... productivity increases will extend workers' consumption into new commodities that were once considered luxury goods (motorcycles, housing materials, and small appliances), which in turn will provide new areas of investment for the indigenous bourgeoisie. It is a class alliance that creates an objective link between indigenous capital and labour and one that is also linked to the progressive features of capitalist development. (Lubeck 1987: 14)

This is a sentiment I strongly agree with, but as an argument it has three problems. First, the opposition between wage-led and externally determined demand is more apparent than real. In all but the smallest countries export success, at least in manufactures, depends largely on a solid domestic market. The interests of the internally oriented bourgeoisie may start with wage-led demand. But as the walls of protectionism have tumbled down in one Third World country after another, under the influence of the World Bank and the WTO, externally determined demand becomes more difficult to ignore. The only way around this is through some sort of arrangement with the TNCs.

Second, Nigeria, like most Third World countries, imports most of its motorcycles and motorcycle parts, non-traditional building materials, and appliances. Import substitution or indigenous investment in these products is not unproblematic. And third, although Lubeck does not actually say it, the implication of his argument is that progressive capitalist development is an indigenous, national project. The gist of my argument is that the capitalist globalization leaves less and less space for exclusively national, capitalist projects. It follows that members of the indigenous bourgeoisie who resist incorporation into the transnational capitalist class are, with few exceptions, going to be trapped in a spiral of declining markets, low technology, and uncompetitiveness.

It is easy to ridicule such an argument by pushing it to absurd limits. To avoid this it is necessary to distinguish foreign and transnational, and also autonomous development and national development. Not all of the practices of the transnational capitalist class are transnational. There is still space for genuinely indigenous economic, political, and culture-ideology practices, but the capitalist global system increasingly marginalizes such practices, making them commercially irrelevant. The transnational capitalist class is a bridge between local communities and the capitalist global system, and the more assiduously its members bring transnational practices into what were once the realm of the regional or the local, then the more faithfully they serve the interests of the system and the more capital they accumulate.

Kitching, in an otherwise excellent analysis of the problem of autonomous development, seems to confuse autonomous and national development when he argues that if there is no national capitalist development then the bourgeoisie must be comprador in character (in Lubeck 1987: ch. 2). Confronting the problem of autocentric development he argues that the 'progressiveness of capitalism' may produce 'genuinely transformatory capitalist development (. . . massively raising productivity and the general income level)' without a national bourgeoisie (ibid.: 50). But this reduces the distinction between the national and the comprador bourgeoisie to a quite arbitrary judgement on what constitutes national development.

This returns us to the notion of the objective interests of the capitalist class. The central and common and defining objective interest of all capitalist classes, whether regional, indigenous, national, foreign, or transnational, is the private accumulation of capital. How individual capitalists or groups of them chose to accumulate will have to be explained in terms of personality, entrepreneurial history, and material conditions. Capitalist globalization theory argues that in the latter part of the twentieth century more and more capitalists came to believe that their objective interests were best served through transnational practices. The evidence for this is the phenomenal growth of the presence and influence of the TNCs both within and outside the countries of the First World, and their political expression, the transnational capitalist class (Sklair 2001).

Most of the scholars contributing to Lubeck's book, while discussing African indigenous bourgeoisies, actually confirm this judgement. Swainson concludes a detailed study of indigenous capitalism in Kenya and the export promotion strategy of the late 1970s as follows: 'At this stage, an indigenous bourgeoisie is unlikely to supplant foreign capital in any Third World country, whatever its level of development. A more likely picture is a varying degree of integration and interpenetration' (in Lubeck 1987: 160). Biersteker argues that 'Indigenization [in Nigeria] thus encourages a comprador role for local business in a society already plagued by strong comprador tendencies' (ibid.: 272) and that 'foreign capital has not been seriously threatened by the indigenization exercise' (p. 275). And Campbell demonstrates that indigenization in the Ivory Coast did not really challenge the dominance of foreign capital because to do so would have been to put the mode of accumulation at risk, as the case of indigenization in Nigeria shows (Chapter 4 above). What these cases suggest is that triple alliances between the state, TNCs, and indigenous capitalists are globalizing.

FROM TRIPLE ALLIANCES TO THE TRANSNATIONAL CAPITALIST CLASS

The concept of the transnational capitalist class can be (and has been) criticized on the grounds that a state bureaucracy cannot be called a class. For example, Embong (2000) argues that the concept is overworked. The Marxist definition of class in terms of private ownership of the means of production used to work well for most First World societies, but it always left much to be desired in the analysis of the Second and Third Worlds, where the larger part of the means of production was owned and controlled not by private capitalists but by state or parastatal enterprises. There is some justification for treating those who control these enterprises as capitalists if they manifest certain characteristics. The term state capitalist has often been used to refer to those who run such enterprises in a manner that is virtually indistinguishable from private enterprises, as Chossudovsky (1986) more or less suggests in the case of post-Mao China.

State capitalists and similar groups are often seen as part of the triple alliance between TNCs, the local bourgoisie, and the state bureaucracy. However, where we cannot identify a triple alliance, a society may still be dominated by a transnational capitalist class whose practices are genuinely transnational, whether or not all three parties are represented. Members of the TCC see their interests bound up not only with particular corporations or states but also with the capitalist global system as a whole and see their mission as organizing the conditions under which capitalist globalization can be furthered locally. Members of the comprador class may have admitted that their interests and those of the foreigners they served were antagonistic to those of their countrymen and women. However, members of the transnational capitalist class conceive of their interests and the interests of the capitalist global system that they serve as essential for national development. Indigenization, such as occurred in Nigeria, had the function of transforming a comprador class and/or a triple alliance, formerly identified with foreign TNC interests, into a transnational capitalist class, increasingly identified with the interests of nominal or actual Nigerian transnational corporations. Ake (1985: 175) put this well when he suggested that indigenization may have 'reinforced the division of labour between the Nigerian bourgeoisie (as specialists in maintaining the political conditions of accumulation) and foreign capital (as specialists in production)'.

Evans (1979) argued that the countries of the capitalist core relied on political stability in the semi-periphery (the NICs), in order to assure the continuing accumulation of capital, and that the triple alliance delivered this primarily through state bourgeoisies and the autocratic regimes that nurtured them. On this thesis, state enterprise is the path to local accumulation, but it falls far short of meeting the needs of the masses. Purging this of its state-centrism, we must ask why those who own and control major capitalist assets rely on stability in the Third World and how the transnational capitalist class, whether in the form of the triple alliance or some other grouping, is used to deliver it. The answers to these questions will be found in the analysis of culture-ideology transnational practices and in particular the culture-ideology of consumerism in the Third World, to which I turn in the next chapter.

NOTES

1. A stratified sample from nine countries in sub-Saharan Africa discovered that 75 per cent could define democracy, though 'while international donors and certain segments within the governments of these nine . . . states may be convinced that democracy and free markets go hand-in-hand, the people remain less than convinced' (Mattes and Bratton 2001: 59).

2. A suit against Unocal for knowingly using slave labour in Burma is going through the courts in the USA as I write (**www.laborrights.org**).

3. Utting makes the provocative suggestion that something akin to the UN Centre on Transnational Corporations, disbanded in 1992, would be more useful.

4. For more on Unilever as a globalizing corporation see Sklair (2001: *passim*).

5. This is not, however, an exclusively Third World issue, as similar conditions do occur in parts of the First World (Mitter 1986, Bonacich and Applebaum 2000). The increasing interconnectedness of these work situations is, of course, a direct consequence of capitalist globalization.

6. Not in all cases, however. For Coca-Cola's violations of labour rights in Guatemala see Gatehouse (in Press and Thompson 1989: ch. 3) and in Colombia, see **www.laborrights.org**.

7. Again, state-centrism reduces the value of the analysis. While average wages clearly differ, many low-wage countries have higher-wage sectors and regions, just as many high-wage countries have lower-wage sectors and regions.

8. The terms export-processing and export-oriented zones are less useful than they were as more of the zones are engaging in manufacturing as well as pure assembly activities, and more governments are granting access to domestic markets for the products of these zones. In 1970 there were about twenty zones in ten Third World countries, by the late 1980s there were more than 260 in more than fifty countries (UNCTC 1988: 169–72), and in 1997 ILO estimated that there were over 850. I use EPZ and EOZ interchangeably.

9. For example, a conference on the Maquila Export Industry held in Tijuana, Mexico (IME2000) had many more positive contributions on the maquilas than had been the case in previous decades. This reflects changes in actual research projects and publications.

10. See Visvanathan *et al.* (1997: part 3). This is also the case, of course, in many other industries, for example in the vineyards of Chile (Bee 2000).

11. This isssue is discussed in Tiano (1986) in the context of three explanations of female industrial employment, the integration, marginalization, and exploitation theses. See also Tiano (1994); Pearson (in Elson 1995: ch. 6); Moghadam (in Simai 1995: vol. ii, ch. 7); and Ladino (1999).

12. In fact, in 1984 the government of Mauritius abolished the minimum wage for men but not for women to correct the female bias in EPZ employment (Nababsing, in Kothari and Nababsing 1996: ch. 3). By 2001, cheaper women workers were being imported from China, encouraging 'jobless growth'.

13. Hirata (in Elson and Pearson 1989) usefully compares female and male workers in the French and Brazilian plants of an electronics TNC. See also Garnsey and Paukert (1987: 29–44).

14. The organizations of women working in the Free Trade Zones in Jamaica and the Dominican Republic show the rich variety of paths to empowerment that can be developed (Dunn 1994). See also historical and contemporary accounts of women organizing in Rowbotham and Mitter (1994).

15. This phenomenon is discussed in Sklair (1993). For critical analyses of some of the problems that export orientation raises, see Kaplinsky (1984) and Amin (1997).

16. From *Fortune* magazine in the USA: 'Even in today's red-hot job market, workers who lose a job earn 6% less on average in the new one they land. Others face pressure to take skimpy raises or pay cuts from employers that threaten to move offshore. Even service and white-collar workers are no longer exempt' (Bernstein 2000: 51).

17. On the class interests involved in the campaign to push through NAFTA and their relations to state structures and agents, see Dreiling (2000), and MacArthur (2000). While neither use the term, this is a clear case of the transnational capitalist class in action.

18. There were also twenty-four food and drug store groups in FG500 (2001) led by Carrefour from France, with revenues of almost $60b., followed by companies from the USA, Netherlands, Germany, UK, Japan, France, Belgium, Australia, Canada, and Switzerland; and six beverage companies, led by Coca-Cola and Pepsico.

19. Other chapters in Bryceson and Jamal (1997) that focus on winners and losers are Y. Habtu on landlessness in Ethiopia (ch. 3), and M. Iliya and K. Swindell on Nigeria (ch. 5). See also Araghi (1995) on de-peasantization and Waters (2000) on the persistence of subsistence.

20. For an illuminating discussion on the usefulness of entitlements see the fierce exchange between Peter Nolan and A.K. Sen in the *Journal of Peasant Studies*, 21 (Oct. 1993: 1–40). Bush (1996) takes this argument further. See also Allen and Thomas (2000), particularly the chapter by Crow.

21. See also the sombre report by the Novartis Foundation (funded by the TNC of the same name), in 2000, 'Food Security for a Growing World Population' (Novartis website). While this is a very informative source it should be noted that Novartis is heavily involved in GM food technology and stands to gain commercially from dramatic statements on food crises.

22. A human rights scholar argues: 'As FIAN [FoodFirst Information and Action Networks] insists, a person who dies as a result of government-induced famine is as equally a victim of human rights abuses as one who perishes as a consequence of extra-judicial execution by agents of the state' (Welch 2001: 275). This is true but reflects the general bias in the human rights field toward crimes of the state and relative neglect of crimes of the private sector (see below, Chapter 11).

23. FAO (2001: 1), downloaded from the FAO website on 22 July 2001.

24. These are, of course, generalizations and there are exceptions to all. For example, the land tenure legislation in Eritrea of 1994 gave all whose main source of income was the land lifetime usufruct rights at age 18, regardless of sex, religion, or marital status. For details of the mixed effects of the Green Revolution for poor women, see FAO (2001) and Arends-Kuenning and Makundi (2000).

25. For analyses of the record of the IMF and the World Bank in Africa, compare World Bank (1994) with Logan and Mengisteab (1993), Brown (1995), and Brydon and Legge (1996).

26. For an ambitious attempt to work out the positive effects of population increase, see Dyson (2001)

27. As there have been in many other countries over similar issues, discussed in Walton and Seddon (1994), Walton (1998), Petras and Harding (2000).

28. The World Food Programme of the UN distributes about $300m. of food for emergencies per annum. While dated, Maxwell and Singer (1979) is still useful theoretically.

29. Dom Helder Camara, the Brazilian priest, famously said: 'When I give food to the poor they call me a saint. When I ask why the poor have no food they call me a communist.'

30. The grain surplus has been a problem in the USA at least since the 1930s. See 'Consumer engineering the grain surplus' in Sheldon and Arens (1932). On Cargill and the grain trade, see Kneen (1995).

31. The ubiquitous industrial hamburger is a poor and unhealthy substitute for high-quality beefsteak. For the globalization of beef, see Gouveia (in Bonanno *et al.* 1994: ch. 5).

32. Because of its proximity to the United States there has been much research on TNC export cash cropping in Mexico. See, for example, the case of strawberry imperialism (Feder 1978), and in general Bonanno *et al.* (1994).

33. See Tullis and Hollist (1986: esp. chs. 9–10) where the accuracy of this statement might be assessed. U. Patnaik describes the Green Revolution in India as 'National self-sufficiency combined with mass poverty' (in Bernstein *et al.* 1990: 82). For an optimistic update from a globalizing bureaucrat, see Conway (1998).

34. For developmental communism see Gills and Qadir (1995), and for the post-developmentalist critique, see Rahnema and Bawtree (1997).

35. The centrality of the electronics and computer industries makes them particularly important for questions of Third World development and globalization (Henderson 1989, Dicken 1998: ch. 11).

36. Brown, in his absorbing book about Sino-Foreign Joint Ventures (1986: 27), identifies one Tong King-sing as the first comprador to the Hong Kong firm of Jardines in 1863. Tong helped to establish the China Merchants Steam Navigation Company, which was instrumental in the creation of the Shenzhen Special Economic Zone on behalf of the Chinese government about 100 years later. Jardine Matheson is one of the twelve TNCs from China in the FG500 for 2001.

37. Kagarlitsky (2000) has many penetrating ideas on the relationship between national interest and globalization but I cannot accept his thesis that the global capitalist class is marginal in most societies.

38. In this paper we analyse FG500 TNCs from the Third World. In 2001, there were thirty-three, plus two from Russia.

39. For substantial evidence that corporate-driven corruption is on the increase globally see CornerHouse (2000). This begins with a 1996 quote from the chief procurement adviser for the World Bank: 'Corruption has been going up geometrically over the past 10 years' and continues 'multinationals, supported by Western governments and their agencies, are engaging in corruption on a vast scale in North and South alike'. See also the interview-based study by Herry-Priyono (2001) on corruption in Indonesia.

40. For evidence that this is happening all over Latin America, where most governments appear to want to join NAFTA, see Ochoa and Wilson (2001) and Petras and Harding (2000).

41. See the thesis on technopols in Latin America in Dominguez (1997) and my discussion of it (2001: 137–8).

42. The contributors to Moran (1993) confirm the trend to more friendly relations between Third World governments and TNCs.

Chapter 7

THE CULTURE-IDEOLOGY OF CONSUMERISM

The dominant paradigm in the study of development in the 1950s and 1960s was modernization theory, based on the polar opposites of traditional and modern. Its underlying idea was that in order to develop, the countries of the Third (and Second) World would have to become more like the countries of the First World in their economic, political, and value systems. The first two requirements seemed theoretically unproblematic. Some form of free enterprise capitalist economy and some form of pluralist democracy were clearly called for. However, apart from some rather vague ideas about the need for individual achievement and entrepreneurial spirit, following the lead of Max Weber, the system of values necessary for development remained elusive. Many theorists put their faith in the virtue of innovation to transform the traditional into the modern, but experiences with innovative doctrines of religious fundamentalism, for example, persuaded most development theorists that it is not innovation as such, but what is being innovated that is the issue.

CONSUMERISM AND PRODUCERISM

It should be obvious from what has been argued above that my own approach to values and development is that the value-system that has been most successfully put in place for the transition to capitalist modernization and subsequently capitalist globalization is the culture-ideology of consumerism. In the 1970s, Wells suggested that the concept of modernization needed to be split analytically and replaced by the concepts of consumerism and producerism. Wells defined consumerism as the increase in consumption of the material culture of the developed countries, and producerism as increased mobilization of a society's population to work, and to work more productively in the non-consumerist sector of the economy. Thus it followed that 'development requires the maximization of producerism' (Wells 1972: 47) and that consumerism is 'basically antithetical to development' (p. 48). He created a useful typology distinguishing four types of societies (p. 195): high producer-consumer (overdeveloped hedonistic), high consumer and low producer (declining parasitic), low producer-consumer (underdeveloped traditional), and high producer and low consumer (ascetic developmental).

In the 1970s it was not difficult to name names. High producer-consumer societies were obviously those in North America and Western Europe who, as we shall see, have now generated politically important movements that have challenged overdeveloped hedonism (culture-ideology of consumerism). Societies low on both measures, particularly the Fourth World of the very poorest countries in Africa and Asia, score low not necessarily because of conscious choice but because of lack of means of production and lack of spending power. Elites in these countries, small as they are, consume prodigiously and their numbers have grown rapidly in recent decades, while the position of the poorest in these countries stagnates or, in some cases, has been deteriorating—the class polarization effects of capitalist globalization. The only type difficult to identify is the high consumer–low producer, the stagnant or declining parasitic society. Some commentators, obsessed with the hollowing out of US corporations, enormous trade deficits, and the loss of some traditional export markets, slapped these labels on the USA, but this is patent nonsense. Although Japan's productivity in the automobile industry, and South Korea's in the steel industry, and Hong Kong's in the apparel industrial may have been superior to the USA at times, at the beginning of the twenty-first century the total GNP of the United States (about ten trillion dollars) was still double that of its nearest challenger (Japan), about as much as the rest of the First World combined, and more than all the economies of the Third World!

The final type of society in Wells's typology was the high producer–low consumer. This is where the most dramatic changes occurred in the last decades of the twentieth century. Some communist and socialist societies, particularly China during the period of the Cultural Revolution (1966–76), North Korea since its establishment, and Cuba during its periods of moral incentives (see Cole 1998), fit the description of ascetic developmentalism. In these cases, high producerism, especially the promotion of heavy industry and capital goods, was combined with low consumerism, the result of policies to hold down increases in the disposable income of the masses (see Gills and Qadir 1995). As we shall see in Chapter 9, since the 1980s a substantial proportion of China's urban and coastal populations have lurched dramatically from a state of low to much higher consumerism while attempting to sustain a high level of producerism. Writing in the 1970s, Wells argued that premature consumerism (an interesting if controversial concept), can never lead to development, even when promoted by an industrial policy based on import substitution. The conclusion that he draws is that those who genuinely want development should encourage coercive producerist elites. There are few today who would consider China's so-called Gang of Four to be a proper model for developmental leadership!

Catholicism and Islam have also preached anti-consumer messages. Pope John Paul II often attacked the spiritual emptiness of consumerist society. In Iran, the Ayatollah Khomeni, the leader of the Shia Muslim community, promoted the concept of *gharbzadegi* (variously defined as Westoxication, Westitis, Euromania, Occidentosis, plague from the West) and this was particularly applied to Westernizing women. Moghadam quotes an Iranian cleric to the effect that Western dress for women 'is a product of the corrupt Western capitalist societies . . . one of the means they use to manipulate human society and stimulate them by this force to become consumers of their products' (Moghadam 1993b: 173). She cites the Preamble to the Iranian Constitution of 1979: 'A woman . . . will no longer be regarded as a "thing" or a tool serving consumerism and exploitation' (p. 174). In Iran and other Muslim countries women were warned that fashion clothing, cosmetics, smoking, drinking, and Hollywood role models 'made her easy prey for commercialization and contamination by the West. The solution to this vulnerability to the slings and arrows of the imperialists was compulsory veiling' (p. 175). Moghadam, in showing how and why many educated 'empowered Islamist women' still accept the logic of this argument, illustrates the complexities of relationships between capitalism, culture, and consumerism.

Wells's own substantive research on the effects of television in Latin America, documents, not surprisingly, that programmes from studios in the USA were a strong influence for consumerism and a very weak influence for producerism in Latin America. Again, we must be careful not to fall into the trap of state-centrism. It is difficult to see how consumerism as opposed to producerism can be said to serve the national interests of the USA in the Third World. However, it is very easy to see how consumerism can be said to serve the interests of the capitalist global system, dominated as it was for much of the twentieth century by TNCs of US (and European) origin. The dynamic for permanently increasing the consumption of the products of capitalist enterprise feeds through the profit-maximizing practices of each individual unit to the system as a whole, irrespective of the consequences for the communities in which it happens to be located or the planet as a whole, and those who lose out in the struggle for decent standards of living (Redclift 1996). Capitalist globalization in the Third World depends on the successful promotion of the culture-ideology of consumerism among people with no regard for their ability to produce for themselves, and with only an indirect regard for their ability to pay for what they are consuming. Development assistance (aid), for example, moves funds from taxpayers in richer countries to consumers in poorer countries, but not always for appropriate forms of consumption, not to speak of what is siphoned off in corrupt deals or stolen. In this sense, consumerism has nothing to do with satisfying biological needs, for people will seek to satisfy these needs without prompting from anyone else, but with creating what can be called induced wants.

Marcuse, in his now neglected classic *One Dimensional Man* (1964), discusses false needs in a similar context. His argument seems to me to betray an intellectual arrogance stretching back at least to Rousseau of forcing people to be free (which I share to some extent) but which must be avoided if the argument has to have any cross-cultural credibility. By induced wants I mean to suggest that after biological needs have been satisfied there is an almost limitless variety of wants that can be induced. Patterns of socialization either structure these wants in the interests of those who wish to exploit them for personal gain, for example the transnational capitalist class or the leaders of other-worldly religions, or encourage individuals and groups to follow their own arbitrary tastes.

The imperative of capitalist globalization implies that people have to be taught how to consume, in the special sense of creating and satisfying induced wants. Advertising, the main channel through which the culture-ideology of consumerism is transmitted, has always projected itself as an educational or at very least an informational practice, and the same claims are made for the Internet. As TV and the Internet continue their apparently relentless penetration of our lives, we can only speculate what Marx would have thought about the fact that in the homes of almost every worker and many peasants there is now a flickering box churning out the words and images of capitalist consumerism day and night, every day and every night. The study of the mass media in the Third World and their relationship with advertising is the obvious place to begin to search out the ways in which the culture-ideology of consumerism works. It is no accident that most of the research on this issue has been done within the framework of theories of cultural and media imperialism.

CULTURAL IMPERIALISM AND MEDIA IMPERIALISM

In capitalist or quasi-capitalist societies, processed food, drink, tobacco, cars, personal and household products, and leisure-related items take up most advertising revenue. Though the patterns differ from country to country and between newspapers and magazines, radio, television, billboard advertising, and the Internet, the vast majority of goods and services advertised are consumer rather than producer goods and services. Most readers will probably react to this statement: so what? If this is indeed the case then it is a measure of the success of consumerism, not a comment on how obvious the statement actually is. Why is it more natural to advertise to persuade people to buy consumer products, particularly when what is being sold are minor differences (what the adpersons call the unique selling point) than to advertise to persuade manufacturers to buy goods and services that would improve their processes of production? Trade journals are full of the latter, but they are a tiny proportion of total advertising expenditures. So consumer advertising is not more natural than advertising producer goods, it only seems so within the culture-ideology of consumerism.

It appears to be even less natural that consumer advertising should so predominate over producer advertising in the Third World because one would suppose that those most likely to be able to purchase goods would be the business community and the government, in the market for producer goods, and not the mass of the population. Nevertheless, consumer goods are just as heavily promoted in the urban areas of some Third World countries as in the First. This apparent paradox is often explained in terms of how cultural imperialism is reproduced through media imperialism. Both of these ideas are highly controversial.

The cultural imperialism thesis argues that the values and beliefs of powerful societies are imposed on weak societies in an exploitative fashion (see, for example, Golding and Harris 1997, Chadha and Kavoori 2000). In its neo-Marxist version, this usually means that First World capitalist societies impose their values and beliefs on poor Third World societies. The thesis has also been used to try to explain the consequences of the deleterious influence of the US media on rich countries, like Canada (Lee 1980: ch. 4), Australia, and the world in general (Tunstall 1977). Kivikuru (1988), in an interesting analysis of media in Finland, suggests that media systems developed relative autonomy through a process of modelling on media in the USA, doing more or less what is done there but with some local variations. Media imperialism follows logically from cultural imperialism. If US or Western control of culture is admitted, then it is clearly achieved through control of the mass media, which creates the conditions for conformity to the dominant culture and limits the possibilities of effective resistance to it. Theories of cultural and media imperialism are strongly held and strongly disputed.[1]

There are four main types of criticisms of cultural and media imperialism theories. First, what is often identified as US cultural and media imperialism is really just advanced professional practice. Second, there are quite different processes at work in different countries and cultural variations can be more important than global patterns. Third, all countries develop internal cultural and media systems that counteract the external influences of cultural products from the USA, Europe, Japan, etc. Fourth, flows from the USA

Figure 7.1 D-Day for cultural imperialism
Source: © Andy Singer (**www.andysinger.com**)

may work for as well as against national autonomy.[2] The cartoon by Singer (Figure 7.1) is an ironic comment on the 'invasion' of cultural imperialism.

It will be immediately obvious that most of this debate is posed within the terms of the state-centrist paradigm and, as such, few could disagree that it is possible to challenge US hegemony successfully in a wide variety of ways. As in most industries, economies of scale tend to lead to the most efficient practices. (Let us not complicate matters at this stage by asking efficient for whom or by noting that even this truism is being challenged by new flexible production methods in some science-based industries.) The largest media industry by far is based in the USA and its practices are invariably taken to be state of the art. In discussing the relationship between US and Third World media, Lee (1980: 82) asserted that: 'coproduction has been largely limited to Anglo-American interests . . . As a mockery to cultural diffusion, the coproduced products have been deliberately Ameri-canized'. He explained this in terms of the triumph of the US-driven commercialization of global TV, one of whose consequences is 'a genuine pressure on local talents to con-form to the arbitrary "world standard" of technical excellence which may be at variance with native cultural needs' (p. 102). This has been changing since Lee wrote.

One can certainly find co-productions that are not particularly Americanized, some national media systems that vary significantly from others in being less Americanized, domestic elements that successfully resist Americanization attempts, and even cases where Americanization does seem to promote cultural autonomy. The glasnost-inspired Americanization of Soviet TV (see Barnathan 1989) and subsequent developments in postcommunist Europe have elements of the latter. The introduction of the VCR into Turkey and its use by the Kayapo people in Brazil have had varying effects on the preservation of local cultures (see Ogan 1988).[3]

If we replace Americanization with capitalist consumerism in the argument, we can see that there is a double process of culture-ideology transformation going on here. Capitalist consumerism is mystified by reference to Americanization, while Americanization, loosely understood as the method of the most successfully productive economy in human history, gives its imprimatur to capitalist consumerism. The centrality of the American dream for the project of capitalist globalization is a staple component of the globalization debate. Contrary to expectations borne of the origins of capitalism in north-west Europe, the USA and not the European core has become synonymous with capitalism in its global incarnation. The globalization of capitalism, thus, is imagined as the Americanization of capitalism, the culture-ideology of consumerism its value-system and rationale. But to identify cultural and media imperialism with the USA, or even with US capitalism, is a profound and a profoundly mystifying error. It implies that if American influence could be excluded then cultural and media imperialism would end. This could only be true in a purely definitional sense. Americanization itself is a contingent form of a process that is necessary to capitalist globalization, the culture-ideology of consumerism.[4] This perspective is supported by the critique of media imperialism in Asia by Chadha and Kavoori (2000). Media imperialism, they argue, ignores the strength of national gatekeeping policies (the Six Nos in China and restrictive legislation in India, Indonesia, *et al.*). It ignores the dynamics of audience preference, demonstrating that local shows are much more popular than imports (this is often a question of language, as the formats of imports are often copied, forcing foreign companies to localize production). Lastly, the local competition to media and electronic TNCs is growing and becoming more sophisticated, as domestic producers export to their diasporas and neighbours (from India and Mexico, for example). The Indian public enterprise Bharat Electronics Ltd, for example, beat off the challenge of companies from Europe, the USA, and the NICs to win a contract to digitalize Nepal TV. However, all that this really shows is that Third World media are becoming more like First World media, 'a pattern of increasing commercialization and a concomitant challenge to public broadcasting . . . audiences are increasingly viewed and targeted as consumers rather than citizens' (Chadha and Kavoori 2000: 428).[5]

However, the thesis of an American-driven cultural imperialism dies hard. The link between Americanization and cultural dependence began with the Hollywood movie industry cartel in the 1920s and the star system on which it was based. The way in which this was achieved is a paradigm case of the interrelationships between the economic, the political, and the culture-ideology spheres, structured by the economic interests of those who owned and controlled the industry and the channels through which its products were marketed and distributed globally (see Maltby 1995). Hollywood and the advertising industry based in Madison Avenue, New York, influenced the early years of mass culture all over the world. Outside the USA, as Smith (1980: 45) argued: 'advertising has been unable to manifest itself as a source of independent patronage of indigenous media because of American dominance in the advertising industry.' The theories of the media produced by Hollywood were based on a single mass market, as later theories of global standardization of production also were. However, this distorts the reality of the Third World, let alone the First and New Second Worlds. Smith (1980) points out that in Asia in the 1970s there were more than 140 English language daily newspapers that soaked up most of the elite-oriented advertising revenue and set the standards of modernization and Americanization for everyone.[6] Today we can add the overwhelming influence of TV, dissemination of Hollywood blockbuster movies, and the Internet. In a penetrating post-colonialist analysis of the media in India, Parameswaran (1997) shows how English-language media discourses contribute to the formation of urban middle and upper classes.

This is nicely, though perhaps unwittingly, illustrated by a study of telenovelas, Latin American soap operas, by Rogers and Antola (1985). They show that in Latin America, hours of imported TV programmes actually declined on average between 1972 and 1982 and that the Peruvian soap opera *Simplemente Maria* enjoyed a phenomenal success all over Latin America. The show was tied in with the sales of Singer sewing machines and this, according to Rogers and Antola, proved that large audiences and profits could be made 'while at the same time promoting an educational theme that contributes to national development' (p. 31). The educational theme was that a slum girl who gets a job with a rich family can become an important fashion designer, but it is not clear exactly how this contributes to national development! Rogers and Antola also comment on the largely Mexican Spanish (language) International Network (SIN), which began to reverse media imperialism by sending Spanish language programmes to US Chicano and latterly wider audiences. This conclusion is true only in the state-centrist sense inherent in the theory of cultural and media imperialism. What the success of *Maria* and SIN actually demonstrates is the triumph of consumerism, whether produced by North or South Americans. The soap opera *Oshin*, from Japan, has been broadcast in around fifty countries and its enthusiastic reception from Iran to Thailand (Singhal and Udornpin 1997) as well as similar successes for soap operas from Brazil, e.g. in Russia (Oliveira, in Nordenstreng and Schiller 1993) reinforce the thesis that it is not only mass market entertainment from the USA or the West that can successfully cross borders.

In a very useful review of what have come to be known as prodevelopment soap operas, Brown (1992) shows how they have become a truly global phenomenon. Created by Miguel Sabido of Televisa in Mexico in the 1960s, the idea was taken up by the Center for Population Communications-International in New York and introduced into India, where *Hum Log* (We People), a phenomenally successful serial, was the result. This was followed, with varying degrees of success by *Cock Crow at Dawn* in Nigeria, *Tushauriani* in Kenya, *Sparrows don't Migrate* in Turkey, *High Stakes* in Brazil, *Daughter of Eve* in Pakistan, and many others, all carrying (more or less) prodevelopment messages. What Brown fails to discuss is the implications of these soap operas for changing consumption patterns and the connection between the new ways of life, sometimes background but often foreground in these stories, and global capitalist consumerism. The evidence provided by Oliveira (in Nordenstreng and Schiller 1993) for Brazil, and Wilk (1993) for Belize, shows that what the success of Maria and most other prodevelopment soap operas actually demonstrates is the triumph of capitalist consumerism, whoever produces them.

Further confirmation of this is provided in research from South Korea which states unambiguously the ambiguous finding that: 'The extensive consumption of material goods, which is a defining characteristic of the Korean middle class, is a contradiction of Korea's Confucian heritage' (Hart 1993: 42). The point is that the culture-ideology of consumerism both neutralizes and reinterprets cultural traditions in a way that stifles popular opposition. This is one of the most effective techniques of capitalist globalization in apparently hostile cultural climates and has been well understood by policy makers in the United States. A report from the US Committee on Foreign Affairs, 'Winning the Cold War. The U.S. Ideological Offensive' (published as long ago as 1964) argued prophetically:

In foreign affairs, certain objectives can be better achieved through direct contact with the people of foreign countries than with their governments. Through the intermediary of the techniques and instruments of communications, it is possible today to reach important and influential sectors of the population of other countries, to inform them, to influence their attitudes, and may be to succeed in motivating them to certain determined actions. These groups, in turn, are capable of exercising considerable pressure on their governments. (Cited in Mattelart 1978: 12)

Almost forty years later we find the same sentiment expressed, this time in connection with the efforts of the US government and major corporations to bring China into the WTO. 'Opening China's Information Technology market will . . . increase the flow of information among Chinese and between China and the outside world, in ways and in such volumes that no amount of censorship or monitoring can totally control. This cannot but promote the right kind of change in China' (White House, **www.chinapntr.gov** 2000, cited in Nolan 2001: 793).

These conceptions of what it takes to win the war for hearts and minds, clearly a product of corporate thinking (see Figure 7.1 above), are breathtakingly simple and cannot be dismissed out of hand for the good reason that they have been proved correct, in the short run at least. The ideology of free choice and consumer sovereignty may seem crude to the Western cynic but to product-starved consumers in postcommunist Europe and the Third World, as the history of the last decades of the twentieth century demonstrated beyond reasonable doubt, it is a potent force. The message of the 'American' or the 'Western' way of life (including, confusingly, elements borrowed from Latin America, China, India, Japan, and so on) has indeed been transmitted over the heads of governments direct to the people.

This, of course, has been made possible by the technical innovations in communications that were discussed in Chapter 5, nowhere more clearly to be seen than in the events that transformed Eastern Europe, particularly the breaching of the Berlin Wall in 1989. The communications revolution promoted the culture-ideology of consumerism even to those for whom the products were not yet available or who could not realistically be expected to be able to buy them.

LATIN AMERICAN RESEARCH ON THE MEDIA

Since the 1970s, there has been a great flowering of research on these issues in Latin America, stimulated intellectually by the sympathetic critical response to dependency theory and politically by the events in Chile during the period of the Popular Unity government led by Salvador Allende, and also media experiments in Cuba (see, for example, Kunzle 1978; Hamelink 1984: ch. 2) and elsewhere. Roncagliolo, an active participant, has usefully summarized this research in a paper on 'Transnational Communication and Culture' (1986) and reference to this source will serve as an introduction to what is a complex and often physically inaccessible body of work.

Three central questions were posed by the researchers: 'What is the place of culture in the transnationalization process and of communication within cultural processes? What does the transnationalization of consumption consist of, if it signifies something more than the homogenization of demand at the international level? Is there such a thing as a transnational culture, or are there simply internationalized patterns of behavior?' (Roncagliolo 1986: 79). In answering these questions several important themes emerged, namely the study of international news flows (a critique of the mercantile concept of news and the idea of information as a social good); transnational culture as universalization of culture promoted by transnationalization of media; new communications technology (how data processing and telecommunications have changed the ground rules for transnational communications); and the prospects for populist alternative communications.

Roncagliolo proposed a set of propositions that summarized the results of the research effort and at the same time represented an attempt to generate a theory of cultural and media imperialism that is neither state-centrist nor locked into the modernization framework. He starts with the rejection of communicationist bias. It is the medium not the communication that is exchanged in the market, and so it is necessary to distinguish three types of merchandise, namely news, medium, and public, and to recognize the predominance of the secondary market (advertising and publicity) over the primary market (messages). Therefore, it is not arbitrary that the media in Latin America pay more attention to the US market than vice versa. This is not to be confused with the question of the free and balanced flow of information that obsesses some communications theorists.

This leads logically to a second proposition, that the 'transnationalization of messages is not a mechanical consequence of a supposed transnationalization of the media, but is a complex process accompanying the transnationalization of the economy and of politics' (Roncagliolo 1986: 82). The crucial paradox is that local media themselves remain relatively impermeable to transnationalization. Generally, TNCs produce the messages and local companies (increasingly connected with globalizing media corporations) distribute them. However, major corporations ultimately control the system through manipulation of the financial sphere, mainly advertising, which imposes a production-financing pincer on local media systems, though it is always liable to a hostile reaction from nationalist and/or popular forces. The new communications technology accelerates the process of transnationalization but also permits new forms of alternative communications. These can only be defined in terms of the national/popular pole, against transnationalization. Defining them in terms of communications themselves (size, technique, politics) is a profound error, because they can rarely defeat the mass media at their own game. Finding the space for counter-hegemonic communications is the real point.

Thus: 'the transnationalization process, far from being a strictly economic phenomenon involving the expansion of corporations, is defined in the political and cultural spheres—that is, in changes within political and civil society' (Roncagliolo 1986: 86). This phase of capitalism is eroding the nation-state, and the transnationalization of communications that it produces is necessary for the creation of phenomena like the global supermarket and the global village. In this phase, the means of communication tend to become the dominant ideological apparatus and partially displace traditional socialization agencies. Echoing media theorists from all points of the ideological spectrum, Roncagliolo argues that 'the scope and intensity of the media presence have endowed the media with an unprecedented socializing efficiency' (ibid.: 87).

I have presented the ideas of Roncagliolo (and those he reports) at such length because they are an unusually clear and early expression of two points that are at the core of my own argument, in contrast to most media research which sidesteps the issues. First, Roncagliolo avoids state-centrism, and this permits a more plausible theory of cultural and media imperialism based not on Americanization, which can easily be disproved, but on the culture-ideology of consumerism, for which the evidence is much stronger. Second, he problematizes the transnationalization of consumption very fruitfully by distinguishing it from the homogenization of international products. In this way he does what I have been trying to do, namely to detach consumerism from the products themselves and to connect it (and them) to the interests they serve in the capitalist global system. Similar themes are developed in a distinctive fashion by Garcia Canclini (2001), adding the dimensions of hybrid cultures, identity as a co-production and the place of the popular in Latin American cultural space.

The cultures of South America are, of course, very heavily influenced by the cultures of North America. One might argue that the culture-ideology of consumerism that I have portrayed here is specific to the American continent. Research from elsewhere suggests that this is not the case. A study of a Cairo neighbourhood by Zayed illustrates the global dimensions of consumerism in an entirely different setting. He argues: 'It is through consumerism that [traditional society] partly becomes westernized and "modernized" . . . incursion of the capitalist system into the periphery entails two processes: growing intensification of market relations, accompanied by the intensification of consumerism and the diffusion of mass culture; the concentration and differentiation of production' (Zayed 1987: 288). In this research site, a mixed poor area of Cairo, the 'flow of foreign commodities plays an increasing role in the satisfaction of the needs of even the poorest strata' (p. 295). The adoption of consumer culture functions on three contradictory levels. First, the choice of cheap imported goods can be economically rational for poor consumers; second, consumerism 'is used by the people whom it subordinates as a veil to obscure the difficult material conditions in which they live' and it functions as a 'symbol of existence in contrast to the process of degradation which is also an outcome of the subordinating nature of consumerism' (p. 299). Zayed's argument implies that once the culture-ideology of consumerism is adopted, poor people cannot cope economically, and a mode of resistance must develop. In the Muslim case this mostly manifests itself in religious extremism, whose target is as often Americanization as it is consumerism as such.

The research of Zayed advances understanding of the culture-ideology of consumerism as a transnational practice one important step. It demonstrates that people are not cultural dopes who mindlessly obey the instructions of an exploitative social order, even when these instructions are effective on a subliminal level. People, particularly poor and enterprising people in the Third World, adopt the culture-ideology of consumerism for easily understandable reasons. In some circumstances, this is the only economically rational option open to them. It is often (perhaps always) a trap but one that is entered not out of stupidity or ignorance but out of a lack of viable alternatives. It is a trap similar to the one that peasants enter when they feed seedcorn to their starving children. They have no viable alternative in the capitalist global system. (And that is why it is urgent to think about alternatives to capitalist globalization.)

The culture-ideology of consumerism lacks this sort of drama and immediacy, of course. It consists of practices that penetrate a society over a long period of time and in a variety of ways. While small minorities all over the world have criticized local versions of consumerism and the culture-ideology that promotes it, it is only very recently that it has been conceptualized as a global problem. This has tended not to happen as a direct critique of consumerism itself, but as a Third World protest at what was referred to above as cultural and media imperialism. One consequence was the call for a new world information order.

THE NEW WORLD INFORMATION ORDER

Research on a new world information and communications order got under way in the 1970s, particularly through agencies such as UNESCO. This was conceptualized as a communications revolution for the Third World, for example in an interesting collection of essays edited by Kumar (1980), which dealt with global knowledge systems and contained discussions on the ways in which TNC control over book publishing, news agencies, vocational training, and education were already having profound effects on Third World cultures. Interest in these questions intensified in the 1980s and the struggle for control of the electronic media was reflected in a growing volume of research on communications in the Third World (see Stover 1984; Jefkins and Ugboajah 1986; Reeves 1993; Boyd-Barrett and Rantanen 1998; Tehranian 1999). Whereas political imperialism and economic neo-colonialism had focused attention on the economic and political consequences of First World hegemony over the Third World countries within their various spheres of influence, the communications revolution of the 1980s focused attention on the culture-ideology sphere (see Becker et al. 1986).

In the field of information technology (IT), in particular, there have been tremendous quantitative and qualitative advances. Innovative technologies have created new services, new occupations, and new cultural goods, such as cable television, video, mobile phones, and the Internet. In their *Global Media Atlas* Balnaves et al. (2001) provide a wealth of data about the extent and rapidity of the diffusion of these media all over the world. Castells's enthusiastically received three-volume work had labelled this the Information Age. Volume One, *The Rise of the Network Society*, prompted the *Economist* magazine, an influential mouthpiece of the transnational capitalist class, to proclaim him: 'the first significant philosopher of cyberspace' (Castells 2000: back cover).[7] In all these areas, the opportunities for hegemonic control are obvious and, indeed, have been enthusiastically seized by major TNCs, and members of the transnational capitalist class and their local affiliates everywhere. In China, though, the situation is less clear-cut (Nolan 2001: ch. 11).

In *Transnationals and the Third World: The Struggle for Culture*, Mattelart (1983) had identified five theoretical stages through which the analysis of the 'Transnational Apparatus of Production of Cultural Commodities' advanced. He conceptualized the stage reached in the second half of the twentieth century in terms of what the writers of the Frankfurt

School had termed the culture industry.[8] Spanning everything from TV through tourism to advertising it seeks to transform the global audience into consumers of transnational commodities through the propagation of a set of self-serving notions of development, communication, organization, daily life, and change (see also Mattelart 2000). There are some who would regard the views of Mattelart (and the Frankfurt School) on this issue as one-sided and lacking in acknowledgement of the relative autonomy of creative talent in the Third World (see Lazarus 1999) and the capacity of institutions and individuals in the Third World to hold on to their own cultures and develop new forms for themselves. Nevertheless, as scholars with professional experience in the media like Bagdikian (1989) and Hermann and McChesney (1997) have documented, by the 1990s the TNCs that largely control the new technologies had created opportunities to reconstruct cultural practices and products on an unprecedented scale in the interests of capitalist globalization. A European Commission study of the mid-1990s 'maps the way in which mergers, acquisitions and partnerships between 1991 and 1994—worth about $90 billion—are linking telecoms network providers with a broad array of new and traditional media, such as electronic information services, publishing, cable television and broadcasting' (Winseck 1997: 242, n. 5, as documented in Table 4.1 above). The extent to which the TNCs have actually seized these opportunities and the extent to which elites and cultural gatekeepers in the myriad communities of the Third World collude or resist the reconstruction of their cultures is still an open question. There has been a considerable amount of research on the issue.

The World of the News study, for example, was carried out by thirteen separate research teams, and another team from the United States covering sixteen different media systems, monitoring newspapers and broadcasting in twenty-nine countries in 1979. Each news item was coded by location, source, position, and nationality of actor, topic, and theme. Politics and regionalism dominated and there was not much cross-bloc coverage. A symposium in a major communications journal on the project usefully illustrated the different conclusions that could be drawn from such research. One participant concluded that the 'overall pattern of attention paid to certain kinds of events was remarkably similar' (Sreberny-Mohammadi 1984: 125); and another claimed that the 'pseudo debate' over media bias was exposed by the research. Lack of interest in what other people are doing rather than a lack of information is the issue, and while coverage may be accurate though unbalanced: 'It is instructive to note how little of the news contained any themes' (Stevenson 1984: 234) proving, presumably, that the objective standards of professional journalism are universally maintained. Stevenson concludes: 'Too much of the New World Information Order debate has focussed on assertions that were probably never true and are certainly no longer true. This study helps clear the air of the pseudo debate' (ibid.: 236).

Nordenstreng, who thought up the project in the first place, clearly disagreed. He complained that 'The final project was dominated by "vulgar" categories that capture ad hoc aspects of the media content, rather than a comprehensive image carried by the content . . . mainly determined by various pragmatic aspects—not least of which was the need to get a minimum common core of hard quantitative evidence across various national media systems' (Nordenstreng 1984: 238). Social scientists will recognize this as the typical positivist dilemma. Nordenstreng demonstrates the point well with his account of qualitative differences between reports in the *New York Times* and *Pravda* of the

SALT II nuclear disarmament negotiations in the 1980s. On the vulgar criteria used in the study, however, the reports were evaluated quite similarly.

In broadcasting, First World TNCs have effectively controlled global flows for decades, and barriers to entry remain formidable (Herman and McChesney 1997). A sixty-nine country study of international TV flows in the early 1980s noted little change from a similar study in 1973, though there were 'greater regional exchanges along with the continued dominance of a few exporting countries' (Varis 1984: 143). Among the more interesting, if hardly surprising, findings of this research were the extent of imported (mainly US) entertainment category programmes in most countries, especially in prime time when advertising revenue is at its highest, and that no programmes originating from socialist countries, or from Third World countries (and very few from other First World countries) were ever shown on prime time US television. The same continues to be true across the mass media.

A symposium on Africa in the Media was told that the numbers of Western correspondents in the Third World and correspondents from the Third World in the West were in decline. In the words of the commentator, 'in a world of satellite technology, this seems absurd' (Palmer 1987: 247). The effects of this are to make it easier for the TNCs to dump cheap news on the Third World, and restrict the flow of news from poor to rich countries, trade practices that the WTO appears not be worried about in this sphere. There are, of course, alternative non-Western sources of news and information and, as critics of the media imperialism thesis always argue, no Third World state is forced to fill its media with material from any particular source. It is easy to forget that it may actually be more cost-effective for a national TV service or a newspaper group from a poor country to buy in regional (let alone overseas) material from sources in the West than to set up its own sources or rely on others as poorly endowed as itself. Where alternative agencies have been created, there are often political forces ranged against them. For example, in a revealing analysis of the Inter Press Service, which was created to provide news for and about the Third World, Giffard (1984) documented how a disinformation campaign against it originating in the USA, which was not supported by the facts about its coverage, almost destroyed the organization. And in a subsequent study of alternative news agencies, Giffard (in Boyd-Barrett and Rantanen 1998: ch. 12) shows that not much has changed since then.[9]

CONTROL OF GLOBAL MEDIA MARKETS

Important as the origin of media content is, it is not the whole story. In a study of TV in Indonesia in the 1970s, where one-quarter of programming was imports (mainly from the USA): 'no case [was found] in any developing countries where television which has been introduced with Western aid has been able to operate completely free of Western influence' (Chu and Alfian 1980: 56). The point is that even if there were no programmes from US or Western sources on Indonesian TV, the culture-ideology of consumerism would still be framing the programming. This is confirmed in a particularly striking fashion by Montoya Martin del Campo and Rebeil Corella (in Atwood and McAnany 1986: ch. 8) in their research on 480 students who watched the Telesecundaria programmes on Mexico's main commercial channel, Televisa. Commercial television 'has become in Mexico a vehicle for the transmission of North American culture, constantly eroding national identity and local cultures. Televisa classifies audiences as "urban", "national middle class", and "Americanized middle class": peasants and Indians are nonexistent in this scheme' (Atwood and McAnany 1986: 147). The selection of messages is not neutral, it rarely is, and ignorance is also an effect of television. The more commercial TV the students watched the more they approved of and accepted as natural and true what they took to be the American way of life, faithfully broadcast by Televisa.

By the 1990s, this problematic had been redefined in global terms, as the study by Fernandes (2000) on media images and the global in India shows. Fernandes asks how globality is 'invented through the deployment of nationalist narratives . . . [via a media-produced] vision of the Indian nation based on an idealized depiction of the urban middle classes and new patterns of commodity consumption' (p. 612), though she does not explain how this is a depiction of the Indian nation. Rajiv Ghandi's slogan of 'A computer for every village' made him a leader who understood the importance of information technology and who saw that the commodities necessary to modernize the country could be produced both by foreign TNCs and Indian companies. This led to a shift in public political discourses away from poverty reduction towards a public culture of consumption. Fernandes (2000: 614) argues that the 'notion that "abroad is now in India" . . . signifies the potential realization of middle-class aspirations of consumption, one that can now take place within India's borders', and she illustrates this through the iconic New Indian Woman, who combines traditional values and modern aspirations.[10]

These research findings from Mexico and India highlight some of the difficulties of the thesis I am arguing, but it highlights even more of the difficulties of the thesis of cultural and media imperialism. It would be possible to construct a project to measure the influence of the TV version of the American way of life in Mexico, or foreign cultural influences in India, or media as a whole. It would be quite possible to do this on a series of variables of which consumerism would be one among many, and perhaps not the most important. But such research, based on a state-centrist methodology, would miss how capitalist globalization works through the culture-ideology of consumerism, rather than through a glorification of the American way of life. There is a parallelism here with the opposition introduced above between the comprador class and the transnational capitalist class. In much the same way as political criticism of global capitalism can be deflected onto a more vulnerable and now dispensable comprador class, culture-ideology criticism of consumerism, as the central value of the capitalist global system, can be deflected onto Americanization, also more vulnerable and perhaps one day dispensable.

Thus, the central idea of the new world information order, that there is a global imbalance in communication, media capacity, and influence (translated into the digital divide today), can be safely taken up by captains of industry and consciousness in the First as well as by radical critics in the Third and New Second Worlds. In Spring 1985, *Journal of Communication* (JC) ran a symposium on the US response to this imbalance, in the light of the decision of the US government to withdraw from what it considered to be an increasingly and unacceptably politicized UNESCO. The Independent Commission for World Wide Telecommunications Development (Maitland Commission), a project to facilitate the progress of global communications in the less-developed countries, played an important part in this.

William Ellinghaus (vice chairman of the New York Stock Exchange and ex-President of AT&T), and Larry Forrester (AT&T International), observed that in the mid-1980s three-quarters of the world's 600 million telephones were in just nine countries. More than two billion people, about half of the global population, shared fewer than 10 million telephones. What, they ask, can be done about this growing imbalance? (*JC* 1985: 14). Maitland suggested a Center for Telecommunications Development and the men from AT&T nominated the US Foundation for World Communications Development (founded in 1984 to collect private sector funds for Maitland) to organize corporations to this end. The public sector would then come in, and (implied but not actually stated) the American way of life could be transmitted, preferably on AT&T equipment, on a truly global scale.

This sentiment is also subtly conveyed in a letter from a United States Department of State official to the Secretary General of the International Telecommunications Union on the subject of the Maitland Report. 'The needs and capacities of each developing country are unique, and for some it may be more beneficial to concentrate first on other tele-communications goals, such as perhaps high speed data access to international commodity markets' (Dougan in *JC* 1985: 21). Michael Gardner, chair of the US Telecommunications Training Institute, suggested that the reasons for the global imbalance were the expense of new communications technology, the low priority that most Third World govern-ments accorded to the sector, and the rapidity of technical change. He argued that US action was needed on grounds of enlightened self-interest, and estimated the global telecommunications market to be worth more than $410 billion. His Institute, set up in 1983 by the private sector and part-funded by the US government (over $100,000 from the US Information Agency), provided free hands-on training for students from the Third World inside US corporations. In its first two years it graduated 373 students from seventy-one Third World countries and aimed to double this output (*JC* 1985: 38). Almost twenty years later, even Bill Gates, founder of Microsoft, told the World Economic Forum at Davos that the digital divide, the new label for these inequalities, was one of the greatest threats facing humankind (certainly it is not good for Microsoft profit forecasts). All these efforts are based on the understandable thesis that enhancing communications improves the prospects for democracy. However, as Winseck (1997) demonstrates, it is easy to confuse the technical and the communicative dimensions of democracy. The major trade agreements of the 1990s (NAFTA and the WTO) largely deregulated private telecommunications networks via the doctrine of the free flow of information, but while this enhanced the technical dimension of democracy (making communication physically easier) it did little for political participation within civil society. Much of what passes for civil society in the USA (and, I would add, many other countries) is actually a process of avoiding politics (Eliasoph 1998).

But how do TNCs actually control media markets? A study of how the Motion Picture Export Association of America operated in India provides one clue. It demonstrates how TNCs from the USA organized a cartel to import and show US films, while Indian (and other Third World-made films) were generally kept out of mass circulation in the United States. The same processes appeared to be in operation for TV and video distribution. The conclusion was that: 'the potential for profits [for the TNCs] and the current open-door policy of the Indian government are encouraging to further transnational involvement' (Pendakur 1985: 70). By the year 2000, the Indian telecommunications market had been almost totally liberalized though it is also true that more films are produced in India (the Bollywood phenomenon) than in any other country in the world (see Gupta 1998). In a comparison of the film industries in Italy and the USA, Waterman and Jayakar (2000) show how from quite different starting points, a roughly similar outcome has occurred. Since the 1970s there has been a substantial decrease in the numbers of Italian-made films on US screens and a substantial increase of US-made films on Italian screens. They explain this in terms of the strength of the domestic film industry in the USA, fostered by the availability of pay TV and the tremendous growth in VCR use. The film industry in Italy, much more reliant on terrestrial channels, could not compete, and the same holds for most other countries. Comparing revenue sources for film distributors in 1995 in Italy and the USA, they found that cinemas accounted for 25 per cent in Italy and 29 per cent in the USA, video 13 per cent and 47 per cent, pay TV 8 per cent and 18 per cent, and broadcast TV 53 per cent and 7 per cent respectively. In 1975 the average major studio film budget was $3.1 billion, by 1997 it was $52.3 billion (Waterman and Jayakar 2000: 520). As pay TV and VCR use increases globally, on this model we might expect the position to change and, indeed, the growth in joint-venture co-productions already blurs the distinctions between film industries in different countries, though Hollywood is still the dominant force (Maltby 1995: ch. 2).

The major mass media—radio, TV, movies, CDs, audio and videotapes, books, magazines and newspapers, and now the Internet—have all expanded in use in the Third World since the 1980s. They are not, however, entirely under formal TNC control. Mass media control can be exercised directly through the production process and indirectly through marketing and distribution. The public media have held out the greatest promise for the Third World in terms of their educational and instructional potential, and it is in this context that opinions are most sharply divided about the new communications technology, the role of the TNCs, and the needs and wants of people.

As has already been suggested, however, research on the mass media in the Third World shows that it is the commercial rather than the educational purposes that are dominant. The record of the TNCs, independent Third World government efforts, or combinations of them, to put the new communications technology to educational and humanitarian use has been spotty, to say the least. The promise of the 1970s that satellite television would revolutionize education, public health, and nutrition, and eliminate illiteracy throughout the urban and rural Third World has been largely disappointed. It will not surprise the cynical to learn that INTELSAT, COMSAT, and other glamorous projects, though they have an impressive spread of participants, have been utilized mainly for elite–elite communications (only those rich enough to send messages speak to those who are rich enough to receive them), the collection of military and commercially relevant information, and for the global transmission of entertainment (Eapen, in Becker et al. 1986, Mansell and Wehn 1998). The alternative media that are somewhat less capital intensive, like desktop publishing, cable television, the video-cassette industry, and the Internet, might in time challenge the hegemony of the TNCs in the mass media of the Third World. The hope of those working in the independent media is that they might furnish more opportunities for independent production and distribution (see Hamelink 1984), but this has not yet happened to any significant degree (M'Bayo 1997, Main 2001).

The enormous growth since the 1980s of culture industries in many parts of the Third World augments the products of Western TNCs with local material, and the two coexist side by side in most marketplaces (see Mowlana 1985, Herman and McChesney 1997). Systems based on television–Internet–mobile phone connections, and the development of wire-less technologies (Bluetooth, Wi-Fi, etc.) promise as yet unrealized potential for social progress all over the world, though the apparent widening of the digital divide suggests that this is a very long-term project for the masses in the Third World. Paradoxically, TNC-generated information technology may increase the penetration of foreign messages and at the same time increase the dissemination of indigenous cultures. In this vein, there are those who argue that IT can make positive contributions to Third World development because of rather than in spite of the technological innovations of the TNCs. Stover (1984: 93–5) pointed out that in the 1980s four trends in IT gave cause for optimism. Computers were becoming increasingly cost-effective, for example a central memory of one million bytes in the 1980s costs far less than 1 per cent of what it cost in the 1960s;[11] miniaturization has made computers more practical for small users; programming advances have increased the adaptation of software to user needs and improved the chances that IT will address the developmental problems of Third World countries. Finally, the integration of television, computers, and telecommunications would permit global networking for the transmission of information and open up new possibilities for resource and technology-scarce countries of the Third World. Again, this is an appealing argument, but, as we have seen, capitalist globalization has created a digital divide, suggesting that the class polarization effect operates in communications as well as in many other areas of day-to-day existence.

Thus, it is too soon to say whether Stover's optimism is justified but the TNCs are already heavily involved in all these developments. The potential benefits for the deprived in the Third World appear to be very minimal compared with the profits to be made by the transnational capitalist class and its local affiliates through the promotion of the culture-ideology of consumerism. The study of advertising in the Third World shows how the culture-ideology of consumerism is expressed and how the new world information order really works.

ADVERTISING AND THE SPREAD OF CONSUMERISM

Transnational advertising agencies (TNAAs) are now big business. As Table 7.1 shows, many have revenues in excess of one billion dollars. They are also increasingly active in the Third World, producing advertisements and marketing strategies often with domestic agencies in joint ventures to promote local and global products and services. Since the 1970s these have taken up more and more Third World radio, TV, and printed media space (Anderson 1984). Studies of the TNAAs, from the USA, Europe, and Japan, provide a good test for the view that we should be looking not at the increase or decrease of Americanization in the Third World but at the inroads that the culture-ideology of consumerism directed by major TNCs is making in Third World societies.[12]

According to Noreene Janus, by 1980 the TNAAs derived more than half of their gross income from overseas, with the Latin American market expanding particularly fast. Brazil, Mexico, and Argentina were among the top twenty advertising markets. Janus's (1986: 128) approach is predicated on the claim that: 'lifestyles promoted in advertising include implicit and explicit agendas for social relations, political action, and cultural change.' In most countries advertising is concentrated on a relatively small group of consumer goods, soaps/detergents, tobacco, drugs, perfumes, deodorants, toothpaste, processed

Table 7.1 Top ten transnational advertising agencies by revenues in $USm. (2000)

Rank	Company	Headquarters	Gross Income	Billings
1	WPP Group	London	7,971.0	67,225.0
2	Omnicon Group	New York	6,986.2	55,651.6
3	Interpublic Group of Cos.	New York	6,595.9	54,828.2
4	Dentsu	Tokyo	3,089.0	21,689.1
5	Havas Advertising	Levallois-Perret (Paris)	2,757.3	26,345.5
6	Publicis Groupe	Paris	2,479.1	29,302.7
7	Bcom3 Group	Chicago	2,215.9	17,932.6
8	Grey Global Group	New York	1,863.2	11,406.3
9	True North Communications	Chicago	1,539.1	13,171.7
10	Cordiant Communications	London	1,254.8	11,256.0

Source: data compiled from *Advertising Age* (23 Apr. 2001); **www.adageglobal.com** (28 Oct. 2001).

foods, alcohol, soft drinks, and cars. Increases in the consumption of these products is less an indicator of level of development than kind of development. All over the world, these products tend to be characterized by high profits, high advertising spend to sales, high barriers to entry, and high levels of penetration by TNCs.[13]

This leads inexorably to the transnationalization of the local mass media. In her own substantive research Janus found that TNCs were responsible for most of the adverts on TV in Mexico and women's magazines in Latin America, and for about one-third of non-government newspaper adverts in Mexico. The next stage in the process, the transnationalization of consumption habits, is not as unproblematic as is sometimes assumed. Janus (1986: 133) argued for a 'perpetual confrontation between transnational expansion and local cultural expansion', and cites as evidence the fact that TNCs such as Gerber (baby food) and Nestlé (instant coffee) have acknowledged that customer resistance is their main marketing problem in Latin America.

It is for this reason that the TNAAs are not only trying to sell specific products in the Third World but are engineering social, political, and cultural change in order to ensure a level of consumption that is 'the material basis for the promotion of a standardized global culture' (Janus 1986: 135). Those who find this difficult to accept might care to look at studies such as Fejes (1980), documenting how the military regimes in Chile and Argentina used TNAAs to clean up their images. Similarly, Jefkins and Ugboajah (1986) in an early study of the media in Africa, illustrate the point with reference to the media-induced following for Western culture heroes and products. And Mattelart shows dramatically how the mass media in Chile changed in the two years after the coup against the Allende government in 1973, when ad agency billings rose tenfold: 'There are no longer any political parties; there is no longer a congress; the mass media naturally become the superstructural party of the dictatorship' (Mattelart 1978: 33). The Pepsi Revolution campaign in Brazil, another telling example, was deliberately designed as an alternative channel of youth protest in a repressive society (Fejes 1980). Similarly, in the US presidential election campaign of 1992, MTV was widely believed to have helped Bill Clinton with a series of adverts framed as pop videos encouraging young people to use their votes. However, the greatest impact of MTV and similar companies is undoubtedly to foster an escapist youth culture globally (see Banks 1997, Barker 1997).[14] With global media corporations taking substantial stakes in TV all over the world the political implications of capitalist globalization in the entertainment industry are substantial (Herman and McChesney 1997).

Writing in *Fortune*, Tully asserts, on the basis of research in which the advertising agency BSB Worldwide videotaped bedrooms of teenagers in twenty-five countries, that 'Teens almost everywhere buy a common gallery of products' (Tully 1994: 90; and compare with Pilkington 1994, on Russian youth). In the early 1990s a South African advertising executive argued that township youth 'may be poor, they may be young and poorly educated, but they have towering aspirations . . . And when they have made it, they want to flaunt it. They want the socially correct brands – Gucci, Dior, Levis, Coca-Cola, Dimple Haig and BMW' (Lascaris 1993).[15] The transition from apartheid to neo-liberalism is well under way in South Africa (Bond 2000). As capitalist globalization intensifies, more and more groups all over the world aspire to similar possessions, and increasing numbers achieve these aspirations, but even more are disappointed and frustrated.

The way that the TNAAs achieve the desired societal changes is through projective advertising, the technique of producing new needs/wants as components of a new life-style, which is replacing suggestive advertising. Janus tries to explain this in historical terms. While Gramsci argued in the 1930s that collective consciousness or common sense is unordered and inconsistent although directed by the dominant ideology, 'the dominant ideology of our times is consumerism and its particular strength may derive from the fact that it helps to order the unordered elements of the collective consciousness' (Janus 1986: 137). She cites Cathelat's idea that advertising is a supralanguage where it is the products' associations rather than the products themselves that are crucial, prior to the use of language (see also Baudrillard 1988). Advertising is a vital link between material and social relations, transforming producers into consumers, by transforming captains of industry into captains of consciousness, as Ewen (1976) argues. In *Learning from Las Vegas* Venturi *et al.* (1977) take this argument into architecture.

Nicholson (1988) reported that while only the United States spent more than 2 per cent of its GNP on advertising in 1986, fourteen other countries spent more than 1 per cent including Argentina, Bolivia, Costa Rica, Dominican Republic, Israel, Panama, and Venezuela. Advertising was also booming in Asia. A table in *Advertising Age* (24 July 1989) showed that at least seven of the top eleven ad agencies in Latin America were then transnational (see also Sinclair 1987). By the year 2000, advertising agencies with trans-national participation topped the list for gross income in 118 out of 124 countries. Independent (local) agencies came top only in Austria, China, Italy, Puerto Rico, South Korea, and Virgin Islands, but in all of these except the last TNAAs dominated the industry ('Top agencies in 124 countries', *Advertising Age*, 23 April 2001: s12–s16). Advertising has become one of the most globalizing industries.

For most people in the First World and for growing numbers in the New Second and Third Worlds, the contradictions of advertising and thus of the culture-ideology of consumerism are blurred by the constant opportunities to consume global brand consumer goods and services. Promotional culture (Wernick, 1991) is a global phenomenon and TNCs have harnessed the new digital technology to drive it all over the world. In India, global media giants like Rupert Murdoch's Star TV and BBC World TV are fighting

Doordarshan, the Indian state network, for market share, but with similar consumerist messages (Herman and McChesny 1997: ch. 6). The tiny English-speaking elite in India actually numbers around twenty million people, a considerable market, while most of the middle class buys global brands as well as electronic goods, cosmetics, and so on made in India. The complexities of the culture-ideology of consumerism are well illustrated by the fact that Doordarshan felt compelled to introduce its own satellite channels showing *Dallas* and *Disney*, while much of the success of Star TV is attributed to local programmes, particularly Indian films (and Chinese films in other Asian markets). The culture-ideology of consumerism thesis argues that global capitalism sells whatever people are willing to buy, whether it be Americanization, kung fu, Hindu musicals, the spicy vegetarian beanburgers or mutton beefburgers of New Delhi's air-conditioned Wimpy bars. Not everyone can afford to buy, but everyone can look and hope to buy some day.

GLOBAL EXPOSURE

The global film, television, and radio broadcasting industries are increasingly organically linked and are still dominated by the commercial interests of US-origin transnationals. Although Hollywood actually produces only a minority of the worldwide total of films and television programmes, its control over marketing and distribution gives it an enormous input onto Third World screens. A report for UNESCO showed that in 1976, 36.5 per cent of Thai TV time was devoted to foreign, mostly US imports; in 1973 almost 90 per cent of the films shown in Argentina were foreign-made, 37 per cent of these from the United States (Guback and Varis 1982: ch. 4). The research of Stover (1984) on the ways in which the new information technology might facilitate cultural dependency, and of Jefkins and Ugboajah (1986: 210 ff.) on the Voice of America fan clubs in Nigeria, illustrate how these trends intensified in the 1980s. The proposition that, in the words of the British media sociologist Jeremy Tunstall, the media are American, became a potent political slogan.

The US–Japanese relationship is of particular significance here. Many in the Third World argue that if the Japanese, so economically powerful, cannot resist American or, more generally, Western consumerism then what chance has anyone else. But the question needs to be reconceptualized in the form: to what extent is the culture ideology of consumerism in Japan an effect of capitalist globalization, or does it have uniquely Japanese (or any other cultural) characteristics? My argument is that the consumerism of capitalist globalization has a universal form but with the permanent potential of national-local cultural contents. A typical, if absurd, example is the new 'fake festival of panty-givers' in Japan. Japanese confectioners take around 10 per cent of their annual sales on St Valentine's Day (whose name was unknown in Japan before the arrival of chocolate). Panty-giving Day 'is an attempt by the lingerie industry to join in the commercial exploitation of fake festivals'. The point is that the culture-ideology of consumerism produces the form, but the content is taken from the film *Working Girl*, whose heroine is given underwear by her boyfriend. Mikiko Taga, the feminist author of a book on *sekihara* (sexual harassment) explains: 'Japanese think this is an American custom and they imitate American actions' (quoted in Sullivan 1990). However, this is driven not by Americanization as such but by the marketing skills of local entrepreneurs. As the contributors to the collection edited by Askenazi and Clammer (2000) show in a variety of ways, consumerism has moved to centre stage in Japanese culture.

There are those who would condemn all US culture products, as there are those who would as uncritically endorse them. This is not the point. The point is that Thailand, Argentina, and Nigeria (and most other Third World countries), as well as Japan and Western Europe, are exposed to media messages of US origin extolling the virtues of capitalist consumerism daily and at a high level of intensity. The balance between US/ European and local-origin mass media communication globally is skewed towards the former, and Third World-origin mass media messages practically never get exposure in the United States or other First World countries. Under the title 'What's hot on TV Worldwide?' *Advertising Age* (1 Dec. 1986: 60) produced a list of the top US and local shows on the television channels of nine Third World and eleven First World countries. Not one of the local shows had ever been networked in the United States. The most popular US shows for the Third World sample were *Knight Rider* (all the way from South Korea to Nicaragua), *The A-Team*, and *Dynasty*. A survey in the *Los Angeles Times* (1992) confirmed the point. In 2001, the shows had changed but the message was similar. All of these programmes, and the many more broadcast in the Third World, present specific messages and convey specific myths about life in the United States and at home (see Barker 1997), as indeed all popular television does in any country. The popularity of such programmes and the annual crop of multi-million-dollar grossing movies that achieve global screening also tell us something about the ways in which the media TNCs have successfully tapped into consumer preferences in the Third World. It must be remembered that these consumers are free to switch on or off, to pay to see films or not. Intellectuals may bemoan the effects of US-influenced public mass media in the Third World, as they bemoan the onward march of the fast food and beverage industries caused by the rise of global franchising, but it cannot be denied that these products of the TNCs are popular and widely sought after all over the world. The inability or unwillingness of local producers, private or state, to compete effectively with the TNCs in these fields does not sufficiently explain the global success that TNC media products enjoy. Further, the Americanization of the mass media is somewhat problematic in light of two facts. First, three of the big five media TNCs (Bertelsman, Vivendi, and NewsCorp) originate in Germany, France, and Australia–UK, and second, many 'American' media companies are actually subsidiaries of these three (Houghton Mifflin publishers, Universal Studios, and Fox, respectively), Sony Corporation from Japan (PlayStation), and others.

DELIVERING THE GOODS

The question of how those driving the culture-ideology of consumerism set about delivering the products that it so assiduously promotes to Third World consumers is rarely asked. Hill and Boya (1987) looked at the ways in which consumer goods are promoted in Third World countries, and provide some interesting information on a sample of sixty-one subsidiaries of nineteen food and drink, pharmaceutical, cosmetics, and general goods TNCs. Many patterns of media use appear to be employed, and they are connected to the diffusion of global retailing techniques to the Third World. Kaynak (1988: ch. 1) describes changes in Third World urban retailing brought about by what I have been conceptualizing as capitalist globalization. This globalizing force is expressed in the decline in the number and competitiveness of small grocery stores, the adoption of self-service techniques, the expansion of large store operations, the differential growth rates of urban and metropolitan as against less urbanized areas, wholesaler-initiated lobbying for a more independent grocery trade, and more focus on operational efficiency. For example, Kaynak noted that shops were upgrading their perishables (fresh meat, fruit, and vegetables), to compensate for the lower margins on groceries resulting from increased competition.

Kacker (in Kaynak 1988: ch. 3) suggests some reasons for increased competition. Some TNCs have been involved in mass retailing in the Third World, for example Bata sold its own shoes, Singer sold its own sewing machines, and Sears, Wal-Mart, and Marks & Spencer between them sell almost everything. The presence of TNCs, he argues, can be very beneficial, by transferring expertise and stimulating local suppliers. This often entails cutting out the middleman, as the experience of IBEC supermarkets in Latin America and MigrosTurk in Turkey showed, and competition between small domestic and larger foreign retailers can also result. The US-based discounter Price Club opened its first S&R Price Membership Shopping store in the Philippines in 2001 'drawing huge crowds' (Canono 2001: 10). Thus, as Kacker (in Kaynak 1988: 40) predicted, by helping to transform retailing: 'Sears, Roebuck [to which we can add Price Club, Wal-Mart, Carrefour and Muji today] is well-known all over the world for making a significant contribution in the creation of a middle class'. Despite the neo-liberal belief in the power of the market to keep prices low, there is no evidence that the revolution in Third World urban retailing has actually reduced or even stabilized the prices of food and other basic goods. Government policies on agricultural incentives, inflation, and reliance on imports are all probably much more important determinants of prices for most people than the retailing system (Walton and Seddon 1994). In addition, there is a good deal of evidence that global brands are just as likely to push prices up, especially for iconic designer labels, than keep them down. What the retailing system certainly does do, however, is to create the infrastructure for the culture-ideology of consumerism to flourish (see Robison and Goodman 1996). Even if the poor urban or rural dwellers cannot afford to buy, they can still gaze in the windows of the boutiques and walk in the shopping malls that have sprung up in all but the very poorest Third World cities in recent decades.

A development central to the culture-ideology of consumerism is the rapid growth of franchising chains all over the world, particularly for fast food. Palmer (1985) argued that the reason why the fast food sector globalized so quickly was because it was seen as non-threatening to the host countries. Fast food franchising outside the USA, he argued, seems to benefit all the players and its success is assured due to 'a growing preference for American fast food over local products' (72). The following comment, in a US government food export magazine, suggests that there may be two factors at work here: 'Parent companies of U.S.-franchise operations may require certain U.S. food ingredients to ensure consistency in quality and reliability' (Canono 2001: 12), shades of the old argument about the difficulty of procuring backward linkages. Catering to local tastes does not necessarily undermine the management philosophy of global standardization if the product itself has a strong enough image and the presence of McDonald's all over the world confirms this. In Eastern Europe, for example, the ecstatic reception of the Golden Arches as communism was crumbling presented some iconic images of the time from Moscow. Another example of McDonald's commercial opportunism was the introduction of the Kiasu Burger in Singapore in 1993, advertising the good qualities of Mr Kiasu, the 'afraid to lose' symbol of the Singapore middle class (Jones and Brown 1994; see also Watson 1997).

The scale of global franchising in fast food and other industries accelerated in the 1980s. *Business America* (3 Mar. 1986: 11–13) reported that about 500,000 outlets employing 6 million people were expected to sell over $US550 billion worth of goods in 1986. Franchising is highly concentrated, with about fifty companies accounting for half of total sales globally. In 1985, thirteen of these were in fast foods and nine in auto dealerships, but only 13 per cent of outlets were in the Third World. The prospects for growth there were considered to be very bright. Kaynak (1988: 50) predicted that 'Franchising is a potent source for socioeconomic development of LDCs'. Postcommunist Vladivostok is an instructive case in point. By 2001 this outpost situated at the junction of the Russian Far East, China, and North Korea (hardly a marketer's dream) boasted the following franchises: Kodak photo and film developing, six Doka-Pizzas (Russian), and various other Russian and Chinese outlets, run by 'a cadre of entrepreneurs and investors' (BISNIS website).

The peculiar significance of fast food franchising is its connection with the home and its effects on the reconceptualization of leisure time and family life. As suggested above, there is no better example of this than the McDonald's phenomenon.[16] In the 1980s a United Nations team researched the fast food industry in the Philippines, Thailand, and Malaysia. Findings from the study of the McDonald's chain in the Philippines highlighted the impact of one globalizing TNC on a society with a long and contentious history of US intervention, some invited and some not. McDonald's opened its first outlet in the Philippines in Manila in 1981, followed rapidly by others. The positive effects on the economy of the Philippines have primarily been in employment (particularly of students), training of staff (McDonald's is renowned for its methods of instilling efficiency), and domestic linkages (the creation and/or encouragement of high-standard local suppliers). The effect on the local Filipino chains was also very interesting. Originally, Filipino hamburger chains marketed their product on the basis of its Americanness. However, when McDonald's entered the field and, as it were, monopolized the symbols of Americanness, the indigenous chains began to market their product on the basis of local taste. Filipino hamburgers are advertised in the context of Filipino lifestyles in contrast to the McDonald's appeal to the 'colonial mentality of the Filipino consumer' (ESCAP/ UNCTC, 1986: 44; see also Sklair 2001: 54–5).[17]

The entry of McDonald's into the Philippines brought competition to a local industry that was satisfying local demand. It was also responsible for an outflow of foreign exchange (repatriated profits) that ordinary people in the Philippines can ill afford. It is possible that hamburgers in the Philippines are more efficiently and hygienically served (and perhaps made) than before, but the impact of McDonald's on the diet of the people is unlikely to have been positive.[18] By 2001, the globalization of the restaurant industry in the Philippines appeared to have moved up a level: 'In fine dining restaurants especially, managers have found that diners are willing to pay more for what they regard as the higher quality and better value of imported foods' (Canono 2001: 12). It is an indication of the class polarization crisis that such judgements can be casually made for many affluent minorities in Third World countries while many more close by go hungry. This is certainly the case in the Philippines.

A study of franchising in Spain (Gamir and Mendez 2000) vividly illustrates the pace of franchising in the 1990s. McDonald's and Kentucky Fried Chicken recorded remarkable growth in Spain in the 1990s, but so did many other franchises in many other product lines. By 1997 there were at least 684 firms with over 20,000 outlets, double the numbers of 1995. Indeed in 1997, the top of the franchise league was occupied by clothing stores (108), followed by catering and restaurants (98), specialized stores (90), and services (82), and real estate/consultancies (40), plus 13 other types (Gamir and Mendez 2000: table 1). Only 44 of these outlets were controlled by US-origin firms, as opposed to 511 from Spain itself, 37 from France, and 22 from Italy (with 14 franchises from other countries represented). This indicates that consumerism is not necessarily all-American.

One flaw in the argument of those who criticize the TNCs and the consumerism that they sustain is the question of consumer sovereignty. As long as consumers have a choice, it may be argued, they are free to buy or not to buy what the TNCs are trying to sell. Advertising may be a hidden persuader, but no one is forced to obey. As long as what the TNCs are trying to sell is not directly life-threatening, the neo-liberal argument claims, surely TNCs are entitled to enter the marketplace. It is important not to fall into the trap of moralizing. Most people in the Third World would be very happy to have the opportunity to share First World lifestyles, animated with the spirit of consumerism, the culture-ideology that encourages us to satisfy more than our biological needs.[19] All consumption due to induced wants has to be driven by external forces. Under the never-ending pressure of consumerism, wants become synonymous with needs. We may pause to distinguish the effects of consumerism in societies where affluence is the norm (though even here some people may be without the necessities of life) and societies where poverty is the norm (though some people may be very affluent). It is only in terms of these distinctions that the creation of new consumption needs by the TNCs in poor countries can be properly evaluated, but even with these distinctions it is difficult, if not impossible, to do more than identify what is happening. Seen in this light, the culture-ideology of consumerism creates a form of cultural dependency. Elizabeth Cardova's definition is poignant, if controversial: 'Cultural dependency means people in our country have to brush their teeth three times a day, even if they don't have anything to eat' (cited in Stover 1984: 31). Most toothpaste and brushes are produced by TNCs.

CASE STUDIES IN GLOBAL CONSUMERISM

THE BABY BOTTLE FEED CONTROVERSY

The controversy surrounding the marketing of the Nestlé infant formula in the Third World is a cause célèbre in the history of both global consumerism and the consumer movement. The case illustrates the stormy history of TNC–Third World relations, and the continuing boycott on Nestlé products points up its continuing significance.[20] Nestlé, SA, a Swiss-based transnational corporation, is the biggest consumer foods company in the world.[21] The company has been marketing in the Third World for many years (see Heer 1991). The public campaign against Nestlé began at a forum on nutrition sponsored by the UN in 1970, where a scientist claimed that the aggressive marketing of infant formula had caused a decline of breastfeeding in many Third World countries. A torrent of scientific and popular publications on the subject began to appear. Over the next few years the belief snowballed that infant formula was actually harmful to babies (Palmer 1993: appendix 1), especially in the sociocultural settings of the Third World. More and more individuals and groups (particularly religious and consumer groups) joined the campaign against the marketing of such products in general and the activities of Nestlé in the Third World in particular. Matters came to a head when a Swiss group accused Nestlé of killing babies. The company sued for libel and in July 1977 an international boycott of all Nestlé products was declared.

The charges of the critics were quite straightforward. The infant formula producers were marketing their products in ways that discouraged breastfeeding, and they were using salespeople dressed like nurses; the companies ignored the fact that many of their Third World customers did not have clean water or hygienic conditions in which to prepare the formula safely and they were not giving sufficient warnings against the dangers of over-dilution; and they were pushing their products through Third World health professionals by methods ranging from excessive pressure to corruption (for one example in the Yemen, see Melrose 1981).

It was becoming increasingly clear that direct contacts between the boycott organizers and Nestlé were unlikely to be productive and both sides made attempts to bring in third parties. The boycott organizers, Nestlé, and other involved parties put their cases to the World Health Organization. In 1981 the WHO promulgated a code for the marketing of breast-milk substitutes that adopted most of the recommendations of the boycotters. The vote was 118 to 1 (the United States), and represented a serious political defeat for Nestlé and the other infant formula companies. After many years of having tried to play down the controversy, Nestlé realized that it needed a more proactive strategy if it was ever to have the boycott lifted. In 1981 it created the Nestlé Coordination Center for Nutrition, Inc. (NCCN), a group of public relations experts with a generous budget to resolve the problem. NCCN, and in the following year the Nestlé Instant Formula Audit Commission (NIFAC), went on the offensive.

By accommodating critics, dividing the opposition, and shrewd targeting of winnable objectives, these bodies began to win the public relations battle and the boycott coalition began to crumble. In 1984 the boycott was called off. This prompted a social marketing expert to comment: 'The lesson to be learned here is that the absence of sophisticated regulatory mechanisms in the Third World should not be misconstrued as an open invitation to free-wheeling marketing behaviour. One suggested rule-of-thumb for international markets: If you can't get away with it at home, it's better not to try it elsewhere' (Manoff 1984: 16, 20). However, the case was not closed. The anti-Nestlé campaigners continued to monitor the situation carefully and throughout the 1980s Nestlé and other TNCs were relentlessly criticized for continued violations of the WHO code of practice. Nestlé hotly disputed these accusations and argued that the campaigners were misinterpreting the WHO code. In 1988 the boycott was reinstated.[22]

What are the lessons of the Nestlé case? Although there is now recognition on the company side that there are questions of morality and social responsibility involved, neither Nestlé nor the infant formula industry has ever seriously acknowledged anything more than free-wheeling marketing behaviour (in Manoff's ambiguous phrase). Nestlé and other companies have never conceded that they owe reparations of any sort to the bereaved parents and stunted children in countries where their (allegedly now discontinued) malpractices actually did lead to death and ill health. Nevertheless, governments and health workers in beleaguered Third World countries still want infant formula, and some seem satisfied that the WHO code sufficiently protects mothers and babies.[23] The lesson for the TNCs is that there are now groups of activists operating transnationally to monitor the activities of the TNCs all the time, particularly where there are health implications for people in the Third World. When the *Wall Street Journal* (25 Apr. 1989, B6) revealed that Nestlé's public relations advisers (the major transnational advertising agency Ogilvy and Mather) had proposed a Proactive Neutralization campaign to infiltrate the company's opponents and discredit them, this caused a storm and boosted the renewed boycott.[24]

Nestlé's heavy involvement in the international food regulatory agency, Codex Alimentarius, which is run jointly by the World Health Organization and the Food and Agriculture Organization, has been documented by Avery *et al.* (1993). At the Codex's 19th session (1989–91), industry representatives far outnumbered the other groups and Nestlé's thirty-eight representatives, the most of any non-governmental organization, dwarfed the eight representatives from public interest groups. These patterns persisted in subsequent Codex sessions. It is not only in the infant formula sector that Nestlé wields considerable power.

Nestle's ongoing response to the boycotts is that though infant formula sales in the Third World are only about 1 per cent of global turnover, the company will not abandon these products and give in to what it considers to be 'misguided attacks' (see Sklair 2001). In parallel with this decision Nestlé has waged a continual, sometimes aggressive, defence of its position against its critics. For example, Nestlé circulated a hostile commentary on the Interagency Group on Breastfeeding Monitoring report, *Cracking the Code* (1997), which made substantive criticisms of Nestlé and other purveyors of infant formula. Nestlé argued that the report did not provide sufficient details of its allegations to enable the industry to check them out. However, many empirical studies have been carried out in various parts of the world (for example, in Poland, Bangladesh, Thailand, and South Africa) to discover the veracity of charges about violations of the International Code of Marketing Breast-milk Substitutes since it was established by the WHO in 1981. The main charges are that the companies are responsible for negative information messages about breastfeeding, and for the distribution of proprietary products and free samples that might discourage breastfeeding. The company have always denied these charges, claiming that any violations were the results of unfortunate misunderstandings and problems in managing local staff. In 1999, the new CEO of Nestlé distributed copies of supportive letters, written by government agencies and medical authorities all over the world, to a wide array of interested parties (including the present writer). However, it was forced to withdraw some of these letters as they were misleading.

The international boycott of Nestlé products and the campaign against violations of the International Code and Nestlé continues.[25] The newsletter of Baby Milk Action (June 2001) reported that the campaign had offices in sixteen countries and supporting groups in more than sixty. Code violations were alleged for Nestlé in Côte d'Ivoire, Milupa in Hong Kong, Wyeth in Uruguay, Abbot-Ross in Canada, Mead Johnson in Taiwan, Heinz in Italy, Cow & Gate (Nutricia) in Russia, Hipp in the UAE, Gerber in the USA, and Danone in Ghana. The marketing of infant formula is global as is the campaign against it.

DRUGS, HEALTH, AND PROFITS

The pharmaceutical-medical drugs industry, for obvious reasons, has also attracted a great deal of attention from those for whom global consumerism is problematic. Medical drug sales in both less-industrialized and advanced industrial societies are often highly controversial (for an extreme case, see Hansson 1989). The pharmaceutical industry claims that its research and development and testing costs put it in a special category compared with most other industries, but critics have drawn attention to the fact that the industry's extremely high ratio of advertising expenditure to sales revenue is what makes it unusual. What is undeniable, however, is that many TNCs in the pharmaceutical industry have over the years adopted systems of differential pricing in different markets, and that consumers in many Third World countries have been paying far more for their internationally branded medicines than consumers in some First World countries. It has also been established that labelling practices vary quite dramatically between markets in rich and poor countries, leading to widespread charges of unethical behaviour against the companies.

The pharmaceutical industry is a special industry (along with other medical and hospital products industries, some of which are integrated with it) in terms of its direct and intimate connection with human life and well-being, but like most other industries it only survives as long as it makes profits. The main contradiction between the activities of the drug TNCs and the needs of the Third World is that the bulk of TNC research and promotional effort is directed towards the relatively expensive drugs designed to combat the perceived health problems of the rich countries, while the poor countries of the world require, for the most part, relatively simple and cheap preparations to cope with the illnesses of the mass of their populations (see Medawar 1984, Chowdhury 1995). A clear illustration of this is the treatment of diarrhoea, a major killer in most Third World countries, and especially dangerous to infants. Pharmacies in some parts of the Third World will routinely recommend expensive antibiotics and anti-diarrhoeal drugs. These are in most cases (though, of course, not in all cases) quite unnecessary and can even be dangerous. One notorious example is the hydroxyquinolines, some of which were withdrawn in the United States in the mid-1970s but continue to be available over the counter in many Third World countries. The best treatment for diarrhoea, universally recognized by health professionals, is a simple rehydration solution (boiled water, sugar, and salt) which most people could prepare for themselves at low cost, even in conditions of substantial deprivation. It is clearly not in the short-term financial interests of the local firms, the TNCs producing the superfluous drugs, or the pharmacies selling them to have these facts widely known though no doubt many pharmacists all over the world freely provide this information. One of the most discussed cases of unethical marketing of such drugs by a TNC in the Third World is that of Searle's Lomotil, documented by Medawar and Freese (1982).

As in the marketing of infant formula, there is also a voluntary International Code of Pharmaceutical Marketing Practices, adopted by the International Federation of Pharmaceutical Manufacturers Associations (IFPMA) in 1981.While consumer groups in many countries have been watching the transnational activities of IFPMA members for decades, three issues have come to the fore: the export of drugs and chemicals banned in their countries of origin, the larger question of inappropriate drugs for the Third World, and the fact that drug companies generally focus on medicines for the affluent rather than the poor. The debate over export to the Third World of products banned in the First World highlights many of the problems surrounding any attempt to evaluate the culture-ideology of consumerism in the Third World. From the point of view of the TNC, if a sovereign state in the Third World allows a product to enter then the attitude of the United States or any other government should be irrelevant. There is even some research suggesting that in the area of environmental pollution some types of TNCs actually have a relatively good record in the Third World, despite tragedies like Bhopal (Leonard 1986). More specifically, it is impossible to ignore the argument that the benefits of malaria control in a Third World country, resulting from the use of a pesticide banned elsewhere, may be sufficient to offset risks to health, and may justify the marketing of hazardous pesticides. Third World governments and planners often accept this privately. Parasitic diseases, notably malaria, kill around one million under-5s every year. From the point of view of First World governments, seriously worried by the loss of markets for manu-factured goods to foreign competition, anything that makes it more difficult for their manufacturers to export is rarely welcomed. Nevertheless, there is clear evidence that Third World consumers have not always been properly served by drug TNCs (Norris 1982).

In the case of the United States, the Food and Drug Administration sets what are probably the most exacting safety standards in the world. It could well be argued that the balances of benefits and costs in poor countries, which have quite different priorities, are not the same as in rich countries. Few Third World (or even First World) countries can reasonably be expected to have the capacity to monitor perfectly the safety of drugs, chemicals, and so on for themselves (Braithwaite and Drahos 2000) despite the increasing global harmonization of law (Wiener 1999). Corporate lobbyists argue that the best sys-tem is to encourage the TNCs to regulate their own activities and so hold themselves responsible for any avoidable mishaps. TNCs argue that they cannot be held responsible for incorrect or inappropriate use of their products and that as long as they are not breaking any rules in the countries in which they are selling, the rules of their home countries cannot fairly be applied to inhibit their business. This is a contentious issue for pharmaceuticals (Chowdhury 1995), as it is for infant formula.

Arguments like these provide the reasoning behind several voluntary codes of conduct that attempt to control the uses of drugs and chemicals. In the case of direct danger to life the issue is straightforward, if often technically very complicated. In the case of appropriateness, it is rarely straightforward. In 1977, the WHO developed a list of between two and three hundred essential drugs to help Third World medical personnel choose from the tens of thousands available on the market. It is a little baffling to learn (from Medawar 1984: 34) that in Norway in the early 1980s there were about 1,000 branded drugs available for prescribing, while in India there were about 15,000. And India is by no means unique in the Third World in this respect. Several Third World countries at one time or another have restricted imports of drugs not on the WHO list (for example, Bangladesh, Zimbabwe, Mozambique). Others (for example, Mexico, Nicaragua, Costa Rica, and Kenya) have developed essential drugs projects through which a small number of the most useful medicines are made available very cheaply through government dis-pensaries in the countryside (Chowdhury 1995). These initiatives are not necessarily antagonistic to the interests of the TNCs as most of the drugs are still imported or, where produced locally, are often manufactured by their local subsidiaries. However, they fundamentally question the way that pharmaceutical companies do business in the Third World, and there is little evidence to suggest that all TNCs are prepared to abandon the questionable business practices that have brought lucrative rewards over the years. It is also the case that in many countries of the Third World cheap generic drugs do not displace the more expensive branded drugs.

With the creation of the World Trade Organization in 1995 and new rules on intellectual property, pharmaceutical companies began to act even more aggressively to capture and secure new markets. The HIV/AIDS epidemic in Africa—responsible in South Africa for 40 per cent of deaths among the 15–49 age group—provided a test case in the late 1990s. The rights of globalizing corporations to extract the full price for their products were challenged by governments in the Third World, who attempted to address the crisis, as the Brazilian government had previously done with some success. A group of pharmaceutical TNCs used the WTO to sue the South African government, which was attempting to provide low-cost treatment to large numbers of those infected with the virus, for violating trade rules. As a result of a global campaign the drug companies withdrew their suit in 2001, but they only conceded the point that the HIV/AIDS epidemic was a national emergency for South Africa (and thus the WTO rule could be waived), not that governments should be permitted to deal with health issues in the most effective way. While it is true that most countries in Africa do not provide general patent protection for the anti-retroviral drugs for treating AIDS, the most effective and popular drugs are protected and they can cost up to three times as much as generic drugs.[26]

The advertising of drugs and health-related products obviously plays a part in this. A study sponsored by the International Advertising Association reviewed the control of pharmaceutical advertisements in fifty-four countries in the 1980s, and found that there was very little serious monitoring of the claims of drug advertisements. Most TNC advertising was devoted to the over-promotion of general health products like laxatives, vitamins, and diet supplements (today we could add impotence and obesity drugs) of doubtful medical value.[27] The bewildering variety of tonics on sale in most Third World countries is testimony to the power of the TNCs and local companies to sell promises in liquid, tablet, and lozenge form. The struggle for global regulation of marketing and sale of drugs and health-related products rests on an uneasy compromise between the TNCs and organizations such as the WHO, with little sign of progress to the point where the real medical needs of the mass of Third World peoples will be adequately met. The situation described by Melrose (1982) has changed somewhat in terms of disease profiles (McMurray and Smith 2001) but has not been dramatically improved overall.

But the most serious criticism of the major drug companies is that they neglect the medical needs of the poor in the Third World by over-concentrating on those of the affluent in the First World. Capitalist globalization, after all, is about maximizing profits globally. A damning report was released by the charity Médecins sans Frontières in September 2001 under the title 'Fatal Imbalance: the crisis in research and development for drugs for neglected diseases' (at **www.msf.org**). Based on responses from eleven major pharmaceutical companies (nine others failed to respond) it revealed that while eight new drugs on impotence and seven for obesity were being actively developed at enormous expense, only about 1 per cent of R&D budgets of these companies were being applied to the major diseases of the poor—TB, malaria, sleeping sickness, and Leishmaniasis (a parasitic disease transmitted by sandflies that disfigures and kills up to half a million people a year in over eighty countries). The report argues that there is plenty of university research on these diseases but that the drug companies fail to develop the drugs as they would not be very profitable.

The solution appears not to be the replacement of the TNCs by indigenously owned drug companies. A study of the Turkish pharmaceutical industry, in which large indigenous and transnational corporations shared the market, demonstrated than in most important respects large drug companies, whether foreign or local, acted in a similar manner. It concluded: 'Both the TNCs and the large comparable local drug firms similarly rely more heavily on the production of those drugs which do not provide cures for the major causes of mortality in the country' (Kirim 1986: 521). Again, capitalist globalization is charged with catering to the needs of the rich at the expense of the needs of the poor.

What, then, is the solution? Claudio Schuftan has suggested delinking, to sever the links between the TNC dominated Western health-care model and the Third World. He argued that in general TNCs and the type of organized medical systems they work through cannot meet the needs of the poor and the sick in the Third World and the treatments that they offer tend to do as much harm as good (Schuftan 1983).[28] Schuftan's approach mirrors the experience of the barefoot doctors in China in the 1960s and 1970s. The fact that the Chinese authorities saw fit to downgrade this experiment should not lead one to suppose that it was a failure or that something better was put in its place.

Once again, dilemmas abound. The TNCs that sell drugs in the Third World have undoubtedly saved countless lives, even if their practices have also caused unnecessary suffering and fatalities. The culture-ideology of consumerism in the Third World holds out a vision of health and bodily well-being, for consumerism would lose much of its positive meaning without this. The drug companies have always been very active in promoting these absolutely commendable values even if the products through which the values are promoted have been found to be wanting in many cases. Medawar (1979) illustrated this in his studies of how health and nutrition themes pervaded processed food advertising, particularly in the Third World. Foods and drinks lacking in nutrition or providing nutrition in an inappropriate and deceptively expensive fashion are, indeed, a highly profitable component of TNC-induced consumerism. The case of 'the other baby killer' (sweetened condensed milk) as researched in Malaysia (Consumers Association of Penang 1981) and junk food-driven obesity diseases in the Third World (McMurray and Smith 2001) are tragic examples of this. The case of the cola beverages is another serious, if less deadly example of the clash between consumerism and inappropriate consumption in the Third World.

COLA WARS

The so-called cola wars provide a telling example of how the TNCs have gone about the creation of a culture-ideology of consumerism in the Third World. Coca-Cola (Coke), the market leader, has been sold outside the United States since the beginning of the twentieth century (Pendergrast 1993). In an article to celebrate the hundredth anniversary of the company and what it stands for, *Beverage World* (May 1986: 48–51) under the revealing title, 'Ambassador to the world', provided an insight into how the industry sees the product. By 1929 Coke was operating sixty-four bottling plants in twenty-eight different countries. Recalling its diplomatic skills and its very special role as a symbol of the

American way of life, the article describes how Coke survived the India–Pakistan War by turning its plants into blood donor stations, how it survived the Arab anti-Zionist boycott, and how it recovered after its major diplomatic setback—losing control of the Russian market to Pepsi. By the mid-1980s Coke was found in 155 countries, over 60 per cent of its sales were outside the United States, and more than 300 million Cokes were drunk every day. By 2000, its worldwide revenues were $35 billion. It is truly globalizing!

Only since the 1980s has the pressure of competition, particularly from its great rival Pepsi, led Coke and its competitors to a more public global strategy and a specific target-ing of Third World markets (see Clairmonte and Cavanagh 1988: chs. 7 and 8). In the early 1980s it was reported that the annual consumption of Coke overseas was 49 6.5 oz-units per person, compared with 272 units in the United States. The potential for growth was thus outside the US market rather than in any major expansion of domestic consumption (*Advertising Age*, 29 Oct. 1983: 2, 86). The cola wars illustrate one phase in the continuing campaign orchestrated by the major beverage TNCs to structure new consumption needs, or more accurately induced wants, particularly in the Third World. The cola wars are particularly intense in the struggle for the teenage market. Coca-Cola was reported to have been researching the global teenager in a nine-country study and to have discovered that music and associated styles of clothing, sport, and consumer electronics are the three parameters of the global teenage market (Tully 1994). Coca-Cola is constantly connected with all of these in a variety of direct and indirect ways (see Sklair 2001: 168–71)

This is true not only for Coca-Cola. Well over half of total world soft drink consumption takes place in the United States. Between the mid-1960s and the late 1980s, per capita consumption of soft drinks in the USA more than doubled while that of water appears to have halved (though sales of bottled water, some of it owned by the cola companies, has reversed this to some extent). Soft drink consumption exceeded that of water, coffee, beer, and milk (*Beverage World*, Feb. 1989: 45). While, no doubt, North Americans can always be persuaded to have another one, the greatest challenge for the TNCs is to persuade consumers elsewhere to develop the same habit. As one industry analyst has proclaimed: 'because the international soft drink market is yet in its infancy, the suc-cesses of both Coke and Pepsi will serve to grow the entire world market. Their success, in part, hinges on their ability to change the way consumers in foreign markets regard soft drinks. . . . So as a strategy, Coke will target an increasingly younger consumer in an attempt to shape his [*sic*] drinking habits to consume more soft drinks instead of alternative beverages' (Hemphill 1986).

One indication that the beverage industry was gearing itself for an onslaught on the drinking habits of the global consumer came in 1984 when InterBev'84 was staged with 15,000 delegates from nearly thirty countries. Two years later, under the slogan 'Selling the World', InterBev'86 brought together 25,000 people from eighty countries to ponder the thought expressed by a prominent industry representative: 'You have billions of people around the world that have yet to be exposed to soft drinks.' In the mid-1980s, even Coca-Cola, the market leader, had half its sales in only five countries (*Beverage Industry*, Sept. 1986: 1ff.). The cola wars were well and truly under way!

Announcing that 'Cola wars move to foreign shores', *Advertising Age* (26 Aug. 1985: 6) described how Pepsi and Coke were locked in global combat in Europe and Asia; in 'Latin soft drink wars' (11 Nov. 1985), how Pepsi's 7UP and Coke's Sprite were engaged in a lemon–lime battle for the allegiance of potential South American consumers; and how

Schweppes was challenging in Australia (18 Dec. 1989). 'Pepsi in China' (*Beverage Industry*, Apr. 1986: 15, 20) recounted how PepsiCo would invest $100m. over ten years to develop the Chinese soft drinks industry, and secure the company's place as the prime purveyor of non-alcoholic beverages in the communist world. PepsiCo has operated a bottling plant in Canton since the early 1980s, and along with its joint venture Happiness Soft Drinks Corporation in the Shenzhen SEZ, serves the Chinese and South-East Asian markets (Sklair 1985). Coke, however, fought back, and the Chinese authorities have had a certain degree of success in playing the two corporate giants off against each other. By the late 1990s both colas were well established in the Chinese market, and *Fortune* reported that Coca-Cola had signed a distribution deal with neighbourhood committees of the Communist Party in Shanghai (25 May 1998).

India, too, has had its own cola war. The Coca-Cola presence in India dates from 1950 and in alliance with a local bottling company aligned with the politically dominant Gandhi family, it prospered until 1977 when it was forced to withdraw rather than give up its total control (as IBM had also done when threatened with indigenization). A local soft drink, 77 Cola, flopped because of marketing and flavour problems, but a rival Coke clone, Campa-Cola, was more successful (*Advertising Age*, 28 Jan. 1985: 63). The cola wars in India were sustained by the bold actions of an Indian entrepreneur, who tried to keep Pepsi out of the country, while sneaking his own brand of fruit juice into the United States (*Forbes*, 22 Sept. 1986: 207; Chakravarty 1989). In July 1994, Hindu fundamentalists in northern India declared a boycott of Coca-Cola and Pepsi-Cola, calling them 'the most visible symbols of the multinational invasion of this country' and threatened a country-wide boycott of foreign consumer goods. The clash of interests between those who want to buy these products, local competitors, and fundamentalists attacking the evils of modern consumerism, is a heady brew, as Figure 7.2 illustrates. By the late 1990s, Pepsi was said to be winning over the key market of some 200 million middle-class youths (*Fortune*, 27 Apr. 1998). And so it goes on!

Figure 7.2 Cola wars in India
Source: Emily Calkins

In Vietnam, Pepsi-Cola's local partner had its products out on the streets of Ho Chi Minh City hours after President Clinton announced the end of the US trade embargo in 1994 which, Reuters News reported, signalled new cola wars for Vietnam's 70 million consumers. Coca-Cola had previously signed joint-venture agreements with two local firms to produce the beverage in Vietnam. Cans of these drinks were freely available in Vietnam, smuggled in from neighbouring countries. When democratic elections removed the pressure to boycott the government in South Africa, Pepsi-Cola announced that it was returning to the country in joint ventures with black partners after decades of anti-apartheid protest. Coca-Cola had divested its interests in 1986, but a local firm which had been left with a bottling licence had captured most of the market.

While Coca-Cola outsells its main rival by a significant amount worldwide, the next phase of the cola wars is likely to feature other products owned by Coke and Pepsi as much as fizzy drinks. Both are heavily involved in the exceptionally lucrative bottled water business, and Pepsi paid $14 billion for the Quaker Oats food group, outbidding Coca-Cola. In Venezuela, however, the domestic Cisneros Group had ended its relationship with Pepsi in that market and joined up with Coca-Cola, which acquired several popular local brands as part of the deal. Coke was beset with many problems at the turn of the century, being sued by black employees at home and by antitrust authorities in Texas and in Europe (*Business Week*, 29 May 2000) and in disputes over predatory pricing by US bottlers exporting to Japan, where Coke derived 20 per cent of its profits on just 5 per cent of its production (*New York Times*, 26 Jan. 2000). *Fortune* has speculated that Pepsi might be winning the cola wars (2 Apr. 2001: 96–7).

There are very few parts of the world in which the effects of the cola wars have not been felt. In even the most remote places Coke and Pepsi and their ubiquitous marketing slogans and logos are acknowledged as symbols of the American way of life. They are also marketed on the prospect that anyone, however poor, who can afford a bottle or a can, can join in the great project of global consumerism, if only for a few moments. The transnational practices of the capitalist global system fade into the background as the joyous promises of 'Coca Cola is It' or membership of the 'Pepsi Generation' or some new slogan flood the foreground.

Now this may be very welcome news for those who oppose the consumption of alcohol by the young, and it may also be good news for those involved in bottling plants and distribution networks. It is hardly up to the outside observer to decide whether one or other or any fizzy drink is appropriate for anyone's consumption. Nevertheless, it is legitimate to draw attention to the massive marketing budgets and the battery of promotional skills put to work by TNCs like Coca-Cola and PepsiCo in poor communities, and to acknowledge that they really can create new consumption needs for nutritionally worthless products, and dictate the means to satisfy them largely on their own terms.

It is not irrelevant that most of the players in this game are connected with TNCs that originate in the United States with eager associates all over the world, and that what is being marketed is not simply a soft drink but a style of life, specifically a (North) American style of life. An executive of a small cola company put the point plainly when he said: 'our emphasis in Third World countries is to reinforce to the consumer that we are an American soft drink and we do have the quality the consumer has been looking for and not always finding . . . there is a tremendous potential for expanding per capita consumption . . . through impacting lifestyles in the same manner that we have here in the U.S.'

(Jabbonsky 1986: 188).[29] This statement epitomizes the relationship between Americanization and the culture-ideology of consumerism in the capitalist global system.

THE GLOBAL SMOKE RING

According to *Fortune* (23 July 2001), the global tobacco industry is dominated by three corporations.[30] Largest by a long way is Philip Morris (PM), no. 34 in the Global 500 with revenues in excess of $63 billion; second is Japan Tobacco, ranked 230 ($20 billion); then British American Tobacco (BAT), ranked 261 ($18b.). Reynolds Tobacco, formerly RJR Nabisco before it sold off its non-US tobacco interests to Japan Tobacco, is still a major force in the USA but is no longer in the FG500. American Brands (acquired by BAT in 1995), Rothmans International, the German firm Reemstma, and several state monopolies make up the strong second tier. The tobacco sector, despite all its woes, had a return on revenues of almost 10 per cent, double the Global 500 industry average. Despite the gathering pace of the anti-smoking movement onslaught on the industry and its continuing legislative successes in many places, there are no definitive signs that the tobacco corporations are collapsing. On the contrary, they are generally doing well.

The world market for tobacco has experienced several transitions (Goodman 1993). By the 1960s the tremendous growth in sales that had seen the cigarette replace all other forms of tobacco consumption had begun to slow down. The tobacco TNCs were still relatively small, with national monopolies in most of the large countries of the world inhibiting their growth overseas. Added to this, health alarms from prestigious sources (the Royal College of Surgeons in the UK, and the Surgeon General in the USA) began to implicate tobacco smoking in cancers, heart diseases, and other medical problems. Though the industry denied these charges, it was later revealed in court that many senior executives and corporate professionals (scientists and lawyers) had been aware of at least some of the health risks and addictiveness of smoking for decades. The evidence was contained in 4,000 pages of documents belonging to Brown and Williamson, the US subsidiary of BAT, delivered anonymously in 1994 to Dr Stanton Glantz, a long-time anti-smoking campaigner. The documents were summarized in a series of articles in the *Journal of the American Medical Association* (see **www.library.ucsf.edu.tobacco**, and Glantz *et al.* 1996). It is pure speculation on my part, but the leaking of these documents may have been provoked by the widely condemned spectacle of senior tobacco executives swearing on the Bible on camera before a Congressional committee that cigarettes were not addictive and that they had no proven link to cancer. In March 1997 in exchange for an end to litigation by twenty-two US states, Liggett (makers of Chesterfield), the smallest of the US tobacco majors, admitted that the industry had lied about its knowledge of the links between smoking and disease and that it had deliberately targeted under-age smokers. The company also agreed to pay the states $25 million and 25 per cent of annual pre-tax profits for twenty-five years as part-payment of Medicare bills incurred by the states to treat sick smokers. Though the other cigarette companies immediately responded by blocking Liggett's release of documents in the courts, by June 1997 the tobacco industry in the USA had agreed to pay $14.8 billion annually over the following twenty-five years to state health authorities, mostly funded from increased cigarette prices. Further curbs on advertising and promotion and industry-funded programmes to help people stop smoking were also part of the settlement. These and other widely publicized events of the summer of 1997 and subsequently have led some to believe that the tobacco industry in the USA and, perhaps, in the rest of the world, is on its last legs. Others (myself included) suspect that this is yet another twist in the continuing story of America's 'Hundred-Year Cigarette War' (Kluger 1997). My analysis of capitalist globalization predicts that the industry, supported crucially by globalizing state officials, politicians, professionals, and consumerist elites, will continue to sell cigarettes and make good profits while the transnational capitalist class and its local affiliates in the Third and New Second World retain their powers. This is despite attacks from other parts of the state apparatus and NGOs on the promotional culture of cigarettes (see below).

Paralleling these developments in the social and legal environments of the industry, there began to occur what Shepherd (1985: 86) describes as the 'virtual disappearance of the private, nationally-owned tobacco company and its replacement by a transnational corporation subsidiary' (see also, Goodman 1993; McGowan 1995: ch. 7). While this judgement may have been a little premature in the 1980s, by the 1990s it appeared much more plausible. PM, BAT, RJR, and Reemtsma more or less bought up the industry in Eastern Europe and the former USSR. Japan Tobacco, previously a state monopoly, responded to the lifting of restrictions on imported cigarettes, which had captured over 20 per cent of the Japanese market by 1996, by aggressively marketing its own brands (notably Mild Seven) abroad and by acquiring all the business of RJR outside the USA. Though the China National Tobacco Corporation has joint ventures with the major tobacco TNCs, the national monopoly looks secure for the time being. The Chinese government raises over 10 per cent of its annual revenues from cigarette taxes. This creates a formidable dilemma, considering that the former Supreme Leader Deng Xiao Ping had famously stopped smoking in a highly publicized gesture at a meeting of the National People's Congress in the early 1990s.

Where country legislation prohibits or imposes high taxes on imported brands smuggling has become a multi-billion-dollar and often violent business. Of the estimated 80 billion foreign cigarettes sold in China in 1994 not a single one had been imported legally (*International Herald Tribune*, 5 Mar. 1997). The smuggling issue was raised in the Philippines parliament where La Suerte Cigar and Cigarette Factory was exposed for selling Philip Morris brands for 15 pesos per pack while the official tax alone on these cigarettes was 66 pesos per pack (*Business Daily* [Manila], 5 Mar. 1997). BAT has also been accused of colluding in the smuggling of its brands, a charge that company documents appear to confirm.

After decades of health scares, increased government taxes, and public anti-smoking propaganda, cigarette sales in First World countries started to decline in the 1990s. Though premium price brands, notably Marlboro, increased their market share all over the world and thus made up for some of the lost revenue in volume, the general decline in the numbers of smokers and the number of cigarettes they were smoking in North America and Western Europe, told the major tobacco companies that industry growth would be much more likely in the Third World and postcommunist Europe. Industry sources (see company Annual Reports) and critics (Nath 1986, Shenon 1994) alike have documented the targeting of Third World (and increasingly New Second World) consumers as a deliberate strategy to compensate for the apparently irreversible decline in revenues anticipated in the First World. By the mid-1990s, PM, RJR, and BAT already had over two-thirds (often more than 90 per cent) of the cigarette market in Barbados, Ghana, Honduras, Hong Kong, Kenya, Morocco, Nicaragua, Sri Lanka, and Turkey (*Tobacco Reporter*, Oct. 1996).

Marlboro is the top selling imported brand all over the world. In the midst of litigation that threatened to cripple the industry financially and media speculation of the actual collapse of the industry, PM announced an increase of 12.5 per cent in fourth quarter tobacco profits in 1996, on a sales volume rise of 4.1 per cent (0.4 per cent for the industry as a whole). Marlboro accounts for about one-third of the total US market for cigarettes. A survey of the world's most valuable brands by share value in 1996 (*Tobacco Reporter*, Sept. 1996) gave Marlboro, valued at $44.6 billion, the top place, closely followed by Coca-Cola (at $43.4 billion) with McDonald's ($18.9 billion) and IBM ($18.5 billion) and the rest some way behind.[31] The size of these markets makes it obvious why so many corporations seek to create global brands. And, of course, to create global brands TNCs need access to all parts of the globe (Sklair 2001: 85–9).

Whereas in 1985 the global tobacco companies had legal access to only 40 per cent of the potential world market for cigarettes, by 1994 this had risen to 90 per cent (Shenon 1994). The reasons for this dramatic increase were the trend to deregulation of foreign investment and trade in general, strategic alliances between local and global cigarette companies and the dilution of government monopolies all over the world. Social factors like increasing prosperity of the new middle classes and the drive to upgrade their consumption patterns like preference for expensive imports over cheaper local cigarettes (see Goodman 1993), the liberation of women to indulge in previously male-dominated pastimes like drinking alcohol (Jernigan 1997) and smoking cigarettes (Greaves 1996), and massive advertising and promotional campaigns by the global corporations (see below), have all contributed to the rapid increase in sales of globally branded cigarettes in the Third World and postcommunist Europe. 'Tobacco companies have poured billions into a frenzied burst of cross-border acquisitions ... profit margins will rise as the cigarette makers persuade increasingly affluent smokers to change from local brands to higher-margin international names' (*Institutional Investor*, 31 May 1996: 37). PM and RJR had actually bartered 34 billion cigarettes with the Russian authorities in 1990, apparently to prevent civil unrest caused by a shortage of local brands. 'Foreign cigarette brands became the leading advertisers on Russian television and radio. Tobacco ad revenues maintained municipal transport systems from St. Petersburg to Sofia, Bulgaria. In Bucharest, Reynolds provided a year's supply of bulbs for traffic lights—in exchange for permission to add the Camel logo to each yellow light' (Rupert and Frankel 1996). The idea of cigarette TNCs as capitalist liberators of postcommunist Europe is not entirely fanciful (K. Krasovsky, in INFACT 1998).

Tobacco transnationals are increasingly targeting the Third World because there are, relatively speaking, fewer smokers of cigarettes there (Frey 1997). The distribution of manufactured cigarette consumption in the 1980s was clearly skewed in terms of the First World/Third World divide. Of the countries represented in the data where average daily consumption was six cigarettes or more per adult only one was in Africa; the four in the Americas included Canada and the USA; nine were in Asia, including Japan, Israel, Hong Kong, Macau, Taiwan, and South Korea; Australia, New Zealand, and the Philippines; and seventeen European countries. Of those countries where fewer than six cigarettes per adult were smoked twenty-six were in Africa, twenty-six in Latin America and the Caribbean, twenty-two in Asia, twelve in Europe, and Fiji (Nicolaides-Bouman *et al.* 1993: table 4).

This pattern is changing rapidly. WHO estimated that in 1995 the average number of cigarettes smoked per day was twenty-two in the First World and fourteen in the Third World, mirroring a decline in the habit of 1.4 per cent per annum in the former but an increase of 1.7 per cent in the latter. However, it appears that while there are fewer smokers in the First World, they may be smoking more expensive brands (notably Marlboro) so tobacco company profits may continue to rise. The WorldWatch Institute Annual Report for 1996 estimated that cigarette production worldwide had reached an all-time peak of more than 5.5 trillion, an increase of 50 billion over 1994. WHO has documented the rise in cigarette smoking per person per year in key Third World markets from the 1970s to the 1990s. In most of the largest countries (China, Indonesia, South Korea, Bangladesh, India, and Thailand) per capita consumption has increased as has the country's rank order in cigarettes smoked per capita on the WHO database of 111 countries. Smoking declined between the 1980s and the 1990s in the Philippines, Singapore, and Malaysia. The latter two are too small to make much difference to cigarette company profits, but highly significant in that both introduced strict controls on advertising and sales to minors in the 1970s and enforced these rigorously, but even here teenage smoking appears to be on the increase again.[32]

Gender, class, age, ethnic, and religious variables would undoubtedly give a sharper picture, but one brute fact remains. The potential for cigarette industry growth lies not in the First World where fewer people are smoking, even if they can be persuaded to smoke more expensive cigarettes, but in the Third World. There, groups that previously were outside the market for manufactured and particularly globally branded cigarettes are rapidly being brought into its orbit. Given the health risks of cigarette smoking, which are widely known, and the increasing levels of local campaigning against these risks (Slama 1995), for the industry to be surviving let alone thriving suggests that it has managed to assemble a powerful coalition of support over a wide range of social groups and institutions, a case of the transnational capitalist class in action all over the world (Sklair 1998: 25–8).

Though direct advertising of cigarettes is gradually being banned in the First World, it is still a powerful force in many Third World countries. Data from the late 1980s showed that one or more of PM, RJR, and BAT occupied a top ten position in advertising revenues in South Africa, Hong Kong, Malaysia, Philippines, Argentina, Chile, Kuwait, Oman, Qatar, Saudi Arabia, and the UAE, while only in Belgium and Luxembourg, New Zealand, and North America in the First World, was this the case (*Advertising Age*, 4 Dec. 1989). Kumar (2001) predicts that if tough health warnings on cigarette advertising are enforced almost all outdoor advertising could disappear in India.

Tobacco sponsorship has grown at the expense of direct advertising globally, providing money for sports, the arts, medical research, and universities. Major tobacco companies give huge amounts of money to charities of various types all over the world. In the 1990s PM disbursed around $50 million in cash annually and tens of millions more in non-monetary support. Other companies also gave substantial amounts. Cohen and Goldstein (1999) termed the consequence of this largesse 'the institutional addiction to tobacco'! One typical example comes from the Group to Alleviate Smoking Pollution (**www.gaspforair.org**) which lists twelve organizations in Colorado (USA) that received sponsorship from the tobacco industry in the years 1995–9. They included the American Indian College Fund, Colorado AIDS Project, Colorado Dance Festival, Denver Art Museum, Network to End Domestic Violence, and Senior Helpings Initiative, all very worthy causes deserving of support. Multiply this thousands of times all over the world and the global institutional addiction to tobacco becomes clear (Cornwell 1997).

The most visible public expression of the cigarette promotional culture is the long-standing and relentless sponsorship of youth-oriented sporting and entertainment events all over the world where glamour, athletic prowess, and sexual success are identified with cigarette smoking. This assertion is supported by a multitude of examples over the last decades: Miss Ghana and Miss Gitanes beauty contests in Africa; cricket in Pakistan; Marlboro and Chinese soccer; BAT 555 Nightman Disco in Beijing. Newsletters of the anti-smoking movement in Asia, AGHAST (Action Groups to Halt Advertising and Sponsorship by Tobacco, a campaign of the International Organization of Consumer Unions, based in Malaysia) and in the USA, the Boston-based INFACT, provide many more.

The PM website asserts: 'Philip Morris International currently participates in more than 130 youth smoking prevention programs in over 70 countries' (accessed September 2001) and all the other cigarette companies make similar claims. However, as with the infant formula companies, the industry stands accused of hypocrisy. For example, in 1997 PM created a new record label for undiscovered female musicians, Women Thing Music (a reference to the Virginia Slims cigarette created for young women). The company's CDs were free with the purchase of two packs of these cigarettes, only available in cigarette outlets. This is a clear and blatant attempt to induce teenage girls to buy these cigarettes and it undermines the FDA regulations to discourage youth smoking. The free entertainment listings magazines that are available in most US cities are full of large advertisements for music events sponsored by the tobacco companies, whose logos are graphically displayed. This is known as brand stretching and Mary Assunta (in INFACT 1998) gives many examples of the practice in Malaysia, notably BAT's Benson & Hedges-branded café, and its website in Poland, purporting to be a guide to night life in the main cities but actually promoting its cigarette brands. The cigarette companies always claim that these activities are intended to persuade smokers to change brands, not to entice young people to start smoking. An epidemiological study of advertising and promotion of cigarette brands in the USA, where restrictions are probably tighter than anywhere else in the world, reports the following results:

We estimated that between 1988 and 1998, there will be 7.9 million new experimenters because of tobacco advertising and promotions. This will result in 4.7 million new established smokers . . . Of these, 1.2 million will eventually die from smoking-attributable diseases: 520 000 from Camel, 300 000 from Marlboro, and the remainder from other brands. (Pierce *et al.*1999: 37)

This can be compared with a report to the government of the Czech Republic in which Philip Morris argued that people dying young save governments money as old people are so much more expensive to look after. PM had taken over the state tobacco company, Tabak, in 1992 and had seized 80 per cent of the market, promoting Marlboro aggressively beside local brands (*Guardian*, 17 July 2001).

Notwithstanding massive financial investments over a wide range of social institutions the most fundamental weapon in the armoury of the cigarette industry may be the social and sexual allure of the cigarette since its introduction as a mass consumer product, commonly dated from its manufacture by the French state tobacco monopoly in 1845 (Goodman 1993: 97 ff.). A young barber from Sichuan province in China expresses the contemporary version of this sentiment: 'I know that smoking is not a good habit, that it's harmful to your health. But I have no choice. To carry on social relationships and to do business, I have to smoke' (quoted in 'The Biggest Habit in the World, the Greatest Risk', *International Herald Tribune*, 22 Mar. 1996).

The industry is supported, often covertly, by an army of lobbyists, publicists, and ideo-logues, working wherever there are potential smokers to target. Among its most effective techniques are the continual defence of smokers' right to smoke wherever they wish, and its attempts to label the smoking and disease connection as controversial. Most promin-ent in this connection is Burson-Marsteller, Philip Morris's PR firm, which has created front organizations, notably the National Smokers Alliance, in the guise of citizen's groups to undermine anti-smoking information. Though most active in the USA, the cigarette lobby has a global reach. One example among thousands: as a US Environmental Protection Agency report on the dangers of passive smoking winged its way around the world, an article placed in *Business Daily* ((Manila) 10 Jan. 1997) reported that 'independent' journalists from the USA and Britain had rushed to attack the anti-smoking lobby.

While it does not have anything like the massive funding of the tobacco industry worldwide the anti-smoking movement, nevertheless, is also well organized, persistent, and clearly prepared for a very long-term campaign. It works through national voluntary associations, most prominently Action on Smoking and Health (ASH) in the UK, USA, and Australia, and many smaller, more focused groups against under-age smoking, smoking in public places, and cigarette advertising. The global centre of the movement is the regular World Conference on Tobacco and Health (WCTH) which, since its first meeting in New York in 1968, has provided a forum for anti-smoking activists, scientists, and practitioners to publicize their activities and to network. A watershed was reached at the Tokyo conference in 1988 when it was decided to ban industry representatives from the next meeting in Perth in 1990. The mood of the WCTH has since hardened towards the tobacco corporations (compare Ramstrom (1980) on the Stockholm conference and Slama (1995) on the meeting in Paris). Hewat (1991) labels the core of the anti-smoking movement, Daube's Dozen, after Mike Daube, formerly director of ASH in London and assistant commissioner for public health in Western Australia, who organized the WCTH in Perth.[33] This organization is growing into a formidable network. Large meetings in Beijing in 1997 and Chicago in 2000 (hosted by the American Cancer Society and the American Medical Association and attended by 4,000 professionals) and an active website (**wctoh.org**) maintain considerable pressure on the tobacco industry and those marketing its products.

By the mid-1990s health authorities all over the world began to speak with increasing regularity and alarm of the epidemic of smoking-related diseases that was sweeping the world. The WHO had been actively supporting the anti-smoking movement in a variety of ways, publishing statistics on smoking-related diseases and death rates, and working with health professionals. In 1999 its governing body, the World Health Assembly, took the dramatic step of proposing a Framework Convention on Tobacco Control. This is the first time that the WHO has ever exercised its constitutional power to formulate a treaty, indicating how seriously it took the crisis of smoking-related diseases. This initiative was widely welcomed by governments, even those of tobacco-growing states, and NGOs. The tobacco companies also joined in the negotiations and, not surprisingly, seek to influence the process, to the dismay of the WHO.

The anti-smoking movement has had many successes. In the USA, an ever-increasing number of smoking notables—the model for the Marlboro cowboy, the grandson of the founder of R.J. Reynolds Tobacco Company, sports bodies, artists and scientists formerly in receipt of tobacco money, and many professional associations—have denounced the habit and the methods the industry uses to promote it. The newsletter of the campaign group INFACT (Summer 2001: 2) reported that in a Harris Interactive poll 16 per cent of respondents who had heard of PM had boycotted their products in the past year. International Weeks of Resistance to Tobacco Transnationals were organized in thirty-five countries (including Honduras, Malawi, and India).

Globalizing bureaucrats who promote the interests of the tobacco industry are opposed by those, mostly in the Health and Education spheres, who are part of the anti-smoking movement. Indeed, the struggle between pro-tobacco government agents and agencies in revenue and industrial departments and anti-smoking activists in health and education appears to be an increasingly global phenomenon.[34] Disagreements at the local and country-wide levels between groups for and those against the tobacco industry have been paralleled internationally through the United Nations system. The FAO has supported the interests of tobacco growers while the WHO, in the interests of disease reduction, has campaigned against the role of tobacco in development (Taylor 1985: ch. 14; Nath 1986; Nyoni 1994).[35] Nevertheless, despite all this practical and ideological mobilization by the anti-smoking movement since the 1960s, more cigarettes are being smoked globally than ever before, the tobacco corporations make large profits, most of their shareholders seem content to take their dividends, and the promotional culture of cigarettes shows no sign at all of abating.

The tobacco industry links directly both with the economic crisis of increasing wealth and increasing poverty, and with the ecological crisis of planetary and individual well-being. The culture-ideology of consumerism promises that global capitalism will deliver prosperity for all and that this prosperity will be sustainable. The tobacco industry, through its marketing of cigarettes, actually does promise both, but in perverse and, ultimately, dishonest forms. Most people, however poor, can afford to smoke cigarettes. The promotional culture of cigarettes connects the consumer, however episodically, with the glamorous world of the adverts and smoking icons. Together with other affordable fashionable consumer goods (access to sports and entertainment through television, global branded soft drinks, fast foods, popular music, counterfeit clothes, and accessories) cigarettes help to mask the increasing gap between richer and poorer all over the world. Billions of small acts of consumption help momentarily to dissolve the economic crisis of global capitalism for individuals while intensifying it for the system as a whole as governments struggle to cope with epidemics of smoking-related diseases.

The promotional culture of cigarettes impacts the ecological crisis in two ways. First, it encourages farmers and governments to grow tobacco on land that could be producing nutritious food crops with less environmental stress. Tobacco prices make it one of the most valuable crops in the global marketplace. Second, tobacco is widely acknowledged to be the most significant cause of death on the planet, and a smoking-disease epidemic is already upon us (even the World Bank admits this). The promotional culture of cigarettes, by enriching those who control tobacco production and glamorizing smoking, helps mask the ecological crisis of global capitalism.

CONCLUSION

These brief studies of global consumerism set out to document the spread of the culture-ideology of consumerism in the Third World.[36] The choice of high prestige, relatively costly non-essentials is deliberate, because it is precisely the contradiction inherent in these mass-luxury global brands that symbolizes the problem that the capitalist global system faces in extending itself globally as competing brands battle for markets. These battles will be fiercely fought all over the world over colas, cars, cigarettes, detergents, toothpastes, movies, mobile phones, drugs, and countless other goods and services, no doubt in some countries where TNC advertising budgets are greater than state expenditures on education, as Figure 7.3 illustrates. The questions remain: can capitalism ever achieve its global goal of addicting all the people of the world to the culture-ideology of consumerism? Can it even meet the basic biological needs of the world's people, let alone their cultural and other needs? Despite the ingenuity of the TNCs, the efforts of the transnational capitalist class, and the hegemony of the culture-ideology of consumerism, the answers are by no means clear.

This sentiment encapsulates what many thinkers in the Third World fear most about the impact of the TNCs on their communities and cultures in the future. The spread of the new international division of labour, in its widest sense, has indeed brought many jobs and a good deal of prosperity to the transnational capitalist class and other groups in the Third World. Nevertheless, many in the Third World believe that, despite the apparent successes of the culture-ideology of consumerism, most of the material benefits, such as they are, will never percolate through to them.

These views range from the cautious to the catastrophic. Twenty years ago James and Stewart (1981: 106) found on the basis of a study of eight products: 'tentatively, that products developed in advanced countries are likely to have inegalitarian effects when introduced to poor countries and may, under certain conditions, cause losses among some or all consumers'. More dramatic is the prediction by Jayaweera that 'capitalism will also have left behind in the Third World, as its most enduring contribution to Third World development, an almost unfettered and wild consumerism, undergirded by the new electronic entertainment technologies'. He concludes on the grim note that 'when production pulls back to the metropolitan centers, and the offshore enclaves are dismantled, those tastes and aspirations will remain, along with the TV and video networks that nourished them' (Jayaweera, in Becker *et al.* 1986: 42–3). Not many people share the view that capitalism in the Third World will end in this way, but most would agree that the TNCs have played a crucial role in raising consumerist expectations that cannot be satisfied within the foreseeable future for billions of people around the world.

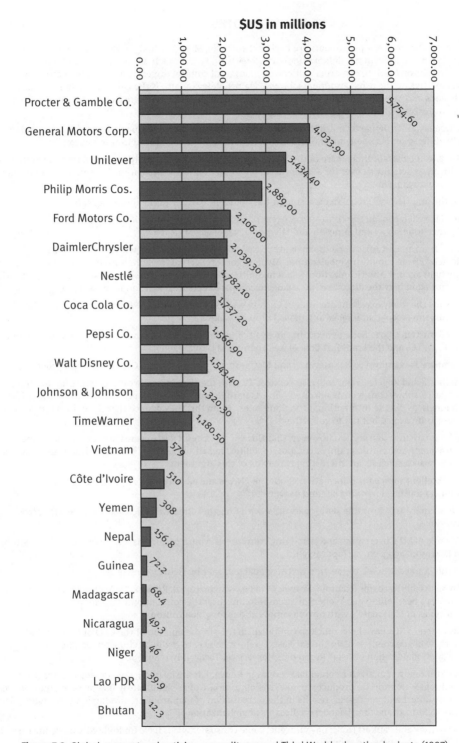

$US in millions

Procter & Gamble Co.	5,754.60
General Motors Corp.	4,033.90
Unilever	3,434.40
Philip Morris Cos.	2,889.00
Ford Motors Co.	2,106.00
DaimlerChrysler	2,039.30
Nestlé	1,782.10
Coca Cola Co.	1,737.20
Pepsi Co.	1,566.90
Walt Disney Co.	1,543.40
Johnson & Johnson	1,320.30
TimeWarner	1,180.50
Vietnam	579
Côte d'Ivoire	510
Yemen	308
Nepal	156.8
Guinea	72.2
Madagascar	68.4
Nicaragua	49.3
Niger	46
Lao PDR	39.9
Bhutan	12.3

Figure 7.3 Global corporate advertising expenditures and Third World education budgets (1997)
Source: advertising budgets from Advertising Age (16 July 2001); education budgets calculated from World Bank and UNESCO data.

NOTES

1. Among the strongest proponents are Becker *et al.* (1986), Mattelart (1983, 2000), Schiller (1981) and Sussman and Lent (1991). Melkote (1991) and Reeves (1993) are much more sceptical and the attempt in Tomlinson (1991) to construct a discourse analysis of cultural imperialism provides a different perspective on the usual arguments for and against. Relevant also is the cultural discount thesis of Hoskins and Mirus (1988: 500), who argue convincingly that 'US dominance follows naturally from the characteristics of television programming, its production and trade'.

2. These headings derive from Lee's discussion (1980), but my interpretations are radically opposed to his. The differences between cultural and media imperialism are not crucial in this context.

3. See also the extraordinary case of the 'pornographic' videotape allegedly smuggled into the Philippines which was actually a cover for a Japanese documentary on the assassination of Benigno Aquino (cited in Mowlana 1985: 88).

4. Zeitlin and Herrigel (2000) make a similar but not identical case in the industrial sphere.

5. See McNeill (2000) on the contested concept of national identity. Most of the contributions in Featherstone (1990) and Jameson and Miyoshi (1998) engage this issue.

6. This, from an East African newspaper editor, articulates well the way in which Americanization becomes detached from capitalist globalization: 'My fight for intellectual freedom is more important to me than the fight against Americanization' (cited in Smith 1980: 40). For insights into First World–Third World cultures and how the discourse has changed, compare Worsley (1984) and Lazarus (1999).

7. Despite the many excellent qualities of Castells's work, I agree with the friendly-critical evaluation by Friedmann (2000) that it lacks any radical utopian vision.

8. See Bernstein (1992). For a penetrating analysis of trade liberalization and culture policy, connecting GATT, WTO, and the Frankfurt School, see Footer and Graber (2000).

9. Compare Samarajiwa (1984), Herman and McChesney (1997: ch. 6), and Curran and Park (2000).

10. Malhotra and Rogers (2000: 408) also connect TV with the New Indian Woman, reporting that Indian-origin TV shows consistently outrated imports in the 1990s: 'Indian advertisers flocked to the private channels, as did the international conglomerates.' From this they deduce that the cultural imperialism thesis is incorrect, but fail to go further.

11. Salinas Bascur (1985) argues, however, that this led to wasteful and expensive over-purchase (and consequent under-utilization) of computer facilities in Latin America. The crash of many e-commerce firms in 2001 suggests an interesting extension of this argument.

12. An excellent source for information about the TNAAs and advertising as a globalizing practice is the industry journal *Advertising Age* and its website.

13. For an analysis of how one senior executive with Colgate-Palmolive conceived this, see Sklair (2001: 259–60).

14. The role of MTV in creating and sustaining consumerist youth cultures is well documented (see Sturmer, in Dowmunt 1993: ch. 4; Gupta 1998).

15. In this connection, see the section on the global teenager in Klein (2000: 118–21).

16. On McDonald's see, for example, Fishwick (1983), Watson (1997). Ritzer's *The McDonaldization of Society* (1996) is a best-selling neo-Weberian attempt to interpret the contemporary world in terms of the principles of McDonald's with obvious implications for globalization.

17. Other food TNCs have been quick to capitalize on this. In the opinion of the CEO of Heinz (which markets in 200 countries): 'In the Far East, Western habits are really catching on' and he can profit from the 'McDonaldisation of Asia ' (quoted in *Management Today*, July 1989: 69).

18. In a still relevant analysis of breakfast cereals in Kenya, Kaplinsky (1979: 90) argued: 'a move from traditional, appropriate products to new, less appropriate ones significantly increases the nutrient cost to consumers and, moreover, results in the introduction of inappropriate production techniques'. See also, McMurray and Smith (2001) on diseases of globalization.

19. As Garnsey and Paukert (1987: 69–70) argue, some consumer goods have undoubtedly made life easier for women in the domestic sphere.

20. This section is based on Pagan (1986); Muskie and Greenwald (1986); Chetley (1986); Heer (1991); Palmer (1993); Sethi (1994); Newton (1999) and Nestlé and campaign group websites.

21. In addition to its most famous product, Nescafé instant coffees, it also owns Perrier, Carnation, Chambourcy, Findus, Libby, Buitoni, Rowntree, and many other brands (see the website of the Baby Milk Action Campaign in the UK). In 2000 Nestlé ranked 41 in the FG500, with almost $50 billion in revenues.

22. Code violation is a controversial question and rests, to some extent, on company claims that they have little control over what actually happens with their products in the Third World. The interested reader is advised to access the Nestlé and Baby Milk Action websites.

23. In an interesting paper, Howard and Mayo (1988) illustrate concretely how the corporations could build in safeguards to prevent misuse of their products. But this would raise costs.

24. Though Nestlé rejected the proposal it retained the advisers! See *Multinational Monitor* (May 1989: 21–3); the sensationally titled, but very informative 'Forget the dead babies. Nestlé's PR firm spins feel-good line', *Voice* (2 May 1989: 14,18); and the Action for Corporate Accountability press release, 'Infant health activists angered by Nestlé's "PR only" response' (26 Apr. 1989).

25. Under the headline 'Food lobby forced PM into u-turn on plan for vaccination', the *Guardian* (8 Sept. 2001) identified Nestlé as the leader of the Food and Drink Federation campaign for the disastrous mass slaughter of cattle during the foot and mouth epidemic in Britain. Nestlé has a powdered milk factory in the north of England, from which 75 per cent of products go to the Third World.

26. But even the generics are too expensive for poor people, for example Cipla in India costs about $350 per person per year. The struggle over AIDS/HIV can be followed on the Internet. See also Baylies and Bujra (2000).

27. The research (reported in *Advertising Age*, 22 Apr. 1985: 55) was carried out by Boddewyn whose 1992 book on self-regulation in the advertising industry in thirty-eight countries is a good guide to the subject.

28. This argument has parallels with Illich's thesis of clinical iatrogenesis and related theories of commerciogenic illness. All are based on the idea that it is profit-inspired medical intervention that is responsible for most illness.

29. Mr Jabbonsky reappears as a spokesman for Pepsi-Cola defending the company's record in marketing in schools (*Beverage World*, 15 May 2001). I discuss this issue in Sklair (2001: 169–70).

30. This is an edited and updated version of part of Sklair (1998). I have adapted the title of the section from Taylor's fine book, *The Smoke Ring* (1985).

31. In a 2001 list from Interbrand based on sales, Marlboro does not make the top ten (Coca-Cola was top at $68.9b.). PM had a market value of $113b. (*Forbes*, 9 July 2001) so Marlboro is clearly still one of the world's most valuable brands. In 2000 PM spent $94m. in promoting Marlboro out of a total advertising budget of $1.8 billion in the USA alone, second only to General Motors who spent $2.8 billion (*Advertising Age*, 16 July 2001: s1–s12).

32. *Business Week* (6 Mar. 2000: 13) reports research by J. Gruber of MIT: 'the sharp reduction in the retail price of cigarettes [in the USA] in the early 1990s accounts for roughly 30 percent of the increase in teen smoking in the years that followed.' This confirms results from other countries.

33. The other eleven were a mixture of writers, medical researchers, and public health activists from Australia, the UK, the USA, Japan, and Hong Kong.

34. The cases of the USA and the UK are now well documented (McGowan 1995, Read 1996) and evidence from the Third World is also building up (see Nath 1986, Frey 1997).

35. The dilemma this poses for development professionals is well expressed in the confused and contradictory 'World Bank policy on tobacco' in the 1993 World Development Report issue on health (World Bank 1993: 89). Since then, the policy has become a little clearer.

36. Space precludes the inclusion of more cases. Suitable candidates for this type of study would include the private car (Newman and Kenworthy 1999); mass tourism to and in the Third World (Harrison 1994; Mullins, in Judd and Fainstein 1999: 245–60, Ghimire 2001); alcohol (Jernigan 1997); and mass media targeted at children (Dorfman and Mattelart 1975, Dorfman 1983, Buckingham 1997).

Chapter 8

CAPITALIST GLOBALIZATION IN COMMUNIST AND POSTCOMMUNIST SOCIETIES

Proletariat of all countries – Sorry!
(Slogan on an independent march in Moscow, Revolution Day, 7 Nov. 1989)

Until 1990, between twenty and thirty countries considered themselves communist or socialist. Economically, they fell into two groups, those that belonged to Comecon and those that did not. The Comecon group comprised most of the Eastern European countries where communism followed the Soviet victory in Europe in 1945, plus Cuba and Vietnam. The other group included Third World countries that opted for some variant of socialism when they were granted independence by the colonial power, like Tanzania, or after revolutionary wars, like China and the African states of Angola, Mozambique, and Zimbabwe.

Prior to the late 1980s when Stalinist communism began to disintegrate, the countries of Eastern Europe and the former Soviet Union were commonly referred to as the Second World, to distinguish them from the First World of the capitalist industrialized countries and the Third World. Though the label of the Second World appears to have fallen very quickly out of use, it may be premature to abandon it altogether and I distinguish here between the Old Second World and a New Second World that has replaced it. The issue of the Old and the New Second Worlds, the transition from communism to postcommunism, the continuities and discontinuities between them, will be taken up later in this chapter. The next chapter focuses on the relationship between China and capitalist globalization.

That leaves a group of countries known as the socialist Third World, a convenient label even if it conceals as much as it reveals. There is a good deal of controversy about these labels and how to categorize communist and socialist societies (Keller and Rothchild 1987, Heath 1993, Gills and Qadir 1995, King 2000).

COMMUNISM AND SOCIALISM DEFINED

There are different ways of defining socialist and communist societies. The terms are sometimes used interchangeably, but usually socialism is seen as a stage on the road to communism, a sort of transitional society. Both these usages can be defended, but the second is more useful. Socialism is defined as the social system based on the principle to each according to work, from each according to ability, while communism is defined by to each according to need, from each according to ability.[1] As will be immediately obvious, while this definition does distinguish socialism from communism, and tells us that no society in the world has achieved communism, it does not really distinguish either from many other social systems. There are, however, several structural features of social-ism that do distinguish it. These would certainly include the attempt to break the power of private capital over the economy and to establish mechanisms of democratic planning for the eventual transition to communism (see White 1983: 1). In addition to these com-mon structural features, there are also many sources of heterogeneity between societies that have embarked on the road to socialism. Among the most important are the widely varying initial conditions of their birth, the brand of socialism adopted, and the point in the socialist development reached at the time of the analysis (Forbes and Thrift 1987: Introduction).[2]

The analysis of Rothchild and Foley (in Keller and Rothchild 1987: 282–4), though intended for the study of Afro-Marxist regimes, has a much wider application. They suggest seven criteria of socialism, as follows:

1. Commitment to a specifically African (or presumably any other regional) scientific socialism but still true to orthodox Marxist-Leninism. (The reference here is to the distinction between revolutionary but petit-bourgeois ideology as in Tanzania and Algeria; and a wider range of revolutionary transformations as in Angola, Mozambique, and Ethiopia);

2. Focus on class analysis rather than a populist analysis based on the people as a whole;

3. The leading role of the vanguard party representing, but not necessarily led by, the working class;

4. Commitment to strengthening the state;

5. Open acceptance of revolutionary transformation to bring about a new social order, using coercion if necessary and including the reduction of the penetration of foreign-based capitalism;

6. Commitment to the creation of social and economic conditions for the redistribution of wealth and the triumph of socialism;

7. Finding natural allies in the socialist bloc.

The contents of this list can be criticized on various grounds, for example that Marxism is actually aimed at the abolition of the state, and that there are problems involved in the relationship between coercion and democracy. But Rothchild and Foley are inclined to argue that these regimes are trying to achieve socialism under very difficult conditions, and that this will inevitably lead to reluctant pragmatism.

An important determinant of reluctant pragmatism is that the socialist societies of the 1980s could no longer operate as if they could insulate themselves from capitalist global-ization, which is what they had previously been trying to do to a greater or lesser extent. While not everyone agrees that the remaining socialist countries now operate within the orbit of global capitalism, few will deny that many economic, political, and culture-ideology practices of capitalist globalization are penetrating socialist (and former social-ist) societies in ways that would have been considered unthinkable not long ago.[3]

Many remarkable developments have occurred in the communist world since the 1980s, notably the opening-up of the People's Republic of China (PRC) and other socialist Third World and Eastern European countries to capitalist transnational practices, particularly in the economic sphere. Political and culture-ideology changes have also been spectacular, but more unpredictable. This chapter will briefly analyse the experiences of some countries in the Americas and in Africa that have tried to implement socialist development strategies of one type or another, in terms of the global forces to which they have been exposed. The New Second World is then discussed and the chapter concludes with an examination of the choices open to socialist and formerly socialist Third World countries in a global system which, in the postcommunist era, is increasingly dominated by capitalist transnational practices.

THE SOCIALIST THIRD WORLD

As discussed above, the socialist bloc of Eastern Europe, led by the Soviet Union, established its own alternative to the capitalist global system, Comecon, though only two Third World countries (Cuba and Vietnam) joined.[4] Comecon had economic relations with most of the countries of the Third World, through its import and export trade and the activities of its transnational corporations (see below). In some countries at some periods, for example in Egypt under Nasser, in Ethiopia, Ba'athist Iraq and Syria, Cuba from the 1960s, North Vietnam in the 1960s and 1970s, Soviet influence was much stronger than Western influence.[5] The most thoroughly researched case of the transnational relations between the Soviet Union and a Third World country is probably Cuba. The issue is usefully posed in terms of the argument that Cuba simply exchanged US imperialist exploitation and dependency for Soviet imperialist exploitation and dependency.

CUBA

When Fidel Castro and his supporters defeated the Batista dictatorship in 1959 it was not at all certain that they would automatically ally with the communist camp. A combination of Cuban and US provocation, however, led gradually to this outcome. Cuba is typical of many Third World countries in that its economy is highly dependent on one product, in Cuba's case sugar. Before 1959 the US government guaranteed a market for Cuban sugar, after 1959 it was the Soviet Union that bought most of it. This brute economic fact makes plausible the conclusion that Cuba exchanged one master for another. This is a very complex question, involving economic, political, and culture-ideology judgements.

We can make no progress until we disaggregate the composite term dependency. Packenham (1992: ch. 7) usefully does this. Table 8.1 is based on his comparison of Cuban dependence between 1959 and the 1980s. Packenham's analysis, useful as it is, begs many conceptual questions about dependency and some substantive questions about how to measure it. There is little disagreement about the details of Cuba's relationships with the Soviet Union, though the interpretations of these details can vary widely. For example, in his analysis of Cuban dependency, LeoGrande shows that for sixteen out of twenty-eight indicators Cuban dependency seems to have declined, though Mesa-Lago pointed out that ten of these sixteen indicators involved trade dependency.[6] The nub of the differences is the view, plausible to some and ridiculous to others, that dependency on the Soviet Union was non-exploitative and more benevolent than dependency on the

Table 8.1 Cuban dependencies after 1959

Monoculture of national production	No change
Overall trade dependency	No change
Monoculture of exports	No change
Trade partner concentration (USA/Comecon)	No change
Trade partner concentrations (USA/USSR)	Less dependent
Capital dependency	No change
Debt dependency	More dependent
Energy dependency	More dependent
Technological dependency	No change

Source: adapted from Packenham (1992: ch. 7).

USA. Fidel Castro himself, and many other Latin American anti-imperialist writers have argued that the influence of the Soviet Union was benign. Whether this is true or not, the fact remains that the Soviet government could have cut off most of Cuba's oil, and a substantial part of its imports of food, raw materials, and capital goods, as well as most of its weapons. The export market for at least half of Cuba's sugar was also vulnerable. However, and this is a central part of the argument, this only proves that the Soviet Union could have exercised policy leverage on Cuba, not that it actually exploited Cuba economically. Indeed, the evidence, complicated as it is, suggests that over the years Cuba may well have earned more from its sugar deals with the Soviet Union than it would have earned on the world market. The fact that after the collapse of the Soviet Union, the Russian government virtually stopped all economic relations with Cuba supports this interpretation (Mesa-Lago 1993: 144 and *passim*, Cole 1998).

There are other considerations, too. Cuba joined Comecon in 1972, and closely followed Soviet planning and organizational methods. The thesis that Cuban society was Sovietized in a variety of ways cannot seriously be denied, and Cuba's domestic social structures, its political and cultural life, and foreign policy, all testified to increasing Soviet and decreasing Western influence from the 1960s to 1990 (Halebsky and Kirk 1992). This changed in the 1990s with the opening up of external and internal economic and social policies (Cole 1998: Brundenius and Weeks 2001: part 1).

It is, however, also difficult to deny that throughout this whole period Cuba was still, in many respects, affected by capitalist globalization. The Sovietization of Cuba thesis may be true, but in common with most other socialist Third World countries, Cuba's links with the capitalist world economy have grown substantially since the 1980s, and the fact that Cuba is now open to selected foreign investment suggests that the trend is set to continue. In the mid-1990s, Old Havana was turned into a virtual free economic zone, run as a business by the city authorities (see Scarpaci, in Scarpaci 2000). In 1995 Cuba passed Law 77 legalizing direct foreign investment and in 1996 Decree 165 authorized free import/export zones in the island. In 1997 individuals were allowed to apply for Internet authorization, but it was priced well above the range of most Cuban workers. The Internet is being mobilized in the service of development, for example through the Infomed health site established with a UNDP grant. Cubans abroad can use the official Cubaweb site to move money into the bank accounts of their relatives on the island.

A judgement expressed in 1980 is still valid: 'Cuba can restrict and regulate, but not eliminate, relations with Western bloc countries. It is socialist in name, ideology, and intent, but it must come to terms with capitalist forces in its international relations' (Eckstein 1980: 270). The economic blockade imposed by the US government continues to undermine economy and society in Cuba. Miami-based Cuban opposition groups gain strength with the prospect of the death of Fidel Castro. The leading opposition group, the Cuban American National Foundation, is already said to be in informal contact with members of the Cuban government. The issue today is not so much that Cuba is being engulfed by capitalist globalization but that its leaders and a substantial proportion of its people have sustained their commitment to socialist development for so long.[7]

NICARAGUA

In 1979, after almost twenty years of struggle against the dictatorship of the Somoza family and their friends, the Sandinista National Liberation Front led by Daniel Ortega launched a civil war, seized state power, and established a revolutionary socialist regime. The Somoza regime had lasted for forty-six years, largely propped up by successive US governments and the transnational corporations that extracted much of the little wealth the country produced. The Sandinista regime was immediately isolated and faced a hostile military, political, and economic threat from elements in the USA. All through the 1980s the Reagan government waged what Walker (1987) termed an 'undeclared war' against the Nicaraguan people, covertly funding the so-called Contras in terrorist activities all over the country.

The option of a close economic relationship with the Soviet Union was not available to the Nicaraguan government. Only two socialist Third World countries, Cuba and Vietnam, had been admitted to Comecon. The rest had to work out their transnational relationships with the Soviet Union and the rest of the world on other terms and for many, the best option appeared to be membership of the Non-Aligned Movement (NAM) at the UN. Nicaragua used its membership of NAM to mediate its relationships with both superpowers.

By 1979, NAM had almost one hundred members, including many in Latin America. The sixth NAM summit meeting in Havana in 1979 provided the ideal base for Nicaragua to seek support from and express support for all those involved in revolutionary struggles. The siting of a NAM Extraordinary meeting in Managua in 1983 was a further indication of the success of its policy, eloquently summarized as the unity of the weak by Daniel Ortega, when he first addressed the United Nations as leader of his country. Membership of NAM (rather than Comecon) afforded Nicaragua a more independent and flexible foreign policy than was possible for Cuba, and this led to a higher level of international support for Nicaragua in the UN and elsewhere. It has even been suggested that this diplomatic and solidaristic activity helped to restrain the USA from actually invading Nicaragua, though not from funding the Contra terrorism that eventually put an end to Nicaragua's experiment with socialism.

Nicaragua, a neighbour of Cuba (another victim of US military as well as economic aggression) also struggled to build socialism from an extremely low base of economic and social resources. The fundamental problem for Nicaragua and for all other small countries seeking to pursue a socialist path to development was the viability of socialism within a capitalist global system. A combination of economic isolation and military intervention, orchestrated and funded by elements in the US state, literally brought this tiny country to its knees. In the elections of 1990 the Sandinistas were defeated by the National Opposition Union (UNO) led by Violeta Barrios de Chamorro (whose family owned the major newspaper in the country). All the indications were that the people of Nicaragua had voted to end the devastation caused by the US-funded Contras, rather than to express any great enthusiasm for UNO. During the 1990s, the Chamorra regime was characterized by rapid encroachment by the TNCs, the emergence of local affiliates for the transnational capitalist class, and the culture-ideology of consumerism via the mass media. There had been genuine progress in the fields of education, health, land reform, and the environment under socialist leadership in the 1980s (Rosset and Vandermeer 1986, Vanden and Prevost 1993), and there have been notable struggles to maintain these gains under the new regime (see Sinclair and Nash 1995).

Robinson (1997) provides a useful analysis of the transition in Nicaragua from the 1960s to the 1990s, showing how capitalist globalization produced changes in the economic model, the political regime, the class structure, and international relations and exchanges. Under the tutelage of the World Bank and USAID the Chamorro government negotiated huge foreign debts, necessitating the restructuring of the economy towards maximizing export earnings to earn the foreign currency to service these debts. Robinson reports that in 1993 while 28,000 small farmers could raise no credit at all, 'just nine newly consolidated capitalist agri-business and export groups monopolised over 30% of all credits' (Robinson: 1997). The banking system, the training of management and administrative personnel, and the structure of imports were all heavily influenced by the international financial institutions. By the mid-1990s 400 state enterprises, comprising 40 per cent of GNP, were privatized, leading to the reconcentration of property ownership and the formation of a modernizing elite that could connect with the transnational capitalist class. In these ways capitalist globalization is transforming Nicaragua from an agro-export system in which producers, middlemen, and buyers are linked in a set of simple exchanges, into a much more complex network of transnational circuits of accumulation.

Changes in the political regime, from authoritarianism through the brief revolutionary period to polyarchic democracy (see Robinson 1996), and in Nicaragua's international relations, particularly through the coordinating role of the UNDP, provide further support for Robinson's thesis that capitalist globalization is rapidly dominating Nicaragua.

These are clearly processes that are at work all over the world but the ways in which they worked out in Nicaragua illustrate the options, or rather lack of options of a small, poor, tropical country. In 2001 with new elections looming, Daniel Ortega re-emerged as a modernized socialist leader of a modernized Sandinista Party, despite damaging allegations of sexual abuse by his stepdaughter and the general opposition of the feminist movement in Nicaragua. He campaigned on the possibilities of working with the new reality of global capitalism against the corrupt political-business elite that was running the country. He championed all those ignored by the regime: the growing numbers of urban poor in barrios without proper sanitation and clean water, the children who look for food in contaminated landfills, and impoverished peasants whose livelihoods are being destroyed by the plunging world coffee price. As in Venezuela, Mexico, Peru, and El

Salvador, the crises of capitalist globalization appear to be giving former socialist revolutionaries a certain appeal in Nicaragua, though Ortega lost the election.

SOCIALISM IN SUB-SAHARAN AFRICA

Although the intensity of capitalist globalization in the socialist Third World countries increased dramatically in the 1980s, the seeds of the process can be quite clearly seen in the 1950s and 1960s when the proclamations of African Socialism rang through that continent. The inability of the African socialist countries either to break from global capitalism or to make domestic political progress led many radical theorists to the conclusion that they never really stopped being dependent underdeveloped societies. It is useful to distinguish between those states that achieved their independence through a process of negotiation with the colonial power in the 1960s (Tanzania is the classic example), and those who liberated themselves through revolutionary struggle in the following decades (for example, the ex-colonies of Portugal, and Zimbabwe). These cases are often referred to as first wave, socialist-humanist and second wave, Marxist-Leninist regimes, a more useful guide to original ideology than actual practices.

Keller and Rothchild (1987) point out that in francophone (Algeria, Mali, Guinea) and anglophone (Ghana, Tanzania) Africa, populist socialist ideas were common in the struggle against colonialism. These were often non-Marxist, and sometimes, as in Kenya, not even anti-capitalist. Lack of effective administrative control (the so-called soft state) made it difficult to put socialist ideas into practice. As populist socialism declined, scientific socialism bloomed. In 1969, President Ngouabi proclaimed the People's Republic of the Congo, the first Afro-Marxist regime to reject populist socialism officially, and many others followed (including Somalia, Madagaskar, Benin, Mozambique, Angola, and Ethiopia). It was not until military interventions of the Cubans in Angola in 1975 and the Soviets in Ethiopia in 1977, that the West began to pay serious attention to communism in Africa.

It is difficult to see how, under the conditions of capitalist globalization, African socialism could be much more than a form of state capitalism where bureaucracies try to run the economy with very limited resources. It is even doubtful that the very restricted level of autonomy they had permitted them to run the system in any very meaningful sense. As Keller argued in the mid-1980s: 'In every case, these regimes are heavily dependent on foreign capital, mostly provided by bilateral and multilateral aid agencies' (in Keller and Rothchild 1987: 16). The key issue in such cases always is: in whose interests do the bureaucrats run the economy and society?[8] From the point of view of the workers and the peasants, state capitalism is similar in at least some of its essentials to private capitalism. The direct producers in the factories and the fields still have to struggle against their bosses. Though they are employees of the state, these bosses may identify more with bosses elsewhere than with the masses in their own country. There are undoubtedly many state and party bureaucrats in the socialist Third World who do take the socialist project seriously (see Forbes and Thrift 1987; and White et al. 1983). Nevertheless, one is left with the distinct impression that, leaving aside the corrosive effects of corruption and nepotism, these socialist entrepreneurs are outnumbered by entrepreneurs and bureaucrats of a more orthodox kind. These latter often become important elements in the emergence of the local affiliates of the transnational capitalist class in the socialist Third World.

Each region has its own structures, institutions, and personnel to promote the global capitalist project. In sub-Saharan Africa, before the accession to power of the African National Congress (ANC), the Republic of South Africa was the core of this system and fulfilled a strategic global function for capitalism in the whole continent. The transnational corporations had for decades used South Africa as their base from which to extract minerals, food, and industrial crops from the region, and from which to sell their goods in regional markets (see Hauck *et al.* 1983).[9] It is sobering to reflect that even the most militant socialist opponents of apartheid in Southern Africa, Mozambique, Angola, and Zimbabwe, were unable to cut themselves free from dependence on capitalist globalization as it operated at the end of the twentieth century through Southern African economies and societies.[10]

With the victory of the nominally socialist ANC led by Nelson Mandela in South Africa's first democratic elections in 1994, the political situation in the whole of Southern Africa changed. In June 1994 South Africa joined the Southern African Development Community (SADC), originally formed in 1980 by nine front-line states to reduce their economic dependence on South Africa, but it achieved very little success. South Africa also had to forge a relationship with the eighteen-member Preferential Trade Area (formed in 1982) that resulted in a Common Market for Southern and Eastern Africa (COMESA). South Africa is said to be a swing economy, meaning that for every 1 per cent its economy grows, the rest of Southern Africa grows several times more. As the World Bank estimated that only in Botswana and Swaziland were people significantly richer in the early 1990s than they were in the early 1980s, there is clearly substantial room for improvement (see Jamal and Weeks 1993, Wilson *et al.* 2000). The effects of these initiatives for the countries of Africa that have had socialist experiments remain to be seen. The cases of two of them, Tanzania and Mozambique, will now be briefly examined.

TANZANIA

The twin necessities of socialism, to create a hegemonic political base, and to seize the commanding heights of the economy from those who own and control them, were never achieved to any great extent anywhere in Africa. Tanzania was created in 1964 out of Tanganyika (granted independence by the British government in 1961) and the islands of Zanzibar and Pemba. The post-independence experience of Tanzania exemplifies these problems. During the height of the Tanzanian experiment with socialism parastatal enterprises, publicly owned but effectively run on private enterprise lines, were controlled by foreign managers and local bureaucrats whose commitment to the goals of socialism were in question at home and abroad. Nationalization in Tanzania was carried out with full and fair compensation, which left the new companies on a feeble economic footing. The belief in neutrality of management and the recipes of foreign consultants (like McKinsey) left little space for socialism. Capital–labour relations likewise were subordinated to management needs (Loxley and Saul 1975).

Where the TNCs initiated their own enterprises, they tended to be relatively capital-intensive projects established to maximize profits, rather than labour intensive projects that served the needs of most Tanzanians. The Mwanza textile mill, for example, was built by French investors, and cost three times as much as the Chinese-built Friendship textile mill. The French project produced the same value of goods with one-third of the workforce, efficient perhaps in narrow economic terms but, many would argue, not as appropriate to the needs of Tanzanians at the time. Increasingly, under the influence of foreign experts, the World Bank, and other purveyors of the capitalist global project, relations between capital and labour in Tanzania were subordinated to the requirements of the external capitalist market. Writing of the silent class struggle Shivji (1976) called the new ruling class the bureaucratic bourgeoisie. In my terms, bureaucratic bourgeoisies often turn into globalizing bureaucrats, politicians, and professionals with a little help from their friends in the transnational capitalist class. This appears to be what happened in Tanzania.

The key to Tanzanian socialism lay in the struggle between two development strategies, neither fully implemented. One, the *ujamaa* (familyhood) tradition was based on an African past (perhaps somewhat idealized), much of which had been destroyed during the colonial period with the intrusion of capitalist agriculture. *Ujamaa* was encapsulated in the call for land to be returned to the communal cultivators. The other strategy, promoted in the First Five Year Plan (commended by a World Bank mission in 1961 which had blamed stagnation on conservative peasants and poor extension services), directed resources to progressive farmers and the resettling of people on more fertile lands. The Arusha Declaration of 1967 was a turning point. The First Five Year Plan had not worked; it simply reinforced the tendencies promoting a classic export-oriented dual economy. In Arusha, President Nyerere identified capitalism as the main obstacle to Tanzania's development, and began a process of nationalization of foreign interests, particularly the banks. The new policy, with the slogan of mass participation and equality in distribution, broadcast throughout Africa a vision of development based on self-reliance and peasant agriculture, but also industrialization (see Mittelman 1981, whose comparison with Mozambique is very instructive).

The Government of Tanzania Guidelines of 1971, partly in response to the military threat posed by Idi Amin in Uganda, went even further. Expensive private houses were expropriated, causing one-fifth of the Asian population to leave and a massive brain drain. All official salaries were reduced. But in 1977, ten years after Arusha, the government was forced to admit that Tanzania was neither socialist nor self-reliant, though it claimed to have halted nascent capitalism.

The *ujamaa* experiment was based on the communal ownership of land. Most small farmers were unwilling to organize in collectives and by 1970 a campaign of persuasion more or less signalled that the voluntary phase of *ujamaa* was over. As long as the government had something to deliver to the villagers they would cooperate, but there were never enough resources. Outright compulsion was introduced after a severe drought in 1973. While villagization did bring some measure of welfare and social services to the countryside, it failed the production test decisively. The subsistence sector has proved peculiarly resistant to marketization (see Waters 2000) though the Tanzanian state was not so resistant. It was, therefore, not surprising that successive governments in Tanzania slowly abandoned socialist policies, threw in their lot with the World Bank and embarked on state expenditure cuts, privatization, and a greater reliance on the market (D. Potts, in Cook and Kirkpatrick 1995). Kivikura (in Boyd-Barrett and Rantanen 1998:

ch. 9) shows how this process worked as the media were deregulated in Tanzania, an essential part of the spread of capitalist globalization and particularly the culture-ideology of consumerism in the Third World.

Between 1967 and 1977, foreign borrowing rose from a quarter of development expenditure to more than half of it. By the 1980s, the World Bank was more or less dictating the country's export and import trade through a system of tied aid. Financial support for village projects was increasingly channelled through World Bank loans and the ujamaa programme became something of a showcase for foreign investment! The decision of the major international financiers to support *ujamaa* villages, once the symbol of creeping African socialism, might be seen as part of an implicit strategy by sections of the transnational capitalist class to keep Tanzania stable and to inhibit the production of manufactures that might cut out First World imports.

In 1991 a Presidential Commission recommended that a multi-party electoral system be established and this led to what looked like fundamental political reform. In a challenging analysis, Vener (2000) explains this in terms of the perceptions of the Tanzanian leadership that more aid would be forthcoming if the political system was liberalized. At that time aid to Tanzania was worth over one-third of GNP, putting the country in the group of highest aid recipients in the world. By the early 1990s all major donors had incorporated democratization into aid conditions. The World Bank was making strong connections between democratization, good governance, and economic development, and this put further pressure on Tanzanian leaders for reform. Although the data suggests that aid flows were actually not much related to democratization as such, Vener shows that politicians in Tanzania (government and opposition) made the connections. So, a complex mix of external rhetorical pressure and internal politics strongly influenced political reforms in Tanzania. This is one of many cases in which globalization has encouraged democratization in one-party states, but the results have sometimes mixed elements of '(Un)Democracy' with democracy (see Scholte 2000: ch. 11). An example of this in Tanzania was the tax revolt in Arumeru District in 1998. Kelsall (2000) shows how the revolt was linked to the introduction of multi-party democracy and the promotion of political reforms by aid donors. But Kelsall cautions against counting this rural mobilization as evidence of a popular movement, explaining it more in terms of the rise of powerful local elites who were able to take advantage of the opening up of the political system. Rimmer (2000) is not alone in arguing that democratization has led to increased rather than reduced levels of corruption in Tanzania and other countries in sub-Saharan Africa.[11]

Meanwhile, as in most of the Third World, the burden of foreign debt remains. According to Jubilee 2000 (the campaign to persuade governments, private lenders, and international financial institutions to wipe out Third World debt), Tanzania owed $7.6 billion in 1998, a debt to exports ratio of 484. This was three times higher than the ratio the World Bank/IMF considered sustainable in the medium term. Debt service rose by 48 per cent in 1998, the largest increase in ten years. The government spent as much to service this debt (over 3 per cent of economic output) as it spent on education and twice as much as it spent on health.[12]

An important aspect of this process is what Bryceson (1981) termed the proletarianization of women in Tanzania. Most Third World policy makers believe that removing people from their means of subsistence and forcing them to become wage labourers will encourage the transition to industrialization. A rather precise sexual division of labour had been imposed on peasant women by the colonial authorities in the 1930s, and some Tanzanian women saw proletarianization as a means of escape from male domination. Since the 1940s women have been migrating to the towns to join their men or to seek work, or both (Tripp, in Beneria and Feldman 1992: ch. 7). Women are part of the small industrial labour force in Tanzania, but tend to be replaced by men when factories are automated (for example, in matchmaking and coffee curing). Bryceson noted that the Maternity Leave Act of 1975 resulted in some employers refusing to hire women (as in China more recently). There are large numbers of unmarried women with children who rely on their own labour power and, to that extent, have escaped from the sexual subordination to which peasant women are often subject. But many of those who cannot find jobs are forced into prostitution by the freedom of the market. Those who remain in the villages grow increasingly reliant on the local informal sector for survival (M. Bagachwa, in Bryceson and Jamal 1997: ch. 8). The programmes of the World Bank appear to have worsened rather than improved the prospects for poor women and their children. Kawewe and Dibie (2000) come to the same conclusions on the impact of the structural adjustment programme in Zimbabwe, another African socialist experiment that failed to materialize. This is a pattern that is by no means unique to Africa or the socialist and Third World for that matter (see Brydon and Chant 1989).[13]

MOZAMBIQUE

An instructive comparison can be drawn between Tanzania, the leading first wave African socialist state, and Mozambique, often identified as a hard-line second-wave Marxist-Leninist state. Their paths to independence could hardly have been more different. For Tanzania, independence was granted by a British government, anxious to rid itself of colonial responsibilities while maintaining the economic stake of 'its' TNCs, while for Mozambique the revolutionary movement, Frelimo, had a long and bloody struggle for freedom from a ruthless but eventually exhausted Portugal.[14]

By the time Frelimo came to power in 1975 the Portuguese farmers who had dominated the economy had largely sabotaged agriculture as they abandoned the country. Food for the cities was the top priority of Frelimo and to achieve this a policy of state farms and agricultural co-operatives, reliant on imported tractors and chemicals, was embarked upon. Mozambique proceeded rapidly to implement socialist policies. The banks were nationalized in 1978 with compensation, and although the government sought to take over the commanding heights of the economy, private property was retained in housing and land. Private medicine, law, and education persisted, as did private business. Dynamizing groups of Frelimo cadres worked at the grassroots, in the countryside and in the towns, where a serious commitment to industrialization was made.

The exodus of the Portuguese colonialists did not, of course, entirely end the influence of Portugal. Policy decisions to support the modern sector and encourage what Raikes (1984) calls an essentially Portuguese urban diet are explicable only in terms of a curious but by no means unusual mixture of communist ideology and the legacy of colonialism on its erstwhile subjects.

It is not only in Mozambique, or even in Africa, that the peasant sector has been starved of resources thanks to an oversimplified conception of agricultural modernization based on foreign rather than local standards of living. The government took the pattern of consumption under colonialism for granted, and tried to maintain European standards, though attempting to establish them as the norm rather than the privilege of the elite. This meant that most of the available resources of the state went to support cash crops (rather than production of food crops) to pay for imports, and to favour relatively expensive rather than basic foods. The inevitable consequence was that the family commercial sector was left to stagnate and resource-wasting state farms took most of the available investment. Peasants were forced to trade on the black market, and state agencies were chronically unable to ensure supplies of food and other essentials to the mass of the population.

The government actually signalled the end of the free welfare state and 'the persistent spirit of getting things for nothing' (to quote the then Finance Minister, Baltazar) in 1984. A free market in a variety of goods and services was announced then, and private foreign investment was heralded as the main engine of change. The official news agency admitted that it would not be easy to defend socialism because capitalists 'leave behind them a petty bourgeoisie and government absolutely corrupted by the crumbs from the neocolonial banquet'. Despite this, the new course was seen as the only prospect for development.[15]

The salience of the official analysis was entirely borne out by the establishment of three agricultural plantations by the British-based TNC Lonrho, representing an investment of $40 million. In at least one of these, the Nhamatanda estate, which grew cotton and food crops in a joint venture with the Mozambique government, the classical conditions of enclave development were reproduced. The estate had its own import and export facilities, and the workers were paid in tokens to be exchanged for goods in the company store. Poor socialist as well as poor capitalist governments are forced into such alliances.[16]

By the mid-1980s the cumulative effects of the terrorist war waged by the South African-funded Renamo dissidents, poor policy decisions by the government, drought, and the consequent near-destruction of the rural and urban sectors, were paralysing the authorities. Between 1981 and 1986 production had fallen by 30 per cent and per capita consumption by 45 per cent. The result was a World Bank/IMF-sponsored Economic Rehabilitation Programme (PRE) that the government of Mozambique had little alternative but to accept (Torp et al. 1989: ch. 3). Contradictions abound. By the late 1980s the minimum wage was less than the cost of the average food basket, let alone other necessities of life, though the urban middle class (including a number of wayward party cadres) was growing. There were luxury goods in the shops for those with money to buy. The new policy subordinated government decisions to market forces, but the basic weaknesses of the economy, low productivity, and imports for consumption financed through aid, all persisted.

The PRE was a typical World Bank restructuring exercise, with devaluation, cuts in state spending, reduction in price subsidies, and investment increased at the expense of consumption. As Torp et al. (1989: 53) explained: 'The programme aims to transfer resources and initiatives from the public sector to the private sector, including the peasant family sector, and to encourage exports.' A massive injection of external resources, spare parts for industry, and consumer goods to stimulate peasant production resulted in some growth. But the urban poor still went hungry, school rolls continued to fall, health facilities closed down, and the prospects for socialism in Mozambique dimmed. All the evidence suggests that the World Bank made the policy for Mozambique, while Frelimo explained it to the masses. By the mid-1990s aid represented more or less 100 per cent of GDP, a condition that led Sidaway and Power (1995) to classify Mozambique as an aid-dependent state. The demand for higher levels of production was gradually being replaced by the demand for the restoration of pre-independence structures, mostly initiatives in the private sector. This was not too difficult a task to accomplish, as most agree that the basics of the colonial capitalist economic system are still in place (Munguambe, in Heath 1993: ch. 9, Cramer and Pontara 1998).[17] For Mozambique, as for much of the rest of Africa, the argument of Logan and Mengisteab (1993: 21) is convincing: 'The simple truth is that economic reform which excludes the activities of a good 70 to 80 per cent of the African population cannot expect to be successful or sustainable.'

The Mozambique government officially abandoned Marxism in 1987 when its World Bank-backed reform programme was established, but, after some early progress, continued civil war and more devastating droughts inhibited economic growth. A UN-US-brokered peace settlement resulted in an agreement between Frelimo and Renamo in 1992, and political pluralism slowly emerged with the formation of new parties. Under the tutelage of the UN, multi-party elections took place and the creation of a government of national unity along the lines of the South African compromise was mooted. Victoria Brittain detailed the atrocities of Renamo and described the forces aligned against the Mozambican government:

600,000 or so Portuguese who fled to South Africa at independence have invested heavily in Renamo, planning to have their farms, ranches, and businesses back. US right-wingers in the circle of Major-General John Singlaub of the World Anti-Communist League, Richard Secord of Iran-contra fame, Sybil Cline of US Global Strategy Council, and businessmen dreaming of making Mozambique the Hong Kong of Africa, were an important part of the mythologising of Renamo as an alternative to a government originally defined as socialist. (*Guardian*, 6 Aug. 1994: 13)

It is, therefore, not surprising that the opposition between settler citizens and native subjects in colonial Mozambique survived the Frelimo victory and the defeat of colonialism and continues to impact economic and political life. Mamdani (1996) argues that it is important to distinguish between market-based identities (including class), a product of commodity relations, and political (legally enforced) identities, a product of state formation. Neither native nor settler is a class identity. As Marx argued, in primitive accumulation the political prevailed over the economic relation (domination over exploitation) and the dynamic of the colonial world was in contradiction between the two, particularly how forced labour was pushed out of the customary sphere into the market. In Tanzania, Mozambique, and other post-colonial societies this inhibits the prospects for democracy. The persistence of the structures that defined the difference between settlers and natives in the colonial period explains this: 'Mozambicans of European, Asian and mulatto origin were disproportionately represented in the political elite and among the new capitalists running trade and taking over privatized state assets' (O'Laughlin 2000: 5).[18]

Frelimo (led by Chissano) narrowly beat Renamo in the 1999 election, but when the Renamo leader refused to accept the result the international donor community backed Chissano.[19] The 'US State Department seems to still be divided, with the old cold warriors still hostile to Frelimo, but with another group supporting Frelimo because of its whole-hearted adoption of capitalism and IMF structural policies' (Hanlon 2000: 593). Frelimo's relatively poor showing in the 1999 elections were due to the feeling of the poor that economic conditions were not improving. 'People see that Maputo [the capital] is a prosperous and expanding city, and they also see how rapidly the gaps between rich and poor are increasing' (p. 596; see also on Maputo, Sidaway and Power 1995). Widespread corruption in the courts and in the privatization process (especially involving banks and government contracts) was also a contentious issue. 'Many government ministers and their families, and President Chissano's family, are involved in businesses which now dominate the local economic scene. Renamo figures such as Raul Domingo are being incorporated into this new politico-economic elite' (Hanlon 2000: 596).[20] Hanlon concludes that the once-Marxist Frelimo needs the once-insurgent Renamo to pre-empt real opposition, possibly from its own disaffected left. In her critical analysis of Mozambique in the 1990s, Ostheimer (2001) terms the system democratic minimalism. Not all those who study Mozambique are as gloomy about its prospects, however. Fieldwork in the urban political centre and in rural areas gave Braathen and Palmero (in Wilson *et al.* 2000: ch. 13) some grounds to argue that there are some signs of what they term pro-poor governance from Frelimo (to whom they give the benefit of the doubt). But even they agree that local democracy and effective poverty alleviation are as yet quite feeble. The floods that devastated the country in 2000 set back an already desperate situation.

The reintroduction of capitalist and colonial practices as a result of capitalist globalization does not effect men and women in exactly the same ways. While Mozambican resistance in the war against Renamo terrorism undermined the patriarchal authority of the home, the persistence of traditional female subservience to men contrasted with a new female sexual self-confidence. The Frelimo socialist project for reconstruction promised to make space for the feminist project of gender equality, as appeared to have been implied by the revolutionary method of self-empowerment, but this did not happen very widely (Urdang 1989). As was argued in an informative study of the Mozambique Women's Organisation (OMM): 'the political programme of modernization and the exclusion of gender struggle often amounts to a tacit support for male power, whether intended or not' (Arnfred 1988: 12). Women in Mozambique made no great leaps forward in the 1990s, though Tripp (2001) does suggest that independent women's movements are stirring all over Africa (see also Basu 1995).

Is there anything left of the socialist project in Africa? Rothchild and Foley, in their analysis of ideology and policy in Afro-Marxist regimes in the 1980s, argued that the experiments of Mozambique and Angola with non-socialist economic practices, like private trading, peasant production, and relations with TNCs, represented 'a shift of emphasis intended to strengthen the country to deal with a hostile environment, not a substantial retreat from basic Marxist-Leninist principles' (in Keller and Rothchild 1987: 311). Mozambique's liberal investment code guaranteed repatriation of profits and compensation against nationalization; and in addition to the plantations revived by Lonrho, General Motors, for example, were contracted to transport coal around the country. In Angola, although the regime remained committed to Marxist-Leninist ideology, they argued: 'it has excellent business relations with a wide array of prominent multinational firms. Angola's state oil corporation, Sonangol, in partnership with Chevron, Texaco, Elf Aquitaine, Conoco, and others, is actively exploring the country's rich offshore deposits, and prominent Western banks such as Chase Manhattan play an important role in financing the country's development' (Keller and Rothchild 1987: 312). This trend has continued.

If Keller and Rothchild are correct for Mozambique and Angola, even allowing for the ravages of the terrorist wars promoted by the apartheid regime in South Africa and the CIA, then prospects for both the TNCs and socialism in Africa are perhaps not quite so bleak as might be imagined. But, it must be said, most scholars today would regard the prospects for the TNCs and the prospects for socialism to be mutually exclusive. However, as we shall see in the next chapter, TNCs and what has come to be known as market socialism, both appear to be thriving in China.

TRANSNATIONAL PRACTICES IN THE OLD SECOND WORLD

On 9 November 1989 the authorities of what was then communist East Germany announced that citizens were at last free to travel to the West. Children, women, and men immediately began to knock down the Berlin Wall, built in the 1960s to prevent spontaneous interaction between the peoples of Eastern and Western Europe and one of the most hated symbols of Stalinist authoritarian rule. Soon, pieces of authentic Berlin Wall were being sold all over the world and Stalinist communism collapsed. East and West Germany were reunited in 1990 and the Soviet Union itself was dissolved in late 1991. The economic, political, and culture-ideology transnational practices that had been permeating Eastern Europe for decades were now being enthusiastically and openly promoted, often by the newly elected governments of the former communist states and their free-market advisers, consultants, and allies from the transnational capitalist class.

All over Eastern Europe, ideologues of communism fell silent and ideologues of capitalism interpreted the collapse of Stalinist communism to mean that everyone in Eastern Europe with, it is fair to note, varying degrees of enthusiasm, had converted to free-market capitalism. The Cold War had been won by the West and the victors felt entitled to celebrate their triumph. There are many examples of the expression of this capitalist triumphalism. One that may be of particular interest to some readers of this book was the statement of Henry Catto, the Director of the United States Information Department, the publishers of the semi-official scholarly journal *Problems of Communism*, whose contributions to research and discussion on the nature and practice of communism all over the world have been substantial. Writing in the last issue, he says: 'With the collapse of communism in eastern Europe, in the former Soviet Union, and in many other countries around the world, the journal may rightly declare its mission accomplished. This May–June 1992 issue will be the last.'

The analysis here will take a different direction for reasons that are quite straightforward. If you analyse the momentous events in eastern Europe in state-centrist terms, as did Mr Catto, then the most important facts are the political changes of regimes in each state from monolithic Communist Party control to more pluralist polities. If, on the other hand, you try to analyse what has been going on in terms of the global forces at work, applying the global system theory outlined in this book, then the change of political regime, while very important, will not be the only phenomenon worth looking at. My argument is that the continuities of the processes of globalization that preceded and in some very critical ways caused the changes in Eastern Europe are just as important as the genuinely new forces at work. This is the reason why it is still useful to talk of the Old and the New Second Worlds. The legacy of communism is not as easy to shut off as the publication of *Problems of Communism*.[21] The idea of the New Second World suggests that without an understanding of the global forces that helped transform the Old Second World our understanding of the New is bound to be flawed. The judgement that introduces a penetrating study of the mass media in post-communist Eastern Europe is most apposite here: 'the ideas of Marxism actually provide the best available account of what the nature of the communist regimes really was, the manner of their decline and fall, and the reasons for the peculiar features of the successor societies' (Sparks 1998: p. xiii).

In the sphere of politics the importance of the structural changes is overwhelming for understanding the social and political complexities of each case, at the regional, national, and local levels. However, these complexities only rarely and temporarily restrain the forces working in the transnational economic, political, and culture-ideology spheres. In much the same way, there are fundamental differences within and between the countries and sub-national levels in postcommunist Europe, indeed some of these former countries (for example, Czechoslovakia) are now different countries (Czech Republic and Slovakia). Nevertheless, the label postcommunist Europe, including all the parts of the former Soviet Union, Poland, Hungary, East Germany, Czechoslovakia, Bulgaria, Romania, and Yugoslavia, still describes a genuine unit of analysis for global system purposes.

Few would have predicted that the two Russian words most broadcast in the world's mass media in the 1990s would have been *perestroika* (restructuring) and *glasnost* (openness). While the first refers to efforts to make the domestic economy and system of administration more efficient, the second came to imply a receptivity to progressive ideas and influences from inside and outside the Soviet Union. Both glasnost and perestroika appeared to be sweeping the whole of Eastern Europe in the direction of global capitalism, or at least towards an opening to the practices of capitalist globalization. Birman's analysis (1989) of the dramatic gaps between personal consumption in the USA and the USSR (and, by implication, the rest of Eastern Europe) makes it less difficult to understand the force of the pent-up consumer demand that propelled these changes so rapidly.[22]

Although these movements appear highly dramatic, unforeseen, even cataclysmic, the historical record shows that as long ago as 1957 Poland attempted to embark on a process of economic reform and was rapidly followed by most of the other members of Comecon (Korbonski 1989). These attempts were not successful, nor were they carried out very systematically. The point, however, is that the classic communist strategies, far from overtaking the prosperity of the capitalist centre, were unlikely even to provide reliably for the necessities of their own citizens. The governments and informed publics of the countries of Eastern Europe did not suddenly wake up in the mid-1980s to find that they were falling behind global capitalism. They had been conscious of this fact at least since the 1960s.

In the 1950s the policy makers of Comecon rejected the global capitalist project, in particular the culture-ideology of consumerism, and therefore could choose to ignore it. By the 1980s the politics and culture-ideology of modernization in the industrial societies of Eastern Europe, combined with the power of capitalism to communicate on a global scale, had changed the situation irredeemably. The political leaders in Eastern Europe could no longer pretend that the West was failing to feed, clothe, and house its people. The aspirations of the masses in the socialist countries began to find a voice in more responsive leaders. After the disasters of the Soviet invasions of Hungary that destroyed the reforming government of Imry Nagy in 1956, and of Czechoslovakia that suppressed the Prague Spring of Dubček and his colleagues in 1968, Gorbachev and other communist leaders in the 1980s were forced to respond to popular pressure for change in order to have any chance of political survival. A central element in this popular pressure was the culture-ideology of consumerism. As *Advertising Age* so unsubtly put it as the Wall came down: Eastern Europe Beckons! (20 Nov. 1989).[23]

TNCs IN THE OLD SECOND WORLD

Though the political changes were sudden, the underlying economic changes have been more gradual. The governments and enterprises in most Eastern European countries had been actively engaged with capitalist globalization for decades (Frank 1977). Since the 1970s transnational corporations from Bulgaria, Czecholovakia, East Germany, Hungary, Poland, Romania, and the USSR had been operating in most countries of the world (McMillan 1987). Indeed, until the 1990s, TNCs from these countries were far more active in the rest of the world than TNCs from capitalist countries were in Comecon countries.

Comecon direct investments (CDIs) tended to be equity investments in locally incorporated joint stock companies. Though banks and insurance companies established branches directly, subsidiaries were more common in most other sectors. McMillan suggested that this was seen as the best way to avoid the hostility in host countries, but subsidiaries themselves often established branches. The equity split was very variable, but the Comecon partner usually took the majority share (for example, in retailing, technical services, banking, and transport). Local personnel were frequently employed.

By 1983, there were CDIs in twenty-three First and seventy-five Third World countries. Comecon investments in the Third World were concentrated by value in a small number of countries. Nigeria, Morocco, India, Singapore, Lebanon, Iran, Mexico, and Peru accounted for about half of the total. Investments in the First World were mainly in support of exports, while those in the Third World were mainly involved in resource exploitation. The typical Comecon TNC tended to be small, between ten and fifty employees (none were found to have more than 500). Like capitalist TNCs in the Third World, they relied largely on the local market for investment funds (McMillan 1987).

In the mid-1980s there were at least 600 so-called red TNCs, with investments of at least one billion dollars. About a third were active in the Third World. However, this represented only about one-tenth of 1 per cent of global foreign investment. The pattern of Soviet-style foreign trade organizations predominated, though manufacturing ventures were on the increase. One survey showed that 377 of 403 Comecon TNCs in the First World in 1986 were in the service and construction industries. The spread in Third World countries was rather more even.[24] There is abundant evidence to suggest that the growth of the red TNCs was a consequence of the even more substantial growth of Comecon trade with the Third World since the 1960s. Nayyar (1977: ch. 1) reported that between 1960 and 1970 the share of the Third World in Comecon exports rose from 8 per cent to 15 per cent and its share of Comecon imports rose from 9 per cent to 11 per cent. Asia took 40 per cent of this trade, while Africa and Latin America took 30 per cent each. However, as with the red TNCs investment was concentrated—only fourteen countries accounted for 70 per cent of the total, with India and Egypt by far the most important trading partners. These two countries received about 30 per cent of socialist bloc aid in this period, which was also very concentrated.

Comecon–Third World trade tended to operate within bilateral agreements for the exchange of commodities, cash transactions being in local rather than hard currencies. This was obviously very useful for most Third World countries, which tend to be short of hard currency. Soviet credits were important for many development projects and contributed to import flexibility for many poor countries.

Trade does not necessarily benefit all parties equally, and there were cases of Comecon countries dumping Third World goods on to the world market that they had received in barter deals. Theoretically, Third World producers could find their exports undercut by their own goods that had already been exported to a Comecon country. This could work both ways. Comecon countries accepted goods that they did not want in order to supply a Third World partner with goods that it could not afford to pay for. However, to the extent that Comecon mainly exported machinery and transport equipment, and other manufactured goods, and imported mainly textiles and raw materials from the Third World, long-term agreements between the parties did tend to lead to more price stability for Third World commodities than they enjoyed in the world market.[25] As noted above, the trade relations between Cuba and Comecon bear this out (see Mesa-Lago 1993).

Opening up to First World TNCs began seriously in the mid-1980s when the countries of Eastern Europe began to respond to the global consensus on the beneficial effects of foreign investment. The Soviet Union made a serious attempt to attract FDI through joint-venture regulations established in January 1987. In an interesting comparison between these joint ventures and the concessions to foreign capitalists during the New Economic Policy period of the 1920s, Gutman (1992) concludes that neither succeeded in attracting the massive amounts of foreign capital hoped for. However, many foreign corporations seemed keen to have a presence in the Soviet market (see, for example, Lindsey 1989; *Management Review* 1990). By March 1987, there were more than 100 applications for FDI in the Soviet Union, about twenty under negotiation, and three already in the stage of filing for endorsement (Ivanov 1987). However, most of the forty or so agreements operational up to mid-1989 were reported to be losing money. One exception was Applied Engineered Systems (AES), a joint venture between a Soviet state firm and Combustion Engineering, a firm from the USA that had been doing business in the USSR for some years (subsequently acquired by the major FG500 company, ABB). Combustion Engineering had something that Soviet policy makers considered essential for their industrial modernization plans, namely process-controlled equipment. The Soviet personnel in AES began by assembling kits of components supplied from the USA, under the management of Combustion Engineering technical staff. They then graduated to assembling whole units by themselves and to manufacturing some of the parts in the Soviet factory. The aim of the company was eventually to manufacture the whole product in the USSR from domestically produced components for the domestic market, and also to export (Copetas 1989).[26]

The first genuine capitalist foreign direct investment in the Soviet Union was announced on 28 November 1989, when Fiat signed a deal worth over a billion dollars for a factory near Moscow to manufacture, market, and export Fiat-badged cars. This was a qualitative step beyond the production under licence through which Fiat already turned out local-badged cars in Russia, Poland, and Yugoslavia. One Fiat executive quoted at the time 'believes eastern Europe will become the new Korea of the motor industry, except this time cheap production will be available on our doorstep' (*Guardian*, 2 Feb. 1989: 4). Volkswagen were also considering East Germany for the same purpose.

Soviet planners were well aware of the economic potential of manufacturing for export. They were also, no doubt, aware of the costs. In 1988 a decree established the Soviet Far East as a special region of joint entrepreneurship and Odessa, Estonia, and Sochi, among other places, were said to be keen to follow suit. Advocates of this opening-up policy spoke of Nakhodka, a port east of Vladivostok, as a new Singapore. In September 1989, at an international meeting in Moscow sponsored by the UNCTC, the creation of three free zones (Nakhodka, Vyborg, and Novgorod) was announced. By 2000, about twenty-five similar zones had been announced, however not one has been very successful, so far.

Parallel initiatives were also to be found in other communist states in Eastern Europe. Nawrocki (1987) describes the history of foreign direct investment (FDI) legislation in communist Poland. In 1976, a regulation permitted FDI in small businesses, but this was restricted to foreign investors of Polish descent. In 1982, shortly after the brutal (but, of course, temporary) suppression of the Solidarity movement, the Law on FDI in Small Industry allowed foreigners or TNCs to set up wholly owned subsidiaries and offered various tax and currency incentives. A Chamber of Industry and Commerce (InterPolcom), set up in 1977, facilitated FDI. The policy had a certain degree of success. From three foreign enterprises in 1977, the total grew to almost 700 in 1986, but total FDI was valued at only $100m. These enterprises employed about 60,000 workers (less than 1 per cent of the total workforce), and over half of these worked in firms with less than fifty workers. They were mainly in textiles and garments, chemicals, wood, and engineering, oriented to the domestic rather than the export market. New laws were passed in 1986 to encourage foreign investment in larger enterprises and in the service sectors, and the efforts of Western state agencies to help the Solidarity government of 1989 encouraged more FDI.[27]

Martonyi (1987) discusses similar moves in Hungary. The legal framework for joint ventures in Hungary dates from the early 1970s, when it was restricted to R&D, commerce, and services. In 1977 it was widened to include manufacturing industry. Foreign interest, however, was slight, growing only from eight joint ventures worth about $10m. in 1980, to sixty-six worth $80m. in 1986. In Hungary the foreign partner was normally permitted a minority of the equity, but there were exceptions, mainly for exporting and high-technology ventures, and in banking and tourism. From 1982 joint ventures were allowed in special zones offering a certain degree of legal extra-territoriality. But the price of isolation in these offshore joint ventures was usually greater than the costs of operating under full domestic regulations.

Measures to promote FDI improved after 1986 as intrusive bureaucracy declined, tax benefits increased, and better legal (especially international) protection for foreign investors was introduced. In the words of a responsible official: 'the policy of promoting joint ventures in Hungary forms an integral part of an economic policy whose main objectives are the further progress of economic reform and a fuller integration of the national economy in the world economy' (Martonyi 1987: 53). The spread of Westernization or, more accurately, capitalist globalization, went further in Hungary than anywhere else in Eastern Europe. Since the first wave of decentralization in 1968, and particularly since the 1980s, new forms of individual and partnership enterprises flourished in many areas of the economy. A new economic zone (which housed a busy branch of Marks & Spencer) was established in Sopron, on Hungary's border with Austria. Only hard (Western) currency was accepted. A visit to this zone led one commentator to suggest that 'unbridled consumerism is what perestroika is really all about'.[28]

Even in Romania, before the Ceauşescu regime was overthrown, the heavy hand of the state was not total, particularly in the retail and professional sectors, where something like a free market existed. In his study of the SKALA Cooperative department store chain in Bucharest, Naor (in Kaynak 1988) showed how entrepreneurial forces worked in the retail sector, for example in the development of franchising.

TRANSITIONS FROM COMMUNISM TO POSTCOMMUNISM

There are many moments around 1990 that are symbolic of the end of the Stalinist form of communism that dominated the history of Eastern Europe and in some respects the whole world from 1945 to 1990. For many, the destruction of the Berlin Wall in 1989 was the defining moment, for others it was the quasi-public execution of the Romanian dictator Ceauşescu and his wife. Yet others would chose the election of the dissident playwright, Václav Havel, as interim president of Czechoslovakia. With the benefit of hindsight, however, we can argue that the real defining moment of the entire historic process was the decision to dissolve the Soviet Union shortly after the attempted coup in August 1991 had failed to impose a military solution onto a political and economic crisis. The Commonwealth of Independent States (CIS), which succeeded the defunct Soviet Union, was clearly an unstable entity, and from the rubble emerged a new Russia, striving for a place in the world as the premier postcommunist power.

While the masses of the population rejected Stalinist communism in the Soviet Union and Eastern Europe the precise modes of rejections and balance of social forces involved were different in each country. Similarly, the nature of the changes since the late 1980s, in particular the pace and scope of marketization and democratization, have varied, sometimes quite dramatically from country to country and within countries. As the contributors to a four-volume collection on postcommunist societies show, each of the twenty-seven states (at last count) that emerged from the transitions in Europe and Eurasia has its own story (Dawisha and Parrott 1997).[29] Most of the research on the subject suggests that there is no significant constituency for a return to Stalinist central planning but that belief in the free market that was introduced to replace it, after widespread initial enthusiasm, has waned.[30] Specialists on the region were not short of explanations of what went wrong with the communist dreams of a better society and advice about what to do next. W.W. Rostow, author of the influential non-communist manifesto of the 1960s, *Stages of Economic Growth*, for example, argued that to continue growing, the Soviet economy in the 1950s and 1960s would have had to develop 'the sectors associated with high mass consumption: those linked with the automobile, durable consumer goods, and the life of suburbia' (in Chirot 1991: 62). He offered an eight-point programme: 'The first requirement is the efficient introduction of, say, fifty large Western and Japanese firms into the Soviet Union, and twenty-five into eastern Europe' (ibid.: 67). Fischer (2000) agreed, proclaiming that FDI is a strategy for industrial recovery.

Since the late 1980s many small, medium, and large foreign firms have shown an interest in markets, natural resources, and labour in Eastern Europe. The Slovenian scholar Svetlicic surveyed the complexities of TNC involvement in what are known for investment purposes as the transitional economies. By 1993, Romania had most contracts with foreign enterprise (26,000) but only $680 million in investments, whereas Hungary had only 15,000 contracts but the largest amount of investment, about four billion dollars. Russia, with more than 5,000 projects and three billion dollars invested was also significant. Of the rest, only Poland and the Czech Republic had more than one billion dollars invested. The data suggest that Russia had the largest investment per project and that foreign direct investment does represent a 'quite substantial part of overall economic activities' in many of these countries (Svetlicic 1993: 16). More recent studies of foreign investment and privatization in the Czech Republic, Poland, Hungary, and Russia (in Artisien-Maksimenko and Rojec 2001) confirm that TNCs continue to be interested in increasing their stake in these economies.

The seriousness with which globalizing politicians and bureaucrats in Russia treated the issue of foreign investments was illustrated in a report of the first meeting of the Consultative Council for Foreign Investments. This was attended by the Russian Premier and representatives of fourteen major TNCs, including Ernst and Young, Coca-Cola, BASF, Procter & Gamble, United Technologies, Mitsui, Mars, and Citicorp. The Russian Economics Minister was quoted as saying that FDI would reach $10–15 bn. per annum by the year 2000 (BBC, Selection of World Broadcasts, Russia, 28 June 1994). By 1995 the Russia Federation had attracted a cumulative total of $5.5bn. in foreign investments, and by 1999 this had risen to $16.5bn., about $2–$4bn. per annum (UN 2000).[31]

The manner of entry of TNCs is always significant. Most companies have entered the New Second World via acquisitions of or joint ventures with local companies and the general pattern is of many small companies with small investments and a few large TNCs with most of the stock (Artisien-Maksimenko and Rojec 2001). Most investments are in manufacturing in all the countries of postcommunist Europe, with consumer goods prominent. Global marketeers talk about 400 million unsatiated customers. Svetlicic (1993) and others, however, reported some local resentment over foreign invasion of these economies in the early 1990s, which led to a gradual elimination of the very liberal incentives for FDI that the investment authorities in many postcommunist countries had rushed to implement, though TNCs still appear to be very welcome.

There is evidence that Russia's indigenous entrepreneurs, many actually former state enterprise managers, were beginning to carve out places for themselves in the new political and economic structures. Lane (1993) reported a reputational study asking forty-eight respondents of note who they thought were the most influential people in Russia. Only fifteen people were mentioned by more than ten of the informants in response to questions on internal politics, the republics, marketization, and influence. All were members of the political elite with the exception of Arkadii Volsky, a former state enterprise manager and president of the All-Russian Union of Industrialists and Entrepreneurs and a key member of various other organizations, who was ranked the fifth most influential person in the country under Boris Yeltsin. In general, the media and the business lobby (in that order) were not seen as very influential, but the bourgeoisie were not surprisingly seen as the group most supporting market reforms and generally seen as quite influential along with the mafia (organized crime rings). The conclusion to this research was that: 'there has been a change in the structure of the elites rather [than] a change of personnel within them' (Lane 1993: 35). Another influential member of the new bourgeoisie Konstantin Zatulin, the leader of Businessmen for a New Russia (fifty-three regional branches by 1993), was of the opinion that Russia's salvation would come from its entrepreneurs. Both Volsky and Zatulin were counted among the richest people in Russia (see Kryshtanovskaya 1994: 12). The relationship between this emerging indigenous bourgeoisie, many of whom are former party officials (the nomenklatura) and the embryonic transnational capitalist class in Russia will undoubtedly play a central role in the future of the country and the region.

Certainly the domestic capitalist elites are beginning to flex their muscles. In August 1998 Russia's leading bankers persuaded the government to default on its debt and thus saved themselves a great deal of money. 'In Russia's current condition, with an atomized society ruled by a corrupt and ineffective state and an unstable economy governed by a weak and deficient legal system, individuals can earn a great deal of wealth and exert great influence on the government' (Stowe 2001: 49). There is very little analysis of business–government relations in Russia, and Stowe correctly asks: 'How can we understand capitalist Russia unless we understand Russia's capitalists?' (p. 50). This is, of course, a question that is equally relevant for many parts of the world.

Marketization, of course, has opened up opportunities for many small entrepreneurs as well. An interesting study of one globally oriented garment-making enterprise (USF) from the Ukraine by Kalantaridis (2000), clearly illustrates how older patterns of transnational business are being transformed by capitalist globalization. USF was established as a state enterprise in 1947, and was privatized in 1994 as a closed stock company (owned by individual employees with varying shares). By 1998 it had tripled its employees to 1,250 plus an additional network of subcontractors employing 1500. Much of this success was attributed to a young energetic director who had made contact with a Slovakian firm that subcontracted for a major UK brand and this led to sub-subcontract work. As a result of her visits to trade fairs, the director forged links with a German firm, and by 1998 the export market of USF (to the UK, France, and Germany) accounted for 65 per cent of its production. However, as it could not raise capital at home it relied on foreign buyers for finance. Its business network with enterprises in Western Europe, and intermediaries in Hungary and Slovakia and other local manufacturers increased its level of dependency. The future is full of promise, but little security, a key aspect of incorporation into the global economy.

Different but just as significant forms of new entrepreneurial activity are the individualized east–west trading networks that have mushroomed since 1990, that Morawska (1998) argues are being dependently incorporated into global capitalism. East European governments encourage income-seeking circular migrations of their citizenry (see also Faist 2000) as a safety valve against popular discontent. These trips are mainly organized around beat-the-system/bend-the-rules activities, reliant on patronage and informal networks and directed towards the personal consumption of the entrepreneurs and their families and friends rather than productive investment. 'A new, locally recognized middle-class replaces or at least significantly dilutes the influence of the old-regime nomenklatura regime' (Morawska 1998: 15) and, of course, it becomes an integral if very junior partner of the local transnational capitalist class.

The postcommunist societies of Europe are certainly in a state of transition, but there is very little agreement about exactly where they have come from and even roughly where they are heading. Despite more or less free elections, there are many who would agree with the assertion of Denitch (1992: p. x) that 'The economies of the post-communist states are uniformly worse at providing necessities, not to speak of luxuries, for their populations as a whole, than the regimes they have replaced' (see also Freeland 2000). While these are not calls for the restoration of the Soviet Union, though such calls have been heard, they are stark reminders of the hollowness of capitalist triumphalism. Most specialists on the region agree that liberalization is not democratization. 'Liberalization involves an expansion of the sphere of public activity and a consequent roll back of regime control, but one which, in theory, does not alter the basic power distribution; the authorities retain the capacity to intervene to change an outcome they do not like. In contrast, democratization involves a fundamental change in the power relationship underlying the regime' (Gill and Markwick 2000: 3, n. 7).

The gender implications of the marketization of postcommunist Europe have attracted a great deal of research attention (for example, Einhorn 1993; Moghadam 1993a; Gal and Kligman 2000). Einhorn puts the issues very clearly: 'despite clear improvements in the civil and political rights associated with democratic citizenship, in the short run at least women in east Central Europe stand to lose economic, social welfare, and reproductive rights. Moreover, a newly dominant discourse threatens to subordinate women's citizenship rights in many cases to the goals of nationalist projects' (Einhorn 1993: 1; see also Posadskaya, in Moghadam 1993a: ch. 7). LaFont (2001) demonstrates that women have not gained (and many may have suffered) politically, economically, and culturally as a result of the end of communism. With the spread of democracy, women have lost out in terms of political representation as quota systems (especially for peasants) have disappeared (in the Russian Federation and five other East European states, women had a lower proportion of parliamentary seats in 1999 than in 1987). Men dominated the occupational system during communism, and this has not changed. LaFont reports that help-wanted ads for foreign joint ventures showed definite bias for male applicants, and in Lithuania gender-specific ads for government jobs actually conflict with the Constitution. Employment rates for women are increasing and new social insurance rules discourage private and public employers from taking on women. However, economic decline intensifies pressure on women to find paid work. 'As the level of inequality throughout the region has grown, there are emerging very evident "winners" and "losers". The winners represent a very small elite group of successful entrepreneurs and those who profit from the "grey economy", while there are millions of "losers" (58 million Russians are living below the poverty line)' (LaFont 2001: 211–12).

These developments have led to a resurgence of nationalist ideology with two main consequences for women. First, the emphasis on women as reproducers of future citizens relegates them to secondary roles and, second, the primacy of the ethno-nation masks growing gender-based and class-based inequalities (ibid.). In the search for explanations of why this has happened in the postcommunist societies the argument of Lapidus on the impact of restructuring on women in the former Soviet Union rings true for most of the New Second World:

The old, almost exclusively male, nomenklatura has largely managed to transform its political power into property rights in the emerging market system, accumulating capital for entrepreneurial activities . . . the voucher system, adopted as an instrument of privatization, is particularly advantageous to the management and employees of well-endowed industrial enterprises who are able to become owners of the newly created joint stock companies, while the largely female-dominated institutions of the cultural establishment or service sector offer no comparable opportunities to acquire potentially valuable property rights. (In Moghadam 1993a: 156)

The implications of such developments for the class structures of postcommunist Europe are profound. It is first necessary to be reminded that there were important differences between the countries and communities of Eastern Europe before they became communist, and that the forms of communism differed in each country. It is also important to distinguish those countries which had brutal authoritarian regimes (Stalinist Russia, Romania from the 1950s) from those that were far less authoritarian (Hungary). Etzioni-Halevy (1993) makes an interesting case, based on her demo-elite theory that the autonomy of business or economic elites stabilizes democracy and so the only way to guarantee democracy in Eastern Europe is the creation of such elites through privatization. This argument is very sensitive to the relations between elites and sub-elites (such as church, trade unions, academic-intellectual groups) and thus connects usefully with the plethora of research on the newly emerging shoots of civil society in the New Second World. Ost (1992) elaborates a complementary argument to the effect that reforms can only succeed where the workers have a stake. He argues: 'Practices that might threaten democratic consolidation [the reference is to Latin American corporatism] can strengthen democracy in eastern Europe' (Ost 1992: 51). Indeed, the thesis that the workers are the only important group in the New Second World who are not politically represented to any significant degree, reinforced by the research of Clarke et al. (1993) on the role of the workers in the transition to capitalism in Russia, gives an ironic twist to the legacy of Stalinist communism.

This has led Ashwin (1998) to pose the important question of why there has been no organized workers' movement and few workers' protests in Russia. The social stability of post-Soviet Russia has been explained in various ways, through theories of social contract, incorporation, or atomization. Ashwin argues, however, that the so-called 'endless patience' of the workers is best understood in terms of the social organization of traditional Soviet enterprises responsible for supplying workers with housing, rest and leisure facilities, kindergartens, health care, allotments, goods in short supply, and loans. This state paternalism rarely worked very well and workers were obliged to cultivate relations with those in a position to help (managers and trade union leaders), thus the typical response to difficulties was individual rather than collective. When the system broke down and marketization began to replace state enterprises, workers already had a repertoire of individualized survival strategies. How long the endless patience of the Russian workforce or postcommunist working classes in general will last is an open question (see also Clarke et al. 1993, Etzioni-Halevy, in Higley et al. 1998: ch. 13). The Russian news agency Interfax reported in January 2000 that average monthly wages had fallen by 10 per cent (from the equivalent of $74 in 1998 to $67 in

1999). About 50 million people received less than the minimum monthly subsistence level (about \$38).

A preliminary attempt to identify the parameters of the new class structure in Hungary in the 1990s focuses on the visible divisions that have emerged with striking rapidity. Kovacs and Maggard (1993) argue that the dream of the new Hungary that triggered the collapse of communism was of a large affluent middle class with few very rich or very poor people. When the existing middle class began to suffer from rising prices and unemployment there was genuine surprise, not only in Hungary but all over the Second World. The second (informal) economy, which had become the norm in the 1970s and 1980s in all communist countries (Łoś 1990), postponed the threatened social disaster by providing income for those who found themselves suddenly in need. Despite this safety net, many middle-class middle-aged people were reported to be on the downward slope. At the other extreme was a new grande bourgeoisie, a combination of old bureaucrats, new managers, and an emerging entrepreneurial class. In light of the history of Europe in the 1920s and 1930s, the conclusion is ominous: 'The emergence of this new class is visible in the conspicuous consumption of luxury goods . . . [evidence of] a rapidly widening gap between social strata in eastern Europe. Sharp class divisions are appearing' (Kovacs and Maggard 1993: 338). In 1987 Mercedes sold only seventy cars in Russia, in 1992 it sold 3,500, mostly to rich 'biznizmen' (Svetlicic 1993: 43, n. 73).

Research on the lifestyles of the rich in postcommunist Russia illustrates the rapid advance of a new class and its implications for the culture-ideology of consumerism. Kryshtanovskaya (1994) reported that while 12 per cent of Moscow millionaires were millionaire-nomenklaturists, young millionaire-parvenus, often with little formal education, were rising fast. Criminal-mafia connections were admitted by 40 per cent of the business sample in this research, and 25 per cent retained criminal connections. The conclusion parallels findings from other postcommunist societies: 'a new social class of entrepreneurs has emerged and is establishing itself in contemporary Russia' against a background of general impoverishment (Kryshtanovskaya 1994: 22).

Łoś and Zybertowicz (2000: 202–3) make a very powerful case for what they term the new reality of the communist capitalist offensive in Poland (and to varying degrees elsewhere) and what is called the Red Web. This cannot be understood in isolation from its police-state roots and the processes of the privatization of the communist state. They argue:

By keeping the educational level of the population low, and by controlling opportunities for foreign travel and contacts, the party/police state promoted and catapulted into the international arena its own elite, who became part of the new international class. Moreover, global technological changes shifted the centre of economic activity to the areas where former secret service operatives and younger, cosmopolitan nomenklatura activists could capitalize on their experience and expertise in fields including (dis)information technologies, languages, foreign banking, economic and technological espionage, advertising, market intelligence, public relations, image-making, security and communications . . . By establishing themselves as proponents of internationalism and openness, and by stigmatizing those who stressed sovereignty and the national interest as backward, parochial and xenophobic, they showed that they were the 'enlightened' elite with whom supra-national organizations and corporations could do business.

So, 'former secret service operatives were in a unique position to become the intermediaries between the global economy and the new Polish economy' (p. 206). Global crime syndicates offer lucrative connections, particularly in the former Soviet bloc, where a new world of largely unregulated global business has given many opportunities for the transnationalization and privatization of the state.[32]

This argument is advanced theoretically and empirically by Hellman and Schankerman (2000) on the basis of the Business and Enterprise Performance Survey carried out under the auspices of the World Bank in 1999. The survey covered more than 3,000 firms in twenty postcommunist countries and was focused on enterprise–state relations and the role of corruption and state capture. While the state no longer plans these economies, it still intervenes in firm decision-making, provision of benefits (notably investment, subsidies, and tax regimes) and has some control over the system of bribery payments. However, all these factors vary by enterprise size and ownership type, and other economy-wide variables. Thus, marketization has changed the form of state intervention but has not necessarily reduced the level (replacing formal control by informal taxes of bribes and red tape). The key variable is state capture by business measured in terms of (a) how far firms and/or other private actors can influence policy by providing benefits to politicians and (b) how far it is concentrated in a relatively small number of firms (compare CornerHouse (2000) and Rose-Ackerman (1999)). While there appears to be some relationship between privatization and good govenance (the strongest rationale for the haste with which these programmes were implemented) this did not hold in high-capture states (notably Russia, Georgia, and Bulgaria). We would expect, under such circumstances, that a large number of new rich business people would flourish.

A central element in the emergence of new classes and status groups is the relations between economic interests, styles of life, and values. Though it would be absurd to claim that the culture-ideology of consumerism was entirely absent from the Old Second World (see, for example, Hernadi 1992), the collapse of communism and the attempts to create market economies and societies almost overnight threw up some interesting issues for global system theory. As the old communist regimes began to break up, those bearing the good news of global capitalism flocked east. Iconic individuals like the blue pimpernels (business consultants) of Prague, spreading the glad tidings of capitalist globalization (Gott 1990), joined the entrepreneurs at the 1990 Leipzig Trade fair where 'The East is Open for Business' (Farr 1990). The staff of the Soros Foundation's International Management Centre, the first to be opened in the communist world (*Economist*, 15 July 1989: 50) mingled with the likes of Mark Palmer, a former US envoy to Hungary who left government service to run the private Central European Development Corporation. Academics from prestigious Western universities were invited to perform economic miracles and transform Old Second World economies into new East Asian-type dragons or, simply, rich Western economies, most of whom were themselves, ironically, in recession at the time.

These people and institutions brought with them not only expertise of various kinds but also cultural values and ideological predispositions. Of direct relevance to my analysis is the ways in which the TNCs in general and consumerist elites in particular organized and transmitted the culture-ideology of consumerism in postcommunist Europe. It is not much of a surprise that in the age of capitalist globalization Russian millionaires spend their money on expensive foreign cars, luxury flats in select areas of Moscow, dachas, property abroad, private education at home and abroad, exotic leisure, and foreign travel.

Global brand consumer goods and services TNCs expanded their activities rapidly in

Eastern Europe in the 1990s (Belk and Shultz 1994). For example, Procter & Gamble took over a detergent factory in Russia in a privatization acquisition, producing both Ariel, the global detergent, and Tix, a local brand. Direct-selling cosmetic firms grew rapidly. Oriflame from Belgium had 20,000 salespersons and Avon UK had 50,000 in Eastern Europe by 1993. The battle for the fast food and beverage markets in Eastern Europe was also joined. Pepsico planned a $500 million investment in Poland over five years, with Pizza Hut, Taco Bell, and Kentucky Fried Chicken opening branches all over the country. McDonald's and Burger King were already in business. Pepsico's joint venture with a major Polish confectionery firm, 40 per cent of which was acquired for $25 million in 1991, was specifically to combat Coca-Cola, which itself announced a $250 million investment plan for the 38 million potential consumers in the Polish market (Reuter News, 10 Aug. 1993).

Cosmopolitan launched its first Russian edition to considerable local acclaim. 'Cosmo Russia says it does not want to preach vulgar, expensive consumerism and is not interested in the "nuvo-rishy" (new rich). But the message is clear—it's alright to have a bit of glamour and making money is no longer a crime' (Reuter News, 27 Apr. 1994). The global confectionery corporation, Mars, announced in 1994 that it would open a $100 million manufacturing plant near Moscow, which led Reuters to comment that 'Mars and Snickers bars, sold in kiosks from St Petersburg to the Pacific island of Sakhalin, have become icons of the new mass consumerism sweeping across Russia. The products are so widely advertised and distributed that politicians joke about the "snickerization" of Russia' (Reuter News, 16 Mar. 1994). Pilkington (1994), writing about Russia's youth, traced the rise of rampant consumerism among some sections of the population from the mid-1980s.[33]

The commercialization of the media in the postcommunist societies took rather different forms in the different countries.[34] This led to debates about a Marshall Plan of the Mind to reinforce capitalist values in Eastern Europe. MTV, for example, was invited into Lithuania to promote democracy (reminiscent of the MTV campaign to young voters in the 1992 presidential election in the USA that was said to have been a factor in propelling Bill Clinton into the White House). The first commercial network in Eastern Europe, Nova TV, began broadcasting in the Czech Republic in February 1994. This was a $45 million venture run by the Central European Development Corporation, headed by the above-mentioned Mark Palmer. In a revealing article, 'Have Contacts, Will Cash In: The Revolving Door Comes to Hungary' (5 Feb. 1990: 45), even *Newsweek* questioned the propriety of recent ex-diplomats like Mr Palmer and Ronald Lauder, the cosmetics heir and himself former ambassador to Austria, engaging in these types of activities. As the fourfold structure of the transnational capitalist class implies, capitalist globalization positively encourages such multiple and/or serial roles.

The hope of the free marketeers is that a higher level of mass consumption will be attained very quickly before social and political pressures destroy the frail shoots of democracy and capitalist enterprise. The prediction of the critics of capitalist globalization is that conditions are liable to get much worse for the mass of the population before they get better, always assuming that they will get much better. The costs incurred by shock treatments and big bangs for the emplacement of a globalizing capitalist market economy and society in Eastern Europe are turning out to be hard to bear for the majority, even if affluent minorities flourish.

There are indications that this was already an issue in the old Soviet Union as it was breaking up. Kagarlitsky (1989) warned that the economic and social reforms would leave large sections of the population behind, as entrepreneurial and opportunistic minorities enriched themselves in a variety of ways. According to Russian survey research (Kryshtanovskaya 1994) this is exactly what happened. Even before the dissolution of the Soviet Union the *Guardian* reported ('The Cult of Russia's New Rich', 4–5 Nov. 1989) on a daily Aeroflot–Pan Am flight 30 from New York to Moscow, known as the flying vacuum cleaner because of the volume of consumer goods that homecoming Russians brought with them. This led to rapid increases in burglary (and the private security industry) in Russia.

An ominous development, noted by many analysts, was the rise of mafia-like structures in Russia (Serio 1992, Varese 2001) and other parts of postcommunist Europe (for example, members of the Stasi, the secret police in the former East Germany, have been implicated in mafia activities).[35] This is not entirely a consequence of the collapse of the Soviet Union, as 'the crime statistics indicate that a degree of societal disintegration had set in substantially before the breakdown of the Communist regime' (Ryan 1993: p. xii). However, organized crime certainly increased in the 1990s. In mid-1994, President Yeltsin announced a war against the Russian mafia because 'Mafia-type crime groups have mushroomed in Russia since the collapse of the Soviet Union, controlling parts of the official economy and tightening their grip on politics' (Reuter News, 24 June 1994). *The Economist*, in an article (one of several in the 1990s) under the title 'Russia's Mafia: More Crime than Punishment' (9 July 1994: 19–22) warned that fighting the mafia may endanger the democratic reforms in Russia. According to Arkadii Vaksberg, journalist and author of a book on the Russian mafia in 1991, it engulfs 'the entire soviet power-system, all its ideological, political, economical and administrative manifestations' (quoted in Varese 2001: 186). Soviet specialists and foreign scholars are agreed that organized criminal activity spread rapidly after 1986. Perhaps 2,600 groups, of which fifty were 'deeply conspiratorial', were discovered by 1990, some territorial, some ethnic, and some named after their leaders. There is no evidence to suggest that they have disappeared in the new Russia (Varese 2001). Under such circumstances it is not surprising that Russia's democracy has been characterized as stillborn (Gill and Markwick 2000), and even a form of postcommunist *caciquismo* (Matsuzato 2001).

Extremist nationalist groups, embittered by the get rich quick mentality that perestroika encouraged, use the weapons of anti-Semitism and pan-Slavism. More and more credit-card-only outlets point up the increasing gap between rich and poor; and there is talk of the possibility of social chaos. President Putin is accused of using the brutal war in Chechnya to distract the population from the failures of the regime. Ironically, in the short run at least, the perestroika and glasnost that flung the doors open to capitalist globalization may have made the societies that emerged from the former Soviet Union and communist Eastern Europe less like the First World it was intended to emulate, and more like the Third World.[36] The judgement of Gustafson (1999: 234), that the 'transition to capitalism Russian-style may not win the hearts of Russians, but it may—just possibly—be tacitly accepted as the system best suited to the urban and middle-class people that Russians have become', while understandable, seems to underestimate the growing gulf between rich and poor.

CHOICES FOR SOCIALIST SOCIETIES

Of the choices facing leading groups in existing socialist societies, and those who wish to create socialist globalization, the utopian communist dream of a classless society is a truly transnationalist humanitarian vision that would obviate the necessity for war, hunger, and deprivation of all sorts. It would also remove the social conditions that aggravate the human predispositions to anger, hate, envy, depression, boredom, and violence, and secure the social conditions that promote the equally human predispositions to tolerance, altruism, love, and enthusiasm. This vision has almost disappeared throughout the world, largely because the state forms that Stalinist communism encouraged led neither to increased human freedoms for their populations nor to general increases in prosperity sufficient to compensate the population for the deprivations they suffered in the revolutionary process. This is, in some cases, a very harsh judgement even if it is true. For example, the people of Nicaragua did not seek the US economic blockade and the CIA-funded Contra terrorism that stifled their revolution. The people of Mozambique did not chose to become embroiled in a war against South African-financed MNR terrorists that almost destroyed the material conditions for the construction of socialism in their country.[37] But that is what happened. The communist parties and governments of Eastern Europe had no such excuses, and many of their peoples appear to have rejected the communist vision too, though it is less clear that capitalist globalization is what they want.

Many Marxists see the main cause of discontent in the socialist world in the absurdity of the idea of socialism in one country created by the Stalinists to sustain the national integrity of the Soviet Union. Communism is a globalizing theory and practice or it is nothing and the prospects for isolated socialist states, breakaway socialism as it is sometimes labelled, in a capitalist global system must always be bleak. As one writer put it in the 1980s: 'the continued strength of world capitalism, especially as it operates in the interstate system, has pushed these [socialist] states in the direction of reintegration as functional parts that reproduce the logic of the capitalist world-economy' (Chase-Dunn 1982: 9).

It may be intellectually sounder to argue that actually existing communist states had no genuine connection with the communist ideal.[38] While the authoritarian Stalinist version of communism appears to have been rejected in all the former communist countries, it is not at all clear what is to replace it. What are the choices open to those who cannot accept capitalist globalization now that Stalinist authoritarian communism has been rejected?

The restoration of some version of capitalism is the obvious choice. It involves a complex set of ideas, particularly in societies that have never really experienced much capitalism. In a very real sense, the tremendous changes that are taking place in surviving communist societies are the results of attempts to come to terms with the economic, political, and culture-ideology practices of capitalist globalization. Capitalist globalization, through the culture-ideology of consumerism, has very successfully projected its vision of the good life (as opposed to the socialist vision of the good society). The globalizing culture-ideology of consumerist capitalism appeals to individualism, private enterprise, and the idea of choice (for those with the money to pay, of course). Most socialist societies, despite some very impressive rates of economic growth in the past, appeared in the 1980s to be in economic crisis. But the economic crises of socialist societies were crises in terms of the criteria of capitalist globalization, namely their inability to satisfy ever-growing demands for consumer goods (see Birman 1989), rather than in terms of their own original ideals, namely the provision of a basic minimum standard of living for everyone as the basis of satisfying lives for all, in contrast to enrichment for the few. The argument is not that the demand for consumer goods creates crises, but that the spread of the culture-ideology of consumerism, based on the creation of artificial wants, as an inevitable consequence of the globalization of the capitalist mode of production, is not sustainable. The class polarization crisis and the ecological crisis are, paradoxically, fatal flaws in both Stalinist socialism in one country and capitalist globalization worldwide. However, it is also true that it is always very difficult to decide in any community where the dividing line between genuine needs and induced wants is, and, indeed, the dividing line may change over time.

The economic reforms in postcommunist Europe and the socialist Third World were typically labelled as moves towards the restoration of capitalism, approvingly by capitalists eager to cash in, and disapprovingly by theoretical communists defending the purity of their beliefs. These judgements of right and left are predicated on conceptions of capitalism that monopolize individual enterprise and entrepreneurship. This has the unfortunate effect of making it virtually impossible to criticize inefficiencies in socialist economic and social planning without appearing to advocate the restoration of capitalism, at one extreme, or sounding hopelessly naive on the question of human motivation, at the other. The simplistic belief that privatization will solve all ills is as false in the New Second World as it is in the other two (Cook and Kirkpatrick 1995, Łoś and Zybertowicz 2000). This goes to the very heart of the dilemma faced by all the socialist societies that embarked on processes of reform in the 1980s. We could ask why it is that almost a century after the Russian Revolution and more than half a century after the Chinese Revolution, few appear to believe that communism works. If the leaders no longer appear to believe, then it is not surprising if no one else does.

The Chinese authorities, as we shall see in the next chapter, have been accused of the restoration of capitalism since 1979. The argument hinges on the extent to which socialist development depends on the promotion of transnational practices that are capitalist in origin. The contradiction here is apparent, not real. Just as socialist practices, like socialized health services and public housing, have a different significance in capitalist and in socialist societies, capitalist practices, like the freedom of employers to fire workers and of owners of firms to declare bankruptcy have a different significance in socialist and in capitalist societies. However, they may not, it is true, have very different immediate consequences for the individual worker or citizen involved.

The need to introduce capitalist practices into socialist societies is due to the political primacy of economic growth, particularly state-sponsored export-oriented industrialization, in current development strategies. This has repercussions for class structure in socialist societies, in terms of the tendencies to favour the urban proletariat over the peasantry, despite communist-populist rhetoric, and the growth of an urban-based (and biased) bureaucracy. Though Marxists argue that under communism the state will wither away, it is precisely in communist societies that state control grew to enormous proportions. The characterization of communist societies as state capitalist began with the labelling of the Soviet Union and since Milovan Djilas wrote *The New Class* in the 1950s the idea of a state bureaucratic ruling class in communist society has been widely discussed inside and outside Marxist circles. What the reforms in the Soviet Union, Eastern Europe, and China in the 1980s introduced to the debate was the idea that an actual capitalist bourgeoisie, as opposed to the party or state bourgeoisie, was emerging in these societies.

Ivan Szelenyi's study of socialist entrepreneurs in rural Hungary during the communist era throws light on this issue. Hungary was the only country where family entrepreneurship actually did re-emerge in communist Eastern Europe, and Szelenyi develops a complex theory to explain how four class processes (proletarianization, the formation of a new working class, embourgeoisement, and cadrefication) took place simultaneously. An elaborate methodology predicted, through life histories and the inheritance of cultural capital, how the new entrepreneurs emerged. Szelenyi (1988: 13) argues: 'The kind of embourgeoisement we are describing here—at least until now [1980s]—has not led to "capitalism." Rather, a new, state socialist type of mixed economy is emerging, with a uniquely new dual system of social stratification. It is as different from laissez-faire or welfare state capitalism as it is from the Soviet style of monolithic, redistributive, state socialism.' (I shall pursue the idea of the socialist entrepreneur with reference to the class structure in China in the next chapter.)

Szelenyi draws two main theoretical conclusions. The transition of class fractions from self-employed petit bourgeois to either capitalist entrepreneur or pure proleratian may not be as simple as Marx imagined; and concepts like market and entrepreneur need to be converted before they can be used for non-capitalist societies, like that of a state socialist mixed economy. In search, albeit ironic, of a Third Way between capitalism and communism, he goes on to develop these ideas in terms of new kinds of small-scale production for specialized consumer goods and agricultural products markets in the new world of flexible specialization, but not many people will believe that the salvation of Eastern Europe lies in the unreliable consumption habits of Western yuppies, though these niche markets certainly enrich some people. Hann also discusses the Hungarian alternative. He argues that what was needed was not total marketization as some new political parties were demanding (and eventually got), but a hierarchy of ownership structures in Hungary and, by implication, all contemporary socialist societies. Hann makes the useful point that the grassroots view of property as a stark alternative between private property or collective property is false. This implies that some real rights did exist under state socialism, at least in Hungary. However, he highlights the problem of reconciling these Third Way ideas and the fact that 'consumerist aspirations to possess more material goods have propelled the economic transformation of the whole country' (Hann 1993: 116).

This is not simply romanticism. As Kovacs and Maggard argue (specifically for Hungary but no doubt true to some extent for the whole of postcommunist Europe): 'Socialism produced not only victims. For many people socialism meant a modest but improving standard of living and some degree of security. Recent developments [the rapid marketization of the early 1990s], however, threaten this "little security" and project an uncertain future' (Kovacs and Maggard 1993: 324). They contrast the ironical freedom that people had not to identify with the old communist system to the feeling of inside but outside the new system, where most are glad of the more genuine pluralism of civil society but feel they have no part in determining how the new system actually works. I shall return to this consequence of capitalist democracy in the concluding chapter.

If the introduction or restoration of capitalist practices into socialist societies does not necessarily mean the restoration of capitalism itself, what does it mean? The answer to this question is one that Third Way theorists often tackle, if obliquely. They argue, usually as a critical response to the excesses of globalizing neo-liberalism, that what is needed to increase human happiness and make societies more efficient is the insertion of some social democratic practices into capitalist societies. In the first and second editions of *Sociology of the Global System* I presented my own version of the Third Way under the rubric of democratic feminist socialism. With the election of New Labour driven by Tony Blair and his group in 1997 the Third Way of Anthony Giddens became something of a political orthodoxy for Blair, the US President Bill Clinton, and many other reforming and to some extent globalizing politicians around the world (see Giddens 2000, and critiques by Callinicos 2001 and Mouzelis 2001). However, with Clinton out of office under a cloud, and Blair's New Labour project in disarray (despite another massive election victory in 2001), the Third Way appears to have been quietly incorporated into the social democratic version of capitalist globalization.[39]

The problem with the version of the Third Way taken up for a time by globalizing politicians, bureaucrats, professionals, and even some TNC executives (in the case of one enthusiast, President Vincente Fox of Mexico, a former Coca-Cola executive) around the world was that it retained the most damaging aspects of capitalist globalization and marginalized some of its more positive consequences. This is most clearly seen in the approach to competitiveness, a central prop of the neo-liberal economic and social theory that underpins capitalist globalization.

For Third Way theorists, competitiveness is a prime economic and social value, not for its intrinsic worth but for its pre-eminent status as the means to the end of social justice. Private business, of course, must be competitive, in order to ensure jobs and prosperity, even when this competitiveness has the direct effect of destroying whole industries and impoverishing whole communities. As many critics of capitalism have pointed out (notably the monopoly capitalism school associated with the periodical *Monthly Review*) the economic efficiency that drives competitiveness operates in a context of supremely biased accounting and serves the interests of specific groups rather than the public as a whole. The cheap food policy, about which there has been so much discussion in the UK, is based on driving down costs and driving up productivity (the essence of economic efficiency) resulting in cost displacement to other groups within the food system. Because of the almost inevitable breakdowns in the system (BSE, foot and mouth disease, and other food and drink hazards) what looks like economic efficiency and benefits for the consumer (apparently cheap food) has turned out to be highly inefficient for the community as a whole, and deadly for some (see Monbiot 2000: ch. 8, Hines 2000: ch. 18, Isserman 2001).

The drive for this spurious competitiveness is directly connected with what has been dramatically termed the dismantling of the welfare state. Shin (2000) puts this in a straightforward manner in the argument that as states compete against each other to attract foreign investment this influences social policy. They do this by presenting themselves as business-friendly. The evidence for this thesis is that there are common trends in most welfare states. They all display to a greater or lesser extent market-conforming policies on business taxation, reduction in employers' contributions for social protection, reduced levels of income security, increased levels of funding for labour market enhancement, and less state intervention in the regulation of the labour market. Shin connects this directly with state responses to globalization. However, as Bowles and Wagman (1997) conclude in their study of the actual responses of First World governments: 'The experience of the 1980s suggests that multiple responses to globalization are possible; the fate of the welfare state appears to depend on institutional structures and policy decisions, rather than on an inevitable capitulation to global forces' (333).[40] This is entirely true. There is nothing inevitable about the dismantling of the welfare state under pressure from capitalist globalization. If it takes place, it is the result of conscious decisions by those who run the government and those who control the state.

Third Ways, therefore, can be of at least two types. They can be based on efforts to make capitalist globalization more humane, more sustainable, and less polarizing, or they can be based on an alternative form of globalization, that is already more humane, more sustainable, and less polarizing. One alternative that has attracted a great deal of critical attention since the 1980s is market socialism, but there has been virtually no attempt to connect market socialism with globalization. Would a theory of market socialism as the socio-economic base of socialist globalization have any better prospects of resolving the twin crises of capitalist globalization than current Third Way theories? This is the problematic that frames the discussion of China in the next chapter.

CONCLUSION

The old Second World and, to a much lesser extent, the socialist Third World, in the past enjoyed a certain measure of autonomy from the capitalist global system. Comecon for some time served to insulate businesses and institutions in Eastern Europe from having to compete on the world stage with those of global capitalism. The available evidence suggests that the countries of the socialist Third World, like those of the capitalist Third World, never really managed to free themselves from global capitalism, and perhaps some of their leaders never intended this in any case. The Soviet Union did achieve a high level of independence in an alternative global system but as the communist project began to collapse, its peoples and its leaders became increasingly attracted to aspects of the global capitalist project, particularly the culture-ideology of consumerism. This is now more or less true in postcommunist Europe and in the Third World as a whole.

The feeling is entirely mutual. Representatives of the transnational capitalist class from all over the world have been flooding into postcommunist Europe and the socialist and former socialist Third World making deals, setting up joint ventures, opening consultancies, and generally teaching erstwhile communists how to operate profitably within the capitalist global system. Illustrations of this are legion: from the entrepreneurs rushing into Vietnam hoping to turn it into another Asian tiger to the World Bank and IMF restructuring of former socialist economies in Africa, from the gradual but apparently inexorable commercialization of Cuba and its growing reputation for the sort of rapacious tourism more commonly associated with Bangkok to the more full-blooded transformation of China. Neither the TNCs nor the politicians nor the ideologues of free enterprise are in any doubt that capitalism has triumphed over Stalinist communism because it has delivered the goods. It satisfies the demands of the consumers. Or that is what it looks like from the East and the South.

In order to spread the culture-ideology of consumerism, the remnants of the socialist Third World appear to need transnational corporations and their local affiliates to produce the goods for domestic consumption and export, and the transnational capitalist class and its local affiliates to organize the system politically. These are emerging, embryonically, in what is left of the socialist Third World, and in the former Soviet bloc. I have argued that all these developments do not necessarily point to the restoration of full-blown capitalism, indeed I find this to be an unlikely scenario in the long term. This is what is suggested by the rather special case of China. So, the most populous country in the world and what *Business Week* (17 May 1993) called 'the emerging powerhouse of the 21st century', beckons.

NOTES

1. For an interesting discussion of the principle of 'distribution according to work' (DATW) see *Social Sciences in China* (1989). Sociologists might like to compare DATW with the functionalist theory of stratification and consider the point that the criteria on which different jobs are evaluated distinguishes capitalism from socialism.

2. Gills and Qadir (1995) is a valuable and more recent source on these regimes. Post and Wright (1989) is an analytic discussion of Third World socialism, that lays out seventeen conditions of socialism, derived from Marxist and post-Marxist experience (11–17).

3. Some far-seeing scholars anticipated the changes. See, for example, Girvan's 1975 essay (reprinted in Sklar 1980); Frank's rousing article (1977); and more generally, Chase-Dunn (1982).

4. Mozambique was denied full membership because the Soviet Union would not commit itself economically as it had done in Cuba and Vietnam (Jinadu, in Keller and Rothchild, 1987: 239–53).

5. See Laiodi (1988) for an unusually interesting collection of essays on how the Soviet Union was perceived in Black Africa, Iraq and Syria, Turkey, the ASEAN Countries, Vietnam, India, and Latin America. This makes a welcome change from the innumerable works that discuss how the Soviet Union treated such countries.

6. For references to these works and further discussion on the issues, see Packenham (1992). Useful collections on Cubanology from opposing perspectives are Roca (1988) and Zimbalist (1988), which provide information on a wide range of issues. On the effects on Cuba of the collapse of the Soviet Union and communism in Eastern Europe, see the volumes edited by Halebsky and Kirk (1992) and Mesa-Lago (1993). Cole (1998) provides a valuable insider's analysis; see also Brundenius and Weeks (2001: Part 1).

7. For some interesting comments on this, see the systematic comparisons of the political economies of Chile, Cuba, and Costa Rica in Mesa-Lago (2000).

8. However, as MacGaffey (1991) argues for Zaire, a prior key issue is whether or not there is an effective state at all in some Third World countries.

9. This helps to explain the struggle over the sanctions weapon against apartheid. For a thought-provoking examination of the question of transnationals in Southern Africa see Seidman *et al.* (1986), which is useful both for South African-based TNC activity and the efforts of socialist countries in the region to resist and create their own structures. Bond (2000) explains what happened in the 1990s.

10. Mezger (1978) clearly illuminates the roots of this dependency for the mining industry in the region.

11. Herbst (2001) makes the point that though adjectival democracy (semi, quasi, real, popular, participatory, limited, liberal, non-liberal, incomplete, etc.) suggests that political systems are on the road to genuine democracy, there is little evidence that this is actually happening in Africa. As in Europe, the process could take a long time and suffer reverses.

12. See the website of Jubilee 2000 (a 'think-and-do-tank' of the New Economic Foundation in London, renamed Jubilee + in 2001) for these figures and data on the debt burden as a whole.

13. On the performance of the Bank see also Fox and Brown (1998) and Laurell (2000) for Latin America.

14. See Mittelman (1981) and Moore-Lappe and Beccar-Varela (1980), for (rather different) systematic comparisons between the two countries. Both works provide background for understanding subsequent developments. Mittelman (2000: ch. 5) is useful, but very pessimistic.

15. Quoted in 'Revolutionary Mozambique puts its money on capitalism' (*Guardian* 9 May 1984: 10). This is by no means a unique case. As Steinberg (1982: 119) commented on Burma: 'Ironically, the attainment of Burma's socialist goals is increasingly dependent on foreign capitalist economies.'

16. Dowden's (1987) conclusion still rings true: 'profitable enterprises are being handed over to foreign companies such as Lonrho. There is no popular capitalism in the privatisation of Africa. Increased production benefits only foreign companies or individuals who do not reinvest their profits locally.' As we see later, this is also the case in postcommunist Europe.

17. The same case can be made for many other Third World socialist countries. Stoneman (1978) makes it for the transition from Rhodesia to Zimbabwe; and Khaing (1986: 41) says of Burma: 'Any time that the inner councils of the state decide to return to capitalism, the people will be ready with the skills they have kept alive, and the wits they have may be even sharper in the pursuit of profit under socialism.' See also Tanaka (1992) for the cases of Vietnam, Mongolia, and North Korea.

18. A critical commentary by Mamdani follows O'Loughlin's article in *African Affairs*. See also Braathen and Palmero, in Wilson *et al.* (2000: ch. 13).

19. Joachim Chissano, President since 1986, was reported to have taken up Transcendental Meditation under the influence of the Maharishi, whose Heaven and Earth Development Corporation [*sic*] had its eye on vast tracts of land in resource-rich Mozambique (Reuters News-Africa, 18 Mar. 1994).

20. It is not only in the postcommunist countries in Africa that corruption and nepotism have accompanied privatization, as the study of Uganda by Tangri and Mwenda (2001) demonstrates.

21. In fact it reappeared under the title *Problems of PostCommunism*, with the reflective statement: 'For ten years academics, policymakers, and other experts have lamented how the post-communist leaders have made a mess of the transition. Few, however, have stopped to consider that some of the problems of post-communism were created by the West. Did Western haste, naivete, or arrogance increase the burden on post-communist societies?' (Editors 2001: 1).

22. That this is not exactly what the original intention of the policy was, is clear from Gorbachev (1988).

23. See also *Advertising Age* (19 Feb. 1990) for more on the Eastern European market. Rosati and Mizsei (1989) discuss the pressures on Eastern European governments to adopt export-oriented industrialization and the capitalist global project.

24. See 'Socialist countries' enterprises abroad: new trends' (*CTC Reporter* (UNCTC) Autumn 1987: 17–22). TNCs from China, as we shall see in Chapter 9, have been particularly active.

25. Nayyar (1977) contains informative essays on trade relations between Comecon and Tanzania, Egypt, Ghana and Nigeria, India, and Pakistan, as well as the impact of Soviet oil, and China's aid and trade with the Third World. See also Skak (in Caporaso, 1987) on East/ South (NICs) economic relations.

26. ABB appears to have acquired the company, but there is no record of it on the ABB website.

27. As King (1986) shows, the Polish government began to market imported global brands aggressively as early as 1985. King's research provides solid evidence for the culture-ideology of consumerism in communist Poland. See also, on rock music, Ryback (1989).

28. Ian Traynor (*Guardian*, 11 May 1989). For a similar situation in Zahony, on the Hungarian-Russian border, see *The Economist* (22 July 1989: 44).

29. In his excellent review and reconceptualization of the literature, King (2000: 154) argues that the idea of postcommunism is 'genuinely useless'. In his view, a more useful question is how did similar systems become so different? He goes on to argue that the importance of region depends on the research question being asked. This is precisely my point. The concepts of New Second World and postcommunism are important for the analysis of capitalist globalization.

30. Although he does not use these terms, Poznanski (1993) makes the argument that the transformation of the Old into the New Second World was more of an evolutionary than a revolutionary change. This would help to explain the apparently peculiar political and electoral events that have taken place.

31. The 1999 total was about the same as the Czech Republic, somewhat less than Hungary, but only about half as much as Poland. China, on the other hand, had over $300bn. in FDI! (UN 2000).

32. In a rather less alarming analysis of elite formation in postcommunist societies, Higley *et al.* (1998: 2) report: 'We find that the most prominent trend is toward more polyarchical constellations of elites . . . elite changes in several countries as still quite open-ended, leading away from the old communist configuration toward several alternative configurations.' Time will tell.

33. As we shall see in the next chapter, China's 'New-new people phenomenon' followed a few years later.

34. Sparks (1998) is a thought-provoking study of the subject drawing important conclusions for media theory in general.

35. In their draconian analysis of postcommunist Poland, Łoś and Zybertowicz (2000) imply that the whole society is best analysed in these terms.

36. Caroline Thomas (1999: 225) argues: 'As we enter the new millennium, the Third World, far from disappearing, is becoming global. The dynamic of economic driven globalization is resulting in the global reproduction of Third World problems.'

37. In the words of a Christian Aid report: 'The objective of the MNR is to make life unbearable for the farmer and the peasant by making it impossible for them to grow their crops and by making them homeless . . . Their paymasters want to point to the chaos in Mozambique . . . where else the bottom line of this war except the survival of white minority rule in South Africa?' (Knight 1988: 14). This is the same so-called low intensity strategy used in Angola and Nicaragua. The white minority government has gone but capitalist globalization is rampant.

38. In the first edition of *Sociology of the Global System* in 1990 I wrote: 'This is my own view, but it is hopeless to try to argue the case with the victims, for they have suffered too much to be willing, far less enthusiastic, to give the communists another chance. This is the message of some of the extraordinary elections in eastern Europe.' The continuing election victories of ex-communists leading parties with new names since 1990 seem just as extraordinary as the elections which threw them out of office. No doubt we are in for many more surprises.

39. See Hoatson (2001) for an instructive analysis of how community development policy and practice in Australia and Britain evolved from the welfare state through the contract state to the Third Way.

40. See also the project of Deacon *et al.* (1997) on connections between the globalization of social policy and the socialization of global politics.

Chapter 9
CAPITALIST GLOBALIZATION IN CHINA

NEW CHINA

The Chinese economic reforms of the late 1970s, the post-Mao economic policies, clearly represented a real shift in strategy for the government of the People's Republic of China (PRC), but whether they represented a real shift in goals is less easy to determine (compare Blecher 1997 and World Bank 1997). Chinese policy, even during its most isolationalist periods, was aimed at harnessing the best of foreign technology and methods. Reluctance to become dependent on foreign capital and technology to the same extent as other Third World countries, at least up to the 1980s, was a result of the bitter experience of the Sino-Soviet split in the late 1950s, and a keen eye for the worst consequences of neo-imperialism elsewhere. The policy of self-reliance did not mean 'rely on ourselves for everything' but 'do not rely on foreigners for anything we can do for ourselves'. Even during the Cultural Revolution, turnkey projects for large chemical fertilizer factories were concluded with foreign companies.[1]

Mao's economic policy was thoroughly tempered by strategic military thinking. Throughout the 1950s and the 1960s China felt threatened by actual wars conducted by the USA and its allies on its borders with the declared aim of defeating communism, and by potential war from a hostile USSR. Regional self-sufficiency in the 1960s was reduced to village level with the exhortation that everyone should 'store grain, and prepare for the eventuality of war'. The military rationale of these decentralizing processes declined in the 1970s as China's entry into the United Nations in 1971 and the Nixon visit to Beijing in 1972 reduced China's isolation. However, exposure of the economic inefficiencies of the policies had to wait until the death of Mao in 1976 and the defeat of the Gang of Four and their followers, who had forced the Cultural Revolution to extremes, shortly after.

THE OPENING DOOR

The economic reforms of the late 1970s inaugurated a process of selective decentralization. By the early 1980s a form of regional decentralization was being encouraged that presaged a radically new theory of development for China, and one that owed little to Mao Zedong. The establishment of the Special Economic Zones (SEZ) in 1979 began the general opening up of the Chinese economy to capitalist globalization, and the subsequent emergence of market socialism.

China is the most populous country on earth, with a population of over 1.2 billion people, most of whom are young. One of the most visible effects of the economic reforms of 1979 and since has been the transformation from a low-income, low-inflation, and low-consumption economy to one in which there are substantially increased incomes for numerous groups, significant inflation, and a veritable consumer boom in the cities and some parts of the countryside. An early sign of these changes was the announcement in 1984 that for the first time peasants were to be subject to personal income tax (previously a fixed percentage of production had been levied as a tax on the collective). The fact that even a small proportion of Chinese workers and peasants had money to spend after they had bought the necessities of life indicated that there were many millions of extra potential consumers in the global marketplace.

The south of the country has always provided the bulk of Chinese emigration, principally to South-East Asia but also much further afield. Apart from Hong Kong, about half of whose people were actually born in the PRC, there are important Chinese communities in Malaysia, Singapore, Thailand, and Indonesia (and, of course, in many other parts of the world). In most of these countries the Chinese are over-represented in business, and they have always been wooed by the authorities in the PRC, who have consistently seen them as economically and politically worthwhile allies. Services and facilities for them constitute a growth industry throughout China. The official interest parallels and is thoroughly nurtured by strong clan, village, and kin links. Many overseas Chinese consider investment in China as both a patriotic duty and a convenient way to help their relatives (Hodder 1996, Yeung and Olds 2000).

From the early 1980s there was a general liberalization of the economy accompanied by changes in political and cultural-ideological practices, some quite incredible from the perspective of previous decades. For example, the lifting of restrictions on various forms of private enterprises led to an embryonic stock market. One manifestation of this was in the attempts by some entrepreneurs to sell shares in public as well as private enterprises. The difference between buying shares in private companies, which no one in China had experienced since the 1940s, and deposits in bank or co-operative savings accounts, which have been widespread and secure throughout the whole period of communist rule, was not at all clear to the uninitiated. As a result, many people lost money, some no doubt cheated by unscrupulous speculators. The official visit of John J. Phelan (then chairman of the New York Stock Exchange) to China in 1987 served to give Chinese stock dealings a measure of legitimacy but this has not been matched by adequate regulatory law.

The first joint-stock company was set up in Shenzhen in 1983, and by the 13th Congress of the Communist Party in 1987 shareholding was deemed 'another form of socialist ownership'. As most shares are state-owned this is not as ridiculous as it sounds. By the end of 1991, there were over 3,000 joint-stock companies, but only 2 per cent issued shares to the general public (Yang, in Heath 1993: ch. 10). Though Shenzhen led the way, the financial capital of China is now undoubtedly Shanghai (Hertz 1998, Olds 2001: ch. 5). The first Chinese interbank currency market in China opened in Shanghai in 1994, joining the pre-existing commodities and gold exchanges. By 1994, the Shanghai Securities Exchange was trading in almost 200 stocks with a total market capitalization of $US40 billion, double that of Shenzhen. Olds (2001: 182 ff.) reports that up to one million Shanghainese trade in the new Shanghai Stock Exchange, relocated to a purpose-built high-tech building modelled on the latest telecommunications centres in Japan. People's Bank and other major Chinese banks were moved from Beijing to Shanghai in the mid-1990s.

In the cities, the economic reforms resulted in tremendous growth in small businesses, particularly personal services. For example, beauty parlours have mushroomed, encouraging an expanding clientele to seek social and psychological fulfilment through cosmetic surgery for the creation of Western facial features. By 1988, it was reported that

20 per cent of all China's doctors and nurses were in private practice, many of them specializing in such fields (Schell 1988). The growth of the tourist industry in China has also been extraordinary, but only in contrast to the situation up to the late 1970s, rather than in comparison with what is common in the rest of the Third World. Now, at sites throughout China, foreign and local tourists are accosted by multitudes of peddlers selling local curios and other objects of uncertain origin, often undercutting the prices of the official state shops. At the most popular attractions, like the Terra Cotta soldiers outside Xian, the Ming Tombs outside Beijing, and of course the Great Wall (see Figure 9.1) large markets catering to the tourist trade have implanted themselves.[2] Whereas visitors in the 1960s and 1970s had complained that the reticence of the salespersons made it difficult to buy anything, now the complaint is that hawkers will not leave them alone. In the mid-1990s, for example, there were at least three glossy free publications advertising luxury goods and services for tourists in Beijing: *Beijing Talk* (the voice of Beijing's expatriate community), *Welcome to China: Beijing* (the Beijing Tourist Authority journal), and *Food Guide* (the Beijing restaurant guide). These were being used by prosperous Chinese as well as foreign tourists (see also Smith, in Scarpaci 2000)

These may be seen as interesting if rather peripheral examples of what has been happening in China since 1978. More central to the future of the society and more salient for the analysis of the impact of capitalist globalization on it, is the open-door policy. In 1988, about ten years into the policy, the east coast open belt (China's gold coast) covered a total area of 320,000 sq. km with a population of 160 million, about 15 per cent of the national total. The open region is made up of three parts, namely the four Special Economic Zones (SEZs), the coastal open cities, and the larger coastal open economic areas (Zheng 1988, Li and Li 1999).

The SEZs were established in south-east China in 1979–80. The largest and most important was at Shenzhen, directly across the border from Hong Kong's New Territories (Sklair 1985, 1991). In order to facilitate the utilization of foreign investment, in 1983 the

Figure 9.1 Consumerism in China
Source: author's photo.

Chinese authorities announced the establishment of eight zones for priority investment. These were large areas, like Beijing– Tianjin–Bohai Bay, the nine municipalities and fifty-seven counties of the Shanghai Zone, the Wuhan Zone, and the Pearl River Delta Zone. As they already contained about 90 per cent of China's foreign investment, the plan was, and largely still is, to concentrate most of the future FDI in these areas where, it is argued, it can be put to the most effective use most quickly (the Chinese version of comparative advantage). Two hundred and twenty-two key cities (later increased to around 300) were designated to transmit development to the backward areas that surround them.

In 1984 fourteen coastal cities were opened up to relatively unrestrained foreign investment. The rationale for this policy was the trickle-down effect, now somewhat discredited in the eyes of most planners. While it would be rash to prejudge the issue, several decades of development planning experience would suggest that this strategy has little to commend it. It is only fair to add, however, that there is no single development strategy with very much to commend it on the available evidence. The choice of investment priority areas and open ports is a predictable first step in any process of contemporary industrialization. In 1985, in yet another open-door initiative, Coastal Open Economic Areas were established in fifty-two Pearl River Delta cities and Yangtze River Delta cities and counties, and in Fujian. In 1994 the Chinese authorities permitted the Singapore government to open an industrial park in Souzhou, followed by another in Wuxi in 1995 (Pereira 2000). In nearby Shanghai, a major urban development with substantial foreign funding was set in motion in the special district of Pudong (Olds 2001). These were already relatively prosperous areas, but links with the outside world through foreign investment and foreign trade have made them even richer.

In the words of an open-door policy maker, the 'long time isolation from the world economy, a product of many historical factors, has become a matter of the past' (Zhang 1988: 70; see also World Bank 1997, Li and Li 1999). However, from the beginning of the open-door policy, more prosperous areas were expected to pay a certain price for their new economic opportunities. In return for greater autonomy each community in the open-door region was expected to:

[1] increase its output of technology intensive products as well as its export of labour in order to earn the foreign currency that China needs to import equipment and materials;

[2] encourage the growth of international as well as domestic cycles of production through the use of both domestic and imported inputs for exports;

[3] increase all forms of foreign investment;

[4] import more foreign technology and use it for both import substitution products and R&D;

[5] selectively learn from foreign managerial expertise;

[6] train various kinds of personnel (Zhang 1988).

The Chinese government invested heavily in infrastructure to improve the foreign investment climate, particularly in Shenzhen, and this provoked a good deal of criticism. One indication of the resentment felt at the over-generous treatment Shenzhen received from the centre can be gauged from the vote at the National People's Congress (China's Parliament) in 1989, on special rights for Shenzhen. These were opposed by 274 out of

2,688 deputies, with 805 abstentions, 'the largest opposition debate and votes in the history of the congress' (*Beijing Review*, 17–23 Apr. 1989: 5). It would be incorrect to see this as a vote against the open-door policy as such. Nevertheless, there has been some criticism of the emphasis on exports, partly because Chinese goods tend to be perceived as low quality, but to a greater extent because the level of unsatisfied domestic demand has been high. However, China, in common with many other Third World countries locked into export-oriented development strategies, considers it necessary to export in order to earn the hard currency to import. One consequence has been a Chinese version of the race to the bottom as Shenzhen and other economic zones competed for foreign investment (see Breslin 1996).

Of particular significance for Shenzhen, and indeed the growth of the whole Pearl River Delta, is the relationship with Hong Kong. There has been a substantial trading link between Hong Kong and the rest of China for decades (see Youngson 1983). Indeed, Hong Kong could hardly have prospered in the way that it has since the 1950s without supplies of relatively cheap food, raw materials, labour, and latterly oil from the PRC. The trade, however, is decidedly two-way. While the value of Chinese exports to Hong Kong increased almost twentyfold between 1960 and 1980, Hong Kong exports to China increased over fifty times in the same period, most of the increase being in the 1970s. Before reunification in 1997, PRC exports to Hong Kong were commonly trans-shipped to third countries, indicating both the shortcomings of the Chinese transportation network, and the residual resistance that some countries still had to doing business with China directly. The volume of trade and trade-related contacts between the south of China and Hong Kong has increased enormously since the 1980s. Most of these contacts take place in Canton, and in the Shenzhen SEZ.

While Chinese society has rarely been as thoroughly egalitarian as some of its more enthusiastic erstwhile supporters have imagined, in general Communist Party policies managed to keep intra-regional inequalities in check more successfully than inter-regional differences (Long and Ng 2001, Blecher 1997). The economic changes since the late 1970s, and particularly the exhortations to the workers and the peasants to enrich themselves as fast as possible within the somewhat elastic bounds of socialist legality, have certainly increased local inequalities. The question that was increasingly posed in the 1990s was whether the overall benefits of the economic reforms were sufficient to compensate for the income and other differentials they were clearly producing. Fan (1997) shows how the ideological and scientific dimensions of the debate over uneven development evolved in China and draws attention to the increasing importance of the role of firms and enterprises compared with state plans and intervention. The fixation on spatial forms and location also explains the relative lack of research on economic sectors. China, in brief, is becoming more like other parts of the world in terms of inter- and intra-regional inequalities. This is effectively illustrated in the fact that there were ten times more telephones per person in urban than rural areas in the mid-1990s (Mansell and Wehn 1998: table 8.3).

While some argue that TNCs have played a muted role in all of this (Sun 1998), I would agree with Li and Li (1999: 10) who show that since 1989 'the role of FDI has been undergoing a radical change: it no longer simply plays a symbolic role in China's opening up to the outside world, it has become one of the key driving forces in the development of the local and national economy'. Much of the foreign investment that flowed into China in the 1980s came from small to medium-sized companies, usually based in Hong Kong and overwhelmingly run by ethnic Chinese. Although sources differ, by the mid-1990s there were probably over 250,000 foreign-invested enterprises in China with registered capital of around $US130 billion (only the USA had more FDI than China in the 1990s). There is a growing body of research on joint ventures in China, indicating interesting differences and interesting similarities with those in other parts of the world (see Beamish 1993). A small number of very large TNCs, for example, PepsiCo from the USA, Sanyo from Japan, and British Petroleum, have invested in Shenzhen SEZ and the adjoining Shekou Industrial Zone (Wong and Chu 1985; Sklair 1991). Outside the SEZs, many large TNCs have been operating since the 1970s. A spate of regulations to encourage foreign investment continually reinforced the impression that, irrespective of what was going on in domestic politics, TNCs continued to be very welcome in China. Corporations like Motorola, Hewlett-Packard, Nestlé, and Sony expanded rapidly in China in the 1990s, often in collaboration with official bodies. Such developments can be followed on the websites of many TNCs, providing solid evidence for the useful distinction between the hard (infrastructure) and soft (social, political, and financial) environment for FDI in China (Li and Li 1999).

The business press regularly reports that global consumer goods brand leaders like Colgate-Palmolive, AT&T, Avon, Motorola, and Coca-Cola, as well as companies in more capital-intensive sectors, like Boeing and General Electric, are investing heavily in the Chinese market. All of these foreign-invested companies, from the global TNCs to the small overseas Chinese enterprises employing family members from the ancestral village, will have some local Chinese managers. A study of managers working in the foreign sector shows some interesting differences between them and managers in the domestic sector. The foreign sector managers tended to have greater job mobility and better benefits and were not so influenced by the party and the dossier system of controlling employees in the state sector (Pearson 1992). This suggests that there is the possibility of a new social group emerging which could ally itself with other groups who see their interests best served by a growing private business sector.

The culmination of the open-door policy came in 1999 when China signed an agreement with the USA paving the way for China to join the WTO (see Lai 2001, Nolan 2001: ch. 11). One of the most despised symbols of the anti-globalization movement (see Chapter 10 below) is now inextricably tied to the political economy of the only remaining great communist power! As always, it is difficult to distinguish the specific impact of the TNCs from the more general effects that arise from any type of contact with capitalist globalization. Nevertheless (as discussed in Chapter 4) there were direct links between TNCs in the China market and state-owned TNCs from China and the internal and international struggles over China's membership of the WTO. The consequences will be felt in China's economic, political, and culture-ideology structures. They can be illustrated through analyses of the labour market (economic TNPs); changes in class structure (political TNPs); and the creation of new consumption needs (culture-ideology TNPs).

THE LABOUR MARKET

Up to the beginning of the 1980s the basis of Chinese communist employment policy was the iron rice bowl. This meant that most work units in China were obliged to employ many more people than they really needed, and to maintain employment irrespective of conditions of operation, both in the urban and the rural economies (see Dutton 1998, Stockman 2000). In addition, many large state corporations provide housing and other benefits for their workers. For example, the major steel producer Shougang housed 20,000 workers' families in new flats between 1979 and 1990, and expanded the living space of 11,000 more (Nolan 2001: ch. 9). Therefore, although many Chinese enterprises achieve high levels of production, very few achieve high levels of productivity per worker. When foreign investors began to do business in China, there were many disputes between them and the Labour Services Bureaux (the state organizations that provide workers to firms) over employment levels and labour discipline. Both sides faced serious problems. The TNCs, most of whom were quite small, had come to China precisely to take advantage of lower wages (as well as more and cheaper land for industrial expansion). Though wages in less industrially advanced areas in China, principally those distant from the coastal regions, are very low, those in the major cities and in Guangdong province, adjoining Hong Kong, where much foreign investment was concentrated, tend to be relatively high. Full wage costs to foreign employers in Shenzhen Special Economic Zone, for example, were about half of those in Hong Kong in the 1990s, and so there were not the huge labour cost savings to be found in some other Third World locations. This meant that the TNCs were less willing to tolerate either excess labour or unsatisfactory workers than they might otherwise have been. Under this pressure cracks appeared in the iron rice bowl. However, Labour Bureaux were still responsible for finding alternative jobs for those allocated to but not employed by factories in the SEZs. Enterprises owned by the state and by local authorities in urban and rural areas shed labour by the millions in the 1980s and 1990s, adding to the demand for these jobs.

From the point of view of workers surplus to requirements and/or those who failed to match up to the demands of TNC labour discipline, this was the thin edge of the wedge. However, it can be argued that it was precisely to learn from foreign capitalists about how to run modern factories and offices efficiently that the economic reforms were introduced and foreign direct investment was encouraged in the first place. It was with this problem in mind that in 1987 a retired West German engineer was appointed general manager of the Wuhan Diesel Engine factory, the first foreigner to run a state factory. The rationalization of labour figures prominently in most Chinese analyses of economic reform, and there is no doubt that practices introduced by foreign companies are beginning to have an impact on employer–employee relations throughout China (see Dutton 1998: 42–61 on the impact of economic reforms on the work units).

One of the most important new social forces to have emerged in the 1990s has been an unprecedented rise of internal migration (Cannon 2000). Tens of millions of Chinese are said to be on the move every day all over the country, mainly leaving their rural homes to seek employment opportunities in the cities. While there are millions who move legally within the work unit system, there are many more who travel without official authorization and who become part of the floating populations that have literally changed the face of many large Chinese cities. The long-term significance of these population movements within China is that the migrants appear to be forming a variety of social and economic groupings that puts them, to some extent, beyond the usual mechanisms of state and party control. Unsurprisingly, many of these unofficial migrants have been labelled as deviants by the authorities and respectable city dwellers alike while, at the same time, their labour is widely used in the booming Chinese informal sectors (see Dutton 1998: part II, Stockman 2000: ch. 3).

It is not only at the worker end of the labour force that the impact of capitalist globalization is being felt. Since the early 1980s a revolution has been going on in the practice of enterprise management, and many academic management theorists and working management consultants (sometimes the same people) have been invited to China to instruct Chinese managers and administrators in the art and science of management. A highly visible symbol of these activities has been the establishment of several US and EEC-sponsored MBA programmes through the Chinese university system and other management training schemes. In an analysis of three such programmes, Zweig (2000: 230) shows that 'donors virtually ran the centres directly for most of the project's life until management was transferred to the Chinese side. . . . Global linkages were also key to their long-term financial viability, as many business opportunities derived from global ties.' In one college, even when staff were being trained to advise township and village enterprises (TVE) on internal management reform, TVE managers were more interested in foreign trade and joint ventures, and would have ignored the centre if this had not been on offer. This research corroborates other studies to show that 'even without privatization, SOEs [state owned enterprises] do respond to the increased marketization of the Chinese economy, especially if their subsidies are cut' (Zweig 2000; 230). Nevertheless, Zweig quotes one foreign expert on a local cadre: 'Anytime we brought up the word "profit-making" or earning a profit in the context of what we were offering here in Chengdu, he, being a good communist and an engineer in a main state-owned enterprise, always would stop and remind us that we weren't in this for the money, and that this was not a profit-making operation. There was always the rider attached. He never ever missed that beat' (p. 223). Gradually, ideas about how to run profitable enterprises and how to build systems of corporate governance are emerging (Mallin and Rong 1998).

This takes us to the core of the fundamental dilemma that a communist society like China faces in its struggle to modernize and in its relations with the TNCs, the bearers (and often the owners) of the technology and techniques that are widely believed to be necessary for modernization. The history of PRC enterprise management has seen violent swings from reds (those with the correct political attitudes) in control, to experts (those with technical expertise irrespective of political attitudes) in control. These two positions were summed up by competing slogans: 'better socialist weeds than capitalist rice' (Gang of Four) and 'it doesn't matter whether the cats are black or white, as long as they catch mice' (Deng Xiaoping)! It would be naive to assume that all enterprise managers in China are now experts, and that the reds have been entirely eliminated (or, for that matter, that these two categories are mutually exclusive or exhaust all the possibilities). TNC operations in other Third World countries have often been seen to depend as much on finding people who know their way around the corridors of power (or, at least, the foreign investment bureaucracy), as on finding indigenous managers who are technically competent. From the point of view of the TNC trying to gain a foothold in China, perhaps the local expert is less vital than the red who can work the political system. From the point of view of the Communist Party cadres who bear the responsibility of enterprise manage-ment in the new conditions of profit and loss accounting, the problem is increasingly: where is the economic liberalization policy leading? Olds's analysis of the project to develop the financial district in Shanghai (2001: ch. 5) shows just how complex this question is.

The other side of the foreign investment coin is, of course, that job creation is often accompanied by job losses elsewhere. Factory relocation from another country to China or any other lower-wage site is a central economic transnational practice of capitalist globalization. Since the 1980s, some jobs have certainly been lost in First World com-munities as TNCs relocated to China, but the greatest impact has been on the hundreds of thousands of jobs shifted from Hong Kong to Shenzhen, and from Shenzhen to the Pearl River Delta and beyond, particularly in the garment, electronics, and toy industries. According to one trade union source: 'workers in Hong Kong helplessly watch their employers move the production lines across the border and gradually their wages eroded since they are paid on piece-rate basis' (Lee 1987). As we have seen, this is a truly global process. The Hong Kong Clothing Union mounted a Job Saving Campaign in the 1980s which, among other things, highlighted the shady practice of keeping plants open for minimal production in Hong Kong to secure false Certificates of Origin, thus making it possible to sidestep First World quotas and to continue exporting to the USA and Europe. The result was under-employment of the workforce rather than mass redundancies. Surveys showed that many employers were routinely deceiving Hong Kong Customs officials. This is yet another case where capitalist globalization has formidable advan-tages in the struggle to destroy labour solidarity. China's accession to the WTO will intensify these pressures on workers.[3]

This is reinforced by the huge scale of internal migration that has occurred in the 1990s as a result of the economic reforms, not least mass redundancies in state-owned enter-prises (Cannon 2000, Nolan 2001: *passim*). Tens of millions of unemployed workers and landless peasants have left their homes in small towns and the countryside and flocked to the major cities in search of work. This has raised the spectre of an new underclass and highlights contentious issues of the class nature of the open-door policy in China.

CLASSES IN THE NEW CHINA

There are those who see the attempted reform of the labour market as a clear indication of the capitalist nature of the PRC. Charles Bettelheim, the noted historian of the Soviet economy, characterized both the Soviet and the Chinese systems as state or party capital-ist. He argued (in Fitzgerald and Wuyts 1988) that despite quite respectable growth of industry between the 1950s and the 1970s, the Maoist strategy was condemned because of poor progress in agriculture, a reduction in the share of services in the national economy, growth in urban unemployment, and a gradual reduction in the marginal efficiency of investment. Communist China, according to Bettelheim, has always been a society ruled by a party bourgeoisie, and since 1978 has embarked on a new road which could lead either to a mixed or a predominantly private capitalist system.

The theme of capitalist restoration (or re-creation) is becoming very familiar in the analyses of all socialist societies. However, not everyone agrees that a capitalist restoration has taken place in China. Solinger, in a closely argued piece of research, labelled the situation at the end of the 1980s, 'Capitalist measures with Chinese characteristics'. She demonstrated that the reforms were, in fact, state-centred, not centred on private enterprise. Their rationale was to recoup state losses incurred over the years as a result of subsidizing inefficient enterprises, and to turn bureaucrats into better managers. Enterprise bankruptcy regulations, takeovers of loss-making companies by profit-making companies, the spread of shareholding and embryonic stock markets, were all responses to the dire lack of state funds. 'There is no privatization of any significance going on' (Solinger 1989: 22).

She shows, for example, the differing significance of shareholding and bankruptcy in communist China and in the capitalist system. The Chinese system of shareholding is based on shares that are really state and enterprise bonds, holding no risks, rather than capitalist-type speculative shares. State enterprises were prohibited from issuing more than 30 per cent of their capital in shares, and these shares were often used as extra welfare payments and bonuses for the workers.[4] The system of official warnings for near-bankrupt state enterprises often leads to firms being turned round rather than going to the wall.

Party bureaucrats in China and other communist countries tolerate such apparently capitalist practices because they provide many commercial opportunities. For example, Solinger shows how those who ran state organizations like material supply bureaux, industrial companies set up by local authorities, trade associations, investment companies, and economic and technical cooperation committees, all stood to benefit from the reforms. She concludes, not unreasonably in my view, that capitalist measures are moulded to adapt to Chinese communism rather than vice versa!

In the culture-ideology sphere, this can be illustrated by the discovery of the New-New People Phenomenon in China, reported in the official Party publication, *Beijing Review* (Lu 2001). This is the generation of Chinese youth born in the 1970s and 1980s. They dye their hair, have rings in their noses and ears and they have mastered computer skills to communicate electronically. Nevertheless, 'It is believed that with correct guidance, most of them will cast off this life and return to normal lifestyle' (Lu 2001: 13). Zhang Yu, aged 16, is a typical example. She goes to an acting school attached to a TV and film company in Beijing, and buys her clothes at the South Korean dress market in downtown Beijing. The school forbids students to dye their hair and to leave the campus more than once a week, but they ignore the rules. 'Their excuse is the rebellious mindset of their generation' (p. 14). They consume as much Korean and Japanese culture, McDonald's food, and foreign films as they can afford. And this generation is not shy about sex. The writer concludes that we should remember the tolerant attitude that Zhou Enlai showed towards American hippies in the 1970s when considering the New-New generation.[5]

Is a new class emerging in China? My own research in the 1980s and early 1990s focused on the Shenzhen SEZ, just across the border from Hong Kong. While the thesis that there is a new class emerging in Shenzhen (let alone in the rest of China) as a consequence of the open-door policy is highly controversial, the thesis that there are new strata (groups that have qualitatively new positions and interests) can hardly be denied. Generalizing from Shenzhen and other areas that are clearly within the orbit of capitalist globalization, there are three new strata from which local affiliates of the transnational capitalist class appear to be emerging. First, there are those officials who have gone into business, opening up potential channels for lucrative dealings with TNCs; second, private entrepreneurs and professionals, some of whom work for and with foreign TNCs in China; third, those who run Chinese TNCs in China, in Hong Kong, and abroad, often combining the roles of globalizing executives and bureaucrats. These groups overlap to some extent and individuals move from one to another, as in the transnational capitalist class.

OFFICIALS

One distinctive feature of Chinese (and Soviet-style) political economy is that officials have enormous power in the economic and commercial spheres. It is common knowledge that the economic reforms in China created opportunities for corruption and nepotism that the government has signally failed to control (for a balanced discussion, see Stockman 2000: 85–90). The special relationships between officials and entrepreneurs (foreign and Chinese) are plain for all to see and this is a major source of corruption. Ding (2000) provides evidence that a form of nomenklatura capitalism is emerging as officials create transnational businesses out of illicitly privatized state firms. These problems are openly discussed in the Chinese media and Shenzhen has often been singled out for criticism in this regard. In 1988, for example, Li Hao, Mayor and Party Secretary of Shenzhen, admitted that corruption had seriously discredited the SEZ with the public—a rhetorical statement that had been heard previously and would be heard many times again. In Shekou, the industrial zone west of Shenzhen, the seriousness of the situation was recognized in early 1989 by the promulgation of four new regulations concerning the widespread phenomenon of public officials involved in private enterprise. The Shekou authorities offered the following conditions: holders of concurrent public and private posts must declare their interests, hand over excess income, and receive half back. Corrupt earnings and brokerage income, if declared and returned, would be excused (*Shekou News*, 6 Feb. 1989).

Although many blamed the SEZ for the rapid increase of corrupt cadre practices, it was clear that such practices had been widespread throughout the country since the introduction of the open-door policy in 1979. The PRC magazine *China Market* (Nov. 1988: 15) for example, reported that many of China's 390,000 companies were briefcase (paper) companies. One such company in Zhejiang province was revealed as having made over one million yuan in its one and only transaction, buying 3,000 tons of urea from the state fertilizer agency and selling it on at 70 per cent above the official price! This phenomenon is commonly known as jumping into the sea, and stories of officials and intellectuals going into business on their own accounts are legion. Dutton (1998: 220–1), for example, reports the extremely interesting case of a female lawyer moving from a university job to private practice in order to work more closely with her husband who happened to be a senior official in the Bureau of Public Security. He wittily refers to this as the one family, two systems phenomenon! Wong (1994) reports a survey showing that about 30 per cent of government officials in China's biggest cities have engaged in part-time business at one time. He distinguishes between two forms of jumping. The first is when government departments set up commercial operations, what he calls a government-linked company

(GLC). Two examples give the general picture. The Department of Public Health in one city set up a medical supply company for hospitals, and the Tax Bureau in another city set up a company to help people process their tax returns. The second form is when senior local officials set up new businesses for themselves, like the Southern Pharmaceutical Company in Shenzhen, headed by the local Communist Party Secretary.[6]

Wong argues that a bureaucratic-business nexus has emerged in China, in which new GLCs are becoming bigger and more diversified, and that TNCs like the New China Hong Kong Group (run by high-level ministers, Hong Kong businessmen, and Singapore state and private entrepreneurs) are emerging. Under the telling title 'Enterprising cadres' the *Far East Economic Review* (16 May 1991) described the activities of Guangdong Enterprises, the Hong Kong-based arm of Guangdong provincial government, a typical transnational GLC. Established in 1981, right at the beginning of the reform period, it was restructured into a holding company in 1986, with dozens of direct subsidiaries and branches in Hong Kong, plus fifteen overseas outlets (including three trading companies and a hotel in Thailand). Revenue in 1990 was in excess of three billion US dollars. Profits were reinvested in steel mills, prawn breeding, and hundreds of smaller projects in Guangdong and a sizeable property portfolio in Hong Kong. In the early 1990s, the company had a near monopoly on tour groups from Guangdong to Hong Kong and supplied most of Hong Kong's vegetables and pond fish. In his monumental study of *China and the Global Business Revolution*, Nolan (2001) shows that what firms are and who owns them is far from clear in China.

The danger here, of course, is that such companies use their political power to distort markets for private ends, just as companies in capitalist systems with near-monopolies do. However difficult it is in practice to do, it is important to distinguish personal from institutional jumping into the sea, indeed Wong (1994) makes a persuasive argument about the beneficial effects of the informal economy when individuals become entrepreneurs. The Chinese government has ordered all state and party organizations to delink from GLCs on several occasions, but this ruling is not enforced universally. Chinese critics argue that such practices are undermining the market for many goods, and though the authorities know about them, they are not cracking down hard enough. These criticisms were given theoretical form by Hua Sheng and his colleagues at the Chinese Academy of Social Sciences, who argue that failure to separate economic from political power is destroying the reforms because bureaucrats monopolizing the supply of raw materials are corrupt, making a rational pricing and allocation policy impossible to put into practice.[7]

PRIVATE ENTREPRENEURS

At the beginning of the reforms in 1978 there were said to be 150,000 households engaged in private businesses. By 1992 the number had risen to 21 million people engaged in fourteen and a half million businesses, 'from restaurants and hairdressers to high-technology, consultancy, advertising, interior design, etc.' (Yang, in Heath 1993: 188). The numbers continue to increase. While most were very small family businesses it is evident that many private individuals in China have made a great deal of money from their entrepreneurial talents. White (1993: ch. 7) connected this with the rise of civil society in China. He identified three types of associations that were filling in the gaps increasingly left by party and state, namely associations of professionals, enterprise managers, and private business people and entrepreneurs based on sector or locality. While some are controlled by the party or the state apparatus, some have a measure of independence. In a complementary study, Unger (1996) shows how new business associations are providing a series of bridges between private business and the government. Some of these associations are clearly creatures of the government (Unger correctly identifies them as corporatist) but not all, and he also sees in them the seeds of civil society in China.

According to Zhang and Qin of the Chinese Academy of Social Sciences, a new social stratum of owners of private enterprises began to emerge in the 1980s and they rapidly became politically organized. One survey in the late 1980s even suggested that 15 per cent of these people were members of the Communist Party.[8] All over the country entre-preneurs' clubs and magazines sprang up and the common consensus was that a new entrepreneurial culture was becoming established in China. Phrases like getting rich quick and putting money above everything, while not entirely unchallenged, were officially legitimized by the view that the pursuit of individual wealth is a necessary precondition of national prosperity in contemporary China. Under such conditions, it is hardly surprising that an entrepreneurial stratum is growing rapidly.

Goodman (in Robison and Goodman 1996: ch. 10) distinguishes between various cat-egories of what he calls China's new rich, on the basis of their wealth and influence and their activities. He identifies the owner-operators of new businesses and highlights their conspicuous wealth; suburban executives control the vast network of rural and township industries and they are forging links overseas; state capitalists and model managers are encouraged to be entrepreneurial as the authorities desperately seek to make their enterprises profitable; wheelers and dealers, for example share traders on the embryonic Chinese stock markets; and trend-setters, symbolized by the mobile phone whose pur-chase and running costs are clear signs that its possessor has lots of money. What is of great significance for my argument in Goodman's work is that all of these types of new rich appear to be forging lucrative relations with TNCs of various types. While there is no suggestion that the only way to make money in Communist China is to be useful for the advance of capitalist globalization, it is clearly a major strategy of the new rich.

Most researchers on China agree that the entrepreneurs and the officials are often the same people. But do they constitute a class, and are they allied with others sharing the same (proto-capitalist) interests? For an answer to this question it is necessary to focus our attention on those who run state-owned TNCs in China, in Hong Kong, and abroad.

GLOBALIZING EXECUTIVES AND PROFESSIONALS

The practices and influence of overseas Chinese capitalists are central for the understand-ing of the progress of capitalist globalization in China. Chossudovsky (1986: 140–4) argued that they played a key role in the process of class formation in the post-Mao period. Overseas Chinese often have close kin connections with what were termed the national patriotic bourgeoisie and have been included in foreign trade and investment policy-making at several levels (for example, in the SEZs).[9] Business Week (19 Sept. 1988: 18–21) had raised the prospect of a Greater China combining the labour force of the PRC, Taiwan's skills, and Hong Kong's financial might in the late 1980s (see also Harding 1993).

Since the mid-1980s there has been an unprecedented level of contact between foreign business people and PRC Chinese, both in China and in Hong Kong, but nowhere more so than through Shenzhen. About 200,000 mainlanders visited Hong Kong between 1983 and 1988, including many young people keen to see capitalism at first hand. In the other direction, the number of ferry passengers between Hong Kong and China rose from 300,000 in 1979 to 2.8 million in 1987. Many of these passengers were foreigners who worked in Shenzhen, some on a very long-term basis.[10] As travelling between Hong Kong and Shenzhen became easier and border facilities became more streamlined (it is about forty minutes by train from Kowloon in Hong Kong to Shenzhen, and about one hour by ferry from Hong Kong to Shekou, the industrial zone to the west of Shenzhen), more and more people commute between Hong Kong and the SEZ. This increases the opportunities for interactions and business. The Shenzhen and Hong Kong media often carry stories of business visitors to and from the SEZ, and there is now more or less a free flow of persons and ideas between Hong Kong, long (though not entirely accurately) regarded as the epitome of free enterprise capitalism, and Shenzhen.

In preparation for 1997, when Hong Kong was reincorporated into China, there was a rapidly increasing body of mainland Chinese living and working in Hong Kong (see Shih, in Kaynak and Lee 1989). Before reunification there were said to be around 4,000 PRC-funded offices in Hong Kong, some very small and some very big. The China Resources Corporation, resplendent in its new office block on the Hong Kong waterfront (representing the Foreign Trade department of the State Council in Beijing) was the largest of the Chinese holding companies. It handled imports and exports between China and the rest of the world through a multitude of subsidiaries. Others like Everbright Holdings, the Bank of China, and China International Trust and Investment Corporation (CITIC), had carved out a substantial chunk of Hong Kong real estate and industry for the Chinese government in the 1980s. The China Merchants Company had represented Chinese shipping in Hong Kong for more than 100 years, and had a direct link with Shenzhen SEZ through its management of the Shekou zone (Sklair 1991).

Resentment built up against PRC cadres working in Hong Kong throughout the 1980s, on matters concerning both their business practices and their personal lifestyles. This came to a head in late 1988 when several scandals rocked the PRC in Hong Kong business community and led the Chinese authorities to demand that all these enterprises be reregistered and thoroughly examined. This was carried out at a high level as it was a very sensitive matter (the military were said to be using these firms for speculative purposes).[11] Chinese working or studying abroad were allowed to bring back eight big things (consumer durables) duty free. The question people asked about the so-called red capitalists was how, on such low salaries, did they find the money (then around $HK25,000) to buy them? This has been connected with the parallel goods market that continues to flood China with goods imported under official licences but sold privately.

Many administrative departments in Hong Kong also run businesses. For example, Xinhua (the official Chinese News Agency), the highest level representative office in Hong Kong, had dozens of enterprises in Hong Kong and Macao. Many ex-Xinhua cadres had retired to Hong Kong and Macao and had run trading companies there, strictly against PRC rules. Such red capitalists were charged with having extravagant lifestyles not only outside the country but when they returned to spend time in China.[12] The problem for China was how to stop the rot in Hong Kong without destroying the confidence of the foreign investors. A complicating factor was that foreign partners in many joint ventures were really Hong Kong affiliates of Chinese state and provincial bodies, acting as brokers rather than genuine traders, whose main function was often to solve foreign currency problems.[13]

The influence of TNCs from Hong Kong (mostly small scale) in Shenzhen is undeniable. The Chinese currency circulates alongside Hong Kong (and US) dollars in the Zone. Many foreign banks have branches there for corporate and personal accounts. Foreign currency is almost indispensable for economic success in Shenzhen and although it is becoming easier to acquire, access to Hong Kong and its unrestricted foreign exchange market is certainly a commercial advantage that many red capitalists use to the full.

It is as well to be clear that the title red capitalist is not always necessarily one of disapproval. To put no finer point on it, these people were sent to Hong Kong and abroad to make money, connections, and trade for the PRC (as indeed are those who work in foreign-related business within China). The problems arise, naturally, when they begin to make money, connections, and trade for themselves. The question of class arises when they begin to make alliances with others whom they perceive to have common interests in the pursuit of private profit through the accumulation of capital.[14] One highly significant source of alliances, common throughout China (and elsewhere) is that the officials, private entrepreneurs, and expatriate red capitalists are often members of the same family. Cadres and their children frequently engage in private business and combine their state and private connections very profitably. The government has publicly condemned this for years, but it is has not yet shown that it has the political will or the bureaucratic muscle to eradicate the corrupt practices that often result from the combination of economic and political power.[15] While in the short term the Party and the government may prevent any or all of these strata from becoming a class for itself, as history teaches, new classes can crystallize independent of official approval.

Remarkable as it may appear, in the 1990s the Chinese state (or rather the globalizing fractions of it) set about deliberately to create a group of 'national champions', enterprise groups modelled to some extent on the Japanese and Korean conglomerates (Sutherland, in Nolan 2001: ch. 3). In 1994 the government established the Association for the Promotion of China's Business Groups, initially with representatives from seventy-four existing groups, but subsequently increased to over 100, permanently located at their Beijing headquarters. Under the slogan 'grasp the large, let go of the small' (Nolan 2000: 69), by the late 1990s these groups accounted for 25 per cent of tax, assets, and sales in China; for 50 per cent of the profits of the state sector; and for over 10 per cent of China's GDP. Six of China's top ten domestic and foreign brands are produced by members of this national team, and many have attracted finance from abroad. (For a list of the 120 largest of these groups, see Nolan 2001: 101–35). One of the stated objectives of the policy was to make China's major enterprises competitive with the leading TNCs in the world. In detailed studies of aerospace, pharmaceuticals, power equipment, oil and petrochemicals, autos and components, steel, coal, and IT, Nolan shows that while China is now a mighty economy, its major business groups are generally uncompetitive, mainly because they have invested very little in R&D. From a relatively weak position in the 1970s, China is now the number one producer of cereals, meat, cotton, fruit, crude steel, coal, cement, and TV sets; and number two in electricity generation and chemical fibres (Nolan 2001: table 14-3). It hopes to challenge in the IT sector, though Nolan argues: 'the conditions on which China has agreed to enter the WTO constitute a dissolution of China's right to implement an industrial policy in this [or, indeed, any other] sector' (p. 792). Big and rapidly expanding, the Chinese companies have a long way to go before they become state-of-the-art.

What the Chinese government has successfully accomplished, however, is the construction of a substantial number of very big business groups. As Table 9.1 shows, by 2001 no fewer than eleven state-owned firms from China had forced their way into the *Fortune Global 500*. While this probably has no immediate consequences for the upgrading of the Chinese economy, it may well have substantial consequences for the emergence of a new class of major globalizing executives and professionals drawn from the ranks of those who run these vast enterprises. There is already evidence that the leaders of Chinese big business look to globalizing corporations from the capitalist core for their inspiration. Nolan cites Ye Qing, one of the most celebrated of the new men, who 'believes that Shenhua [a major coal conglomerate] must replicate the structure of the global mining giants, such as Rio Tinto, by developing mining businesses other than coal' and cutting costs of production (Nolan 2001: 735). If the transnational capitalist class is to have a component in China, then it will be largely located among these people.

Table 9.1 State-owned companies from China in the *Fortune* Global 500 (2001)

Company (FG500 Rank)	Revenues ($bn.)	Industry	Employees
Industrial and Commercial Bank (213)	22.1	Banking	471,123
Bank of China (251)	19.5	Banking	203,070
China Construction Bank (411)	12.7	Banking	420,000
Ag Bank of China (448)	11.7	Banking	500,000
China National Petroleum (83)	41.7	Energy	1,292,558*
Sinopec (68)	45.3	Petroleum	1,173,901
China Telecom (228)	20.8	Telecomms.	588,882
China Mobile (336)	15.0	Telecomms.	118,824
Sinochem (276)	18.0	Trading	8,619
Cofco (414)	12.5	Trading	28,000
State Power (77)	42.5	Utilities	1,137,025

* largest employer in the world

Notes: Jardine Matheson, also included under China, is a private Hong Kong based company (ranked 494), with revenues of $10.4bn., in the food stores category employing 150,000 people.

Source: data compiled from *Fortune* Global 500 (23 July 2001)

IS THERE A TRANSNATIONAL CAPITALIST CLASS IN CHINA?

So, is there a new capitalist class emerging in China that could facilitate capitalist globalization? And if there is, is it in any sense a transnational capitalist class? If a new class is emerging out of these strata it is most likely to be based on an alliance between private capitalists and entrepreneurs who have a connection with the state and/or party apparatus and, in places like Shenzhen, Chinese who are part of the transnational economic relations network. The foreign direct investment at work in China is still quite limited relative to the size of the economy, though it is massive in global terms (as noted, second only to FDI in the USA in the 1990s). While most of the TNCs in the country are actually small overseas Chinese operations, there is no doubt that those at the centre of economic power of the capitalist global system have considerable interest in China, both as a source of cheap labour and as a potential market. This was clearly expressed in a UN China Round Table on Foreign Direct Investment held in Beijing in 1987: 'Once having abandoned the ideological hang-ups against accepting the role of foreign direct investment that have inhibited so many developing countries, China is likely to want to continue to take advantage of it' (Richardson, in Teng and Wang 1988: 25). The haste with which the TNCs have flocked to China since then suggests that the sentiment is mutual. Even the terrible events of June 1989 (see Mok 1998) had little effect on the resolve of the Chinese government and the TNCs to accelerate capitalist globalization in China.[16]

The reality of corruption highlights the potential effects of such a new class. The next stage in Chinese development could bring the clash between groups of quasi-capitalist entrepreneurs seeking to build up their own wealth and new socialist entrepreneurs dedicated to the creation of wealth for all the people without exploitation and excessive differentiation between the richer and the poorer groups. It would be unduly cynical to define the quest for efficiency among the Chinese managers and technicians in foreign-invested enterprises in a way that contradicts the as yet only vaguely formulated notion of socialist entrepreneur.[17] While interesting, research on TNCs and local embeddedness in Shanghai is inconclusive on this issue. Yeung and Li (2000) argue that two relatively understudied factors pertaining to the performance of joint ventures with foreign companies are the previous economic strength of the local partners, and the large domestic market in China. Site interviews with fifteen large manufacturing equity joint ventures showed that these factors do affect local involvement in management, industrial linkages, and technology transfer. Shanghai Bell Telephone Equipment Manufacturing Co. (China Posts and Telecommunications with Alcatel Bell and the Belgian government) and Shanghai VW Automotive both had local majority ownership, while DuPont Agricultural Chemicals was foreign majority owned. All three of these joint ventures had strong local partners, in fact the size of the local market encouraged DuPont to establish a research laboratory in Shanghai, the only DuPont laboratory in the Asia-Pacific region in 1997. Similarly, there have been some successful joint ventures in the automobile industry in China (Sit and Liu 2000). The senior executives of the Chinese partners of these companies could form a nucleus for a transnational capitalist class or they could be anti-capitalist socialist entrepreneurs. At present, this does not seem to be a question in urgent need of an answer in China. The point is whether or not they run their businesses efficiently and profitably. What also appears clear is that foreign enterprises do not necessarily improve labour relations in China. There is evidence of a low level of unionism, general lack of protections for workers, and inadequate working environment in these joint ventures. Zhu (2000) argues that the situation in China is a warning to workers in Third World states not to become too dependent on foreign investment and globalization from above.

If a transnational capitalist class is emerging, global system theory predicts that one consequence would be an increase in class polarization, and this appears to be happening (see below). Therefore, the future of the urban working class and workers and peasants in rural areas will be a key issue. We can only speculate that some workers might resist private entrepreneurs as their working conditions worsen, while others might take advantage of the new opportunities that economic and social changes bring. White (in Fitzgerald and Wuyts 1988) made the plausible suggestion that the labour reforms might well produce a more militant labour force and a more organized managerial response (see also Zhu 2000). The presence of tens of millions of migrant workers from rural areas on the fringes of the labour force in the formal sector has already created unstable situations in many parts of the country (Cannon 2000: part I). If this instability spills over into the settled population, and there are some signs that this is happening in the cities, then the open-door policy will have had the totally unintended consequence of sharpening a class struggle that the Chinese authorities had hoped to bury in the 1980s.

The emergence of housing classes is also a distinct possibility. Freese (2001) reports that the average price for a single family unfurnished apartment in Shangai and Beijing is around $50,000 and that the market for home furnishings is booming. At the other end of the scale, as Smith (in Cannon 2000) and Dutton (1998: part II) both argue, a migrant underclass has been created. Members of this class can find little work that is entirely legal, which encourages criminality and heavy reactions from the police.[18] Dutton uses the events of the successful campaign of the Beijing authorities to clean up Zhejiang village (a hotbed of crime and deviance named for its inhabitants, mainly rural migrants from Zhejiang province) to frame a not entirely ironic thesis on the communities these migrants are creating all over China.

From these stories, one begins to realize that the 'sunny side up' face of China is changing. This change is bringing forth a new phenomenon, which, in other circumstances, we might mistake for the birth of the working class. Socialist China finally has the class it has desired for so long, yet the reforms ensure that this emerging class is treated in a manner whereby we really can . . . close our eyes and think of (Victorian) England. (Dutton 1998: 130)

However, as research on the informal sector has demonstrated, capitalist globalization provides opportunities for enrichment even for apparent social deviants living on the fringes of respectable society.

Empirical evidence strongly confirms the class polarization thesis for China, between provinces and within provinces, cities, and rural areas. Survey data for the whole of China indicates that the income of the top quintile (20 per cent) was four times that of the bottom quintile in 1990. By 1993 the differential had risen to 6.9, and by 1998 it was 9.6. The top quintile received over 50 per cent of total income in 1998, compared to 5.5 per cent for the bottom quintile (Guan 2000: table 3). A careful study of Jiangsu province confirms the broad trend, showing that since the reforms: 'the philosophy of China's regional development has experienced a significant change, moving away from socialist idealistic egalitarianism to pragmatic uneven development which emphasises on [sic] efficiency and output. Uneven regional development is regarded as an inevitable stage in the development process, and it is an objective rule, not a problem' (Long and Ng 2001: 215). This has led, not surprisingly, to increases in intra-provincial inequalities. Jiangsu is, typically, divided into poorer areas and faster growing areas, mainly those along the coast, close to cities, and with long histories of township and village enterprises. Economic and political decentralization has encouraged local protectionism, and rent-seeking has increased for the benefit of investors. This has weakened the ability of the government in Beijing to redistribute resources (see also Breslin 1996).

This decline in redistribution is reflected in changes to the system of social policy in

China since market reform. The welfare state in China before 1978 was quite comprehensive, and though there were some differences between urban and rural areas (see Guan 2000: table 1) socialist economic policy and socialist ideology had some successes in narrowing traditional gaps between richer and poorer. Public ownership of the means of production (state and collective), a centrally planned economy (making it relatively easy for government to mobilize resources), and an egalitarian ideology supported high expectations that government would intervene to help the disadvantaged. Welfare system reform was undertaken for two main reasons, to promote economic efficiency and to change the culture of dependence on the iron rice bowl.

The main lines of reform were a societalization of the welfare system to reduce the role of government, to increase the role of NGOs (resident community associations and special agencies for the elderly), and to reduce the role of urban work units. By the 1990s, the universal welfare system had been replaced by marketization and privatization of services (notably urban housing),[19] beneficiaries' payment for services (some social insurance, higher education), and some means-tested benefits. In the main cities a minimum standard of living is financed by local government, but relatively few are covered. In rural areas, the traditional Five Guarantees, mainly for old people living alone, is still to some extent financed by county-level pooling of resources. Guan (2000) shows the effects of these changes on urban inequality, which increased dramatically from 420 per cent (top to bottom quintile) in 1990 to 960 per cent in 1998 (in 1990 the top 20 per cent received 38 per cent of all income, the bottom 20 per cent received 9 per cent; by 1998, as noted above the proportions were 52.3 per cent to 5.5 per cent). Public opinion surveys show that over 80 per cent of the population now consider social inequality as a big problem.

So, despite the Chinese economic miracle, the effects of market socialism may well be a class polarization similar to that being created by capitalist globalization. This baleful conclusion is in line with what we know about the consequences of the economic reforms on the sexual division of labour in the workplace. The status of women in the domestic economy has been affected where they have come into close contact with the open-door policy and the TNCs. In Shenzhen, unlike most other zones around the world, the numbers of female and male workers have been roughly equal (Sklair 1991) and this reflected Chinese employment practices at that time, the mediating effects of the labour supply authorities, and the mix of industries. It is also worth noting that the urban Chinese household, while not by any means free from patriarchal domination, might be somewhat more sexually democratic than households in other Third World countries. However, as both domestic and foreign invested enterprises became more profit conscious, the relatively generous maternity and other benefits that women have enjoyed began to work against them.[20]

These issues were highlighted by Chinese media reports in the late 1980s of a village where 95 per cent of the employed women were said to have returned to the home as a result of the economic reforms. Most rural women over 40 were said to have given up their paid jobs, and even for young women, doing housework took on a new meaning, namely 'doing special labor as the masters of society and the household rather than slaves'. Is going to the city to be a housekeeper an advance over staying at home and being a housemaker? For one uneducated woman: 'it was a great pleasure for her to see that her husband eats and dresses well, to raise her child, and to keep her home in good order. Can we say she is ideologically backward or that she has backtracked to the status of household slave? I am afraid we cannot say so.' The (male) commentator concluded, if women have the choice and they chose to stay in the home, this can be socially useful.[21] The tremendous rise in the migration of rural women into the cities in the 1990s must be considered in this context. Studies by Chinese researchers on the occupations of these women (many as household workers and nannies, some as prostitutes) paint a considerably less positive picture, of exploitation and sad lives (translated in Dutton 1998: 132–44 and *passim*).

THE CULTURE-IDEOLOGY OF CONSUMERISM IN CHINA

While China is still a very poor country, with large pockets of absolute deprivation in its vast hinterland, there is no doubt that in the 1980s a huge urban and rural-suburban consumer demand was created as a result of government policies (Chai 1992). Since 1978, the responsibility systems in the factories and in the countryside, under which people and enterprises paid the costs and reaped the rewards of their own economic actions, and official encouragement for individual enrichment have started to transform the whole country. Millions of small family businesses have been permitted to flourish, serving needs that had either been suppressed or neglected in the previous period. Western styles of clothing, personal goods, and a wide variety of consumer durables can be seen on the streets and in homes in all the coastal cities, and increasingly in the countryside too (Sklair, in Belk and Schultz 1994: 259–92; Goodman, in Robison and Goodman 1996: ch. 10; Zhao 1998; Dutton 1998).

Prior to 1978 there were relatively few retail outlets in China. Of those shops that did survive the destruction wreaked by the Japanese and the civil war, most were closed down in favour of the new state-run marketing and supply co-operatives. It is estimated that between 1957 and 1978 the number of retail outlets in China fell from 2.8 to 1.3 million; outlets per 1,000 persons in urban areas fell from 10 to 1.5; and employment in distribution fell from 1.4 to 1 per cent of the total workforce (Mun, in Kaynak 1988: ch. 15). Thanks to the policy of transforming what had been consumer cities into socialist producer cities, and also to some extent to the traditional Chinese downgrading of traders and merchants, there was little notion of consumer sovereignty in the PRC. Since the late 1970s the most important changes in the distribution of goods and services have been the re-emergence of the rural markets, particularly in the suburbs of cities, the rocketing numbers of individuals and families that have become traders, the growing demand for better-quality products (not unconnected with the one-child family policy), and the growth of multiple sources of goods, both for stores and their customers. For example, in the course of the 1980s the much visited Nan Fang Department Store in Canton increased the numbers of its suppliers from 20 to 1,000, and the products it sold from 19,000 to 27,000.

The number of supermarkets in China is increasing by leaps and bounds. Apart from the new shopping malls in the big cities, most Chinese stores are relatively small and with a very limited range of customer services. Shopping malls tend to be more expensive than small stores, as they are targeted at better-off and better-educated people, who are prepared to pay higher prices. The goods they sell are not necessarily imports, but they are often in foreign styles. These stores are sometimes restricted to customers who have Foreign Exchange Certificates or hard currency, like the so-called Friendship Stores specifically designed for foreign tourists and expatriate Chinese.[22]

Retailing in China (and in most other communist countries) differs from retailing in other parts of the world on several counts. First, there is controlled market entry, which makes it difficult if not impossible for private individuals to open shops (as opposed to small-scale family concerns). China relaxed controls considerably in this respect in the 1980s, but the enormous increase in retailing outlets has come from market stalls and itinerant traders rather than from shops as such, though the state and the municipalities have opened more shops than in previous decades and foreign stores (like B&Q from Britain) have been encouraged to expand. Second, China has an irregular supply of consumer goods, especially high-quality goods. This is a result of the traditional over-emphasis on heavy industry as against light industry, and the rigid state control of foreign trade, particularly the import of consumer goods. However, both these policies have been changing since 1978. During the 1980s the government committed itself to increasing supplies of the big consumer durables (washing machines, refrigerators, TV sets), and by partially decentralizing foreign trade it opened the door to local imports of consumer goods, particularly from Japan and other countries whose products were trans-shipped through Hong Kong. Finally, until recently, TNCs had no consumer goods manufacturing facilities in China to serve the Chinese market.

The TNCs have clearly been observing these developments with great interest. Both Coca-Cola and PepsiCo have bottling plants in the PRC. Foreign soft drinks are widely available though fairly expensive in relative terms, but a cheaper local soft drink Xingfu Cola (Lucky Cola), a blatant copy is, as it were, softening up the market. The fast food industry is also growing rapidly in China, and chains such as Kentucky Fried Chicken, Pizza Hut, and McDonalds (see Yunxiang Yan, in Watson 1997) have all successfully negotiated franchise agreements with the Chinese authorities. The Chinese welcome companies such as these into the country for the advanced technology that they bring to this and other sectors, and they are being used to upgrade local industries (see Li and Li 1999, Sit and Liu 2000, Yeung and Li 2000). The Chinese authorities consider that the risks involved in exposing the population directly to products that are global symbols of advanced capitalism's favoured lifestyles, are more than offset by the potential industrial benefits. The cola wars (discussed in Chapter 7) have been fought in China since the 1980s.

Most global brand consumer products are now available in China. These include the beverages and fast foods of the franchisers, the soaps, toothpastes, and cosmetics of the leading TNC manufacturers, the consumer electronics from which no part of the world is entirely immune and, increasingly, fashion garments and accessories with Japanese, European, and American labels. Century 21, the real estate franchise, is operating in Beijing. This flood of Western goods and services (a convenient if inaccurate label because so many of them come from Japan and other Asian sources, including China itself) is most noticeable in the big cities, but it is evident to a greater or lesser extent all over the country. With it has come a perceptible change in the appearance and values of the Chinese people, particularly cultural elites and the young (Wang 1996, Dutton 1998, Lu 2001). How much this is due to the impact of capitalist globalization is very difficult to say, though we can assert that the most important bearers of these influences as they affect China are the consumerist elites (merchants and mass media). These include a mixture of many very small companies (mainly from Hong Kong) and a few very large TNCs (mainly from the USA, Japan, and Europe).

Some of the largest TNCs active in China are the transnational banks. Although several of them have had representative offices in the major Chinese cities for some time, the lucrative credit card business was closed to them until 1986, when the Mastercard and Visa networks, followed rapidly by American Express, were granted access. In 1988 China had fewer than three thousand credit card outlets and very few state enterprises were willing to accept them. Total credit card turnover in China was worth only about 10 per cent of Hong Kong's, with a population two hundred times greater (Lim 1988). However, the introduction of MasterCard's Great Wall card and others that followed undoubtedly increased their use, and they play a part in the onward march of capitalist globalization in China.

The culture-ideology of consumerism places all poor countries in a terrible dilemma, and China is no exception. The official policy of concentration on heavy industry and producer goods that drove the economy and politics during the Maoist era meant that China, once it started to change its economic priorities, was under the most intense pressure to supply its people with consumer goods. Since the 1978 reforms the government has proclaimed a policy of rising standards of living for the masses. In order to carry out the policy, some local authorities and state enterprises awarded pay rises on declining revenues. This led to great increases in personal consumption in many places, a phenomenon encapsulated in the slogan: 'Celebrating the Spring Festival at the expense of the state' (meaning that food was sold at prices subsidized by the work unit at holiday times).

In urban areas production more or less doubled in the 1980s, money income more than doubled, and purchasing power rose about three times. This was achieved by printing money and by foreign loans, and inflation naturally followed, a situation not improved by chronic waste of resources. As a Chinese researcher put it, the Japanese mentality of 'living in a poor nation' seems to have vanished in China![23] The three most prized consumer items of the 1960s and 1970s, watches, sewing machines, and bikes, were replaced in the 1980s by refrigerators, washing machines, TVs, and radio-recorders and, in the 1990s, by colour TVs, videos, fridge-freezers, washer-driers, stereos, and electronic cameras. Now, mobile phones, smart apartments, and private cars are likely to be on the shopping list of the most affluent Chinese. In the rush to modernize, the local and global environmental consequences of a mass automobile culture in China have little priority. Indeed, while official and popular Green movements are growing in China (see Lo and Leung 2000), there are also signs of an impending ecological crisis as capitalist globalization and developmentalism penetrate ever deeper (Cannon 2000: parts 2 and 3).

The crisis of ecological unsustainability is precisely summed up in the subtitle of a volume of the Harvard University Committee on Environment China Report, *Reconciling Environmental Protection and Economic Growth* (McElroy *et al.* 1998). This is the dilemma, sometimes bitterly expressed in the First World–Third World disputes over the Kyoto global warming treaty. The Harvard group of US and Chinese scholars leaves no doubt that there is a problem and, significantly, they make connections between what I have called the crises of class polarization and ecological unsustainability when they argue: 'It is typically true not just in China that the poor disproportionately suffer pollution damages, potentially exacerbating class resentment and social discontent' (McElroy *et al.* 1998: 55, n. 7). Rapid industrialization in China's booming cities is accompanied by rapidly expanding use of chemical inputs in agriculture. Thus in the view of Sanders, 'farming has become increasingly dependent upon techniques which undermine sustainability' (in Cannon 2000: 233). The water table in north China is said to be dangerously depleted. These developments are clearly related to what I have termed the culture-ideology of consumerism in China.

Throughout the 1980s the Chinese government was ever announcing its intention to control more strictly the import of consumer goods like wines, cigarettes, canned drinks, cars, and household electrical appliances. In the words of a high-level Chinese research team: 'In recent years, a consumer psychology has been created by the premature consumption, and a high-level consumption drive has been touched off by the "demonstration effect" of opening to the outside world' (Xia and Li, in Reynolds 1987: 105). This thesis raises an issue that has been seized upon by the critics of the culture-ideology of consumerism in communist China, namely the polluting influence of Western capitalist values. In 1983–4 the Chinese government unleashed a campaign against spiritual pollution in an attempt to foster its alternative, socialist spiritual civilization. The targets of the campaign were, confusingly, the remnants of the Gang of Four and those who were accused of spreading corrupting capitalist practices through foreign investment and superfluous foreign trade. The campaign trod a very narrow path. While the authorities did not want to scare off foreign investors they did want to send signals to them and their Chinese associates that the open-door did impose some restrictions, though these were not always very clearly specified. The campaign against spiritual pollution did not last very long but others like it have reappeared in various guises. In particular, attempts to apply the brakes on internal reforms that were evident in 1986–7, and since June 1989, and the ongoing campaigns, sometimes explicit and sometimes implicit, against bourgeois liberalization, keep up the pressure to ensure that the open-door does not let everything in (Stockman 2000: ch. 7). An example from Shenzhen will illustrate the complex issues involved. In 1988 *China Youth News* reported that ten Shenzhen massage parlours had advertised in Changsha (a city in central China) for masseuses, and this had outraged the local people. On investigation, the parlours turned out to be perfectly respectable. However, these investigations revealed that conditions in many TNC assembly plants in Shenzhen were 'unbelievably bad' and child labour and excessive compulsory overtime were also found. The local cadres were accused of 'doing anything for money' (Becker 1988). It is as if direct attacks on capitalist economic practices themselves are prohibited by the open-door policy, but the culture-ideology of consumerism can be attacked, and through it, capitalist economic practices can be challenged.

This raises the issue of human rights, and the crucial distinction between how they are seen and dealt with in China and how they are seen and dealt with from the outside. In his penetrating study of this question, Wachman (2001) concludes that the Chinese Communist Party and state have not been shamed into making concessions but have sometimes acted for strategic geopolitical reasons. He discusses the claims in the official Beijing White Paper on Human Rights of February 2000 that much progress had been made since 1949 and that the Western concept of human rights is not universally acceptable. 'For developed Western states to focus on civil and political liberties is fine, considering that these states have already developed a high degree of prosperity and stability. The PRC does not discount the possibility of striving towards the same ends, but puts the need to reach a higher level of economic development first' (Wachman 2001: 271). Nolan (2000: 915) expresses a similar sentiment: 'China's masses had achieved huge advances in their "human rights" to live a decent and fulfilled life.' As we shall see in Chapter 11, arguments such as these are frequently employed in the field of human rights.

The connections between this and the democracy movement, its violent suppression in June 1989, and subsequent events are highly convoluted, but it is surely of great significance that the first public statement of Deng Xiaoping after the killings in Tiananmen Square was to reassure foreign investors that the open-door policy was unchanged and would continue. As I argued in a previous chapter, the interests of the TNCs are best served by a stable business climate that gives opportunities for individual and corporate wealth creation, and that the TNCs are generally indifferent to democracy. The Chinese authorities realize this. There is little evidence to suggest that foreign TNCs play any direct part at present in Chinese domestic politics, though there is certainly a rapidly growing stratum of Chinese whose interests, both private and public, are identified with the success of the open-door policy and by implication with the advance of capitalist globalization in China. Whether this stratum will develop into a transnational capitalist class is a question that still waits for an answer. If such a class ever becomes established in China it will probably be within the state apparatus as much as outside it. In this case its political influence and the political influence of the TNCs in China will be powerful.

MEDIA IN CHINA

One of the most visible changes in China since 1979, directly connected with the impact of the TNCs and the creation of new consumption needs, is in the extent, forms and contents of the mass media. The advertising industry is a good place to start to evaluate this. From the mid-1960s until the late 1970s, there was practically no product advertising in China. Anderson (1984) presents a rare glimpse into the rebirth of the advertising industry in the PRC. Radio commercials first appeared in January 1979, and in March 1979 a TV commercial (for Lucky Cola) was broadcast. The first commercials for foreign products were shown in April on Canton TV (for US cigarettes and Japanese watches) and many more followed. In 1982, CBS made a deal with the Chinese authorities by which the Chinese gave 320 minutes of air time for commercials on Chinese TV in exchange for sixty hours of US television programmes. This opened the floodgates for the rapid expansion of the Chinese advertising industry, which rocketed from ten (state-run) agencies in 1980 to 7,000 (mostly not state-run) in 1988 (Schell 1988).

Large advertising billboards are now a common sight in Chinese cities, and the once-austere *Beijing Review* (the main print vehicle through which the Chinese government communicates to the world in several languages) has been carrying vivid advertisements for some time. By the mid-1980s, some of the world's largest advertising agencies had a presence in China. The Japanese agency Dentsu, one of the biggest, has been in association with the Shanghai Advertising Corporation since 1979 and the giant Young and Rubicam began training Chinese advertising staff in New York in 1980. McCann-Erickson, also of New York, has handled the Coca Cola account in China and the China National Airline account abroad, and Ogilvy & Mather handled the first Chinese advertising campaign (for Chinese herbs and drinks) in the USA (Anderson 1984: ch. 9). By 2001, a Hong Kong based agency, Ion Global, was the biggest profit-maker in the industry, though Ogilvy & Mather's two companies in Hong Kong and Beijing/Guangzhou/Shanghai had billings of $370 million (no billings were available for Ion Global). Over forty agencies had billings of more than $10 million, fourteen in excess of $100 million (*Advertising Age*, 23 Apr. 2001: s12). Symbolic of these changes brought by market socialism, in 1987 thousands of selected foreigners received a Confidential letter from Zhao Ziyang, Premier of China, inviting attendance at the 1987 Beijing International Advertising and Marketing Congress. The Chinese here, as in other areas, are careful to point out the difference between socialist and capitalist practice. Whereas under capitalism, it is argued, advertising is mainly devoted to ensuring that a product or service fights off its competitors, under socialism advertising is more of an educational and informational medium. There are contradictions in this view for all parties. As Hansen (1974: 6) said in his early and still useful study of advertising and socialism: 'It is not so obvious how advertising fits into an economy of the Soviet type.'

The central contradiction revolves around the very valid point that though a consumer revolution has occurred in China, to the present it has reached a relatively small proportion of the population (probably fewer than 25 per cent, mostly concentrated in and near the coastal region). White (1993: 204–5) described the phenomenon of red-eye disease (social envy) of those who see others with more consumer goods than they have and the consequent ratcheting discontent of those who, even though they are doing well, always want to do better. Studies of the media leave no doubt that something like a culture-ideology of consumerism is gathering pace in China. A telling indication of this was that in 2000, amid a blaze of publicity, the government extended the May Day holiday to a full week to encourage consumer spending.

One measure of the spread of the culture-ideology of consumerism (in China as in other relatively poor countries) is the creation of wants for acquiring expensive foreign consumer durables. More and more Chinese citizens are travelling abroad and bringing such goods home with them. China does not seriously regulate the personal imports that individuals carry on entry to the country. Hundreds of thousands of Chinese (mostly, but by no means exclusively, from Hong Kong) have brought many consumer goods for their relatives and friends in the PRC. Many TNCs have found it worthwhile to advertise to create product differentiation for PRC citizens likely to want such products. Now Chinese television not only advertises products of joint venture TNCs but also competing Chinese products, and what was not so long ago a chronic shortage of consumer goods in the shops has become in some places a glut.

Advertisements for global brands bring in foreign currency to China, and they also nurture more modern styles of mass media to create a more consumer-oriented public (Sklair, in Belk and Schulz 1994). The government and party are as aware as anyone else of the merits (some might argue the necessity) of communication skills for internal social control and external public relations. Advertising TNCs are widely seen as the vehicles through which these skills are generated and perfected. In the short-term, therefore, the socialist purpose of advertising is lost in the rush to master techniques. It is worth remembering, too, that most advertising executives when in philosophical mood will claim that their practice is educational and instructional, though not necessarily directed towards socialist goals.

There are several long-term contradictions likely to be created by the impact of the capitalist globalization brought by TNCs and broadcast by the mass media in China. The first is a consequence of the fact that for the foreseeable future there will be little mass consumer market for non-essentials outside the main coastal cities and a few other prosperous parts of the country. Second, a market for what are defined, at least for contemporary urbanites, as essentials is certainly growing all the time but this is seen by many Chinese as being out of step with the general level of development of the economy and society. (Recall the comment from the 1980s about the Japanese mentality of living in a poor nation having vanished in China.) Third, the policy to encourage some people to get rich quick has not yet come to terms with the fact that, increasingly, a small but rapidly expanding stratum is already in the market not simply for inessentials but for luxury goods while perhaps as many as one hundred million people in China are still malnourished and living below the poverty line. Zhao (1998: 151–2) indicates how the media in China handle what I would not hesitate to call a class polarization crisis. While the 'current news media scene in China can be explained neither by the Party principle nor by market forces alone . . . [before the reforms] access to the system was determined almost exclusively by those with political power. Now, it is available to those with economic power, a power the majority of workers and peasants do not possess.' This reflects increasing class divisions in China.

The media pay little attention to ordinary workers and peasants and the unemployed, and none at all to strikers. For example, newspapers failed to take up the cause of peasants whose land was being seized to build golf courses but they did celebrate the openings of the golf clubs. Local and city TV stations also indicate that a commercialized media sector is emerging within the Party-controlled system. This is reflected in a new discourse that luxury consumption is serving the people, an interesting consumerist slant on the Maoist mass line! Thus the oppositional character of commercialized media is oppositional in only a very restricted meaning of the term. In the words of the publisher of a successful pioneering newspaper (*Beijing Youth News*): 'Marketization and political orientation of the news are not incompatible. The key lies in the perspectives of news workers' (quoted in Zhao 1998: 149). This interpretation is confirmed, significantly, by a correspondent from the *People's Daily* writing in *Media, Culture and Society* (Hong 1998). Since the 1980s, the state has stopped subsidizing the press and forced it to rely on the market. By 1994, there were almost 2,000 newspapers in China and subscription wars affected them all. The rapid growth of TV has also had a serious impact on the press, and many evening and weekend papers have appeared to compete in the light entertainment sector. The new trend to self-distribution (papers being sold in the streets rather than being delivered to workplaces) to some extent has brought journalists in closer touch with their readers. The introduction of the five-day week in 1995 meant much bigger markets for weekend leisure pursuits, and weekend fever gripped all parts of the press. A new journalistic ideology emerged that the press should speak for the people and reflect the people's character, but in practice increasingly the press 'speak for the ever more powerful business interests, rather than for "the people". Economic reforms have fundamentally changed the way the press exists' (Hong 1998: 36). The press now reflects the role of money in the Chinese value-system through adverts, newspapers becoming involved in other commercial interests, and the creation of newspaper conglomerates. Notable in this respect is the *Guangzhou Daily*, which has substantial property, printing, advertising, and paper interests. In most capitalist societies major corporations aided by the media tend to orient themselves to the strata with purchasing power, and the China of market socialism appears to be heading in this direction.

The Internet presents a particularly difficult challenge for party control (see Chinadotcom 2000). Despite regular crackdowns, Internet cafés in their thousands are flourishing all over the country and they do provide many outlets for cultural and even political opposition to government policies. In a study of media commercialization in Taiwan, South Korea, Singapore, and Hong Kong, Hong and Hsu (1999: 225) argue that 'the most profound significance of media commercialization in the Asian political and social context is an alternative or indirect way to achieve media democratization, which is the first step towards political and social democratization'. It remains to be seen if this is what will happen in China.

NOTES

1. All unattributed Chinese language sources were translated by Dr Huang Ping, formerly a research student in the Sociology Department, London School of Economics. I have also used translations from the US-based *Foreign Broadcast Information Service* (*FBIS*) and the BBC's *Summary of World Broadcasts* (*SWB*) series.

2. See also Dutton (1998: 231 ff.) on theme parks, and the cult of the Mao badge.

3. In this context, see Chossudovsky (1986: chs. 7–9) on China's limited capacity to resist the overtures of the TNCs. In Mexico, the maquilas are accused of causing massive job losses in US manufacturing industry (Sklair 1993). See also on TNCs in Germany, Gensior and Scholer (in Elson and Pearson 1989). Many jobs migrated from west to east and south Europe in the 1990s and many workers travelled in the opposite direction (Faist 2000).

4. This was the case in the Beijing Minibus Company whose leading management group I interviewed in April 1989 with the help of Huang Ping.

5. This article is lavishly illustrated (note that no. 22 of *Beijing Review* for 2001 is no. 21 in the North American edition). See also Wang (1996) on 'high culture fever' in China.

6. Mok (1998) in his study of the intellectuals and the democracy movement, presents information on the perceptions of intellectuals about jumping into the sea (table 8.1) and valuable empirical confirmation of the substantial rise in household incomes of such people (table 8.2).

7. I am grateful to Dr Huang Ping for this information, and to him and other members of the editorial board of the journal *Chinese Social Sciences Quarterly* for sessions in Beijing in 1993, and to the organizers of the conference on 'Globalization and China' in Hainan Island in 2000, where research on these issues was discussed.

8. In 'Features, practice of private economy viewed' (in *FBIS*-235, 7 Dec. 1988: 32–6). See also Rosen (1987/ 1988) and White (1993: ch. 6). For a revealing account of one entrepreneur with transnational connections, see 'Going it alone' *Beijing Review* (27 Feb.–5 Mar. 1989: 19–22) and many similar cases in Dutton (1998) and Stockman (2000). Nolan (2001) discusses several globalizing entrepreneurs/bureaucrats who have created major corporations.

9. Though Chossudovsky gives no source for this assertion, I can confirm it from my own interviews with entrepreneurs active in the Shenzhen SEZ during the 1990s. The discourse of Overseas Chinese, however, does need deconstructing, as Olds (2001: 58–63) suggests.

10. In 1986 there were 2,300 non-PRC specialists working in the SEZ, most from Hong Kong. See 'Outside experts aid Shenzhen', *China Daily* (17 Feb. 1986). For the travel data, see *FBIS*-192 (4 Oct. 1988: 73, 74). The numbers have increased considerably since then.

11. The People's Liberation Army is said to have 15,000–20,000 enterprises (military converted to civilian and new businesses), to employ 3 million workers, and to produce about 10 per cent of China's gross industrial output value (including 10 per cent of pharmaceutical drugs, 20 per cent of cars and trucks,

and 50 per cent of motorbikes). It is also active in the hotel, telecommunications, and smuggling industries (Nolan 2001: ch. 5).

12. For example, the director of Xinhua in Hong Kong in summer 1994 still kept his job while: 'On a salary of just HK$5,000 a month, he bought a villa outside Peking worth HK$177,000. It was seized by the authorities earlier this month, along with a satellite dish, whose ownership is a sure sign of membership of the elite in China' (*Observer*, 31 July 1994).

13. Rose-Ackerman (1999) like most other World Bank influenced writers on the subject, lays most of the blame for corruption on rent-seeking government officials, but as Herry-Priyono (2001) demonstrates in his thesis on Indonesia, private businesses often initiate the process.

14. For a discussion on the attitudes of enterprise cadres by the Chinese Economic System Reform Research Institute, see Yang *et al.* (in Reynolds 1987: ch. 5). Dutton (1998) shows how some work units began to change in the 1990s from welfare-oriented institutions to businesses. See also Baek (2000).

15. In August 1989, and regularly thereafter, relatives of the top Chinese leaders (the 'new princes') were said to have given up their private business interests. Whether they have all actually done so is another question.

16. See 'Turmoil won't close open-door' (*Beijing Review*, 26 June–2 July 1989). Predictions inside and outside China after June 1989 that the open-door policy might be seriously curtailed came to nothing.

17. I have in mind those Chinese managers and officials I interviewed in 1983–4, 1988–9, 1993, and 2000 in Shenzhen, Beijing, and Hainan Island who saw no contradiction between efficient enterprise and the goals of socialism. However, the stock market speculators that Hertz (1998) studied in Shanghai are probably more numerous.

18. Dutton (1998: 99) gives some remarkable figures on the residency fees that the Beijing municipality levied on rural migrants in the mid-1990s. These ranged from the equivalent of $US1,200 per head for residency in an outer county or rural area to an almost unbelievable $US12,000 per head for groups of ten or more people wanting to live together in the inner-city or inner-suburbs. However, these figures only seem remarkable; in other countries the private housing market levies its own fees through differential rents and other charges.

19. In the 1990s government agencies began to sell off apartments to private individuals fuelling a boom in private (and some public) housebuilding (Freese 2001), though as noted above some state enterprises still house thousands of their workers.

20. See 'Paper urges solving women employment problems', translated in *FBIS-165* (25 Aug. 1988: 42–3). LaFont (2000) shows this also to be true in postcommunist Eastern Europe.

21. Quotes from 'New Thinking' on women's liberation', *FBIS*-189 (29 Sept. 1988: 51–3). On more general issues of gender and family in China, see Stockman (2000: esp. ch. 5).

22. For an insight into the development of an urban mega-project in Shanghai, see Olds (2001).

23. From 'Article says consumption "running wild" ', *FBIS*-172 (6 Sept. 1988: 37–8).

Chapter 10

CHALLENGES TO CAPITALIST GLOBALIZATION

The period from 1995 to the beginning of the twenty-first century was a turning point for capitalist globalization and perhaps it will be seen some day as a turning point for humanity. In 1995 the World Trade Organization opened its doors for business (the ambiguity is intended) and the OECD began, with very little publicity, to plan for a Multilateral Agreement on Investment (MAI). Both these institutional movements signalled the intent of the transnational capitalist class to pursue its agenda of capitalist globalization on behalf of those who own and control the transnational corporations and their allies in state and international politics, bureaucracies, the professions, and consumerist elites.

Those who were running the WTO and planning the MAI paid little attention to genuinely democratic procedures. The WTO had emerged from the GATT negotiations and the initiative for the MAI came from the Business and Industry Advisory Committee of the OECD (see below). As most writers on global trade acknowledge, these matters are normally decided by politicians, bureaucrats, and lobbyists for corporate interests. What they fail to recognize is that they are normally decided by members of the transnational capitalist class, a combination of corporate executives, globalizing bureaucrats, politicians, professionals, and consumerist elites. The scope and level of organization and the ferocity of opposition on the streets in sites of resistance all over the world to various manifestations of capitalist globalization caught the pundits by surprise. Pundits, of course, are usually surprised because the nature of modern mass media gives them little time and incentive for reflection. Sound bites, rapid flows of images, and instant journalism are the enemies of the understanding that sober reflection can bring. In the second part of this chapter I shall try to explain the defeat of the MAI and the significance of the battle of Seattle (and subsequent battles) against capitalist globalization. In order to do this, it is necessary to consider what led up to these two defining moments, namely the counter movements that began in the 1960s[1] against the status quo, against a multitude of ills of modern society, and the gradual emergence of movements against capitalist globalization as such. My problematic is capitalist globalization and its alternatives, so it makes sense to combine analysis of campaigns, networks, and movements and not to make too fine a distinction between them here.

The concept of social movement can be usefully understood in a very general sense as well as in a more precise, technical sense. Here social movements against the status quo are to be understood in general terms to include campaigns, networks, counter movements of various types with varying degrees of organizational capacity and with varying, sometimes competing, goals. The following section on the anti-globalization movement (in the singular) argues the thesis that there is emerging a coherent movement against globalization that is beginning to identify the target of capitalist globalization rather than globalization as such. However, the strong and mostly positive influence of the counter movements from before 1995 has led to some confusion over strategy and tactics in the anti-globalization movement.

The contours of three counter movements will be sketched in to provide a background for a more extensive discussion of the rise of anti-globalization movements. While none of the three counter movements mounted a coherent challenge to capitalist globalization, they all contributed to what is now, undeniably, a variety of anti-globalization movements with the potential to become a serious movement offering a serious alternative to capitalism (Singer 1999). The struggle to resist globalization from above through globalization from below has begun (Falk 1999). The three counter movements are protectionism (an important source for the localizing challenge to globalization); social movements of various types, particularly the New Social Movements that became an important source for identity-based challenges to the status quo (see Calhoun 1994); and Green movements (explaining and politicizing the ecological crisis). The radical wings of these movements have campaigned against the crises of class polarization and ecological unsustainability.

COUNTER MOVEMENTS

PROTECTIONISM

Protectionism is, of course, not a new phenomenon. Indeed, the most potent argument against it may be that we know only too well how protectionism contributed to the great worldwide depression of the 1930s. Nevertheless, as the World Bank and other august proponents of the perpetual increase of global trade never tired of reminding us throughout the 1980s, many First World governments began to step up protectionist measures in that decade and continue to do so when it serves the interests of big capital.[2] The free entry of goods (particularly consumer goods) from abroad is frequently a contentious feature of global trade. Restrictive measures have been directed at Third World manufacturers whose electronic and electrical products, garments, shoes, toys, sporting, and household goods were said to be unfairly flooding vulnerable First World markets. The interesting twist to this issue is that it was Japan, clearly now a First World country and undoubtedly the most dynamic economic power in the world between 1970 and 1990, that was often identified in the United States and in Europe as the worst offender, with the four East Asian NICs not far behind. The Asian Tigers, ironically, all prospered from protected markets in the USA as did, to some extent, the economies of Third World countries in the British Commonwealth and the French overseas empire, from various forms of trade preference.

There are two main varieties of protectionism. The first comes from within the capitalist mode of production, conceptualized and popularized in terms of the special interests of local business groups as opposed to the systemic interests of capital as a whole. This form I label selective protectionism. The second form is what Lang and Hines (1993) call the new protectionism. Hines (2000) has developed this into a more fully localized alternative. A parallel thesis, labelled the subsistence perspective (Mies and Bennholdt-Thomsen 1999), is a more direct alternative to the culture-ideology of consumerism, and thus to capitalist globalization. These will be discussed as part of the anti-globalization movement below.

The tendency to selective protectionism is increased by the belief that a substantial part of TNC manufacturing industry is footloose, i.e. liable to move around the globe to maximize its profits with scant regard for the welfare of the workers in abandoned factories and their communities. This is quite ironic, as selective protectionism was often used by governments in the Third World to entice TNC investment with the guarantee of protected markets. Import substitution industrialization, for example, frequently relied on what Evans (1979) labelled the triple alliance between the state, local capital, and multinational corporations. As transnational corporations tend increasingly to integrate their production and trading processes into globally organized networks (Dicken 1998) the barriers to footloose corporations are reduced. Offshore plants tend to be financially controlled from abroad, they are often rented rather than owned, and their managers tend to have cosmopolitan rather than local perspectives. All of these factors weaken the ties that such businesses have with the communities in which they are located and make it less difficult for them to close down and/or relocate if and when business conditions deteriorate in one site relative to other sites. This happens all over the world, though workers and communities in the Third World tend to enjoy fewer legal protections against redundancy than those in the First World. For example, when the UK-based retailer Marks & Spencer announced in 2001 that it was closing down all its branches in France, it was forced by French and EU legislation to offer fairly substantial compensation to its former staff. This does not often happen in the Third World. The mobility of the TNCs, the job losses that usually follow, and the comparison of cheap imports with goods previously produced at home, increase protectionist pressures among labour and small local capitalists alike. Many local struggles are inspired by this selective form of protectionism.

Selective protectionism is not a wholesale challenge to the status quo though the threat of it is ever present as a reminder that the orderly progress of global trade in the interests of capitalist globalization is from time to time disturbed by voracious TNCs and local capitalists in collusion with government agencies and organized labour. This works both ways. Genuine free traders argue that if Third World markets are to be open to goods and services from the rest of the world then those markets should also be open to them. The protectionist policies towards domestic agriculture in the USA and Japan, and the Common Agricultural Policy of the EU, linger on as good examples of how powerful local interests can resist the general globalizing trend (Bonanno et al. 1994). With the creation of the WTO the pressures for free trade and open borders increased dramatically for governments all over the world. And as we shall see below, opposition to this version of free trade has become one of the central pillars of the anti-globalization movement.

The growing realization of the connections between globalization and free trade, and the groups that oppose free trade and protectionism are well illustrated in a study of the middle-class reaction to the economic crisis in Brazil in the 1980s and 1990s. The hyper-inflation of the 1980s created shortages and those who could afford to pay outrageous prices did so, thus fuelling the crisis. Social solidarity declined, and a dog-eat-dog mentality became the norm. The protectionism that had characterized the Brazilian economy led to an impasse in which some social groups turned to the left politically, and others went right 'toward globalization, a term with wholly positive connotations: it is seen as the antithesis of the "archaic" and corrupt "traditions" of Brazilian business. Brazil's problem was not [seen as] capitalism but bad government and business' (O'Dougherty 1998: 168).

Protectionism is frequently conceptualized by members of the transnational capitalist class as archaic, and its ideology is identified with corrupt traditional practices. All parties realize this, and so selective protectionism acts as a bargaining counter for the rich, and a bluff for the poor, and mainly comes to life in its use as a rhetorical device to satisfy local constituencies. For example, desperate politicians tend to fall back on it to appease working-class voters all over the world. As Aaronson (2001) convincingly argues, it is emotive issues like food safety, the environment, and labour standards that bring people out on to the streets against so-called free trade. Many protests and some social movements contain strong elements of selective protectionism.

NEW SOCIAL MOVEMENTS

Social movements, under a variety of labels, have always been of interest to social scientists. It is significant that social movements research, previously rather marginal, has been gradually drawn into the centre of social theory, particularly under the rubric of new social movements (Scott 1990). The argument that even when they are not apparently interested in seizing state power, new social movements (NSM) can still be as interesting as revolutionary movements, has in some ways liberated the study of them.[3]

Globalization is often seen in terms of impersonal forces wreaking havoc on the lives of ordinary and defenceless people and communities. It is not coincidental that interest in globalization since the 1960s has been accompanied by an upsurge in NSM research. NSM theorists, despite their differences, agree that traditional labour movements based on class politics have won substantial gains for workers (especially in the First World) but have generally failed to transform capitalist societies. A new form of analysis based on identity politics (notably of gender, sexuality, ethnicity, age, subcultures, community, and belief systems of a bewildering variety) has developed to document and explain the movements dedicated to effective resistance against sexism, racism, environmental damage, warmongering, capitalist exploitation, and other forms of injustice. While its star appears to be waning, as so often happens in social research many of its insights have been incorporated into the orthodoxy that has relegated it to the sidelines.[4]

There are, however, three types of social movements that do tend to get singled out for special treatment, probably because of the volume of research that has been devoted to them and the institutional structures (funding support, research centres, conferences, publications, formal and informal networks) that have grown up around them. They are the women's movement, the human rights movement, and the Green movement. I shall consider the human rights movement (and the women's movement as a central part of this) in the next chapter.

GREEN MOVEMENTS

Of all the social movements, the Green (environmental) movements present the greatest contemporary challenge to capitalist globalization. This is paradoxically confirmed by the fact that capitalists, politicians, and ideologues (and some scientists) have all tried to jump onto the Green bandwaggon and to appropriate their policies for themselves (see McCormick 1992, McManus 1996, Sklair 2001: ch. 7). This is not surprising because Green movements are largely based on a straightforward conception of planet earth and what needs to be done at the local and global levels to sustain human life on it.[5] The challenges that Green movements posed to capitalist globalization (and state socialism) concerned the consumption of non-renewable resources and the impacts of industrialization. While Green movements operate on the belief that the resources of the planet are finite and have to be carefully tended, capitalist globalization is predicated on the belief that the resources of the planet are virtually infinite, thanks to the scientific and technological ingenuity released by the capitalist system. This belief system argues that there is unlimited potential for replacement or substitution of resources as they are used up and that we will always find ways of coping with our waste and repairing the planet. This, of course, underpins the culture-ideology of consumerism.

I have elsewhere tried to analyse how we can make an analogy between the capitalist global system and what can be termed the global environmental system (in Redclift and Benton 1994). In particular, we can hypothesize that the transnational capitalist class has helped create a global environmental elite which has been more or less incorporated into the transnational capitalist class and thus is becoming further and further distanced from anti-capitalist deep greens. These deep greens (shorthand for a range of radical ecological views) are diametrically opposed to the business proponents of sustainable development led by TNC reformists. The mission of the sustainable development histor-ical bloc that these TNC reformists have created is to ensure that development (almost entirely defined in terms of economic growth) and sustainability (heavily conditioned by the technical capacities of capitalist globalization) are inextricably linked (Sklair 2001: ch. 7). All that is possible is done to distance global capitalism from the sources of environ-mental problems and, in particular, to insulate the culture-ideology of consumerism from such criticism. The relative success of the transnational capitalist class in this endeavour is the reason why it is analytically more useful to conceptualize Green move-ments in the plural, rather than as a movement in the singular and to see the movement–movements relationship as dialectical, not static. Not all Green movements have thrown in their lot with the sustainable development historical bloc, though most of the major Green movements and many of the smaller local ones have some relations with it. There is a good deal of funding for Green groups that play the capitalist game and there can be a good deal of trouble for those that do not (see Rowell 1996).

The arguments between corporations and their critics on the environmental impact of capitalist globalization were supposed to have been brought out into the open by the United Nations Conference on Environment and Development, the Earth Summit in Rio in 1992 (see Redclift 1996: ch. 2, Panjabi 1997). Problems were identified particularly in the spheres of production and trade. However, what actually happened in the opinion of many radical environmentalists was the corporate capture of the Earth Summit by the TNCs led by the Business Council for Sustainable Development under the dynamic lead-ership of Stephan Schmidheiny with the active support of Maurice Strong, the secretary general of the conference. This coalition blocked any major threat to the interests of global capitalism at Rio. Environmental discourse is a powerful weapon for all sides in disputes over Green issues (see Holzer 2001) and the corporations used it to good advantage, particularly in the elaboration of the sustainable development historical bloc (Sklair 2001: ch. 7).

It is certainly remarkable how quickly so many corporate executives and other members of the transnational capitalist class actively sought Green credentials (Robbins 2001). We can divide these into at least two groups, the critical optimists and the cynical optimists. The critical optimists, like Schmidheiny himself, have done an excellent job of working out what is necessary, individually and collectively, to ensure that the planet will continue to be habitable at ever-improving standards of living. The cynical optimists, on the other hand, see sustainable development as a series of good business opportunities. In the shameless words of an executive from Loblaw, Canada's major food distributor, to an environment summit sponsored by *Advertising Age*: 'If we made a lot of money destroying this planet, we sure can make money cleaning it up' (quoted in Vandervoort 1991: 14). Waste management is one of the fastest growing industries of the current period.

Some Green movements are closely connected with the critical consumer movement. The idea of consumerism has experienced an important dialectical inversion in recent years. It is commonly used in two senses. In this book it is used to denote an uncritical obsession with consumption. It is, however, also commonly used in an opposite sense, as in the consumer movement's version of consumerism, to denote suspicion of consumer goods, a wish to know more about how they are produced and who produces them. This version of consumerism can lead to a radical critique of consumption. To minimize confusion, I shall use consumerism where I mean the first, and the consumer movement to denote the second.[6]

Kaynak (1985: 15) defines the consumer movement 'as a movement seeking to increase the rights and powers of buyers in relation to sellers' and presents a useful historical account from the first co-operative society, founded in Scotland in 1769, to the present (see also Birchall 1997). He connects the rise of consumer movements in different countries with the position of the country in the world market, but from the marketing rather than political economy point of view. This may explain why his discussion of consumer movements in the Third World confuses the two meanings of consumerism. Food riots in North Africa, he writes, 'are examples of what LDC consumers are concerned with—the right to consume' (Kaynak 1985: 20). But this misses the real distinction between diametrically opposed beliefs based on entirely different conceptions of the satisfaction of human needs, between the quest for the good life promoted by capitalist globalization and the quest for the good society at the base of radical alternatives to capitalist globalization. This is one of the central issues around which the embryonic anti-globalization movement is coming together as it emerges out of protectionism, new social movements, and Green movements.

THE ANTI-GLOBALIZATION MOVEMENT

As I argued in Chapter 3, the fatal flaws of capitalist globalization are the class polarization crisis and the crisis of ecological sustainability. The focus of most contemporary social movements has been on either what I have identified as polarization issues (though not usually class polarization) or ecological issues, but connections between them have rarely been made. The successes of the anti-globalization movement, in the short time since its emergence, have been due to its capacity to make these connections.

The globalization of social movements involved the establishment of transnational networks of people with similar interests and, to some extent, converging identities outside the control of international, state, and local authorities. There is a substantial volume of research and documentation on such developments (see, for example, Keck and Sikkink 1998, Smith *et al.* 1997, Cohen and Rai 2000). Some of these new movements were established as a result of and/or in direct response to state and inter-state initiatives. For example, UN conferences such as UNCED in Rio in 1992 and the Women's Conference in Beijing in 1995 spawned thousands of official and alternative organizations and movements (Vig and Axelrod 1999: part III, O'Brien *et al.* 2000). Such movements flourished outside the UN system too. The Zapatista movement that rose up in Chiapas (Mexico) is a prime example of how identity-based collective action in even a remote community can successfully connect polarization and ecological crises in a way that attracts significant transnational support (see Nash 2001, Schulz 1998).

The challenges to capitalist globalization can be usefully distinguished in terms of the economic, political, and culture-ideology spheres. Concretely, these are challenges to the TNCs, to the state and inter-state fractions of the transnational capitalist class, and to the culture-ideology of consumerism. Challenges to the TNCs usually involve disrupting their capacity to accumulate private profits at the expense of their workforces, their consumers, and the communities that are affected by their activities. An important part of economic globalization today is the increasing dispersal of the manufacturing process into many discrete phases carried out in many different places (global commodity chains). Being no longer so dependent on the production of one factory and one work-force gives capital a distinct advantage, particularly against the strike weapon that once gave tremendous negative power to the working class. Global production chains can be disrupted by strategically planned stoppages, but this generally acts more as an inconvenience than as a decisive weapon of labour against capital. The global division of labour builds flexibility into the system so that capital can migrate anywhere in the world to find the cheapest reliable efficient sources of labour.[7] At the level of the production process, globalizing capital has all but (though not quite) defeated labour.

Capitalist globalization, if we are to believe its own propaganda, is continuously beset by opposition, boycott, legal challenge, and moral outrage from the consumers of their products, and occasionally by disruptions from their workers. There have been some notable economic successes for labour movements in many countries in achieving rela-tively high standards of living for their members and political successes in establishing genuinely democratic practices. The emergence of new transnational networks of work-ers, through established unions and by other means, has been happening quietly. For example, Murray (2000) describes how transnational labour movement organizations (the ILO and the ICFTU) have begun to use the Internet for organizational, educational, and campaigning purposes through the interactive Organized Labour 2000 conference, what Shostak (1999) terms CyberUnion. New technologies also bring new resources for peasant organizations (Edelman 1998). Initiatives like these have led some researchers to argue that the prospects for labour to play a more important role in the struggle against capitalist globalization may be improving (see, for example, Walker 1999, Munck and

Waterman 1999). On the basis of research on European Works Councils, Wills (1999) concludes that TNC-driven economic globalization may actually improve the prospects for transnational labour organization (compare Leisink 1999).

'Nationalization—the use of national political and regulatory resources to constrain the boundaries of markets to overlap with actual national geographical frontiers—leaves labor deeply committed to the nation as its home, however. This is the nub of labor's problems today' (Ross 2000: 89). Apart from a rather hopeful nod towards labour legislation in the EU, Ross gives no clear idea of how these problems can be resolved, though there are signs that labour movements, notably in the USA and Europe, are beginning to grapple with these issues. For example, a study to evaluate the place of globalization and international solidarity in ten leading worker education programmes in the USA usefully distinguished accommodatory education from transformatory education (Salt *et al.* 2000). This highlights the contradiction between those who chose to work within and for the system for their own benefit and those who attempt to globalize labour resistance to capitalism. While a viable alternative to capitalist globalization is unlikely to come primarily from the labour movement in the near future, the active practice of transformatory education (on the shop floor and in the office as well as in the classroom) is necessary for this ever to take place. It is clear that no viable alternative to capitalist globalization can be created without the active participation of a significant part of the labour movement, globally. This moves us on from challenges to the TNCs to challenges to the state and inter-state fractions of the transnational capitalist class.

The issue of democracy is central to the advance of the forces of globalization and the practices and prospects of movements that oppose them, local and global. The rule of law, freedom of association and expression, freely contested elections, as minimum conditions and however imperfectly sustained, are as necessary in the long run for mass market-based global consumerist capitalism as they are for alternative social systems.[8] In the next chapter I problematize the globalization of human rights, but here I focus on the analytically (though not necessarily temporally) prior issue of democratization as a channel for movements that challenge the state and inter-state fractions of the transnational capitalist class.

A significant analytic feature of these movements (and the new theoretical frameworks being developed to research them) is the critique of state-centrism. For example, the collection edited by Smith *et al.* (1997) is subtitled *Solidarity Beyond the State*. The idea of solidarity beyond the state, so difficult for traditional political scientists, sociologists, and International Relations theorists to comprehend, connects at many points with the critique of state-centrism that lies at the heart of genuine theories of globalization.

Working along similar lines, Cohen and Rai (2000: 8–10) highlight six factors that make movements go global. The first and most powerful is that a global age requires global responses; this is facilitated by cheap communications that permit a transnational level of organization; governments have to adapt to the increasing powers of other actors, notably TNCs and social movements; these movements (particularly environmental) have been forced to adopt a global logic for the reason that environmental problems respect no state frontiers; in movements focused on human rights there is an implied universal logic by virtue of human qualities; and there is some convergence on values (notably democratization). This last factor is, in my view, the fundamental link between transnational movements and the anti-globalization movement.[9]

Not all movements need to, want to, or actually do become transnational to achieve their aims. What Smith *et al.*, Cohen and Rai, and many others are really getting at is that more and more social movements need to, want to, and actually do become transnational (or global) for good reason. Precisely because capitalist globalization works mainly though transnational practices, in order to challenge these practices politically, the movements that challenge them have to work transnationally too, confronting officials and politicians at all levels in towns and cities, in the countryside, and in sites of symbolic significance for the state and inter-state system. For example, opposition to what are seen as unnecessary, ecologically unsustainable and class polarizing mega-dam projects in India (Dwivedi 1998), China (L. Sullivan, in Vig and Axelrod 1999: ch. 14) and elsewhere (*New Internationalist*, July 2001) has involved struggles with local officials, state agencies, and international financial and other institutions. By making transnational connections, movements against local injustices can become part of an anti-globalization movement, and if the correct diagnosis of the problems is made, part of a movement offering an alternative to capitalist globalization. This refers back to the dialectical relationship between movements in the plural and a movement in the singular.

A notable example of this process of connecting movements and a movement and, at the same time, the local and the global, was Global View 2001. This was a campaign of twenty-four well-known NGOs working in the UK and worldwide for all-party action during the 2001 general election in the UK. The platform of the campaign was extremely wide, covering aid, health and education, HIV/AIDS, debt and poverty reduction, reform of the IMF/World Bank/WTO, investment, labour standards, corporate responsibility, capital flows, climate change, GMOs, conflict prevention and resolution, arms, and asylum seekers. While most of the NGOs supporting the campaign were specialized in only one or two of these issues as separate movements, they could all work together within a movement. As Figure 10.1 illustrates, the focus of the campaign was that the British people should think about how their votes could help to end world poverty and promote human rights. While there is no explicit anti-globalization (or anti-capitalist) message here, there is clearly a critical subtext.

Tarrow (1998: ch. 5) provides a useful framework within which to analyse the ways in which campaigns, organizations, and movements can lead to substantive changes. From the study of the emergence of the politics of contention in the former Soviet Union, he demonstrates the importance of political opportunities in transforming mobilization into action. He highlights the following dimensions: (1) opening of access to participation for new actors; (2) evidence of political realignment within the polity; (3) emerging splits within the elite and the appearance of influential allies (Tarrow treats these separately); and (4) decline in the state's capacity or will to repress dissent.

Let us examine each of these in turn with respect to the emergence of an anti-globalization movement and struggles against capitalist globalization.

(1) Increasing access: Tarrow suggests that the easiest way to open up access to participation for new actors is through elections, and historically this is certainly true. As we shall see in the explanation of the defeat of the MAI below, the threat that they would lose votes and find it more difficult to be re-elected was crucial in the decisions of the governments that abandoned the MAI. The role of the Internet, and to some extent increasing access to the mass media, means that different publics can make their voices

Figure 10.1 Vote for Me

© Oxfam, reproduced with permission of Oxfam Publishing, 274 Banbury Road, Oxford, OX2 7DZ.

heard, both to other publics with whom they share interests and to political leaders and gatekeepers of public opinion (Walch 1999).

(2) Shifting alignments: in his study of the short-lived alliance between Greens and organized labour in the USA from 1948 to 1970, Dewey (1998) demonstrates the potency of this alignment and the importance that the TCC attached to destroying it. My argument is that the alliance between Greens and labour is crucial for the success of the anti-globalization movement.[10] In many (perhaps most) places around the world the labour unions and the Green movements have more members and are better organized and funded than any other movement. The networks and alliances that sprang up around the anti-globalization movement in the 1990s brought many activists involved in the new social movements based on identity politics into close contact with labour and Green activists (some activists are members of multiple organizations, of course). While not wishing to minimize the significance of the destructive sectarian splits that have under-mined the effectiveness of many radical movements throughout history, an anti-globalization movement built on these alliances will help to focus opposition to capitalist globalization more clearly than has been possible in the past. This has certainly been the case with support networks around the Zapatistas in Mexico and many other indigenous

groups (Starr 2000: ch. 3), and the global coalitions against the MAI and the WTO etc. (see below).

(3) Divided elites and influential allies: if one factor is to be singled out as the most important spur to the creation of an anti-globalization movement since 1995, it is surely the divisions that appeared to be growing in the transnational capitalist class. Splits have emerged within the corporate elite (particularly over climate change and sweatshops) and within the globalizing bureaucracies of the World Bank and other parts of the international financial establishment (particularly over the Asian financial crisis). While the modest Tobin tax proposal (Tobin 2000, Wachtel 2000) to recoup a little of the enormous profits of global financial transactions for social ends has not yet proved acceptable to those who own and control private finance, discussion of it has had a certain shaming effect.[11]

Globalizing and more sceptical members of the OECD and the G7 have also disagreed over globalization, and the UN system has seen some important internal struggles over closer links with corporate partners. At Davos, and even in the articulation of various Third Ways, the capitalist triumphalism that greeted the collapse of communism in Eastern Europe and the Soviet Union has diminished. Prominent individual members of the transnational capitalist class have broken ranks, even if only temporarily, to deplore the negative consequences of capitalist globalization. For example, Bill Gates is on record as a critic of the digital divide, George Soros has criticized the globalization of finance, Sir John Browne (the chief executive of BP) has defended the environment. Ravi Kanbur of Cornell University resigned as author of a World Bank report on poverty and Joseph Stiglitz departed as chief economist at the World Bank, all contributing to the ever-growing critique of the so-called Washington Consensus (see Makinson 2000) from within the capitalist system. Even the WTO has a rather defensive website item on ten common misunderstandings: 'Is it a dictatorial tool of the rich and powerful? Does it destroy jobs? Does it ignore the concerns of health, the environment and development? Emphatically no. Criticisms of the WTO are often based on profound misunderstandings of the way the WTO works.' A rather bemused feature in *Business Week* expressed the mood well:

It's hard to figure how a term that once connoted so much good for the world has fallen into such disrepute. In the past decade, globalization—meaning the rise of market capitalism around the world—has undeniably contributed to America's New Economy boom. It has created millions of jobs from Malaysia to Mexico and a cornucopia of affordable goods for Western consumers. It has brought phone service to some 300 million households in developing nations and a transfer of nearly $2 trillion from rich countries to poor through equity, bond investments, and commercial loans. It's helped topple dictators by making information available in once sheltered societies. And now the Internet is poised to narrow the gulf that separates rich nations from poor even further in the decade to come. (6 Nov. 2000: 41).[12]

Sophisticated social scientists may be forgiven for a touch of scepticism on the severity of these splits and the extent to which these people and institutions can be considered as useful allies.[13] This is not the point. The significance of these public demonstrations of divisions over globalization is that they send messages of confusion to the public at large, and the anti-globalization movement can use them to great advantage. Ashwin (2000: 110) argued that 'governments and the international financial institutions are in the midst of a mini-crisis of confidence regarding the potential negative effects of liberalization [meaning capitalist globalization]'. The mini-crisis has been escalating ever since, particularly in light of fears of a global recession combined with revelations about state-sponsored brutality against peaceful protesters against globalization, particularly in Genoa in the summer of 2001.

There are at least two ways to read this evidence. The first is the cynical view of co-option and selling-out. Certainly, my thesis of the creation of the sustainable development historical bloc might err on the side of cynicism. Members of the transnational capitalist class who appear to take sustainable development seriously and who appear to acknowledge ecological crisis (like Sir John Browne and those other CEOs who took their companies out of the Global Climate Coalition), may simply be playing at gesture politics. The second view is the thesis of organizational learning. This means that movements might actually convert some influential members of the transnational capitalist class to their views on important issues. In his critique of what he terms predatory globalization, for example, Falk (1999) argues that neo-liberals have undermined the social contract between state and society. In his view, a global civil society based on normative ideas of sustainable development, human rights, and cosmopolitan democracy (not to be confused with what he calls 'closet Marxism') can replace globalization from above.[14]

This analysis suggests that not all victories and defeats are matters of crude power struggles but that ideals matter. In their discussion of the role of NGOs in the human rights field, Steiner and Alston argue that these organizations have had some real successes, notably the 1997 Ottowa Landmine Treaty, the 1998 Rome Statute on the International Criminal Court, and (less convincingly) the 1999 Seattle WTO meeting.

Perhaps most significant is the blurring of the distinction between the insiders and the outsiders as NGO representatives have become part of governmental delegations. They have also increasingly become key partners in the delivery of humanitarian and other forms of development assistance, partners with government in performing a variety of functions such as human rights education, the monitoring of voluntary codes of conduct and even the delivery of basic social services, and even partners with business and labour unions in various areas. (Steiner and Alston 2000: 940–1)

While it seems unlikely to me, it is certainly possible that as many members of the transnational capitalist class are influenced by the anti-globalization movement as vice versa. Time will tell!

(4) Repression and facilitation: In a striking and rather frightening forecast of what capitalist globalization could become, Jones argues:

There is some reason to believe that the globalization process (and the modernization project) will be less integrative in the future than in the past, thereby leaving space for cultural integrity in the many backwaters of what I term Blade Runner [after the dystopian Ridley Scott film] capitalism. This is primarily due to the fact that the organizational drivers of the international economy and the globalization process, are impelled by a strict and simple logic: to improve their cost and revenue structures. If a site has nothing to offer these firms, they will bypass it. Many lesser developed countries and indigenous cultures fit this profile. (Jones 1998: 288)

In Blade Runner capitalism the techno-economy of the formal sector needs the grunge economy of the informal sector. Here I focus on the violence and polarization implicit in the Blade Runner scenario rather than on Jones's confidence that it has potential for saving indigenous cultures.[15] The vision of Los Angeles, where the film is set, is not too far distant from many cities of the present: sharp high-tech corporate and official architecture interspersed with piles of discarded people and garbage, policed and menaced by ruthless killers operating under no recognizable rule of law. It would be an exaggeration to characterize the sites of resistance since 1995 in these terms. However, one of the enduring symbols of the anti-globalization movement is the picture of heavily-armoured militia protecting Niketown in Seattle, an image straight out of *Blade Runner*.

In democracies, even the flawed democracies of the First World, the costs of repression for the authorities (official or, on occasion, corporate) should not be under-estimated. There is no doubt that the costs of the repression of protests against the Vietnam War in the 1960s and 1970s were an important factor in persuading the US government and their allies to disengage. The same can be said about the anti-Poll Tax protests in Britain, anti-World Bank and IMF food riots in the Third World, and many other movements. To these we can add the costs to transnational corporations and local officials of repressing protests against dams and involuntary relocation of large numbers of people (in India and China, for example), industrial pollution hazards (all over the world), controversial power stations (Enron in India), and threats to the habitats of indigenous peoples (in Nigeria, for example). The great transformation that occurred in the 1990s was the speed and scale of communications making almost instantaneous information available through what Langman and his colleagues (2002) have termed cyberactivism. As all these social movements and protests become transnationalized, as they become parts of many interlocking global networks and, simply, as they spread the word about the real nature of how the transnational capitalist class reacts when challenged, the potential for a movement against capitalist globalization increases. The section on the battle of Seattle below examines some possible consequences of the violent repression of protesters as members of the various fractions of the transnational capitalist class (mostly peace-loving men and women in their own spheres) were besieged in cities all over the world.

Tarrow argues that any decline in the state's capacity or will to repress (though it is not only the state that can repress) will lead to more political opportunities for contentious social movements to exploit. The first decade of the twenty-first century will probably be decisive in at least one respect, namely the extent to which political leaders in each state are prepared to ignore the rule of law in order to discourage protests against globalization.[16] If the rule of law prevails then this will undoubtedly facilitate the movement. I shall argue this in the context of the globalization of human rights in the next chapter.

The evidence does suggest that we are entering a new transnational cycle of contention.[17] However, the question of exactly what these movements are trying to achieve needs to be addressed. For this we must move on to studies of anti-corporate movements. The key issue, according to the analysis of their programmes by Starr (2000), is the unaccountability of global institutions, particularly globalizing corporations.[18] However, anti-corporate, for critics of globalization, does not necessarily mean anti-capitalist. Starr argues that the foundational logic of the dominant global system is not necessarily capitalist, but involves a complex of factors including economic growth; enclosure of the commons and the increasing concentration of economic power in the hands of bigger and bigger corporations; dependency; colonialism; and anti-democratic tendencies (as consumerism replaces the rights of citizenship). This is a very mixed bag but certainly all these and more are to be found within anti-globalization movements.

It is easy to draw the conclusion from all this that it is not capitalism that is the enemy, but big business, whether private or state. Economic globalization driven by major corporations (or faceless bureaucracies) is an easy target, made even easier by the fact that the ownership class has been transformed. Small capitalists are gradually being squeezed out of the system, families are being replaced by unrelated blocks of stockholders, and human corporate owners are being replaced by non-human computer programmes that move investment funds around according to abstruse formulas, enriching the few while destroying lives and communities.

Starr's analysis covers a bewildering variety of anti-corporate movements and protests, from those involved in the struggles against structural adjustment, for peace and human rights (for example, the Permanent People's Tribunal on TNC violations of human rights), and for land reform. The US Greenbelt Alliance asks: 'Imagine your metropolitan area if you had to get all your food and take all your vacations within a fifty mile radius' (Starr 2000: 63). The cyberpunk hackers, crackers, phreakers, cyphers, and cyberchic not only expose corporate crimes and misdemeanours, they also penetrate corporate and governmental computer systems and cause occasional havoc (pp. 73–8). But generally these groups do not articulate an alternative vision.

Through delinking and relocalization, the refusal of distant authority can become a reality, the first step in creating an alternative to globalization. Pacione (1997) shows how Local Exchange Trading Systems (LETS) are already beginning to do this. Anarchism, while it has failed to discard its bad but not totally fair reputation for chaos and violence, has created movements that focus on small-scale local autonomy against socialist and capitalist statism that have inspired many others. Movements for local sustainable development (for example permaculture), groups organized around the small is beautiful approach, bioregionalism, urban agriculture, farmers' markets, sustainable cuisine from the Chefs' Collaborative, small business groups growing out of anti-WalMart campaigns, local barter economies (Ithaca HOURS, LETS, Grain de Sel in France, for example) and sovereignty movements of indigenous peoples and even religious nationalists, all offer alternatives in their own spheres to a corporate world (Starr 2000: ch. 4).[19] However, capitalist globalization could accommodate and subvert most of these initiatives and turn them into variations on the consumerist theme.[20]

Starr not unreasonably concludes that the only viable alternative is some kind of post-corporate relocalized economy, but the politics of the transition to this are, as yet, difficult to discern. The modern capitalist state obviously could not lead humanity to this destination, even if most of us wanted to go there.[21] Localism, therefore, appears the more convincing strategy, for example shortening food links would be one way to undermine globalization of agriculture, retailing, and trade. Starr commends the principle of site here to sell here (Lang and Hines 1993). This new protectionism is a challenging set of ideas that presents, in theory at least, a viable alternative to globalization, though not to capitalism.

Hines has developed this thesis under the somewhat playful title *Localization: A Global Manifesto* (2000). He defines globalization narrowly as: 'the process by which governments sign away the rights of their citizens in favour of speculative investors and transnational corporations' (p. 4) and argues that it leads to the erosion of wages, welfare, and environmental protection. His alternative is localization. Globalization, therefore, is delocalization. Actually, most studies of globalization, including my own work on global-izing corporations and the transnational capitalist class, suggest that exploiting local workforces, resources, environments, symbols, and cultures is the basis of corporate profits. This exploitation is not new though the scale of it is, and it does not necessarily destroy the local, which changes anyway.

Localization for Hines does not mean overpowering state control, 'merely that gov-ernments provide the policy framework which allows people and businesses to rediver-sify their own local economies' (Hines 2000: 29). There is one important question that needs to be asked here. Why are governments not doing all this now? (Most would claim they were.) Hines proposes ten criteria of a sustainable community: basically good facil-ities accessible to all; good education, work and local economy; ecology; lifestyles, infor-mation, culture, participation, and ongoing improvements. Against this is the triple threat of globalization: more international competitiveness and less public expenditure and community activity; opening of government procurement to international competi-tion that disadvantages local providers; and competitive agribusiness that undermines agriculture to feed people locally (ch. 5).

How are all these admirable goals to be achieved? Hines argues that single-issue groups will never achieve much unless they challenge the need to be internationally competitive in the interests of regional and national self-reliance. International development requires that the WTO be revised to become a General Agreement for Sustainable Trade (not an easy task when companies have to site here to sell here).[22] While the critique of inter-national competitiveness is a very significant part of the alternative to capitalist global-ization, it is not exactly a rallying cry that is likely to mobilize the population and, as Hines conceptualizes it, the implications for workers and farmers in the Third World are far from clear. So, it is not surprising that such views are usually seen as variations on the old imperialist protectionism rather than a genuinely new version.

The same can be said for the subsistence perspective of Mies and Bennholdt-Thomsen (1999). The title of the original German edition was *A Cow for Hillary*, referring to the deprived condition of the wife of the then President Clinton when she met some women in Bangladesh. Poor Hillary, no cow, no income of her own, and only one daughter! This true story teaches us five lessons:

(i)   the importance of the view from below;

(ii) the importance of people's control over their means of subsistence;

(iii) the fact that such control gives women pride, dignity, courage, and a sense of equality (the Bangladeshi women felt no inferiority to Hillary);

(iv) the positive mindset of the women in Bangladesh (and, potentially, people everywhere); and

(v)   the need to abandon First World/Third World schizophrenia. We know that it exists, they say, but we need not accept it. (Mies and Bernholdt-Thomsen 1999: 4).

The subsistence perspective (SP) explicitly rejects the developmental model of catching up. Rather than poor people being brought to the destructive and unsustainable stand-ards of living of the rich, everyone should be encouraged to live a subsistence existence. Mies and Bennholdt-Thomsen are realistic about this apparently absurd thesis. They describe a Women and Ecology congress in Cologne in 1986 where speaker after speaker brought up objections to the SP. It was criticized for being unfriendly to women (who would be the first to make sacrifices); for being too moralistic (economics, after all, is about interests); for being good for the rich in the First World who can afford to buy ethically (but not for the poor); that it sounded like a fascist blood and soil ideology; it was Luddite; it might work for small groups, but cannot destroy capitalism; and, the final barb, it is apolitical, a 'patchwork quilt of a thousand subsistence communes or eco-villages' (quoted in Mies and Bernholdt-Thomsen 1999: 15). The authors naturally argue energetically against all these objections. The central analytical thrust in the SP is the critique of the concepts of need and sufficiency and this leads to a critique of the culture-ideology of consumerism (though not in these terms). Chapters on subsistence and agriculture, the market, the city, the commons, wage labour, women's liberation, and politics, while not totally convincing are no less so than most rather more sensible alternatives to capitalist globalization. Both the localization and the subsistence perspectives have added vital components to the intellectual armoury of the movement against capitalist globalization. This is evident in the two defining campaigns that are examined next.

THE DEFEAT OF THE MULTILATERAL AGREEMENT ON INVESTMENT (MAI)

Though the OECD had been discussing ways of freeing the TNCs from restrictive legislation for decades (many would argue that by the 1990s there were few serious restrictive regulations left), negotiations to establish the MAI were opened in 1995. The MAI was a series of proposals to do for foreign investment what the WTO was doing for trade, namely to abolish barriers, to establish level playing fields, and to ease the progress of capitalist globalization. Similar proposals had been mooted in the fledgling WTO, but had run into opposition led by representatives from India and Malaysia. In any case, those pushing it thought that the OECD, dominated by First World governments and corporate lobbies, was perhaps a more suitable venue for these matters. Generally, OECD member states irrespective of which political party was in government had been content to rely on toothless voluntary agreements on the conduct of what the organization chose to call multinational enterprises (considered to be less threatening than transnational corporations).[23]

Business input to OECD negotiations had been institutionalized in 1962 with the creation of the Business and Industry Advisory Committee (BIAC), through which the interests of business (dominated unsurprisingly by big business) were channelled. As with the international body for food, Codex Alimentarius, there is a peculiar relationship between official governmental participation (like Codex, the OECD is an inter-governmental organization) and what can be labelled official adjunct personnel and organizations. In the USA the body responsible for input to the BIAC on behalf of the US government was the private interest group, the US Council for International Business. The Confederation of British Industries, the private interest group that speaks for big business in the UK, was responsible for BIAC input on behalf of the British government, and the powerful employers organization, Keidanren, ran BIAC Japan. There were similar arrangements in other member countries.[24]

Formal discussions on the MAI began at the OECD in May 1995. The existence of the proposals was known to few people outside the narrow confines of the specialist trade and investment communities until a leaked report on the MAI was posted on the Internet in 1997. Many environmental, consumer, labour rights, and development groups rapidly began to alert the wider public to the possible dire consequences of the Agreement. In response, some details of the negotiations were posted on the OECD Internet site, and the OECD published a Policy Brief on it (No. 2, 1997) and wider consultations began. A contentious NGO/OECD Consultation was followed by a Joint NGO Statement extremely hostile to the MAI, released in Paris on 27 October 1997, and rereleased in an updated form on 11 February 1998.[25] Two days later a full-page advertisement making the case against the MAI, supported by 600 organizations in sixty-seven countries, appeared in the *New York Times*, *International Herald Tribune*, and other opinion-forming newspapers. While it is true that the USA and Canada between them provided over 200 of these organizations, substantial support also came from many other countries. These included 15 organizations from Australia, 15 from Austria, 10 from Brazil, 10 from Germany, 16 from Italy, 12 from Japan, 65 from Mexico (many also involved in the struggle against NAFTA), 18 from the Netherlands, 10 from Russia, and 13 from the UK. Most prominent in this initiative were the international environmental organization, Friends of the Earth plus Public Citizen and the Sierra Club (both US-based).

The central theme of the advertisement was the role of the major corporations in promoting and influencing the MAI. The headline, 'Top Secret: New Mai Treaty. Should Corporations Rule The World'[26] (*New York Times* 13 Feb. 1998), alerted a mass audience that something important was afoot. The campaign against the MAI in the USA is an object lesson in how global corporations can be challenged through global-local action by using the democratic system. The Boston Area MAI Action Groups, for example, created a website (available through the MAI portal) that successfully connected national conferences on MAI with local action. 'So please, call your representative and senators. (Call the Capitol switchboard at 202–225–3121.) Talk with the aide who deals with "international trade and investment." . . . Ask for your representative's position on "full debate," and how he [*sic*] intends to deal with a fast-track proposal when it does come up. Then ask for his mailing address and write a letter to confirm the conversation. See our sample letters.' (Underline in original, to access sample letters.)

Crucial in this campaign was the work of Robert Stumberg, a law professor at George-town University. His research was instrumental in mobilizing local and state officials all over the USA against the MAI on the (very real) grounds that it would seriously limit the already limited autonomy of municipal and state authorities in the realms of economic, environmental, and social affairs. It is likely that pressure from these officials on the Federal government, already embroiled in various trade and investment disputes with the EU and with international bodies, heightened its awareness of the political risks involved in the MAI.[27]

The British government was also ambivalent on the issue, as was made clear in the debate on MAI reported in *Hansard* (23 Feb. 1998: 147–54). It is an interesting comment on New Labour to note that the debate was secured by Dr Nick Palmer who was both a consultant for the major pharmaceutical TNC, Novartis (his former employer), and a member of the World Development Movement, who spearheaded the campaign against the MAI in Britain. Dr Palmer (who noted that the Conservative benches were entirely empty) was extremely hostile to the MAI. The Labour government had given it a guarded welcome while noting that there was a growing public hostility to some of the provisions in the proposed agreement. As in the USA, campaigners in Britain also had some success in connecting the local, the national, and the global. For example, according to the MAI Coalition, in mid-1998 around twenty local authorities in England (including Birmingham City Council, Oxfordshire County Council, and Bournemouth Borough Council) had passed resolutions expressing concern about the local impacts of any MAI. Links had also been forged with the churches, trade unions, academic researchers, and political parties (see *MAI Coalition Newsletter* July 1998). This rapid growth of local, national, and global campaigns against the MAI was not good news for those working quietly behind the scenes to prepare public opinion in the USA, Europe, and elsewhere for what they hoped would be more or less a *fait accompli*, MAI by stealth.

The official US government-nominated representative on the BIAC was, as noted above, the United States Council for International Business (USCIB), a membership-based organization comprising more than 300 corporations and interested parties. In fact, USCIB has had the official role of representing US business on international issues since 1947. It is also the official US representative on the ILO and other international bodies.[28] While nominally representing the interests of the US government (and, presumably, the people), the focus of the work of the USCIB since the 1980s has been on open markets and level playing fields for trade and investment in the interests of major US corporations. To this end, USCIB participated in BIAC informal working groups of experts who met with OECD negotiators regularly in Paris. USCIB also advised the US Trade Representative and the State Department and met with them regularly on MAI and other matters. At the crucial January 1998 consultation between BIAC and OECD negotiators where, presumably, the growing campaign against the MAI was high on the agenda, the Executive Director of USCIB and his equivalents from Canada, Britain, France, Germany, and other member countries met with senior OECD personnel. Also included in this meeting were executives from ten individual corporations, seven of these ranked in the top 100 investors in the world (Shell, Volkswagen, GE, Nestlé, Unilever, Texaco, and Kobe Steel).

The problem for USCIB (and its partners in BIAC) was that no senior politicians had backed the MAI publicly. In my terms, many globalizing politicians realized the potential for political damage inherent in the MAI and, though they wanted it, they wanted it without too much fuss and, of course, their first priority is usually to win elections. In the USA, the problems of the IMF and other more specific trade and investment issues had higher priority for politicians than the MAI in the latter part of the 1990s. The pro-MAI coalition in and around the OECD had planned to complete the Agreement for signing at the OECD Ministerial meeting in April 1998, but this was postponed and more consultations took place. It was becoming clear that the MAI was in trouble. In September 1998 a report by Catherine Lalumière, a European deputy from France, suggested that the negotiations should be moved to the WTO. The French government took this as its cue to withdraw from the increasingly unpopular MAI process and finally in December 1998 the OECD officially abandoned it. Some governments (Japan, for example) welcomed the suggestion that the matter should be taken back to the WTO, probably under a new name. Given the coalition against the WTO which arose in the late 1990s (and which shows no sign of abating in the early years of the new century) this seems an unlikely prospect in the near future. A Statement against the WTO and the deregulation of the global economy organized by Friends of the Earth brought together almost 800 organizations from over seventy-five countries (4 Aug. 1999) in anticipation of the Seattle meetings. However, it should also be noted that there are many more countries in the WTO system than there are in the OECD. In the long term most major TNCs are probably just as interested in investing in developing countries as in the rich and to some extent investment-saturated economies of the OECD. This is the case for the tobacco TNCs, as we saw in Chapter 7.[29]

The debate over the MAI (and over the WTO) rapidly migrated from elite circles to the public domain via the Internet and the mass media. This demonstrates that relatively obscure trade and investment debates can be successfully politicized by those who abhor the consequences of capitalist globalization, and the role of distant international bodies and familiar globalizing corporations. Both the class polarization crisis and the crisis of ecological unsustainability were laid at the doors of the World Bank, IMF, WTO, and other official bodies and their corporate friends. Even though the early negotiations were largely unnoticed (they were never secret as some of their critics have claimed, though the OECD did not exactly mount a public awareness campaign), MAI was clearly of great significance as the first truly global attempt to establish binding norms for foreign investment. However, it was not an attempt to regulate foreign investors but an attempt to regulate those who might try to interfere with foreign investment, namely community, municipal, and national governments. That was its fatal flaw. Therefore, the failure to establish the MAI is a valuable comment on the spheres in which corporations are replacing states as the dominant forces in the governance of the global economy and the spheres in which they are not.

The message of the BIAC Chairman in the 1998 Annual Report attributed the failure to push through the MAI to the financial crisis that began to sweep through Asian and other emerging markets in 1997, and had 'fanned the flames of opposition to globalization and amplified the chorus of criticism of liberalised trade and investment rules'. But this seems to miss the point. It was not the flames of opposition to globalization that destroyed the MAI, it was the fact that even globalizing politicians in the governments of OECD member countries saw the MAI as a vote-loser. For politicians in these countries the MAI was seen as a further and more menacing threat to their autonomy vis-à-vis global capital.

If my explanation is correct, and the coalition of globalizing bureaucrats and corporate executives inside and outside the OECD was defeated by a coalition of national and local politicians (not necessarily all of the same political parties) and a wide variety of transnational and local campaigning groups, then we can learn important lessons about globalizing politics from this case. Tactically, while many intellectuals are sceptical if not cynical about elections and popular sentiments, if national and local politicians can be persuaded that policy decisions such as the implementation of MAI could seriously damage them in electoral terms, then this democratic tactic can be powerful. Thus, even left-leaning governments (to stretch the term unbearably) like New Labour under Blair and the Democrats under Clinton began by supporting the MAI in the OECD and were only persuaded to abandon it by the apparent groundswell of popular and political opinion against it. It is very probable that a new form of the MAI will be reintroduced when conditions are ripe, for example if and when rising inflation and/or rising unemployment undermine the opposition to foreign investment and the jobs that major corporations always offer. Relying solely on governments of whatever political party to defend the popular classes (to use an old-fashioned but apt term) while the hegemony of global capital continues to be exercised through the transnational capitalist class is not a viable long-term strategy, but it can be a useful tactic.

THE BATTLE OF SEATTLE AND AFTER

Walden Bello was not alone when he stated: 'The last year will probably go down as one of those defining moments in the history of the world economy, like 1929' (Bello 2001: 71). The year in question began in December 1999 with a WTO summit meeting in Seattle. Despite many differences among the protesters, Bello claims that 'most of them were united by one thing: their opposition to the expansion of a system that promoted corporate-led globalisation at the expense of social goals like justice, community, national sovereignty, cultural diversity and ecological sustainability' (p. 72). In other words, the many anti-globalization movements that had been fermenting over the last decades of the twentieth century were transforming themselves into a singular movement against capitalist globalization.[30]

The WTO was born with a reputation for lack of transparency, undemocratic pro-cedures, and an inbuilt susceptibility to corporate lobbying (Barker and Mander 2000). Its meeting in Seattle was well publicized and it was evident that those promoting capitalist globalization saw it as a good opportunity for positive media coverage, after all, the mission of the WTO was to make us all prosperous (Dunkley 2000, O'Brien *et al.* 2000: ch. 3). The organization of the protest against the WTO in Seattle has now passed into activist folklore, and with the help of the capitalist-controlled mass media, into the collective memories of people all over the world. The presence of hundreds of thousands of pro-testers confronting large numbers of heavily armoured police forced the WTO to aban-don the meeting and beat a hasty retreat. Some violence occurred, mostly to property, and groups of protesters attacked global brand stores, such as McDonald's and Nike.[31] This demonstration of opposition to capitalist globalization was rapidly followed in the first half of 2000 by tens of thousands of people protesting at the World Bank/IMF head-quarters in Washington DC, and by about 2,000 protesters who asked the leaders of the Asian Development Bank to leave Chiang Mai in Thailand. The Bank belatedly established an NGO Task Force to deal with the issue. Bello observes that poor Thai farmers had joined with middle-class youth in Chiang Mai and that this was one link in the worldwide chain of protest against globalization. By September, the focus had shifted to Melbourne, site of the World Economic Forum Asia-Pacific Summit. This attracted around 5,000 pro-testers, and street battles erupted that forced delegates to be moved around the city by helicopter. Later in September, 10,000 people demonstrated in Prague, where World Bank leaders were besieged and their meeting abandoned. In Prague, as in many other places, the struggle against imperialism was identified with opposition to McDonald's franchises (see Figure 10.2). Czech Republic President Václav Havel hosted a consultation between leaders of the World Bank and the IMF, the financier George Soros, and representatives of various NGOs (the voice of civil society), but nothing came of it.

The leaders of the World Economic Forum in Davos in January 2001, one of the loudest voices of capitalist triumphalism in the early 1990s, visibly shaken, put reform of the global system at the top of its agenda. But this agenda was discussed behind a high fence and massive police presence to shut out thousands of protesters. A platform was given at Davos to anti-globalization activists and many fine words were exchanged between them

Figure 10.2 McDonald's in Prague
Source: James Gleeson

and members of the transnational capitalist class, but little action followed. An alternative Davos met at the same time with an impressive array of anti-globalization organizations discussing resistance and struggles all over the world. The G7 plan to lessen the burden of debt-servicing of the forty-one poorest countries, a key demand of the protesters, had delivered only one billion dollars of relief between 1996 and 2000 (3 per cent of the total).[32] Despite trying to sound conciliatory, the World Bank, the IMF, and the WTO all dug in their heels, dismaying prominent World Bank and other reformers. Much of the focus of protests was on the abuse of power by TNCs (many of whom were named by well-informed campaigning groups).

New and more ominous elements were to emerge in 2001. In June a large protest took place in Gothenburg and a protester died. And in July during even larger demonstrations during the G8 summit in Genoa a protester, Carlo Giuliano, was killed by a military conscript (he was then run over by a police vehicle as he lay dying, the driver pleading panic). Later that night, hundreds were beaten as they slept in a school in the city that was being used by the Genoa Social Forum, a peaceful group well known to the authorities. Some protesters were later tortured by police and militia units. Disturbing and incontrovertible evidence quickly came to light that the authorities had ignored self-styled anarchist groups with public policies of violence who had already demonstrated violently. Instead, they attacked peaceful protesters. This appeared to be a deliberate tactic of terrorizing innocent people in order to scare off protestors in the future. The political opportunity for this tactic to succeed, of course, was the original pre-publicized violence of a tiny minority of the protestors. This permitted leaders such as Tony Blair to continue to condemn the entire anti-globalization movement as violent and irrelevant and to remain silent about the state-sponsored violence that had occurred in Genoa (and elsewhere).[33]

The catalogue of protest from Seattle to Genoa (and beyond, without any doubt) is difficult to fit into a neat analytical framework. It is clearly a real movement against globalization. The work of Starr illuminates both the variety of anti-corporate and anti-globalization movements, and the most potent themes that inspire them and could focus their opposition to appropriate targets. What appears to be happening is that these movements and protests are becoming more and more clearly focused on the four fractions of the transnational capitalist class. The movement against major corporations is clear for all to see. As has been documented at various points in this book, and as is frequently reported even in mainstream mass media, the practices of companies like Exxon, McDonald's, Nike, The Gap, BP, Shell, Nestlé, Monsanto, Philip Morris, BAT, Mitsubishi, and many others are closely monitored all over the world and their wrongdoings exposed. Globalizing bureaucrats like those who run the WTO, World Bank, IMF, OECD, and so on are clearly targets, as are the globalizing politicians who lead the governments of G7 and other countries. Globalizing professionals are more difficult to identify, though the neo-liberal think tanks and some scientists who provide them with reassuring evidence on the safety of GM crops and evidence against the existence of global warming certainly qualify. So do the legions of professional lobbyists, consultants, and PR people who are often the mouthpieces of TNCs, states, and inter-state bodies. Finally, and significantly, the movement has focused specifically on consumerist elites (merchants and media) in many sites of resistance, targeting many global brand names, despised symbols of capitalist globalization, and places where they are sold.

Those sympathetic to global capitalism and respectful of their governments and inter-state institutions will quite properly observe that this is a one-sided picture of Seattle and after. For these people, and there are very many of them, the most important single fact about anti-globalization protests is their violence against global leaders, those whose duty it is to maintain law and order, and their destruction of public and private property. The violence gives the transnational capitalist class and those who speak for them the perfect excuse for marginalizing, sometimes avoiding entirely, most of the issues that the anti-globalization movement is raising. Corporate executives, globalizing bureaucrats, politicians, professionals, and consumer elites are all appalled by acts of violence and random destruction that they can attribute to protesters, but have been notably silent about similar corporate and state-sponsored acts, precisely the type of hypocritical behaviour that many of the protesters are campaigning against.

What the twentieth century taught us is that revolutionary social change brought about principally by violent means is unlikely to produce democratic outcomes, although some violent overthrows of dictatorships have brought improvements to the lives of ordinary people. Nevertheless, non-violence is the only long-term strategy for the construction of any viable alternatives to capitalist globalization.[34]

THE NONVIOLENT ALTERNATIVE TO CAPITALIST GLOBALIZATION

'In the twentieth century, nonviolence became more of a deliberate tool for social change, moving from being largely an ad hoc strategy growing naturally out of religious or ethical principles to a reflective, and in many ways institutionalized, method of struggle' (Zunes *et al.* 1999: 1).[35] These tactics include strikes, boycotts, mass demonstrations, popular contestations of public space, tax refusal, destruction of symbols of government authority (like official identification cards), and, more positively, creations of alternative institutions. The power of non-violent social movements is based on non-cooperation with the authorities, to undermine their legitimacy.

There is a good deal of research and opinion poll evidence that shows a declining level of support in societies with democratic institutions for the aims of protesters who are identified with violent tactics, and an increasing level of support for those who are not (della Porta and Diani 1999: 182; see also Tarrow 1998: 95–6). Therefore, it is obviously to the advantage of the targets of movements and protests to label protestors as violent. And just as obviously, it is to the advantage of movements and protestors who wish to win mass support to avoid violence. In two cases related to the movement against capitalist globalization that have been discussed above, opposition to the Enron project in India in the 1990s and the protest against the G8 summit in Genoa in 2001, the issue of violence loomed large. In both cases there is at least prima facie evidence of the use of provocation and intimidation by the authorities, and this is a very alarming prospect for parliamentary democracies. The case for non-violence in the movement and protests against capitalist globalization is overwhelming.

Organized non-violence was a twentieth-century innovation. Boulding describes how this was largely due to Gandhi, who was responsible for the transition from informal and unorganized to formal and organized non-violence as a political strategy. One development of this is defensive defence, i.e. disarming behaviour without threat to the threatener (in Zunes *et al.* 1999: ch. 1). In a textbook from the 1970s, Gene Sharp identified three tactical categories: non-violent protest and persuasion (petitioning, picketing, demonstrating, and lobbying); non-violent non-cooperation (boycotts, strikes, tax resistance); and non-violent intervention (physical obstruction, blockades, civil disobedience, sit-ins). In all, Sharp lists 198 tactics.[36]

History is replete with convincing and inspiring examples of the successes, usually under-reported, of non-violent social movements. Perhaps the most publicized case in which a non-violent movement defeated an authoritarian leader and paved the way for the transfer of state power was the people's movement in the Philippines in 1986 (Zunes *et al.* 1999: ch. 7). What the media dubbed '77 hours that toppled Marcos' have been analysed by many, but Zunes demonstrates that the decades of non-violent education and movement-building that made it possible have been largely ignored. He utilizes the framework of Lakey to analyse five theoretical stages of non-violent revolution. The categories would be similar everywhere, but the details of course differ from place to place. The first stage is cultural preparation (in the Philippines this involved the Catholic Church and various left-wing and student organizations). Second, organization-building (this must be accomplished across sectors, and deep into the grassroots, 'vast networks of decentralized popular organization'). Third is the propaganda of the deed (massive public demonstrations, people's strikes that were organized by 500 and more grassroots organizations claiming 1.5 million members and crossing class and ethnic lines). The fourth stage is massive non-cooperation that makes it difficult for the authorities to govern (for example, disrupting government-controlled banking services, and delaying payment for public-utility charges). Last, and decisive if a real revolution is to occur, is the establishment of parallel institutions (what Gramsci called counter-hegemony). In the Philippines, a network of rural co-operatives, alternative educational institutions, and an alternative election commission partly fulfilled this role.

The spark that ignited this organizational and ideological tinder was the assassination of the popular reformer, Benigno Aquino, by agents of the state. This brought middle-class non-violent opponents of the regime into the struggle in greater numbers. However, Zunes argues, 'it is highly unlikely that most of them [opponents of Marcos] considered themselves pacifist in orientation. It appears, then, that most of the non-violent activists favored nonviolence on largely pragmatic grounds' (p. 139). The Tagalog expression for non-violence is *alaydangal*, meaning to offer dignity, contrasting Ghandian active non-violence to Christian passive non-violence, turning the other cheek. All commentators are agreed that the very high level of non-violent discipline meant that the US government and military, up until then largely uncritical backers of the regime, found it impossible to support Marcos in the face of popular opposition. The courage of the people on the streets and their level of non-violent organization were the key factors.[37]

Zunes asks: why did this strategy succeed in the Philippines while it failed or was not even attempted elsewhere? He cites the importance of a relatively free press and freedom of movement, nominally democratic institutions, and the power of the Church. All these (plus, of course, the unwillingness of the US government even under the hawkish Reagan administration, to intervene) made continued repression unworkable. This reasoning, which is not wholly convincing, does highlight one factor of particular relevance for the study of capitalist globalization and the struggle against it, namely that free markets and neo-liberal political doctrine do entail a minimal level of state intervention, in theory if not always in practice. This is historically associated with the processes of democratization and redemocratization that have occurred all over the Third World and postcommunist Europe while capitalist globalization has been gathering pace there. Parliamentary democracies, for all their failings, tend to be less violent than authoritarian states. Though armed intervention in the affairs of sovereign states still goes on, it is not these cases but that of the Philippines that will most likely provide the model for the future of intervention. Non-violence, therefore, gives social movements much more prospect of spreading their message and achieving their ends without repressive outside intervention.

The movement against capitalist globalization appears to present a dilemma for this analysis, as intervention is hardly likely to come from outside the planet. However, this dilemma is more apparent than real. The movement is global, but its activities are always local, always in one or more sites of resistance. Certainly many members of the state militia in Seattle and Genoa were from outside the city (as were many of the demonstrators). It is a commonplace that civil disturbances are best repressed by forces from outside the locality. Determined active non-violence will always be an effective challenge to parliamentary democracies because most politicians want to be re-elected and we must assume that they would want to avoid excessive state violence against ordinary people protesting peaceably on their streets. As long as the movement against capitalist globalization can be convincingly characterized as violent and chaotic, the authorities need not worry very much about their repressive violence.

The membership of the anti-globalization movement is at present split between small violent minorities (some of whom correctly see violence as an attention-getting tactic, some of whom indulge in violence for cathartic reaons as well) and a huge non-violent majority. As with most large gatherings, there are usually hangers-on whose presence at demonstrations has little to do with the movement.[38] At all the major protests, groups specializing in non-violence have attempted to teach their tactics and inculcate their ideology as far and as wide as possible. In Seattle and Prague they achieved a good measure of success.

Slowly, labour, environmental, and other movements are being drawn into the non-violent fold.[39] An inspiring example is the tens of thousands of Nicaraguans, both former Contras and Sandinistas, who protested against austerity measures in the spring of 1997. Just as militarism and corporate capitalism have become global, so must non-violent movements. The future success of the movement against capitalist globalization and the viability of an alternative to it ultimately depend on the victory of non-violence as a universal principle. The growing influence of the globalization of human rights in movements against global capitalism is a positive contribution to these ends. In the next chapter I explore how non-violence and human rights can provide the underpinning for a powerful, perhaps an irresistible alternative to capitalist globalization.

NOTES

1. The global movement for nuclear disarmament (and the associated movement against nuclear power) began in the 1950s, but subsequently fed into a more general peace movement (Mattausch, in Cohen and Rai 2000: ch. 12).

2. The literature on protectionism is enormous. A useful study that airs the key First–Third World issues is Yoffie (1983). See also, Aaronson (2001) on 'America First'.

3. The literature on social movements grew rapidly in the 1990s; della Porta and Diani (1999) is a good survey that tries to connect research from Europe and the USA; Hamel et al. eds. (2000) includes work from the influential Social Movements Research Group of the International Sociological Association; see also della Porta et al. (1999). For the transnationalization of social movements, see Smith et al. (1997), Tarrow (1998), and Cohen and Rai (2000). Zunes et al. (1999) is an important study of non-violent social movements and I return to this at the end of the chapter.

4. As Starr (2000) observes, many apparently identity-based NSM are in fact class-based (see Calhoun 1994). While social movement theorists generally restrict their attention to underdog movements, Boies and Pichardo (1993–4) develop a theory of elite social movement organizations and I have generalized this (sadly, without much approval from social movement scholars) into a theory on social movements for global capitalism (Sklair 1998, 2001 passim).

5. There are, of course, many important differences between different Green movements and associated ad hoc groups. See Redclift and Woodgate (1995), Yearley (1996), Peet and Watts (1996), Dobson (1998).

6. The inversion is nicely illustrated by Editors of Fortune (1972), a critique of the consumer movement on behalf of the prime ideologues of consumerism. See also Sinclair (1987: 65). Ewen (1988: ch. 10) notes the same inversion for environmentalism.

7. Few workforces can any longer decisively 'hold capital to ransom' by withdrawing their labour. Tarrow, however, argues that when in early 1997 Renault announced the closure of a plant in Belgium, the Eurostrike was born (Tarrow 1998: 176).

8. I say in the long run. In the short term, authoritarian regimes can ignore demands for democratization and push forward consumerist market reforms. It is by no means obvious that everyone in the world prefers democracy to economic prosperity, if that is the choice they are persuaded to accept.

9. It has to be noted, however, that many important social movements advocating democracy often lack much democracy in their own organizations. Fennema and Tillie have a point when they argue with respect to political participation in Amsterdam: 'To have undemocratic ethnic organisations is better for the democratic process than to have no organisations at all' (1999: 723, italics in original).

10. Reisner (2001) shows the potential for such mobilization against genetic engineering.

11. The growing transnational network of the Association for Taxation of Financial Transaction to Aid Citizens (ATTAC) promises to make this issue more visible than it is at present. I am grateful to Susan George for information about its work.

12. It had previously run a powerful cover story arguing that: 'The [anti-globalization] protestors have tapped into growing fears that U.S. policies benefit big companies instead of average citizens—of America or any other country' (Bernstein 2000: 50). *Fortune*, *The Economist*, and others also joined in.

13. Higgot and Phillips (2000) make a strong argument that these splits have long-term significance for the future of capitalist globalization. We shall see!

14. Risse *et al.* (1999) show how what they call 'international human rights norms' can promote domestic change.

15. Jones (1998: 293) makes the unusual argument that this is less of a threat to indigeous cultures than either Fordism or state socialism. 'The threat globalization poses to indigenous cultures is thus overrated—in fact it seems (in retrospect) that the modernist obsession with developing the Third World reached its peak in the 1970s and has been receding ever since (except in a relative handful of NICs).' This, he suggests, opens the way for recombinant local cultures as hybrids upon which consumer capitalism can be overlaid. The research of McGuckin (1997) on the Tibetan refugee carpet industry is a challenging test of this thesis.

16. The 'war against terrorism' declared by the US and UK governments after 11 September 2001 clearly introduced important and unpredictable new factors into the practice of the rule of law globally.

17. For some relevant case studies in Latin America, see Petras and Harding (2000).

18. One example indicates the tone: 'Monsanto should not have to vouchsafe the safety of biotech food. Our interest is in selling as much of it as possible. Assuring its safety is the FDA's [US Federal Food and Drug Agency] job' (Director of Corporate Communications, quoted in Starr 2000: 9). See also, Lappe and Bailey (1999), Sklair (2001: esp. 224–7).

19. Enthusiasm is infectious, but for a sobering assessment of thirty comprehensive community plans for sustainable development in the USA, see Berke and Conroy (2000).

20. Raynolds (2000) shows how major food TNCs (Dole for example) are already moving into organic production and ethical trading. Barrientos (2000) calls ethical trade a 'paradox of globalization'.

21. Starr, of course, is not the only writer who finds this difficult. Held *et al.* (1999: table C.1) in their apparently more sophisticated model of three political projects for globalization—liberal-internationalism, radical republicanism, and cosmopolitan democracy (their preference)—list many factors but fare no better. For my own preference (socialist globalization of human rights) see the next chapter.

22. For a sharp critique of WTO neglect of human rights and how it can be reformed (less convincing) see Petersmann (2000).

23. Compare the OECD and Global Trade Watch websites, Balanya *et al.* (2000: ch. 12), Smythe (in Higgott *et al.* 2000: ch. 4), and Wood (2000). My own interpretation of the movements for and against MAI derives from interviews and information-gathering in Washington DC in 1998 and in London since 1997.

24. I am grateful to the BIAC office in Paris, and to officials in the relevant US and UK organizations for information. The trade union movement is also officially represented in the parallel Trade Union Advisory Committee, but this was much less influential.

25. In November 1997, for the first time in sixty years the US Congress threw out an expansion of free trade bill (to fast track NAFTA provisions). This clearly indicated growing disquiet about free trade.

26. This borrowed the title of the popular anti-corporate book by David Korten, *When Corporations Rule the World* (1995). Korten was a member of the influential International Forum on Globalization that helped to orchestrate the campaign against the MAI (and subsequent events in Seattle and after).

27. This interpretation is supported by a rather defensive letter from Timothy Deal, senior VP of the USCIB (*Washington Times*, 26 Dec. 1997), in response to a front-page article in *The Times* that had discussed the case against the MAI. Mr Deal ended his letter with a plea to take the debate 'out of the feverish atmosphere of Internet chat rooms'! His worries were justified: the 'Annotated list of worldwide MAI Websites' on the Corporate Watch website in mid-1998 ran to ten pages.

28. Including official negotiations on Customs Modernization, Bribery and Corruption, EMU, WTO Telecommunications Agreement, and Climate Change (see USCIB 1996–7 Annual Report, Table on 'Meeting Business Needs: Examples of USCIB's Global Network at Work').

29. For the influence of Philip Morris and RJR in the MAI campaign, see INFACT (1998).

30. There is a particularly rich variety of websites on the topic (notably **indymedia.org**). While the mass media focus is usually on one place at a time, the protests are often in many places simultaneously. However, as Fox and Brown (1998: 30) argue in their collection on NGOs and the World Bank, many networks are 'fragile fax-and-cyberspace skeletons'. See also Smith (2001*b*), Smith (2001*a*), and Langman *et al.* (2002), and the special issue of *Monthly Review* (July/Aug. 2000).

31. This had already happened in other cities, see Klein (2000: ch. 13) on the 'Reclaim the Streets' movement in London in the 1990s. See also Hamel *et al.* (2000) on urban social movements.

32. The Jubilee 2000 Campaign had campaigned in over forty countries since 1996 for debt forgiveness. See also Dent and Peters (1999).

33. The Italian government carried out a rapid inquiry into these events. Predictably, this found no evidence of official wrongdoing.

34. The suicidal destruction in New York and Washington in September 2001 and the military campaign that followed only deepens my conviction that this is true, though I have no easy solutions.

35. Zunes *et al.* appears to me to be the best recent collection on the subject, combining theoretical reflections with case studies from the Middle East, Europe, Asia, Africa, Latin and North America.

36. As reported by McAllister (in Zunes *et al.* 1999: 22–3). McAllister highlights the centrality of women in the history of non-violence but their relative invisibility in textbooks about it.

37. The presence of brave foreign NGO personnel has provided some degree of safety for local activists in many other non-violent struggles, for example with the Zapatistas in Chiapas (Nash 2001: ch. 4), Peace Brigades International in Sri Lanka (Coy, in Smith *et al.* 1997: ch. 5), and SERPAJ in Latin America (Pagnucco in ibid.: ch. 7).

38. See Smith (2001*a*) and a multitude of evidence from websites, notably **www.indymedia.com**.

39. The thesis of Bayat (2000) that global restructuring is transforming the urban poor in the South from dangerous classes into quiet rebels deserves more empirical research.

Chapter 11

FROM CAPITALIST TO SOCIALIST GLOBALIZATION THROUGH THE TRANSFORMATION OF HUMAN RIGHTS

Capitalist globalization is failing on two counts, fundamental to the future of most of the people in the world and, indeed, to the future of our planet itself. It cannot resolve either the class polarization crisis or the crisis of ecological unsustainability and may well be intensifying both. However, globalization should not be identified with capitalist globalization, though capitalist globalization is its dominant form in the present era. This makes it necessary to think through other forms of globalization, forms that might retain some of the positive consequences of capitalism (in so far as they can exist outside capitalism) while transcending it as a socio-economic system in the transition to a new stage of world history. The two crises of capitalist globalization cannot be resolved within capitalism.

Here I shall explore one path out of capitalism through the connections between capitalist globalization (where we are), what can be termed cooperative democracy (a transitional form of society), socialist globalization (where we should be heading), and what can be termed the culture-ideology of universal human rights. Such a transformation could be achieved by the gradual elimination of the culture-ideology of consumerism and its replacement with a culture-ideology of human rights. This means, briefly, that instead of our possessions being the main focus of our cultures and the basis of our values, our lives should be lived with regard to a universally agreed system of human rights and the responsibilities to others that these rights entail. This does not imply that we should stop consuming. What it implies is that we should evaluate our consumption in terms of our rights and responsibilities.[1]

The main thrust of this argument is that by genuinely expanding the culture-ideology of human rights from the civil and political spheres, in which capitalist globalization has often had a relatively positive influence, to the economic and social spheres, which represents a profound challenge to capitalist globalization, we can begin seriously to tackle the crises of class polarization and ecological unsustainability. But political realism dictates that this change cannot be accomplished directly; it must proceed via a series of transititional stages. Capitalism and socialism, as we have seen in the case of China, are not watertight categories. Capitalist practices can and do occur in socialist societies (for example, making workers redundant to increase profits) just as socialist practices can exist in capitalist societies (for example, ensuring that everyone in a community enjoys a basic decent standard of living). The issue is hegemony, whose interests prevail, who defends the status quo (even by reforming it), and who is pushing for fundamental change. And, of course, other people may have other names for what I call 'socialism'.

These are historically specific questions and realistic attempts to answer them must begin from the actually existing conditions of societies. We can distinguish three general types of societies: first, relatively rich parliamentary democracies (however flawed they may be), second, relatively poor authoritarian states, and third, poor weak states. The first group consists of the countries of the First World plus some of the NICs of Asia and Latin America. The second group consists of the remaining communist and non-democratic strong states. The third group consists of the rest of the world (many small, poor countries). It is pointless to speak of any type of genuine socialism without first having a certain level of economic development, whether this is achieved through colonialism, small-scale indigenous capitalism, the dependent development of capitalist globalization, capitalist globalization itself, or even some distorted form of socialism or communism.[2]

Communities in the First World and the NICs are theoretically in a position in terms of resources, potential for social mobilization, and openness of their political systems to begin the transition from capitalist globalization to a transitional stage in which the market is controlled by democratically elected authorities for the benefit of the community as a whole. Of the second group, China has already achieved a form of market socialism though, as we have seen, the combination of market socialism and capitalist globalization in China has led to an intensification of the crises of class polarization and ecological unsustainability. For the third group, the weakness of states and poverty of societies mean that it is difficult to plan but, paradoxically, it may be easier for some communities to innovate to solve communal problems in appropriate ways. However, it is unlikely that many of these poor weak countries will be able to develop economically to any satisfactory degree unless, paradoxically, capitalist globalization can be made to work properly or can be successfully challenged. The challenges I have in mind are, for example, ensuring that fair prices are paid to the direct producers of food and industrial crops, and ensuring that foreign investments benefit the less well off rather than, as at present, the already better off in poor countries. Under the conditions of capitalist globalization it is extremely unlikely that communities in the rest of the world could achieve these transformations without support from powerful groups in the First World, for example radical elected governments.

ALTERNATIVES TO CAPITALIST GLOBALIZATION

The main popular alternative to capitalist globalization is a variety of forms of co-operative democracy that are alive and well all over the world but mostly in small scale enclaves (Birchall 1997, Shuman 1998, Mies and Bennholdt Thomsen 1999, Hines 2000). Co-operative socialism has a long history though I am not aware of any attempt to connect it systematically with globalization. The agenda for self-reliance and localization, discussed in the previous chapter, loses what is most valuable about capitalist globalization, its sociocultural cosmopolitanism and its potential (usually unrealized) for sustainable economies of scale.

Thinking about how co-operative democracy could be extended globally has been stimulated by theory and research on market socialism. Schweickart (in Ollman 1998)[3] elaborates three central pillars of market socialism as follows:

(i) Market socialism eliminates or greatly restricts private ownership of the means of production and substitutes state or worker ownership. Here we must be careful to distinguish between nationalization of utilities or manufacturing industries on the British or French model, and socialization, on the model of producer–consumer co-operatives for goods and services (hereafter P-CCs). As many commentators point out, one of the main reasons why the Chinese experiment with market socialism has been successful in terms of economic growth is that the government de-nationalized large numbers of state enterprises and devolved ownership and/or control to their managers, workers, and other interested parties. While the Chinese model may not have many positive lessons for the First World (and, of course, it started from conditions of extreme poverty), the negative lesson that very large-scale state enterprises are usually very inefficient in authoritarian societies is valuable.

(ii) Market socialism retains but restricts the power of the market. Naturally, market socialism would be absurd without the market, but the idea of 'restricting the power of the market' is not entirely clear. There are two obvious meanings. First, the power of the market can be restricted by legislating that some sectors of the economy are off-limits for private ownership, as was the case until recently for public utilities (for example, water, gas and electricity, telephones, and railways) in most countries. These were usually state monopolies, though they were often run like private companies and were often very unpopular with consumers. (The so-called private-public initiative of the New Labour government in Britain was an innovative attempt to ensure that the public pays the costs and private capitalists retain the profits in such ventures.) Second, market power can be restricted by governments controlling the prices of some goods and services provided by private companies (again, attempted at various times by governments all over the world). Experience shows that neither of these forms of restricting the power of the market works well because they tend to lead to rent-seeking and/or corruption. What I have in mind is restricting the power of the market on the basis of enterprise size (see below).

(iii) In some forms, market socialism may replace wage labour with workplace democracy, leading eventually to worker self-management as the mode of organization of whole societies. There is a wealth of experience, some successful, some less successful, that already exists all over the world in workers' control and self-management. Bayat (1991) usefully distinguishes state-led, union-led, and autonomous forms of workers' participation in the control of the workplace and connects these to the roads to various types of socialism. Research suggests that producer co-operatives are almost always as efficient as joint-stock capitalist enterprises. The most widely studied case is that of the Mondragon network of co-operatives in Spain but there are many more (see Shuman 1998, Mies and Bennholdt-Thomsen 1999: ch. 4).[4] They are also superior to TNCs in eliminating inequalities, they are more democratic, and they challenge the hypermobility of capital. Markets need not be identified with capitalism in the sense that though capitalism is impossible without the market, markets can exist without the capitalist mode of production or capitalists. As Schweickart pointedly argues: capitalists are 'functionally obsolete. Capitalists are no longer needed to raise capital, manage industries, or create new products or technologies. There are other, better ways, of performing these functions' (in Ollman 1998: 20). This argument, common amongst market socialism theorists mirrors the argument that while capitalism needs to globalize, globalization need not be capitalist.

There is certainly no reliable blueprint for bringing about market socialism or making it succeed on any scale (as there is none for capitalism). To distinguish it from capitalism, however, the absolute minimum condition is that private ownership of the means of production, distribution, and exchange is restricted to small-scale enterprises, in order to prevent the emergence of a transnational capitalist class and its local affiliates. There are two further reasons why private ownership must be restricted to small-scale enterprises. First, only in this way can there be any realistic prospect of diminishing and eventually eliminating the culture-ideology of consumerism and replacing it with a culture-ideology more conducive to human rights and responsibilities. What drives capitalist globalization is the constant need for corporations to accumulate capital for their owners and to get bigger and more profitable all the time. The damage their growth might inflict on the people who work in them, the communities in which they operate, and the planet as a whole (intensifying the crisis of ecological unsustainability) is not irrelevant, but it is certainly not their top priority. Second, major TNCs tend to create class polarization (through the race to the bottom) while smaller interrelated communities of co-operatives may or may not reduce polarization. The test comes when the best endowed of these communities combine to create genuine economic efficiencies. But this would not, in my view, really be a form of market socialism at all. The transitional stage between capitalist and socialist globalization, where private ownership and control are restricted to small enterprises, and where larger enterprises are genuinely socialized, can be termed co-operative democracy.[5] In principle, there is no reason to doubt that majorities in democratic political systems could vote for parties that promise radical redistribution, sharing, and the type of restrictions on the power of the market discussed above. This is even likely if progressive politicians and the gatekeepers of the mass media start to realize the connections between capitalist globalization and its most undesirable consequences: the crises of class polarization and ecological unsustainability.[6] As I argued in the previous chapter, this is what the movement against capitalist globalization has forced onto the mainstream agenda. But what lies beyond co-operative democracy, even if the tiny shoots that already exist should grow?

SEEDS OF SOCIALIST GLOBALIZATION

Socialist globalization is a system of transnational practices in the economic, political, and culture-ideology spheres. In a society organized on the principles of socialist globalization, the characteristic institutional form for economic transnational practices would be producer-consumer co-operatives (P-CCs) of various types, not cartel-seeking conglomerate transnational corporations. Just as major TNCs have many shareholders and some of them will have interests in several TNCs, so socialist globalization will encourage some people to be involved in several P-CCs. This is similar in practice to the stakeholder concept that is so influential in contemporary discussions of corporate citizenship (see Warhurst 2001). Where this is taken seriously (it rarely is) it could create something like a socialist practice in capitalist societies.

There are many examples of tiny seeds of socialist globalization struggling to flower in capitalist societies. One such experiment that has attracted the attention of scholars and activists alike is the popular participation introduced by the Brazilian Workers' Party (PT) that mobilized more than 50,000 households to take part in decision-making on the budget in the city of Porto Alegre.[7] Despite all the predictable difficulties of time, energy, skills, and motivation, Porto Alegre proved that some measure of genuine democracy can be won by individuals, groups, and elected authorities who have the political will to develop the administrative expertise. The experience of one woman speaks volumes:

After starting to participate in the forum of cooperatives, I started to become involved with the community leaders and wound up being elected as the Delegate of the Participatory Budget. At first, I did not understand much but with time I started to get it. I got a group together from our cooperative to come at a regular basis. I then was elected to the Council. There it was that I really learned what is a movement, what a community leader does. It was an incredible learning experience becoming a community leader. (quoted in Baiocchi 2001: 58)

While this has not destroyed capitalism in Brazil and the movement may have its weaknesses, it has demonstrated that such expansions of what Fung and Wright (2001) call 'empowered participatory governance' are possible.[8]

Many other small-scale communities organized along co-operative democratic lines already exist (Shuman 1998, Hines 2000). The Women's Support Network of the Self Employed Women's Association (SEWA) in India (Rose, in Visvanathan *et al.* 1997: 383) is a very fine example (see Figure 11.1). While this may appear to have little relevance for more prosperous communities in the First World, a good deal of sociological research indicates a connection between small business, civic engagement, and well-being wherever it occurs. Tolbert *et al.* (1998), for example, cite findings reported to the US Senate Small Business Committee in the 1940s showing that cities characterized by small business enjoyed higher levels of well-being than big business cities. This and subsequent research, they argue, represents a challenge to the promise of global capitalism. The importance of civic engagement goes back to de Tocqueville and the early Chicago School, and more recent arguments about third places between the home and the workplace (though in many communities today this third place is likely to be the shopping mall). Socio-economic well-being was measured by income, inequality and poverty rates, and unemployment; civil society was measured by third places, the presence of small manufacturers, family farms, associations, and religious denominations. On a data set of more than 3,000 counties in the USA, a significant connection was found between well-being and civil society, consistent with the explanation that local businesses and associations are much more likely to be embedded in the community than large transnational corporations. This finding will ring true to many people around the world whose communities have been destroyed by the presence or relocation of TNCs. Socialist globalization means that people's economic and social rights (to a decent level of socio-economic well-being) are part of their civil and political rights, and vice versa.[9] The local capitalism that Tolbert *et al.* commend has more in common with producer-consumer co-operatives than the global capitalism of the major TNCs, but both require the support of wider societal authorities.[10]

In China, a nominally communist society, the case of rural women's co-operatives supports this view. Chen (1999) studied the first women's credit co-operatives and their

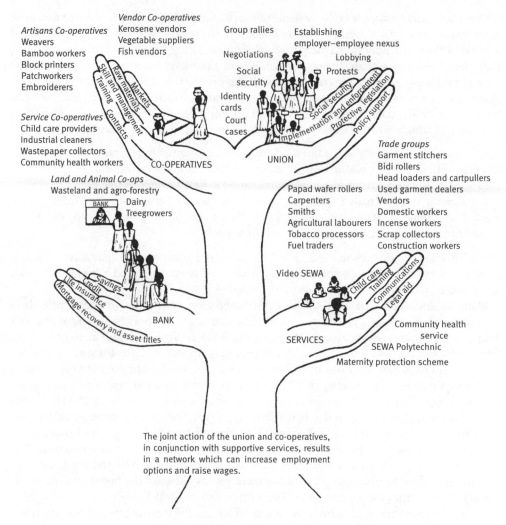

Figure 11.1 The SEWA Tree: A Women's Support Network
Note: for more information see the SEWA International website.
Source: Kalina Rose, in Visvanathan (1997: 383) © 1997 Zed Books (London) and Kalina Rose.

support organization, the International Committee for the Promotion of Chinese Industrial Co-operatives. Chinese women joined co-operatives to help solve problems of access to resources, notably land, credit, jobs, training, and information. Chen shows that equitable relations between the local co-operatives, the International Committee, and the All-China Women's Federation (the party organization) were crucial to the success of these co-operatives, particularly for the issue of banks that would lend to women. However, in the absence of a national legal framework, the future of the co-ops is not assured. Where there is a strong state, it is necessary to formalize and coordinate local economic initiatives, but the local state can act if its leaders have the political will (as in Porto Alegre and Brasilia).

The characteristic institutional form of political transnational practices for socialist globalization would be self-governing communities of P-CCs who enter into larger political and/or economic units on the basis of genuine democratic decision-making, not the transnational capitalist class focused on organizing the global system for private profits. And in the culture-ideology sphere, the characteristic culture-ideology transnational practices of socialist globalization would provide spaces for a wide variety of cultural and ideological practices and values that positively encourage universal human rights and ecological sustainability, not a culture-ideology that subordinates almost every practice and value to consumerism.

The comparison between capitalist and socialist globalization, therefore, is stark. Whereas transnational corporations are undemocratic, unrepresentative entities whose prime purpose is to make profits for those who own and control them globally without due regard for the welfare of the communities affected by their behaviour, P-CCs will be organized to improve the welfare of their own communities of origin and communities they are making alliances with. Under capitalist globalization, millions of people (and hundreds of TNCs) seem prepared to share a part of their wealth with the under-privileged and less fortunate at home and abroad (corporate philanthopy). Therefore, it is not entirely unrealistic to assume that these philanthropic and altruistic practices could be organized more efficiently and even spread more widely in the social climate that socialist globalization would encourage. There is no reason why transnational P-CCs organized along socialist lines could not operate for the benefit of producers, consumers, and the environment.

Whereas the transnational capitalist class operates to further its sectarian economic interests through political influence, self-governing communities and their larger political units are more likely to manage better the balance between individual interests (for example the special interests of individuals and families at different stages in the life cycle), community interests (in terms of different resource endowments), and the interests of larger collectivities. Whereas the culture-ideology of consumerism encourages consumption with little regard for the resources or the carrying capacity of the planet, a culture-ideology of human rights[11] would encourage genuine efforts to meet the basic needs of everyone in the world and start to give a realistic framework for people with different histories, capacities, preferences, and beliefs to have pleasurable and satisfying lives.

This alternative to capitalist globalization, of course, sounds very utopian.[12] Many would agree with its desirability but most would question its practicality. This forces us to look at our own societies and to identify those practices and values on which these changes can be built. As argued above, we must start from where we are and where the present writer is at present is in one of the relatively rich countries of the First World. Typically, this is a society where most people enjoy the fruits of the culture-ideology of consumerism but also appear to be worried about various aspects of the ecological crisis, where the general level of prosperity is high but where there are constant reminders of the class polarization crisis. How could such a society begin the movement from capitalist to socialist globalization, and why would its members want to do this? In the previous chapter evidence on anti-capitalist and anti-globalization movements and networks suggested that there is clearly a great deal of dissatisfaction about the way we live (revolving around the emotional and spiritual crises of the rich, and the material and educational deprivation of the poor). While they propose alternatives to capitalist globalization, most of these movements tend to focus either on issues of class or regional polarization (First World against Third World) or on ecological unsustainability (Green movement), rarely connecting both crises. This is why many consider that there is no adequate focal point for these movements and networks. This is precisely the reason why it is necessary to introduce the discourse and organization of universal human rights.

The globalization of human rights is the logical and substantive link between co-operative democracy and socialist globalization. If we can demonstrate that the achievement of universal human rights is not possible under the conditions of capitalist globalization (capitalism can only justify itself in the long run by its alleged superiority in providing better lives for all) then it follows that some other form of globalization will be required if universal human rights are to be realized for all peoples. However, as Pateman (1996: 10) reminds us, this could raise the paradox that on the one hand a global language of democracy is being created, and on the other 'the idea of universal human rights is under theoretical attack by the proponents of the local, the particular, and social and cultural differences'. Democratic systems have been used to persecute minorities. Only if P-CCs could avoid such outcomes would they stand any hope of persuading most people that this is an alternative to capitalist globalization. Socialist globalization, under these circumstances, could provide a convincing framework for overcoming the crises of class polarization and ecological unsustainability. Doing nothing will not be a viable option in the long run.

Substantively, taking the globalization of human rights seriously means eliminating the radical distinction that exists between civil and political rights on the one hand, and economic and social rights on the other. Doing this systematically undermines the three central claims of capitalist globalization: namely that globalizing corporations are the most efficient form of production, distribution, and exchange; that the transnational capitalist class organizes communities and the global order in the best interests of everyone; and that the culture-ideology of consumerism will satisfy our real needs. In order to demonstrate the theoretical superiority of socialist over capitalist globalization it is, therefore, necessary to analyse in some detail the discourse and organization of universal human rights, a system that emerged in parallel with capitalist globalization itself in the second half of the twentieth century.

THE GLOBALIZATION OF HUMAN RIGHTS

In their comprehensive survey of human rights, Steiner and Alston (2000: 2) write: 'Over a mere half century, the human rights movement that grew out of the Second World War has become an indelible part of our legal, political and moral landscape.' This is no doubt true for those who write and read such books, but certainly not for everyone everywhere (as the book so fully describes). Neither is it irreversible for those who enjoy protection of their rights for most or all of the time.

Scholars and activists generally distinguish between two categories of rights.[13] The first is *civil and political rights*, like freedom from torture, equal protection before the law, and the right to free speech and political association. The second category is *economic and social rights*, for example, rights to food, health care, education, and shelter. The legal basis of all these rights is the United Nations Charter, and associated regional agreements.[14] The Universal Declaration of Human Rights was proclaimed in 1948, followed by the International Covenant on Civil and Political Rights (hereafter ICC) and the International Covenant on Economic, Social and Cultural Rights (hereafter ICE) in 1976. Most states have signed these legal codes, though many have reserved their positions on one or more items. One further pillar in the UN system of human rights is the Convention on the Elimination of All Forms of Discrimination against Women (CEDAW). Pride of place belongs to the Universal Declaration of Human Rights, a document that still has its 'place of honor in the human rights movement. . . . It proceeded to work its subversive path through many rooted doctrines of international law, forever changing the discourse of international relations on issues vital to human decency and peace' (Steiner, quoted in Steiner and Alston 2000: 139).

The period immediately following 1945 was a watershed for the emerging human rights movement. Though the Nuremberg Trials were not the first occasion in history when the victors passed moral judgements on the vanquished, the enormity of Nazi crimes against humanity appeared to justify moral as well as legal penalties. It is not to deny other previous and subsequent holocausts to argue that the holocaust in Europe perpetrated by the Nazis made many people in all walks of life rethink the seductive appeal of cultural relativism (insightfully discussed in Clendinnen 1999). UN-sponsored Tribunals on former Yugoslavia and Rwanda further reinforced the idea of crimes against humanity as crimes for which the international community would not excuse the perpetrators. Such crimes became absolutized, they became acts which no exceptional circumstances would justify. But not entirely![15] The Pinochet case (Steiner and Alston 2000: 1198–216) opened up spaces for bringing those with ultimate responsibility for gross violations of human rights to the bar of international justice. The first conviction for genocide was handed down by the War Crimes Tribunal in The Hague in the summer of 2001—forty-six years in prison for the Bosnian Serb general Krstic. Truth commissions had been established in formerly authoritarian states in Latin America, Asia, Africa, and Europe (UNDP 2000a: table A3.1 lists fourteen). In particular, the Truth and Reconciliation Commission in South Africa started a long, incomplete, and painful process of bringing abusers and abused face to face to establish 'truth' and seek reconciliation (see Henderson 2000). It also condemned some acts against the oppressors.

Parallel with the UN Charter, the Universal Declaration of Human Rights, the ICC, and the ICE, a series of specific human rights treaties has emerged. The most important of these treaties are the 1951 Convention on Genocide (130 states signatory by 2000), the 1969 Convention on Racial Discrimination (155 states), the 1981 CEDAW, the 1987 Convention on Torture (118 states), and the 1990 Convention on Rights of the Child (191 states). Therefore, it can be argued that there are in place adequate numbers of legal instruments to protect human rights and that most states in the world have committed themselves to uphold them. Nevertheless, many states, including some of the richest, for example the USA and the UK, as well as some of the poorest, for example China and Myanmar (Burma), have at one time or another been investigated and/or named and shamed for human rights violations at the UN. Two mechanisms of the UN Commission on Human Rights provide such opportunities. Items under the 1503 procedure (examination of complaints) rose from 25,000 per annum in the mid-1980s to 300,000 in 1993 (much of this was organized letter-writing) and stabilized at around 50,000 in 2000.

Since 1972, seventy-five states have been investigated. However the process of investigation under 1503 is secret, leading Amnesty International and other human rights organizations to charge that it was as much an instrument for concealing as exposing violations (Steiner and Alston 2000: 618). The 1235 procedure gives governments and/or NGOs a public opportunity to name and shame violators at Commission meetings (eighteen such investigations were being conducted in 2000). Usually governments defend themselves vigorously (Iran, China, and others have done so). Why do they take the trouble? The answer suggests that for governments, even the most repressive, the human rights movement is significant all over the world, particularly when it draws in transnational economic practices like trade and investment.

With few exceptions all these UN Conventions and treaties establish positive rights for individuals and positive duties for states to protect these rights. However, and we could argue that this is actually the central feature of the system, all these Conventions and treaties have limitation clauses that qualify the rights of individuals and dilute the duties of states under exceptional circumstances like public emergencies. As a result, these Conventions and treaties have rarely been allowed to challenge the autonomy of governments to do exactly as they please. State sovereignty remains the general principle on which the inter-state system rests (Buzan and Little 2000: 337 ff., Halliday 1999: 12 ff.). Connected with this issue is the debate contrasting indivisibility (all human rights are equal in importance) with hierarchy (some rights are more important than others). Though there is a good deal of controversy, most writers and practitioners do accept that there is a hierarchy of rights, with civil and political rights at the top and economic and social rights some way behind or, in some theories, not proper rights at all. For example, since CEDAW was created in 1981 there has been much debate over women's rights. Some complain that women's rights are being prioritized unfairly above all others, while others argue that women's rights are ghettoized within CEDAW. More states have entered reservations to the ratification of CEDAW than to any other human rights treaty.[16]

Economic and Social Rights (herafter ESR)—usually defined as the duty of the state 'primarily to provide material resources to the rights-bearer, like housing or food or health care' (Steiner and Alston 2000: 183)—are at the centre of the argument between supporters and opponents of capitalist globalization. While capitalists, imbued with neo-liberal values and the culture-ideology of consumerism, tend to accept that civil and political rights (or, more rhetorically, freedoms from state interference) need to be protected to guarantee a minimum of social order, economic and social rights are more problematic for them. Neo-liberals argue that the sanctity of private property, paradoxically the core economic right, is the only basic human right essential to a market-driven society, while the provision of goods such as housing, food, education, and health care are not human rights at all, but commodities allocated like all other commodities by the market. This view is enshrined in the rhetoric of neo-liberalism in homilies of the type: 'no one owes you a living' (interestingly close to the Soviet principle of 's/he who does not work does not eat'), and 'there is no such thing as society' (individuals have to take responsibility for themselves and their families). Opponents (socialist or not) of capitalist globalization argue that everyone, irrespective of circumstances, has the right to a basic level of economic and social well-being (as enshrined in Articles 23 and 25 of the Universal Declaration of Human Rights).

The origins of the ESR system are to be found in the International Labour Organization, created in 1919 as an associate agency of the League of Nations to serve as a bulwark against the appeal of Bolshevism to workers all over the world. The ILO articulated the principles that people everywhere were entitled to a decent standard of living and that workers were entitled to some basic rights. From the 1940s on these principles gradually evolved into a vague and general right to development as decolonization loomed. The paternalistic impulse of this movement can be gleaned from the fact that what we now know as 'development' appears in Chapter IX (International Economic and Social Co-operation), Article 55(a) of the UN Charter, where the UN committed itself to promote higher standards of living, full employment, and conditions of economic and social progress and development for all the peoples of the world. Struggles over the establishment of a single human rights Covenant foundered on cultural differences of various types (related to gender, religion, ethnicity, etc.) so two separate conventions, the International Covenant on Economic, Social and Cultural Rights and the International Covenant on Civil and Political Rights (as noted above) resulted. This outcome sent the message to the international community that there were two categories of human rights. Entitlement to economic and social rights generally were seen as subject to available resources, and the obligations of states to achieve them was, thus, not absolute but something that might be accomplished sometime in the future.[17]

However, the issue of who, exactly, was responsible for ensuring that rights were established and protected was still blurred. Those in control of the political system in some countries, for example the USA, have tended to pay less attention to providing for economic and social rights, while those in other countries, for example China, have tended to pay less attention to civil and political rights. A central principle of socialist globalization is that neither of these sets of rights can be fully realized without the other. Having the right to vote in freely contested elections has a very different meaning for well-fed people compared with starving people, just as having a satisfying job that pays for a decent standard of living has a very different meaning for someone under threat of arbitrary arrest all the time compared with someone who can generally rely on the rule of law. The role of the state should be central to this analysis in the sense that states that actually do guarantee civil and political rights might be also expected to guarantee economic and social rights. But this has not always been the case and, under the neo-liberal disciplines of capitalist globalization, civil and political rights have gradually been disconnected from economic and social rights. This is the socio-legal aspect of class polarization under capitalist globalization. Steiner and Alston (2000: 300) express this rather diplomatically: 'Pressures to reduce the size of the public sector, to privatize various functions previously performed by governments, and to stimulate growth by reducing taxes, all render governments less able to accept responsibility for economic and social rights.'[18] Governments, of course, normally do have choices in these matters, but those under the disciplines of the World Bank, the WTO, and the TNCs for the most part choose not to prioritize economic and social rights.[19]

What the Indian Constitution of 1950 called 'directive principles of state policies' illustrates this clearly. Baxi (in Steiner and Alston 2000: 283–4) shows how these principles have been put into practice in terms of social action litigation, when ordinary people write to the Courts about violations of the human rights of impoverished groups in Indian society. This means, in Baxi's view, that 'The law of standing, that is persons who can bring complaints of rights-violation, has been thus revolutionised; and access to constitutional justice has been fully democratised'. The Courts commission and fund researchers to find out the facts, in Baxi's striking phrase, to 'provide the material for doing justice', and compensation and detailed measures of rehabilitation for victims are accorded the status of a constitutional right (Steiner and Alston 2000: 285). Examples abound. The Supreme Court of India monitors the treatment of the blinded of Bhagalpur, relief and medical treatment for the victims of Bhopal, the administration of the Agra Protective Home for Women, and prison administration in the State of Bihar. No doubt there are very many more examples of violations of rights that go unrepaired and remain invisible in India (the Enron case and the Narmada dam, for example), but social action litigation shows what is possible. So, while quite realistic about the limited impact of social action litigation in India and the ongoing struggle between the judiciary and the executive, and specific courts and specific institutions in violation of people's rights, Baxi does show how a large and relatively poor state could nurture a legal system that turns abstract rights into economic and social realities. This puts to shame the feeble protestations of capitalist globalizers that the rich states of the First World cannot afford to protect economic and social rights for all.[20]

Despite the onward march of capitalist globalization, states (or, more to the point, governments) could restructure their priorities in the direction of satisfying the economic and social rights of the large majority of the people while, at the same time, enhancing their civil and political rights. In the richest countries, where average per capita income according to the World Bank is around $25,000 (World Bank 2001: 14) the resources are already available to provide proper diet, housing, education, health care, and environmental security for everyone who wants them. This, however, would necessitate higher taxes and reduced consumption of luxury goods and services. There is no reason in principle why a political party could not campaign on such a programme and win. However, under the conditions of capitalist globalization, driven by the culture-ideology of consumerism, this seems unlikely to occur. Realistically, such a programme is more likely to be forced on rich countries by a combination of the effects of the twin crises of ecological unsustainability and class polarization. This could happen gradually or catastrophically, depending on various factors, including mass mobilization and political leadership.

In poor countries, those with an average per capita income of around $420 in 1999 (World Bank 2001: 14),[21] the issues are similar in principle, but differ in practice. Democratic political systems, even in poor countries with weak states, do not exclude the election of governments that genuinely set out to redistribute societal resources to benefit their poorer citizens and give them the tools to improve their own conditions. However, it rarely happens to any significant degree, despite the sometimes quite radical programmes that various Third World governments put forward. The Structural Adjustment Programmes of the international financial agencies are both a real constraint on progressive policies of genuinely radical governments and a convenient excuse for revolutionary poseurs.

Table 11.1 records the present priorities under capitalist globalization contrasted with the priorities of a world of socialist globalization based on the globalization of human rights. The first column lists policies that promote capitalist globalization and would encourage class polarization and ecological unsustainability, while the second column lists policies that promote more equitable distribution, more characteristic of socialist

Table 11.1 Reallocating resources from the priorities of capitalist globalization to the priorities of socialist globalization

From Capitalist Globalization	To Socialist Globalization
Export-orientation	Revival of local economy
Foreign borrowing to service debt	Renegotiate foreign debt
Austerity measures to pay the debt	Local economic expansion
Shrinking state	Community control of the local economy
Export zones processing imported components	Exports linked to local economy
Race to the bottom for wages and conditions to attract investment	Increased wages to stimulate local economy
TNC and finance-driven economy	Economy driven by producers and consumers co-operatives
TCC-driven competing states system	Democratic unions of producer-consumer co-operatives
Culture-ideology of consumerism	Culture-ideology of human rights on a global scale

globalization. The point, of course, is not that all the priorities of capitalist globalization should be ignored, but that even in rich countries there are substantial areas of neglect that need to be addressed and that can only be dealt with by setting priorities on the basis of the needs of the whole community not, as at present, on the basis of what the most powerful groups want. It is important here to distinguish clearly between what I am conceptualizing as the culture-ideology of consumerism and rights to adequate consumption. The human right to adequate consumption (we can define this as the basic minimum level that even averagely well-off people would settle for) properly conceived, entails the social responsibility of those who are democratically elected to make such decisions to ensure that this is available to all. The crisis of ecological unsustainability dictates that this will entail reductions in consumption for better-off people all over the world. These are the responsibilities involved in the globalization of human rights, responsibilities that people in a society based on the principles of socialist globalization will gladly teach their children and perhaps in the short term, more reluctantly, practice themselves.

HUMAN RIGHTS AND SOCIAL RESPONSIBILITIES

The discourse and organization of human rights provokes a series of fundamental questions on how we think about justice in the global system. Why does the language of rights rather than responsibilities (or duties) dominate treaties, constitutions, and political debate? In what ways, if any, is it superior to the language of responsibilities? Would the values and goals of a human responsibilities movement be different from those of the human rights movement? The question that is most often posed, particularly by those who wish to highlight the importance of cultural difference rather than universality, is whether, and to what extent, does the language of rights entail what are considered to be rights? This is an indirect expression of the thesis that the language and the substance of the Western liberal tradition appear to dominate both the discourse and the organization of the human rights movement.[22]

In the Western liberal tradition rights tend to be conceptualized individualistically, but the duties and responsibilities of individuals tend to be marginalized or excluded entirely from consideration. As discussed above, the fact that the international human rights movement originated within and through the inter-state system and the efforts of those who were representatives of it, means that the discourse and the movement have always carried the tensions inherent in trying to reconcile individual rights and state sovereignty (Forsythe 2000: ch. 2). Despite what is written down in treaties and conventions and the laws of individual countries, even when they are generally upheld, rights are never absolute even in the most democratic societies. This is partly because parliamentary democracies are so imperfect, and partly because the agencies of the state, even in parliamentary democracies, always place their own security above all rights.[23] Under the conditions of capitalist globalization what state functionaries consider vital to the national interest is much more likely to be driven by the interests of those who own and control big business (as interpreted and implemented by their allies in the bureaucracy and government at all levels) than those of ordinary people or the principles of ecological sustainability. Thus, capitalist globalization encourages states to reduce their duties and responsibilities to their citizens, and to restrict them to the protection of those rights compatible with or not hostile to the interests of big business.[24] A good example of this process is the way in which many states have restricted the right to protest against globalization (as in Davos, the First of May 2001 in London, and in Genoa, discussed in chapter 10).

Different cultures predispose their members to see the world differently and the idea that individuals have duties and responsibilities to each other is far more common in some cultures than others. For example, according to Jomo Kenyatta, the Gikuyu people in Kenya live on the basis that 'collective activities make heavy tasks easier' (quoted in Steiner and Alston 2000: 346). Principles such as this logically and emotionally lead to a greater belief in the virtues of communities based on the duties and responsibilities of people to each other as well as their rights.[25] Significantly, the first human rights treaty to highlight duties as well as rights was the African Charter on Human and People's Rights of 1986, though in practice human rights are no better (in many cases much less) protected for the poor and under-privileged in Africa than elsewhere. By 2000, fifty-three states in Africa had signed up to the Charter but, as with all other Human Rights treaties, the signatories included many parties that appeared to routinely violate the very rights they were obliged to protect. Nevertheless, it is important to seek a balance between utter cynicism and utter naivety in this as in other fields. The world would not necessarily be a better place if there was no international human rights legislation and is not necessarily a worse place because of it.

One of the reasons why politicians who adopt the main tenets of neo-liberal capitalist globalization have been so successful in parliamentary democracies all over the world is precisely because of the appeal of responsibility over rights rhetoric for so many of those who bother to vote. In relatively rich societies poor people whose rights are violated often lack public sympathy, typically orchestrated by the mass media, because they are perceived as making little positive contribution to society (the unemployed) at best, or as being a drain on society (so-called welfare scroungers and bogus asylum seekers) at worst. These popular idioms are consistently used to justify reductions in welfare services or to exclude some services as rights altogether. The right to suitable employment, enshrined in many international treaties and national constitutions, is a good case in point. Work-share programmes that have been introduced in the USA, Canada, and the UK appear to recognize that the state has some obligation to ensure adequate employment or provide unemployment benefits for adults but, as Peck and Theodore (2001) argue, while these programmes rarely produce many good jobs they do depress welfare claims. Usually the unemployed must accept the responsibility of taking any job deemed appropriate by the authorities that is offered to them. There is no easy solution to this problem. It appears intuitively obvious that small communities organized through something like producer-consumer co-operatives are better suited to solving it than very large societies centrally organized on the basis of individuals and their households.

Responsibilities and rights are two sides of the same coin; each right implies a responsibility, each responsibility implies a right. It would be entirely illogical to assert the right for everyone to have a satisfying job without asserting the responsibility for someone or some institution to ensure that jobs exist. But this is exactly what most international human rights treaties and conventions, and national laws do. Generally, they assert these rights without specifying who or what has the responsibility for delivering them. The state, of course, is usually intended to be the institution responsible for delivering rights but even where the state has the resources to do this there is always a let-out (exceptional circumstances, usually defined by the state) and specific agencies and agents are very rarely held responsible. It is rare even in the most democratic states for individuals to be held responsible for violations of rights, and when violations are dealt with in the courts, it is the system rather than agencies or agents that is, abstractly, held responsible. This line of argument leads radical critics of the discourse and organization of human rights to argue that the human rights system acts as much to protect the violators as to protect the violated. Certainly, the UN Commission on Human Rights has been criticized on the grounds that states vie to place their representatives on the Commission not to pursue abuses but to ensure that their own abuses and those of friendly states are spared embarrassing exposure. The official human rights movement is not without its critics.

THE OFFICIAL HUMAN RIGHTS MOVEMENT

While the UN human rights organizational structure is very complex (see above, and the diagram of the system in Steiner and Alston 2000: 598), there is general consensus that it became more effective in the 1990s. During his term of office Secretary-General Boutros-Ghali opposed the creation of a High Commissioner for Human Rights. His successor, Kofi Annan, appointed one and earned a reputation for having mainstreamed human rights throughout the UN. In the judgement of Steiner and Alston (2000: 599), UN 'bodies dealing with issues from economic development to peacekeeping and beyond have been encouraged to address systematically the human rights dimensions of their mandates'. One significant innovation has been the establishment of field operations in about twenty countries to combine the monitoring of human rights with technical co-operation and peacekeeping, though lack of resources has reduced the effectiveness of these interventions.[26]

This is of course very sensitive and difficult work. UN agencies have to balance universal human rights with the principle of non-interference in the internal affairs of member states. Kofi Annan has stressed that the UN Charter was issued in the name of the peoples not the governments of the United Nations, but this obviously conflicts with

Article 2(7) of the UN Charter: 'Nothing contained in the present Charter shall authorize the United Nations to intervene in matters which are essentially within the domestic jurisdiction of any State ... but this principle shall not prejudice the application of enforcement measures under Chapter VII [threats and aggression]' (Steiner and Alston, 2000: 588). The problem is that it is never those people whose rights are being violated who get to decide which matters are 'essentially within the domestic jurisdiction of any State'. The fundamental flaw in the UN-oriented human rights approach is that most individuals are not in a position to dictate what their rights should be. Responsibilities and rights have a different logical and practical status. Logically, most people are in a position to decide what their own responsibilities to specified others are and should be and to act on these decisions. Practically, only in very extreme cases is the full weight of the law used to punish people for evading their responsibilities (for example, those of parents to look after their children). The responsibility of corporate executives, politicians, and officials for ensuring that private and public goods and services are safe is practically never enforced in court.[27] The responsibility of the community to ensure that everyone in the community has enough to eat is more realistic, even when there is not much food to go round, than a statement that individuals have the right to have enough to eat.

Globally, the main institution charged with the responsibility for delivering human rights is the UN Commission on Human Rights (UNCHR), established in 1946. It consists of representatives from around fifty member governments and meets annually in Geneva for six weeks every year. Since 1992 extra emergency sessions have been held to deal with widely publicized human rights crises. (There are, of course, other human rights crises that are not widely publicized and fail to attract much attention in the UN system.) Over 3000 people participated in the deliberations of the Commission in 1999, including 587 officials representing 53 member states, 586 officials representing 91 other states, and 1,824 persons representing 212 NGOs (some of these in a quasi-official capacity). Steiner and Alston, both of whom have been intimately connected with the work of the Commission, note three significant features of the UN human rights system. It is concerned with (i) civil and political rather than economic and social rights, (ii) gross and noticeable violations rather than persistent violations of a lower visibility, and (iii) issues rather than consciousness-raising and education. This last task has largely been left to international, national, and local non-governmental organizations (NGOs).

NGOS AND CIVIL SOCIETY

As indicated in the previous chapter, human rights NGOs are part of a broad range of organizations and movements, variously referred to as transnational advocacy networks (Keck and Sikkink 1998, Fox and Brown 1998), transnational social movements (Smith *et al.* 1997), and even a nascent transnational civil society (Guidry *et al.* 2000). These umbrella terms generally exclude official governmental bodies (including the UN and other inter-state networks) and those attached to the private economic sector (Welch 2001). Steiner and Alston (2000: 939) list the alphabet soup of organizations that make up this complex.

NGOs and INGOs (international NGOs) . . . CSOs (civil society organizations), CBOs (community-based organizations), PVOs (private voluntary organizations), GROs (grassroots organizations), QUANGOS (quasi-NGOs), GONGOs (government organized NGOs), BINGOs (business and industry [sometimes

Big International] NGOs), DONGOs (donor organized NGOs), and DNGDOs (domestic nongovern-mental development organizations).

At the UN Beijing World Conference on Women in 1995, for example, 40,000 people representing thousands of these groups attended the NGO forum.

The mainstream view of global civil society is that it is what is left over when we abstract all the organizations of the state and private business. As there has been phe-nomenal growth in NGOs all over the world it is said that global civil society has grown with them. Anyone who has been at all persuaded by the main argument of this book will immediately see global civil society defined in this way as a flawed concept. The power and influence of the TNCs and their local affiliates in economic life, of the transnational capitalist class in political life, and of consumerism in culture-ideology, ensure that the spaces for global civil society to exist free from the influences of capitalist globalization (including globalizers in the state) are strictly limited. Thus, excluding groups attached to private economic interests from civil society seems to me a serious error as there is a mass of evidence to suggest that private economic interests wield increasing influence in what are often misleadingly termed public interest groups (see Boggs 2000, Sklair 2001). This does imply the strong thesis that for there to be a genuine global civil society its institutions and actors must oppose capitalist globalization and for them to be effective, they have to have something convincing to put in its place. As argued above, it is time to start to think the unthinkable and to work out how the capitalist inter-state system can be replaced while we are monitoring it to prevent and/or make restitution for abuses. No doubt there are many theoretical possibilities, and the socialist globalization I propose in this book is one of them.

The polarization effect of capitalist globalization expresses itself to some extent in the way that the global human rights movement operates. Wichterich (2000) probes the fact that is it acceptable for experts to jet around the world networking but it is usually considered a waste of time and resources for slum dwellers to do the same. What she labels the New International Women's Politics is largely based on global networks of women's groups dominated by organizations based in First World countries, often pursu-ing a single issue and missing the bigger picture. She identifies the US-based WEDO (Women's Environment and Development Organization) as a paradigm case of the conference-centred political process, modelled on the structures of male-dominated international politics and NGO practice. Early formal successes in establishing organiza-tions and gaining entry to the corridors of power proved to be an illusion, as evidence mounted that nothing much has changed in the lives of most of the women on whose behalf the organizations were set up in the first place.[28] This casts doubts on the effectiveness of the monitoring method, as women's NGOs followed structures and pro-cedures that the World Bank, UN, and other powerful organizations laid down for them. 'This professionalization has brought to the fore a new transnational and transcultural class of lobbyists, who appear really on top of their subject and tools, competent and eloquent, who tour the world with a high salary, a high expense account, and an equally high appraisal of themselves' (Wichterich 2000: 157). This has led to a hierarchical differentiation among the women's NGOs.

Such phenomena are not restricted to the women's movement. In his quite positive discussion of the role of INGOs in the successful campaign to ban the use of landmines (the Ottawa Convention), Anderson comments that most of the organizations involved were fundamentally elite organizations. While they obviously did essential work they talked mainly to each other and did little to reduce the democratic deficit. His conclusion is that this form of civil society is not really part of democracy, rather it is a substitute for democracy. The ability to be a pressure group, not democratic legitimacy, is the hallmark of INGOs (in Steiner and Alston 2000: 950–3). Similar organizations working with similar agendas on other issues have also had some real successes. For example, the equally elitist campaign that led to the creation of the 1998 Rome Statute on the International Criminal Court resulted in some important war crimes trials. One might even argue that the coalition of NGOS that disrupted the 1999 Seattle WTO meeting and subsequent events in the capitalist globalization calendar would have had an even more dramatic effect in raising consciousness if they had been more elitist and less libertarian. Steiner and Alston, as insiders, are more optimistic about the benefits that NGOs can deliver than Wichterich, a radical journalist.

Mutua (in Welch 2001: 152) locates the problem in what he terms the conventional doctrinalist nature of Western human rights groups that tend to focus on human rights abuses in repressive foreign countries, leaving civil rights groups to focus on domestic issues. 'Until recently, and to a large extent even today, none of these American INGOs focused on human rights issues in the United States, except to seek the reform of U.S. foreign policy and American compliance with aspects of refugee law.' The careers of the founders and current luminaries (even the non-white non-Westerners) of all the major Western INGOs illustrate the dominance of the conventional doctrinalists. Apart from Amnesty International, they all take funds from foundations and corporations; and their fund-raising 'gimmicks' (annual awards dinners where rich supporters buy tables for their associates) reinforce their image with the great and the good. Conventional doctrinalists stress a narrow range of civil and political rights, and Mutua shows that: 'In a reflection of this ideological bias, INGOs mirrored the position of the industrial democracies and generally assumed an unsympathetic and, at times, hostile posture towards calls for the expansion of their mandates to include economic and social rights' (in Welch 2001: 155). Recent rhetoric on the indivisibility of rights, he claims, has not been matched by action, though this may be changing.[29]

Under the conditions of capitalist globalization the ever-closer connections with officialdom is a mixed blessing for NGOs, and the evidence on such collaborations suggests that it is the agenda of globalizing business and governments, often mutually reinforcing, that drives the process.[30]

Most prominent human rights organizations face the problem of representation, a central issue of democratic politics. Who, speaks for whom, and with what right? Among the thousands of campaigns and movements working for human rights locally and/or globally (see Smith et al. 1997, Keck and Sikkink 1998), two stand out. The biggest is Amnesty International (AI), founded in 1961. AI now has around one million members in more than 160 countries, and national sections in fifty-six countries. Its budget of $25 million is raised from individual subscriptions and funding from private foundations. It does not accept money from governments. The other is Human Rights Watch, founded in 1988. It began its existence as Helsinki Watch, established to monitor the human rights commitments of the superpower agreement of 1975 (the Helsinki Accords). In contrast to AI, Human Rights Watch is a non-membership organization with regional divisions and a budget of around $16 million. It has prime access to the mass media, particularly in the USA, and its regular reports of abuses of human rights all over the world are highly visible and, like AI, often controversial. Both AI and Human Rights Watch have influential websites that are heavily used, and both have been the subject of a good deal of academic research (see Welch 2001: part I). Despite the powerful work they do, in some respects these are both elitist organizations that have ambiguous positions with respect to capitalist globalization.[31] Perhaps the point is that in order to achieve much within the confines of capitalist societies it is easier to be an elitist movement.

PROTECTING HUMAN RIGHTS

Despite the enormous amount of international, regional, national and local legislation, and political agitation on their behalf, many people in the world suffer violations of one or more of their economic, social, civil, or political rights on a daily basis. Therefore, we must pose the question: how far have states, individually or as part of the UN system, acted as effective protectors and enforcers of human rights over the last few decades? There are two dimensions to this question. First, radical political change can transform a society from one in which most human rights are routinely violated to one in which most human rights are generally protected, or vice versa. South Africa in the 1990s was widely regarded as a notable success story of radical political change for human rights. State policy deliberately sought to bring about a transition from a society based on racist denial of human rights for the majority of the people to one in which the protection of human rights for all was forced onto the political agenda. A good example of the opposite process was the military coup against the democratically elected government of the Chilean President Allende in 1973, and the subsequent military dictatorship of General Pinochet based on gross violations of human rights.

Second, states can for a variety of reasons change their attitudes towards human rights violations in other states and begin to exert pressure for change in these other states. Again, this can work both ways. Governments can decide to stop tolerating or to start tolerating human rights abuses in other countries. The US government and the European Union are the most visible, simply because they usually have the most clout internationally. The Carter Presidency (1976–80) when US foreign policy was used aggressively to target states that abused human rights, stands out in this respect. Even here, while eight abusing states (all in Latin America) had their security assistance (arms supplies) terminated, many other gross violators, for example Indonesia, Iran, South Korea, the Philippines, and Zaire, did not suffer this penalty (see Cohen, in Steiner and Alston 2000: 1096–9). Indeed, it may be nearer the mark to argue that despite the high level of rhetoric from successive US and other First World governments on the sanctity of international human rights, they have more often found excuses for gross violators (like national interest, employment in the domestic armaments industry, constructive engagement) than actually punished them in any way.[32] It is difficult to escape the conclusion that this is inherent in the structure of the inter-state system with its inbuilt rhetoric of international competitiveness. This manifests itself in relatively harmless ways (in sport, for example), through its more serious forms (trade) to its most destructive (wars and proxy-wars). Given the infrequency with which states in the capitalist global system act decisively against even the most blatant violations of human rights, for example freedom from torture, let alone what are usually seen as more contentious rights, for example to a decent standard of living and a healthy environment, it is likely that the type of co-operative democracy proposed here will do better. Not for the first time, it is the nature of the state itself in capitalist globalization that comes under scrutiny.

This is another invitation to think the unthinkable, namely of a world that has gone beyond the separate states of the inter-state system in which most of us live. It is neces-sary to phrase the issue in this way to highlight two important facts. First, there are many millions of stateless people today (for example, refugees and asylum seekers); and second, there are many more millions who live within the borders of so-called nation-states but find this problematic (for example, indigenous peoples, progressive-minded people who are repelled by nationalism, and people with transnational loyalties and identities). If a global society is to be created on the foundations of a transnational network of intercon-nected producer-consumer co-operatives organized into mutually supportive com-munities then rights and responsibilities at all levels would be more closely connected. The existing state system encouraged by capitalist globalization has proved itself incap-able of dealing with the rights of minorities on too many occasions to inspire much confidence that it is a satisfactory political form. Rosalyn Higgins unwittingly confirms this when she expresses the liberal view on the problem of the relationship between states and the minorities that reside within them. Minority rights, she argues, are not necessarily people's rights, entailing self-determination and rights of secession.

Because I believe in diversity, and plurality, and tolerance, and mutual respect, I favour multi-culturalism and multinationalism. The use of force is appalling, indiscriminate barbarity unforgiv-able. But the move to uninational and unicultural states that constitutes postmodern tribalism is profoundly illiberal. The attempt to legitimate these tendencies by the missapplication of legal terms runs the risk of harming the very values that international law is meant to promote. (in Steiner and Alston 2000: 1286)

This reasoning, however understandable, is quite arbitrary in that it tends to limit the number of states to roughly the number we have now, most of which were founded on the violation of the rights of some groups. A more radical solution is to question the assumption that the state and the current inter-state system, based on more or less exclusive nationalisms, are the best available forms of political life and to think through alternatives to them. This is the political project of socialist globalization. But we still have to work out how to get from here (and here is many places) to there (and that might be many places too).

There is a growing consensus that development does connect with human rights, but not exactly how.[33] One of the clearest expressions of the connections between human rights and human development served as the introduction to the UNDP Human Devel-opment Report for the year 2000:

Human rights and human development share a common vision and a common purpose—to secure the freedom, well-being and dignity of all people everywhere. To secure:
Freedom from discrimination—by gender, race, ethnicity, national origin or religion.
Freedom from want—to enjoy a decent standard of living.

Freedom to develop and realize one's human potential.

Freedom from fear—of threats to personal security, from torture, arbitrary arrest and other violent acts.

Freedom from injustice and violations of the rule of law.

Freedom of thought and speech and to participate in decision-making and form associations.

Freedom for decent work—without exploitation. (UNDP 2000a: 1)

As I argued in the previous chapter, and as this statement from the UN confirms, there is widespread agreement on what changes are desirable to improve the lives of the majority of the people around the world. In this age of apparently relentless globalization, change is clearly in the air. Despite rising aspirations, development and freedoms are not happening quickly enough for most people.

Global systems like capitalism are not born and do not die in the course of a few generations, but they do change. New generations face new challenges and meet them or fail to meet them and this changes the conditions for how the next set of challenges will be met by subsequent generations. Of course, how the future will turn out is a matter of conviction and cannot be predicted with any scientific precision. And of course, political will, while not the only factor, cannot be discounted in the creation of a better future just as lack of political will or political will of an evil sort can be a factor in the creation of a worse future. Socialist globalization or any other alternative to capitalist globalization will have to be created by people working together. What I have been arguing in this chapter is: (i) that capitalist globalization cannot resolve the crises of class polarization and ecological unsustainability; (ii) that the gradual elimination of privately owned big business and its replacement by producer-consumer co-operatives is more likely to resolve these crises than muddling through with capitalist globalization; and (iii) that the globalization of human rights can play a powerful part in this transformation.

The many radical movements that were discussed in the previous chapter feed into an emerging anti-globalization movement. As this movement inspires ever larger numbers of people to become active in the pursuit of human rights and the social responsibilities that are an integral part of them, we can begin to work out alternatives to capitalist globalization. Socialist globalization is one of many alternative paths.

NOTES

1. The supposed rise of postmaterialism, even in its extended form as propounded in the work of Inglehart (1997) in no way challenges this view. Most green consumers like most green corporations (see Robbins 2001) are not opposed to the culture-ideology of consumerism.

2. Thus I accept Warren's (1980) version of Marxism to the extent that socialism is impossible without the development of the productive forces, but reject the implication that there is only one way for the productive forces to develop.

3. This is one chapter in the collection edited by Ollman (1998) that serves as a sound critical introduction to debates on market socialism. However, the contributors (for and against) focus mainly on what can be termed 'market socialism in one country' and do not discuss the issue of globalizing it.

4. See the website of the Centre for the Study of Co-operatives at the University of Saskatchewan (**cop-studies.usask.ca**), for theoretical discussion and concrete cases.

5. Roemer's model (in Ollman 1998) is based on the redistribution of stocks and shares and proposes that companies be nationalized when they reach a certain size.

6. The problem of how to deal with those who refuse to accept the will of the majority has to be confronted in any theory of democracy, mine included (see Fennema and Maussen 2000).

7. It should be noted that Porto Alegre is a relatively prosperous city. See, R. Abers (in Douglass and Friedmann 1998: ch. 4) and Baiocchi (2001). Heller (2001) usefully compares Porto Alegre with cases in South Africa and Kerela.

8. Another example of effective democratic political action, from the Federal District of Brasilia is the policy of scholarships for poor families to ensure that their children graduate from school. The policy has been adopted widely throughout Brazil (see Buarque 1999). Whether capitalist globalization in Brazil can provide enough satisfying jobs for millions of extra educated youths remains to be seen.

9. Mattes and Bratton (2001: 52) report that only 5 per cent of respondents in a sample from nine African countries saw democracy in terms of social and economic development.

10. Note, however, the argument of Eliasoph (1998) that 'avoiding politics' is a rule of the game of most voluntary associations in the USA. Further, local small-scale capitalism can also be vicious at times.

11. Adding ecological sustainability will be superfluous when ecological human rights are granted their proper place in the pantheon of human rights and social responsibilities, as exemplified in the theoretical and practical work of the environmental justice movement (see Westra and Wenz 1995, Dobson 1998).

12. For an inspiring defence of utopian thinking, see Friedmann (2000). Singer(1999) and Mouzelis (2001) both offer a realistic utopianism. Some of the poverty-reduction proposals of the World Bank and various other agencies over the last fifty years appear even more utopian than my modest proposals.

13. This section is largely based on Steiner and Alston (2001). This book of almost 1,500 pages skilfully blends commentaries, and scholarly and official sources into an encyclopedic narrative of international human rights. Most of the sources directly quoted are written or cited by Steiner and Alston.

14. As of 2000, the European Convention on Human Rights had been adopted by forty states, the American Convention on Human Rights by twenty-five and the African Charter on Human and People's Rights by fifty-three.

15. For an even-handed commentary on Nuremberg and some critical arguments of the process and outcomes, see Steiner and Alston (2000: ch. 3, D). Nothing in human experience, it seems, can be absolute when we start to analyse it.

16. See Steiner and Alston (2000: ch. 6, A), especially the discussions on the apparently unambiguous question of female circumcision.

17. As noted above, by the 1990s, under the impact of a capitalist globalization that was obviously failing to deliver on its promises, the World Bank and various UN agencies began to set targets and timetables for the achievement of various economic and social rights. My argument is that capitalist globalization (locked into crises of class polarization and ecological unsustainability) will never achieve these targets.

18. The attack on the welfare state is a common target of critics of capitalist globalization (see, for example, Deacon *et al.* 1997).

19. For an interesting contrast between ILO and WTO approaches to trade and labour rights see McCrudden and Davies (2000).

20. To put this in context, justice is generally slow in India, where there are twenty-three cases pending per 1,000 persons, over 2,000 per judge (and Bangladesh has more than twice as many), according to a report cited by UNDP (2000a: 101)

21. Data for purchasing-power parity brings the low income average up to to $1,870. The middle group of countries have average per capita income of $1,980 ($5,200 at PPP). As I argue in Chapter 2, these figures need to be deconstructed.

22. This is one, albeit crucial, part of the general problem of Orientalism and postcolonialism (how First World elites structure ideas of the Third World). Lazarus (1999) is an insightful if controversial guide whose starting point is 'hating tradition properly' (from Adorno).

23. This is often taken to ridiculous extremes. For example, the authorities in Britain have at one time applied the Offical Secrets Act to welfare system classifications, and at another declined to force food companies to divulge information that would assist in the struggle against foot and mouth disease.

24. See the interesting and by now quite typical argument of Cragg (2000) in the *Journal of Business Ethics* that

business needs a new social contract with the state on human rights. For a more nuanced version of this argument see Falk (2000). Neither of these see capitalism as such as the problem.

25. See the discussion of the *ujamaa* principle in Tanzania (above Ch. 8). The Confucian value system in China and elsewhere (see Kim, in Sklair 1994: ch. 5) is also frequently cited in this context. However, the key issue is the connection or disconnection of values and practices in real life situations.

26. What is coming to be termed the globalization of violence forces us to recognize the centrality of wars and peacekeeping for understanding the discourse and organization of many human rights. See Kaldor (1999) and Held *et at.* (1999: table 2.2 and ch. 2 *passim,*).

27. Major exceptions appear to be the product liability suits brought against tobacco (and other) companies in the USA but, as I have argued (Sklair 1998), individuals are rarely held responsible and the companies usually survive and prosper. Corporate executives are much more likely to go to jail for financial crimes than for causing death and disease.

28. On this sweeping judgement, compare Wichterich (2000) with the opposite but less convincing view that the position of women (and everyone else) has dramatically improved under capitalist globalization, in Easterlin (2000). For a more balanced view on this and other aspects of class polarization, see UNDP (2000*b*). To reiterate: the class polarization thesis maintains that the rich are getting richer and the poor are getting poorer. However, the conditions of the much larger middle groups do impact the averages on all measures, and these vary from place to place.

29. However: 'The current human rights movement in Africa—with the possible exception of the women's rights movement and faith-based social justice initiatives—appears almost by design to exclude the participation of those people whose welfare it purports to advance . . . Instead of being the currency of a social justice or conscience-driven movement, "human rights" has increasingly become the specialized language of a select professional cadre with its own rites of passage and methods of certification' (C.A. Odinkalu, in Steiner and Alston 2000: 946-7). Compare Tripp (2001).

30. Good examples of this process are the growing UN/TNC links (see, Lee *et al.* 1998, Karliner 1999, Utting 2000) and the Codex Alimentarius system.

31. I do not make this criticism lightly (being a fully paid-up member of AI and its Urgent Action network), but in the spirit of Belton (1998), whose biography of Helen Bamber (founder of the Medical Foundation for the Care of Victims of Torture) is an insightful account of varieties of human rights movement experiences, explaining why Bamber and others left AI.

32. The argument continues between those who believe in constructive engagement as against positive sanctions as the best way to change regimes that grossly violate human rights. The defeat of apartheid in South Africa suggests that selective sanctions that damage those in power and those who most benefit from the regime (often difficult to target accurately) rather that blanket sanctions that emiserate the masses (as in successive US government policies towards Cuba and Iraq) are most effective in the long run. The value of encouraging and materially supporting human rights organizations within these countries cannot be overstated. The case of Burma (Ch. 4 above) shows there are no easy answers.

33. It is significant that Steiner and Alston, who devote the last chapter of their book to 'Globalization, Development, and Human Rights', chose to locate a discussion of the controversies over human rights abuses by TNCs here (ch. 16, E). In addition to several established journals on business ethics, the *Journal of Corporate Citizenship* (Issue 1, Spring 2001) promises to be a useful source. For my own analysis of the issues see Sklair (2001: chs. 6 and 7).

Chapter 12

CONCLUSION: THE END OF CAPITALIST GLOBALIZATION AND ALTERNATIVE FUTURES

SOCIALIST GLOBALIZATION?

I have argued that there is an alternative, socialist globalization, but that as a global project it has hardly begun to make an impact in either material, political, or ideological terms, in comparison with the bounding successes of capitalist globalization. Indeed, the whole book has been organized around the premise that, despite serious challenges and widespread cynicism, no other world-view has come anywhere near the ideological force or the practical achievements of capitalist globalization.

Nevertheless, a sober recognition of how the crises of class polarization and ecological unsustainability are gradually undermining the power of the global capitalist system gives confidence that the search for alternatives is not futile. There is a long-standing and lively debate that has been energized by the collapse of communism in Eastern Europe, both by those who reject capitalism and those who are simply sceptical, about what to put in its place. My argument is that socialist globalization is not only possible but necessary. While the version outlined in Chapter 11 is certainly not a blueprint for the transition from what we have now to what we ought to be aiming for, my contention is that it does raise the central issues of this transition: democracy, human rights, and socialism. All these terms are highly controversial and hotly contested.

DEMOCRACY

Democracy, of which capitalism claims a monopoly, has at least two senses, namely parliamentary democracy (the capitalist sense) and participatory democracy (the socialist sense). The differences between these two types of democratic practices are profound. Parliamentary democracy is based on a system of professional political parties whose activists organize candidates to compete for the votes of the electorate at (generally) fixed intervals. Once the election has decided a winner, often a winning coalition of losers, the electorate is expected to withdraw from active politics and let their representatives get on with the job, until the next election. While extra-parliamentary activity is usually legal, it is rarely encouraged and only when it becomes violent is it given much attention in the mass media. Democracy here means the freedom of the individual to help choose who is to govern and, under certain circumstances, to become a candidate for election.

Participatory democracy is based on the concept that people should not cease to be politically active or aware between elections. On the contrary, people as individuals and as members of interest groups, through those they delegate to act for them, are entitled to have an ongoing voice in what is done in their names. Thus, while participatory democracy has need of parliaments (or similar bodies) it is people rather than parliaments that are supreme. Therefore, sub-parliamentary bodies are necessary to act as channels of communication and decision-making (in both directions) between people and government. Characteristics of this type of democracy are frequent reporting back of delegates, representations of popular opinion to policy makers, open government, and referenda on important questions. This is exactly what is meant by the idea that the basic units of socialist globalization would be self-governing producer–consumer co-operatives.

Of course, this is a very cumbersome system and its critics argue that under such constraints nothing would ever be accomplished. As it has never been tried on a large scale, it is not possible to know with any degree of certainty whether it would actually be any less efficient than the gargantuan bureaucracies that govern most contemporary states. A somewhat less efficient system might be a bearable price to pay for an increase in the volume and quality of democratic practices. Here we have much to learn from the proponents of localization and self-sufficiency. The optimum scale of the basic unit of society is a critical question and one that parliamentary systems are often forced to grapple with, particularly when there are apparent conflicts between majority and minority rights.

HUMAN RIGHTS

The human rights project, as discussed in the previous chapter, is problematic. For a variety of reasons that competing theories have tried to explain biologically, historically, sociologically, and psychologically, there are few if any societies that have delivered genuine equality of opportunity and commonly accepted fairness in outcomes in the economic, political, and culture-ideology spheres. Structured social inequalities are so institutionalized that the terms used to label them, notably sexism for the oppression of women and girls (sometimes of men and boys), and racism for the oppression of ethnic minorities (sometimes majorities) are now part of everyday discourse. Many more are also oppressed by homophobia, ageism, discrimination against the disabled, the uneducated, or the poor in general. Individual women and members of oppressed ethnic and other groups, of course, have succeeded in their chosen fields, but in general all over the world the dominant groups earn more than the oppressed groups for comparable work, enjoy more positions of political power, and are more influential in culture and ideology. Although capitalism clearly did not create all these inequalities, historically it has reinforced and channelled them, albeit in different ways. Capitalist globalization, however, may be changing this for educated members of some of these groups because of its demand for their specialized labour, and for those with sufficient spending power because of its reliance on their consumption (culture-ideology of consumerism).

Many progressive writers simply incorporate the liberation of women, or ethnic, or other minorities into the democratic and/or socialist project, arguing that sexist, racist, or other minority forms of democracy is no democracy at all. The histories of women's movements and the struggle for the emancipation of people of colour, nationally and internationally, suggest that this is not good enough. I have already commented critically on the widespread assumption that modernization and the penetration of capitalist globalization would inevitably bring equality of opportunity for women, and similar arguments have been made by modernization theorists about people in the Third World. Evidence from the First World and the richer parts of the Third World shows that this is not necessarily the case. Marxists, under the influence of the Engels thesis (that exploitation by sex is a consequence of the more general division of labour, particularly under capitalism, and will disappear when capitalism is transcended) would obviously not be surprised by the inability of capitalism to eradicate sexism or racism. The evidence from socialist and communist societies suggests that women may well have improved their positions compared with the previous regimes, but by no stretch of the imagination does it permit us to draw the conclusion that socialism liberated women.

Capitalism gives a definite, though sociologically ambivalent, place to most women and men, and ethnic and other minorities in terms of their class positions. It may well be the case that the low level of support that feminist socialism has won from working-class women (let alone men) is due to their perception that they might have more to lose than to gain from it. This is why the human rights component of socialist globalization is so important.

SOCIALISM

The socialist part of the project is the most difficult to specify with any degree of plausibility. The question is whether there are any viable alternatives to big business and its local affiliates in the economic sphere, to the transnational capitalist class in the political sphere, and to the culture-ideology of consumerism in the sphere of values. As Chapters 8 and 9 documented, the communist ideal has faded, but the Third Way as popularly formulated cannot be untangled from its capitalist roots. Such attempts maintain coherence only through the device of ignoring the conflicts of interests that persist between labour and capital, in their many forms, even after centuries of stunning capitalist material progress. I am fully aware that most of the conflicts in today's world appear to be based on issues of personal identity, notably race, religion, and nationalism, rather than class. It would take quite another book to argue the view that these are secondary rather than primary causes. Nevertheless, it is true to say that there is no adequate theory of how class relates to race, religion, and nationalism in the economic, political, and culture-ideology spheres, nationally or transnationally.

I would argue that conflicts of race, religion, and nationalism, real as they are, actually stand for something else even where they obviously take on lives of their own. What they stand for is the fear of the opposing groups that their conditions of existence are at risk. These are material conditions, and they reverberate in all spheres. Enthusiasts for capitalist globalization argue that only it can develop the productive forces to a level that would begin to offer material security to most of the people of the world. However, as I have argued, it does this under constant conditions of class and other types of struggle, sometimes violent, but mostly peaceful, if robust. This is the opening that anti-globalization movements have exploited. Because I cannot accept the optimistic hope that capitalism can become much more humane globally than it already is, or that Stalinist communism can ever produce a decent society, in my view the next step in the quest for human progress has to be in the transformation of capitalist globalization into socialist globalization through the globalization of human rights.

The socialism that seems most likely to emerge out of the global capitalist system is not going to come about as a result of a revolutionary seizure of state power (this method has failed miserably wherever it has been tried), but as a result of a successful period of social experimentation in which the hegemony of global capitalism is increasingly and effectively challenged by a combination of local and transnational democratic social movements (in the very wide sense of the term that I have been using). Although there can be no specific formula for the transition to socialist globalization there are many ideas about how capitalist economies could be transformed to produce, eventually, fairer and more socially efficient societies. The contributions to the debate around market socialism discussed in the previous chapter bring out many of the issues that would have to be addressed to make the transition. The balance between economic and social efficiency is clearly central to these analyses.

Paradoxically, the ideological onslaughts on socialism in the freemarketeering 1980s and 1990s were accompanied by many instances of capitalist-led initiatives to democratize the workplace. The fundamental issue is the connection between power in the workplace and the right of capitalists and their agents to dispose of the profits of enterprises as they see fit. The challenge of socialism is precisely the challenge of socializing profits through the abolition of private ownership of the major means of production while leaving the minor means of production (small workshops, personal services, and other economically marginal activities) in the hands of individuals. Socialist entrepreneurs would be responsible for the efficient and socially beneficial maximizing and socializing of surpluses from all other enterprises. A central problem of socialist politics is to prevent the workers (including socialist entrepreneurs) from creating tyrannies of producers.

What capitalist globalization fails to provide are genuine opportunities for people to make their own choices about whether to live in a forever increasingly marketized society where fewer and fewer things and experiences escape commercialization. While the culture-ideology of consumerism provides ever-expanding apparent choices of goods and services, there is little or no choice about whether or not we wish to live in the consumerist lifeworld. Capitalism takes the global system to the level of material abundance for some, but unrestrained consumerism creates environmental degradation and resource scarcity and still fails to raise the living standards of all to anything like a satisfactory degree. Socialist globalization would eventually raise the quality of life (rather than the standards of living set by consumerist capitalism) of everyone and render the culture-ideology of consumerism superfluous by establishing other less destructive and polarizing cultures and ideologies in its place. There is no blueprint for this—if we want such a world we will have to create it by trial and error.

As long as the mass media are directly, or indirectly through commercial leverage, under the control of the transnational capitalist class, it is difficult to see how the socialist project can get a fair and balanced hearing in the newspapers, on television and radio, or anywhere else. Nevertheless, and not for the first time, global capitalism is caught in a contradiction of its own making, namely its commitment to freedom of choice in the marketplace. This ensures that alternative points of view do get heard and seen, even if not often on prime time or on the front pages. The digital divide exists, but it contains the seeds of its own transcendence.

What is more difficult to imagine is the idea of socialist economic transnational practices. This raises the question of whether or not the transnational corporation is inherently a capitalist phenomenon. As I argued in previous chapters, much transnational trade, commerce, and production is highly exploitative, particularly where organized TNCs are dealing with unorganized producers. It is not clear how genuinely socialist transnational practices could prevail with the current system of states. Theoretically, socialist globalization would make the nastier side of nationalist ideologies unnecessary but, practically, the way to achieve this is far from clear at this point in time.

Socialist globalization is one alternative to capitalist globalization. It is an organic project and while no one part can be entirely detached from the whole, it is still possible to observe the roots and shoots of socialist globalization in the edifice of global capitalism though, at present, it appears to pose no serious practical threat to it. However, capitalist globalization, though dominant, is not entirely coterminous with the world as it is today. Even if it was once believed, few now imagine that the streets of Tokyo, New York, Paris, or London (or anywhere else) are paved with gold. The settlements of poverty and dreadful deprivation jostling for survival in the richest cities of the richest countries (the class polarization crisis) are visible daily on the same screens and pages that advertise the consumer goods that the poor are encouraged to covet. Perhaps not as visibly as the symbols of consumerism, nor as ubiquitous, but the same 'freedom of choice' that propagates the culture-ideology of consumerism also propagates its negations: sexism, racism, child abuse, drug addiction, violence, unhappiness, hopelessness. It is not unreasonable for the poor, as well as the rich, to want the best of all worlds. This being so, it is reasonable to assume that poor people will want a better standard of living and prefer the system that delivers it as long as it does. Thus, the triumph of global capitalism is the triumph of the transnational capitalist class in selling the culture-ideology of consumerism and delivering the goods through the transnational corporations and other economic institutions. It is ironic that this can be observed as clearly in socialist and postcommunist societies as in the capitalist world in the twenty-first century.

I have tried to show how development strategies driven by the material demands of capitalist globalization have created a transnational capitalist class. But this class is not simply an effect of the global system, for it also embodies the histories, cultures, and practices of its members and their institutions and groups. These groups can turn the developmental strategies of global capitalism to their own purposes and even, on occasion, challenge those who wield central power in the system. In doing this they create their own contradictions, throw up opposing classes, provoke class struggles, set in train economic, political, and culture-ideology changes. History, far from being at an end, has hardly begun!

REFERENCES

Aaronson, S. (2001). *Taking Trade to the Streets: The Lost History of Public Efforts to Shape Globalization.* Ann Arbor: University of Michigan Press.

Abel, C., and Lewis, C. (eds.) (1985). *Latin America, Economic Imperialism and the State.* London: Athlone Press.

Adikibi, O. (1983). The Transfer of Technology to Nigeria: The Case of Tire Production. In C. Kirkpatrick and F. Nixson (eds.), *The Industrialization of Less Developed Countries.* Manchester: Manchester University Press.

Ake, C. (ed.). (1985). *Political Economy of Nigeria.* London: Longman.

Al-Moneef, M. A. (1999). 'Vertical Integration Strategies of the National Oil Companies'. *The Developing Economies,* 36 (June), 203–22.

Alamgir, M., and Arora, P. (1991). *Providing Food Security for All.* London: Intermediate Technology Publications for International Fund for Agricultural Development.

Allen, T., and Thomas, A. (eds.) (2000). *Poverty and Development into the 21st Century.* Oxford: Oxford University Press with the Open University.

Amin, A. and Thrift, N. (eds.) (1994). *Globalization, Institutions, and Regional Development in Europe.* Oxford: Oxford University Press.

Amin, S. (1997). *Capitalism in the Age of Globalization.* London: Zed Books.

Anderson, M. (1984). *Madison Avenue in Asia.* London: Associated University Presses.

Andrae, G., and Beckman, B. (1985). *The Wheat Trap.* London: Zed Books.

Ang, I. (1990). 'Culture and Communication: Towards an Ethnographic Critique of Media Consumption in the Transnational Media System'. *European Journal of Communication,* 5, 239–60.

Anker, R., and Hein, C. (eds.) (1986). *Sex Inequalities in Urban Employment in the Third World.* London: Macmillan.

Apeldoorn, B. van (2000). 'Transnational Class Agency and European Governance: The Case of the European Round Table of Industrialists'. *New Political Economy,* 5/2: 157–81.

Appadurai, A. (1996). *Modernity at Large: Cultural Dimensions of Globalization.* Minneapolis and London: University of Minnesota Press.

Araghi, F. (1995). 'Global Depeasantization, 1945–1990'. *Sociological Quarterly,* 36/2: 337–68.

Arends-Kuenning, A., and Makundi, F. (2000). 'Agricultural Biotechnology for Developing Countries: Prospects and Policies'. *American Behavioral Scientist,* 44/3: 318–49.

Armstrong, W., and McGee, T. (1985). *Theatres of Accumulation: Studies in Asian and Latin American Urbanization.* London: Methuen.

Arnfred, S. (1988). 'Women in Mozambique: Gender Struggle and Gender Politics'. *Review of African Political Economy,* 41(Sept.): 5–16.

Artisien-Maksimenko, P., and Rojec, M. (eds.) (2001). *Foreign Investment and Privatization in Eastern Europe.* Basingstoke: Palgrave.

Ashkenazi, M., and Clammer, J. (eds.) (2000). *Consumption and Material Culture in Japan.* London and New York: Kegan Paul International.

Ashwin, S. (1998). 'Endless Patience: Explaining Soviet and Post-Soviet Social Stability'. *Communist and Post-Communist Studies*, 31/2: 187–98.

Atkinson, A., and Bourguignon, F. (eds.) (2000). *Handbook of Income Distribution*. Amsterdam and New York: Elsevier.

Atwood, R., and McAnany, E. (eds.) (1986). *Communication and Latin American Society: Trends in Critical Research 1960–1985*. Madison: University of Wisconsin Press.

Aufderheide, P. (1999). *Communications Policy and the Public Interest*. New York: Guildford Press.

Avery, N., Drake, M., and Lang, T. (1993). *Cracking the Codex: An Analysis of Who Sets World Food Standards*. London: National Food Alliance.

Backman, M. (1999). *Asian Eclipse: Exposing the Dark Side of Business in Asia*. Singapore: John Wiley.

Baek, S. W. (2000). 'The Emerging Capitalist Spirit of Private Enterprises in China: Capitalism with Chinese Characteristics'. *Asian Perspective*, 24/3: 61–80.

Bagdikian, B. (1989). 'The Lords of the Global Village'. *The Nation*, 1–2 (June): 805–20.

Bailey, P., Parisotto, A., and Renshaw, G. (eds.) (1993). *Multinationals and Employment: The Global Economy of the 1990s*. Geneva: International Labour Office.

Baiocchi, G. (2001). 'Participation, Activism, and Politics: the Portoalegre Experiment and Deliberative Democratic Theory'. *Politics and Society*, 29/1: 43–72.

Balanya, B., Doherty, A., Hoedeman, O., and Ma'anit, E. (2000). *Europe Inc*. London: Pluto Press.

Balnaves, M., Donald, J., and Donald, S. H. (2001). *The Global Media Atlas*. London: British Film Institute.

Banks, J. (1997). 'MTV and the Globalization of Popular Culture'. *Gazette*, 59/1: 43–60.

Barker, C. (1997). *Global Television*. Oxford: Blackwell.

—— and Mander, G. (2000). *Invisible Government. The World Trade Organization: Global Government for the New Millennium*. San Francisco: International Forum on Globalization.

Barnathan, J. (1989). 'News in the Soviet Union'. *Television/Radio Age* (4 Sept.), 42–4.

Barnes, J., and Kaplinsky, R. (2000). 'Globalization and the Death of the Local Firm? The Automobile Components Sector in South Africa'. *Regional Studies*, 34/9: 797–812.

Barnet, R., and Muller, R. (1974). *Global Reach: The Power of the Multinational Corporation*. New York: Simon and Schuster.

Barrientos, S. (2000). 'Globalization and Ethical Trade: Assessing the Implications for Development'. *Journal of International Development*, 12: 559–70.

Bartlett, C. A., and Ghoshal, S. (1989). *Managing Across Borders: The Transnational Solution*. Boston: Harvard Business School Press.

Bassett, T. (1988). 'Development Theory and Reality: The World Bank in Northern Ivory Coast'. *Review of African Political Economy*, 41 (Sept.): 45–59.

Bassiry, G., and Dekmejian, R. (1985). 'MNCs and the Iranian Revolution: An Empirical Study'. *Management International Review*, 25/2: 67–75.

Basu, A. (ed.) (1995). *The Challenge of Local Feminisms: Women's Movements in Global Perspective*. Boulder, Colo: Westview Press.

Baudrillard, J. (1988). *Selected Writings*, ed. M. Poster. Oxford: Blackwell.

Bayat, A. (1991). *Work, Politic, and Power: An International Perspective on Workers' Control and Self-Management*. London: Zed Books.

—— (2000). 'From "Dangerous Classes" to "Quiet Rebels": Politics of the Urban Subaltern in the Global South'. *International Sociology*, 15/3: 533–57.

Baylies, C., and Bujra, J. (2000). 'HIV/AIDS in Africa: Global and Local Inequalities and Responsibilities'. *Review of African Political Economy*, 27/86: Special Issue.

Beamish, P. (1985). 'The Characteristics of Joint Ventures in Developed and Developing Countries'. *Columbia Journal of World Business*, (Fall): 13–19.

—— (1993). 'The Characteristics of Joint Ventures in the People's Republic of China'. *Journal of International Marketing*, 1/2: 29–48.

Beck, U. (1999). *World Risk Society*. Cambridge: Polity Press.

Becker, D., Frieden, J., Schatz, S., and Sklar, R. (eds.). (1987). *Postimperialism*. Boulder: Lynne Rienner.

Becker, J. (1988). 'China's Experiment with Capitalism Comes up against Free Market Vices'. *The Guardian* (5 Sept.).

Becker, L., Hedebro, G., and Paldan, L. (eds.) (1986). *Communication and Domination*. Norwood, NJ: Ablex.

Beder, S. (1997). *Global Spin: The Corporate Assault on Environmentalism*. Totnes, Devon: Green Books.

Bee, A. (2000). 'Globalization, Grapes and Gender: Women's Work in Traditional and Agro-Export Production in Northern Chile'. *Geographical Journal*, 166: 255–65.

Beeson, M. (2000). 'Mahathir and the Markets: Globalisation and the Pursuit of Economic Autonomy in Malaysia'. *Pacific Affairs*, 73/3 (Fall): 335–52.

Belk, R. (1988). 'Possessions and the Extended Self'. *Journal of Consumer Research*, 15 (Sept.), 139–68.

—— and Shultz, C. (eds.) (1994). *Consumption in Marketizing Economies*. Westport, Conn.: JAI Press.

Bello, W. (2001). '2000: The Year of Global Protest'. *International Socialism*, 90: 71–6.

—— and Rosenfeld, S. (1990). *Dragons in Distress: Asia's Miracle Economies in Crisis*. San Francisco: Institute for Food and Development Policy.

Belton, N. (1998). *The Good Listener. Helen Bamber: A Life against Cruelty*. London: Orion Books.

Beneria, L., and Feldman, S. (eds.) (1992). *Unequal Burden*. Boulder, Colo: Westview Press.

Bennet, D., and Sharp, K. (1985). *Transnational Corporations versus the State: The Political Economy of the Mexican Automobile Industry*. Princeton: Princeton University Press.

Berger, P., and Hsiao, H.-H. M. (eds.) (1988). *In Search of an East Asian Development Model*. New Brunswick, NJ: Transaction Books.

Bergson, C., Horst, T., and Moran, T. (1978). *American Multinationals and American Interests*. Washington: Brookings.

Berke, P., and Conroy, M. M. (2000). 'Are We Planning for Sustainable Development?' *Journal of the American Planning Association*, 66/1: 21–33.

Bernstein, A. (2000). 'Backlash: Behind the Anxiety Over Globalization'. *Business Week (24 Apr.)*.

Bernstein, H., Crow, B., Mackintosh, M., and Martin, C. (eds.) (1990). *The Food Question: Profits versus people?* London: Earthscan.

Bernstein, J. (ed.) (1992). *The Culture Industry: Selected Essays on Mass Culture*. London: Routledge.

Bhalla, A. (ed.) (1998). *Globalization, Growth and Marginalization*. London: Macmillan.

Birchall, J. (1997). *The International Co-operative Movement*. Manchester: Manchester University Press.

Birman, I. (1989). *Personal Consumption in the USSR and the USA*. London: Macmillan.

Blakely, E., and Snyder, M. (1997). *Fortress America*. Washington: Cato Institute.

Blecher, M. (1997). *China against the Tides*. London: Pinter.

Boddewyn, J. (1992). *Global Perspectives on Advertising Self-Regulation*. Westport, Conn: Quorum.

Boggs, C. (2000). *The End of Politics: Corporate Power and the Decline of the Public Sphere*. New York: Guildford Press.

Boies, J., and Pichardo, N. (1993-4). 'The Committee on the Present Danger: A Case for the Importance of Elite Social Movement Organizations to Theories of Social Movements and the State'. *Berkeley Journal of Sociology*, 38: 57-87.

Bonacich, E., and Applebaum, R. (2000). *Behind the Label: Inequality in the Los Angeles Apparel Industry*. Berkeley and Los Angeles: University of California Press.

Bonanno, A., and Constance, D. (1996). *Caught in the Net: The Global Tuna Industry, Environmentalism and the State*. Lawrence, Kan: University Press of Kansas.

—— Busch, L., Friedland, W., Gouveia, L., and Mingione, E. (eds.) (1994). *From Columbus to ConAgra: The Globalization of Agriculture and Food*. Lawrence Kan: University Press of Kansas.

Bond, P. (2000). *Elite Transition: From Apartheid to Neoliberalism in South Africa*. London: Pluto Press.

Boorstin, D. (1968). 'The Consumption Community'. In G. McClellan (ed.), *The Consuming Public*. New York: Wilson.

Booth, D. (ed.). (1994). *Rethinking Social Development*. London: Longman.

Bornschier, V., and Chase-Dunn, C. (eds.) (1999). *The Future of Global Conflict*. London: Sage.

Boserup, E. (1989). *Woman's Role in Economic Development*. New York: St Martin's Press.

Bowles, P., and Wagman, B. (1997). 'Globalization and the Welfare State: Four Hypotheses and Some Empirical Evidence'. *Eastern Economic Journal*, 23/3: 317-36.

Boyd-Barrett, O., and Rantanen, T. (eds.) (1998). *The Globalization of News*. London: Sage.

Braithwaite, J., and Drahos, P. (2000). *Global Business Regulation*. Cambridge: Cambridge University Press.

Branford, S. (2001). Bean stalked. *Guardian* (Society section), (5 Sept.): 8.

Brecher, J., and Costello, T. (1994). *Global Village or Global Pillage: Economic Reconstruction from the Bottom Up*. Boston: South End Press.

Brenner, R. (2001). 'The World Economy at the Turn of the Millennium toward boom or Crisis?' *Review of International Political Economy*, 8/1: 6-44.

Breslin, S. (1996). 'China: Developmental State or Dysfunctional Development?' *Third World Quarterly*, 17/4: 689-706.

Brewer, A. (1990). *Marxist Theories of Imperialism* (2nd edn.). London: Routledge and Kegan Paul.

Brewer, T., and Young, S. (1998). *Multilateral Investment System and Multinational Enterprises*. Oxford: Oxford University Press.

Brower, M., and Leon, W. (1999). *The Consumer's Guide to Effective Environmental Choices*. New York: Three Rivers Press.

Brown, C., Waltzer, H., and Waltzer, M. (2001). 'Daring to be Heard: Advertorials by Organized Interests on the Op-Ed Page of *The New York Times*, 1985-1998'. *Political Communication*, 18: 23-50.

Brown, D. (1986). *Partnership with China*. Boulder, Colo: Westview Press.

Brown, M. B. (1993). *Fair Trade: Reform and Reality in the International Trading System*. London: Zed Books.

—— (1995). *Africa's Choices: After Thirty Years of the World Bank*. Harmondsworth: Penguin Books.

Brown, W. (1992) 'Sociocultural Influences of Prodevelopment Soap Operas in the Third World'. *Journal of Popular Film and Television*, 19 (Winter): 157-64.

Brundenius, C., and Weeks, J. (eds.) (2001). *Globalization and Third World Socialism: Cuba and Vietnam*. London: Macmillan.

Bryceson, D. (1981). 'The proletarianization of women in Tanzania'. *Review of African Political Economy*, 17 (Jan.–Apr): 4–27.

Bryceson, D. F., and Jamal, V. (1997). *Farewell to Farms: De-agrarianisation and Employment in Africa*. Aldershot: Ashgate.

Brydon, L., and Chant, S. (1989). *Women in the Third World*. London: Edward Elgar.

—— and Legge, K. (1996). *Adjusting Society: The World Bank, the IMF and Ghana*. London: I.B. Tauris.

Buarque, C. (1999). *Abolishing Poverty: A Proposal for Brazil*. Brasilia: Mixed Commission, National Congress of Brazil (trans. Linda Jerome).

Buckingham, D. (1997). 'Dissin' Disney: Critical Perspectives on Children's Media Culture'. *Media, Culture and Society*, 19: 285–93.

Buckley, P., and Clegg, J. (eds.) (1991). *Multinational Enterprises in Less Developed Countries*. London: Macmillan.

Burton, J. (1972). *World Society*. Cambridge: Cambridge University Press.

Bush, R. (1996). 'The Politics of Food and Starvation'. *Review of African Political Economy*, 68: 169–95.

Buzan, B., and Little, R. (2000). *International Systems in World History: Remaking the Study of International Relations*. Oxford: Oxford University Press.

Calhoun, C. (ed.) (1994). *Social Theory and the Politics of Identity*. Oxford: Blackwell.

Callinicos, A. (2001). *Against the Third Way*. Cambridge: Polity Press.

Cannon, T. (ed.) (2000). *China's Economic Growth: The Impact on Regions, Migration and the Environment*. London: Macmillan.

Canono, J. (2001). 'Philippine Market Blends Eastern Traditions, Western Tastes'. *AgExporter (FAS online)*, 13 (Sept.): 8–13.

Caporaso, J. (ed.) (1987). *Changing International Division of Labor*. Boulder, Colo: Lynne Rienner.

Cardoso, F., and Faletto, E. (1979). *Dependency and Development in Latin America*. Berkeley: University of California Press.

Carr, M., Chen, M., and Tate, J. (2000). 'Globalization and Home-Based Workers'. *Feminist Economics*, 6/3: 123–42.

Castells, M. (1997). *The Power of Identity*. Oxford: Blackwell.

—— (2000). *The Rise of the Network Society* (2nd edn.). Oxford: Blackwell.

Chadha, K., and Kavoori, A. (2000). 'Media Imperialism Revisited: Some Findings from the Asian case'. *Media, Culture and Society*, 22/4: 415–32.

Chai, J. (1992). 'Consumption and Living Standards in China'. *China Quarterly*, 131 (Sept.), 721–49.

Chakravarty, S. (1989). 'How Pepsi Broke into India'. *Forbes* (7 Nov.): 43–4.

Chaplin, S. (1999). 'Cities, Sewers and Poverty: India's Politics of Sanitation'. *Environment and Urbanization*, 11/1: 145–58.

Chase-Dunn, C. (1982). *Socialist States in the World System*. Beverly Hills, Calif: Sage.

—— (1989). *Global Formation*. Oxford: Blackwell.

Chataway, J., Levidow, L., and Carr, S. (2000). 'Genetic Engineering of Development? Myths and Possibilities'. In T. Allen and A. Thomas (eds.), *Poverty and Development into the 21st Century* (469–84). Oxford: Oxford University Press.

Chen, L. (1999). 'Expanding Women's Co-operatives in China through Institutional Linkages'. *Development and Change*, 30: 715–38.

Cherry, C. (1978). *World Communication: Threat or promise*. (Rev. edn.). London: John Wiley.

Chetley, A. (1986). *The Politics of Baby Food*. London: Pinter.

Chinadotcom (2000). '(Inter)connecting China'. *Cambridge Review of International Affairs*, 14/1: 323–30.

Chirot, D. (ed.) (1991). *Crisis of Leninism and the Decline of the Left*. Seattle: University of Washington Press.

Chossudovsky, M. (1986). *Towards Capitalist Restoration? Chinese Socialism after Mao*. London: Macmillan.

Chowdhury, Z. (1995). *The Politics of Essential Drugs*. London: Zed Books.

Chu, G., and Alfian. (1980). 'Programming for Development in Indonesia'. *Journal of Communication* (Autumn): 50–74.

Ciccantell, P. (2001). 'NAFTA and the Reconstruction of U.S. Hegemony: The Raw Materials Foundations of Economic Competitiveness'. *Canadian Journal of Sociology*, 26/1: 57–87.

Cioffi, J. (2000). 'Governing Globalization? The State, Law, and Structural Change in Corporate Governance'. *Journal of Law and Society*, 27/4: 572–600.

Clairmonte, F., and Cavanagh, J. (1988). *Merchants of Drink: Transnational Control of World Beverages*. Penang: Third World Network.

Clarke, S., Fairbrother, P., Buroway, M., and Krotov, P. (1993). *What about the Workers? Workers and the Transition to Capitalism in Russia*. London: Verso.

Clendinnen, I. (1999). *Reading the Holocaust*. Cambridge: Cambridge University Press.

Cohen, J., and Goldstein, A. (1999). 'Institutional Addiction to Tobacco'. *Tobacco Control*, 8 (Spring), 70–4.

Cohen, R. (1997). *Global Diasporas: An Introduction*. London: UCL Press.

—— and Rai, S. M. (eds.) (2000). *Global Social Movements*. London: Athlone Press.

Cole, K. (1998). *Cuba: From Revolution to Development*. London: Pinter.

Conway, G. (1998). *The Doubly Green Revolution: Food for All in the 21st Century*. Harmondsworth: Penguin.

Cook, P., and Kirkpatrick, C. (eds.) (1995). *Privatization Policy and Performance: International Perspectives*. Hemel Hempstead: Prentice Hall/Harvester Wheatsheaf.

Cooley, A. (2001). 'Booms and Busts: Theorizing Institutional Formation and Change in Oil States'. *Review of International Political Economy*, 8 (Spring), 163–80.

Copetas, A. (1989). 'Perestroika's Yankee Partner'. *New York Times Magazine (11 June)*, Part 2: 120–2, 130, 132.

CornerHouse. (2000). *Exporting Corruption*. Sturminster Newton, Dorset: Cornerhouse Research Unit.

Cornwell, T. B. (1997). 'The Use of Sponsorship-Linked Marketing by Tobacco Firms: International Public Policy Issues'. *Journal of Consumer Affairs*, 31/2: 238–53.

Cowie, J. (1999). *Capital Moves: RCA's 70-Year Quest for Cheap Labor*. Ithaca, NY: Cornell University Press.

Cox, R. W. (1987). *Production, Power, and World Order: Social Forces in the Making of History*. New York: Columbia University Press.

Crabtree, J. (1987). *The Great Tin Crash: Bolivia and the World Tin Market*. London: Latin American Bureau.

Cragg, W. (2000). 'Human Rights and Business Ethics: Fashioning a New Social Contract'. *Journal of Business Ethics*, 27: 205–14.

Cramer, C., and Pontara, N. (1998). 'Rural Poverty and Poverty Alleviation in Mozambique: What's Missing from the Debate?' *Journal of Modern African Studies*, 36/1: 101–38.

Curran, J., and Park, M.-J. (eds.) (2000). *De-Westernizing Media Studies*. London: Routledge.

Currie, J. (2002). 'Globalization and Universities'. *Higher Education: Handbook of Theory and Research* XVIII. New York: Agathon Press.

Davis, S. (1996). 'The Theme Park: Global Industry and Cultural Form'. *Media, Culture and Society*, 18: 399–42.

Dawisha, K., and Parrott, B. (eds.) (1997). *Democratization and Authoritarianism in Postcommunist Societies*. Cambridge: Cambridge University Press.

Deacon, B., Hulse, M., and Stubbs, P. (1997). *Global Social Policy: International Welfare Organizations and the Future of the Welfare State*. London: Sage.

della Porta, D., and Diani, M. (1999). *Social Movements: An Introduction*. Oxford: Blackwell.

—— Kriesi, H., and Rucht, D. (eds.) (1999). *Social Movements in a Globalizing World*. London: Macmillan.

Denitch, B. (1992). *After the Flood: World Politics and Democracy in the Wake of Communism*. London: Adamantine Press.

Dent, M., and Peters, B. (1999). *The Crisis of Poverty and Debt in the Third World*. Aldershot: Ashgate.

Dewey, S. (1998). 'Working for the Environment: Organised Labor and the Origins of Environmentalism in the United States, 1948–1970'. *Environmental History*, 3 (Jan.): 45–63.

Diaw, K., and Schmidt-Kallert, E. (1990). *Effects of Volta Lake Resettlement in Ghana: A Reappraisal after 25 Years*. Hamburg: Institut fur Africa-Kunde.

Dicken, P. (1998). *Global Shift: Transforming the World Economy* (3rd edn.). London: Paul Chapman.

Ding, X.-l. (2000). 'Informal Privatization through Internationalization: The Rise of Nomenklatura Capitalism in China's Offshore Business'. *British Journal of Political Science*, 30/1: 121–46.

Dobson, A. (1998). *Justice and the Environment*. Oxford: Oxford University Press.

Dockemdorff, E., Rodriguez, A., and Winchester, L. (2000). 'Santiago de Chile: Metropolization, Globalization and Inequality'. *Environment and Urbanization*, 12/1: 171–83.

Dollar, D., and Svensson, J. (2000). 'What Explains the Success or Failure of Structural Adjustment Programmes?' *Economic Journal*, 110 (Oct.): 894–917.

Dominguez, J. (ed.) (1997). *Technopols: Freeing Politics and Markets in Latin America in the 1990s*. University Park, Pa: University of Pennsylvania Press.

Doran, C., Modelski, F., and Clark, C. (eds.) (1983). *North–South Relations. Studies of Dependency Reversal*. New York: Praeger.

Dorfman, A. (1983). *The Empire's Old Clothes: What the Lone Ranger, Babar and Other Innocent Heroes Do to our Minds*. London: Pluto Press.

—— and Mattelart, A. (1975). *How to Read Donald Duck: Imperialist Ideology in the Disney Comic*. London: International General.

Douglass, M., and Friedmann, J. (eds.) (1998). *Cities for Citizens: Planning and the Rise of Civil Society in a Global Age*. Chichester: John Wiley.

Dowden, R. (1987). 'Disturbing Echoes of the Pre-colonial Era in Africa'. *Independent* (14 Oct.).

Dowmunt, T. (ed.) (1993). *Channels of Resistance: Global Television and Local Empowerment*. London: BFI/Channel Four.

Drakakis-Smith, D. (2000). *Third World Cities* (2nd edn.). London: Routledge.

Dreiling, M. (2000). 'The Class Embeddedness of Corporate Political Action: Leadership in Defense of the NAFTA'. *Social Problems*, 47/1: 21–48.

Drèze, J. and Sen, A. (ed.) (1991). *The Political Economy of Hunger* (Vol. iii). Oxford: Clarendon Press.

Dror, D. (1984). 'Aspects of Labour Law and Relations in Selected Export Processing Zones'. *International Labour Review*, 3 (Nov.–Dec.), 705–22.

Dunkley, G. (2000). *The Free Trade Adventure: The WTO, the Uruguay Round and Globalism, a Critique*. London: Zed Books.

Dunn, L. (1994). 'A Sociological Analysis of Methods of Organizing Used by Women in Caribbean Free Trade Zones: Implications for Development'. Ph.D. thesis, London School of Economics.

Dunning, J. (1981). *International Production and the Multinational Enterprise*: Allen and Unwin.

—— (ed.) (1992–4). *United Nations Library on Transnational Corporations*. London: Routledge.

—— (1997). *Alliance Capitalism and Global Business*. London: Routledge.

—— and Sauvant, K. (eds.) (1996). *Transnational Corporations and World Development*. London: International Thomson.

Durning, A. (1992). *How Much is Enough*. London: Earthscan.

Dutton, M. (1998). *Streetlife China*. Cambridge: Cambridge University Press.

Dwivedi, R. (1998). 'Resisting Dams and "Development": Contemporary Significance of the Campaign against the Narmada Projects in India'. *European Journal of Development Research*, 10/2: 135–83.

—— (2001). 'Environmental Movements in the Global South: Livelihood and Beyond'. *International Sociology*, 16/1: 11–31.

Dyson, T. (2001). 'A Partial Theory of World Development: The Neglected Role of the Demographic Transition in the Shaping of Modern Society'. *International Journal of Population Geography*, 7: 67–90.

Easterlin, R. (2000). 'The Worldwide Standard of Living since 1800'. *Journal of Economic Perspectives*, 14/1: 7–26.

Eckstein, S. (1980). 'Capitalist Constraints on Cuban Socialist Development'. *Comparative Politics* (Apr.): 253–74.

Edelman, M. (1998). 'Transnational Peasant Politics in Central America'. *Latin American Research Review*, 33/3: 49–86.

Einhorn, B. (1993). *Cinderella Goes to Market: Citizenship, Gender and Women's Movements in East Central Europe*. London: Verso.

Eisenstadt, S. (ed.) (1970). *Readings in Social Evolution and Development*. Oxford: Pergamon.

Eliasoph, N. (1998). *Avoiding Politics*. New York: Cambridge University Press.

Elson, D. (ed.) (1995). *Male Bias in the Development Process* (2nd edn.). Manchester: Manchester Univerity Press.

—— and Pearson, R. (eds.) (1989). *Women's Employment and Multinationals in Europe*. London: Macmillan.

Embong, A. R. (2000). 'Globalization and Transnational Class Relations: Some Problems of Conceptualization'. *Third World Quarterly*, 21/6: 989–1000.

Emmanuel, A. (1972). *Unequal Exchange: A Study of the Imperialism of Trade*. New York: Monthly Review Press.

Enderwick, P. (ed.) (1994). *Transnational Corporations and Human Resources* (vol. xvi, United Nations Library on TNCS). London: Routledge.

Errington, D., and Gewertz, F. (1997). 'The Wewak Rotary Club: The Middle Class in Melanesia'. *Journal of the Royal Anthropological Institute' (n.s.), 3 (June): 333–53.

ESCAP/UNCTC. (1986). The Socio-economic Impact of Transnational Corporations in the Fast Food Industry: Some Findings from a Case Study of McDonald's Corporation in the Philippines'. *Asia-Pacific TNC Review* (Jan.) 40–1.

Esteinou Madrid, J. (1986). 'Means of Communication and Construction of Hegemony'. In R. Atwood and E. McAnany (eds.), *Communication and Latin American Society: Trends in Critical Research, 1960–1985*. Madison: University of Wisconsin Press.

Etzioni-Halevy, E. (1993). *The Elite Connection: Problems and Potential of Western Democracy*. Cambridge: Polity Press.

Evans, P. (1979). *Dependent Development: The Alliance of Multinational, State and Local Capital in Brazil*. Princeton: Princeton University Press.

—— (1995). *Embedded Autonomy*. Princeton: Princeton University Press.

—— Rueschmeyer, D., and Skocpol, T. (eds.). (1985). *Bringing the State Back In*. Cambridge: Cambridge University Press.

Ewen, S. (1976). *Captains of Consciousness*. New York: McGraw-Hill.

—— (1988). *All Consuming Images: The Politics of Style in Contemporary Culture*. New York: Basic Books.

Faist, T. (2000). *The Volume and Dynamics of Migration*. Oxford: Oxford University Press.

Falk, R. (1999). *Predatory Globalization: A Critique*. Cambridge: Polity Press.

—— (2000). 'Humane Governance for the World: Reviving the Quest'. *Review of International Political Economy*, 7/2: 317–34.

Faltermayer, E. (1991). 'U.S. Companies Come Back Home'. *Fortune* (30 Dec.), 88–92.

Fan, C. C. (1997). 'Uneven Development and Beyond: Regional Development Theory in Post-Mao China'. *International Journal of Urban and Regional Research*, 21/4: 620–39.

FAO (1999). *Food Insecurity Report*. Rome: Food and Agriculture Organization.

—— (2001). *FAO Focus: Women and Food Security* (www.fao.org/focus/e/women).

FAO/WHO (1999) *Understanding the Codex Alimentarius*. Rome: FAO/WHO.

Farr, M. (1990). 'East is Open for Business'. *Guardian (12 Mar.)*.

Fath, J. (1985). *Women and the Growth of Agro-industries in Developing Countries*. Vienna: UNIDO, mimeo.

Featherstone, M. (1987). 'Consumer Culture, Symbolic Power and Universalism'. In G. Stauth and S. Zubaida (eds.), *Mass Culture, Popular Culture, and Social Life in the Middle East*. Boulder, Colo: Westview Press.

—— (ed.) (1990). *Global Culture: Nationalism, Globalization and Modernity*. London: Sage.

Feder, E. (1978). *Strawberry Imperialism*. London: America Latina.

Fejes, F. (1980). 'The Growth of Multinational Advertising Agencies in Latin America'. *Journal of Communication*, 30 (Autumn): 36–49.

Fennema, M., and Maussen, M. (2000). 'Dealing with Extremists in Public Discussion: Front National and "Republican Front" in France'. *Journal of Political Philosophy*, 8/3: 379–400.

—— and Tillie, J. (1999). 'Political Participation and Political Trust in Amsterdam: Civic Communities and Ethnic Networks'. *Journal of Ethnic and Migration Studies*, 25/4: 703–26.

Ferdinand, P. (ed.) (2000). 'The Internet, Democracy and Democratization'. *Democratization*, 7/1: whole issue.

Fernandes, L. (2000). 'Nationalizing "the global": Media Images, Cultural Politics and the Middle Class in India'. *Media, Culture and Society*, 22/5: 611–28.

Field, J. (1973). 'Transnationalism and the New Tribe'. In R. Keohane and J. Nye (eds.), *Transnational Relations and World Politics*. Cambridge, Mass.: Harvard University Press.

Fieldhouse, D. K. (1986). 'The Multinational Corporation: Critique of a Concept'. In A. Teichova, and M. Levy-Leboyer, and H. Nussbaum (eds.), *Multinational Enterprise in Historical Perspective*. Cambridge: Cambridge University Press.

Findlay, M. (1999). *The Globalization of Crime: Understanding Transitional Relationships in Context*. Cambridge: Cambridge University Press.

Fischer, P. (2000). *Foreign Direct Investment in Russia: A Strategy for Industrial Recovery*. London: Macmillan.

Fisher, K., and Urich, P. (2001). 'TNCs: Aid Agents for the New Millennium?' *Development in Practice*, 11/1: 7–19.

Fishwick, M. (ed.) (1983). *Ronald Revisited: The World of Ronald McDonald*. Bowling Green, Oh: Bowling Green University Popular Press.

Fitzgerald, E., and Wuyts, M. (eds.) (1988). *Markets within Planning: Socialist Economic Management in the Third World*. London: Cass.

Flora, C., and Flora, J. (1978). 'The Fotonovela as a Tool for Class and Cultural Domination'. *Latin American Perspectives*, 1 (Winter): 134–49.

Footer, M., and Graber, C. B. (2000). 'Trade Liberalization and Cultural Policy'. *Journal of International Economic Law*, 3/1: 115–44.

Forbes, D., and Thrift, N. (eds.) (1987). *The Socialist Third World: Urban Development and Territorial Planning*. Oxford: Blackwell.

Forsyth, T. (2001). 'Environmental Social Movements in Thailand: How Important is Class?' *Southeast Asian Journal of Social Science*, 29/1.

Forsythe, D. (2000). *Human Rights in International Relations*. Cambridge: Cambridge University Press.

Foster, H. (ed.) (1985). *Postmodern Culture*. London: Pluto Press.

Fox, J., and Brown, L. D. (eds.) (1998). *The Struggle for Accountability: the World Bank, NGOs, and Grassroots Movements*. Cambridge Mass: MIT Press.

Frank, A. G. (1977). 'Long Live Transideological Enterprise! The Socialist Economies in the Capitalist International Division of Labour'. *Review*, 1 (Summer): 91–140.

—— (1984). *Critique and Anti-Critique*. London: Macmillan.

Frank, T. (1998). *The Conquest of the Cool: Business Culture, Counterculture, and the Rise of Hip Consumerism*. Chicago: University of Chicago Press.

Freeland, C. (2000). *Sale of the Century: The Inside Story of the Second Russian Revolution*. London: Little, Brown.

Freese, R. (2001). 'China's Construction Market: A New Star in the East'. *AgExporter* (FAS online), 13 (Jan.): 1–4.

Frey, R. S. (1997). 'The International Traffic in Tobacco'. *Third World Quarterly*, 18/2: 303–19.

Friedmann, J. (2000). 'The Good City: In Defense of Utopian Thinking'. *International Journal of Urban and Regional Research*, 24/2: 460–72.

Fröbel, F., Heinrichs, J., and O. Kreye, (1980). *The New International Division of Labour. Structural Unemployment in Industrialized Countries and Industrialization in Developing Countries*. Cambridge: University Press.

Fung, A., and Wright, E. (2001). 'Deepening Democracy: Innovations and Empowered Participatory Governance'. *Politics and Society*, 29/1: 5–41.

Gail, B. (1978). 'The West's Jugular Vein: Arab Oil'. *Armed Forces Journal International* (Aug.): 18–32.

Gal, S., and Kligman, G. (eds.) (2000). *Reproducing Gender: Politics, Publics, and Everyday Life After Socialism*. Princeton: Princeton University Press.

Gamir, A., and Mendez, R. (2000). 'Business Networks and New Distribution Methods: The Spread of Franchises in Spain'. *International Journal of Urban and Regional Research*, 24/3: 653–74.

Ganguly-Scrase, R., and Scrase, T. (1999). 'A Bitter Pill or Sweet Nectar?: Contradictory Attitudes of Salaried Workers to Economic Liberalization in India'. *Development and Society*, 28/2: 259–83.

GAO (2001). *International Monetary Fund: Efforts to Advance U.S. Policies at the Fund* (GAO-01-214). Washington: General Accounting Office.

Garcia Canclini, N. (2001). *Consumers and Citizens* (trans. G. Yudice). Minneapolis: University of Minnesota Press.

Garcia-Johnson, R. (2000). *Exporting Environmentalism: U.S. Multinational Chemical Corporations in Brazil and Mexico*. Cambridge, Mass.: MIT Press.

Garnsey, E., and Paukert, L. (1987). *Industrial Change and Women's Employment: Trends in the New International Division of Labour*. Geneva: International Institute for Labour Studies.

Gereffi, G. (2001). 'Shifting Governance Structures in Global Commodity Chains, With Special Reference to the Internet'. *American Behavioural Scientist*, 44/10: 1616–637.

—— and Kaplinsky, R. (eds.) (2001). 'The Value of Value Chains'. *IDS Bulletin*, 32/3: whole issue.

—— and Korzeniewicz, M. (eds.) (1994). *Commodity Chains and Global Capitalism*. Westport, Conn: Praeger.

—— and Wyman, D. (eds.) (1990). *Manufacturing Miracles: Paths of Industrialisation in Latin America and East Asia*. Princeton: Princeton University Press.

Gerlach, M. (1992). *Alliance Capitalism: The Social Organization of Japanese Capitalism*. Berkeley and Los Angeles: University of California Press.

Gershenberg, I. (1987). 'The Training and Spread of Managerial Know-how: A Comparative Analysis of Multinational and Other Firms in Kenya'. *World Development*, 15 (July), 931–9.

Geyikdagi, Y. (1984). 'Attitudes towards Multinationals: The Middle East in the World Context'. *Management Decision*, 22/3: 14–21.

Ghimire, K. (ed.). (2001). *The Native Tourist: Mass Tourism within Developing Countries*. London: Earthscan.

Gibbs, D. (2000). 'Globalization, the Bioscience Industry and Local Environmental Responses'. *Global Environmental Change*, 10: 242–57.

Giddens, A. (1990). *The Consequences of Modernity*. Cambridge: Polity Press.

—— (2000). *The Third Way and its Critics*. Cambridge: Polity Press.

Giffard, C. (1984). 'Inter Press Service: News from the Third World'. *Journal of Communication*, (Autumn): 41–59.

Gill, G., and Markwick, R. (2000). *Russia's Stillborn Democracy?: From Gorbachev to Yeltsin*. New York: Oxford University Press.

Gill, S. (ed.) (1993). *Gramsci, Historical Materialism and International Relations*. Cambridge: Cambridge University Press.

Gillespie, K. (1984). *The Tripartite Relationship*. New York: Praeger.

Gills, B., and Qadir, S. (eds.) (1995). *Regimes in Crisis: The Post-Soviet Era and Implications for Development*. London: Zed Books.

Girvan, N. (1976). *Corporate Imperialism: Conflict and Expropriation*. New York: Monthly Review Press.

Glantz, S., Slade, J., Bero, L., Hanauer, P., and Barnes, D. (eds.) (1996). *The Cigarette Papers*. Berkeley and Los Angeles: University of California Press.

Goldfrank, W., Goodman, D., and Szasz, A. (eds.). (1999). *Ecology and the World-System*. Westport, Conn.: Greenwood Press.

Golding, P., and Harris, P. (eds.) (1997). *Beyond Cultural Imperialism: Globalization, Communication and the New International Order*. London: Sage.

Goodman, J. (1993). *Tobacco in History: The Cultures of Dependence*. London: Routledge.

Gorbachev, M. (1988). *Perestroika*. London: Collins.

Goss, J. (1993). 'The "Magic of the Mall": An Analysis of Form, Function and Meaning in the Contemporary Retail Built Environment'. *Annals of the Association of American Geographers*, 83/1: 18–47.

Gott, R. (1990). 'The Blue Pimpernels'. *Guardian (15 Jan.)*.

Grabowski, R. (1994). 'The Successful Developmental State: Where Does It Come From?' *World Development*, 22/3: 413–22.

Graham, R. (1982). *The Aluminium Industry and the Third World*. London: Zed Books.

Graham, S. (1999). 'Global Grids of Glass: On Global Cities, Telecommunications and Planetary Urban Networks'. *Urban Studies*, 36/5–6: 929–49.

Greaves, L. (1996). *Smoke Screen: Women's Smoking and Social Control*. London: Scarlett Press.

Green, C. (1998). 'The Asian Connection: The U.S.-Caribbean Apparel Circuit and a New Model of Industrial Relations'. *Latin American Research Review*, 33/3: 7–47.

Grieco, J. (1984). *Between Dependence and Autonomy: India's Experience with the International Computer Industry*. Berkeley: University of California Press.

Guan, X. (2000). 'China's Social Policy: Reform and Development in the Context of Marketization and Globalization'. *Social Policy and Administration*, 34/1: 115–30.

Guback, T., and Varis, T. (1982). *Transnational Communication and Cultural Industries*. Paris: UNESCO.

Guerlain, P. (1997). 'The Ironies and Dilemmas of America's Cultural Dominance: A Transcultural Approach'. *American Studies International*, 35/2: 30–51.

Guidry, J., Kennedy, M., and Zald, M. (eds.) (2000). *Globalizations and Social Movements: Culture, Power, and the Transnational Public Sphere*. Ann Arbor: University of Michigan Press.

Gupta, N. (1998). *Switching Channels: Ideologies of Television in India*. New Delhi: Oxford University Press.

Gustafson, T. (1999). *Capitalism Russian-Style*. Cambridge: Cambridge University Press.

Gutman, P. (1992). 'The Opening of the USSR to Foreign Capital: From Concessions during NEP to Joint Ventures under perestroika'. In M. Lavigne (ed.), *The Soviet Union and Eastern Europe in the Global Economy* (ch. 9). Cambridge: Cambridge University Press.

Habermas, J. (1976). *Legitimation Crisis* (trans. T. McCarthy). London: Heinemann.

—— (1989). *Lifeworld and System: A Critique of Functionalist Reason* (vol. ii of *The Theory of Communicative Action*) (trans. T. McCarthy). Boston: Beacon Press.

Halebsky, S., and Kirk, J. (1992). *Cuba in Transition: Crisis and Transformation*. Boulder, Colo: Westview Press.

Hall, T. (ed.) (2000). *A World-Systems Reader*. Lanham, Md.: Rowman and Littlefield.

Hall, T. and Hubbard, P. (1998). *The Entrepreneurial City*. New York: John Wiley.

Halliday, F. (1999). *Revolution and World Politics: The Rise and Fall of the Sixth Great Power*. London: Macmillan.

Hamel, P., Lustiger-Thaler, H., and Mayer, M. (eds.) (2000). *Urban Movements in a Globalising World*. London: Routledge.

Hamelink, C. (1984). *Transnational Data Flows in the Information Age*. Lund: Studentliteratur.

Hanlon, J. (2000). 'Violence in Mozambique: In Whose Interests?' *Review of African Political Economy*, 27/86: 593–8.

Hann, C. (1993). 'Property Relations in the New Eastern Europe: The Case of Specialist Cooperatives in Hungary'. In H. De Soto and D. Anderson (eds.), *The Curtain Rises: Rethinking Culture, Ideology and the State in Eastern Europe* (ch. 5). New Jersey: Humanities Press.

Hansen, P. (1974). *Advertising and Socialism*. London: Macmillan.

Hansson, O. (1989). *Inside Ciba-Geigy*. Penang: International Organization of Consumer Unions.

Harding, H. (1993). 'The Concept of "greater China": Themes, Variations, and Reservations'. *China Quarterly*, 136 (Dec.), 660–86.

Harmes, A. (1998). 'Institutional Investors and the Reproduction of Neoliberalism'. *Review of International Political Economy*, 5 (Spring): 92–121.

Harrison, B. (1994). *Lean and Mean: The Changing Landscape of Corporate Power in the Age of Flexibility*. New York: Basic Books.

Harrison, D. (1988). *The Sociology of Modernization and Development*. London: Macmillan.

Hart, D. (1993). 'Class Formation and Industrialization of Culture: The Case of South Korea's Emerging Middle Class'. *Korea Journal*, 33 (Summer): 42–57.

Hart, M. (1997). 'The WTO and the Political Economy of Globalization'. *Journal of World Trade*, 31 (Oct.): 75–93.

Harvey, D. (1989). *The Condition of Postmodernity*. Boston: Blackwell.

Hauck, D., Voorhes, C., and Goldberg, C. (1983). *Two Decades of Debate: The Controversy over U.S. Companies in South Africa*. Washington: Investor Responsibility Research Center.

Heath, J. (ed.) (1993). *Revitalizing Socialist Enterprise: A Race against Time*. London: Routledge.

Heer, J. (1991). *Nestlé 125 Years 1866–1991*. Vevey: Nestlé SA.

Heilman, B., and Lucas, J. (1997). 'A Social Movement for African Capitalism? A Comparison of Business Associations in Two African Cities'. *African Studies Review*, 40/2: 141–71.

Held, D., McGrew, A., Goldblatt, D., and Perraton, J. (1999). *Global Transformations: Politics, Economics and Culture*. Cambridge: Polity Press.

Heller, P. (2001). 'Moving the State: The Politics of Democratic Decentralization in Kerala, South Africa and Porto Alegre'. *Politics and Society*, 29/1: 131–63.

Hellman, J., and Schankerman, M. (2000). 'Intervention, Corruption and Capture: The Nexus between Enterprises and the State'. *Economics of Transition*, 8/3: 545–76.

Hemphill, G. (1986). 'Selling the World: Soft Drink Potential is Staggering'. *Beverage Industry* (Sept.): 1–124.

Henderson, J. (1989). *The Globalisation of High Technology Production*. London: Routledge.

Henderson, W. (2000). 'Review Article. Metaphors, Narrative and "Truth": South Africa's TRC'. *African Affairs*, 99: 457–65.

Herbst, J. (2001). 'Review Article. Political Liberalization in Africa after Ten Years'. *Comparative Politics*, 33/3: 357–75.

Herman, E., and McChesney, R. (1997). *The Global Media: The New Missionaries of Corporate Capitalism*. London: Cassell.

Hernadi, A. (ed.) (1992). *Consumption and Development: Economic, Social and Technical Aspects*. Budapest: Hungarian Scientific Council for World Economy.

Herod, A. (2001). *Labor Geographies: Workers and the Landscapes of Capitalization*. New York: Guildford Press.

Herry-Priyono, B. (2001). 'The Predicament of a Rent-Seeking Society: A Sociology of Business-Government Relations in Indonesia'. Ph.D. thesis, London School of Economics.

Hertz, E. (1998). *The Trading Crowd: An Ethnography of the Shanghai Stock Market*. Cambridge: Cambridge University Press.

Hewat, T. (1991). *Modern Merchants of Death*. Victoria: Wrightbooks.

Hicks, N., and Streeton, P. (1979). 'Indicators of Development: The Search for a Basic Needs Yardstick'. *World Development*, July: 567–80.

Higgott, R., and Phillips, N. (2000). 'Challenging Triumphalism and Convergence: The Limits of Global Liberalization in Asia and Latin America'. *Review of International Studies*, 26: 359–79.

—— Underhill, G., and Bieler, A. (eds.) (2000). *Non-State Actors and Authority in the Global System*. London: Routledge.

Higley, J., Pakulski, J., and Wesolowski, W. (eds.) (1998). *Postcommunist Elites and Democracy in Eastern Europe*. London: Macmillan.

Hildyard, N. (1996). 'Public Risk, Private Profit: The World Bank and the Private Sector'. *Ecologist*, 26 (July/Aug.), 176–78.

Hill, H. (1982). 'Vertical Inter-firm Linkages in LDCs: A Note on the Philippines'. *Oxford Bulletin of Economics and Statistics*, 44 (Aug.): 261–71.

Hill, J., and Boya, U. (1987). 'Consumer Goods Promotions in Developing Countries'. *International Journal of Advertising*, 6: 249–64.

Hill, P. (1986). *Development Economics of Trial*. Cambridge, Cambridge University Press.

Hill, R. C., and Kim, J. W. (2000). 'Global Cities and Developmental States: New York, Tokyo and Seoul'. *Urban Studies*, 37/12: 2167–95.

Hiller, H. (2000). 'Mega-Events, Urban Boosterism and Growth Strategies: An Analysis of the Objectives and Legitimations of the Cape Town 2004 Olympic Bid'. *International Journal of Urban and Regional Research*, 24/2: 439–58.

Hines, C. (2000). *Localization: A Global Manifesto*. London: Earthscan.

Hirschman, A. (1958). *The Strategy of Economic Development*. New Haven: Yale University Press.

Hirst, P., and Thompson, G. (1996). *Globalization in Question: The International Economy and the Possibilities of Governance*. Cambridge: Polity Press.

Hoatson, L. (2001). 'Community Development Practice Surviving New Right Government: A British and Victorian Comparison'. *Community Development Journal*, 36/1: 18–29.

Hodder, R. (1996). *Merchant Princes of the East: Cultural Delusions, Economic Success, and the Overseas Chinese in Southeast Asia*. New York: John Wiley.

Holzer, B. (2001). 'Transnational Subpolitics and Corporate Discourse: A Study of Environmental Protest and the Royal Dutch/Shell Group'. Ph.D. thesis, London School of Economics.

Hong, J., and Hsu, U-C. (1999). 'Asian NIC's Broadcast Media in the Era of Globalization: The Trend of Commercialization and its Impact, Implications and Limits'. *Gazette*, 61/3–4: 225–42.

Hong, L. (1998). 'Profit or Ideology? The Chinese Press Between Party and Market'. *Media, Culture and Society*, 20/1: 31–41.

Hood, N., and Young, S. (eds.) (2000). *The Globalization of Multinational Enterprise Activity and Economic Development*. New York: St Martin's Press.

Hoskins, C., and Mirus, R. (1988). 'Reasons for the US Dominance of the International Trade in Television Programmes'. *Media, Culture and Society*, 10: 499–515.

Howard, D., and Mayo, M. (1988). 'Developing a Defensive Product Management Philosophy for the Third World Markets'. *International Marketing Review*, 5: 31–40.

Howells, J., and Wood, M. (1993). *The Globalization of Production and Technology*. London: Belhaven Press.

Hughes, J. (2000). *Ecology and Historical Materialism*. Cambridge: Cambridge University Press.

Ihonvbere, J., and Shaw, T. (1988). *Towards a Political Economy of Nigeria: Petroleum and Politics at the (Semi-)Periphery*. Aldershot: Avebury.

ILO. (1984). *Technical Choice and Employment Generation by Multinational Enterprises in Developing Countries*. Geneva: ILO.

INFACT. (1998). *Global Aggression: The Case for World Standards and Bold US Action Challenging Philip Morris and RJR Nabisco*. New York: Apex Press.

Inglehart, R. (1997). *Modernization and Postmodernization: Cultural, Economic, and Political Change*. Princeton: Princeton University Press.

International Confederation of Free Trade Unions (ICFTU) (1983). *Trade Unions and the Transnationals, Export Processing Zones* (Bulletin, Special Issue March no. 3, mimeo). Brussels: ICFTU.

Isserman, A. (ed.) (2001). 'Genetically Modified Food: Understanding the Societal Dilemma'. *American Behavioral Scientist*, 44/8: whole issue.

Ivanov, I. (1987). 'Joint ventures in the Soviet Union'. *TNC Reporter*, 23 (Spring): 49–51.

Jabbonsky, L. (1986). 'Double Cola Seeks a Place in the Third World'. *Beverage World* (Sept.): 186–90.

Jacobson, T. (1993). *Waste Management: An American Corporate Success Story*. New York: Gateway Business Books.

Jamal, V., and Weeks, J. (1993). *Africa Misunderstood or Whatever Happened to the Rural-Urban Gap?* London: Macmillan.

James, J. (1983). *Consumer Choice in the Third World*. London: Macmillan.

—— (2000). *Consumption, Globalization and Development*. London: Macmillan.

—— and Stewart, F. (1981). 'New Products: A Discussion of the Welfare Effects of the Introduction of New Products in Developing Countries'. *Oxford Economic Papers*, 33: 81–107.

Jameson, F. (1991). *Postmodernism, or, The Cultural Logic of Late Capitalism*. London: Verso.

—— and Miyoshi, M. (eds.) (1998). *Cultures of Globalization*. Durham, NC: Duke University Press.

Janus, N. (1986). 'Transnational Advertising: Some Considerations on the Impact on Peripheral Societies'. In R. Atwood and E. McAnany (eds.), *Communication and Latin American Society: Trends in Critical Research 1960–1985* (ch. 7). Madison: University of Wisconsin Press.

Jefkins, F., and Ubgoajah, F. (1986). *Communications in Industrializing Countries*. London: Macmillan.

Jenkins, R. (1987). *Transnational Corporations and Uneven Development*. London: Methuen.

Jernigan, D. (1997). *Thirsting for Markets: The Global Impact of Corporate Alcohol*. San Rafael, Calif: Marin Institute.

Jodice, D. (1980). 'Sources of Change in Third World Regimes for Foreign Direct Investment'. *International Organization*, 34 (Spring): 177–206.

John, N. (2000). 'The Campaign Against British Bank Involvement in Apartheid South Africa'. *African Affairs*, 99: 415–33.

Jomo, K. S. (1998). *Tigers in Trouble*. London: Zed Books.

Jones, D., and Brown, D. (1994). 'Singapore and the Myth of the Liberalizing Middle Class'. *Pacific Review*, 7: 79–87.

Jones, M. (1998). 'Blade Runner Capitalism, the Transnational Corporation, and Commodification: Implications for Cultural Integrity'. *Cultural Dynamics*, 10/3: 287–306.

Joshi, A. (forthcoming). 'Globalization, Agribiotechnology and Sustainable Development'. Ph.D. thesis in progress, London School of Economics.

Journal of Communication (1985). 'What Now? Telecommunications Development. The U.S. Effort'. *Journal of Communication*, 35 (Spring): 8–51.

—— (1989). 'The Information Gap'. Summer, special issue.

Judd, D., and Fainstein, S. (eds.) (1999). *The Tourist City*. New Haven and London: Yale University Press.

Kagarlitsky, B. (1989). 'The Market instead of Democracy'. *International Socialism*, 45: 93–104.

—— (2000). *The Twilight of Globalization* (trans. R. Clarke). London: Pluto.

Kalantaridis, C. (2000). 'Globalization and Entrepreneurial Response in Post-Socialist Transformation: A Case Study from Transcarpathia, Ukraine'. *European Planning Studies*, 8/3: 285–99.

Kaldor, M. (1999). 'Transnational Civil Society'. In T. Dunne and N. Wheeler (eds.), *Human Rights in Global Politics* (195–213). Cambridge: Cambridge University Press.

Kaplinsky, R. (1979). 'Inappropriate Products and Technique: Breakfast Food in Kenya'. *Review of African Political Economy*, 14 (Jan.–Apr.): 90–6.

—— (ed.) (1984). *Third World Industrialisation in the 1980s: Open Economies in a Closing World*. London: Cass.

Karliner, J. (1997). *The Corporate Planet: Ecology and Politics in the Age of Globalization*. San Francisco: Sierra Club Books.

—— (1999). 'Co-opting the UN'. *Ecologist*, 29 (Aug./Sept.), 318–21.

Kaufman, E. (1988). *Crisis in Allende's Chile*. New York: Praeger.

Kawewe, S., and Dibie, R. (2000). 'The Impact of Economic Structural Adjustment Programs [ESAPs] on Women and Children: Implications for Social Welfare in Zimbabwe'. *Journal of Sociology and Social Welfare*, 27/4: 79–107.

Kay, C. (1989). *Latin American Theories of Development*. London: Routledge.

Kaynak, E. (1985). 'Some Thoughts on Consumerism in Developed and Less Developed Countries'. *International Marketing Review* (Summer): 15–30.

—— (ed.) (1988). *Transnational Retailing*. Berlin: Walter de Gruyter.

—— and Lee, K. (eds.) (1989). *Global Business: Asia-Pacific Dimensions*. London: Routledge.

Keck, E., and Sikkink, K. (1998). *Activists Beyond Borders: Advocacy Networks in International Politics*. Ithaca: Cornell University Press.

Keller, E., and Rothchild, D. (eds.) (1987). *Afro-Marxist Regimes: Ideology and Public Policy*. Boulder, Colo: Lynne Rienner.

Kelsall, T. (2000). 'Governance, Local Politics and Districtization in Tanzania: The 1998 Arumeru Tax Revolt'. *African Affairs*, 99: 533–51.

Keohane, R., and Nye, J. (eds.) (1973). *Transnational Relations and World Politics*. Cambridge, Mass: Harvard University Press.

Khaing, M. M. (1986). 'Entrepreneurs within a Socialist Economy—Burma'. *Southeast Asian Business*, 11 (Fall): 36–41.

King, A. (ed.) (1991). *Culture, Globalization and the World-System*. London: Macmillan.

King, C. (2000). 'Post-Postcommunism: Transition, Comparison, and the End of "Eastern Europe" (Review Article)'. *World Politics*, 53/1: 143–72.

King, R. (1986). 'Aggressive Promotion of Imported Consumer Products by a Socialist State Enterprise'. Paper presented at the Proceedings of the 1986 Conference of the American Academy of Advertising.

Kirim, A. (1986). 'Transnational Corporations and Local Capital: Comparative Conduct and Performance in the Turkish Pharmaceutical Industry'. *World Development*, 14 (Apr.): 503–21.

Kivikuru, U. (1988). 'From Import to Modelling: Finland—An Example of Old Periphery Dependency'. *European Journal of Communication*, 3: 9–34.

Klein, N. (2000). *No Logo*. London: Flamingo.

Kluger, R. (1997). *Ashes to Ashes: America's Hundred-Year Cigarette War, the Public Health and the Unabashed Triumph of Philip Morris*. New York: Knopf.

Kneen, B. (1995). *Invisible Giant*. London: Pluto Press.

Knight, D. (1988). *Mozambique: Caught in the Trap*. London: Christian Aid.

Knox, P., and Taylor, P. (eds.) (1995). *World Cities in a World System*. Cambridge: Cambridge University Press.

Kobrin, S. (1980). 'Foreign Investment and Forced Divestment in LDCs'. *International Organization*, 34 (Winter): 65–88.

—— (1988). 'Expatriate Reduction and Strategic Control in American Multinational Corporations'. *Human Resource Management*, 27 (Spring): 63–75.

Korbonski, A. (1989). 'The Politics of Economic Reforms in Eastern Europe: The Last Thirty Years'. *Soviet Studies*, 41: 1–19.

Korten, D. (1995). *When Corporations Rule the World*. San Francisco: Kumarian Press.

Korzeniewicz, R. P., and Moran, T. P. (1997). 'World-Economic Trends in the Distribution of Income, 1965–1992'. *American Journal of Sociology*, 102 (Jan.): 1000–39.

Kothari, U., and Nababsing, V. (eds.) (1996). *Gender and Industrialisation: Mauritius, Bangladesh, Sri Lanka*. Mauritius: Éditions de l'Océan Indien.

Kovacs, D., and Maggard, S. (1993). 'The Human Face of Political, Economic, and Social Change in Eastern Europe'. *East European Quarterly*, 28 (Sept.): 317–49.

Kowaleski, D. (1982). *Transnational Corporations and Carribean Inequalities*. New York: Praeger.

Kryshtanovskaya, O. (1994). 'Rich and Poor in Post-Communist Russia'. *Journal of Communist Studies and Transition Politics*, 10 (Mar.): 3–24.

Kumar, A. V. R. (2001). 'Tobacco Use: An Urgent Health Concern'. *Economic and Political Weekly* (17 Feb.): 530–2.

Kumar, K. (ed.) (1980). *Transnational Enterprises: Their Impact on Third World Societies and Cultures*. Boulder, Colo.: Westview Press.

Kunzle, D. (1978). 'Chile's La Firme versus ITT'. *Latin American Perspectives*, 16 (Winter): 119–33.

Ladino, C. (1999). 'Maquiladora Employment, Low Income Households and Gender Dynamics: A Case Study of Ciudad Juarez, Mexico'. Ph.D. thesis, London School of Economics.

LaFont, S. (2001). 'One Step Forward, Two Steps Back: Women in Post-Communist States'. *Communist and Post-Communist Studies*, 34: 203–20.

Lai, H. H. (2001). 'Behind China's World Trade Organization Agreement with the USA'. *Third World Quarterly*, 22/2: 237–55.

Laiodi, Z. (1988). *The Third World and the Soviet Union*. London: Zed Books.

Lall, S. (ed.) (1983). *The New Multinationals: The Spread of Third World Enterprises*. Chichester: John Wiley.

—— (1985). *Multinationals, Technology, and Exports*. London: Macmillan.

Lane, D. (1993). 'Political Elites and Leadership under Yeltsin'. *RFE/RL Research Report*, 2/30: 29–35.

Lang, T., and Hines, C. (1993). *The New Protectionism: Protecting the Future against Free Trade*. London: Earthscan.

Langman, L., Morris, D., and Zalewski, J. (2002). 'Globalization, Domination, and Cyberactivisim'. In W. Dunaway (ed.), *The 21st Century World-System: Systemic Crisis and Antisystemic Resistance*. Westport, Conn.: Greenwood Press.

Lappe, M., and Bailey, B. (1999). *Against the Grain: The Genetic Transformation of Global Agriculture*. London: Earthscan.

Lascaris, R. (1993). 'Report on Advertising around the Globe: The New Third World'. *Campaign* (24 Sept.).

Lasserre, P. (1982). 'Training: Key to Technological Transfer'. *Long Range Planning*, 15/3: 51–60.

Laurell, A. C. (2000). 'Structural Adjustment and the Globalization of Social Policy in Latin America'. *International Sociology*, 15/2: 306–25.

Lavelle, K. (2001). 'Ideas within a Context of Power: The African Group in an Evolving UNCTAD'. *Journal of Modern African Studies*, 39/1: 25–50.

Lazarus, N. (1999). *Nationalism and Cultural Practice in the Postcolonial World*. Cambridge: Cambridge University Press.

Lechner, F., and Boli, J. (eds.) (2000). *The Globalization Reader*. Boston and Oxford: Blackwell.

Lee, C.-C. (1980). *Media Imperialism Reconsidered: The Homogenizing of Television Culture*. Beverly Hills, Calif.: Sage.

Lee, C. (1987). 'Hong Kong Clothing Union: Job Saving Campaign'. *TUEC Bulletin* 3: 2–3.

Lee, K., Humphreys, D., and Pugh, M. (1998). 'Privatization in the United Nations System: Patterns of Influence in Three Intergovernmental Organizations'. *Global Society*, 1/3: 42–54.

Leisink, P. (ed.) (1999). *Globalization and Labour Relations*. Cheltenham: Edward Elgar.

Leonard, R. (1986). 'After Bophal: Multinationals and the Management of Hazardous Products and Processes'. *Multinational Business*, 2: 1–9.

Leopold, M. (1985). 'The Transnational Food Companies and their Global Stategies'. *International Social Science Journal*, 105: 315–30.

Li, F., and Li, J. (1999). *Foreign Investment in China*. London: Macmillan.

Liebes, T., and Katz, E. (1990). *The Export of Meaning. Cross-Cultural Readings of Dallas*. New York: Oxford University Press.

Lim, L. (1985). *Women Workers in Multinational Enterprises in Developing Countries*. Geneva: ILO.

Lim, P. (1988). 'Credit Goes Charging into China'. *China Trade Communique* (June): 4–16.

Lindsey, M. (1989). *International Business in Gorbachev's Soviet Union*. London: Pinter.

Lloyd, P. (1982). *A Third World Proletariat?* London: Allen and Unwin.

Lo, C. W. H., and Leung, S. W. (2000). 'Environmental Agency and Public Opinion in Guangzhou: The Limits of a Popular Approach to Environmental Governance'. *China Quarterly*, 163 (Sept.): 677–704.

Logan, I. B., and Mengisteab, K. (1993). 'IMF-World Bank Adjustment and Structural Transformation in Sub-Saharan Africa'. *Economic Geography*, 69/1: 1–24.

Long, F. (1986). *Employment Effects of Multinational Enterprises in Export Processing Zones in the Caribbean* (Working Paper No. 42). Geneva: ILO/UNCTC Multinational Enterprises Programme.

Long, G., and Ng, M. K. (2001). 'The Political Economy of Intra-provincial Disparities in Post-reform China: A Case study of Jiangsu Province. *Geoforum*, 32/2: 215–34.

Łoś, M. (ed.) (1990). *The Second Economy in Marxist States*. London: Macmillan.

—— and Zybertowicz, A. (2000). *Privatizing the Police-State: The Case of Poland*. London: Macmillan.

Loxley, J., and Saul, J. (1975). 'Multinationals, Workers and the Parastatals in Tanzania'. *Review of African Political Economy*, 2 (Jan.-Apr.): 54–67.

Lu, P. (2001). 'New-New People, A Special Lifestyle'. *Beijing Review* (31 May): 13–17.

Lubeck, P. (ed.) (1987). *The African Bourgeoisie*. Boulder, Colo: Lynne Reinner.

Lyddon, D. (1996). 'The Myth of Mass Production and the Mass Production of Myth'. *Historical Studies in Industrial Relations*, 1 (Mar.): 77–105.

MacArthur, J. (2000). *The Selling of 'Free Trade': NAFTA, Washington, and the Subversion of American Democracy*. New York: Hill and Wang.

MacBride Commission (1980). *Many Voices, One World*. Paris: UNESCO.

McCarthy, S. (2000). 'Ten Years of Chaos in Burma: Foreign Investment and Economic Liberalization under the SLORC-SPDC, 1988–1998'. *Pacific Affairs*, 73/2: 233–62.

McCormick, J. (1992). *The Global Environmental Movement: Reclaiming Paradise*. London: Belhaven.

McCormick, P. (1997). 'Telecommunications Divestment: An Erosion of Democracy in the Caribbean'. *Gazette*, 59/2: 91–104.

McCrudden, C., and Davies, A. (2000). 'A Perspective on Trade and Labor Rights'. *Journal of International Economic Law*, 3/1: 43–62.

McElroy, M., Nielson, C., and Lydon, P. (1998) *Energizing China: Reconciling Environmental Protection and Economic Growth*. Cambridge, Mass: Harvard University Press.

MacGaffey, J. (1991). *The Real Economy of Zaire: The Contribution of Smuggling and Other Unofficial Activities to National Wealth*. Philadelphia: University of Pennsylvania Press.

McGowan, R. (1995). *Business, Politics and Cigarettes: Multiple Levels, Multiple Agendas*. Westport, Conn: Quorum Books.

McGrew, T. (1992). 'A Global Society'. In S. Hall (ed.), *Modernity and its Futures*. Cambridge: Polity Press/Open University.

McGuckin, E. (1997). 'Tibetan Carpets: From Folk Art to Global Commodity'. *Journal of Material Culture*, 2/3: 291–310.

McKendrick, N., Brewer, J., and Plumb, J. H. (1982). *The Birth of a Consumer Society: The Commercialization of Eighteenth-century England*. London: Hutchinson.

McLuhan, M. (1987). *Understanding Media: The Extensions of Man*. London: ARK.

McManus, P. (1996). 'Contested Terrains: Politics, Stories and Discourses of Sustainability'. *Environmental Politics*, 5/1: 48–53.

McMichael, P. (ed.). (1994). *Global Restructuring of Agro-Food Systems*. Ithaca, NY: Cornell University Press.

McMichael, P. (2000). *Development and Social Change: A Global Perspective* (2nd edn.). London: Sage.

McMillan, C. (1987). *Multinationals from the Second World*. London: Macmillan.

McMurray, C. and Smith, R. (2001). *Diseases of Globalization*. London: Earthscan.

McNeill, D. (2000). 'McGuggenisation: National Identity and Globalisation in the Basque Country'. *Political Geography*, 19: 473–494.

Madden, C. (1977). *The Case for the Multinational Corporation*. New York: Praeger.

Madeley, J. (1999). *Big Business, Poor Peoples: The Impact of Transnational Corporations on the World*'s Poor. London: Zed Books.

Madon, S. (2000). 'The Internet and Socio-economic Development: Exploring the Interaction'. *Information Technology and People*, 13/2: 85–101'.

Maex, R. (1983). *Employment and Multinationals in Asian Exporting Zones*. Geneva: ILO.

Maguire, J. (1999). *Global Sport: Identities, Societies and Civilizations*. Cambridge: Polity Press.

Main, L. (2001). 'The Global Information Infrastructure: Empowerment or Imperialism?' *Third World Quarterly*, 22/1: 83–97.

Makinson, D. (ed.) (2000). 'The Development Debate: Beyond the Washington Consensus'. *International Social Science Journal*, 166: whole issue.

Malhotra, S., and Rogers, E. (2000). 'Satellite Television and the New Indian Woman'. *Gazette*, 62/5: 407–29.

Mallin, C., and Rong, X. (1998). 'The Development of Corporate Governance in China'. *Journal of Contemporary China*, 7/17: 33–42.

Maltby, R. (1995). *Hollywood Cinema*. Oxford: Blackwell.

Mamdani, M. (1996). *Citizen and Subject: Contemporary Africa and the Legacy of Late Colonialism.* Princeton: Princeton University Press.

Mander, J. (1978). *Four Arguments for the Elimination of Television*. New York: Quill.

Mander, J., and Goldsmith, E. (eds.) (1996). *The Case against the Global Economy. And for a turn Toward the Local.* San Francisco: Sierra Club.

Manoff, R. (1984). 'Learning a lesson from Nestlé'. *Advertising Age* (13 Feb.): 16–20.

Mansell, R., and Wehn, U. (1998). *Knowledge Societies: Information Technology for Sustainable Development.* Oxford: Oxford University Press.

Manser, R. (1993). *The Squandered Dividend: The Free Market and the Environment in Eastern Europe.* London: Earthscan.

Mara, D., and Feacham, R. (2001). 'Taps and Toilets for All: Two Decades already, and Now a Quarter Century More'. *Water*, 21 (Aug.), 13–14.

Marcuse, H. (1964). *One Dimensional Man*. London: Routledge.

Marcuse, P., and Kempen, R. van (eds.). (2000). *Globalizing Cities: A New Spatial Order.* Oxford: Blackwell.

Marjoribanks, T. (2000). *News Corporation, Technology and the Workplace*. Cambridge: Cambridge University Press.

Martonyi, J. (1987). 'The Legal Framework for Joint Ventures in Hungary'. *CTC Reporter*, 23: 52–3.

Massie, R. (1997). *Loosing the Bonds: The United States and South Africa in the Apartheid Years*. New York: Doubleday.

Matsuzato, K. (2001). 'From Communist Boss Politics to Post-communist Caciquismo—The Meso-elite and Meso-governments in Post-communist Countries'. *Communist and Post-Communist Studies*, 34: 175–201.

Mattelart, A. (1978). 'The Nature of Communications Practice in a Dependent Society'. *Latin American Perspectives*, 1 (Winter): 13–34.

—— (1983). *Transnationals and the Third World: The Struggle for Culture.* South Hadley, Mass: Bergin and Garvey.

—— (2000). *Networking the World: 1794–2000* (trans. L. Carey-Libbrecht and J. Cohen). Minneapolis: University of Minnesota Press.

Mattelart, M. (1986). *Women, Media and Crisis*. London: Comedia.

Mattes, R., and Bratton, M. (2001). 'Africa's Triple Transition: Popular Perspectives'. *African Security Review*, 10/1: 49–59.

Maucher, H. (1994). *Leadership in Action: Tough-Minded Strategies from the Global Giant* (trans. B. J. Perroud-Benson,). New York: McGraw-Hill.

Maxfield, S., and Schneider, B. R. (1997). *Business and the State in Developing Countries*. Ithaca, NY, and London: Cornell University Press.

Maxwell, S., and Singer, H. (1979). 'Food Aid to Developing Countries: A Survey'. *World Development*, July: 225–47.

M'Bayo, R. (1997). 'Africa and the Global Information Infrastructure'. *Gazette*, 59/4–5: 345–64.

Medawar, C. (1979). *Insult or Injury*. London: Social Audit.

—— (1984). *Drugs and World Health*. London: Social Audit.

—— and Freese, B. (1982). *Drug Diplomacy*. London: Social Audit.

Mehta, A. (2000). *Power Play: A Study of the Enron Project*. New Delhi: Orient Longman.

Meijer, I. C. (1998). 'Advertising Citizenship: An Essay on the Performative Power of Consumer Culture'. *Media, Culture and Society*, 20: 235–49.

Melkote, S. (1991). *Communication for Development and the Third World Poor*. London: Sage.

Melrose, D. (1981). *The Great Health Robbery: Baby Milk and Medicines in Yemen*. Oxford: Oxfam.

—— (1982). *Bitter Pills. Medicines and the Third World Poor*. Oxford: Oxfam.

Merkle, J. (1980). *Management and Ideology: The Legacy of the International Scientific Management Movement*. London: University of California Press.

Mertz, H. J. (1984). *Peace and Affluence through the Multinational Corporations*. Bryn Mawr: Dorrance.

Mesa-Lago, C. (1993). *Cuba after the Cold War*. Pittsburgh: University of Pittsburgh Press.

—— (2000). *Market, Socialist and Mixed Economies: Comparative Policy and Performance of Chile, Cuba and Costa Rica*. Baltimore: Johns Hopkins University Press.

Mezger, D. (1978). 'How the Mining Companies Undermine Liberation'. *Review of African Political Economy*, 12 (May–Aug.): 53–66.

Mies, M. (1998). *Patriarchy and Accumulation on a World Scale: Women in the International Division of Labour*. London: Zed Books.

—— and Bennholdt-Thomsen, V. (1999). *The Subsistence Perspective: Beyond the Globalised Economy* (trans. P. Camiller, M. Mies, and G. Weih). London: Zed Books.

Miller, D., and Slater, D. (2000). *The Internet: An Ethnographic Approach*. Oxford: Berg.

Minor, M. (1994). 'The Demise of Expropriation as an Instrument of LDC Policy: 1980–1992'. *Journal of International Business Studies*, 25: 177–88.

Miozzo, M. (2000). 'Transnational Corporations, Industrial Policy and the "War of Incentives": The Case of the Argentine Automobile Industry'. *Development and Change*, 31: 651–80.

Mittelman, J. (1981). *Underdevelopment and the Transition to Socialism*. New York: Academic Press.

—— (2000). *The Globalization Syndrome: Transformation and Resistance*. Princeton: Princeton University Press.

Mitter, S. (1986). *Common Fate, Common Bond*. London: Pluto Press.

Mlinar, Z. (ed.) (1992). *Globalization and Territorial Identities*. Aldershot: Avebury.

Moghadam, V. (ed.) (1993a). *Democratic Reform and the Position of Women in Transitional Societies*. Oxford: Clarendon Press.

—— (1993b). *Modernizing Women: Gender and Social Change in the Middle East*. Boulder, Colo.: Lynne Rienner.

Mok, K.-H. (1998). *Intellectuals and the State in Post-Mao China*. London: Macmillan.

Monbiot, G. (2000). *The Captive State*. London: Macmillan.

Monga, Y. D. (2000). 'Dollars and Lipsticks: The United States through the Eyes of African Women'. *Africa*, 70/2: 192–208.

Moody, R. (1998). *Mining and the Politics of Risk*. New York: International Publishers.

Moore-Lappe, F., and Beccar-Varela, A. (1980). *Mozambique and Tanzania: Asking the Big Questions*. San Francisco: Institute for Food and Development Policy.

Moran, T. H. (1974). *Multinational Corporations and the Politics of Dependence: Copper in Chile*. Princeton: Princeton University Press.

—— (ed.). (1993). *Governments and Transnational Corporations* (vol. vii, United Nations Library on TNCs). London: Routledge.

Morawska, E. (1998). *The Malleable Homo Sovieticus: Transnational Entrepreneurs in Post-Communist East Europe* (RSC No.98/53). Florence: European University Institute.

Morgan, G. (2001). 'Transnational Communities and Business Systems'. *Global Networks*, 1/2: 113–30.

Mouzelis, N. (2001). 'Reflexive Modernization and the Third Way: The Impasse of Giddens' Social-Democratic Politics'. *Sociological Review*, 49/3: 436–56.

Mowlana, H. (1985). *International Flow of Information*. Paris: UNESCO.

Munck, R. (1989). *Latin America: Transition to Democracy*. London: Zed Books.

—— and Waterman, P. (eds.) (1999). *Labour Worldwide in the Era of Globalization*. London: Macmillan.

Muniz, A., and O'Guinn, T. (2001). 'Brand Community'. *Journal of Consumer Research*, 27: 412–32.

Murray, J. (2000). 'Labour Faces the Future: The Online Conference on Organised Labour in the 21st Century'. *International Journal of Comparative Labour Law and Industrial Relations*, 16/1: 103–7.

Murray, W. (1998). 'The Globalization of Fruit, Neo-liberalism and the Question of Sustainability: Lessons from Chile'. *European Journal of Development Research*, 10/1: 201–27.

Muskie, E., and Greenwald, D. (1986). 'The Nestlé Infant Formula Audit Commission as a Model'. *Journal of Business Strategy*, 6: 19–23.

Nash, J. (2001). *Mayan Visions: The Quest for Autonomy in an Age of Globalization*. London: Routledge.

—— and Fernandez-Kelly, M. P. (eds.) (1983). *Women, Men, and the International Division of Labor*. Albany, NY: SUNY Press.

Nath, U. R. (1986). *Smoking: Third World Alert*. Oxford: Oxford University Press.

Nawrocki, I. (1987). 'Foreign Enterprises in Poland: Ten Years of Experience'. *TNC Reporter*, 24 (Autumn): 49–50.

Nayyar, D. (ed.) (1977). *Economic Relations between Socialist Countries and the Third World*. London: Macmillan.

Nettl, P. (1969). *Rosa Luxemburg* (abridged ed.). Oxford: Oxford University Press.

Newfarmer, R. (1985). *Profits, Progress, and Poverty*. Notre Dame, Ind.: University of Notre Dame Press.

Newman, P., and Kenworthy, J. (1999). *Sustainability and Cities: Overcoming Automobile Dependence*. Washington: Island Press.

Newton, L. (1999). 'Truth is the Daughter of Time: The Real Story of the Nestlé Case'. *Business and Society Review*, 104/4: 367–95.

Nicholson, P. (1988). 'Asia's Space Invaders'. *South* (May): 12–13.

Nicolaides-Bouman, A., Wald, N., Foley, B., and Lee, P. (1993). *International Smoking Statistics*. Oxford: Oxford University Press.

Nolan, P. (2001). *China and the Global Business Revolution*. Basingstoke: Palgrave.

Nordenstreng, K. (1984). 'Bitter Lessons'. *Journal of Communication*, Winter: 138–42.

—— and Schiller, H. (eds.) (1993). *Beyond National Sovereignty: International communications in the 1990s*. Norwood, Mass: Ablex.

Norris, R. (ed.) (1982). *Pills, Pesticides and Profits: The International Trade in Toxic Substances*. New York: North River Press.

Norwine, J., and Gonzalez, A. (eds.) (1988). *The Third World: States of Mind and Being*. Boston: Unwin Hyman.

Nyoni, N. (1994). 'Kicking the Habit: Dependence on Tobacco Crop Poses Third World Dilemma'. *Ceres*, 26/3: 15–16.

O'Brien, K., and Leichenko, R. (2000). 'Double Exposure: Assessing the Impacts of Climate Change within the Context of Economic Globalization'. *Global Environmental Change*, 10: 221–32.

O'Brien, R., Goetz, A. M., Scholte, J. A., and Williams, M. (2000). *Contesting Global Governance: Multilateral Economic Institutions and Global Social Movements*. Cambridge: Cambridge University Press.

Ochoa, E. C., and Wilson, T. D. (eds.) (2001). 'Mexico in the 1990s: Economic Crisis, Social Polarization, and Class Struggle'. *Latin American Perspectives*, 28/3, special issue.

O'Connor, M. (ed.) (1994). *Is Capitalism Sustainable?* New York: Guildford Press.

O'Connor, E. (1999). 'The Politics of Management Thought: A Case Study of the Harvard Business School and the Human Relations School'. *Academy of Management*, 24/1: 117–31.

O'Donnell, G. (1979). *Modernization and Bureaucratic-Authoritarianism: Studies in South American Politics*. Berkeley: University of California Press.

O'Dougherty, M. (1998). 'The Devalued State and Nation: Neoliberalism and the Moral Economy Discourse of the Brazilian Middle Class, 1986–1994'. *Latin American Perspectives*, 26 (Jan.): 151–74.

Ogan, C. (1988). 'Media Imperialism and the Videocassette Recorder: The Case of Turkey'. *Journal of Communication*, 38/2 (Spring): 93–106.

O'Hearn, D. (1998). *Inside the Celtic Tiger: the Irish Economy and the Asian Model*. London: Pluto.

Ohmae, K. (1995). *The End of the Nation State*. New York: Free Press.

Okada, Y. (1983). 'The Dilemma of Indonesian Dependency on Foreign Direct Investments'. *Development and Change*, 14: 115–32.

O'Laughlin, B. (2000). 'Class and the Customary: The Ambiguous Legacy of the *Indigenato* in Mozambique'. *African Affairs*, 99: 5–42.

Olds, K. (2001). *Globalization and Urban Change: Capital, Culture, and Pacific Rim Mega-Projects*. Oxford: Oxford University Press.

Ollman, B. (ed.) (1998). *Market Socialism: The Debate among Socialists*. New York and London: Routledge.

Onimode, B., Ohorhenvan, T., and Adeniran, T. (1983). *MNCs in Nigeria*. Ibadan: Les Shyraden Nigeria Ltd.

Ost, D. (1992). 'Labor and Societal Transition'. *Problems of Communism*, (May–June): 48–51.

Ostheimer, A. (2001). 'Mozambique: The Permanent Entrenchment of Democratic Minimalism?' *African Security Review*, 10/1: 25–36.

Otobo, D. (1987). *Foreign Interests and Nigerian Trade Unions*. Oxford: Malthouse.

Owen, R., and Sutcliffe, B. (eds.) (1972). *Studies in the Theory of Imperialism*. London: Longman.

Owusu, J. H. (2001). 'Determinants of Export-Oriented Industrial Output in Ghana: The Case of Formal Wood Processing in an Era of Economic Recovery'. *Journal of Modern African Studies*, 39/1: 51–80.

Pacione, M. (1997). 'Local Exchange Trading Systems as a Response to the Globalization of Capitalism'. *Urban Studies*, 34/8: 1179–99.

Packenham, R. (1992). *The Dependency Movement: Scholarship and Politics in Development Studies*. Cambridge, Mass.: Harvard University Press.

Pagan, R. (1986). 'The Nestlé Boycott: Implications for Strategic Business Planning'. *Journal of Business Strategy*, (Spring): 12–18.

Palmer, G. (1993). *The Politics of Breastfeeding*. London: Pandora Press.

Palmer, J. (1985). 'Consumer Service Industry Exports'. *Columbia Journal of World Business*, 20/1 (Spring): 69–74.

Palmer, R. (1987). Africa in the media. *African Affairs*, 86 (April): 241–7.

Pang, E. (2000). 'The Financial Crisis of 1997–98 and the End of the Asian Developmental State. *Contemporary Southeast Asia*, 22/3: 570–93.

Panjabi, R. K. L. (1997). *The Earth Summit at Rio: Politics, Economics, and the Environment*. Boston: Northeastern University Press.

Parameswaran, R. (1997). 'Colonial Interventions and the Postcolonial Situation in India: The English Language, Mass Media and the Articulation of Class'. *Gazette*, 59/1: 21–41.

Parker, B. (1998). *Globalization and Business Practice: Managing Across Boundaries*. London: Sage.

Pateman, C. (1996). 'Democracy and Democratization'. *International Political Science Review*, 17/1: 5–12.

Pearson, M. (1992). 'Breaking the Bonds of "Organized Dependence": Managers in China's Foreign Sector'. *Studies in Comparative Communism*, 25 (Mar): 57–77.

Peck, J., and Theodore, N. (2001). 'Exporting Workfare/Importing Welfare-to-work: Exploring the Politics of Third Way Policy Transfer'. *Political Geography*, 20: 427–60.

Pedler, R. H., and Van Schendelen, M. (1994). *Lobbying the European Union: Companies, Trade Associations and Issue Groups*. Brookfield, Vt., and Aldershot: Dartmouth Publishing.

Peet, R., and Watts, M. (eds.) (1996). *Liberation Ecologies: Environment, Development, Social Movement*. London: Routledge.

Pena, D. (1997). *The Terror of the Machine*. Austin, Tex.: CMAS Books.

Pendakur, M. (1985). 'Dynamics of Cultural Policy Making: The U.S. Film Industry in India'. *Journal of Communication*, 35 (Autumn): 52–72.

Pendergrast, M. (1993). *For God, Country and Coca-Cola*. New York: Macmillan.

Pereira, A. (2000). 'State Collaboration with Transnational Corporations: The Case of Singapore's Industrial Programmes (1965–1999)'. *Competition and Change*, 4: 423–51.

Petersen, K. (1993). *The Maquiladora Revolution in Guatemala*. New Haven: Yale Law School, Center for International Human Rights.

Petersmann, E.-U. (2000). 'The WTO Constitution and Human Rights'. *Journal of International Economic Law*, 3: 19–25.

Petras, J., and Harding, T. (2000). 'Introduction: The Radical Left Response to Global Impoverishment'. *Latin American Perspectives*, 27/5: 3–10.

—— and Veltmeyer, H. (2001). *Globalization Unmasked: Imperialism in the 21st Century*. London: Zed Books.

Pierce, J., Gilpin, E., and Choi, W. (1999). 'Sharing the Blame: Smoking Experimentation and Future Smoking-Attributable Mortality due to Joe Camel and Marlboro Advertising and Promotions'. *Tobacco Control*, 8: 37–44.

Pilkington, H. (1994). *Russia's Youth and its Culture*. London: Routledge.

Poon, J., Thompson, E., and Kelly, P. (2000). 'Myth of the Triad? The Geography of Trade and Investment "Blocs"'. *Transactions of the Institute of British Geographers*, 25/4: 427–44.

Portes, A., and Castells, M. (1989). *The Informal Sector*. Baltimore: Johns Hopkins University Press.

Portes, A. (ed.) (2001). 'New Research and Theory on Immigrant Transnationalism'. *Global Networks*, 1/3: special issue.

Post, K., and Wright, P. (1989). *Socialism and Underdevelopment*. London: Routledge.

Poznanski, K. (1993). 'An Interpretation of Communist Decay: the Role of Evolutionary Mechanisms'. *Communist and Post-Communist Societies*, 26 (Mar.): 3–24.

Press, M., and Thomson, D. (eds.) (1989). *Solidarity for Survival: The Don Thomson Reader on Trade Union Internationalism*. Nottingham: Spokesman.

Preston, P. (1998). *Pacific Asia in the Global System*. Oxford: Blackwell.

Pries, L. (ed.). (2000). *The Emergence of Transnational Social Spaces: International Migration and Globally Operating Companies in the Early Twenty-First Century*. London: Routledge.

Radice, H. (2000). 'Responses to Globalization: A Critique of Progressive Nationalism'. *New Political Economy*, 5/1: 5–19.

Rahnema, M., and Bawtree, V. (eds.) (1997). *The Post-Development Reader*. London: Zed Books.

Raikes, P. (1984). 'Food Policy and Production in Mozambique since Independence'. *Review of African Political Economy*, 29 (July): 95–107.

—— and Gibbon, P. (2000). ' "Globalisation" and African Export Crop Agriculture'. *Journal of Peasant Studies*, 27/2: 50–93.

Ramstrom, L. (ed.). (1980). *The Smoking Epidemic: A Matter of Worldwide Concern*. Stockholm: Almqvist and Wiksell.

Randall, V., and Theobold, R. (1998). *Political Change and Underdevelopment* (2nd edn.). London: Macmillan.

Rao, S. L. (2001). 'Dabhol, Godpole Report and the Future'. *Economic and Political Weekly* (12 May).

Raynolds, L. (2000). 'Re-embedding Global Agriculture: The International Organic and Fair Trade Movements'. *Agriculture and Human Values*, 17: 297–309.

Read, M. (1996). *The Politics of Tobacco: Policy Networks and the Cigarette Industry*. Aldershot: Avebury.

Redclift, M. (1996). *Wasted: Counting the Costs of Global Consumption*. London: Earthscan.

—— and Benton, T. (eds.) (1994). *Social Theory and the Global Environment*. London: Routledge.

—— and Woodgate, G. (eds.). (1995). *The Sociology of the Environment*, 3 vols. Aldershot: Edward Elgar.

Reeves, G. (1993). *Communications and the 'Third World'*. London: Routledge.

Reisner, A. E. (2001). 'Social Movement Organizations' Reactions to Genetic Engineering in Agriculture'. *American Behavioural Scientist*, 44/8: 1389–404.

Reynolds, B. (ed.) (1987). *Reform in China*. Armonk, NY: M. E. Sharpe.

Rimmer, D. (2000). 'Review Article. Aid and Corruption'. *African Affairs*, 99: 121–8.

Risse-Kappen, T. (ed.) (1995). *Bringing Transnational Relations Back In: Non-State Actors, Domestic Structures and International Institutions*. Cambridge: Cambridge University Press.

Risse, T., Ropp, S., and Sikkink, K. (eds.) (1999). *The Power of Human Rights: International Norms and Domestic Change*. Cambridge: Cambridge University Press.

Ritzer, G. (1996). *The McDonaldization of Society* (revised edn.). Newbury Park: Sage.

Robbins, P. (1996). 'TNCs and Global Environmental Change: A Review of the UN Benchmark Corporate Environmental Survey'. *Global Environmental Change*, 6/3: 23–44.

—— (2001). *Greening the Corporation*. London: Earthscan.

Roberts, J. T., and Hite, A. (eds.) (2000). *From Modernization to Globalization: Social Perspectives on International Development*. Boston: Blackwell.

Robertson, R. (1992). *Globalization: Social Theory and Global Culture*. London: Sage.

Robinson, M., and White, G. (eds.) (1998). *The Democratic Developmental State: Politics and Institutional Design*. Oxford: Oxford University Press.

Robinson, W. (1996). *Promoting Polyarchy*. Cambridge: Cambridge University Press.

—— (1997). 'A Case Study of Globalisation Processes in the Third World: A Transnational Agenda in Nicaragua'. *Global Society*, 11/1: 61–91.

Robison, R., and Goodman, D. S. G. (eds.) (1996). *The New Rich in Asia: Mobile Phones, McDonald's and Middle-Class Revolution*. London: Routledge.

Robson, P. (ed.). (1993) *Transnational Corporations and Regional Economic Integration* (vol. ix, United Nations Library on TNCs). London: Routledge.

Roca, S. (1988). *Socialist Cuba: Past Interpretations and Future Challenges*. Boulder, Colo.: Westview Press.

Rogers, E., and Antola, L. (1985). 'Telenovelas: A Latin American Success Story'. *Journal of Communication*, 35 (Autumn): 25–35.

Roncagliolo, R. (1986). 'Transnational Communication and Culture'. In R. Atwood and E. McAnany (eds.), *Communication and Latin American Society: Trends in Critical Research 1960–1985*. Madison: University of Wisconsin Press, ch. 4.

Rosati, D., and Mizsei, K. (1989). *Adjustment through Opening of Socialist Economies* (Mimeograph): United Nations University.

Rose-Ackerman, S. (1999). *Corruption and Government: Causes, Consequences and Reform*. Cambridge: Cambridge University Press.

Rosen, E. (2002). *Making Sweatshops: The Globalization of the US Apparel Industry*. Berkeley and Los Angeles: University of California Press.

Rosen, S. (1987/88). 'The Private Economy'. *Chinese Economic Studies*, 2 parts, 21 (Fall and Winter).

Ross, G. (2000). 'Labor Versus Globalization'. *Annals of the American Academy of Political and Social Science*, 570 (July): 78–91.

Ross, R., and Trachte, K. (1990). *Global Capitalism: The New Leviathan*. Albany, NY: SUNY Press.

Rosset, P., and Vandermeer, J. (eds.) (1986). *Nicaragua: Unfinished Revolution*. New York: Grove Press.

Rothstein, F., and Blim, M. (eds.) (1992). *Anthropology and the Global Factory: Studies of the New Industrialization in the Late Twentieth Century*. New York: Bergen and Garvey.

Rowbotham, S., and Mitter, S. (eds.) (1994). *Dignity and Daily Bread. New Forms of Economic Organising among Poor Women in the Third World and the First*. London: Routledge.

Rowell, A. (1996). *Green Backlash: Global Subversion of the Environmental Movement*. London: Routledge.

Rowley, C., and Benson, J. (eds.) (2000). *Globalization and Labour in the Asia Pacific Region*. London: Frank Cass.

Rubinoff, J. A. (2001). 'Pink Gold: Transformation of Backwater Aquaculture on Goa's Khazan Lands'. *Economic and Political Weekly* (31 Mar.).

Rueschmeyer, D., Stephens, E., and Stephens, J. (1992). *Capitalist Development and Democracy*. Oxford: Polity Press.

Rupert, J., and Frankel, G. (1996). 'In Ex-Soviet Markets, US Brands Took On Role of Capitalist Liberator'. *Washington Post* (19 Nov.).

Russett, B. (1984). 'Resource Dependence and Analysis'. *International Organization*, 38/3: 481–99.

Ryan, M. (1993). *Social Trends in Contemporary Russia: A Statistical Source-Book*. London: Macmillan.

Ryback, T. (1989). *Rock around the Bloc*. New York: Oxford University Press.

Salinas Bascur, R. (1885). 'Information in the Third World: Adjusting Technologies or Strategies'. *Media, Culture and Society*, 7: 355–68.

Salt, B., Cervero, R., and Herod, A. (2000). 'Workers' Education and Neoliberal Globalization: An Adequate Response to Transnational Corporations?' *Adult Education Quarterly*, 51/1: 9–31.

Samarajiwa, R. (1984). 'Third-World Entry to the World Market in News: Problems and Possible Solutions'. *Media, Culture and Society*, 6: 119–36.

Sanderson, S. (ed.) (1985). *The Americas in the New International Division of Labor*. New York: Holmes and Meier.

Sano, H. (1983). *The Political Economy of Food in Nigeria 1960–1982: A Discussion on Peasants, State and World Economy*. Uppsala: Scandinavian Institute of African Studies.

Sassen, S. (2000a). *The Global City: New York, London, Tokyo* (new edn.). Princeton: Princeton University Press.

—— (2000b). 'Territory and Territoriality in the Global Economy'. *International Sociology*, 15/2: 372–93.

Scarpaci, J. L. (2000). 'On The Transformation of Socialist Cities'. *Urban Geography*, 21/8: 659–69.

Schell, O. (1988). 'Capitalist Birds in a Socialist Bird Cage'. *California Business* (July), 34–47.

Schiller, D. (1999). *Digital Capitalism: Networking the Global Market System*. Cambridge, Mass.: MIT Press.

Schiller, H. (1981). *Who Knows: Information in the Age of the Fortune 500*. Norwood, NJ: Ablex.

Scholte, J. A. (2000). *Globalization: A Critical Introduction*. London: Macmillan.

Schor, J. (1991). *The Overworked American: The Unexpected Decline of Leisure*. New York: Basic Books.

Schuftan, C. (1983). 'De-Westernizing Health Planning and Delivery through Consumer Participation: Some Lessons from Chile and Tanzania'. In J. Morgan (ed.), *Third World Medicine and Social Change*. Lanham, Md.: University Press of America.

Schulz, M. (1998). 'Collective Action Across Borders: Opportunity Structures, Network Capacities, and Communicative Praxis in the Age of Advanced Globalization'. *Sociological Perspectives*, 41/3: 587–616.

Scott, A. (1990). *Ideology and the New Social Movements*. London: Unwin Hyman.

Seidman, A., Seidman, R., Ndlela, D., and Makamure, K. (eds.) (1986). *Transnationals in Southern Africa*. Harare: Zimbabwe Publishing House.

Senauer, B., and Sur, M. (2001). 'Ending Global Hunger in the 21st Century: Projections of the Number of Food Insecure People'. *Review of Agricultural Economics*, 23: 66–81.

Serio, J. (1992). 'The Soviet Union: Disorganization and Organized Crime'. In A. Lodl and L. Zhang (eds.), *Enterprise Crime: Asian and Global Perspectives* (155–170). Chicago: Office of International Criminal Justice.

Servan-Schreiber, J.-J. (1968). *The American Challenge*. Harmondsworth: Penguin.

Sethi, S. P. (1977). *Advocacy Advertising and Large Corporations*. Lexington, Ky.: D. C. Heath.

—— (1994). *Multinational Corporations and the Impact of Public Advocacy on Corporate Strategy: Nestlé and the Infant Formula Controversy*. Boston: Kluwer.

Shannon. (1996). *An Introduction to the World-System Perspective* (2nd edn.). Boulder, Colo: Westview Press.

Shaw, R. (ed.) (1993). *The Spread of Sponsorship in the Arts, Sports, Education, the Health Service and Broadcasting*. Newcastle: Bloodaxe Books.

Shaw, M. (ed.) (1999). *Politics and Globalization*. London: Routledge.

Sheldon, R., and Arens, E. (1932). *Consumer Engineering: A New Technique for Prosperity*. New York: Harper Brothers.

Shenon, P. (1994, 15 May). 'Asia's Having One Huge Nicotine Fit'. *New York Times* (15 May), Section 4: 1, 16.

Shenton, B., and Freund, B. (1978). 'The Incorporation of Northern Nigeria into the World Capitalist System'. *Review of African Political Economy*, 13 (May–Aug.): 8–20.

Shepherd, P. (1985). 'Transnational Corporations and the International Cigarette Industry'. In R. Newfarmer (ed.), *Profits, Progress and Poverty* (ch. 3). Notre Dame, Ind.: University of Notre Dame Press.

Shin, D.-M. (2000). 'Economic Policy and Social Policy: Policy-Linkages in an Era of Globalisation'. *International Journal of Social Welfare*, 9: 17–30.

Shiva, V., and Moser, I. (eds.) (1995). *Biopolitics: A Feminist and Ecological Reader on Biotechnology*. London: Zed Books.

Shivji, I. (1976). *Class Struggles in Tanzania*. London: Monthly Review Press.

Short, J. R., and Kim, Y.-H. (1999). *Globalization and the City*. London: Longman.

—— Kim, Y., Kuus, M., and Wells, H. (1996). 'The Dirty Little Secret of World Cities Research: Data Problems in Comparative Analysis'. *International Journal of Urban and Regional Research*, 20/4: 697–717.

Shostak, A. (ed.) (1999). *CyberUnion: Empowering Labor through Computer Technology*. Armonk, NY: M. E. Sharpe.

Shuman, M. (1998). *Going Local: Creating Self-Reliant Communities in a Global Age*. New York: Free Press.

Sidaway, J. D. (1998). 'The (Geo)politics of Regional Integration: The Example of the Southern African Development Community'. *Environment and Planning D: Society and Space*, 16: 549–76.

—— and Power, M. (1995). 'Sociospatial Transformations in the "Postsocialist" Periphery: The Case of Maputo, Mozambique'. *Environment and Planning A*, 27: 1463–91.

—— and Pryke, M. (2000). 'The Strange Geographies of "Emerging Markets"'. *Transactions of the Institute of British Geographers*, 25: 187–201.

Sigmund, P. (1980). *Multinationals in Latin America*. Madison: University of Wisconsin Press.

Simai, M. (ed.) (1995). *Global Employment: An International Investigation into the Future of Work*. London: Zed Books.

Sinclair, J. (1987). *Images Incorporated: Advertising as Industry and Ideology*. London: Croom Helm.

Sinclair, M., and Nash, J. (eds.) (1995). *The New Politics of Survival*. New York: Monthly Review Press.

Singer, D. (1999). *Whose Millennium? Theirs or Ours?* New York: Monthly Review Press.

Singhal, A., and Udornpim, K. (1997). 'Cultural Shareability, Archetypes and Television Soaps: "Oshindrome" in Thailand'. *Gazette*, 59/3: 171–88.

Sit, V., and Liu, W. (2000). 'Restructuring and Spatial Change of China's Auto Industry under Institutional Reform and Globalization'. *Annals of the Association of American Geographers*, 90/4: 653–73.

Sklair, L. (1985). 'Shenzhen: A Chinese "Development Zone" in Global Perspective'. *Development and Change*, 16: 571–602.

—— (1988a). 'Transcending the Impasse: Metatheory, Theory and Empirical Research in the Sociology of Development and Underdevelopment'. *World Development*, 16 (June): 697–709.

—— (1988b). 'Foreign investment, Irish development and the International Division of Labour'. *Progress in Planning*, 29/3: whole issue.

—— (1991). 'Problems of Socialist Development: The Significance of Shenzhen for China's Open Door Development Strategy'. *International Journal of Urban and Regional Research*, 15/2: 197–215.

—— (1993). *Assembling for Development: The Maquila Industry in Mexico and the United States* (2nd enlarged edn.). San Diego: University of California Center for US–Mexican Studies.

—— (ed.). (1994). *Capitalism and Development*. London: Routledge.

—— (1998). 'The Transnational Capitalist Class and Global Capitalism: The Case of the Tobacco Industry'. *Political Power and Social Theory*, 12: 3–43.

—— (2001). *The Transnational Capitalist Class*. Oxford: Blackwell.

—— and Robbins, P. (2002). 'Global Capitalism and Major Corporations from the Third World'. *Third World Quarterly*, 23/1: 81–100.

Sklar, H. (ed.) (1980). *Trilateralism: The Trilateral Commission and Elite Planning for World Management*. Boston: South End Press.

Slama, K. (1995). *Tobacco and Health*. New York: Plenum.

Slater, D. (1997). *Consumer Culture and Modernity*. Cambridge: Polity Press.

Smith, A. (1980). *The Geopolitics of Information: How Western Culture Dominates the World*. London: Faber.

Smith, J. (ed.). (2001a). 'Globalization and Resistance'. *Mobilization*, 6/1 whole issue.

—— (2001b). 'Globalizing Resistance: The Battle of Seattle and the Future of Social Movements'. *Mobilization*, 6/1: 1–19.

—— Chatfield, C., and Pagnucco, R. (eds.) (1997). *Transnational Social Movements and Global Politics: Solidarity beyond the State*. Syracuse, NY: Syracuse University Press.

Smith, P., and Guarnizo, L. (eds.) (1998). *Transnationalism from Below*. Brunswick, NJ: Transaction Books.

Social Sciences in China. (1989). 'Forum on DATW in a socialist commodity economy'. *Social Sciences in China* (Mar.), 9–19.

Solinger, D. (1989). 'Capitalist Measures with Chinese Characteristics'. *Problems of Communism*, (Jan.–Feb.): 19–33.

Sorkin, M. (ed.) (1992). *Variations on a Theme Park*. New York: Noonday.

Sparks, C., with Reading, A. (1998). *Communism, Capitalism and the Mass Media*. London: Sage Publications.

Spybey, T. (1996). *Globalization and World Society*. Cambridge: Polity Press.

Sreberny-Mohammadi, A. (1984). 'The "World of News" Study: Results of International Cooperation'. *Journal of Communication*, 34 (Winter): 120–34.

Stallings, B. (ed.) (1995). *Global Change, Regional Response: The New International Context of Development*. Cambridge: Cambridge University Press.

Starr, A. (2000). *Naming the Enemy: Anti-Corporate Movements Confront Globalization*. London: Zed Books.

Steif, W. (1989). 'Financial woes in Egypt'. *Multinational Monitor*, (Mar.): 23–5.

Steinberg, D. (1982). *Burma: A Socialist Nation of Southeast Asia*. Boulder, Colo: Westview Press.

Steiner, H., and Alston, P. (eds.) (2000). *International Human Rights: Law, Politics, Morals* (2nd edn.). Oxford: Oxford University Press.

Stevenson, R. (1984). 'Pseudo Debate'. *Journal of Communication*, (Winter): 134–8.

Stewart, F. (1978). *Technology and Underdevelopment*. London: Macmillan.

Stockman, N. (2000). *Understanding Chinese Society*. Cambridge: Polity Press.

Stoever, W. (1989). 'Foreign Collaborations Policy in India: A Review'. *Journal of Developing Areas*, 23 (July): 485–504.

Stoneman, C. (1978). 'Foreign Capital and the Reconstruction of Zimbabwe'. *Review of African Political Economy*, 11: 22–83.

Stopford, J., and Strange, S. (1991). *Rival States, Rival Firms: Competition for World Market Share*. Cambridge: Cambridge University Press.

Stover, W. (1984). *Information Technology in the Third World*. Boulder, Colo: Westview Press.

Stowe, R. (2001). 'Foreign Policy Preferences of the New Russian Business Elite'. *Problems of Post-Communism*, 48 (May/June): 49–58.

Strange, S. (1996). *The Retreat of the State: The Diffusion of Power in the World Economy*. Cambridge: Cambridge University Press.

—— (1998). *Mad Money*. Manchester: Manchester University Press.

Sugden, J., and Tomlinson, A. (1998). *FIFA and the Contest for World Football*. Cambridge: Polity Press.

Sullivan, K. (1990). 'Fake festival of Panty-Givers'. *Guardian*, (14 Mar.).

Sun, H. (1998). *Foreign Direct Investment and Economic Development in China, 1979–1996*. Aldershot: Ashgate.

Sussman, G., and Lent, J. (eds.) (1991). *Transnational Communications. Wiring the Third World*. London: Sage.

Svetlicic, M. (1993). *Foreign Direct Investment and the Transformation of Central European Economies, mimeo*. University of Ljubljana.

Swasy, A. (1994). *Soap Opera: The Inside Story of Procter and Gamble*. New York: Simon and Schuster.

Szelenyi, I. (1988). *Socialist Entrepreneurs. Embourgeoisement in Rural Hungary*. Cambridge: Polity Press.

Tanaka, A. (1992). 'Socialism in East Asia: Vietnam, Mongolia, and North Korea'. In G. Rozman (ed.), *Dismantling Communism: Common Causes and Regional Variations* (ch. 7). Baltimore: John Hopkins University Press.

Tangri, R., and Mwenda, A. (2001). 'Corruption and Cronyism in Uganda's Privatization in the 1990s'. *African Affairs*, 100: 117–34.

Tarrow, S. (1998). *Power in Movements: Social Movements and Contentious Politics* (2nd edn.). Cambridge: Cambridge University Press.

Taylor, J. (1979). *From Modernization to Modes of Production*. London: Macmillan.

Taylor, P. (1985). *The Smoke Ring: Tobacco, Money and Multinational Politics*. London: Sphere.

—— (2000). 'World Cities and Territorial States under Conditions of Contemporary Globalization'. *Political Geography*, 19: 5–32.

Tehranian, M. (1999). *Global Communications and World Politics*. Boulder, Colo.: Lynne Rienner.

Teichova, A., Levy-Leboyer, M., and Nussbaum, H. (eds.) (1986). *Multinational Enterprise in Historical Perspective*. Cambridge: Cambridge University Press.

Teltschler, S. (1994). 'Small Trade and the World Economy: Informal Vendors in Quito, Ecuador'. *Economic Geography*, 70: 167–87.

Teng, W., and Wang, N. T. (eds.) (1988). *Transnational Corporations and China's Open Door Policy*. Lexington, Mass.: Lexington Books.

Teubner, G. (1997). *Global Law Without a State*. Aldershot: Dartmouth.

Thacker, S. (1999). 'NAFTA Coalitions and the Political Viability of Neoliberalism in Mexico'. *Journal of InterAmerican Studies and World Affairs*, 41/2: 57–89.

Thomas, C. (1999). 'Where is the Third World now?' *Review of International Studies*, 25: 225–44.

—— (2001). 'Global Governance, Development and Human Security: Exploring the Links'. *Third World Quarterly*, 22/2: 159–75.

Thomas, P. (1999). 'Trading the Nation: Multilateral Negotiations and the Fate of Communication in India'. *Gazette*, 61/3–4: 275–92.

Thusu, D. K. (2000). *International Communication: Continuity and Change*. London: Arnold.

Tiano, S. (1986). 'Women and Industrial Development in Latin America'. *Latin America Research Review*, 21/3: 157–70.

—— (1994). *Patriarchy on the Line*. Philadelphia: Temple University Press.

TIE (1985). *Meeting the Corporate Challenge*. Amsterdam: TIE.

Tinker, I. (ed.) (1990). *Persistent Inequalities. Women and World Development*. New York: Oxford University Press.

Tobin, J. (2000). 'Financial Globalization'. *World Development*, 28/6: 1101–4.

Tolbert, C., T. Lyson, and Irwin, M. (1998). 'Local Capitalism, Civic Engagement and Socioeconomic Well-Being'. *Social Forces*, 77/2: 401–28.

Tomlinson, J. (1991). *Cultural Imperialism*. London: Pinter.

Torp, L., with Denny, L., and Ray, D. (1989). *Mozambique, Sao Tome and Principe*. London: Pinter.

Townsend, A. (2001). 'Network Cities and the Global Structure of the Internet'. *American Behavioral Scientist*, 44/10: 1697–716.

Tripp, A. M. (2001). 'Women's Movements and Challenges to Neopatrimonial Rule: Preliminary Observations from Africa'. *Development and Change*, 32: 33–54.

Tsikata, F. (ed.) (1986). *Essays from the Ghana-Valco Renegotiations, 1982–85*. Accra: Ghana Publishing Corporation.

Tullis, F., and Hollist, W. (eds.) (1986). *Food, the State and International Political Economy: Dilemmas of Developing Countries*. Lincoln, Nebr.: University of Nebraska Press.

Tully, S. (1994). 'Teens: the Most Global Market of All'. *Fortune* (16 May), 90–7.

Tunstall, J. (1977). *The Media are American*. New York: Columbia University Press.

UN (2000). *World Investment Report*. New York and Geneva: United Nations.

UNDP (1993). *Human Development Report*. New York: United Nations Development Programme.

—— (2000a). *Human Development Report*. New York: United Nations.

—— (2000b). *Overcoming Human Poverty*. New York: United Nations Development Programme.

Unger, J. (1996). ' "Bridges": Private Business, the Chinese Government and the Rise of New Associations'. *China Quarterly*, 147 (Sept.): 795–819.

United Nations Centre on Transnational Corporations (UNCTC). (1988). *Transnational Corporations in World Development*. New York: UNCTC.

UNRISD. (2000). *Visible Hands: Taking Responsibility for Social Development*. Geneva: United Nations Research Institute for Social Development.

Urdang, S. (1989). *And Still they Dance: Women, War, and the Struggle for Change in Mozambique*. London: Earthscan.

Utting, P. (2000). 'UN-Business Partnerships: Whose Agenda Counts?' *UNRISD News*, 23 (Autumn/ Winter): 1–4.

Vaitsos, C. (1974). 'Employment Effects of Foreign Direct Investments in Developing Countries'. In E. Edwards (ed.), *Employment in Developing Nations*. New York: Columbia University Press.

van der Pijl, K. (1998). *Transnational Classes and International Relations*. London: Routledge.

Vanden, H., and Prevost, G. (1993). *Democracy and Socialism in Sandinista Nicaragua*. Boulder, Colo.: Lynne Rienner.

Vandersluis, S., and Yeros, P. (eds.). (2000). *Poverty in World Politics*. London: Macmillan.

Vandervoort, S. S. (1991). 'Big "Green Brother" is Watching: New Directions in Environmental Public Affairs Challenge Business'. *Public Relations Journal* (Apr.): 14–27.

Varese, F. (2001). 'Is Sicily the Future of Russia?' Private Protection and the Rise of the Russian Mafia'. *European Journal of Sociology*, 42/1: 186–220.

Varis, T. (1984). 'The International Flow of Television Programs'. *Journal of Communication*, 34 (Winter): 143–52.

Vener, J. (2000). 'Prompting Democratic Transitions from Abroad: International Donors and Multi-partyism in Tanzania'. *Democratization*, 7/4: 133–62.

Venturi, R., Brown, D. S., and Izenour, S. (1977). *Learning from Las Vegas: The Forgotten Symbolism of Architectural Form* (rev. edn.). Cambridge, Mass.: MIT Press.

Vernon, R. (1971). *Sovereignty at Bay: The Multinational Spread of U.S. Enterprises*. New York: Basic Books.

Vig, N. J., and Axelrod, R. S. (eds.) (1999). *The Global Environment: Institutions, Law and Policy*. London: Earthscan.

Visvanathan, N., Duggan, L., Nisonoff, L., and Wiegersma, N. (eds.) (1997). *The Women, Gender and Development Reader*. London: Zed Books.

Wachman, A. (2001). 'Does the Diplomacy of Shame Promote Human Rights in China?' *Third World Quarterly*, 22/2: 257–81.

Wachtel, H. (2000). 'Tobin and Other Global Taxes'. *Review of International Political Economy*, 7/2: 335–52.

Wade, R. (1990). *Governing the Market*. Princeton: Princeton University Press.

Wagle, S. (1996). 'TNCs as Aid Agencies? Enron and the Dabhol Power Plant'. *Ecologist*, 26 (July/August): 179–84.

Walch, J. (1999). *In the Net: An Internet Guide for Activists*. London: Zed Books.

Walker, R. (1999). 'Putting Capital in its Place: Globalization and the Prospects for Labor'. *Geoforum*, 30: 263–84.

Walker, T. (1987). *Reagan versus the Sandinistas: The Undeclared War on Nicaragua*. Boulder, Colo.: Westview Press.

Wallach, L., and Naiman, R. (1998). 'NAFTA: Four and a Half Years Later: Have the Promised Benefits Materialized'. *Ecologist*, 28 (May/June): 171–6.

Wallerstein, I. (1974, 1980, 1988). *The Modern World-System*, 3 vols. New York and San Diego: Academic Press.

—— (1991). *Geopolitics and Geoculture*. Cambridge: Cambridge University Press.

Walton, J. (1998). 'Urban Conflict and Social Movements in Poor Countries: Theory and Evidence of Collective Action'. *International Journal of Urban and Regional Reserach*, 22/3: 460–81.

—— and Seddon, D. (eds.) (1994). *Free Markets and Food Riots: The Politics of Global Adjustment*. Oxford: Blackwell.

Wang, J. (1996). *High Culture Fever: Politics, Aesthetics, and Ideology in Deng's China*. Berkeley: University of California Press.

Warhurst, A. (2001). 'Corporate Citizenship and Corporate Social Investment: Drivers of Tri-Sector Partnerships'. *Journal of Corporate Citizenship*, 1 (Spring): 57–73.

Warren, B. (1980). *Imperialism: Pioneer of Capitalism*. London: New Left Books.

Waterman, D., and Jayakar, K. (2000). 'The Competitive Balance of the Italian and American Film Industries'. *European Journal of Communication*, 15/4: 501–28.

Waters, M. (1995). *Globalization*. London: Routledge.

Waters, T. (2000). 'The Persistence of Subsistence and the Limits to Development Studies: The Challenge of Tanzania'. *Africa*, 70/4: 614–52.

Watson, J. (ed.) (1997). *Golden Arches East: McDonald's in East Asia*. Stanford, Calif.: Stanford University Press.

Watts, M., and Goodman, D. (1997). *Globalising Food: Agrarian Questions and Global Restructuring*. London: Routledge.

Weeks, G. (2000). 'Waiting for Cincinnatus: The Role of Pinochet in Post-Authoritarian Chile'. *Third World Quarterly*, 21/5: 725–38.

Welch, C. (ed.) (2001). *NGOs and Human Rights: Promise and Performance*. Philadelphia: University of Pennsylvania Press.

Wells, A. (1972). *Picture-Tube Imperialism? The Impact of U.S. Television on Latin America*. Maryknoll, NY: Orbis.

Wernick, A. (1991). *Promotional Culture: Advertising, Ideology and Symbolic Expression*. London: Sage.

West Africa (1980). 'Imperialism and the Volta Dam.' *West Africa*, 31 (24 Mar.): 518–23.

Westra, L., and Wenz, P. (eds.) (1995). *Faces of Environmental Racism: Confronting Issues of Social Justice*. Lanham, Md.: Rowman and Littlefield.

White, G. (1993). *Riding the Tiger: The Politics of Economic Reform in Post-Mao China*. London: Macmillan.

—— Murray, R., and White, C. (1983). *Revolutionary Socialist Development in the Third World*. Brighton: Wheatsheaf.

Wichterich, C. (2000). *The Globalized Woman: Reports from a Future of Inequality* (trans. P. Camiller). London: Zed Books.

Wiener, J. (1999). *Globalization and the Harmonization of Law*. London: Pinter.

Wignaraja, P. (1993). *New Social Movements in the South: Empowering the People*. London: Zed Books.

Wilk, R. (1993). ' "It's Destroying a Whole Generation": Television and Moral Discourse in Belize'. *Visual Anthropology*, 5: 229–44.

Willetts, P. (1982). *Pressure Groups in the Global System*. London: Pinter.

Williams, W. (1991). *Third World Cooperation: The Group of 77 in UNCTAD*. London: Pinter.

Wills, J. (1999). 'Taking on the CosmoCorps? Experiments in Transnational Labor Organization'. *Economic Geography*, 75: 111–30.

Willums, J. O., and Goluke, V. (1992). *From Ideas to Action: Business and Sustainable Development*. Oslo: International Chamber of Commerce.

Wilson, F., Kanji, N., and Braathen, E. (eds.) (2000). *Poverty Reduction—What Role for the State in Today's Globalized Economy?* London: Zed Books.

Winseck. (1997). 'Contradictions in the Democratization of International Communication'. *Media, Culture and Society*, 19: 219–46.

Wong, J. (1994). 'Power and Market in Mainland China: The Danger of Increasing Government Involvement in Business'. *Issues and Studies*, 30 (Jan.): 1–12.

Wong, K., and Chu, D. (eds.) (1985). *Modernization in China: The Case of Shenzhen SEZ*. Hong Kong: Oxford University Press.

Woo-Cumings, M. (ed.). (1999). *The Developmental State*. Ithaca, NY: Cornell University Press.

Wood, D. (2000). 'The International Campaign against the Multilateral Agreement on Investment: A Test Case for the Future of Globalisation?' *Ethics, Place and Environment*, 3/1: 25–45.

World Bank (1993). *World Development Report: Investing in Health*. New York: Oxford University Press.

—— (1994). *Adjustment in Africa. Reforms, Results and the Road Ahead*. New York: Oxford University Press.

—— (1997). *China Engaged: Integration with the Global Economy*. Washington: World Bank.

—— (2001). *World Development Indicators*. New York: Oxford University Press.

World Resources Institute (1992). *World Resources 1992–93*. Oxford: Oxford University Press.

—— (2000). *World Resources 2000–2001*. Washington: World Resources Institute.

Worsley, P. (1984). *The Three Worlds*. London: Weidenfeld and Nicolson.

Yearley, S. (1996). *Sociology, Environmentalism, Globalization*. London: Sage.

Yeung, H. (1994). 'Third World Multinationals Revisited: A Research Critique and Future Agenda'. *Third World Quarterly*, 15: 296–317.

—— and Olds, K. (eds.) (2000). *Globalisation of Chinese Business Firms*. London: Macmillan.

Yeung, Y., and Li, X. (2000). 'Transnational Corporations and Local Embeddedness: Company Case Studies from Shanghai, China'. *Professional Geographer*, 52/4: 624–35.

Yoffie, D. (1983). *Power and Protectionism*. New York: Columbia University Press.

Youngson, A. (ed.) (1983). *Hong Kong and China: The Economic Nexus*. Hong Kong: Oxford University Press.

Zaalouk, M. (1989). *Power, Class and Foreign Capital in Egypt: The Rise of the New Bourgeoisie*. London: Zed Books.

Zapata, F., Hoshino, T., and Hanono, L. (1990). *Industrial Restructuring in Mexico: The Case of Auto Parts*. Tokyo: Institute of Developing Economics.

Zayed, A. (1987). 'Popular Culture and Consumerism in Underdeveloped Urban Areas: A Study of the Cairene Quarter of Al-Sharrabiyya'. In G. Stauth and S. Zubaida (eds.), *Mass Culture, Popular Culture, and Social Life in the Middle East*. Boulder, Colo.: Westview Press.

Zeitlin, J., and Herrigel, G. (eds.) (2000). *Americanization and its Limits: Reworking US Technology and Management in Post-war Europe and Japan*. Oxford: Oxford University Press.

Zeitlin, M., and Ratcliff, R. (1988). *Landlords and Capitalists: The Dominant Class of Chile*. Princeton: Princeton University Press.

Zelezny, L., and Schultz, P. W. (2000). 'Promoting Environmentalism'. *Journal of Social Issues*, 56/3: 365–71.

Zhang, G. (1988). 'The Formation and Growth of an Open Belt along China's Coast'. *New China Quarterly* (Aug.): 69–71.

Zhao, Y. (1998). *Media, Market and Democracy in China: Between the Party Line and the Bottom Line*. Urbana, Ill.: University of Illinois Press.

Zheng, Y. (1988). *Business Guide to China's Coastal Cities*. Beijing: Foreign Languages Press.

Zhu, Y. (2000). 'Globalisation, Foreign Direct Investment and their Impact on Labour Relations and Regulation: The Case of China'. *International Journal of Comparative Labour Law and Industrial Relations*, 16/1: 5–24.

Zimbalist, A. (ed.) (1988). *Cuban Political Economy: Controversies in Cubanology*. Boulder, Colo.: Westview Press.

Zunes, S., Kurtz, L., and Asher, S. B. (eds.) (1999). *Nonviolent Social Movements: A Geographical Perspective*. Oxford: Blackwell.

Zweig, D. (2000). 'Foreign Aid, Domestic Institutions and Entrepreneurship: Fashioning Management Training Centers in China'. *Pacific Affairs*, 73/2: 209–31.

INDEX